JERRY HOFMANN ON
FINAL CUT PRO® 4

Jerry Hofmann

New Riders

800 East 96th Street, 3rd Floor, Indianapolis Indiana 46240

Jerry Hofmann on Final Cut Pro 4

Copyright © 2004 by New Riders Publishing

International Standard Book Number: 0-7357-1281-6

Library of Congress Catalog Card Number: 2001099403

Printed in the United States of America

First edition: October 2003

07 06 05 04 03   7 6 5 4 3 2 1

Interpretation of the printing code: The rightmost double-digit number is the year of the book's printing; the rightmost single-digit number is the number of the book's printing. For example, the printing code 03-1 shows that the first printing of the book occurred in 2003.

Trademarks

Warning and Disclaimer

Trademarks

Associate Publisher
Stephanie Wall

Production Manager
Gina Kanouse

Executive Development Editor
Lisa Thibault

Senior Project Editor
Kristy Hart

Copy Editor
Gayle Johnson

Indexer
Larry Sweazy

Proofreader
Debbie Williams

Composition
Amy Hassos
Gloria Schurick

Manufacturing Coordinator
Dan Uhrig

Interior Designer
Louisa Adair

Cover Designer
Alan Clements

Media Developer
Jay Payne

Marketing
Scott Cowlin
Tammy Detrich
Hannah Onstad Latham

Publicity Manager
Susan Nixon

Dedication

For my wife, best friend, and soul mate, Julie, for without her unconditional love and support, this book would not exist.

Contents at a Glance

Table of Contents

About the Author

During his 33-year show business career, **Jerry Hofmann** has become an award-winning theatrical actor, TV and film editor, writer, director, and producer.

His show business career began when he was 5. He was a singer, dancer, pianist, and actor. He was performing professionally by the time he was 18. For the next 10 years, he wrote, directed, and performed in more than 2,000 live sold-out theatrical performances that he coproduced with his wife of now 29 years.

In 1978, Hofmann and his wife moved from Colorado to Los Angeles. There, he began his odyssey in video production, selling equipment for the largest color broadcast equipment VAR in LA. His territory was Burbank and Hollywood. This experience gave him valuable insight into new methods of telling stories with mass communication technologies.

He founded his first television production company in Los Angeles in 1983. During the next eight years, he produced hundreds of TV commercials and industrial films. His clients ranged from Fortune 500 companies to Hollywood studios and advertising agencies.

In 1989, Hofmann obtained one of the first Avid nonlinear disk-based editors in Los Angeles and became a pioneer in the technology. He has been a beta tester for Avid Technology over the years, helping them develop one of the world's premier nonlinear editing solutions.

In 1993, he relocated to Colorado to raise his growing family. He edited the only feature film shot there that year and freelanced as an Avid editor, director, and producer along the front range of the Rockies. He has produced and directed more than 600 projects and has edited many more.

In 1999, Hofmann started teaching part-time at the Colorado Film and Video Instructional Studios, a facility used by the University of Colorado and Aurora Community College. There are 18 Final Cut Pro bays in his classroom and another 24 nonlinear editing bays in the facility. At CFVI, he has post-supervised hundreds of short films produced by his students.

Currently, he has his own company, jlh productions, and he is a partner in Bat-Mann Productions, both located in Denver, Colorado.

Hofmann is a team leader in the Final Cut Pro forum at www.creativecow.net. He also is a designated helper in Apple Computer's Final Cut Pro discussion group and is a frequent visitor at 2-Pop's discussion groups.

He received a BA in theater and a BA in communications (with emphasis on TV and film production) from the University of Denver.

About the Technical Reviewers

These reviewers contributed their considerable hands-on expertise to the entire development process for *Jerry Hofmann on Final Cut Pro 4*. As this book was being written, these dedicated professionals reviewed all the material for technical content, organization, and flow. Their feedback was critical to ensuring that *Jerry Hofmann on Final Cut Pro 4* fits our readers' need for the highest-quality technical information.

Phil Hodgetts has more than 20 years of experience in writing, producing, directing, editing, and motion graphic design across the production spectrum. He is president and CEO of Intelligent Assistance, Inc., which has offices in LA and Newcastle. The company creates a new generation of knowledge tools for digital media practitioners. They are becoming increasingly web-enabled, with classes streamed directly to a custom "floating" application. Outside his primary professional life, Hodgetts writes How2s and reviews for websites and magazines. He also is one of the "DV Guys"—a weekly Internet radio show for digital storytellers at DVGuys.com.

Paul Vachier wears many hats. As a web designer, he got his start designing web articles for *Word* magazine, a groundbreaking early e-zine. Later he worked with the staff at Salon.com to launch their first few online issues. He also served various web design and production stints at companies such as Symantec, @Home, Om Records, Macromedia, Lynda.com (Lynda Weinman's training center), and GoLive Systems. At GoLive Systems he was hired as webmaster and oversaw the creation and maintenance of the company's website during the CyberStudio 3 and CyberStudio 4 product launches. He attended many trade shows, gave many demos, and uploaded lots of web pages to the company servers. He also wrote the original documentation for developing third-party actions and has written many of the actions that ship with GoLive today.

Vachier taught web technologies for a while at San Francisco State University's Multimedia Studies program and at the Academy of Art College in San Francisco. He has coauthored several software- and Internet-related books, including *Plug-N-Play JavaScript* (New Riders), *DeBabelizer: The Authorized Edition* (Hayden), and *Dreamweaver 3 and 4 for Dummies* (Hungry Minds).

Vachier received a BA in anthropology and history from Montclair State University in New Jersey and did graduate studies at UCLA. Today he lives in Santa Fe, NM, where he devotes his time to additional activities such as art, bicycling, skiing, amateur DJing, martial arts (Niseido Ju-Jitsu), and trying to learn Final Cut Pro.

He can be contacted at golivemagic@transmitmedia.com. Websites include http://www.transmitmedia.com, http://www.noendpress.com, and http://www.santafedojo.com.

Acknowledgments

As with any film project, many people's contributions added to this book. Thanks to Ron and Kathlyn Lindeboom for urging me to write it in the first place and for introducing me to the fabulous folks at New Riders. The Creative Cow has been my virtual home since my work with Final Cut Pro began and will continue to be the place you'll find me hanging.

Thanks to the folks at Pearson and New Riders: Jeff Schultz for his encouragement, Kate Small for her gentle persistence, Lisa Thibault for her super editorial ideas and general support—you are the best. Linda Bump for her professional attitude and support. All the folks at New Riders have been simply the best to work with.

I must acknowledge the tips and tricks from my technical editor Philip Hodgetts, whose support and input have been wonderful. Paul Vachier, my other technical editor, supplied invaluable input. I had the best pair of technical editors in the business, and their contributions cannot be minimized. Philip, a true Final Cut Pro guru and teacher, and Paul, a very talented professional, both contributed many things that made the book better. Thanks, fellas.

Without the contributions of the director and producer of "The Midnight Sun," there would also have been a lesser effort for this book. Thanks for your talent and wonderful working relationship, Larry and Colleen McLaughlin. Their efforts three years ago really had a lot to do with this book indirectly and made writing the book a joy.

A million thanks to Chad Roark at Videografx in Denver for his wonderful design and talent, which are evident in the production company logo used at the end of the film. A big thank you to Jon and Heath Firestone at Firestone Studios, whose special-effects work created for the film and this book were just right. Thanks to Randy Hanson at Fanfare in Denver. Randy kept all the audio on a backup system so we could repurpose it for this book, and his professional attitude (and wonderful mixing talents) created the audio track originally for the movie.

I'd also like to thank all the teachers, staff, and students at the Colorado Film and Video Instructional Studios for their support during this effort. I appreciate Frederic Lahey's encouragement in particular, when I was experiencing "When will I ever get this done?" syndrome. Thanks to all the students who gave me very valuable insight into how to approach this topic in general.

This book wouldn't exist without Apple Computer and the folks who have supported this effort. Thanks to Erin McKay Skitt and the rest of the Final Cut Pro team, whose efforts with the software have brought it to a whole new level with Final Cut Pro 4. Thanks to Patty Montesion's encouragement and the good folks who run the discussion group there for FCP, allowing me to learn how to teach, giving me insight into how readers learn. Thank you, one and all.

Thanks to my mother, Nina Christy, and to my late father, Jack Hofmann, for encouraging me throughout my life and preparing me to succeed in this crazy business.

Thanks to my children, Jesse and Taylor, for putting up with Dad in general. My daughter Taylor's gentle reminders to finish the book, and my son Jesse's general support, have served me very well. I love you two very much.

Most importantly, I must acknowledge my best friend, wife, and soul mate, Julie Hofmann. Without her love, support, and encouragement, I would never have been able to write this book. I've dedicated this book to her.

Tell Us What You Think

As the reader of this book, you are the most important critic and commentator. We value your opinion and want to know what we're doing right, what we could do better, what areas you'd like to see us publish in, and any other words of wisdom you're willing to pass our way.

As the Executive Development Editor for New Riders Publishing, I welcome your comments. You can fax, email, or write me directly to let me know what you did or didn't like about this book—as well as what we can do to make our books stronger. When you write, please be sure to include this book's title, ISBN, and author, as well as your name and phone or fax number. I will carefully review your comments and share them with the author and editors who worked on the book.

Please note that I cannot help you with technical problems related to the topic of this book, and that due to the high volume of email I receive, I might not be able to reply to every message.

Fax: 317-428-3280

Email: lisa.thibault@newriders.com

Mail: Lisa Thibault
         Executive Development Editor
         New Riders Publishing
         800 East 96th Street
         3rd Floor
         Indianapolis, IN 46240 USA

Foreword

The Creative Cow Final Cut Pro (FCP) users' forum leadership team includes some of the top names in the world of FCP. If you visit, you'll find a team that includes FCP legends like Philip Hodgetts, Tom Wolsky, and Michael Horton. To hold your own in this group and to excel in such illustrious company is tough because each of these guys enjoys a level of respect given to few FCP users. To join their ranks is not an easy task and requires the kind of expertise and authoritative voice that you'll find in Jerry Hofmann.

When we asked Jerry Hofmann at the 2001 National Association of Broadcasters (NAB) convention to join our FCP team, he laughed and said: "I don't think so! You've already got an incredible team. You are kidding, right? I've respected people like Philip Hodgetts and Michael Horton for a long time—they're heroes of mine. How on earth can I add anything to that kind of line-up?" We told him that he already did and that if he'd go back to the forum and look at the posts and the answers there, he'd see that he was already developing an authoritative voice equal to any on the board. It took a few weeks to convince him, but once Jerry joined the team, he became the hinge on which the community functioned.

Today, Jerry is one of the true luminaries in the FCP skies. When he gives you an answer, you know you've been given the definitive answer. The community members respect him because they know these answers come from a long and storied career spanning decades of film experience. Jerry is also a people person whose teaching style is unthreatening—even to net newbies. And he laughs more than any two people we know combined. He's a great man in the truest sense of the word—a man who really cares about people, and it shows.

Jerry has had a long career in the entertainment industry both in front and behind the camera, working as an actor, a director, and an editor. He's also worked as a stand-up comedian whose shows were sold out weeks in advance. Speaking of his film work, the project that forms the subject matter of this book was an award-winning short film at the Rhode Island Film Festival.

Recently, Jerry decided to take his experience back to school, where today he works as an instructor at a film school in Colorado. His experience in nonlinear video editing on computers dates back to the first Avid systems, where his serial number was 004.

Few users we know of can communicate the editing process as straightforwardly as Jerry or with as much passion on the subject. Jerry loves film. He loves filmmaking. He loves the art and the craft of storytelling and all that goes into it. And when you hear him talk, you know that you've been blessed to get decades of this man's experience, highly compressed in a version so much faster than it took to get him to you. Think of Jerry as "faster than realtime" learning—it would take you years to learn the kinds of things that he gives you in the time that it takes for you to read this book.

If you want to master little-known areas of FCP or you want to edit a film successfully, this is the book for you. Although Jerry covers many of the basics and sets a solid foundation in this work, he gives you so much more than the many FCP books written by those with far less than his own incredible experiences in the world of filmmaking. This book might be built around FCP, but we even recommend it to people who use tools other than FCP. It's *that* good.

The best always,

Ron and Kathlyn Lindeboom
Founders, `creativecow.net`

Preface

During the last 10 years, digital nonlinear editing (DNLE) systems have undergone tremendous development. All the core components that make up a DNLE have seen vast improvements. From 32MHz computers, we now have 3GHz computers. From $15 per megabyte of disk storage, we are now hovering close to one-third of one cent per megabyte. From 4Kbps AppleTalk networks to 800Mbps FireWire networks, we are in an ever-progressing phase of technological advancements.

One of the primary benefits of this technology path is that performance and power have risen sharply while costs have dropped considerably. Today, the power of an uncompressed Standard or High-Definition DNLE is—minimally—10 times more than just five years ago. Simultaneous to the hardware improvements, we've seen a significant growth in the power of DNLE software. DNLEs can now run on the host computer without any additional hardware add-in cards and are still capable of amazing performance. Digital video (DV) cameras have undergone tremendous development, and HD-DV cameras are now on the market for less than $4,000.

The prime benefit of these terrific tools and systems is that with standard computing platforms, readily available and affordable software, and powerful and compact cameras, individuals who might not have a filmmaking background can now easily acquire, edit, and produce content and can do so with relative ease. It's easy to burn these stories to DVD and share them. Posting content to a website allows filmmakers to reach a global audience.

Given all this change, is critical to become educated. What you are about to read was written by a long-time filmmaking and technology professional who is dedicated to educational and practical, hands-on approaches to using these toolsets. Herein you will find a comprehensive, step-by-step approach to working in a nonlinear environment and will be guided toward the various (and best) ways of accomplishing your goals.

Given time, you'll be a master of the software. What you choose to create and what makes it special is not a matter of any tool, but of your imagination.

Tom O'Hanian
Co-Inventor Avid Media, Film, Multicamera Systems
Providence, Rhode Island
July 2003

Introduction

From reading literally thousands of posts and teaching hundreds of people Final Cut Pro and editing aesthetics over the past few years, I've come to the conclusion that learning by doing is the quickest way to master Final Cut Pro (and it's just plain more fun). After you've mastered the tool, it becomes much more enjoyable to express yourself through your edit decisions. Furthermore, several areas or concepts seem to give new editors and even experienced editors problems. So in response to this, I wrote this tutorial. It's really for any editor who would like to learn a logical way to make edit decisions, as well as expedient ways to perform them with Final Cut Pro. In many cases, I talk about workflow that applies to any editing application, because they are as similar as they are dissimilar.

This is not only an attempt at teaching the software. To you it is also an attempt to teach you a technique for editing any project in such way that its goal is reached successfully. The same principles expressed during this tutorial apply to any project you might do, be it a narrative film (like we'll edit together here) or any other form of communication, entertainment, or even a commercial project, such as a television commercial or an industrial marketing video.

I've always felt that editing is very similar to creative writing. Editing is the final rewrite of the script. When editing a documentary, it is very common for the script to be written in the editorial stage. Certainly, when editing anything shot without a script, such as a wedding or other social event, it is in the editing bay where the story is written or rewritten from what actually happened. I believe there is story in every use of the medium. It's your job as an editor to write with pictures and sound the story that might or might not have been written before the shooting took place.

I've attempted to write not only for beginners, but for experienced users of Final Cut Pro as well. If you have some experience with Final Cut Pro or are coming from another editing application, you might find some of the material here familiar. I suggest, though, that you not skip areas of the tutorial you feel you know already. I've purposefully peppered this tutorial with techniques you might not have known Final Cut Pro can do, even in "basic" areas of the software. Just as important, the story-building techniques this book covers are cumulative. The technical editors of this book were amazed that there was still something to learn, even in areas of the software they thought they knew or had mastered. The text also includes a narrative on my cognitive process as I edited the film; hopefully the techniques I employed will help you with your projects when you make edit decisions. At the very least, I hope you gain the ability to know how to approach any project, by simply asking yourself the questions I asked and answered as I edited "The Midnight Sun." You'll not only get a solid foundation in how Final Cut Pro works, but you'll also see how to edit more successful programs. This is my hope for anyone who works with this book.

Having the basics down will serve you well as you learn to use the higher-end features of Final Cut Pro. This tutorial assumes that you've completed the earlier chapters. The first time you start using this tutorial, go through the entire tutorial from the beginning. If you get confused or don't understand an instruction, to check out how any edit or effect should look, simply open the finished sequence file that is included with the tutorial's project file to see how the finished step should look. When you have finished the tutorial, use the book as a reference in the future. Unlike a user's manual, this book is intended to serve as a way of learning the interface, because you need to learn it to finish editing the film.

I've included on the DVD all the available material that was used to edit "The Midnight Sun." Refreshingly, there wasn't a large shooting ratio. After you've finished the tutorial, I think it's a wonderful idea to reedit the program in the way you find most effective. Giving the same source material to different editors in my classrooms over past few years has opened my eyes to the fact there isn't a *single* way to edit a program or movie. The editor's personality and expressions show through the edit decisions each editor makes. It's exciting to see a different point of view, especially when it's expressed with the same source material. So by all means, play with the material, use different shots or shot order, and experiment with the footage to teach yourself how edit decisions affect the story's emotional impact. Enjoy yourself; let your imagination take you places in your mind you didn't know existed. I hope you surprise yourself.

I hope you learn to look at your work from a fresh perspective each time you start another editing session.

What Is Nonlinear Editing?

I think everyone knows the difference between typing on a typewriter and working with a word processor. Many of the differences between these two tasks are the same differences you find with editing with linear and nonlinear editing systems. Like using a typewriter (typing words in the order they must appear on the finished page), when you are editing in a *linear editing* system, you need to record from a source tape to an edited master tape each shot as it comes in the program and for the duration it lasts. If you make a change to these shots after you have edited past them, you have to rerecord every shot past that change to move it either later or earlier on your edited master. Linear editing is constrained to this method. If you decide to delete one of the shots (or erase a word), you have to record over it with the next shot and rerecord all the following shots (just as you would do if you wanted to change a sentence on a typewriter).

Nonlinear editing is more like working on a word processor. If you delete a word, all the rest of the words move over next to the last word you typed before the deleted word. You can do the same thing with shots on your computer in a disk-based nonlinear video editing program such as Final Cut Pro. If you want to move any shot or even groups of shots, you can do so without any of the penalties associated with linear editing. No rerecording is involved. You just delete the offending shot and play back the new sequence without it.

How is this accomplished? Nonlinear editors don't rerecord anything until you export the edited sequence from the computer to the output medium of your choice. This is much like printing a document from a word processing program. Nothing is complete until you've printed the document. The same is true of nonlinear editing. You can make changes anywhere in your program until you are ready to show it to the world. You can do this because you are simply asking the computer to *play back* the shots or parts of shots in the order you have programmed them with your editing software.

A Little History on the Art of Filmmaking

In the old days—about 1989—video editing was a matter of rerecording a source shot (from a camera master) onto a different tape (edited master) in position next to its previous shot, following that with another, and so on. As I have mentioned, this was called linear editing. The editor needed to think about the order and length of shots in the finished program before committing to an edit.

All of this was time-consuming and artistically limiting. The broadcast-quality video editing systems of this era could cost upward of $1 million at the high end and at least $250,000 to do much of anything other than a series of cuts. It was an endeavor that few could afford. These limiting cost/time factors made post production difficult and expensive. Post production drove up the cost of finished production, decreased the number of productions made in the first place, and basically left the option of communication through moving pictures only in the hands of producers with a lot of resources. Only companies with a large budget would even consider communicating this way, be it for an industrial program or a feature film.

To be precise, nonlinear editing started before linear editing. Film editing has always been a nonlinear process. If you wanted to take out the 50th shot, you just physically cut it out and added the remaining shots to the first 49 shots. You did not have to add shots to the film in any particular order, so it was nonlinear. Editing was—and is—fast and relatively intuitive. But it remained daunting to trim just a frame or two from a shot. The editor needed to save these frames, so the edit room became full of little pieces of film all over the place. The invention of film bins came along to help organize the apparent chaos.

For years, this is how film editors worked. Editing was viewed as a painstaking process that few could imagine doing. We either lived with the limitations of linear editing in video or hired assistants to keep track of all those frames of costly celluloid. If you worked in television and your medium was video, you didn't have a choice.

The Emergence of Nonlinear Editing

Tape-based, nonlinear video editing changed all this. Instead of rerecording shots, the computer-controlled systems of yesteryear played back shots from a series of video-tape machines in the order the editor programmed them via a *sequence timeline*. Because this timeline was not a rerecording, the editor could change any shot and see the sequence played back with the new edit decision almost immediately. After initi-ating a playback command to the system, the editor waited for a series of videotape machines to cue to the first series of shots in the timeline. Machine 1 would go to shot 1, machine 2 would cue up shot 2, and so on. The timeline's influence on the art and craft of editing cannot be minimized. Suddenly, the speed at which edit deci-sions could be previewed accelerated tremendously.

Early nonlinear video editing systems were based on videotape. You needed six or eight source video machines loaded with identical copies of source footage—controlled by a computer to access shots in the programmed order—and you simply played them back as the editor intended. While one machine played back a shot, the other machines searched for the incoming shots. Shots could be dropped or added with relative ease, but the high cost of these systems still kept them away from lower-budget producers.

Other nonlinear video-based edit systems were based in videodisk source machines. To be fast enough to let you view a playback of a series of shots, the system had to have copies of the same material pressed onto multiple videodisks; that way, access time to each shot could be accomplished much like the aforementioned videotape-based systems. These videodisk-based systems were used mainly in Hollywood to edit high-end projects, and they were relatively expensive. Cutting with quality video pic-tures in a nonlinear fashion was accomplished, but the cost of editing didn't decrease much. The TV show *Star Trek: The Next Generation* was edited this way for a number of seasons.

In 1988, a company called EMC^2 released the first nonlinear computer disk-based video editing station, based on a PC. A year later, Avid Technology came out with a more attractive one, based on a Macintosh computer. Both stations addressed the issues of not having to rerecord all the shots past a change in a sequence. In addition, they did not require a series of duplicated source material played back on multiple video players. Instead, the editor digitized footage from a videotape machine and "copied" this footage to a hard disk drive. This was cost-effective, but the quality of these early, digitized pictures playing back from hard disk drives was so poor that these pictures could be used only to make edit decisions. This process was called *offline editing*. The editor was free to make changes as often as he wished, making the decision-making process faster, easier, and less costly. As a result, lower-budget programs became better edited.

Video and film editors suddenly had extra time to try what-ifs. What if I tried it this way? What if I tried it that way? No longer worried about how long it might take to see a change, people tried more changes, and the art of program editing took a quantum leap in quality if for no other reason than the time savings involved. These first computer disk-based edit systems cost about $65,000 and could be used to create only edit decision lists, not finished programs. The editor still had to take his computer-generated edit decision list to those million-dollar rooms to create a finished program in a linear editing format. This was called an online edit session.

note   As a side note, what you got for your investment of $65,000 in 1989 (in the case of the Avid product) was a top-of-the-line Macintosh FX, two computer monitors, a 10MB startup disk, 1 or 2GB of media storage, and the necessary software and hardware to digitize from a source machine, which was an added expense. You could use this equipment to make cuts, dissolves, and wipes only, or high-quality cuts-only versions of your edited master if you had two serial-controlled video machines. But few people bothered to do this, because most users took their edit decision list to an online linear bay to complete the edited master tape.

Nothing short of an editing revolution began to take place. Even though you couldn't really finish anything with these early computer disk-based nonlinear editors, you could spend the allotted time given a project to come up with a much better edit. And notably, the cost of these systems made them accessible to more projects. I bought the first Avid product delivered to Los Angeles that year. I saw video playing back on computer monitors at the National Association of Broadcasters (NAB) show in Atlanta in April 1989 and was bowled over by the technology. I wasn't the only one, either. Avid's booth was about 25 feet by 25 feet, and I think the entire company was there hawking the product—all 12 of them. By 1995, Avid had the largest booth at the NAB convention. It was an amazing accomplishment.

Avid became the standard-issue equipment for many years. Thousands of editors everywhere started using Avid's equipment. Along the way, notable contenders such as Media 100 popped up, but never did the bulk of the industry really stray far from Avid's Media Composers and Film Composers. Costs went up as the resolution went up, but by 1994, with the advent of Avid's "high-enough resolution," finishing on these systems became commonplace. Yet, to really do it right, an editor needed to work with a system that ran about $125,000, plus video monitors and source video machines—still out of reach for the masses. Overall post costs went down a bit, but not enough to really cause a revolution in communication through motion pictures.

DV Cameras and Digital Editing Systems

The revolution in production really began with the introduction of digital video (DV) cameras and editing systems such as Final Cut Pro. Final Cut Pro, released in 1999, opened the doors to cost-effective, intuitively accomplished video editing for the masses. Quickly embraced by many professionals, Final Cut Pro's acceptance by thousands has been nothing short of a phenomenon. It is now possible to produce programming with broadcast-quality pictures shot with cameras that cost less than a new luxury car. For as little as $7,000 or less, communicators, educators, entertainers, and even just excited amateurs can produce feature-length programs on their desktops with broadcast-quality pictures.

The Benefits of Final Cut Pro

Final Cut Pro's intuitive interface led me to forsake far more expensive edit stations when I realized it let me accomplish the vast percentage of the work I needed to do with speed and efficiency. Final Cut Pro is a mature program whose widespread acceptance by editors, directors, and producers everywhere has made it a hit in the nonlinear editor (NLE) world. It can feel as comfortable as an old shoe after the first and only learning curve is past. Most importantly, Final Cut Pro is not tied to proprietary hardware other than Macintosh. It's both hardware- and resolution-independent. With off-the-shelf hardware additions, not only can you finish an uncompressed 4:3 top-of-the-line National Television System Committee (NTSC) or Phase Alternating Line (PAL) video project, you can even finish an HDTV-quality program. An HDTV editing station for less than half the cost of that first Avid. Amazing.

One thing that's happened to me is that I no longer have to maintain an office with an expensive NLE in it. For the first time in more than 25 years, I work completely from home. Final Cut Pro has made this possible. I always felt it best to have my own offline editing equipment. Loving the freedom and creativity offered by nonlinear editing, I owned systems that required that I keep them in an office outside my home. These systems' expensive upkeep and payments required that they had to be shared with other editors. Or they were just too large to keep at home. My whole lifestyle changed when I bought my first Final Cut Pro system. My wife is no longer an "editor's widow," and I've become better acquainted with my children. Dad no longer comes home late after everyone has gone to bed. I'm sure my story isn't unique.

The Future of Filmmaking

What might the future hold? What will we do with all this super low-cost, high-quality equipment? Whenever someone tells me the future will be this way or that way, I'm skeptical. But one thing is for sure. I doubt that anyone would disagree that a picture is worth a thousand words, and moving pictures tell you even more. With generations having been weaned on moving images transmitted via television, it's become more than just entertainment. Never forget that more than 80% of interpersonal communication is nonverbal. What we see communicates more than what we read or hear. It's become the most successful and reliable medium of information gathering and dissemination.

With that point in mind, think of the future possibilities that information, education, marketing, and entertainment hold. Videophones are a given (witness the live coverage of the Iraqi war), but the advent of the Internet is already revealing new and exciting pathways for video programs to be distributed. Whether these productions are commercial, educational, or entertaining, not only has the cost of production come down, but extremely low-cost worldwide distribution is already taking place. What will change the most is not what we produce as much as how many people produce. I can't imagine what some folks are thinking up, but no doubt they wouldn't even consider it without the recent cost savings represented by products such as Final Cut Pro.

With more production comes more distribution and more use of the medium in general. In fact, I see the largest growth in information sharing via video than at any time in its history. How about birthday greetings transmitted via wireless Internet to Dick Tracy-style watches? It's all accessible; it's all possible.

No one doubts that the Internet is the most important communication advancement since the printing press. People are viewing video production with it now. With the Internet's broadband capabilities, streaming content created by desktop video production systems is becoming an everyday event. Production is begetting more production. For example, if one company puts a marketing video on the Internet, its competitor might put one up too, if for no other reason than to stay competitive. I've seen this happen.

All this new distribution of video content is being accomplished with equipment at the lowest cost-to-quality ratio in the history of video production. Better stated, all this is being made possible and, in fact, is happening because of these new and inexpensive production and distribution systems. Final Cut Pro is leading the way. Editing on a laptop computer anywhere on the planet is possible at a cost less than yesteryear's basic professional videotape machine.

Files Created and Used by Final Cut Pro

Three basic files are created by editing with Final Cut Pro. The first is the *project file*. This is where all your logging and editing decisions are stored. The project file is best kept on your startup disk as opposed to your media disk so that you can have the benefit of more than one disk drive working for you. With only this file, you can recapture/digitize all the footage again some other time, on some other machine, or in a higher resolution. It is a database of your clips' time code, logging information such as reel or tape names, and your edit decisions.

The second major type of file created by Final Cut Pro is a *media file*. It contains the pictures and sound files you edit your program from. These files are created when you capture or digitize footage with Final Cut Pro. They are QuickTime movies for the most part. Media files can be quite large, and for best performance, they should be kept on a disk separate from your startup disk. You will learn more about this in Chapter 1, "Essential Equipment."

The last major type of file created by Final Cut Pro is a *render file*. This file is a composite of some sort. A *composite* is two or more images combined into one. This type of file is similar to a media file. Render files are large because they are picture or sound files. These files, too, should be kept on your media drive because they are media files, and you need to have a fast and dedicated drive to play them back.

The Overall Process of Editing in Final Cut Pro

When you use Final Cut Pro to edit a program, the first file you create is the project file. It contains references to media files and provides the interface to control video machines from which you capture or digitize source material for use in your program. These media files are represented as clips within the project file. A *clip* in Final Cut Pro is a "pointer" file to the actual QuickTime movie or other computer-generated file, like a Photoshop file. It's not the file itself; it's a reference to it, stored as reference information within your project file.

After deciding which video resolution you will work with, the project file is where you work until you are finished editing. Think of the process like this:

1. Create a project.
2. Copy your footage into your computer.
3. Import footage to your project file by means of reference files (clips). Most of the time, this is part of the logging and capturing process.
4. Cut and paste your clips much like a word processor does with words (keeping this edit decision information in your project file as well).

5. Record it back out to your master tape, or export it as a movie file for use on DVDs, CDs, or the web.

    Delete the large media files (so that you free up disk space to work with a new project), keeping the project file as a backup in case you want to recapture footage later and restore your program to your computer.

This process is nondestructive in nature. This means that the captured footage on your computer is not modified in any way during the process. For example, if you changed the color characteristics of a given shot, the computer would not alter your original file in any way. You might have to render this change, and the computer would create another media file, which is a copy of the original with the color corrections. Rest assured that if all is set up properly and you have a fast-enough Mac, you won't have to render every file or effect you decide to use in your program. When you play your edited sequence, Final Cut Pro plays this rendered file instead of the original media file only if you have programmed a change in that original file's appearance and your computer isn't fast enough to create this new effect without rendering it to a new media file. Thus, if you add a cross-dissolve from one shot to another, only the dissolve might need to be rendered.

What you create with Final Cut Pro is really a list of commands instructing the computer to play back specific files in a specific order, whether they are the original media files or the newer, modified rendered files. This is why it's best to keep your project files on a physically different disk drive than the one your media files are played back on. You get the benefit of more than one disk drive accessing and playing your program.

After you've edited your program and you are satisfied, you go through a process of recording this finished program on a videotape, or you output compressed media files for use on the web, a DVD, or a CD (or even all of these for the same program). Final Cut Pro 4 adds a new program to its arsenal of tools called Compressor for the creation of these *distribution* files.

Different Macintoshes and Real-Time Effects

One thing holds true with most digital video editors. Faster computers make for a more satisfying editing experience. This is more relevant in Final Cut Pro 4 than in previous releases. With this release of Final Cut Pro, Apple has "loosened" the reigns on real-time effects. Real-time effects are any effect or set of effects that you don't have to render in order to see the effect's playback.

The faster and more powerful the CPU, disk drives, and video display card you have installed on your Macintosh, the more real-time effects you can experience. Not only can you see more in real time, but you render considerably faster, too. In a professional situation, this can become crucial.

You can use many combinations of real-time effects (those listed in bold type in Final Cut Pro) and still have real-time playback, depending on the speed and number of processors in your computer. Final Cut Pro 4's new rendering engine allows you to attempt to play back any number of layers of real-time video and audio effects. Computers with dual processors have a definite performance advantage over those with single processors. Each effects operation you apply to a clip or layers of clips makes more (or fewer) demands on your computer's processing capabilities, depending on the effect (some make more demands on your computer than others). When the total processing demands of all combined effects exceed your system's capabilities, you need to render before you can play back.

Each user needs to experiment to see where the threshold of his or her computer makes it necessary for a render to take place.

Learning OS X

You must run OS X to even install Final Cut Pro 4. In fact, you must be running system 10.2.5 or later. Apple's new operating system is no less than a triumph. It's easy to learn and far more stable than any of its predecessors. I highly recommend that you learn this OS and use it to run all your Macintosh applications. OS X is more intuitive, it manages your memory much better than earlier versions, and it's much easier on the eyes. I recommend that you buy a book on OS X and learn how to use it. You will be a better editor and technician for it. Because this is a highly technical field of endeavor, your skills as an editor will be greatly enhanced by your knowledge of your computer and how its operating system works.

Let me give you a scenario. You are working on an edit for a client who is sitting with you in your editing bay. Your computer acts up, or one of its settings is not allowing you to do the work at hand. Rather than wait for tech support, which might come too late, your knowledge of how your operating system works comes to the rescue. Your client is impressed. As desktop video editors proliferate (and they are by the thousands these days), editors who have a working technical knowledge of their systems will be in high demand. Clients will trust that you can get the work done on time, and within budget, if they also know that your computer skills are top-notch. This means repeat and referral business for you. Most of the business I've garnered over the past 25 years or so came to me from repeat and referrals. That's just how show business works.

About the Project

Throughout this book, we'll edit an entire dramatic short film together. Based on Robert W. Service's poem "The Cremation of Sam McGee," "The Midnight Sun" is a 12-minute story. Shot entirely in Colorado on 16mm film, the story is one of those "wild-west ghost stories" that occupy the American literary tradition. I've always loved surprise endings, and this film has a good one. I also hope to give you some pointers on organizing your work in the most convenient and efficient way possible, which will carry over into your future projects for the rest of your editing experience on any nonlinear platform. I also hope to impart some editing aesthetics to help you learn to make your contribution to the storytelling process more valuable to you or your clients in your editorial future.

We'll tell our story with pictures, composites, voice-over, sound sync, dialog, wild sound, a Foley track, and, of course, music. This sounds like a lot of audio tracks, but in reality, the pictures tell the story in this movie. We'll use jump cuts, L cuts, matching action cuts, and transitional effects to aid this process. We even have to do some compositing to keep our producer's budget down. In short, you'll learn the mechanics of Final Cut Pro and how to use them most effectively with any project.

In all, there are about 300 edits to program. You'll work with all the major tools, including color correction, keys, titles, filters, audio filters, and more to make the finished movie.

I hope it's as entertaining for you to edit as it was for me.

Storytelling Without Much Dialog

Motion pictures are called that because the most important aspect of this medium is what we see. It's not that what we hear is unimportant—it is. However, what is shown visually has more impact on the viewer's emotions than what he hears. What the viewer hears should enhance what he sees. First and foremost, we'll edit the picture track for this reason. As an editor, your job is to perform the final rewrite of the script. It's the editor's responsibility to enhance what was originally written and what was originally shot.

Any film needs to be edited visually to the story's rhythm. This story-enhancing rhythm also is part of any video program. Even a documentary or marketing program needs to find its rhythm and never stray from its story. Pacing and timing are *everything* in storytelling with motion pictures, just as they are with a standup comedian, Shakespearian tragic actor, or great cellist or rock guitarist. What fascinates and engages us much of the time is not just what the story is about, but how it is told. This is really evident in the telling of a joke. We've all seen two people who tell the same joke, where one person is funny and the other person is not. It's all in the timing, the pacing, the rhythm of the delivery, and the emotion displayed.

The editor holds the keys to the timing of every event we see and hear in any motion picture. I will pass on some tips on achieving the critical knowledge of what, when, where, and how to make that cut.

I've always thought that moving pictures cut together with emphasis on story are an invaluable asset to a finished project, whether it's a feature film, instructional video, wedding video, TV spot, marketing video, or something else. The medium is one of pictures and sound, and it's the editor's province to pull all these elements together in a way that enhances the *story*. The editor has as much impact on the project's success as the writer's vision and the director's execution of it, because the editor has much to do with setting the project's pacing, timing, and rhythm. In this vein, the project hopefully will teach you not only which buttons to push, but when to make an effective and story-enhancing edit, whether it is a picture or a sound edit.

Who Is This Book For and How Do You Use It?

From reading literally thousands of posts, and directly teaching hundreds of people Final Cut Pro and editing esthetics over the past few years, I've come to a conclusion that learning by doing is the quickest way to master Final Cut Pro (and it's just plain more fun). After you've mastered the tool, it becomes much more enjoyable to express yourself through your edit decisions. Furthermore, there are consistent areas or concepts that seem to give new editors and even experienced editors problems grasping. So in response to this, I wrote this tutorial. It's really for any editor who would like to learn a logical way to make edit decisions, as well as expedient ways to perform them with Final Cut Pro. In many cases, I've talked about workflow that would apply to any editing application, as they are as similar as they are dissimilar.

Not only is this then an attempt at teaching the software to you, it is also an attempt to teach you a technique for editing any project in such way that its goal will be reached successfully. The same principles expressed during this tutorial will apply to any project you may do, be it a narrative film (like we'll edit together here) or any other form of communication, entertainment, or even a commercial project, like a television commercial or an industrial marketing video.

I've always felt that editing was very similar to creative writing. Editing is the final rewrite of the script. When editing a documentary, it is very common for editorial to be where the script is actually written. Certainly, when editing anything shot without a script such as a wedding or other social event of some kind, it is in the editing bay where the story is written. I believe there is story in every use of the medium. It's your job as an editor to write with pictures and sound the story that may or may not have been written before the shooting took place.

I've attempted to write not only for a beginner, but for experienced users of Final Cut Pro as well. If you've some experience with Final Cut Pro or are coming from another editing application, you may find some of the material here already familiar. I suggest though, that you don't skip areas of the tutorial that you feel you know already. I've purposefully peppered the entire tutorial with techniques that you may have not known that Final Cut Pro could do even in what would be considered "basic" areas of the software, and just as important, the discussion of the story-building techniques the book covers, are cumulative. The technical editors of this book were amazed that there was still something to learn even in areas of the software that they suspected that they had previously known or mastered. The text also includes a narrative on what my cognitive process was *as* I edited the film; hopefully the techniques that I employed will help you with your projects when making edit decisions. At the very least I hope you gain the ability to know how to approach any project you may ever do, by simply asking yourself the questions that I asked and answered to myself as I edited "The Midnight Sun." You'll not only get a solid foundation in how Final Cut Pro works, but how to edit more successful programs at the same time is my hope for anyone who works with this book.

Having the basics down will serve you well as you learn to use the higher end features of Final Cut Pro and this entire tutorial assumes that you've completed the earlier chapters. The first time you start using this tutorial, go through the entire tutorial from the beginning. If you get confused or don't understand an instruction, to check out the way any edit or effect should look, simply open the finished sequence file that is included with the tutorial's project file to see how the finished step should be. When you have finished the tutorial, use the book as a reference in the future. Unlike a user's manual, this book is intended to serve as a way of learning the interface as you need to learn it to finish editing the film.

I've included all of the available material that was used to edit "The Midnight Sun" on the DVD. Refreshingly, there wasn't a large shooting ratio Once you've finished the tutorial, I think it's a wonderful idea to re-edit the program the way that you find the most effective. Giving the same source material to different editors in my classrooms over past few years has opened my eyes to the fact there isn't a *single* way to edit a program or movie. The personality and expressions of the editor will show through the edit decisions each editor makes, and it's exciting to see a different point of view especially when expressed with the same source material. So by all means, play with the material, use different shots or shot order and experiment with the footage to teach yourself just how edit decisions affect the emotional impact of this story. Enjoy yourself; let your imagination take you places you simply didn't cognitively realize that existed in your mind. I hope you surprise yourself.

I hope you learn to look at your work from a fresh perspective each time you start another editing session.

What's on the DVD

The DVD contains all the pictures and sound files that you'll use to edit "The Midnight Sun." It also contains some goodies I've found to share with you. Be sure to look in the Goodies folder. Also included is the complete and finished sequence of the movie you'll edit step by step. It's always available to refer to or use when you get to any phase of the editing process.

CHAPTER 1

Essential Equipment

- Minimum System Requirements
- Editing in DV (NTSC and/or PAL)
- Additional Equipment to Think About
- Higher-Quality Video Editing
- Which Setup Is Best?
- Workshop 1: Set Up and Double-Check Your System

Minimum System Requirements

The minimum system requirements to run Final Cut Pro (FCP) 4 and work with this book are as follows:

- A Macintosh computer with a PowerPC G4 or faster processor and an Accelerated Graphics Port (AGP) graphics card
- A 350MHz or faster processor
- 384MB of random-access memory (RAM); 512MB is recommended for Soundtrack and for using RT Extreme or working on long projects in Final Cut Pro
- A DVD drive
- A 6GB audio/video-rated disk drive (20GB or greater is recommended)
- A digital video (DV) source, such as a camcorder or deck, connected to your computer via a FireWire port (also known as i.LINK or IEEE 1394)
- The correct FireWire or device control cable and any additional cables you might need to connect your deck or camcorder to your computer

The software requirements are as follows:

- Mac OS X v10.2.6 or later
- QuickTime 6.3 or later

note

To use Soundtrack or RT Extreme in Final Cut Pro, you must have a Power Macintosh computer with a 450MHz or faster dual processor or a 500MHz or faster single processor.

These are the *minimum* system requirements; it is highly recommended that you exceed them. Final Cut Pro uses the additional resources and runs better and faster on a Dual G4 or G5 computer, because Final Cut Pro is dual processor-aware. Rendering times, which are CPU-intensive tasks, become shorter when the computer can process more quickly. Opening and running large projects also is easier and faster with additional RAM installed. In addition, it's possible to run third-party applications at the same time you are running Final Cut Pro if RAM is available to run them with.

Furthermore, real-time effects become more reliable and robust the faster the computer is. For example, you achieve no real-time playback of clips with effects applied to them with single-processor G4 computers that are slower than 500MHz. As you add more power to the system, you gain more and more real-time playback of these effects. Final Cut Pro 4's real-time rendering engine, called RT Extreme, opens more capabilities in this area as you add power to your system in the form of processor speed, media disk speed, and display card power. Even though you might be able to play back effects without rendering them, they might not play back smoothly or in full resolution until you render them. The idea here is to check the settings used for these effects to make sure they are what you intended without rendering them first.

A G4 PowerBook runs FCP 4 quite nicely. The G4 in the PowerBook allows for some real-time effects and also captures in the Photo-JPEG format for offline. A PowerBook, any eMac, or a G4 iMac will certainly run FCP 4, but they don't allow for robust real-time effects. The minimum requirement for any RT Extreme effects on a G4 PowerBook is 500MHz. An advantage of the PowerBook over the eMac is the availability of an additional external independent computer display. RT Extreme requires a G4 processor and 1MB of level 3 cache to work as well, so you don't get any real-time effects with the currently shipping eMacs or iMacs. This shouldn't stop you from running FCP 4 on them, though. Real-time effects are nice and increase workflow some, but they are not necessary to produce a fine program by any means. The workflow improvements in FCP 4 over FCP 3 are so valuable, I believe they outweigh any earlier loss of real-time effects. Furthermore, your editing workflow and overall experience are greatly enhanced by running Final Cut Pro 4 rather than Final Cut Pro 3. This upgrade is by far the largest and most compelling upgrade in the short history of the software.

At the present time, no iBook runs Final Cut Pro 4. (They won't until they are supplied with G4 processors.)

You need about 650MB of free space for the project and media files that are associated with this book. You also need a Mac that can run FCP.

A Word About Internet Access

I highly recommend that you have Internet access. In most circles of opinion, it is mandatory. The most compelling reason to have Internet access is to stay up to date with your software. In fact, when FCP 3 was introduced, you couldn't even install it without this access, because you needed to download OS updates for OS X! This situation is likely to continue. Internet access has become as common as the telephone, and software makers rely on it to keep their users up to date with their software upgrades. If you are running on an older computer than what is currently being shipped by Apple, you will most likely need Internet access to do this sort of download if you want to run OS X. Furthermore, future releases of OS X, QuickTime, and FCP updates will most likely require Internet access.

Having Internet access also enhances your learning process. Appendix E, "Other Resources," lists web sites that I highly recommend you visit. Some of these sites even give you software, music, picture files, and more for free. Learning software of this nature is difficult enough on your own. This is a great community of users supporting each other online. I'll point you to some sites that also have information on hardware, companion software, music, stock footage, and other resources. Don't forget to check them out!

With Internet access, you can also chat with me at http://www.creativecow.net in the Final Cut Pro forums there, as well as through Apple's Final Cut Pro discussion group. Sometimes you might have questions about the process we will go through together, and I really would like to help you directly in any way I can.

Editing in DV (NTSC and/or PAL)

The most basic Final Cut Pro setup requires only a G4-based Mac with an AGP and built-in FireWire, a computer display, a mini DV or Digital 8 camera, and a FireWire cable to control the camera and capture its audio, video, and timecode information. I cannot stress this enough: Check with Apple's Internet site, `www.apple.com/finalcutpro/qualification.html,` for a list of compatible devices. It's updated from time to time. You access it through the Final Cut Pro area or from the FAQs in Apple's discussion group area. If you own a VHS camera or need to work in this format, solutions are available. If your camera or videotape recorder (VTR) is not on Apple's qualified device list, another way to check whether a proposed camera or deck will work well with Final Cut Pro is to ask in the various forums dedicated to Final Cut Pro users (see Appendix E). Someone is usually available who has already tried or is currently using any given deck or camera you might be interested in using. Sometimes, certain devices need a bit of a workaround to use, and it's best not to be the first one to try it.

As an alternative to this simple setup, you could add an analog-to-digital or DV converter and capture footage from an analog source such as a VHS machine or camera. This analog converter might not be necessary if your DV or Digital 8 camera can serve to accomplish digital-to-analog (D/A) and analog-to-digital (A/D) conversions for you. Most DV decks' and cameras' analog inputs and outputs allow for A/D and D/A conversion, which would forego the use of a capture card or an external A/D-D/A converter. However, remember that you will be tying up your DV camera for this purpose, and you won't be able to capture or record to tape without it. I advise that you use either a deck or an A/D converter to capture DV footage from an analog source, especially if you need to keep that camera working while you are editing.

The only disk drive considerations you should have are either a FireWire drive or another internal ATA 7200rpm disk drive for media storage. FireWire drives work best when they are 7200rpm drives that contain the Oxford 911 ATA-to-FireWire bridge or later, such as the Oxford 922 chipsets used in FireWire 800 drive setups. Apple currently does not recommend FireWire drives for use with FCP, although many users have good luck with them, and they might be your only choice if you are using one of the laptops. Just look for the Oxford Bridge chipset and buy 7200rpm drives, or drives with a minimum of 8.5MBps sustained transfer rate. Building your own by buying an enclosure (which should have the specified bridge) and a fast ATA drive is a good solution, and you will be sure to get a fast-enough drive. Prepackaged drives don't always have the same exact disk drive in them from run to run of the manufacturer.

The only drives that Apple has recommended to date for use as disks for storage of media files are Small Computer Systems Interface (SCSI) drives. That is not to say that ATA drives won't work, but the faster the drives you work with, the fewer the problems you will encounter, and the more reliable and powerful RT Extreme effects will operate.

FireWire 400 enclosed ATA disk drives (which is what "FireWire drives" are) take a bit of a performance hit when running externally (most likely the reason that Apple has never officially recommended them). The same ATA drive (which is what is supplied with "FireWire" drives) mounted internally is about 25% faster. So if you have a tower, you are better off mounting internal ATA drives (7200rpm with 8MB buffers) than running with the same drive mounted in a FireWire enclosure. It's best to populate your G4 tower with internals first if you can. It's not a tough thing to do. Apple has instructions on its support site for the procedure. And you'll do fine with these drives if you are working in DV or lower data rate resolutions.

As I write this, FireWire 800 drive enclosures are appearing. They will improve data throughput. The bottleneck with all FireWire enclosures has been the chipset used to turn the ATA data into data that can be transmitted via FireWire to your computer. The newest Macs all have FireWire 800 ports and can take advantage of the latest FireWire 800 drive enclosures utilizing the new Oxford 922 chipsets. They likely will "bridge" the ATA to FireWire data so quickly that these external drives will perform as well as they would if they were mounted internally. They will be ideally suited to work with a PowerBook that has a FireWire 800 port. On the other hand, unless you need to be portable with your project and its associated media files, you will save some expenditure if you can add ATA internal disk drives to your PowerMac, and you will not gain any performance using external FireWire drives. With the advent of FireWire 800 drives, though, the performance bottleneck might well be the ATA drives themselves. Faster drives will no doubt come along and improve this situation.

Additional Equipment to Think About

You can expand your system to do any level of picture quality and to a higher "professional" level. Much of the following might be more than you need or even want, but much of it is mandatory for a broadcast-quality finishing setup. Chances are, if you are a professional, you will need some, if not all, of the equipment discussed. One of Final Cut Pro's better features is that it is resolution-independent editing software. *Resolution independence* means that with this single version of software that Apple supplies, you can upgrade your hardware to edit video all the way from low data rate motion JPEG to High Definition video and all points in between. No data rate is too large or too small for this software to handle *if* the proper hardware is installed.

In the past, you needed proprietary hardware to upgrade the picture quality of most edit systems. Professionals had to spend tens of thousands of dollars to upgrade from an offline to an online broadcast-quality system. In addition, the editing software had to be upgraded. Final Cut Pro, in contrast, is resolution- and hardware-independent software. The only hardware requirement is a G4 Mac!

State-of-the-Art Drives

State-of-the-art disk drives are getting extremely large and extremely fast. Macintoshes are also becoming faster, as are SCSI specifications and throughput. A year from now, the recommendations in this chapter might be outdated. It's important to understand that because technology is constantly shifting into higher gears, other and newer solutions to run faster systems that can handle uncompressed video might come about, or more real-time effects. However, sometimes it's dangerous to constantly push the envelope, especially if your livelihood depends on how stable and reliable your system is. Be careful. Investing in untried solutions until they really are "tried and true" can be dangerous to your blood pressure, and even your career.

Another point of view expressed often is just the opposite. Buy the biggest, fastest, and latest system you can, because it will last longer. I actually believe that the middle ground is probably the wisest choice. Even if you have state of the art today, you won't have it in six months. It's far more important *what* you put into your program than how fast you can get it done. Content is king. This is not to say that picture quality isn't important—it is. Still, a more compelling program is what you as an artist, technician, and creator should be most concerned with.

An example of pushing the envelope was seen at NAB 2003 in Las Vegas. AJA was showing its new Io product (a wonderful converter, and a next-generation device, I might add) working with a 17-inch PowerBook using two FireWire 800 400GB drives striped in a RAID 0 configuration, recording and playing back uncompressed video with Final Cut Pro 4. It seemed to work. But I'd certainly let time go by and let the "envelope pushers" work out any problems that might occur in a real-world environment before I based my livelihood on this sort of setup. Pretty amazing, though. Imagine, an uncompressed solution on a PowerBook!

Additional RAM

An adage states that you can't be too thin or too rich or have too much RAM. RAM allows your computer to run multiple applications at one time; therefore, it will ease your workflow. Remember, too, that software sellers always list the *minimum*. Most software runs faster and is more stable with more physical RAM installed in your computer.

I suggest that 512MB of installed RAM is the *minimum* you should be running in any modern OS today. However, the more you have, the merrier your computing experience will be. Some third-party capture cards require more RAM. With the recent price drop worldwide in RAM prices, this is an excellent, powerful, and relatively inexpensive upgrade. Additional RAM affects not only Final Cut Pro's performance, but also the rest of the software on your machine. Apple's G5 computers hold a total of 8GB of RAM, and the performance boost to your workflow now and later will definitely be enhanced with more (and faster) RAM.

Storage Space Requirements

Each user must determine just how much storage space for media files he needs for his given workflow. The new requirements for a full install of everything supplied with FCP 4 are larger than ever before. You'll need 1GB of storage just to install the FCP application files. You'll need an additional 14GB of storage for all the media files supplied with LiveType and Soundtrack.

You needn't install these additional media files if you don't intend to use them, but I think you'll find that these wonderful additions to the suite of programs that FCP 4 supplies are very useful indeed. They are tremendously powerful applications (and are a lot of fun to work with), and they further define Final Cut Pro as the best value in editing software. In the case of LiveType, you don't need to install all the media files associated with it; you just install them when you want to use them. However, this requires that you have the additional DVDs handy and available when you want to use these files. If you will edit short-form material, such as a TV commercial or short industrial film, you don't need nearly the space that a feature film editor or documentary editor might need. I once edited a 4-minute short documentary program that used more than 35 hours of source footage! In DV terms, this would require that you have about 1GB of storage for every 4.7 minutes of source footage. In many cases, a shooting ratio of 10:1 (10 minutes of source material shot for each minute of finished program) is common. Therefore, if you are aiming for a 30-minute program, you probably should be looking at storage for 5 hours of source material. In DV terms, this computes to about 100GB of storage.

Running out of storage space for your source material is not always an easy thing to overcome. You can manage media with management tools that Final Cut Pro supplies. You can delete media you've captured that you no longer need or are not using in your program, but it's a far better plan to keep all your source material available for editing and reediting or revising.

Many editors want and should have the ability to capture or digitize *all* or most of the source material that was shot or otherwise created for their project. Revisions are much easier this way. Having to delete material to make room for more material is time-consuming; therefore, it's not cost-effective. Just when you thought you wouldn't need that particular shot, you actually end up needing it and having to capture or digitize it all over again. Needless to say, the workflow becomes tedious if you are constantly spending time deleting, only to have to do more recapturing later.

The DV OfflineRT functions introduced in Final Cut Pro 3 might help here. In short, this format captures media files at a lower resolution, which saves storage space. This is discussed in Chapter 14, "Managing Large Projects." Third-party analog and digital capture cards also have lower-resolution capture capabilities and also might come into play as you plan your storage strategy. In brief, you can capture video at lower resolutions that require smaller amounts of storage space. With the smaller storage space, you can keep more media on your computer's media storage disk. The method here is to capture all your footage, edit in this lower or offline resolution, and then recapture only your edited program in higher or online resolution for final output. This might not be acceptable for some situations, though. One example is when the total editing time has to be as fast as possible, such as when you need a news story to be on the air ASAP.

Another issue to keep in mind is that you need space for any render files you might include in your program. These files are approximately the same size as their duration demands in any given resolution. In an effects-intensive program, you definitely need to plan for these files. You also should not plan to completely fill up the disk drive. Disk drives simply don't perform as well when they are full. I suggest that you keep at least 50 to 100MB of any disk drive's space unused.

Disk Drives for Editing Mini DV, DVCAM, and DVCPRO25 Formats

It is highly recommended that you add an additional ATA 66/100 7200rpm disk drive(s) with 8MB of disk cache to the basic DV Mac setup to use solely as a storage disk for FCP media files. Final Cut Pro calls this disk drive the *scratch disk*. If your intention is to capture or work in higher resolutions, you might need higher-end disk drives. (See the later section "Disk Drive Considerations for Higher-Quality Video Editing.")

You need at least an 8.5MBps sustained transfer rate to reliably capture and play back DV files. Faster is better. If you plan to use a Mac with internal expansion capabilities and you add internal ATA disk drives to it, this is the lowest cost per gigabyte of storage that can record and play back DV media files.

The reason you want a separate drive for use as a scratch disk is that video applications such as Final Cut Pro require tremendous disk drive speeds to play back these large files. Editing DV requires a sustained transfer rate of about 3.6MB per second just to play back the picture and sound files within your computer. Therefore, asking the computer to access the OS, application, project files, and media files from the same physical disk drive is a daunting request indeed.

Partitioning the startup disk, leaving a partition for media files, is only a halfway measure and is not recommended because the same physical drive is still being asked to do it all. Partitioning would result in the development of dropped frames and poor playback performance if you are capturing to the only drive on your Mac. Partitioning disk drives slows down performance as well and really should be avoided for an optimal setup.

Rest assured, though, you can run the lower-resolution files for this tutorial on any disk drive. Because their data rate is lower, you needn't worry about the performance of the files you'll use in conjunction with this book. Also keep in mind that if you capture OfflineRT files instead of full-resolution DV, partitioning a G4 PowerBook or other G4 computer's only internal drive (the startup disk) works great. This is because the data rate needed to play back these media files is about one-third the amount of a full-resolution DV file. It works fine. I *highly recommend* this format for mobile offline editing stations. It renders extremely fast, too!

Disk drives seem to become less expensive, faster, and larger on a weekly basis, so you have little excuse for not setting up your system right from the beginning. However, just how much space do you need? That depends on how much you intend to capture. Keep in mind that many shoots have at least a 10:1 shooting ratio. That is, every minute of finished video has at least 10 minutes shot. Table 1.1 shows just how much storage you might need.

Table 1.1   System Storage Needs

Video Data Rates	1 Minute	30 Minutes	1 Hour
1MBps, offline-quality Photo-JPEG	60MB	1.8GB	3.6GB
3.6MBps, DV-format video	216MB	6.5GB	13GB
24MBps, uncompressed video	1.4GB	43.2GB	86.4GB

As you can see, your storage needs could be large indeed. For DV, you need a whopping 13GB of fast disk drive storage to work with a 10:1 shoot (where you have 10 hours of camera master material), resulting in a 1-hour program if you are capturing most of what was shot. For uncompressed video, you need almost a terabyte, or 1000GB! This is storage just for your camera masters. You need even more room for your rendered effect files. Keep in mind that you should try to have at least another 5 to 10% more storage space for these files, plus space for additional music or graphics files you might use.

Again, more is better, but it isn't necessary in order to start up or use the project in this book. The project is designed to run on the lowliest of minimum requirements. All you need is a 350 G4 computer with AGP graphics or a G4 PowerBook or eMac or G4 iMac with about a gigabyte of free storage space, Final Cut Pro 4, and the will to learn.

FireWire Drives

If you will edit on a PowerBook, iMac, or eMac, your only choice for additional storage space in the newer Apple portables is external FireWire drives. Apple currently does not support their use. If you intend to use a portable and you need more space, look for FireWire drives with fast, sustained transfer rates. For the present, 7200rpm drives with the Oxford 911 ATA-to-FireWire converter chipsets are the most reliable because their sustained transfer rates are fast enough. If your computer supports it, FireWire 800 drives with then-newer chipsets are even better. They seem to be about the same speed as the same drive internally mounted would be.

FireWire RAID systems that might solve this historically unreliable storage device are beginning to appear. Even though FireWire can support transfer rates much faster than is necessary, FireWire drives use internally mounted ATA disk drives. The limitations of the FireWire bridge and the fact that ATA disk drives just aren't that fast keep them from utilizing all the theoretical speed of the FireWire bus. The data has to be bridged by a chipset for the FireWire bus to use it. That's why it's important to note a FireWire drive's specifications if you need to use one.

A Video Deck Instead of a Camera

A camera's tape transport for recording and playing back your material is not nearly as robust as those used by a deck (or VTR). The constant searching and shuttling of the tape as you log, capture, and possibly recapture your footage wears out a camera's tape transport much faster than transports used in desktop video machines. It's a matter of deciding how much you'll use your camera for this purpose. Light use is one thing, but daily and heavier use is quite another.

Video recorder/player decks have a much longer life and allow editing to occur at the same time a shoot might be happening. Furthermore, they search tape as much as 10 times faster than a camera does. In general, video recorder/play decks also give you more features and functions for recording and playing material than cameras do. Some might have audiometers, headphone jacks, multistandard playback and record capabilities, and more. They are required if you plan to edit from something other than VHS or DV.

Betacam machines, DVCAM or DVCPRO machines, and HD machines are an obvious upgrade to consider. To use them, you need serial device control for not only physical control of the machine, but for all the time code information as well. Betacam machines use RS-422 control, for example, and Apple recommends USB serial adapters for this purpose. An alternative is a Stealth Port that Gee Three supplies. (Check out Appendix E to learn more.) The Stealth Port replaces your internal 54Kbps modem on a G4 tower. Many users report better results using the Stealth Port over the use of a USB serial adapter. However, if you have a Mirrored Drive Door Mac, the Stealth Port should be avoided. And it's unavailable for a PowerBook or iBook, so you will need the USB adapter for a portable workstation. Those made by KeySpan seem to be the preferred USB adapter. KeySpan also makes a PCI card, supplying multiple ports for the addition of machines.

Other manufacturers of capture/converter equipment, such as AJA and others, might also have a solution for serial control built into their products. For example, AJA's Io product supplies this port, so check out what you get from your specified capture card or converter supplier for the latest on their recommendations for serial control devices you might need.

Video Monitor

Monitoring your video with an NTSC or PAL video monitor from your computer is also highly recommended. The computer's display shows colors differently than a video monitor or videotape playback does, and it does not display all the resolution of the actual video files intended to be recorded back to tape. When you monitor video with Final Cut Pro, you see all of the raster of the recorded material. TV sets crop up to 10% of the image on all four sides, and the video monitor keeps you apprised of this. They are great for making sure that your titles will be seen.

You can connect a video monitor to your computer through a camcorder or deck that is connected to the FireWire port of your Macintosh when editing DV in either NTSC or PAL formats. Third-party capture cards and media converters also provide this function.

When you set the system to view your source footage or edited program externally on a video monitor, you are better prepared for color corrections, as well as a host of other operations, which are better served by viewing the video the way it will be seen by others when you are finished with your program. Titles, in particular, look a lot better on an external NTSC or PAL monitor. It is probably the single most important addition to your system. Professionals would *never* work without one.

You can even buy a video monitor that displays multiple formats, such as 16:9 display and multiple television standards. HDTV monitors might be a bit pricey, but they probably will become less costly as more users buy them. A quality video monitor can last for years, and it will not go out of date as quickly as your computer or other video equipment such as a camera will.

Expect to pay from two to 10 times as much for higher-end (and, no doubt, better) professional video production monitors. Each of the major companies that make video equipment has pro and prosumer quality equipment. The current crop of CRTs is the culmination of years of research and development. Multistandard versions are your best bet. Look for digital input availability. You'll own this device for years as a professional. Look for monitors that feature SMPTE-C phosphors, which are color-calibrated to a standard. (This feature is not available in consumer TV sets.) These professional monitors can display component, Y/C, and SDI. Even FireWire inputs are arriving.

That said, a consumer TV set with monitor inputs will serve you better than not having an external video monitor at all. But without a blue-only switch (which none of these television sets provides), you cannot set up these monitors ideally for color. There is a way, though. I've heard of putting gel in front of a non-blue-gun-only monitor. I haven't experimented. Having a large gel around is pretty cumbersome.

External Speakers/Headphones

External computer speakers allow you to monitor audio at much higher quality than the speakers that are usually in your computer. To accurately hear the relative volume of your program's various audio tracks to adjust for mixing the proper levels or adjusting audio filter settings, you should use a set of external audio speakers. You can also listen to your audio playback with a quality set of headphones instead of external computer speakers. However, any audio engineer would tell you not to mix with these headphones, because you should do this with external speakers. In a classroom situation that has more than one edit system going at the same time, this is essential.

In Final Cut Pro 3, when you view external video via a FireWire output, you must have a way to monitor the audio, because it is not mirrored on your computer's speakers.

In other words, your computer's speakers are muted when you view your program externally. No longer is this a limitation with Final Cut Pro 4. You set audio and video outputs independently from each other within the application, and they play in sync using *internal* speakers used by your computer system while playing externally on a video monitor, for example.

You can use most external speakers supplied by a video monitor or TV set, but they are not as accurate at monitoring audio as a set of headphones or high-quality computer-driven speakers would be. Various capture cards can provide external monitoring of video and audio as well. These settings can be set separately from each other. A second set of self-powered speakers can be a welcome addition to your system just for monitoring your audio as you watch your video on an external video monitor. These speakers require only a line level input supplied from the output of your DV camera, converter, or capture card.

Audio Mixers

Adjusting audio levels is enhanced by the use of *audio mixers*. You can monitor your output from your computer with mixers and adjust the levels to suit yourself. Moreover, audio mixers allow for more input and output options in your system. To monitor from a DV-based system, you can send out your audio via the FireWire port and connect your media converter's, camera's, or deck's audio output to a mixer. You can also use this mixer to fine-tune audio levels for recording to analog devices, such as a Betacam SP machine or even a VHS machine. In systems that have capture cards, you can send your card's audio signals to a mixer and accomplish the same thing during the recording process. You might even use mixers to monitor your audio with headphones while you view your video externally.

More Desktop Space

If your computer has open PCI expansion slots, or if you have a dual computer display card, you can add a second or even a third computer display. The added screen space is especially welcome if you are running more applications than just Final Cut Pro at the same time. Working with Final Cut Pro on a single 15-inch computer display is difficult at best. A 12-inch PowerBook might be quite compact and a possible candidate for portability, but you'd definitely want a second display if you were to use this machine as your everyday editor.

Professionals typically use two computer displays: one for the Timeline window, Viewer, and Canvas, and the other for the Browser. Some capture cards provide this function as well. If you have never experienced multiple displays, you really don't know what you're missing. After one day, you will wonder how you ever did it without the added screen space.

Many users (including me) consider Apple's Cinema Displays the very best solution for working with Final Cut Pro. These displays are considered among the finest LCD computer displays in the world, and their fairly recent price cuts make them very attractive. Cinema Displays' pixels also stay on until they are told to change their values, whereas "regular" LCD monitors strobe constantly at a high rate, adding to eyestrain. Having a longer timeline is a real time-saver. Less scrolling around within the application makes for a happy, more productive editor and a more satisfying experience in general.

I also recommend flat panel displays over CRT displays for use with any NLE or computer for general purposes. Many studies show that looking at CRT displays for extended periods of time is extremely hard on your vision. Constant eyestrain might become part of your life if you intend to do this for a career. Moreover, LCD screens provide the added advantages of extra workspace and lower power consumption. Let's face it: They are just plain cool, too.

Higher-Quality Video Editing

For many applications, you'll want to edit with higher-quality video than DV. Final Cut Pro's features and functions work much the same regardless of the format you are working with. However, your program can have higher-quality composites and overall picture quality if you start acquiring your material with higher-quality video camera masters or telecine transfers (film to videotape), such as digital Betacam, and DVCPRO50 or even HD cameras. (However, with DVCPRO50, you don't need an additional capture card, because it has a FireWire 400 port.) To preserve all of this better quality, you also must add a capture card or higher-end converter to digitize or capture and maintain this higher quality. In digital video, the higher the quality you maintain, the more disk space that is necessary for the files. Faster speed from your media storage disks is also required.

Higher-End Capture Cards and Io

To capture or digitize video and audio from a Betacam machine or IMX format or any higher-than-DV-quality machine, you need a capture card or AJA's Io or a DV camera, media converter, or deck. Keep in mind, though, that if you use DV captures for these higher-quality formats, you lose some of the available color information and resolution that is recorded in the format. It's best to use a capture card or converter that is designed for uncompressed digitizing or capture to maintain the higher picture quality these formats provide. Final Cut Pro works with these formats as well as high-definition television formats. All of this also holds true for digital Betacam and other digital formats that other manufacturers make, such as the higher-end DVCPRO formats that Panasonic produces.

Currently the only format that is a definite step up in quality from the DV-25 formats that does not require a capture card is Panasonic's DVCPRO50 format. This format's machines supply a FireWire port to capture the video (which is a cost savings in and of itself).

If you intend to work with higher-quality digital video such as digital Betacam or IMX, you really should use a capture card designed for the input of the format you are working in. This usually means you need a serial digital (SDI) input to your Mac. Some cards have component, S video, composite video, and SDI inputs and outputs all in one system. These cards also supply balanced XLR inputs for audio.

Several capture cards are made for use with Final Cut Pro. Pinnacle's CineWave line of cards, Aurora Video Systems, Blackmagic Design, Digital Voodoo, and AJA all make quality cards for this purpose. Each manufacturer has its champions, but any of these cards works well with Final Cut Pro. Each of these systems provides different feature sets, so it's advisable to do some research and learn about these differences before you purchase.

The newest addition to Final Cut Pro 4's technology for capturing uncompressed video is AJA's Io. This revolutionary box takes advantage of Apple's standard FireWire technology. This converter box, about the size of an inexpensive consumer VHS machine, doesn't require a PCI card. Instead, it converts all analog and digital video formats, including uncompressed video, internally in the box. It sends the results of this conversion through a single FireWire cable to your Macintosh (including serial control for your professional machines). Your Macintosh supplies the ability to compress this uncompressed signal into a lower-quality format for use in an offline edit, allowing you to capture more video per gigabyte of storage space. Then, when you are done editing, you can recapture in full resolution, performing your "online" edit.

Appendix E has the web addresses of these companies.

Even within the different manufacturers' lines of cards and boxes, there are different cards for different qualities of video capture. It is outside the scope of this book to explain them all, but you should be aware that typically the more you spend, the higher the quality or the more versatility you get within each of these different lines of capture cards. Prices range from less than $1,000 to well over $10,000.

Some of these systems supply real-time effects (such as dissolves or titles) that might exceed the capabilities of FCP's own internal RT Extreme software technology on your particular CPU, and some don't (such as AJA's Io). It is best to check with the individual manufacturers when you are ready to set up one of these systems. The technology here is changing rapidly, and if I were to mention specifics, they would be outdated in no time. It's always best to consult Apple's device qualifications, found on its web site at http://www.apple.com/finalcutpro/qualification.html.

Each user's particular needs will more than likely determine the right setup for high-quality video work. For example, if you need more real-time effects, the added cost of these systems might be cost-effective. I think your workflow will determine the best setup for your particular needs.

Regardless of the card or box you decide to use, you'll need to support these larger video file sizes with much faster disk drives than those used for DV material. Generally, with more quality comes larger per-minute file sizes for the media files these systems work with.

Disk Drive Considerations for Higher-Quality Video Editing

Apple's recommended hard disks for higher-quality video editing are SCSI disk drive arrays. Either Ultra 2 LVD SCSI or 160M SCSI, which is the faster of the two, is necessary to capture higher-quality video.

I recommend that you use the Ultra 160M SCSI setup or faster. You can have a faster data rate with this format, the cost differential is minimal, and the array's performance can double. That said, you need a SCSI PCI controller card to control these super-fast drives. ATTO Technologies makes my favorite controller card. Their web site is listed in Appendix E.

SCSI disks that are paired in RAID 0 configurations need to match each other's size and speed for optimal performance. In addition, they are necessary to digitize or capture uncompressed video. To ensure the best performance and to be able to capture uncompressed video, SCSI disks need to be 10,000rpm drives or faster, and they should match their interface to the controller card. SCSI controller cards are backward-compatible, but the idea here is to get the fastest throughput possible. Therefore, you should use disk drives with an Ultra 160M SCSI interface. Several manufacturers make them, and they all have their champions. However, most users look to IBM, Maxtor, or Seagate for their disk drive needs. Your desktop or tower Mac can handle two or three of these drives internally, depending on the model. You can check the Hardware area of Apple's web site for specifications for the different towers for current-model Macs and the Support area for older Macs. As I write this, these requirements couldn't be muddier. Four or more ATA internal drives are being striped in a RAID 0 configuration successfully working with uncompressed video, for example.

For more storage space than the few internal drives can provide, external solutions are available. You can build your own array with various enclosures housing SCSI drives or fast ATA drives. Several companies make SCSI solutions that are more or less turnkey, including Apple, with its X Serve RAID, which uses a 2GB Fibre Channel connection. Additionally, Huge Systems, Rorke, ATTO, and Medea also market turnkey disk arrays. Some manufacturers are beginning to develop FireWire array-based solutions. Regardless of how you intend to design your system, you need a sustained transfer rate much higher than DV's requirements to capture and play back uncompressed NTSC or PAL. You need at least an 80MBps sustained transfer rate. (Again, faster is always better.) Ultra 320 SCSI arrays are also quite popular and reliable.

Currently, Pinnacle, AJA DeckLink, and Digital Voodoo make the only HD editing solutions on the market for Final Cut Pro. The data rate requirements that are needed to capture and edit this format are enormous. Think in terms of sets of many drives striped in a RAID 0, Ultra 160M SCSI configuration or faster—a very high transfer rate indeed. Apple's X RAID or Huge Systems' Dual Max SCSI array would be perfect for this purpose.

Some RAID systems offer redundant storage options too. This means that if you lost one of the internal drives, you wouldn't lose any data or media files. This is the optimal setup to choose. A JBOD (Just a Bunch of Disk Drives) RAID doesn't necessarily offer this protection, and if one of the drives fails, you lose all the information on any of the drives it's paired with.

Which Setup Is Best?

There isn't a "best" setup for every user, but there definitely is a *right* setup for each user. Each user must decide which system is best for him or her. Professionally, it's usually wisest to choose a system that will have a fast return on investment. You need to answer many questions before deciding how best to set up a system.

What's your budget? Are you a hobbyist, or will you do this as a professional? How much rendering do you plan to do? Do you need to be portable? Do you plan to work with something other than DV material? You must answer all these questions before you can decide which Macintosh and peripheral equipment is right for your situation.

PowerBooks are wonderful for editing on the go. OfflineRT-quality files from DV sources are perfect companions to these machines. You don't even need external FireWire drives if you have enough space for these OfflineRT files.

Other than the portability factor, eMacs also work well with OfflineRT files stored on their internal drives. I still recommend external FireWire drives for full-resolution DV captures for eMacs, iMacs, and PowerBooks, though.

There has been some experimentation with a PowerBook with two FireWire 800 drives striped in a RAID 0 configuration, which supports the capture of uncompressed video with AJA's Io for the transcoding and capturing. This configuration was shown at NAB in Las Vegas in 2003. This configuration currently is not qualified by Apple. But it's quite possible that it will become commonplace. Wow—a portable computer recording, editing, and playing back uncompressed video!

If you need to edit only DV, if you don't plan to render a lot of effects, if you don't need to be able to offer higher-quality video to clients, if you will mainly do cuts and simple transitional effects and titles, and if you have no need or desire to compress video for the Internet on a regular basis, the highest-end Macintosh is probably more than you need. It certainly won't hurt you in any way, but a limited budget might be better spent another way. You're better off spending the extra money on a quality NTSC monitor or deck than on that somewhat-faster CPU in many cases.

Even as Macs become more powerful (and this latest crop of G5s are certainly a quantum leap in performance), the process of using them to edit video can still be taxing on them. In my opinion, you can't have a computer for editing that is too fast. Faster computers make the whole editing process more enjoyable, and they allow more real-time effects. Rendering times become shorter and less necessary with RT Extreme on faster machines. A tower configuration is probably more advisable when working with uncompressed video, because you need the expandability that open PCI slots provide and the power that their architecture provides. You might want a tower for editing, because you don't want to use FireWire drives (currently not the fastest), and you want an internally mounted solution. Apple typically bundles DVD-R drives with higher-end machines. This is a necessity for those who might want to deliver DVDs.

Workshop 1: Set Up and Double-Check Your System

If you are upgrading from an earlier version of Final Cut Pro, you must have purchased a full version of Final Cut Pro in any release. When you install the upgrade, you'll be asked to enter the serial number of any full version of FCP you have previously purchased.

I strongly suggest that you run Software Update from your System Preferences to make sure you have the very latest versions of QuickTime and Mac OS. Final Cut Pro 4 requires 10.2.5 or later and QuickTime 6.1.1 or later. If Final Cut Pro 4 has an update posted on the Apple web site, be sure to run it. Be sure to check Apple's Final Cut Pro discussion group, or http://www.creativecow.net in the Final Cut Pro forum, or http://www.macfixit.com for reports of any problems or software updates. You never know when a new bug might be introduced with an upgrade that fixes other problems.

In this regard, if you are using any third-party capture card or device, you should check that you have the latest drivers for the device if necessary. DV cameras and video machines don't require this check, but a capture card does.

When you are ready to run Final Cut Pro, check your hardware setup. You need to be able to capture and play back video in the format you are working in.

You might be using a capture card, Io converter, camera, deck, or other A/D converter. If so, you might need to check the literature that came with your equipment for the exact settings you need to use. These capture cards' settings are supplied by the card manufacturers. You can access them by opening the Audio/Video Settings window found on the Final Cut Pro menu or by pressing   +ª +Q. Click the A/V Devices tab and select the appropriate output for your setup.

If you are bringing your video in and out via your computer's FireWire port, you can simply set your playback output to be Apple FireWire NTSC for this tutorial's files. Make sure that your device that converts to and from analog signals, such as a DV camera, is connected to your computer and powered up. You need to restart Final Cut Pro to recognize this FireWire device. Connect cables to the analog outputs of your conversion device (even a DV deck or Digital 8 camera), and run them to your external video monitor's inputs. Don't forget to select the proper input on your monitor for the inputs you are using.

Now that you are running an NLE, you will find that it will serve you well to become fairly computer-savvy. Knowing your software's capabilities is one thing, but not running an optimal system setup will quickly make your editing life an unhappy one.

It's been said that if you are working with state-of-the-art video editing on a computer-based system, you are constantly working in beta software. I tend to believe this is true. Keeping this in mind, a book on OS X and general Mac maintenance is a wise thing to keep around. You really must know your tools hardware- and software-wise to be a competent video editor. Otherwise, you need to work in a facility or environment where a technician is nearby who understands your system's setup. More than one client I've worked with expected me to know all about my tools. When I did, I was definitely admired. Can't have too much of that, now, can you?

Getting to know the most efficient way of utilizing customer support from the manufacturer of any given part of your editing system is something to investigate. Each manufacturer handles customer support differently, and the more you understand a manufacturer's methods, the quicker help can come your way. Remember that luring help with a kind attitude will go a long way toward getting you help quickly. Be sure to visit Apple's online support system at http://www.apple.com/support. It contains thousands of articles on solving hardware and software problems that stem from known issues, or common problems stemming from faulty installation or settings.

If you can't get fast-enough help directly from the manufacturer, another user probably has experienced your problem. The solution might be posted at http://www.creativecow.net in the FCP forum or in Apple's discussion group. The Creative Cow has dedicated forums for AJA, Pinnacle, and Aurora system users and more. You'll find me helping at the Cow and in the discussion group in Apple's support area. I'm always happy to help a new user optimize his or her system for a stable and effective setup.

I suggest that you investigate these sites and become part of the best virtual group of users on the Internet. They offer wonderful free help on learning your system's finer points, and they are very helpful and eager to see that you are *editing* and not *troubleshooting*.

It's impossible to cover every scenario or use of Final Cut Pro 4 in one book, but I've tried to write a book that will more than get you well on your way to a lifetime of happy editing. Hang in there. You don't learn how to edit on an NLE overnight. But if you have a desire to learn, I'm confident you will be able to use your software in short order, and have a great time getting there!

CHAPTER 2

Specifying Setups, Settings, Presets, and Preferences

- About All Those Resolutions
- Easy Setups
- Setting User Preferences
- Changing System Settings
- Changing Settings Using the Audio/Video Settings
- Workshop 2: Investigate the Settings

About All Those Resolutions

Final Cut Pro is *resolution-independent*. That means that it can work with DV, Photo JPEG, and quite a few other formats, including NTSC and PAL—even in uncompressed formats right through to various HDTV formats.

The more third-party equipment you add to the software, the more video formats FCP will be set up to handle, but it comes ready to accept and work great with DV and a Photo JPEG format that FCP calls OfflineRT, as long as you have a G4 and a FireWire port. In fact, the files you are using for this chapter are OfflineRT, so you need to learn how to set up sequence presets correctly and so forth just so you don't render everything you put in the sequences you are building.

Because of this resolution independence, you need to tell Final Cut Pro what format you will work in. The strategy to think about here is that you don't want to do much, if any, *rendering*, which in this case is the processing and render file creation that the computer must perform to change the images from one file format to another. In other words, if you set your capture presets to be one format and your sequence presets to be another, you have to render each edit as you make it in the Timeline. This isn't too efficient.

Even if you eventually will compress the video to another format for another medium, such as the web, you should *edit your project in its native format for best results*. If you are editing from DV material, you want to select the capture and sequence settings to be DV. If you are editing another format, you need to do the same—match your sequence settings to your capture presets.

If you are working with more than one source material format, choose the format that the majority of the source material is in.

Most users use DV as source material. The settings for this are presets already included in FCP 4. They are the DV NTSC (or PAL) Capture and Sequence presets. If you set up your system this way, you should be able to quickly start using your software for DV work. For the tutorial files included with this book, though, the presets should be OfflineRT NTSC for your sequence settings.

About Preferences

Preferences are settings files that store how you last worked with their associated application. This includes things such as capture presets, sequence presets, Favorite effects, media disk (scratch disk) settings, and more. Final Cut Pro stores these files and opens a new project with the settings as each OS X user left them last as the default setting. These files are stored in User>Library>Preferences>Final Cut Pro User Data>Final Cut 4.0 Preferences.

These files are changed each time you change a setting or preset. Each time you start Final Cut Pro, it is set up the same way you last saved it. This behavior doesn't present a problem or require any action on your part after you've set up your "normal" working environment, unless you're getting ready to work on a new project, which might need to be handled differently from the previous one you worked on.

Let's say you last worked on a project that was DV NTSC, and now you want to work on a project that is based on a Photo JPEG compression such as OfflineRT. You need to check your Audio/Video Settings to be sure that everything is set up to be what you need it to be. For example, you'll want to set a capture preset to capture OfflineRT-quality media files and create sequences that match these settings.

Another problem might arise if you open Final Cut Pro after a different editor has been working with the same computer and the same user's account in OS X. Another editor could have set up the preference files differently from the way you need to work with them. If you work in this sort of environment, check your settings each time you begin working on a current or new project. Otherwise, you could do things such as capture to the wrong scratch disk or type of media file.

Different preference files can be saved for each individual user if you set up a Mac OS X user account for each user. The preferences for each user are found in User>Library>Preferences>Final Cut Pro User Data>Final Cut Pro 4.0 Preferences. These preference files can become corrupted or might occasionally need to be reset to the factory settings. Simply trashing them from the desktop results in the factory settings being reestablished when you launch Final Cut Pro again.

Final Cut Pro has many settings for capturing and editing and interfacing your video equipment.

A *setting* adjusts a specific feature of Final Cut Pro, such as a sequence's frame rate.

A *preset* is a predefined group of settings that configure a particular function in Final Cut Pro. There are three types of presets: sequence presets, capture presets, and device control presets. A device control preset consists of approximately 10 settings for controlling your video equipment. When you select a device control preset, all 10 settings are automatically selected.

To change a preset, you change the settings in that preset.

An *Easy Setup* is a group of settings that includes all three presets plus the settings found in the A/V Devices tab. When you choose an Easy Setup, Final Cut Pro automatically adjusts all settings of all presets so that you don't have to adjust them individually.

To change your Easy Setup, select Easy Setup from the Final Cut Pro menu and pull up either a predefined set that comes with Final Cut Pro or a custom Easy Setup you've created.

Easy Setups

The first time you open Final Cut Pro, it asks you to choose an Easy Setup, a scratch disk, and a user mode (see Figure 2.1). This tells Final Cut Pro how you will use it.

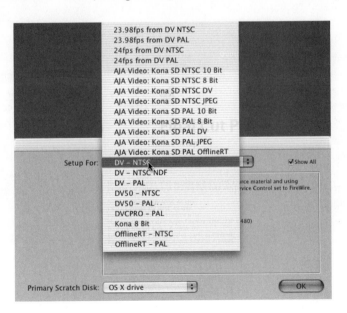

FIGURE 2.1 *Choosing an Easy Setup.*

The pop-up menu allows you to choose a custom setup (a preset you've created) or basic setup (a setup that comes with Final Cut Pro). Final Cut Pro refers to these selections as *Easy Setups*. Easy Setups create a quick work environment for your project. They contain a set of instructions that tell Final Cut Pro which editing environment you will work in. Depending on the FCP version you are working with, the minimum number of presets is four. For most users, this is DV NTSC or DV PAL. You can create your own set of Easy Setups to add to the four that ship with Final Cut Pro. If you have a capture card such as AJA's Kona SD card, you can select these Easy Setups as well, and a check box in the Choose Setup window lets you access these setups.

The first two of these standard Easy Setups, DV NTSC and DV PAL, are digital copies of DV recorded material. The second two are designed to edit compressed versions of these same two formats, which streamlines the operation of changing back and forth between setups. See the later section "Changing Settings Using the Audio/Video Settings."

After you choose a standard setup and scratch disk and click OK, Final Cut Pro opens, as shown in Figure 2.2. After you have this set up, you can access the Easy Setup window from the Final Cut Pro menu or by pressing Ctrl+Q.

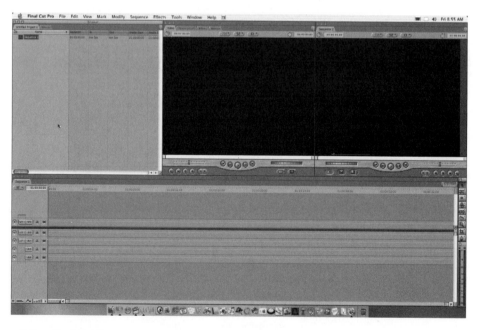

FIGURE 2.2   *Final Cut Pro.*

Setting User Preferences

On the Final Cut Pro menu, you'll find the first of three settings windows, User Preferences (see Figure 2.3). (You also can open this window by pressing Opt+Q.) This set of settings controls how FCP works with you, the user. Notice the set of tabs across the top of the User Preferences window. By clicking a tab, you can access the various settings, the first of which is General User Preferences.

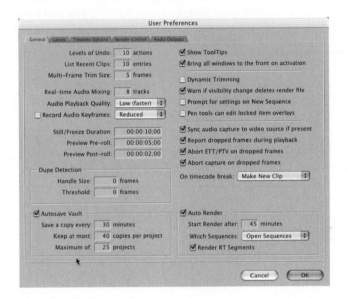

FIGURE 2.3   *The User Preferences window.*

Understanding the Settings in the General User Preferences

Levels of Undo sets the number of actions the computer keeps in memory, allowing you to press Cmd+Z to undo actions in the order you performed them, up to a total of 99.

List Recent Clips is the number of clips that have been loaded into the Viewer.

Multi-Frame Trim Size sets the number of frames you can quickly trim using the trimming tool that is included with Final Cut Pro. You can trim up to 99 frames.

Real-time Audio Mixing sets the number of tracks you will attempt to monitor and mix in real time without mixing them down. The faster your machine, the more you can hear and mix in real time. If you experience dropped frames during playback, you can lower this setting and possibly eliminate them.

Audio Playback Quality sets the quality of the conversion of mixed audio sampling rates within the same sequence (mixing 41kHz from CD music with 48kHz sound sync audio, for example). If you set this to lower than High, you can play back more tracks at one time at the expense of the playback quality. With Low selected, you might hear clicks or pops in the playback. Use lower quality while doing the general edit and higher when you are ready to focus on audio quality or audio editing. Mixing down the audio always results in high quality.

When the Record Audio Keyframes box is checked, keyframes are recorded whenever audio level or panning controls are adjusted. The pop-up menu defines how detailed keyframe automation is when recorded using the Audio Mixer or audio filter controls:

- All records all the keyframes while you move a channel strip's fader or panning slider. The end result is a precise re-creation of the levels you set using the Audio Mixer. The negative thing about this setting is that it might record a single keyframe for each frame, creating a situation in which adjusting these keyframes manually isn't easy.

- Reduced reduces the number of recorded keyframes that are created when you move a channel strip's fader or panning slider. The resulting level or panning overlay in the Timeline or Viewer is an accurate reproduction of the levels you set, but it is easier to edit using the Selection or Pen tool.

- Peaks Only records the fewest number of keyframes necessary to approximate the levels you recorded when moving a channel strip's fader or panning slider. Keyframes recorded using the Peaks Only option reflect only the highest and lowest levels that were recorded.

Still/Freeze Duration sets default In and Out points when you create a still. It also sets the duration of an imported image file.

Preview Pre-roll and Preview Post-roll set the amount of pre-roll and post-roll when you preview an edit from the Trim window.

Dupe Detection Handle Size and Dupe Detection Threshold affect when and how frames are used more than once in the same sequence shown in the Timeline. Dupe Detection Handle Size adds frames to the beginning and end of the clip regions, which are used for comparison to determine whether to display duplicate frame indicators. The default setting is 0. Dupe Detection Threshold allows you to set the minimum number of frames that must be duplicated before a duplicate frame's indicator appears. By default, this is set to 0 so that all instances of duplicated frames are indicated. You can set it as high as 99 frames. In this case, there would have to be a minimum of 99 consecutive duplicated frames before a duplicate frames indicator would appear.

The Autosave Vault lets you access earlier saves of your project files. You set the location of these files by selecting it in the Scratch Disks tab of the System Settings window.

Show ToolTips can be activated to turn on the small yellow boxes that name each of the buttons in the interface. Many of the ToolTips include the keyboard shortcut used for the function.

If the Bring all windows to the front on activation box is selected, and Final Cut Pro is in the background behind another window or application, clicking one FCP window to bring it to the front brings all FCP windows to the front. If this option is not selected, only the window you click is brought forward.

Dynamic Trimming allows for edit points in the Trim Edit window to follow the playhead's position. If this selection is chosen using the J, K, and L keys, the edit points move automatically with the playhead's position. When you press J, for example, pressing K when you see a new edit point automatically moves the edit point to the playhead's position in the Trim Edit window.

Warn if visibility change deletes render file activates a warning dialog box if you turn off a track's visibility or turn off your monitoring of any track. When you turn off track monitoring in Final Cut Pro, you can lose render files. You can bring back renders if you've turned off a track's visibility by performing an Undo (press Cmd+Z).

Prompt for settings on New Sequence displays a Settings dialog box when you ask the software to create a new sequence. This is handy if you want to double-check the sequence settings before you create a new one or if you're using mixed sequences in a project, such as OfflineRT and DV.

Pen tools can edit locked item overlays can allow you to use keyframes and change opacities of video clips and levels of audio clips in tracks you have locked. Locked tracks are tracks of video or audio that you have put in a locked mode; you cannot edit these tracks or change them in any other way with the exception of this particular preference setting.

When capturing audio from a controllable deck for the purpose of synchronizing it with a video clip to create a merged clip (such as syncing sound from a DAT recorder used on the set while shooting film), audio sync can be ensured only if the audio deck is genlocked to a video capture interface connected to your computer. Turning on the Sync audio capture to video source if present option ensures that the sync of audio captured from a genlocked audio deck is accurate. You can genlock a deck to a video capture card by connecting them both to a black burst generator.

Report dropped frames during playback opens a dialog box to let you know that frames were dropped during a playback.

Abort ETT/PTV on dropped frames aborts Edit to Tape or Print to Video operations if the computer drops frames during playback.

Abort capture on dropped frames does just that. It stops the capture but saves all media captured to that point. All media with accurate timecode is saved, and a clip that references this media is saved in the Browser.

The On timecode break pop-up menu has three options to choose from when FCP encounters a timecode break during capture:

- Make New Clip is the default setting. It's new to Final Cut Pro 4. Video that has been captured is saved as a single clip with its Out point set to the last frame of video that has correct timecode. FCP then continues capturing past this break, giving the clip the same name you logged it to be, adding a dash and a number at the end. This is great for capturing whole tapes that might have timecode breaks. You can be assured that all clips captured have accurate timecode.

- Abort Capture stops the process when broken timecode is detected, saves the capture up to that point, and stops the capture process.

- Warn After Capture sets FCP to capture over a timecode break. New to Final Cut Pro 4, this option causes an incorrect timecode to be logged after any break in the code. This keeps you from later recapturing the clips with accuracy.

The Auto Render area of the General User Preferences is a new feature in FCP 4. You can set FCP to automatically begin rendering the sequence(s) you've selected through the pop-up menu, and you can select whether to include segments that contain real-time effects.

Labels

You can use the label settings, shown in Figure 2.4, in a number of ways. You can Ctrl-click a clip, a still image, or a sequence and change its icon display color in the Browser window. Here, you can change what the label color stands for by typing in the box next to the color. When you Ctrl-click a clip or other item in the Browser, you can select from the list of colored representations.

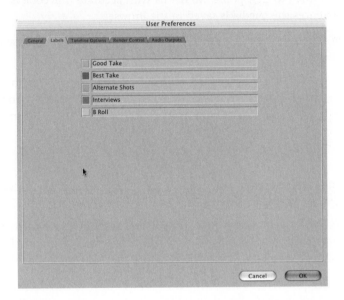

FIGURE 2.4   *The Labels tab.*

Timeline Options

Figure 2.5 shows the window for setting the way your default Timelines are displayed. You can also open this window with the current sequence settings displayed and editable from the Sequence menu. If you change the Timeline Options here, only *new* sequences will be created with these parameters. If you open a current sequence's settings, you can change its parameters by highlighting it in the Browser and pressing Cmd+0.

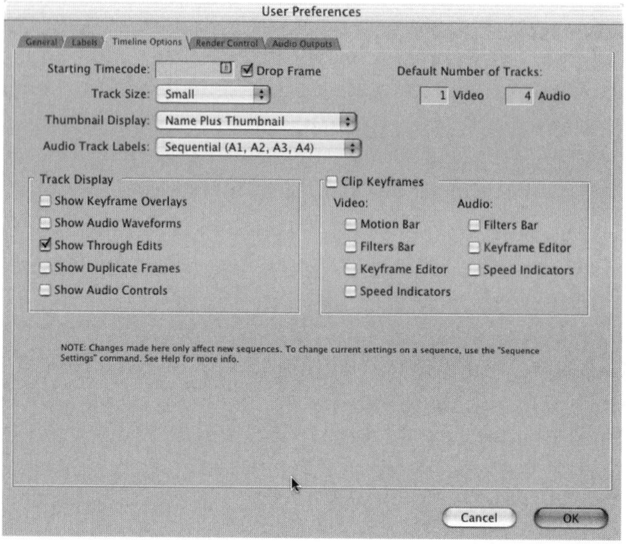

FIGURE 2.5   *The default Timeline Options.*

Starting Timecode provides a box to set the timecode numbering that is used in your sequences. This is handy when you need to have your program start at a given time-code. Many master tapes start at 00;58;30;00 to make room for bars and tone, slate, and black before the program starts at 1:00:00;00.

The Drop Frame check box determines whether the sequence uses drop or nondrop frame timecode. When you edit in NTSC, turning this on lets you determine how long a sequence actually lasts. It accounts for the fact that NTSC video plays at 29.97 frames per second (fps) and not 30fps. It doesn't drop frames; rather, it adjusts for this by dropping frame numbers.

Track Size provides a pop-up menu from which you can set a default track size width. Possible widths are Reduced, Small, Medium, and Large.

Thumbnail Display sets the options of displaying the name only, the name plus the thumbnail (a representative frame of what the clip contains), and a filmstrip display (which displays a set of stills throughout the Timeline).

Audio Track Labels offers two choices. Sequential simply numbers the tracks in order, and Paired labels the audio tracks in pairs such as A1a, A1b, A2a, and A2b. It makes sense to use these pairs if all your audio will be stereo.

Show Keyframe Overlays creates new sequences whose overlays are turned on. You can toggle this feature on and off by pressing Opt+W with any sequence in the Timeline window.

Show Audio Waveforms creates sequences whose audio waveforms appear in the audio clips. You can toggle this feature on and off by pressing Opt+Cmd+W with any sequence in your Timeline window.

Show Through Edits turns on or off the feature of displaying in the Timeline edits between consecutive frames within the same clip (see Figure 2.6). You can delete these edits to make a clip become whole-looking in the Timeline if you Ctrl-click this edit and choose Join Through Edit or select the edit and press Delete. The little triangles on either side of a through edit are red in the Timeline window.

The parameters for Show Duplicate Frames are set in the General User Preferences. This feature warns you if you've used frames more than once. (You might not want to repeat a shot.) If you see a duplicate frame line in a clip, you can Ctrl-click that clip and select Dupe Frames (X) and the clip name and instantly move the position indicator to the clip containing the duplication.

FIGURE 2.6
Red triangles displaying a through edit.

Show Audio Controls shows the solo (all tracks are muted except the selected track) and mute (turns off the sound of that particular track) buttons to the left of each audio track in the Timeline window. You also can turn these buttons on and off by toggling the speaker icon in the far-left corner of the Timeline window.

Clip Keyframes creates new sequences that open with additional space below each video and audio track. Within this new space, you can Ctrl-click to view, add, or modify keyframes set for any given clip for each of the parameters you specify. If these are checked, they are displayed under the clip that these keyframe events have been ascribed to. Within this box are check boxes for Motion Bar, Filters Bar, Keyframe Editor, and Speed Indicators. You can change the Timeline's display to show motion keyframes, filter keyframes, and others by Ctrl-clicking in the area under any clip. New to FCP 4, this feature allows you to adjust your clip's keyframes directly in the Timeline window.

Render Control

The Render Control tab in the User Preferences, shown in Figure 2.7, controls how FCP attempts to play back real-time and unrendered effects. It might be useful for workflow reasons not to render all effects or to render them with a lower resolution or frame rate. If the Filters, Frame Blending For Speed, and Motion Blur check boxes are not checked, FCP plays through any clips containing these effects without attempting to render these CPU-intensive effects in real time. The same can be said of the Frame Rate and Resolution pop-up menus. You can lower these settings to help with real-time playback of your sequence. Of course, if you render all these effects, these settings are ignored.

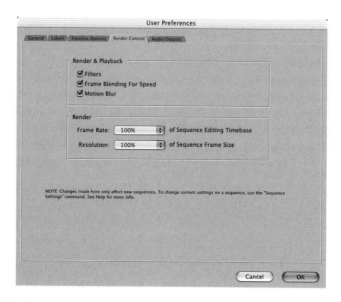

FIGURE 2.7   *The Render Control tab.*

Audio Outputs

The Audio Outputs tab, shown in Figure 2.8, is where you can select the number of audio tracks your system sends out. Depending on your audio hardware, you can select as many as 24 audio tracks. You need third-party audio cards to take advantage of this new feature in Final Cut Pro 4. Again, changing this setting from the User Preferences affects only new sequences created with any changes you've made. You can, however, change these settings on a current sequence by highlighting it in the Browser, pressing Cmd+0, and opening the sequence settings for that sequence.

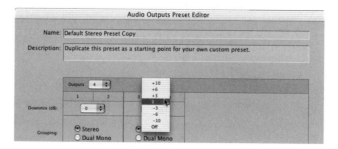

FIGURE 2.8   *The Preset Editor's interface set up for a four-track output.*

By duplicating the Default Stereo Preset, you can create a new preset containing your changes to the standard two-track output. Figure 2.8 shows the Preset Editor's interface set up for a four-track output. You can also downmix tracks (change their levels up or down at the same time).

Changing System Settings

The System Settings set of tabs is new to Final Cut Pro 4. It contains settings that affect how your computer is set up to operate Final Cut Pro. The first of the five tabs is Scratch Disks.

Scratch Disks

Figure 2.9 shows the first tab in the System Settings window. *Scratch disks* are disk drives and partitions that are selected for the storage of media files. Final Cut Pro 4 supports settings for up to 12 scratch disks at one time. Video files, audio files, and all render files can be set to be stored there. When the first disk is nearly full (as set in the Minimum Allowable Free Space On Scratch Disks box), the disk with the most available space is used next, and so on. It's recommended that you leave at least 50 to 100MB of any disk drive's capacity free.

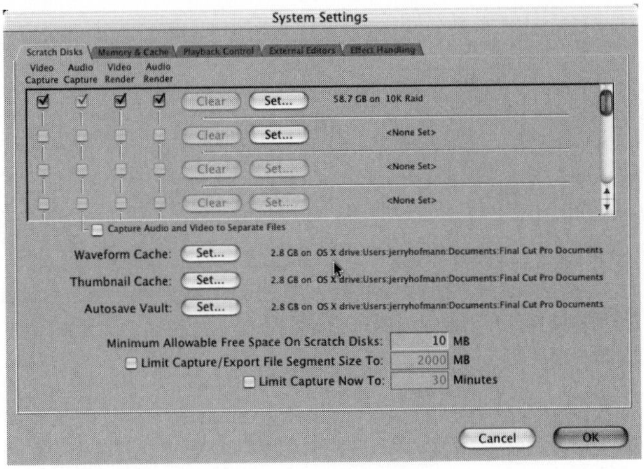

FIGURE 2.9   *The Scratch Disks tab.*

You can select a button in this window to capture audio and video to separate files. This might be useful if you will capture in low-resolution video but you intend to keep high-quality audio files that won't have to be captured again. This is called *offline editing*. Offline editing allows you to capture a lot more footage than you might otherwise be able to. When you are finished with your editing, you can simply recapture only the media that was used in your final sequence.

Waveform Cache refers to the place where you set the audio waveform files to be stored. The same is true of the Thumbnail Cache (frames of video used to display representative frames of clips in the Browser and Timeline) and Autosave Vault location (automatic saves of your project file). These three file types are best left away from the drives you intend to use for media files; typically, this is your startup disk. The reason is that they get rewritten often and might cause fragmentation on the disks you use for media files, thus affecting performance.

You can also limit the Capture/Export file segment size here (if you will send files to a system with file size limitations) and limit the Capture Now command (used in the Log and Capture window) to times and sizes. This might be a more efficient way to manage your media files. Setting a limit to your capture durations allows a large disk array to find the disk space required more efficiently.

note
If scratch disks are unmounted when you launch FCP, and they are specified in your scratch disk settings, Final Cut Pro 4 opens a dialog box allowing you to quit without changing these settings, reset scratch disk settings, or check again, allowing you to mount them (such as mounting a FireWire drive you forgot to mount before you launched Final Cut Pro).

Memory & Cache

Figure 2.10 shows the Memory & Cache tab. With this set of controls, you can control the amount of RAM assigned to Final Cut Pro, the Still Cache setting for RAM, and the Thumbnail Cache settings for disk and RAM.

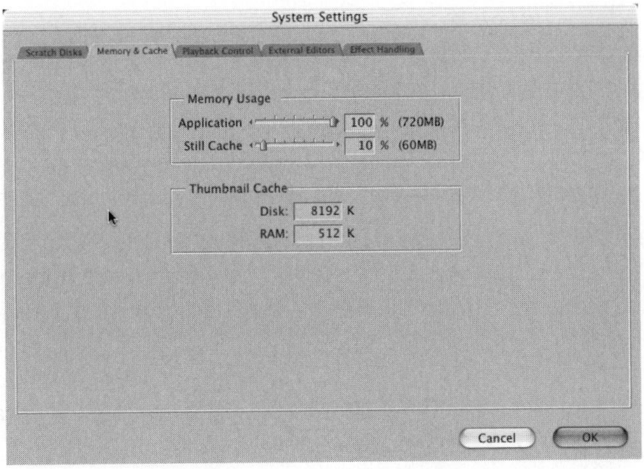

Figure 2.10   *The Memory & Cache tab.*

The total amount of RAM available is displayed on the far right of the first slider. Moving the sliders changes the amount of RAM used. By limiting the amount of RAM used by FCP, you can maintain performance by keeping Mac OS X from using virtual memory. This becomes more important if you are running multiple applications while running Final Cut Pro.

Adding still cache to your system lets you play back more frames of stills in real time with your system. Thumbnail Cache (for disk or RAM) sets the amount of memory used to store thumbnails, which are pictures of your clips viewed from the Browser or Timeline window. Raising the levels of this memory used keeps you from rebuilding them as often. After the levels are built, they are available instantly if you access them again. Sometimes you'll use a lot of thumbnails. You can achieve greater performance of their redisplay by using higher settings for thumbnail storage.

If you are not using a lot of stills, you might want to keep this setting lower and give more RAM resources to Final Cut Pro or another application you might be running.

Much the same can be said of adding disk cache for thumbnails and RAM. RAM stores these and retrieves them for viewing faster than setting this cache to be stored on disk. When your available RAM for thumbnails is used up, FCP begins storing them on your disk.

How much RAM your computer has dictates your optimal settings. Experimenting with these settings in your workflow will reveal the optimal settings for your computer setup. But there's no doubt that more RAM on your machine improves your system's overall performance.

Playback Control Settings

The Playback Control settings, shown in Figure 2.11, are yet another way to set up your system for real-time playback parameters. They are split into two sections—Playback and Record. These settings are system-wide (as opposed to the ones selected in the Render Control tab found in the User Preferences) and affect all sequences played back in your system. With these settings, you decide whether it's more important to play back with higher quality or to play back more real-time effects at the same time.

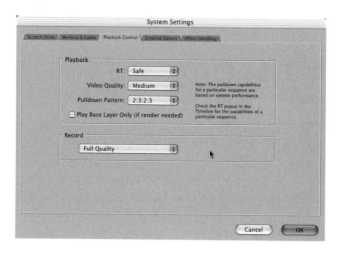

FIGURE 2.11   *The Playback Control tab.*

If you select Unlimited from the RT pop-up menu and set Video Quality to High, you ensure the highest playback quality for your video, but you might not be able to play back as many real-time effects reliably, for example. You can change these settings at any time and experiment with them to see what works best for your particular workflow and computer.

Beneath these pop-up menus is another menu to select a pull-down pattern. These settings are for use when you are editing a 23.976fps timebase and you want to send 29.97fps out the FireWire for recording or viewing on an external video monitor but you want to edit using the 23.98fps your camera records. If you have a DV device that records at 23.976, you need to select one of these pull-down patterns for proper playback at 29.97fps.

You can either select Full Quality as the Record setting or match the setting used in the Playback section. If you select Full Quality, you might have to render some of your effects for a reliable recording to take place without dropping frames. If you choose to match the Playback settings, recordings will follow the parameters you've set in the Playback settings (which might be fine for offline preview tapes, for example).

Experimenting with your particular computer setup is key here. You'll find your optimal setting by trying different settings and seeing which one suits your particular needs or workflow.

External Editors

With the External Editors tab, shown in Figure 2.12, you can set which other applications (any third-party application, in fact) open upon command to edit stills, video files, and audio files, as well as open LiveType files, Apple's new animated titling program, from within Final Cut Pro.

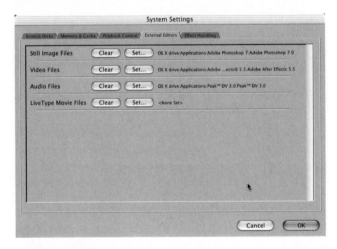

FIGURE 2.12   *The External Editors tab.*

To designate an application as an "editing" application for the different types of media files you might be working with, you simply click the Set button to navigate to it.

To open one of your clips in the assigned program ready for alteration, simply Ctrl-click it and select Open in Editor. The clip opens in the appropriate application for further alteration. You might want to open a still image in Photoshop, for example.

The great thing about this new feature is that when you are finished modifying the clip or still you've edited in the other application, the saved changes can be imported into Final Cut Pro and are applied to all the clips in your project that reference this altered media file. It's great for streamlining a process you need to do to an audio track or video image.

Effect Handling

Part of Final Cut Pro's RT Extreme's new open architecture allows you to set the system to use RT Extreme for computation of real-time effects (Final Cut Pro), or you can select another device, possibly to handle your real-time effects (see Figure 2.13).

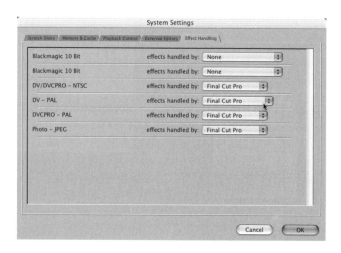

FIGURE 2.13   *The Effect Handling tab.*

Each codec can be assigned its own handler for real-time effects with the Effect Handling settings. Do you want Final Cut Pro to use its own code for real-time effects handling, or do you want to use your video board or capture card's possible real-time effects?

If your capture card can perform any real-time effects for a given codec you have installed, this shows up in the pop-up menu next to the codec's name. You should check with your card's manufacturer for the specifics of what that particular card can do. Many times a new software driver release for a capture card unleashes new real-time effects, so it's best to consult with the maker of your hardware card to keep up to date.

Changing Settings Using the Audio/Video Settings

Before you start a new project, you need to tell Final Cut Pro what format of material you are going to work with so that it can operate properly. The shortcut command is Opt+Cmd+Q.

You can change your presets or create a custom setup from the Audio/Video Settings. The Summary window, shown in Figure 2.14, is always presented first; it summarizes the settings you are currently running. Notice that at the bottom of this window you can select the summary of settings you want to save as an Easy Setup.

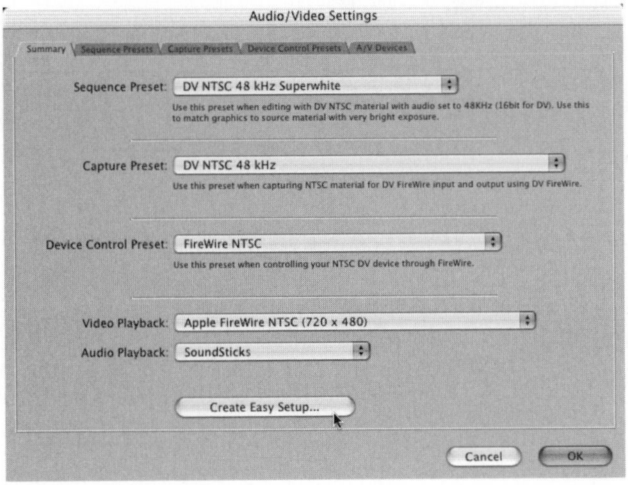

FIGURE 2.14   *The Audio/Video Settings Summary tab.*

The setting displayed in Figure 2.14 is a typical setup for DV NTSC editing with a DV camera or source deck attached to your Mac with a FireWire cable.

Notice that the names next to the pop-up menus here match the names of the four other tabs across the top. You click the button at the bottom to create Easy Setups. After you've been through the four other windows and (possibly) have created a new and custom preset, you can come back to this screen, check the summary to make sure it is correct, and create and name a new Easy Setup if necessary.

If you created custom setups for any of the four settings, you will see its name in the appropriate pop-up menu here in the Summary window. If you are working in DV NTSC, Figure 2.14 is the correct setting for most Sony FireWire-controlled equipment.

Sequence Presets

You can create custom setups for each of the categories by clicking the appropriate tab. The Sequence Presets tab is shown in Figure 2.15.

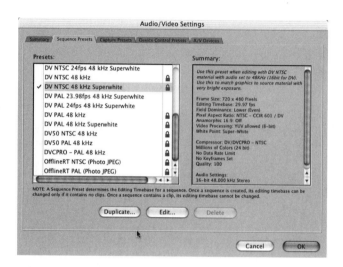

FIGURE 2.15   *The Sequence Presets tab.*

Nine different sequence presets are included with the software. They appear in the white box on the left. Notice that these presets have closed locks. This means that they are "standard" presets that cannot be edited directly. You can duplicate and edit these presets by clicking the Duplicate button in the bottom area of the window. After you have saved a custom sequence preset, it appears in the list on the left. If you make a mistake or you want to create a slightly different setup, you can edit these new presets—they are not locked.

Also notice the check mark next to the DV NTSC 48 kHz Superwhite preset. This check mark shows which default preset you are working with. You can change this default preset by clicking in the blank column next to its name. Many editors like to use multiple sequences while they work. If you tell Final Cut Pro to create a new sequence, the one with the check mark is the default sequence format that is created. This is important to understand if you have selected the option not to prompt for new settings upon creation of a new sequence in the General User Settings window. If you have selected for this prompt to happen, all saved presets show up on the resulting prompting window's pop-up menu.

The summary of each preset is contained in a gray box on the right. Click each preset to see its summary. Each preset has a combination of settings suitable for a specific use: frame size, codec and frame rate, and more.

tip

It's best to set your sequence presets to as high a quality as possible even if you will deliver in a multimedia format or a stream for the Internet. You should edit in your native format and then process the appropriate compression after editing is complete. If you've shot DV, for example, edit in the DV format you shot in (NTSC or PAL) and use the appropriate and "matching" sequence preset.

If you highlight the DV NTSC 48 kHz preset and then click the Duplicate button near the bottom of this window, the Sequence Preset Editor opens, as shown in Figure 2.16. Here you can create custom sequence settings. For example, suppose you have video from DV sources, but all your audio was recorded at 41.1kHz. A "standard" 48kHz setting might tax your computer, because it needs to "up-convert" the native 41.1kHz audio to 48kHz to play it back in a DV NTSC or PAL 48kHz "standard" setting. You can relieve this computer overhead by setting up a 41.1kHz sequence setting during the editing process.

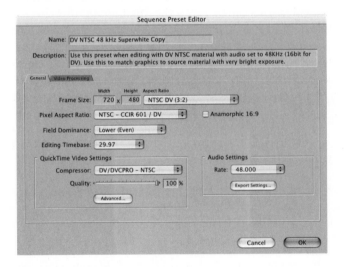

FIGURE 2.16   *The Sequence Preset Editor.*

Creating a Custom Sequence Preset

When creating a custom sequence preset, the first thing to do is give it a new name by typing it in the Name field. The Description field provides a place for a more-detailed description. Take a moment to investigate the pop-up menus on this screen to see which parameters you can change. There are a lot of them. Note that by checking the Anamorphic 16:9 check box, you can create a 16:9 anamorphic setup.

Many cameras shoot in this relatively new format. You can view a widescreen format on newer widescreen TV sets. The aspect ratio of what is viewed on the sets that we all are familiar with is 4:3—that is, four units wide and three units tall. Anamorphic 16:9 video stretches this picture so that squeezing it produces this new widescreeen aspect ratio.

Here's a list of the most common video frame sizes:

- 640×480—A 4:3 ratio for square pixel multimedia video.
- 720×480—A 4:3 nonsquare pixel video frame size used for DV-NTSC video. This can be 16:9 if the Anamorphic 16:9 check box is checked. The pixel count does not change.
- 720×486—A 4:3 nonsquare pixel video frame size used for standard CCIR 601-NTSC video. This can be 16:9 if the Anamorphic 16:9 check box is checked. The pixel count does not change. This requires additional hardware.
- 720×576—A 4:3 nonsquare pixel video frame size used for CCIR 601-PAL or DV-PAL video. This can be 16:9 if the anamorphic 16:9 check box is checked. The pixel count does not change. This requires additional hardware.
- 1280×720—A 16:9 square pixel resolution used for HDTV 720p. It requires additional hardware.
- 1920×1080—A 16:9 higher square pixel resolution used for HDTV 1080i. It requires additional hardware.

The 16:9 aspect ratio is the standard aspect ratio that HDTV uses. It gives the pictures a more "cinematic" look. It also does not crop the films we've enjoyed over the years in movie theaters. Soon, this 16:9 aspect ratio will be the standard that we all accept as normal, and the 4:3 ratio will go the way of the rounded TV screens of the early 1950s.

You can change frame size, pixel aspect ratios, field dominance, editing timebase, and compressors for the video side of things. The video has an Advanced button to add even more options. The QuickTime audio settings can be changed here as well. Figure 2.17 shows the video settings, and Figure 2.18 shows the sound export settings.

The Sequence Preset Editor has two tabs: General and Video Processing (see Figure 2.19).

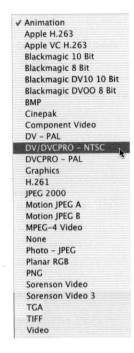

✓ Animation
Apple H.263
Apple VC H.263
Blackmagic 10 Bit
Blackmagic 8 Bit
Blackmagic DV10 10 Bit
Blackmagic DVOO 8 Bit
BMP
Cinepak
Component Video
DV – PAL
DV/DVCPRO – NTSC
DVCPRO – PAL
Graphics
H.261
JPEG 2000
Motion JPEG A
Motion JPEG B
MPEG–4 Video
None
Photo – JPEG
Planar RGB
PNG
Sorenson Video
Sorenson Video 3
TGA
TIFF
Video

8.000
11.025
16.000
22.050
24.000
32.000
44.100
✓ 48.000

FIGURE 2.17
The advanced video settings.

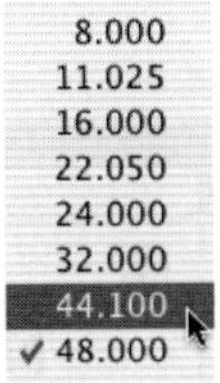

FIGURE 2.18
The sound settings.

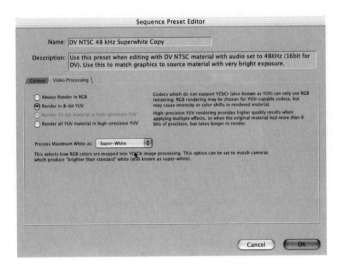

FIGURE 2.19   *The Video Processing tab.*

If the codec you are using (such as the DV NTSC codec) supports the YUV color space, you have options here to select RGB or YUV. A *codec* describes the compression/decompression extension used with QuickTime to allow Final Cut Pro to capture, play back, and record to tape different video file formats. These files can have different amounts of compression applied to them. The more the file is compressed, the smaller the file size, but also the lower the video quality. Uncompressed video is the highest quality and can be edited with Final Cut Pro and the appropriate additional hardware.

When Always Render in RGB is enabled, you force the rendering to happen in this color space instead of in YUV. The reasoning is that the renders of the two types of color space are slightly different. This option might cause subtle color changes in your rendered material. Use this option if you want to accomplish a specific compositing task and you think color clamping in the RGB color space might give you a better result than if you used the straight YUV color space. For example, if you are adding filters (such as those supplied by After Effects) that render only in RGB, you might want to add Final Cut Pro filters (which process in the YUV color space) to the same clips, thereby keeping the look of the renders the same.

When you're editing DV, the Always Render in RGB box should usually remain disabled. When it is enabled, renders of DV video change the look of the original video. If your capture card doesn't support YUV rendering, you don't have the Always Render in RGB option.

The other options in the Video Processing tab are as follows:

- Always Render in RGB forces codecs that normally process color using the YUV color space to process using the RGB color space instead. If selected, this option cause subtle changes in color in your rendered material. If the video capture codec you're using doesn't support YUV rendering, this option is unavailable. Use this option if you want to accomplish a specific compositing task and you think color clamping in the RGB color space might give you a preferred result over using the straight YUV color space. For example, if you're mixing After Effects filters, which process in RGB color space, with Final Cut Pro filters, which process in YUV color space, choosing this option ensures a consistent look.

- Render in 8-bit YUV enables 8-bit rendering using the YUV color space. This is the setting for footage captured from DV-25 source material, such as mini DV and DVCAM tape, or with third-party capture cards that capture 8-bit video in the YUV color space using an appropriate YUV-compatible codec such as cards sold by Aurora Video Systems or the Kona SD card from AJA.

- Render 10-bit material in high-precision YUV enables 10-bit rendering using the YUV color space. This is appropriate for footage captured from third-party capture cards that support capturing 10-bit video in the YUV color space using an appropriate YUV-compatible codec, such as AJA's Io or Kona SD card.

Third-party capture cards capable of 10-bit YUV video let you capture clips with much more color detail, as well as with greater contrast ratios from blacks to whites, than do 8-bit sources. Final Cut Pro can capture and output from such a card using this higher level of quality. Selecting this option allows certain effects such as transitions and filters to be rendered at this quality.

- Render all YUV material in high-precision YUV enables 10-bit rendering even when you use 8-bit source clips. Sometimes, such as when you apply multiple filters to a clip, a higher bit depth improves the quality of the rendered file even though the original clip has only 8 bits of color information. The trade-off is that 10-bit rendering is slower than 8-bit rendering. Selecting this option improves the quality of rendered effects that support 10-bit precision.

The pop-up menu near the center of the window allows you to change the process that Final Cut Pro uses with whites. DV camcorders can record whites higher than 100 IRE—the brightest "legal" measure of the video signal shown on a waveform monitor. These levels above 100 IRE are called *SuperWhite,* and they are brighter than what is legal. If you intend to broadcast your video, it's recommended that you use the other available setting here: White. The White setting ensures that all your video renders are broadcast-legal, effectively limiting the luminance to 100 IRE. Your existing footage will not change and will still be at whatever level it was shot at. If your levels then are higher than 100 IRE, you would see a shift in luminance when the render file played back. IRE stands for the measurements of these signals as set by the Institute of Radio Engineers.

Camera Masters Shot at Higher Than 100 IRE

If your material was shot in DV and you have white levels higher than 100 IRE, I recommend using the SuperWhite setting to avoid clamping and getting sudden changes until you have achieved picture lock or close to it. During color correcting within Final Cut Pro, *picture lock* is achieved when few changes will be made to the video tracks. Any rendering done then will be part of a correction process toward the end of your workflow. This effectively keeps any shifts of luminance that show up during any part of the process at the same time.

As part of the color correction/legal video pass, you also can nest the sequence and apply a Broadcast Safe filter to the nest.

After you've set up the new preset, click the OK button. If you add a capture card, the card manufacturer supplies a new preset, which shows up in the Sequence Preset window after installation.

The Capture Presets Tab

The Capture Presets tab is shown in Figure 2.20. It looks similar to the Sequence Preset tab. It opens with locked presets that determine how you control the capture of your media. Two are for DV (NTSC and PAL), two are for OfflineRT (NTSC and PAL), and one is a Generic Capture Template (used to create custom presets).

tip

If a preset is not selected as a default, the Delete button becomes active. You cannot delete a locked preset.

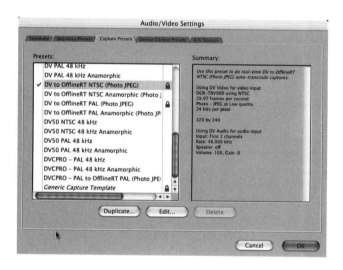

FIGURE 2.20   *The Capture Presets tab.*

note   It's recommended that you capture your media with the highest quality you can and compress it later for delivery in multimedia formats. The idea is to process all your material in as high a quality as you can for as long as you can until you finally have to create the lower-resolution pictures and sound, which should be the last thing you do.

The Capture Presets tab works much the same as the Sequence Presets tab. You must duplicate the locked "standard" settings to create custom ones. The check marks set the default setting, and the Summary on the right summarizes the settings of the highlighted preset. A Generic Capture preset is available for this purpose, but you can duplicate the locked ones you start with as well and customize them.

If you choose the DV NTSC 48 kHz preset and click the Duplicate button, the Capture Preset Editor window opens, as shown in Figure 2.21. You can change the name to better explain what the preset is. You can also type in the Description box a new description that might include the new feature of hearing the audio through your computer's speakers when viewing tapes with Final Cut Pro, for example. In this Editor window, you can change all the properties that make up a digital video file.

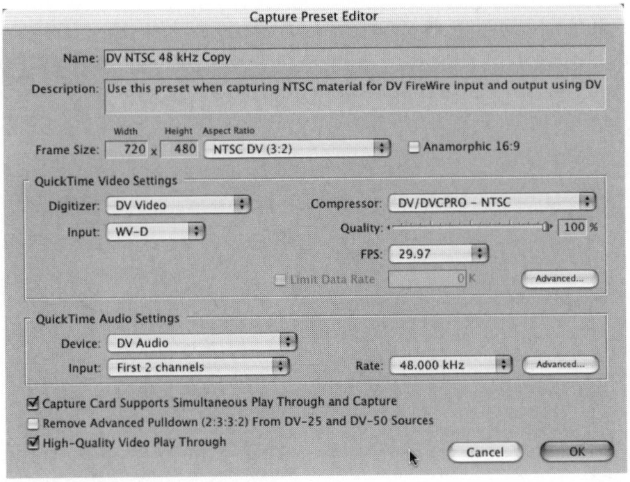

FIGURE 2.21   *The Capture Preset Editor window.*

Investigate the pull-down menus to look at all the options. You see many of the same options found in the Sequence Preset Editor window. More-detailed information about all these settings is available in the Final Cut Pro Help that comes with your software.

One QuickTime Audio setting that needs looking into is Rate (the record setting in kHz). Many cameras can record in more than one kHz setting. If you record material in the 12-bit recording mode, you need to change the standard setting of 48kHz to 32kHz. If you have recorded at the 16-bit setting, you use the 48kHz capture setting. This is especially important with DV material. If you mismatch these settings, your media that contains audio will have popping sounds and audio that drifts out of sync with clips that have synchronized audio and video. Even though you might have recorded in 12-bit mode with your camera, you should set the Audio kHz Rate setting to 16-bit 32kHz, because no 12-bit depth recording rate is available in Final Cut Pro.

Whatever settings you choose, they should match your sequence settings; otherwise, you'll have to render each edit as you place it in the Timeline. Again, if you have installed a capture card, the manufacturer will have supplied presets appropriate for the use of that card, its codecs employed, frame sizes, and QuickTime Audio Settings.

Note that an Anamorphic check box is available in the event you've shot in an anamorphic version of one of the sequence presets. The Anamorphic check box on the footage is automatically tagged as Anamorphic on capture.

Device Control Presets

The Device Control Presets tab, shown in Figure 2.22, sets up the deck control protocol you're getting ready to control your video device with, such as a camera or deck. Different machines use different control settings, and you might need to consult your deck's manual to find out which one it uses so that you can control your source machine or camera. Apple lists the compatible devices on its web site at `http://www.apple.com/finalcutpro/qualification.html`. It's recommended that you consult this web page before you buy a camera or deck to determine whether it will work with Final Cut Pro, but most do.

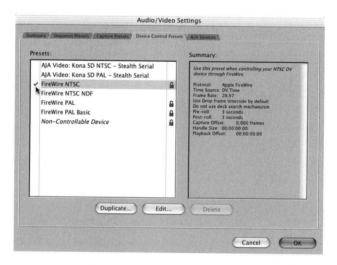

FIGURE 2.22   *The Device Control Presets tab.*

Notice that four standard presets are locked: FireWire NTSC, FireWire PAL, FireWire PAL Basic, and Non-Controllable Device. Each can be duplicated and its copies edited to suit your particular deck or camera's needs. Non-Controllable Device is used when you cannot control the source deck or camera. It allows you to capture video from a deck such as a consumer VHS machine or any other device that cannot be controlled by your Final Cut Pro setup, and devices that do not have timecode recorded on their source material.

If you have a FireWire-connected DV camera, you will probably use NTSC or PAL. However, if you are using certain DV cameras, you might have to duplicate this setting and make changes accordingly. For example, some cameras use a FireWire Basic setting. Apple's device qualification list lets you know how to set up these special cases. This list is accessible from the Final Cut Pro website (`www.apple.com/finalcutpro/ qualification`). Some devices need extra scripts that can be added easily. Consult the list of qualified devices at the Final Cut Pro website.

If you click the Duplicate button on the FireWire NTSC setting, you see the Device Control Preset Editor, shown in Figure 2.23. You can rename this new preset, give it a description, and change its protocol.

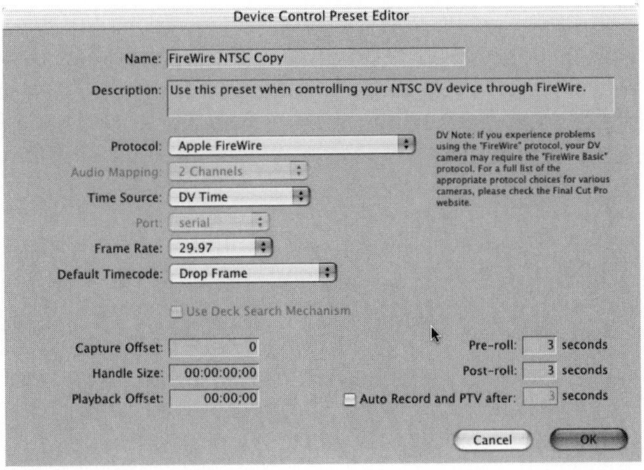

FIGURE 2.23   *The Device Control Preset Editor.*

You can reset frame rates, specify a default timecode, and more to match the source device (a camera or videotape machine). Refer to the manual that came with your video device for more information on what type of control it uses. Many Sony machines use RS-422 controls, but most DV decks use one of two FireWire controls you'll find here (see Figure 2.24).

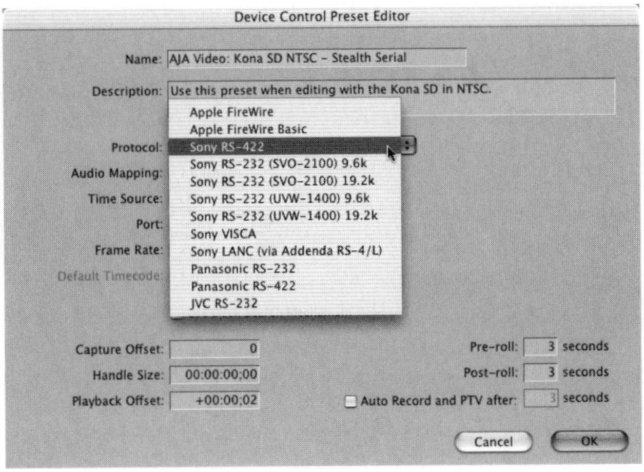

FIGURE 2.24   *RS-422 control.*

When you use a serial control such as RS-422, you might have to account for a time-code capture offset. You do this by obtaining a source tape that has a window burn of timecode that matches its actual timecode, or display of the true timecode associated with the tape superimposed on the picture. Some videotape machines do this by digitizing a video signal with the machine's "Super" output. When you capture this material with this window burn, you might see a slight discrepancy of a few frames between the true timecode on the tape (as seen in the window burn) and what Final Cut Pro reports as the source's timecode. If so (and this is very likely to happen), you can adjust for this discrepancy in the Capture Offset box in the Device Control Preset Editor.

You need a serial adapter for your Mac to control videotape or audio source and record machines with RS-422 or RS-232 remote control capability. Consult your owner's manual for the exact specifications your machine uses. A company called Gee Three sells a great solution for this adapter (http://www.geethree.com). Gee Three calls this a Stealth Port. If you are using a PowerBook, you need a USB serial adapter for serial control. Keyspan (http://www.keyspan.com) sells these adapters. Some capture cards include a serial port for control as well. If they do, the port they supply is listed in the white box of the Device Control Presets tab.

You can also change the standard pre- and post-roll settings with the Device Control Preset Editor for your machine. This becomes important in certain cases. It's much easier to successfully capture video from a videotape machine or camera with a bit of pre-roll. *Pre-roll* means that the source device is given time to start rolling and getting up to speed with stability before the capture process really starts and you are creating a media file. You usually need at least 3 seconds for this to take place, and timecode breaks cannot exist in the timecode during this pre-roll. Thus, if you have material at 00:5:00:00, you must have consecutive timecode before that number. The camera or deck needs to find timecode number 00:4:57:00 and have no break of timecode between this number and the rest of your clip. Otherwise, the timecode that is recorded for that clip will be incorrect and could cause you headaches later if you need to recapture the material.

If you have material at 0:00:00:00 (the start of a tape), you will not be able to capture much before 0:00:03:00. Keep this in mind when you shoot a new tape. Workarounds are available. If you must have this material, you can capture without logging the clip using Capture Now, but it's better to have recorded a bit of video at the start of a tape that you know you will not use and to have reserved this material for pre-roll time. Recording color bars here is your best bet, but rolling your camera on any unneeded material works as well.

tip   Keep in mind that the head of the tape gets extra wear because it's loaded and unloaded into videotape devices more often. Keeping usable material from this area of the tape is a good idea for this reason alone.

The A/V Devices Tab

The last tab in the Audio/Video Settings is the A/V Devices tab, as shown in Figure 2.25.

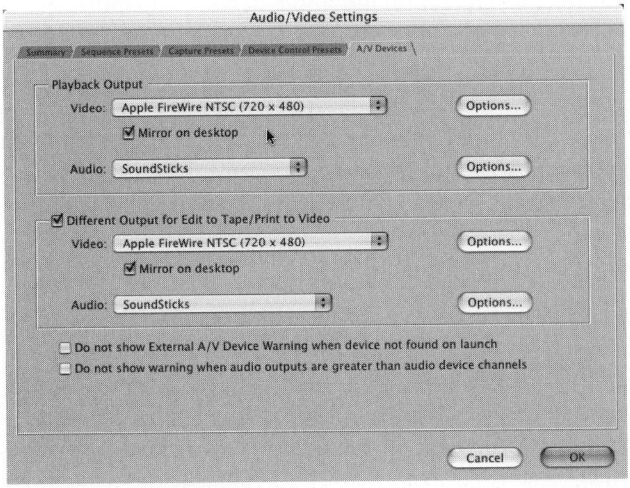

FIGURE 2.25   *The A/V Devices tab.*

On the A/V Devices tab, you can set up how your system views playback externally on a video monitor. You also can set up a different pathway out of your computer for recording video externally. If your system is set up to edit any of the DV formats, you should select Apple FireWire (NTSC or PAL). Additionally, you can click the option to set up a Different Output for Edit to Tape/Print to Video.

These two major areas of the A/V Devices settings can be independent of each other. For example, you might want to view your video externally during playback but monitor your audio with your computer's speakers. When you are ready to record, you will want different settings so that your audio is sent out the FireWire port or capture card set up to record to your tape with the video.

Two Mirror on desktop check boxes are on this screen as well. Clicking either check box allows the video to run on your computer's display at the same time you are viewing your video externally or recording it to tape with the Edit to Tape or Print to Video functions. If these check boxes are checked, you see the video play back in both places. This is handy if you cannot see the "client monitor" at the same time you are operating your system.

This option taxes your computer, so experimenting with slower systems might be in order to make sure that your Mac can do this without stutters, especially if you depend on RT Extreme to send out real-time effects during the recording process. Turning off Mirror on desktop relieves your computer's overhead during the recording and playback process.

If you have a third-party capture card, its audio and video outputs show up as an option in the pop-up menus as well.

Two selectable options appear at the bottom of the A/V Devices window. The first instructs FCP not to warn you if an A/V device is not found upon launching FCP. The second allows you to defeat the warning that audio outputs are greater than the audio device channels available.

Workshop 2: Investigate the Settings

Take some time now to go through the settings on your own system. You might even read back through this chapter as you open the different windows. After you have a handle on these settings, your whole experience with Final Cut Pro will be enhanced greatly. Many folks have a tough time with this part of the learning curve. It's essential for you to understand the basics of this area of the software.

Let's set up a capture setting that allows you to hear the audio recorded on a source tape through the Log and Capture window while you view, log, and capture video from a DV source. Otherwise, you'll be able to hear the audio playback of your tape only externally when capturing and logging your clips later.

1. Make sure your DV camera is connected to your system via a FireWire cable and is turned on. If it is not, close Final Cut Pro, connect your DV device, and restart the application.

2. Open your Audio/Video settings from the Final Cut Pro menu, or press Opt+Cmd+Q.

3. Click the Capture Presets tab.

4. Click the Duplicate button for DV NTSC 48 kHz or DV PAL 48 kHz to open the Capture Preset Editor.

5. Rename this preset DV NTSC 48 kHz (or DV PAL 48 kHz) Hear Audio.

6. In the Capture Preset Editor window, in the QuickTime Audio Settings section, click the Advanced button. This opens the Advanced Sound Settings dialog box.

7. On the right is a Speaker pop-up menu. Click it, and set the speaker to On. Then click OK.

8. Click OK in the Capture Preset Editor window. Notice that this setting is now available on the Capture Presets tab.

9. Click the Summary tab. Take a look at the pop-up menu next to Capture Preset; your new setting is in the list.

10. You can take this a step further. Select the new preset from the Capture Preset pop-up menu. Create an Easy Setup for it by clicking the Create Easy Setup button.

Using this preset in the future will allow you to hear audio playback while viewing source videotapes with DV captures. Creating your own custom presets is as easy as this one was. As soon as you have a handle on this area of the software, the most technical end of your learning curve is over.

CHAPTER 3

Understanding Final Cut Pro's Interface: An Overview

- Activating Windows
- The Browser Window
- The Viewer Window
- The Canvas Window
- The Timeline Window
- The Tool Palette
- Workshop 3: Load the First Project and Become Familiar with the Navigational Controls and Window Arrangement

Activating Windows

Clicking various windows activates them. The Canvas and Timeline activation commands and some of the commands in the drop-down menus across the top are gray and unavailable if the proper window is not activated. You can see which window is active by looking at the title bar at the top of each window. The activated window has a lighter gray color in its header than the other windows' headers.

A great way to activate any of the four major windows is to use the appropriate keyboard shortcut:

- +1 activates the Viewer window.
- +2 activates the Canvas window.
- +3 activates the Timeline window.
- +4 activates the Browser window.

What you do in each window can affect what happens in another. Figure 3.1 shows an alternative view of the interface, created by simply dragging the four windows around and resizing them accordingly.

FIGURE 3.1   *The four major windows.*

The first window we'll discuss in greater detail is the Browser window, which you can see by pressing   +4.

The Browser Window

The Browser window, shown in Figure 3.2, is where you organize your source material and keep your edited sequences. It's a visual list of records that is displayed as icons next to names. This window also contains information about your source material and your edit decisions. These records are not the media files; they are pointer files to the separate media files you have captured, digitized, or copied into your computer's hard drives for use in your project.

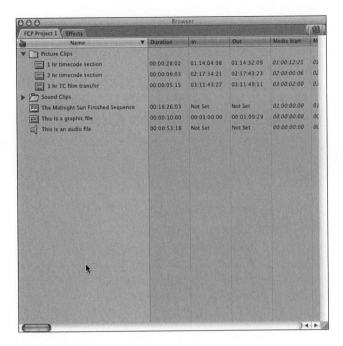

FIGURE 3.2   *The Browser window.*

The Browser window stores a reference file to every element your project contains. You'll probably also end up storing elements you didn't use in your finished program here. You drag these clips around the interface to move shots or elements into your edited program.

There are two tabs in the most basic setup of this window. One is the Project tab (named "FCP Project 1" in Figure 3.2), which contains the pointer files, and the other is the Effects tab, which contains a logically sorted list of available effects. If the Effects tab is not present, you can activate it from the menus by selecting Window, Effects or by pressing   +5. You can bring it forward in the Browser by clicking its tab (see Figure 3.3). Your project will have its own tab at the top of this window.

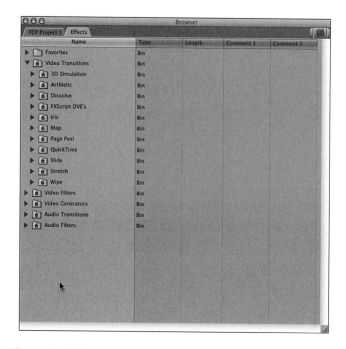

FIGURE 3.3 *The Effects tab in the Browser window.*

You can have as many projects open at the same time as you want, and you can edit between them. You can close these tabs by Ctrl-clicking (click while holding down the Ctrl key) the tab and invoking the Close Tab command (see Figure 3.4). The Close Tab menu is just one of many pop-up context menus that are available in many places around the interface. We'll explore them as we edit our movie. You can close the whole Browser window by clicking the button in the upper-left corner.

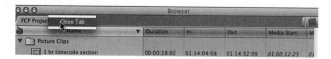

FIGURE 3.4 *The Close Tab menu.*

Types of Reference Files

Many types of elements are contained in the Browser window, as shown in Figure 3.5. Each element has its own icon (the little picture to the left of the clip name). An audio-only clip (the little speaker), a graphic clip (the little square with ABC on it), and a still frame of video each has its own icon, giving you a visual reference as to what type of element it is.

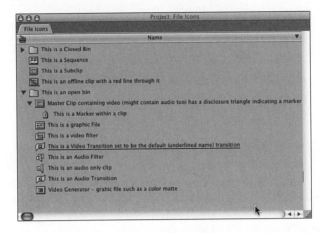

FIGURE 3.5 *The Browser window with all types of elements referenced in Final Cut Pro.*

Clips are reference files that reference individual moving picture, still, and/or sound elements such as QuickTime files, CD audio files, and still frames. Master clips have square icons. These square clips contain video and might or might not contain audio. If they do contain audio, it is usually the sound that was recorded at the same time the pictures were recorded (sync sound).

There is a way to "marry" an audio clip to a video clip. New to FCP 4 is the ability to merge clips. A *merged clip* is typically an audio file you've "married" to a video file. You can merge as many as 24 audio tracks to a single video file, for example. A great use of this feature is to sync your sound to a video clip, such as in the case of a film shoot where you've recorded audio on a DAT machine. When you edit with a merged clip, the synchronized audio and video act as if it was a single media file. You can merge up to 24 different audio tracks to one another without a video track.

To merge a clip, highlight the video (or audio) clip in the Browser and an audio clip you find useful for a merge, and Ctrl-click one of the two or more selected clips. The Merge Clips window opens, as shown in Figure 3.6. Select the appropriate method for FCP to merge the clips, and click OK. Final Cut Pro creates a new clip that, when opened, acts like a single audio/video file. It also renames this new clip with the video file's name with the word "merged" added to the end. In the case of merging only audio clips, the topmost clip's name is used, with the word "merged" added to the end.

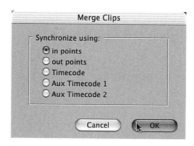

Figure 3.6   *The Merge Clips dialog box.*

After they are created, the only change you can make to these clips is a subframe audio slip. A way to re-create a merged clip is to edit it into a sequence and then delete the original merged clip in the Browser. Then, unlink the items in the Timeline and make any sync changes. (To unlink clips in the Timeline, use the toggle button in the top-right area of the Timeline window, or press Shift+L.) Relink the clips (just click the linking button again or press Shift+L) and then drag them back into the Browser from the Timeline to create a new merged clip.

Sequences contain these clips, all your edit decisions, and your finished program. A sequence icon is a box with yellow and blue boxes within it. You can create as many sequences and clips as you want. This comes in handy for different edited versions of the same material or different areas of your finished programs. You can use multiple sequences in many other ways, such as for a series of similar shots or a sequence for each scene of your feature film.

You can edit from sequence to sequence too, not just from clips. One way is to copy and paste a clip or set of clips between sequences. You can even add an entire sequence to another sequence by dragging its icon to the other sequence in the Timeline window, creating a nest. A *nest* appears to be a single clip, but it contains the contents of its source sequence. It's similar to what After Effects calls a *precomposition* and similar to what happens in Avid when you *collapse* a sequence. When you add an entire sequence by dragging its icon to another sequence, you see a single clip, but if you double-click this nested clip, its source sequence of clips opens in the Timeline window. Any changes made to this source sequence are reflected in the nested clip that is contained in the sequence you add it to.

A *subclip* is a portion of a clip you've set apart as an element you can quickly access. For example, this could be a single shot from a media file or a *master clip* (any original media file) that began as an entire tape with many shots. The subclip icon has serrated edges. You can make subclips from subclips. You can make subclips from audio-only clips, but their icons remain the same as what the audio-only master clip uses (the speaker icon). We'll use subclips extensively as we edit the film.

When clips are offline, they have a red line through them. *Offline* in this context means that no picture or sound files (media files) connect to them.

The rest of the icons are as follows (see Figure 3.5):

- Video transition—An effect between clips, such as a dissolve
- Audio transition—An effect between audio clips, such as a fade or audio dissolve
- Video filter—An effect applied to a video clip
- Audio filter—An effect applied to an audio clip
- Video generator—Effects that Final Cut Pro makes, such as to a title or color bar
- Marker—A reference point within a clip
- Graphic file—Pict files or tiffs are examples
- Audio-only clip—Contains no video

The Browser window also can contain *bins*. They are represented by blue folders that can contain clips, sequences, subclips, or even more bins to reduce clutter and organize your source material.

Also notice in Figure 3.5 the little triangles next to the bins and one of the master clips. These collapsible triangles, called *disclosure triangles,* open and close the bins or open and close the list of markers contained in a clip or subclip. Triangles that point down are open. Triangles that point toward the icon are closed. The bin or clip closes and opens another area for viewing items simultaneously. To open and close them, simply click them.

You can have as many sequences and clips stored in the Browser window as you want, but for good order, you should store clips in a logical bin structure. The icons are actually buttons you click to command Final Cut Pro to call up the media files to play for you in the Viewer window or Canvas window. (See the sections "The Viewer Window" and "The Canvas Window.") If you click the names of these items, you can type a name for them. When clicking the icon of these files, you can drag them or open them in the Viewer, Canvas, and Timeline windows.

This entire display of references (clips, sequences, and effects), as stored and displayed in the Browser window and project settings, comprises the content of the project file. Because the project files are only text files, you can easily back them up on all sorts of different media *away* from the computer. A large project file might be 15MB in size. Backup has to be a way of life for intensive work such as editing. You definitely don't want to lose the log or the editing that's been done. It's a great habit to back up your project file at the end of each session on media that can be stored away from the computer.

The Importance of Backing Up Your Project File

A word to the wise: More than one editor has lost his job because he failed to back up his project file. Think of what could happen if you edited something for months and then lost the use of your project file. I never want to be in that position, and I'm sure you don't either. Disaster happens from time to time during the life of any nonlinear editor (NLE), so don't get caught on this one. Backing up is absolutely the most important computer chore for anyone.

Final Cut Pro can open a saved project file and recapture it on any Mac that runs the same or a newer version of Final Cut Pro. It recaptures all time-coded source material contained in these logs automatically in a process called batch capture. You can find further discussion of backup and recapture strategies in Appendix C, "Solving Common Problems." Media files such as video captures are quite large and might be too cumbersome to back up. Project files, though, are much smaller and can easily be backed up on a Zip disc or CD. If you lose your media drives, you can restore your media files from a backup of your project file. You also can restore all the work you've done with sequences.

There is an auto backup feature within Final Cut Pro called the *Autosave Vault,* but you probably will save these backups to your startup disk, and you could lose that disk, so it's still best to back up on a Zip disc or a CD at the end of each session. The worst case is that you could lose a day or two of work, not months' worth.

Clip Information

Clip information can include reel number, media start and end points, tracks contained, file format information, and more. Clip information is stored in the columns to the right of the clip names. Figure 3.7 shows only a portion of them; you can use the arrows or the bar at the bottom of the Browser window to scroll through them. I grabbed the handle on the bottom-right corner to expand the Browser.

FIGURE 3.7   *An expanded view of the Browser.*

Table 3.1 is a complete list of what clip information can be stored in the columns.

Table 3.1   Columns in the Browser Window

Column	Information
Name	The clip's name as you entered it.
Media Start	The time code where your clip begins on your source tape.
Media End	The time code where your clip ends on your source tape.
Length	The duration of the entire media file.
In Point	The time code position that is set after you select an edit start point in the Viewer or Canvas window.
Out Point	The time-code position that is set after you set an edit ending point in the Viewer or Canvas window.
Duration	The duration of the In point to the Out point in hours, minutes, seconds, and frames.
Tracks	Video and/or audio tracks.
Good	A check mark to quickly sort the best takes feature.
Audio	Specifies whether the clip is stereo, for example.
Frame Size	Expressed as pixels, such as 720×480.
Compressor	Which compressor or codec the clip or sequence uses.
Data Rate	Expressed in kilobytes per second (KBps).
Audio Rate	The clip's sample rate in KHz.
Video Rate	Expressed in frames per second (fps).
Audio Format	Expressed as bits and format.
Alpha	Displays the type of alpha that FCP detects.
Reverse Alpha setting	Can be set to yes or no. A check mark reverses the current setting to invert the alpha channel.
Composite	Expressed as a type that is selectable.

continues

Table 3.1   continued

Column	Information
Pixel aspect	Expressed as a ratio.
Anamorphic	A check mark indicates whether the medium is anamorphic. You also can set this to force this condition.
Description	A user-entered phrase, for example.
Scene	A place where scene descriptions or numbers can be kept.
Shot/Take	A column for shot or take numbers.
Reel	The number or name of the tape the clip is from.
Last Modified	A date and time.
Aux TC 1	User-assigned auxiliary time code number 1.
Aux TC 2	User-assigned auxiliary time code number 2.
Type	A sequence, clip, subclip, or bin.
Log note	Another place to keep notes.
TC	Where the time code is from.
Size	The media file size in bytes. This is great for media-management decisions.
Label	User-selectable.
Source	Where the medium is stored on your disk drive.
Thumbnail	A user-selectable still frame that displays a user-selectable frame that the clip contains.
Comment columns	You can have custom names for four user-definable comments columns. You can change their names by selecting Edit, Project Properties.

Quite a bit of information is stored in these columns. The information is arranged much like a spreadsheet, with column headings at the top and the data that's particular to each clip in the rows and columns beneath the top row of column headers. What's exciting is that all the information is sortable and searchable. Furthermore, Final Cut Pro gathers much of the information stored here automatically. This automation is a necessity if you are editing a feature-length program with thousands of clips.

To sort a column, click its header name at the top of a bin or the Browser window. Click again to reverse the sort. To find a clip, select Edit, Find or press   +F. You can also use the up and down arrows on the keyboard to move the highlight from element to element in this project/display—again, much like a spreadsheet. Pressing letter keys moves the highlight between clips whose name starts with that letter. When the clip or sequence is highlighted, you can press the Return key to load the clip or sequence from the Browser into the Viewer, Canvas, and Timeline windows.

By dragging the column name headers, you can move the columns to the position of your choice. This powerful feature allows you to quickly view the information of your choice next to the Name column, for example.

You can also add or take away columns from your view by Ctrl-clicking any column header. A context menu opens, as shown in Figure 3.8. You also can save and restore custom column layouts from this menu. These layouts are saved in the User>Library>Preferences>Final Cut Pro User Data>Column Layouts folder. New in Final Cut Pro 4, these layouts can be moved from system to system.

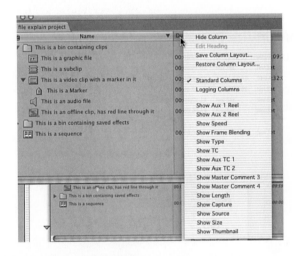

FIGURE 3.8 *The Browser Column context menu.*

You can resize the Browser window by dragging the lower-right corner of the window or clicking its green expansion button to expand its view. Keep the Browser window handy, because you select all source material for your sequence or edited show from this window. The sidebar gives you a quick lesson on some automatic arrangements that can come in handy.

Arranging Those Four Windows
Using the Window menu, you can arrange Final Cut Pro in many ways. Saving frequently used window arrangements for tasks you perform often enhances your monitor setup. If you have multiple monitors or a cinema display, your standard window arrangements

continues

might be different from a person who has just one 15-inch monitor. Accessing these window arrangements is a snap. Just pull down the Window menu to access some arrangements that Final Cut Pro supplies, and then start with one you like. Modify the arrangement by dragging the windows to where you want to work with them, and then -click and select Window, Arrange, Save Custom Layout 1 or 2. Alternatively, you can set this new custom arrangement to be accessed through keyboard shortcuts.

Final Cut Pro then has this setting available when you work in this *particular* project. If you want to use this setting in any or all projects, you need to create a custom layout. After you've set up the windows as you want them to be, save them by selecting Window, Arrange, Save Layout. After you have saved the windows, you can restore them in any project by selecting Window, Arrange, Restore Layout. When you select this command, you see a window that allows you to select any of the saved layouts you've created for this or earlier projects.

Viewing Options in the Browser Window

There are four ways to look at items in the Browser: the List View, and three different icon views. Figure 3.9 shows the Large Icons view. To access the context menu shown in Figure 3.9, Ctrl-click a blank area of the Browser or an open bin. Note the Arrange option. Selecting this in one of the three icon views forces the pictures to fit into the Browser.

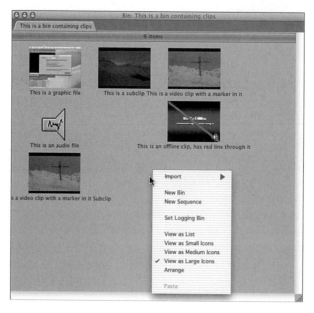

FIGURE 3.9   *The Large Icons view.*

Three other views are listed in the context menu shown in Figure 3.9: Small Icons, Medium Icons, and Large Icons. Experimenting with them is your best bet. When you select these views, the clip information is replaced by a representative frame of the clip in the case of video clips and by larger views of the icons in the case of the other types of files.

You can open a separate bin window by double-clicking its icon in the Browser. You can use all but the List view to arrange your clips in a certain order by dragging them around and then dragging them as a group to the Timeline in order from left to right and then top to bottom. It's sort of like creating a storyboard and then dragging it to the Timeline in the order of your choice. You can trim these complete shots with the tools supplied by Final Cut Pro.

The Arrange selection in the pop-up menu arranges the icon views to fit the pictures into the window shape you are currently working in.

One other context menu can be opened from this window. If you Ctrl-click a clip icon, you can pull up a set of commands to use on that selection, as shown in Figure 3.10.

FIGURE 3.10   *The context menu containing commands available for an item in the Browser.*

The Effects tab, shown in Figure 3.11, contains all the effects you have at your disposal within Final Cut Pro. They are organized into six folders. If you open the triangle next to one of the folders, you can see the list of effects that can be applied to your clips and edit points.

The difference between a filter and a transition, whether it's video or audio, is in how it's applied. A *filter* applies to a clip or a portion of a clip (such as a color correction), and a *transition* is an effect used between two clips (such as a dissolve). Some are audio-only filters and transitions, and some are video-only filters and transitions.

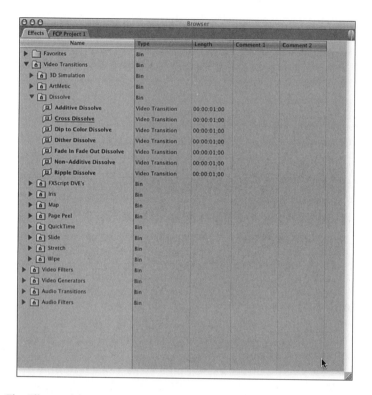

FIGURE 3.11   *The Effects tab.*

In the Favorites folder, you can drag any effect you have customized for quick access as you edit. In the Video Generators folder, you can access all the elements you can create from within Final Cut Pro, such as titles, shapes, gradients, highlights, noise, and audio tone. There are also plug-ins that can be added to Final Cut Pro, such as Boris's Graffiti and Boris's Red. They too show up in this window as generators if they have been added to your system. Note that there are no audio + video filters. Each of these elements must be affected separately.

You can add plug-in effects such as After Effects filters, which show up and are sorted into the appropriate effect categories accessed under this tab.

To add a filter or transition to audio or video, drag the effect from the Effects tab to the clip or cut point you want to affect.

The Viewer Window

The Viewer window, shown in Figure 3.12, is like a QuickTime movie player on steroids. Not only can you view clips and have full VTR-like controls while viewing them, but you can also modify any clip's playback, view source time code, edit from it to a sequence in various ways, and modify all your program's effects. Durations of transitions, amounts of color changes you make, keying parameters, and more are programmed from this seemingly simple window. Used primarily for viewing and marking source material to be added to your program, this window is where you can edit most parameters of all the elements in your finished program, whether they are clips or effects.

FIGURE 3.12   *The Viewer window.*

You can open clips into the Viewer window from the Browser by simply dragging them from the Browser to the Viewer or by double-clicking them. You can load sequence clips from your current sequence for further editing, adding, and modifying of effect parameters by double-clicking them in the Timeline window. Also you can open sequences in the Viewer by dragging them from the Browser to the Viewer.

Buttons in the Viewer Window

The controls and buttons in this window look familiar. They work much like the controls a videotape recorder (VTR) uses (see Figure 3.13). The round center button turns playback on and off. The button to the right of it is "Play Around Current Frame." This button lets you go back a bit, play through the current position, and then play past it a bit. How far it goes back and then plays past your current position depends on what you've set in the User Preferences General window in the preview pre and post roll boxes. It's a quick way to play before and through an edit point (if a sequence is loaded in the Viewer) or any position you might be sitting on to check just the footage around it.

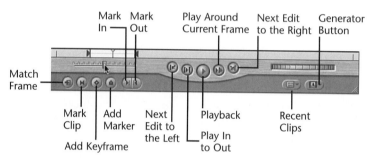

FIGURE 3.13   *Controls used in the Viewer window.*

The next button on the right is the Next Edit button. It moves the position indicator to the next edit to the right. The button on the far left moves you to the next edit point to the left of your current position.

The button with the triangle between two lines is Play In to Out. This button plays your clip from your set In point to your set Out point. The shuttle control on the left scans your material forward or backward; the farther you move from center, the faster the playback goes in either direction. The control on the far-right is the jog control. It performs much slower searching.

The scrubber bar resides just above these VTR controls. It represents the clip's entire duration. The yellow position indicator resides here as well; it's also called the *playhead*. You can click anywhere in this bar to quickly move about within the clip you are working with.

The buttons along the bottom left are as follows:

- Match Frame—Pulls up the same frame if it's in the current sequence into the Canvas window.

- Mark Clip—Selects the clip's boundaries to set an In point at its beginning and an Out point at its end.

- Add Keyframe—Adds a keyframe at the current position. *Keyframes* are markers that set certain frames to become a start, an ending, or even a midpoint for an effect to start or end.

- Add Marker—Adds a marker to the current position. This button has many uses that are explored throughout this book.

- Mark In—Sets the clip's In point at the current position, where you want to see it start in your edited program.

- Mark Out—Sets the clip's Out point at the current position, where you want playback of this clip to end in your edited program.

The two buttons on the bottom right are Recent Clips and Generator. The Recent Clips button, on the left, lists the clips you've recently loaded into the Viewer window. You set the number of clips displayed in the User Preferences General window, but this number is lost each time you close Final Cut Pro. The Generator button is quite a different animal. It lists items you can create in Final Cut Pro. You can open titles, bars, tone, gradients, matte colors, and more in the Viewer window by selecting them here. This is discussed in detail in Chapter 11, "Video Filter Effects and Basic Compositing."

At the top of this window are two time-code displays, three buttons, and a series of tabs. The right time-code display shows the duration of an unmarked clip. It changes to show the duration between an In point and an Out point. Ctrl-click it to pull up a pop-up menu, as shown in Figure 3.14. You can display the time as Drop Frame, Non-Drop Frame, or Frames. The sidebar explains the differences between the two time-code formats. Selecting Frames counts the number of frames from in to out or for the duration of the clip if you have not set these points yet. Durations can also be used to define in and Out points. When you set either point and then type a duration into the box, FCP sets the companion point (in or out) for you.

FIGURE 3.14 *The time-code views context pop-up menu.*

The left time-code display shows the time code that is associated with the current frame you are viewing. It also works as a time-code locator. Type in the time code you want to go to, and as long as the clip in the Viewer contains that number, the Viewer displays the frame stamped with that number. You don't need to type the colons or semicolons. FCP knows that the colons and semicolons are part of the number you are looking for. For example, if you want to type 1 minute, type **10000** for 1 minute, 0 seconds, and 0 frames. If you like, you can avoid adding the 0s by typing periods. For example, 1. equals 1 second, 1.. equals 1 minute, and 1... equals 1 hour.

Drop Frame and Non-Drop Frame Time Codes

Professional videotape formats include a time code, which is a unique number "stamped" on each frame of video. It is displayed as hours, minutes, seconds, and frames: 00:00:00:00. The difference between the Drop Frame and Non-Drop Frame time codes is that Non-Drop Frame (expressed as colons between the numbers) counts each frame of video in ascending order, changing over the count from 00:00:00:29 (29 frames) to 1 second, expressed as 00:00:01:00. The problem is that NTSC video is not 30 frames per second. It's 29.97 frames per second.

If you used the Non-Drop Frame code to set an in point at the beginning of your finished program and an out point at the end to have Final Cut Pro calculate your project's duration, using the Non-Drop Frame code would result in an incorrect duration. This could be disastrous for editing programs that must come to definite time durations, as all broadcast programs must do.

Enter the Drop Frame time code, which is expressed as pairs of numbers separated by colons, but with *semicolons* at the end in Final Cut Pro. At each minute changeover, the numbering system drops the numbers between the fifty-ninth second and the twenty-eighth frame and the next minute point, which starts at that minute and one frame. This numbering scheme "drops" two frame numbers. Thus, frame number 00;00;59;28 is followed by frame number 00;01;00;01. This numbering system skips the dropping scheme at each 10-minute changeover. If you do the math, this works out over a period of *actual* time, and you can rely on the duration of your edited sequence to be the actual time that is calculated using this form of time code. Most professionals use the Drop Frame code, so this "real" time problem doesn't exist. FCP can search for clips if you enter time-code numbers. If you are using Drop Frame by entering time-code numbers, and you enter a number that is not in the sequence because it was dropped, FCP displays a frame assigned with the next-higher number.

As long as your sequence uses the Drop Frame time code, it doesn't matter if your source material uses Non-Drop Frame. The timing will still be correct as long as the sequence uses the Drop Frame code.

PAL video is always 25 frames per second and always uses the Non-Drop Frame time code.

The three oval buttons near the top of the Viewer window in the middle control different viewing options as well as a new behavior that Final Cut Pro 4 introduces. (We'll discuss these buttons in depth as we edit our movie.) The button on the left zooms in or out on your clip. It invokes a command to automatically fit to the window size you've set up for viewing purposes. The button on the right selects options such as time-code overlays and title safe. The new button, in the center (it looks a bit like football goalposts), selects playback behaviors. It's called the Playback Sync button, and it has four options, as shown in Figure 3.15:

- Off—This is the default behavior. The Viewer and Canvas windows play independently from each other.

- Follow—Playback in the Viewer is locked to the playback of the Canvas window. Viewer and Canvas display the *same frame*. As you move the Canvas's playhead, the same frame appears in the Viewer. This is called *ganging*. Note that if the source clip is not already loaded into the Viewer, the Viewer's playhead does not follow along.

- Open—This is similar to the Follow option, except that it automatically loads any clip in the Viewer that the playhead of the Canvas or Timeline is currently viewing. This can be useful for quick alterations to various clips next to each other in your sequence that need to be colorcorrected, for example. The active tab in the Viewer stays open, but the clips loaded in the Viewer match the clips you currently are viewing in the Canvas, and what you see in the Viewer is the color correction visual controls of the Canvas's clip.

- Gang—When this option is chosen, the offset between the position of the playhead in the Canvas and the position of the playhead in the Viewer is maintained as both playheads move together. This mode can be useful for editing operations in which you want to mark in or Out points using durations defined by clips already in the Timeline.

FIGURE 3.15 *Options on the Playback Sync pop-up menu.*

For example, suppose that before you turn on this option, you set an In point in a source clip and set the Canvas's playhead to the In point you want to use in the sequence as a reference. Moving the Canvas's playhead to the Out point you want to reference moves the Viewer's playhead the same amount forward in time, allowing you to set or preview in the Viewer the default Out point that will be used, maintaining the duration you moved the playhead in the Canvas. This is similar to Avid's phantom marks. It allows you to see a clip's default Out point or In point determined by the in or out of a clip already in your sequence.

Tabs in the Viewer Window

The Viewer window has a number of tabs. To open a tab, click it. The Video tab shows the video that's in the clip. The Audio tab displays audio waveforms and allows you to change levels, edit with keyframes, and pan your sound. There might be two of these tabs if your clip contains two separate tracks. A single Stereo Track tab is also seen if the source clip has stereo audio captured with it. In the case of merged clips, you have as many tabs as you have merged audio tracks with a video track. In the case of audio-only clips, you see only an Audio tab and an Effects tab.

The Filters tab is where you access controls of effects (filters) you've added them to. They can be audio filters or video filters or both. There also might be a tab for the Color Corrector, Color Corrector 3-way, and Keyer if you've added one or more of these to the clip that contains them.

Clicking the Motion tab (shown in Figure 3.16) brings up a set of standard tools you can use on any clip. These include Scale (size), Rotation, Center (determines the frame's center point), Anchor Point (the point in the frame that it is set to rotate around), Crop (where you can cut off some of the picture), Distort (where you can change the placement of the frame's four corners), Opacity, adding a Drop Shadow or Motion Blur to your clip, and Final Cut Pro 4's new Time Remap feature. I've stretched the window to reveal the entire contents of this tab. The Motion tab is the basic area for effects. It's available for use on any video clip.

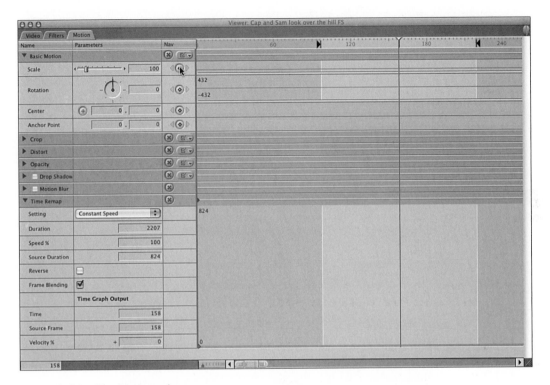

FIGURE 3.16 *The Motion tab.*

The upper bar across the top of the Viewer is a button bar. Here you can drag buttons for quick access to any command from the button list (press +J). Just select the button from the list and drag it to the small "button bounders" in the upper right of the window. These icons bookend your buttons.

The area next to the controls is a Timeline that represents the duration of the clip currently being worked with as it appears in the Timeline. After you add a clip to the Timeline, you double-click it to open it in the Viewer, click the Motion tab, and start creating effects. Keyframes are added to the light-colored area on the right side of Figure 3.16. You can add those familiar triangles next to the different effects to a clip. If you click the triangles, the controls appear, like the Basic Motion effects that are open in Figure 3.16. As we edit our movie, we'll use these effects.

When a clip is opened from the sequence Timeline, the part of the clip that is present (trimmed) in the Timeline is highlighted, but the clip's duration is available on the Motion tab. Note too that the scrubber bar has sprocket hole representations in it when you address the clip as it is present in the Timeline.

The Canvas Window

The Canvas window, shown in Figure 3.17, has many of the same controls as the Viewer window, but it functions as a window that only plays back and modifies the clips as edited in your edited sequence. You can have more than one sequence open at one time, and you can select the active one by clicking its tab at the top of the Canvas window. You can even have more than one sequence accessible here as well. You can drag its tab away from the Canvas and view two sequences side by side, playing them one at a time. Any sequences open in the Timeline window have corresponding tabs to view them from in the Canvas.

Figure 3.17   *The Canvas window.*

You can think of the Viewer window as a source playback or a single clip viewer, and you can think of the Canvas window as a playback monitor for your edited masterpiece. The Canvas window's content is completely tied to your edited sequence. When you play back edited material, it plays back in the Canvas window. When you close the Canvas window, you also close the Timeline window. Final Cut Pro assumes that if you don't want to view a sequence, you don't need the Canvas window open. If the Canvas window is closed, you can open it by double-clicking a sequence in the Browser. Both the Timeline window and the Canvas window open.

All the buttons that look the same as in the Viewer have the same uses, but there are some notable differences in the Canvas window. On the bottom left are three buttons. They represent edit commands, invoked after you select source material to add to your sequence that's active in the Timeline window. The first button inserts the source material into the edited show, the second overwrites material, and the third replaces material:

- The Insert edit command adds material selected with in and Out points from the Viewer to anywhere in your sequence. It also moves all material later than your selected In point to accommodate this new element. Therefore, an Insert edit command lengthens the duration of the sequence of shots.

- The Overwrite edit command covers up older material with the new material selected with in and Out points from the Viewer. The Overwrite edit command does not lengthen the duration of your sequence.

- The Replace edit command is similar to Overwrite because it covers up material, but it works a bit differently. The Replace edit puts a new clip in your sequence by replacing the frame you are currently viewing in the Viewer with the frame you are currently viewing in the Canvas.

The duration of the edit is calculated in one of two ways: in the sequence in and Out points you've made, or, if none have been set, in the duration of the clip you are viewing. You must keep in mind that you must have enough source material before and after the Viewer's frame to cover up the old clip. This does not change the Timeline's duration.

The blue Replace button has a small triangle. This triangle opens a pop-up menu with even more ways of adding material to your sequence, as shown in Figure 3.18.

FIGURE 3.18   *Pop-up edit command buttons.*

Here are the options from left to right:

- Fit to Fill—A four-point edit that calculates the speeding up or slowing down that is necessary for a source clip's in and Out point to become the duration you've selected for it by setting in and Out points in your sequence. For example, if you mark a duration of 1 second in the Viewer and mark an in and Out point with a duration of 2 seconds in the Canvas, Final Cut Pro places a 2-second clip, which is a 50% playback speed of your source clip.

- Insert with Transition—Adds the default transition you've selected. Final Cut Pro defaults to a 30-frame dissolve centered on the edit point, unless you've changed the default transition, as discussed in Chapter 5, "Basic Editing."

- Overwrite with Transition—Does the same as the Overwrite edit, but Overwrite with Transition adds the default transition you've selected. Final Cut Pro defaults to a 30-frame dissolve centered on the edit point, unless you've changed the default transition.

The Canvas Window Overlay

The Canvas window overlay, shown in Figure 3.19, lets you access the same functions as with the Canvas window's edit buttons. To activate these functions, you drag a clip from the Browser or Viewer window to the Canvas window and the appropriate overlay, to either insert, overwrite, replace, or fit to fill. You also can add the user selectable default transition at the same time. This transition will be at the beginning or In point of the edit. When the ghost image is dragged to one of the edit commands, a highlight will appear over the command.

FIGURE 3.19   *The Canvas window overlay.*

Match Frame and Mark Clip Differences

For the most part, the rest of the icons in the Canvas window, which match those in the Viewer, do the same things as those described for the Viewer window, except that they work on your sequences. However, the Match Frame and Mark Clip buttons have different functions. The Match Frame button pulls up the source clip containing the frame you are currently paused on in the Canvas and puts it in the Viewer. The Mark Clip button marks only the clip you are currently paused on and only the top track of audio or video you have targeted by clicking the yellow track indicators on the left side of the Timeline window.

The Timeline Window

The Timeline window, shown in Figure 3.20, displays the clips you have edited in your sequence. This window can contain more than one sequence. You can switch between sequences by clicking the tab at the top of the window, just as you can click the tab at the top of the Canvas window.

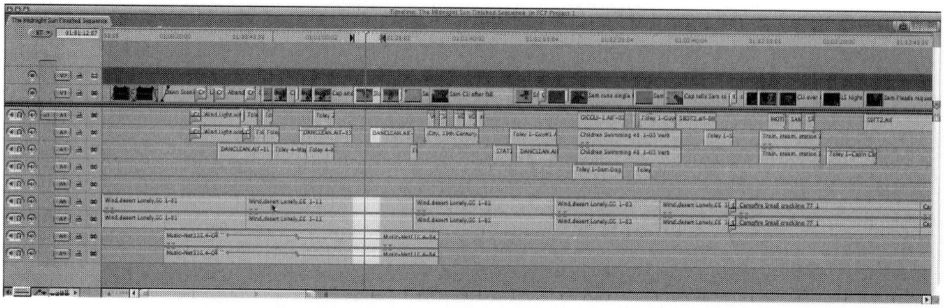

FIGURE 3.20   *The Timeline window.*

You can create a new sequence at any time by pressing ⌘+N. The default number of tracks that this new sequence contains is set in the User Preferences on the Timeline Options tab (activated from the Final Cut Pro menu). Final Cut Pro defaults to one track of video and two tracks of audio.

You can add a clip to a sequence contained in this window by either dragging the clip from the Browser to the sequence or from the Viewer to the sequence, or by marking the clip in the Viewer and editing it to the Canvas window. There's not really a best way. A lot depends on your perception of the easiest way to do this. As we edit the movie, you'll discover and use all the ways you can edit from the Browser to your sequences in the Timeline window.

The Buttons in the Timeline Window

In the upper left of the Timeline window is a pull-down menu that sets the preferences for FCP 4's RT Extreme, as shown in Figure 3.21. It allows you to set the playback quality of FCP's real-time effects. Using these options, you can determine what playback quality you want to work with. You can change it if you'd rather see the RT play back differently. In other words, you can turn on Unlimited RT and maximize your computer's power until you start to drop frames, or you can select Safe RT and have a reliable, high-quality playback.

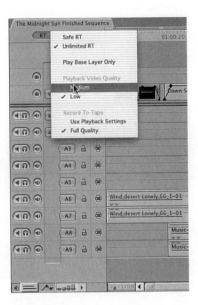

FIGURE 3.21   *RT Settings in the Timeline window.*

Real-time effects are listed in bold on the Effects menu and on the Browser's Effects tab. The number of simultaneous effects that play back in your computer is determined by the size of your CPU's Level 3 cache and the speed of your computer's CPU, memory bus, hard disks, and graphics card. (Open GL is used to speed up real-time display and playback.) The faster your machine, the more you get, basically.

The positive side of this is that it might not matter how reliable playback quality is if you simply want to check out your effects *before* you render them. No longer do you have to render, change parameters, and then render again to check your changes.

As soon as you reach your computer's limits, you either have to reduce the playback quality using the RT pop-up menu or render the clips you want to view in high quality.

note   Some capture cards offer some real-time effect support. You can select them from the User Preferences window in the Playback Control tab. From this window, you can let FCP handle the effects, or you can let your capture card handle them.

Just to the right of the RT pop-up menu is the time-code display. It shows the current time code your playhead is at in the Timeline and Canvas. You can enter a time code here to quickly jump to a specific time in your sequence.

Below the RT menu is a list of the tracks your sequence contains (see Figure 3.22). Here you "target" the tracks you will edit. The track name buttons on the right display your source material's tracks (the clip or sequence loaded in the Viewer; notice that they are lowercase on the left for your source material's track names, and uppercase on the right). The track names buttons on the right represent the tracks your sequence contains.

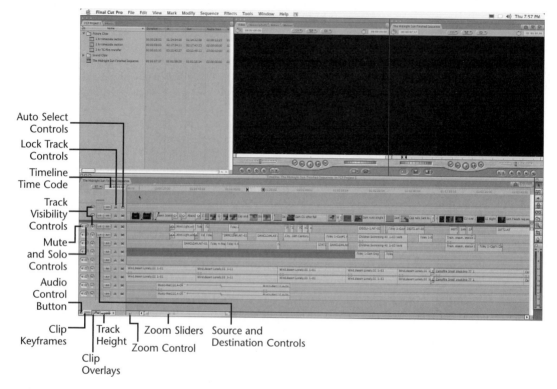

FIGURE 3.22   *Track controls in the Timeline window.*

All you need to do to put, say, a video clip from your Canvas on the V2 track of your sequence is to drag its track name to be next to the V2 sequence track. The same is true of audio clips. If your source material contains audio you don't want to edit into your program, simply slide the audio track's source control to the right to "disconnect" it. The same is true of source video tracks you might not want to include in the edit.

To add tracks to your sequence, simply Ctrl-click in this area and select Add Track. The same context menu deletes tracks and resets your target tracks to the default of v1 to V1, a1 to A1, and a2 to A2. This is handy when you have so many tracks working at once that scrolling around to change the target track settings isn't easy.

The round green buttons with the film or speaker icon just to the left of the Destination and Source Controls column select which tracks should be played back or "monitored" when you play your sequence.

Just to the right of the Destination and Source Controls column is a series of locks. If you click one or more of these locks, those tracks become "locked" and can't be edited or changed without being "unlocked." When you lock a track, a serrated line is drawn through it. Locking your tracks can be useful if you don't want your work to be altered inadvertently. You can, however, add keyframes and set audio levels or video opacities in the User Preferences General window.

To the right of the locks are Auto Select buttons. Auto Select controls have many uses. Clicking these buttons determines which track is "match framed." The highest button active (lit) is the track that is matched in the Viewer if you invoke the Match Frame command in the Canvas. These buttons also denote which tracks you'd like to make a cut with using the Ctrl+V command, which creates an edit point in the middle of a clip already in your sequence. Final Cut Pro calls these *through edits*.

Auto Select controls also allow the contents of the selected tracks to be selected via the Timeline or Canvas windows' in and Out points. For example, a portion of a clip is selected to have a filter applied to only that portion, much like a range selection. But if you use a range selection, these AutoSelect controls are ignored in favor of the selection made with the Range Selection tool. When you use the Auto Select controls, you can add filters to the area selected or delete these selections from your sequence.

On the far left in the audio track section are two buttons contained in an oval. The speaker icon is a Mute control for its associated track, and the headphone icon is a Solo control. *Soloing* an audio track means playing only that track and muting all others. You can solo more than one track at a time by clicking the solo light of another track. (This is much faster than clicking a lot of green monitoring lights in order to focus on two of your possible 99 tracks.)

If the Timeline window doesn't show these far-left buttons, you can modify it so that it does by clicking the Audio control (the speaker icon) in the bottom left of the Timeline window.

In the bottom-left corner of the Timeline are six more buttons:

- Audio control—This is the square button with a speaker icon. It toggles the visibility of the Audio Mute and Solo controls.
- Clip Keyframes control—These are the green and blue lines. Clicking this button adds a row under each video and audio track to indicate whether an effect has been applied to any clip (see Figure 3.23). If a filter has been added or you've created a motion effect (or both), you can manipulate its parameters in

the Timeline window as well as from the filter's tab in the Viewer after double-clicking the clip from the sequence. A green line near the top area means that a filter has been applied. A blue line indicates that a motion effect has been applied.

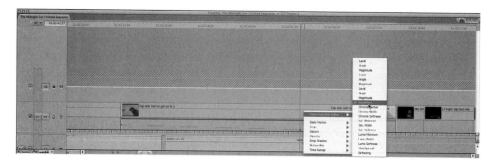

FIGURE 3.23   *The Clip Keyframe area of the Timeline window.*

Keyframes added to these filters show up in the bold colored lines. The default keyboard commands to navigate between keyframes are Shift+K to move your playhead to the next keyframe later in your sequence and   +K to move your playhead to the next earlier keyframe.

Figure 3.23 also shows how you bring up any filter or motion settings you want to manipulate. In the figure, the saturation (amount of color) is set to start at full color and then slowly drop to black and white from the starting keyframe to the ending one.

Only one of these keyframeable lines can be open at a time, but it's a snap to change which parameter from any number of filters or motion effects you've applied. Just Ctrl-click in the Clip Keyframes area and select the parameter from the context menu that appears. You can use the pen tool (p) to add, move, raise, or lower the parameter settings of any give keyframe. You can also use the Selection tool to raise or lower the level for an entire clip without adding any keyframes.

In the case of audio, green lines representing filters applied are the only colored lines. Simply put, if there is a line under your video or audio clip, the Timeline indicates the presence of an effect. If you've added keyframes to the effects, they are displayed here as well, and you can change their parameters from the Timeline window. We'll experiment with these controls as we build the movie together.

■   Clip Overlays control—This button looks like a line graph. It turns on or off a black line that runs inside a video clip and a red line that runs inside an audio clip (see Figure 3.24). In the case of audio, this keyframeable line sets the audio level. In the case of video, it sets the video's opacity. You can use the mouse to set these parameters by selecting the appropriate tool from the Tools palette.

Use the selection tool to raise or lower this line between keyframes, and use the pen tool to add, raise, and lower keyframes. Figure 3.24 shows an audio clip's levels lowering for a time and then coming back up.

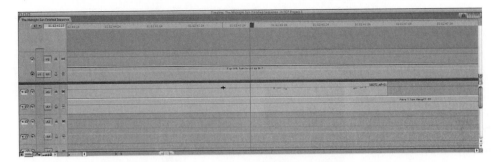

FIGURE 3.24 *Clip Overlay activated.*

■ Track Height control—This button offers four different heights you can select for viewing your tracks. If you have many tracks, it might be most convenient to look at them with a short height to see more tracks at once. If you do this, though, you can't see things such as audio waveforms inside your audio clips or precise indications of the clip overlays and their keyframes. So you'll probably change this view when you need to for these adjustments to be easier. Pressing Shift+T repeatedly toggles between the four different widths.

New to FCP 4 is another way to create different track heights. To change a track's width, just click between the track names (on the black line between them) and drag. In Figure 3.25, the audio track A1 has been expanded to show its waveform better. You can change the height of any audio or video track. If you   -click a track to create a different track height, you can change all tracks of that type at the same time. In other words, if you   -click to change a video track height, all video tracks follow suit. The same is true of audio track height adjustments.

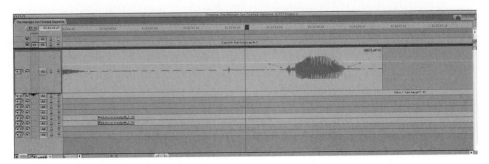

FIGURE 3.25 *Individual track height adjustment.*

■ Track Layout menu—As shown in Figure 3.26, this pop-up menu lets you select ways to change your view of the Timeline window. The selections are pretty self-explanatory, but note that you can save and restore custom layouts of the Timeline window from this menu. These files are saved in the User>Library>Preferences>Final Cut Pro User Preferences>Track Layout folder. These user preferences can be copied from one computer to another for a quick "custom setup."

FIGURE 3.26   *The Track Layout pop-up menu.*

■ Zoom control and the zoom sliders—The small box with an arrow and tick marks is the Zoom control, and the sliders go across most of the bottom of the Timeline window. Both are used to navigate around your sequence. Experimenting with them is probably the best way to get a handle on them. You activate the Zoom control by clicking and dragging the gray pointer to the left to zoom in and to the right to zoom out. The zoom sliders to the right of the Zoom control provide more control. The handles on the end of the gray bar do the zooming in and out. Clicking and dragging the bar itself moves your Timeline left and right, as do the arrows at either end of this control.

Across the top of the window is a ruler with time-code numbers to give you a rough idea of the Timeline's time code. When you click here, your playhead jumps to where you click, as shown in Figure 3.27. If you zoom all the way into your sequence at the playhead's position, you see a shaded line next to it. This line represents the duration of a single frame. This extreme zooming in helps you when you do audio intraframe editing, for example. The waveforms displayed here are much easier to edit when they are zoomed all the way in.

FIGURE 3.27   *Timeline ruler, snapping, and linking controls.*

The default setting of Final Cut Pro 4 has two buttons in the upper-right corner of the Timeline. The one with the arrows turns snapping on and off. If it's on, the position indicator jumps into position at edit points, markers, and in and Out points. With it turned off, you have more precise control of areas near these points.

The icon that looks like an 8 leaning over is the Linked Selection control. Clicking a clip's audio or video track selects any item that is linked to that clip if the Linked Selection button is activated. For example, if you click a video clip that has sync sound associated with it, the sync sound item also is highlighted. It's a way to keep edits you make that might affect sync to keep you in sync, or a way to move a video clip whose audio needs to go with it. For more information on the use of linking, see Chapter 8, "Audio Filters, Timeline Editing, and Keeping Sync." There will be times when you don't want to select linked audio and video at the same time, such as when you want to keep video but lose the sync sound or vice versa. Turning off this option lets you do so.

The controls on the far right, below the two buttons we just discussed, let you scroll up and down to reveal more tracks of audio or video (see Figure 3.28). The center controls move the divider around. It can be placed in various places in the Timeline. For example, you can separate the video from the audio or slide the divider to be between another set of tracks for organizational purposes. If you are viewing all the tracks in your sequence, the sliders disappear. They reappear if you add more tracks that remove some of your tracks from the viewing area. In the lower-right corner is a handle that sizes the whole window. Simply click and drag to resize. Hopefully you might begin to see the advantage of a larger screen space. The larger the Timeline window, the quicker you can navigate it, because you can see more of it at one time.

FIGURE 3.28   *Controls along the far right of the Timeline window.*

The Tools Palette

Figure 3.29 shows the Tools Palette. Final Cut Pro gives you seven different ways to select objects with your interface. The first three buttons are all types of selection tools. Press A on the keyboard or click the first button to activate it. You use this tool to click icons, command buttons, clips in the Canvas, and more. Its use is familiar. In some instances, when another selection tool is chosen, if you move the mouse from the area of its unique use (usually the Timeline), the selected tool defaults back to this tool.

FIGURE 3.29   *The Selection tool.*

The next tool down, shown in Figure 3.30, is another set of selection tools that work only in the Timeline window. Notice that this button has a small arrow in the upper-right corner. In fact, all the buttons beneath the first one have these arrows. They indicate that if you click and hold the button, more buttons pop up.

FIGURE 3.30   *Specialized selection tools.*

When you click the second button from the top, you have three choices: the Edit Selection tool, the Group Selection tool, and the Range Selection tool. The last tool selected in the group remains on the top of the Tool window until another is selected. Pressing G on the keyboard toggles through the selections. You press G once for the Edit Selection tool, again for the Group Selection tool, and again for the Range Selection tool.

The Edit Selection tool selects the edit point closest to the playhead's position and opens the Trim Edit window. You also can activate this tool by pressing V on the keyboard. The Group Selection tool selects whole clips or sets of clips. The Range Selection tool selects an area of material not limited to whole clips. You can select frames of a single clip or set of clips with the Range Selection tool.

Below the Edit Selection tools is a set of Track Selection tools (see Figure 3.31). They allow you to select whole or large parts of tracks or clips. When you click in the Timeline with one of these tools, the clip under where you click and all clips in the direction of the selection tool's arrow are selected. The single arrows select single tracks, the double arrows select all tracks, and the two-headed arrow selects entire single tracks per click. Say you want to select two entire video tracks out of five. You'd use the two-headed arrow to select the first track, hold down the   key, and then select the other track. We'll experiment with these tools in the Workshop. Linking is discussed in detail in Chapter 8.

FIGURE 3.31   *The Track Selection tools.*

The next set of buttons, shown in Figure 3.32, are Trimming Edit tools. With them you can perform a ripple or roll edit in the Timeline and in transitional effect windows. Ripple edits perform moves on edit points that affect the length of the Timeline. As you add or subtract frames, the Timeline "ripples" shorter or longer. You can add a frame to a clip, move all clips down the Timeline a frame, and so on. Roll edits move an edit point sooner or later in your sequence, adding and subtracting frames at the same time on each side of the edit point. This procedure does not lengthen the sequence. Instead, it shortens one side of the edit as you lengthen the other side, keeping your sequence the same length.

FIGURE 3.32   *The Ripple and Roll edit tools.*

Below the Ripple and Roll edit tools are the Slip and Slide tools and the new Time Remap tool (see Figure 3.33). The Slip tool slips a previously edited clip's contents later or earlier without changing the clip's duration. The Slide tool preserves the clip's contents but changes where the clip resides in your sequence, moving the clip's In and Out points simultaneously. Neither tool lengthens the duration of the sequence, because they don't change the clip's duration.

FIGURE 3.33   *The Slip and Slide tools and the Time Remap tool.*

With the Slide Edit tool, the in and Out points of the clip you are affecting stay constant while the clip's position relative to the clips on either side of it changes as the fixed duration clip moves earlier or later in the sequence. With the Slip Edit tool, the Out point of the clip before is fixed, as is the In point of the clip following, but the clip being slipped moves past the opening between the Out and In points of the clips on either side of it.

The new Time Remap tool applies a variable-speed effect to your edit. It works in forward or reverse motion. This new effect is a real-time effect, whereas the constant-speed changes in earlier releases are not. Constant-speed changes alter a clip's duration. Variable-speed changes applied with the Time Remap tool do not change the clip's duration.

There are four places you can make a variable-speed change with the Time Remap tool: in the Timeline, in the Viewer's Motion tab, in the Motion bar under the clip, and in the Timeline's keyframe editor time graph. Making these changes in the Timeline is probably easiest. You can choose to display speed indicators and a keyframe graph under the clip you are affecting in the Timeline. We'll experiment with this tool in the Workshop to get a handle on it.

Next in line are the Razor Blade tools, shown in Figure 3.34. They are fairly straightforward. The single blade splices and creates a new edit point within a clip on a single track in your sequence, and the double blade slices edit points through all tracks. You could use this tool to slice a portion of a clip to remove that portion, for example. Pressing Ctrl+V accomplishes the same function on any targeted video or audio tracks at the playhead's position. Keep in mind that the double razor creates a new edit point on all tracks.

FIGURE 3.34 *The Razor Blade tools.*

The next tools are the navigational tools (see Figure 3.35). The magnifying glasses zoom in or out in the Timeline and in the Viewer and Canvas windows. The magnifying glass with a plus sign zooms in, and the magnifying glass with a minus sign zooms out. The plain hand tool moves your image around in the Canvas, Viewer, and Timeline windows. The hand with the arrows scrolls through video in the Timeline's and Browser's thumbnail pictures when you view your clips as small, medium, or large icons.

FIGURE 3.35 *Navigational tools.*

Next are the Crop and Distort tools (see Figure 3.36). The Crop tool (the one select-ed in the figure) hides or cuts off a portion of your picture for final viewing. The Distort tool drags any or all of the four corners of your image to any point on the screen. The Distort tool is useful for mapping a picture to a billboard that is shot at an angle, for example. These tools are used in either the Viewer or Canvas window when they are viewed in the Wireframe or Image + Wireframe views. These two tools parallel the numeric entries in the Motion tab.

FIGURE 3.36   *The Crop and Distort tools.*

The last set of tools in the Tools Palette is the Pen tool set, shown in Figure 3.37. There are three of them. The plain one sets keyframes in the Viewer, Canvas, and Timeline. The pen tool with the minus sign removes keyframes. The pen tool with the inverted U is the Pen Smooth tool. Smoothing keyframes creates a change between two keyframes that is not linear in its movement between the smoothed keyframe and the next one. The Pen Smooth tool adds bezier handles to the keyframe in the Canvas and Viewer, to keyframe markers in the Motion and Filter tabs, and to the Timeline keyframe graphs.

FIGURE 3.37   *The Pen tools.*

What Are Tooltips?

Tooltips are small yellow boxes that appear when you hold the selection tool over them for a few seconds. These are the Tooltips referred to on the General tab of the User Preferences window. Each name has a letter and/or number after it. These are the default keyboard shortcuts for these tools. Tooltips appear as long as you've set this function in the General tab of the User Preferences. In most cases, the cursor needs to be over the button for the Tooltip to appear, but for tools that aren't the default tool, you need to click and hold. But in most cases you don't need to click at all. Most of the buttons on the interface use Tooltips. It's a great way to learn the default keyboard commands. As you work with Final Cut Pro, you'll discover Tooltips and how they operate. Note that for a Tooltip to show for a specific control, the window that contains the control must be active.

While we're on the subject, I'd like to share with you my view on using the mouse versus the keyboard shortcuts. When you are new to a piece of software, the mouse can be your best friend. You like having a visual way of commanding the software to do what you want it to do. With the new keyboard remapping feature (discussed in Chapter 4, "Organization and Basic Editing"), this might be the way you always want to control Final Cut Pro. But after you've learned what your software can do, it's a huge timesaver to use keyboard shortcuts. There are hundreds of them. A partial list of them appears in Appendix D, "Keyboard Shortcuts." As we edit the movie, we'll discover some of them. But there is no doubt that you should learn to use them. The new keyboard remapping feature can make this a very personal way of working with Final Cut Pro.

Postproduction is always the last thing that happens in the process of producing shows. Unfortunately, it is the editor who usually delivers the final product and is up against the final deadline. If you are fast at using your edit tools, one of two things happens. If you bid your work as a flat fee, you make more per hour. But far more importantly, if you have a deadline that cannot be moved, when you are fast at commanding your computer to do what's needed, you have more time to try what-ifs: What if I edited this way or that way? You end up with a better edit if you have more time to experiment. Each time you move your hands from the keyboard, you lose time. Over a period of hours, this really adds up. After you've spent time thinking about what you want to do, why waste time getting it done? Time is a killer. You'll be hired more often and be viewed as an expert instead of an amateur if you use keyboard commands.

Learning keyboard commands is a one-at-a-time process. After you've learned to mouse to commands, it might feel awkward to learn keyboard shortcuts. Just learn one or two each session. Continue until they become like riding a bike. You won't regret it; I promise. Any seasoned producer will appreciate your speed. I'm talking about getting rehired for the next job. In the long haul, you'll spend about a fifth as much time using a keyboard command than you will using the mouse to get to the menu or button that invokes it.

continues

Here's one other thought: You can be more likely to get carpal tunnel syndrome from repeated mouse movements than from using keyboard shortcuts. In fact, the keyboard commands used in the process of editing are very unlike a straight typing job. A letter command now and then is just not as stressful as typing something like this book or data entries. You can't get away from using the mouse entirely (nor should you), but you certainly can minimize its use.

Workshop 3: Load the First Project and Become Familiar with the Navigational Controls and Window Arrangement

Learning to navigate easily and efficiently with the default set of windows should be the first task you really feel comfortable with. You'll use these windows so much that mastering the navigation techniques becomes mandatory. As you edit the movie, you'll find lots of ways to ease your workflow as soon as you understand workspaces you can create. In this workshop, you'll open and save the project files as well.

Load the Project's Files

The first thing to do is load all the DVD's project and media files onto your computer. They are located in two folders—Project Files and Media Files. If your computer has only one hard drive, click each folder one at a time from the DVD, and unstuff (decompress) them to your hard drive in a place that makes sense to you. If you have more than one drive, click the Project Files folder and drag it to your startup disk, and drag the Media Files folder to your second disk, which usually should be reserved for holding media files only.

1. Open Final Cut Pro. If you have a project already started, Ctrl-click its tab in the Browser window, and close it. Press   +O or select File, Open. Open the project file called Project 1.

2. Final Cut Pro warns you that it's missing media files. All the clips are offline, with red Xs in them. You need to reconnect them to the media files you copied in Step 1. Remember, they are just *reference* files that point to the actual media files. You know that the media files are there. It's just that they are not in the same place they were the last time this project was opened, so you need to tell Final Cut Pro where they are stored now. The same thing will happen if you move media files in the future or rename their folders from the Mac desktop. Highlight everything in the Project file's Browser (just click on the Brower and type command + a) and select "Reconnect Media" from the File menu to reconnect these reference files to the place you installed the media files when you copied their folder from the DVD. Another way to reconnect files is to highlight them in the Browser, Ctrl-click one of them, and select Reconnect Media.

Final Cut Pro's dialog boxes will ask you to find three files. The first of these is the "Boat Composite." You'll find this file in the "Compositing Material" file folder. When you open the folder, you'll see it at the top of the list, click on the "Matched Name Only" selection and also the "Reconnect All files in Relative Path" selection, then Click "Choose." Do the same dor the second file "1 hr timecode section" you'll find in the "Picture Clips" folder, and the same for the "B-Last Poem Clean" clip you'll find in the "ALL Sound Clips" folder. The rest of the files will reconnect automatically. As you import files, these three folders are where you'll find the media files.

3. Now all the entries in your Project 1 file are online, meaning that they are pointing to actual media files on your computer and are ready and available for use within your project. They should not have red lines through them (see Figure 3.38). Highlight the Browser window and select File, Save Project As. Rename this project file Project 1 (*your name*).

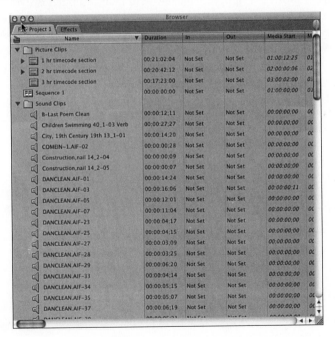

FIGURE 3.38   *The Browser after reconnection.*

4. Double-click "The Midnight Sun Finished Sequence" if it is not already open in the Timeline. This is the sequence you will build. It's included with the project file for reference if you need to look at it. We'll use it now to learn some navigation and viewing techniques. You may have to render everything in the sequence in order to play it back, and you should do so now.

The way to render everything is to open the "Midnight Sun Finished Sequence" by double clicking its Icon in the Browser. It opens in the Timeline Window. With the Timeline window active, type **Command+A**. Open the Sequence Menu and turn on every item in the "Render All" submenu (the check marks for each item will appear one by one). After you've selected them all, type **Option+R** to begin the rendering. Watch the movie so you know where we are headed, and familiarize yourself with the footage at the same time.

Arrange Windows and Viewing Options

1. The most efficient way to ease your workflow is to select the Window, Arrange command. A pop-up menu reveals a list of standard arrangement views and a way to customize window arrangements you want to use in this or any project (see Figure 3.39). The figure shows the options available with dual computer displays. FCP recognizes your computer's setup. Familiarize yourself with the standard setups available on your system by clicking each of the standard arrangements your setup provides. Especially note the new Multiple Edits arrangement and the Audio Mixing arrangement, which introduces FCP 4's Audio Mixer. We'll use it in many later Workshops.

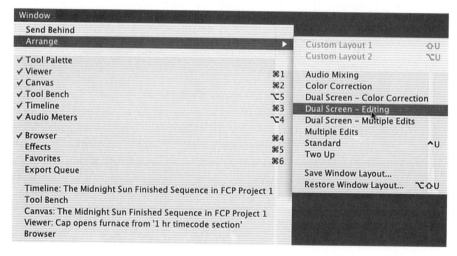

FIGURE 3.39   *Options available for dual computer displays.*

2. Select the Multiple Edits arrangement (Figure 3.40) and experiment with the views available in the new Frame Viewers (see Figure 3.40). Note that there are still Viewer and Canvas windows in this arrangement, but two Frame Viewers are present in Tool Bench windows. Tool Bench windows can contain other tools as well, notably the set of Video Scopes and the new Audio Mixer. We'll use these tools as we edit the movie, but experiment with the Frame Viewers now. Frame Viewers can display side-by-side views of two different clips at the same time. Note that if you are

working on a display that cannot display higher resolutions than 1280×854, the Multiple Edits arrangement is unavailable. If so, select Tools, Frame Viewer or press +7. Pressing +7 again opens a second Frame Viewer. You can drag the tab of the Frame Viewer from the Tool Bench window to see more at one time.

Frame Viewers are particularly helpful when you're color matching two clips. In fact, you can have many of them open at one time to see a whole range of clips in your sequence at once. You can even select the same frame to make one side a "before the filter is applied" view and the other side an "after the filter is applied" view.

Figure 3.40 shows five consecutive edits in the Timeline and a standard Viewer window. The current frame of the Timeline's playhead is displayed in the Canvas. Moving the Canvas's playhead updates all five frame views. The "standard" Viewer is left unchanged.

FIGURE 3.40   *The Multiple Edits arrangement.*

3. The pop-up menus on the bottom of the Frame Viewers allow you to split two picture views vertically or horizontally, as selected by the buttons at the bottom of the Frame Viewer. You can see various clips side by side this way. You can even swap which clip is displayed on which side by clicking the Swap button. This is perfect for matching color corrections, for example. Click and drag the green or blue buttons in a corner of one of the Frame Viewers to do your own "split screen" shapes of the two clips being viewed.

4. In the Frame Viewer on the far right in the Multiple Edit arrangement is a tab that reveals FCP's Video Scopes. You will read more about them later, but note that they are part of this window arrangement. Click the Video Scopes tab to look at these scopes. If you are working on a system that cannot display this arrangement, open the Video Scopes by pressing +9 or by selecting Tools, Video Scopes. As with Frame Viewers, you can open more than one set of Video Scopes.

5. Activate the Hand tool by dragging one of the two clips in a Frame Viewer. You can even drag which portion of a clip is being viewed, and can resize the split screen effect by dragging on one of the colored corners in this window.

6. When you are done experimenting, select Window, Arrange, Standard or press Ctrl+U.

Resize the Windows

1. Customize the arrangement of these four windows. Play with the sizing buttons. Start with the three buttons in the upper left of each window. Each of the four big windows has a handle in the lower-right corner. This handle sizes the window individually when you drag it. The only way to drag and move an entire window is by grabbing its uppermost bar. If you double-click this bar, the window is minimized to the dock. Clicking it again brings it back to its last position. You might want to do this to access the desktop, for example.

2. When you're done, reset the arrangement to the standard arrangement.

3. Final Cut Pro 4 adds a new way to arrange windows. If you move the mouse pointer *between* any two windows and then click and drag, you can resize all (or some of) the other major windows at the same time, making room for the window you want to enlarge. The currently selected tool changes to a resize pointer when you move it between any two of the four major windows. Try this between the Viewer and Canvas, and then between the Canvas and Timeline or Browser and Timeline windows. Pretty cool, eh?

4. When you are done, reset your arrangement to Standard again.

Save Window Arrangements

1. The Window, Arrange submenu has two ways to save arrangements. The first is to use the options Custom Layout 1 and Custom Layout 2. To save a layout, arrange your windows, hold down the   key, and select Window, Arrange, Set Layout 1 or 2. You can save two different layouts, and they will be tied to this project file only. You can start by arranging the windows in the standard way. Set up an arrangement that maximizes the Browser's size and diminishes the size of the other windows using the resize pointer. Then save this view as Custom Layout 1.

2. If you want to save a view for use in all projects, select Window, Arrange, Save Layout. After you have named and saved a view, Restore Layout brings up this arrangement of windows in any project you work on in the future. You can then start a new project and restore these saved layouts whenever you need them.

3. While using FCP, you might inadvertently hide a window. Restoring layouts or recalling the standard set of arrangements brings them forward, as does calling up custom window arrangements and layouts. Where many users get confused is when they close the Canvas window and the Timeline window closes with it. Double-clicking a Sequence icon in the Browser opens these two windows, with the sequence in the Timeline window. Open the Browser window by dragging it to the top left of the display, and then drag its lower-right corner until it fills the display.

4. Then select one of the arrangements to quickly put it back in its place and reveal all the earlier hidden windows.

Navigate the Browser

Because you use the Browser to locate all your source material, it's wise to learn how to navigate it with ease. Using the techniques described below should get you on your way.

1. Click the arrow (the disclosure triangle) next to the Picture Clips folder (bin) to open and close this bin from within the Browser window. Double-click the Picture Clips folder (bin) icon and open it in its own window. Drag the tab in this window to the Browser window's tab area. You can now access this bin from the Browser by clicking its tab. It's a great way to access often-used bins. This is important if you have a lot of them. Documentary and feature editors will appreciate this. Ctrl-click the Picture bin's tab to close it from the Browser's tabbed area. It's still accessible from the Browser and its window. Try it.

2. Hold down the   key while you double-click the Sound Clips bin in the Browser. It opens as a tabbed bin in the Browser. Either Ctrl-click its tab to close it from the tabbed area of the Browser or open it from the Browser's list and close it from the tabbed area.

3. If you close or hide one of the six major windows, you can open it again from the Window menu. Notice that most of the window names have keyboard shortcuts listed next to them. These shortcuts are displayed next to all commands that have them in all the pull-down menus. This is a great way to learn the keyboard shortcuts for the commands you use frequently. Close the Viewer window, and then open it again by pressing   +1. Close the Tools Palette, and then reopen it by selecting Window, Tools. Try closing the other windows and using the Window menu to open them back up. Be sure to close the Timeline window and then reopen it by double-clicking "The Midnight Sun Finished Sequence" in the Browser. One anomaly of this behavior is when you close the Canvas. The Timeline window also closes, but double-clicking any sequence opens them both back up.

4. Open the Picture Clips bin by double-clicking it. Ctrl-click the light gray area away from a clip's name, but within the Name column. You see the pop-up menu shown in Figure 3.41. If the bin is not opened as large as it is in the figure, there might be little arrows at the top and bottom so that you can scroll through this menu. Near the bottom of this menu is a set of four viewing commands. Click each to discover how it changes your view of this information. Choose View as Large Icons, and Ctrl-click the window's gray area between two clips to access the pop-up menu again. This time, select Arrange. If some of the clips were off the picture before, they might come into view. This can be helpful when you have many clips.

FIGURE 3.41   *The context menu found in a bin or in the Browser.*

5. Close the Picture Clips bin. Use the disclosure triangles next to the Sound Clips bin in the Browser to reopen it. Use the scrolling bar across the bottom to drag through all the information kept for each clip. Try clicking a column's name heading to sort that column's data in ascending or descending order. The arrow in the column name header tells you the sort order and which column you are sorting, as shown in Figure 3.42. Adjust the width of the Name column by clicking in the area next to its divider mark at the top between the Name column and the column to its right, as shown in Figure 3.43, and drag with the resize tool (which automatically appears) to increase or decrease the column width. Also note that you can drag the column names to rearrange their order, as shown in Figure 3.44.

FIGURE 3.42   *The sorting arrow display.*

FIGURE 3.43   *Sizing column widths by dragging the line between them in the column heading with the resize tool.*

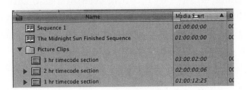

FIGURE 3.44   *Click and drag the column name to reposition the order of the columns.*

6. Ctrl-click these top column names. A context menu allows you to show more or different columns, as shown in Figure 3.45. You can choose from a Standard or Logging setup. This can help if you have many clips.

FIGURE 3.45   *The Column Names context menu.*

7. Open the Sound Clips bin by double-clicking its icon. Then maximize the bin window to reveal as much of it as possible by clicking the green maximize button. To move the Tracks column next to the Name column, click the Tracks column name and drag it to the left, next to the Name column. Then Ctrl-click each of the columns except Name, Tracks, Duration, Media Start, Media End, and Size, and select Hide until only these six columns remain.

8. Ctrl-click the Tracks column and select Save Column Layout. Name the layout "minimal layout," and click Save. Restore the Logging column's layout by Ctrl-clicking the Tracks column heading and selecting Logging Columns.

9. Ctrl-click the Media Start column and select Standard Columns to restore it to its original set of columns. You can also save a column layout that includes only the information you need to quickly review, such as a Label or Scene Number column.

It's important to know that you can minimize what you must view in order to locate source material quickly. Sorting columns also can help you find just what you're looking for. You can sort any column by clicking its column heading. Also keep in mind that you can start with the Standard or Logging layouts and customize them. When you are done with this exercise, select Window, Arrange, Standard to put your view of the interface in order again.

Navigate the Viewer and Canvas Windows

After you've selected what you want to edit by finding it in the Browser, you need to understand how to get around the Viewer and Canvas windows. The following exercises get you on your way.

1. From the Picture Clips bin, open the disclosure triangle next to the 1 hr time-code section Master clip, and then double-click the "Cap up mtn side dusk" marker. (We'll discuss markers in the next chapter. In this case, it was added as a mark you can quickly navigate to from within a clip.) The clip opens in the Viewer window. Play it by pressing the spacebar, clicking the play button in the Viewer window, or pressing the L key. The K key stops playback, and the J key plays backwards. Pressing the L key twice plays double speed, three times plays triple speed, and four times plays quadruple speed. The same goes for the J key, except that the video plays in reverse. Holding down the K key and the J or L key plays the footage forward or backward at about half speed. If you press L four times and then press J twice, you slow down forward playback to double speed, thus allowing you to decrease the speed as you approach the area you're looking for.

2. Holding down the K key while pressing the J or L key moves the video one frame at a time. This is a great way to "creep up on" a frame. Take some time to use all the navigation buttons immediately below the scrubbing bar. Click around the scrubbing bar to quickly navigate through the clip in the Viewer. You can scan by clicking and dragging through the scrubber bar as well. Keep in mind that you can do all these things in the Canvas window too as long as it's the active window. Spend some time with all these navigational techniques to become more familiar with them. Try them all and learn them. If you use the keyboard commands to navigate in the Viewer and Canvas windows, you will find the frames you're looking for much more efficiently.

If your mouse has a scroll wheel, you can use it to navigate through any active window that has vertical scroll bars, such as the Browser or the Timeline window, when working with more tracks than you can see at one time. You can use the scroll wheel to scroll up and down to reveal tracks hidden by a Timeline window that is too small to display them all. You can use a second (or third) monitor to display the Timeline and make it as tall as the monitor. This is wonderful when you're working with many audio and video tracks.

Navigate the Canvas and Timeline Windows

When you navigate in the Canvas or Timeline window, you navigate in both windows, because they are tied to each other. Moving the playhead in the Canvas moves it in the Timeline, and vice versa. You need to master the navigation of these windows. The following exercises get you started.

1. Double-click the sequence titled "Sequence 1" in the Browser window if it is not already the open sequence in the Timeline window (it should be an empty sequence). You mark clips for editing with the two buttons in the Viewer and Canvas windows or with the I or O key. Mark an In point and an Out point for a short duration in the "Cap up mtn side dusk" contained in the Viewer. Set an In point (I) near the beginning of the actor's walk up the hill at 01:13:24:04. Type +3622 in the upper-right time-code display box to jump 36 seconds and 22 frames farther into the clip. Type an Out point (O). Notice that the upper-left time-code display now shows a duration of 36:22. Click in the center of the picture in the Viewer window, and drag the ghosted square from there to the Canvas window highlighting the Insert command. Click the center of the Viewer window and drag directly down to the Timeline window, placing the clip in your sequence just past the earlier clip. Either dragging to the Canvas overlay or directly to the Timeline Window puts your material in your sequence. Highlight the first clip and press the Delete key. Now you have only the second clip. Take some time to navigate the Canvas window with this clip in it. All the same techniques of navigating in the Viewer work in the Canvas and therefore in the Timeline window as well.

2. Settle on a frame somewhere in the middle of the shot in the Canvas, and click the Show Match Frame button (in the lower-right corner of the Canvas window) or press the F key. The same frame appears in the Viewer window. Now move the Viewer's clip somewhat and press F again. The same frame appears in the Canvas. You can use this command to see if you've already used material in the sequence (in the case of match framing from the Viewer) or to pull a clip into the Viewer from the Canvas for viewing purposes.

3. Click the Toggle Timeline Track Height button. The four track height selections are shown in the lower left of the Sequence menu. Notice that they can easily be changed. You can also press Shift+T repeatedly to toggle through the different track heights. Wherever you navigate in the Canvas window, you also navigate at

the same time in the Timeline window. You can use the earlier controls in the Canvas, or you can click the ruler in the top of the sequence in the Timeline window to move around. You can also move around the Timeline by clicking around the scrubber bar at the bottom of the Canvas window.

4. If it isn't already open, open "The Midnight Sun Finished Sequence" by double-clicking it or by clicking its tab in the Canvas or Timeline window if it is already open. Experiment with the navigational sliders at the bottom of the Timeline window. Pay close attention to the handles at either end of the bar. If you move them, you expand or contract the view of the Timeline. If you slide the slider, you move earlier or later in the Timeline.

5. Press   +3 to make sure the Timeline window is active. Press Shift+Z to fill the Timeline window with the entire sequence. Press Z to activate the Zoom tool. Draw a box starting in the area above all the tracks in the Timeline and "lasso" a few clips in the center of the sequence. Note that you just zoomed in on that particular set of clips.

6. Press Shift+Z again to zoom back out. You see the entire sequence, no matter what size the Timeline window is set to. I find this the most efficient way to zoom in and out of the sequence in the Timeline window. Using the Zoom tool in the Timeline, Viewer, and Canvas windows zooms in. Pressing Shift+Z with one of these three windows active zooms back out. In the case of the Canvas and Viewer, this sets them to be "Fit to Window." You'll find that the most reliable playback of your clips and sequences happens when these windows are set to Fit to Window.

CHAPTER 4

Organization and Basic Editing

- The Editing Workflow
- Organizing Source Clips
- Setting In Points and Out Points
- Making Subclips and Their Properties
- Alternative Methods of Organizing Material
- Workshop 4: Organize and Begin Picking Shots

The Editing Workflow

The editing workflow in Final Cut Pro is very customizable. You organize your footage in the Browser, view clips in the Viewer, and then add them to the Timeline or Canvas for inclusion in your sequence (your finished program). You can edit entirely with the mouse, or you can edit entirely with the keyboard. It's up to you, but most editors seem to use a combination of both. Experiment to find your optimal setup for any particular job.

Customizing the Interface

Final Cut Pro 4's keyboard and interface mapping opens a world of possibilities. FCP 4 allows you to map virtually every menu command, keyboard command, and button in any or all of the four major windows discussed in Chapter 3 "Understanding Final Cut Pro's Interface: An Overview," as well as in the Tool Bench window. Buttons can simply be dragged and dropped onto the button bars located at the top of the windows. You also can map any of the 600 commands to your keyboard. Furthermore, you can save the settings of different interface layouts and even move them from editing station to editing station. It might be advantageous to have different layouts for different jobs, because one particular edit might not be the same as the next.

Mapping the Keyboard

You can activate the customizable Keyboard Layout window using the Tools menu or by pressing Opt+H. When you activate this new feature for the first time, the default keyboard layout opens. Thereafter, it opens with the custom keyboard layout you have set up.

Figure 4.1 shows the default keyboard layout. If you are familiar with FCP 3, the keyboard shortcuts are nearly the same in FCP 4, so don't worry that your old keyboard shortcuts won't work any more. Notably, though, Redo has changed. Undo is still Cmd+Z, but Redo is now Shift+Cmd+Z. Default keyboard shortcut layouts can always be recalled by clicking the Reset button, so don't be afraid to experiment.

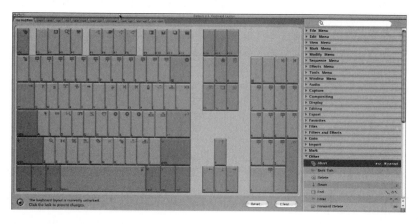

FIGURE 4.1   *The default keyboard layout window.*

Setting up a custom keyboard layout is easy. The right side of the window lists the various commands, organized by menu or category. First, unlock the keyboard by clicking the lock button in the bottom left of the window. Then drag the icon of a command from the list and drop it on the keyboard.

Because there are about 600 different icons, you can't memorize them all. If you hold the mouse over an icon that's already mapped to the keyboard, you see a ToolTip (small yellow box) that describes what the icon stands for.

Notice the search box in the top right of the window. When you type a search word, such as "audio," any command having to do with audio is listed on the right of the window. If you are unsure of which menu or category a certain command is in, the search box helps you narrow down the list. What's even more convenient is the fact that as you type the word you are searching for, the list changes accordingly. For example, to find all the audio commands, you really only need to type **au**. However, doing so lists any command that includes a word starting with "au," such as "auto" for the commands that Auto Select tracks. If you type **aud**, the "auto" commands disappear from the list. To go back to the "standard" listings, just click the X button in the search box.

Even if you don't change the default keyboard setup, you can see what keyboard commands might already be built into the default setup. This is especially useful when you repeatedly use the same command or set of commands.

You can clear the entire keyboard by clicking the Clear button in the lower right of the keyboard display. A total rewrite of the keyboard shortcuts can be especially useful for an editor who is used to different keyboard shortcuts from a different NLE application. I found myself using Avid keyboard shortcuts early on when I was learning FCP (to no avail, of course). I might have become more productive sooner if I had this ability then.

Notice the tabs above the keyboard layout. Clicking any of them opens another keyboard layout, allowing you to use modifier keys (such as Command, Shift, Option, and Ctrl) in your setup. Ten different modifier keystrokes are available for mapping. You cannot drag a shortcut from one modifier keyboard to another.

If you assign a new keystroke to a command, and it is already assigned in the current or default setup, Final Cut Pro asks you if you want to reassign the shortcut. Any assigned shortcut, whether a default one or one you've created, appears next to the command in the list on the right.

After you have remapped your keyboard, you can save the new layout for recall at any time on any edit station, including the present one. Select Tools, Keyboard Layout, Export. This layout is then saved in the User>Library>Preferences>Final Cut Pro User Data>Keyboard Layouts folder. You can recall it by selecting Tools, Keyboard Layout, Import. You can transport this file to another FCP station. I think one of the USB keychain-like memory devices might be just the ticket for this transportation.

Another feature available is to print these layouts. You can save a layout as a text file by selecting Tools, Keyboard Layout, Save grid as Text. This file can then be opened in a text editor or word processor. Because it's a tab-delimited text file, you can also open it in a spreadsheet program and print the layout for a "cheat sheet" that shows you only the commands you have remapped. Pretty cool.

Choosing the other options listed on the Keyboard Layout submenu results in different columns and formats for the text files created:

- Save Menu Commands as Text creates a text file that lists all the commands on the File, Edit, View, Mark, Modify, Sequence, Effects, Tools, and Window menus. (Choosing this option doesn't list the command groups, such as Compositing and Editing.)

- Save Command Groups as Text saves all commands on the Audio, Capture, Compositing, Display, Editing, Export, Favorites, Files, Filters and Effects, Goto, Help, Import, Mark, Other, Project, Render, Search and Replace, Settings, Timecode, Tool palette, Tools, Transport, and Windows command groups. Commands in the text file are listed by command group in the same order they are listed in the Command list area. (This option does not let you save menu sets, such as File and Edit.)

- Save All Commands as Text saves all the sets of mapped keyboard commands (command groups and menu sets), with commands listed alphabetically.

- Key Table as Grid exports as tab-separated variables for import to a spreadsheet.

- The Menu command list is simply a list of menus and the commands and keyboard equivalents that are associated with them. The command is tab-separated, so it forms its own column if it is imported to a spreadsheet (otherwise, it would print with a gap). Organization is by menu.

- Command Groups as Text is essentially the same as the menu commands but is organized by function, such as Audio and Compositing, instead of being based on a menu.

- All Commands as Text organizes the information alphabetically.

The last three commands are essentially the same—a list of commands and keyboard equivalents currently assigned, separated by a tab. All that differs is their organization—by menu, by command group (functions), or alphabetically.

Mapping Buttons to the Button Bars

You can map the command icons to many places in the interface. The Browser, Viewer, Canvas, Timeline, and Tool Bench windows contain a button bar at the top right where you can add these commands. The Timeline window's button bar already contains two commands—the Snapping icon and the Linked Selection icon. Clicking them activates these commands or turns on or off a condition they invoke, such as snapping.

You can map from the Keyboard Layout window's list of mappable commands. You also can open a command by itself for the task by selecting Tools, Button List, by pressing Opt+J, or by Ctrl-clicking a button bar to open the button list. The same button list found in the Keyboard Layout window opens by itself, and the same search box is there as well. If you drag an icon and drop it on one of the button bars in any of the four windows, it's added to the button bar. To remove it, drag it off the button bar, or Ctrl-click it and select Remove from the context menu that appears.

Figure 4.2 shows the context menu that opens when you Ctrl-click any button. This menu allows you to add a spacer between buttons (possibly to group them), colorize the button (to further delineate its category), remove it or all of the buttons in the button bar, open the Keyboard Layout window, and save or restore a button set. These files are much the same as the keyboard layout saves described a moment ago. They are kept in the User>Library>Preferences>Final Cut Pro Users Data>Button Bars folder. Button bar layouts can be moved from station to station. Freelancers will really like this new feature. Create a CD that contains all your custom settings, and load it onto another computer to feel right at home.

FIGURE 4.2
A button's context menu.

Using a Multibutton Mouse

There is an enormous advantage to adding a multibutton mouse to your setup. Many context menus are opened by a Ctrl-click (a right-click on a multibutton mouse), and a mouse's scroll wheel scrolls all the windows vertically in FCP 4. This enhances your workflow tremendously. Scrolling through a Browser or bin full of clips is faster this way.

Ctrl-clicking is best accomplished with a two-or-more-button mouse. I think that the single-button mouse is quaint, but hardly efficient. I heartily recommend a multifunction mouse for use with Final Cut Pro. There are context menus all over the interface you can activate by Ctrl-clicking. You can get to them much quicker than with a keyboard command and a single button mouse click, and you click just once with a multibutton mouse programmed to be a Ctrl-click. You'll be amazed how much easier it is to right-click instead of holding down the Ctrl key and clicking. Ctrl-clicking is akin to right-clicking on a Windows machine, and it's built into many Mac programs, so you'd use it for more than just Final Cut Pro. It's a necessity.

Organizing Source Clips

It's a terrible thing to continually have to interrupt your creative flow because you can't find the clip you know will work really well. The best way to make your workflow fluid is to get your source clips into a manageable order. By doing so, you also refamiliarize yourself with the source material. As you watch it, you begin to formulate a strategy for editorial. Some projects have very little source material and don't really call for a lot of organization, but projects of any length really benefit from it. Think of editors who work with thousands of source clips! The last feature-length project I worked on had about 3,500 individual takes of about 1,000 different setups. Looking for specific takes without organization would have been a waste of time.

Take a look at Figure 4.3. It's the source footage you are about to edit. It doesn't look like too much to sort through, right? It's deceiving, though. The audio clips have some strange names, for one thing. These names are those used by the recording facility where the audio was recorded. They were not captured from tape. They were created as digital files and were sent to editorial with the names and audio formats they were recorded under. So they came to the editor with odd names created by someone else. The three large video files have pretty nondescriptive names (other than the time-code hour that is tied to them), and they contain many shots and more than one take of those setups. Sorting through nearly an hour of footage cut into only three different picture clips would be a huge waste of time.

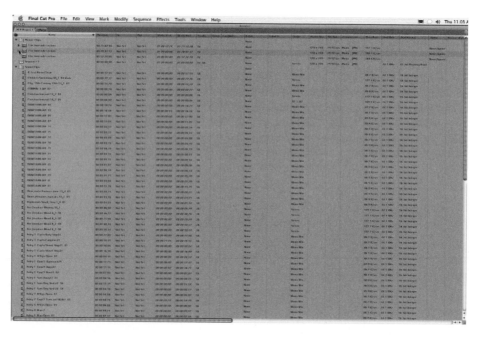

FIGURE 4.3   *The open Browser window.*

As in the case of this tutorial, if you didn't shoot the source footage, you had one look at the source material when you captured the footage or viewed the footage once for this tutorial, but I'll wager that although you noted many of the shots in your memory, you can't remember exactly which clip they are in right now. It's time to subclip them and organize them into bins that contain either the scenes they belong to or a category for the type of element they are. The same can be said for the audio files. We will begin to do this in this chapter's workshop.

Editing Aesthetics

No two films are exactly alike, but all of them have similarities. Everyone grows up watching motion pictures, and we've become accustomed to certain conventions used in the language of film. Hopefully, we get so wrapped up in watching a film that we don't notice how we are manipulated by the filmmaker. The moment an editor misuses this language, we lose interest, or, just as bad, we get confused and lose track of the story.

What are aesthetics, and how do they apply to the art of motion pictures? The dictionary defines this term as follows:

1. The branch of philosophy dealing with the study of values such as the beautiful and the sublime

2. The study of the rules and principles of art

3. A particular idea of what is beautiful or artistic

4. How something looks, especially when considered in terms of how pleasing it is

Every filmmaker strives to create art, but what is art? Back to the dictionary:

1. The creation of beautiful or thought-provoking works, such as in painting, music, or writing

2. Beautiful or thought-provoking works produced through creative activity

3. A branch or category of art, especially one of the visual arts

4. The skill and technique involved in producing visual representations

5. Creation by human endeavor rather than by nature

6. The techniques used by someone in a particular field, or the use of those techniques

7. The skill or ability to do something well

8. The ability to achieve things by deceitful or cunning methods

Enough of Webster. As a filmmaking storyteller, it's your job to use all these definitions of aesthetics. We'll use these definitions and show, at least with this particular project, how they apply. Hopefully you'll keep these tenents in mind when you edit your next project.

The first of my "live and die" rules of editing aesthetics is that storytelling is paramount. If a writer creates the story on paper, it's the director who does the first "transfer" of the story to motion pictures. The editor does the last rewrite of the story using pictures and sound instead of verbs and nouns.

What keeps us involved in a good story? A good story keeps our attention; isn't so familiar a story that the outcome is never in doubt; keeps us entertained, possibly by telling an older story in a fresh way; and keeps our minds on the subject at hand, not

continues

boring us with unimportant details. There are lots of different views of editorial technique, and there are many different styles, but one that everyone can agree on is that a setting must be established first.

Usually, when you tell a well-constructed story, you don't start with what happened until you establish where, when, and in what climate or atmosphere it takes place. This sets a mood. It prepares the viewers for an emotional reaction you are trying to get them to feel, so that as the story is told, they identify with your characters. Hopefully your viewers will get so emotionally involved with the characters that they feel fear or joy, just as the characters do. When telling a story with pictures, this is called an *establishing shot* (or group of shots). Let your viewers know where and under what conditions the story begins. When telling stories that jump from place to place, it's often a good idea to use at least one shot that tells the viewers where you've taken them so that they are emotionally set up to participate.

Another thing to think about with a group of establishing shots is that each one should build on the next. Each shot should tell the viewers a little more about the setting of your story or scene. "The Midnight Sun" takes place in an incredibly cold place, and it involves death, struggle, and promises made and kept. It sounds sort of sad, lonely, serious, and tragic. Actually, this movie is a comedy! Like a great joke, this movie needs to be set up so that the viewer thinks we are going in one direction when in fact we end up in quite another.

An editor's job is to get the audience to *participate emotionally* with the story. That's what keeps them involved and entertained. If you present them with an edit that misuses the language of motion pictures or that makes the audience *aware* that they are being emotionally manipulated, you lose them. They get bored; they turn off the movie or go to the snack bar. In artistic and even financial terms, this loss of interest spells disaster. If the audience loses interest in your TV spot, you don't sell product. If they lose interest in your instructional video or documentary film, they don't learn, and they don't become productive with new knowledge. When they don't get involved with your story, they don't recommend your movie to another potential moviegoer.

When editing a narrative film like "The Midnight Sun," another important technique to employ is what I call "organic editing." These motivated edits feel natural to the viewer because they are much like *what the viewers would be motivated to look at if they were watching the scene in real life.* The actors usually establish a rhythm for a scene; this can be enhanced by the editor's edit decisions. As you edit a story, you'll find that the story contains a beat, just as if it were a piece of music. Actually, there is a rhythm to everything in life. We like rhythm. It reminds us of the most comforting time of our existence—the time when all we had to do all day was listen to our mother's heartbeat. Each of us has an internal clock as well. Its tempo differs from person to person. Your edit decisions sometimes reflect your personality. Some folks talk really fast, and others don't. But when you include a beat between speeches, for example, that character's own rhythm should be reflected in the amount of time you choose to use as a beat between lines. A character's rhythm also reveals itself in the speed between different actions he or she performs.

Think of your own heartbeat and what happens to it when you're scared (or feeling any emotion, actually). A chase scene might excite you enough to make your heart start racing. Reflecting this, you might choose to show cuts of shorter and shorter duration to reflect the emotions onscreen. Put yourself in these emotional moments, and your own personality will begin to show through the edit decisions you make. When you get excited, the edits come faster, and when you relax, they slow down, but only within the context of the story at any given time. Don't show a single frame the audience doesn't need to see, and do show all the frames they must see to understand the story each shot has to tell. After it has been told, get off the shot. Don't bore the audience with redundancies or information that doesn't have much to do with the story being told. Just because it's a pretty shot doesn't mean it adds to the story.

To perform an edit that keeps the viewer involved, start by organizing what the director has shot. If you can't find a certain shot (or worse, you aren't even aware of it), you can't use it effectively when you get to where it should be in your sequence. Just breaking long clips into smaller bites also helps familiarize you with the footage, and that leads to better edit decisions. You don't want any of the footage to be "out of sight, out of mind."

Setting In Points and Out Points

You can set an In point in the Viewer, Canvas, or Timeline window by clicking the appropriate button under the Viewer (if you are setting a source clip's starting point) or the Canvas and Timeline (if you are setting where it starts in the sequence). Out points are set the same way, with the respective Mark Out buttons in the Viewer or Canvas. The keyboard shortcuts are the best way to set In and Out points in the Viewer, Canvas, or Timeline. Press I for in and O for out. The I and O keys are right above the J, K, and L keys, used to shuttle the video in all three windows. You should get into the habit of using these five keys to move, mark, and creep through the footage (L or J +K) to mark your In and Out points most of the time. If you have timecode numbers, such as those given for the Workshops in this book, you can either type them in or get used to using the J, K, and L keys to shuttle to them. Also don't forget that pressing the J or L key more than once speeds up the shuttling process (L for play and J for reverse). By pressing the left or right arrow key, you can go through your footage backward or forward a frame at a time to locate just the right frame at which to set an In or Out point.

tip   You don't have to pause to set an In or Out point. You can set it as you play the video or audio in either the Viewer or the Canvas. You can continually press I to update the Mark In point or keep pressing the O key to keep updating the Mark Out point as you watch the video. Each time you press I or O while you watch the video, the new point gets set. This is great for getting a quick update or making a change as you watch the video play. A constant updating of the In or Out points really helps move your editing along. This works well when you don't know exactly where a pan might end or a zoom or dolly might end or start. It also helps you set the pacing and timing of edits (finding the rhythm of the beats, as mentioned in the sidebar). In the case of an interview, it's great to update an Out point when the next sentence is finished. As soon as you start setting points this way, you'll see the advantages. Try it. You'll like it.

You can't set more than one In point or Out point in the Viewer unless the source material contains audio and video. If the clip contains more than one track of media, you can perform split edits. With split edits, multiple-track source clips (such as sound sync audio and video clips) are marked so that the audio and video are edited into your sequence at different times. For example, you show the video and then add the audio a bit later, or you hear the audio before the video that syncs with it.

However, there's a way to perform split edits more intuitively. First, you cut the audio track the way you want to hear it using audio/video cuts along the way (it helps to set your timing and the scene's rhythm too). After you have performed this rough cut, unlink the synchronized audio from the video clip it's associated with by pressing the unlink button in the upper-right corner of the Timeline window or by pressing Shift+L. Then perform roll edits on the video track. Roll to the left or right. The split edit then gets performed in this manner. An even faster way is to use the Roll edit tool while holding down the Option key. This temporarily unlinks the video clips from their linked audio.

Making Subclips and Their Properties

You can make subclips from any sort of clip, including other subclips. The idea is to spend no more time than necessary to locate a specific shot or moment in what could possibly be an entire tape's clip. In other words, if you find it once, finding it again is a snap.

After you open Project 1, supplied on the DVD, you see that two of the three video clips currently in the Browser window have disclosure triangles next to their names. If you click one of them, it opens to show you the markers I've placed in them. Markers in this case are used to begin the sorting of all the footage that was shot for "The Midnight Sun."

If you double-click one of these clip markers, the footage marked between the position of the marker and the next marker opens in the Viewer window. You can actually edit from this portion of the *master clip* (the original captured video clip that the marked footage is a part of). But you'd still have to sort through a lot of names and open and close the master clips to locate the footage. It's still not as efficient as it could be. The markers are still really a part of a master clip organizationally. Also, in most cases, not all of the clips for a specific scene are together. So to work on a given scene, you still have to sort through a lot of clips to find the appropriate one.

You can turn these markers into a *subclip* and drag and drop this subclip into bins you've created to further organize the footage. The clip named "3 hr timecode section" contains no markers, so it doesn't have a disclosure triangle next to its name. You'll create subclips and markers in this chapter's Workshop and finish the job.

To mark a subclip without using markers, set an In point where you want the subclip to begin, and set an Out point where you want it to end. Then select Modify, Make Subclip, or press Cmd+U. *The subclip is created in the same bin that the master clip it was created from resides in.* If you make a mistake with a subclip, simply highlight its icon in the Browser and press the Delete key to start over, or drag it to the bin it should be in. Again, you are making reference or *pointer* files; you aren't deleting any media.

A problem can arise later if you don't plan ahead as you make edits. The same problem arises if you make edits using marked clips. Final Cut Pro assumes that there is no media on either side of the start point or end point you used when you created a subclip. It's treated as its own capture (media file) from tape and not as part of the "real" media file it was taken from, which might indeed have frames before and after it. If you can't lengthen or create a transitional effect such as a dissolve between two shots because you used this subclip in your sequence, highlight it in the sequence and choose Modify, Remove Subclip Limits. This releases Final Cut Pro to use the frames before or after those contained in the subclip.

tip

Limiting media file access might seem awkward, but it has a definite benefit. If you make subclips a bit on the "fat" side, meaning that you subclip *all the possibly usable footage* even if you think or know you won't use it, removing subclip limits then usually becomes a nonissue, *because you wouldn't want to use media past what you've marked.* The benefit is that this method of "fat" subclipping also lets you know later you can't use the media before or after the subclip because it would cause a camera's cut (the take before or after the current subclip) to show up in the middle of a transitional effect—something you want to avoid.

In other words, when you edit from a subclip to your sequence, you run the risk of not being able to apply a transitional effect (such as a dissolve between two shots) where you want to if you created a subclip with *only* the footage you think you want to use in your sequence. In most cases, don't use subclipping to set your *actual* edit points; go "fat" and subclip the entire bit of footage that relates to a particular shot or take. If you are subclipping from a slate, which is an ideal way to shoot in preparation for logging, start with the slate and end when the camera cuts or even at the beginning of the next slate, not before and not after. You'll never want to show a slate in a scene, so subclipping from slate to slate will never set up a situation where you need to remove subclip limits.

Alternative Methods of Organizing Material

There are alternative ways to break down material for quicker access. For example, you can place it in the Viewer, set In and Out points, and drag it from the Viewer to the Browser. The benefit is that you don't have to worry about removing subclip limits if you edit from these "subclips." They allow you to access certain shots quicker than just searching long clips, and you can rename them as well. But they are not true subclips; they are copies of your master clip with In and Out points. The use of the scrubber bar becomes more problematic, because it is tougher to scroll within objects created this way, especially if it's a short subclip contained in a very long source clip. If you use the method described in the Tip, you gain the ability to scrub more efficiently, and you won't be bothered with removing subclip limits.

There is another negative thing about organizing using any other method. Methods other than creating true subclips leave items with the wrong icons—master clip icons. You never want confusion about this. If clips have similar names, they could be confused with master clips.

When you make subclips from subclips, you retain the ability to see a proper icon. Removing subclip limits also allows this new subclip to access all the media associated with the original medium of the capture it's contained in, not just the media from its original subclip.

Workshop 4: Organize and Begin Picking Shots

Final Cut Pro contains a set of tools that help you get organized and break down your source material to group related clips. Sorting the material saves you a lot of time during the edit and reacquaints you with the material. The Browser is where source material is organized.

1. Open Project 1. You will preserve this original project file and create another one for your own use. That way, you can always start over if you need to without reloading everything from the DVD. Select File, Save Project As. Type **FCP Project 1** *"your name"* in the Save As: field. It's OK to put this file in the same folder as the original, or you can put it in a new folder, as shown in Figure 4.4. Keep this file on your startup disk, not your media disk (if you have one).

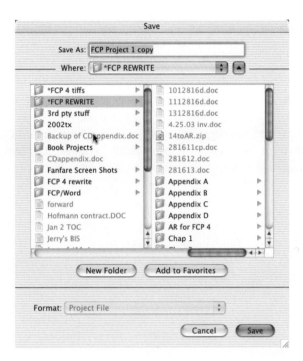

FIGURE 4.4   *The Save dialog box.*

2. Click the triangle next to the Picture Clips bin in the Browser. It opens, and
    its contents are revealed, as shown in Figure 4.5. Double-click the Picture Clips bin's
    folder to open it in its own window, as shown in Figure 4.6. This also closes the bin in
    the project window. Arrange this new window to the side of the Browser window if
    it's not already there so that you can see its tab and the other tabs in the Browser at
    the same time and so that clicking either does not hide the other. Drag the tab near
    the top of the Picture Clips bin to the area where the FCP Project 1 and Effects tabs
    are. The bin's tab should now be part of a set of three tabs contained in the Browser,
    as shown in Figure 4.7. Clicking a tab is a quick way to get to a particular bin. If you
    Option-click a bin, it opens as a tab in the Browser.

    If you have 30 or 40 bins, this might save you a lot of time searching for the one
    or two bins you are currently using. Leave it open for now, but to close the tab in
    the Browser, Ctrl-click the tab and choose Close Tab. You can also put bins inside
    bins. Let's say you have a set of bins broken into scenes. Within these scenes are
    clips of an on-camera host and shots to illustrate the points the speaker is talking

about (these shots are often called b-roll). You could keep the host in the scene bin in another bin created inside the scene bin and the b-roll shots in another. The more organized you are, the easier and quicker it is to make edit decisions. Also, you're less likely to miss a really wonderful edit because you forgot about that special element or couldn't find it.

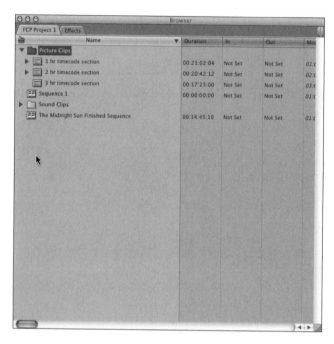

FIGURE 4.5   *Opening a bin with the disclosure triangle.*

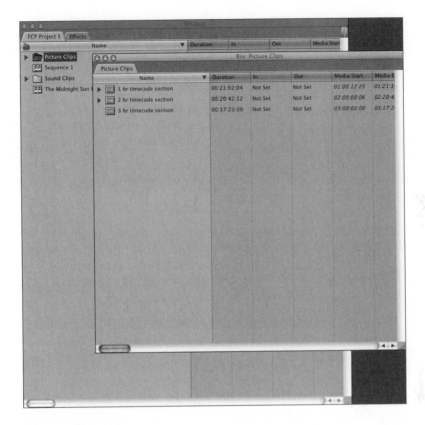

FIGURE 4.6   *The open bin window.*

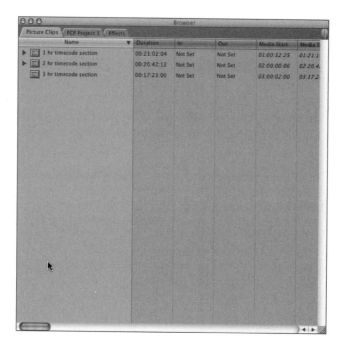

FIGURE 4.7   *The quick access tab.*

3. Click the FCP Project 1 tab. Create a new bin in it by selecting File, New, Bin or by pressing Cmd+B. Notice that the bin's name is highlighted and ready to change, as shown in Figure 4.8. You don't need to delete the old name; just start typing. Type **Scene 1** and Press Enter. You'll look for opening or "establishing" shots to set the movie's mood.

FIGURE 4.8 *Renaming bins.*

4. Open the Picture Clips bin and click the disclosure triangle next to "2 hr timecode section." You see the markers I've placed there for you. Highlight the marker named Abandoned Rags and press Cmd+U. A new subclip with the same name is created in the Picture Clips bin. It might be out of view, so scroll down to find this new subclip.

5. Drag the tab in the Browser of the Picture Clips bin to the side so that it opens in a second window and reveals the rest of the Browser's contents in the first window. Then drag this new subclip, named "Abandoned Rags from '2 hr time-code section' Subclip," to the Scene 1 bin in the first window. Clicking the disclosure triangle next to the Scene 1 bin reveals that the subclip is now there, as shown in Figure 4.9. Notice its serrated clip icon.

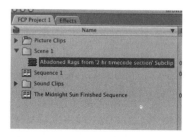

FIGURE 4.9   *The Scene 1 bin containing a new subclip.*

6. Let's do another subclip from marker creation. Open the "1 hr timecode section" disclosure triangle by clicking it, and reveal the markers contained in it. Locate the marker named "Cap up mtn side dusk," which starts at 1:13:03:22, and press Cmd+U. Then drag this new subclip to the Scene 1 bin.

note   The source footage from the film transfer used throughout this book is nondrop frame timecode. Also note that none of the film transfers have any audio tracks. Sync sound can't be recorded to the film. For what little sync sound is used in the film, you'll have audio files that were created from the Nagra that recorded the sound.

7. Drag the "Cap up mtn side dusk" marker from the Scene 1 bin to the Viewer, or simply double-click it. Either way, it opens there. The reason to use this copy is that you will create subclips from it. They will appear in the Scene 1 bin as you make them, not in the Picture Clips bin, where I find it convenient to store all master clips. Subclips are created in the same bin in which the clips or subclips they are created from reside. You are primarily looking for establishing shots for the opening of the movie.

8. Click the Play button in the Viewer. You see a few false starts, and then two takes of Cap pulling Sam's body up a hill, followed by some scenic long shots of snow-covered mountains. The most vivid color in these shots is the sky behind the mountains in Cap's takes, but unfortunately there is not much footage in this shot without Cap walking through it. These were the only long shots taken for an establishing shot for the story, so you'll use a frame of Cap's background without Cap in it and freeze it.

I rather like the balance of the frame at 01:14:04;04. Click the time-code display in the upper right of the Viewer, type **1140404** in the time-code display box, and press Enter. The Viewer displays that frame. There's no need to type the colons, the semicolons, or the first 0. Final Cut Pro adds 0s to the beginning of any time-code numbers so that they contain a total of eight numbers, which all time-code numbers contain. If you typed **1000**, the Viewer would display code at 00:00:10;00 (as long as that time-code number is in the clip you are navigating with).

9. Select Modify, Make Freeze Frame or press Shift+N. A freeze frame with this background is created, with a default duration of 10 seconds from its In point to its Out point. This duration is as it was set in the General tab of the User Preferences window. This freeze's full duration is 2 minutes. Open the Scene 1 bin by double-clicking it. Click and drag the clip from the center of the Viewer back to the Scene 1 bin. (Drag it to the Name column.) As you drag, you see a ghosted version of the clip drag with the mouse. When you let go, a graphic clip is saved in your bin that is this freeze frame, as shown in Figure 4.10. Notice that the frame's timecode number becomes part of its name, and it has a new icon, indicating that it is a graphic file, as shown in Figure 4.11.

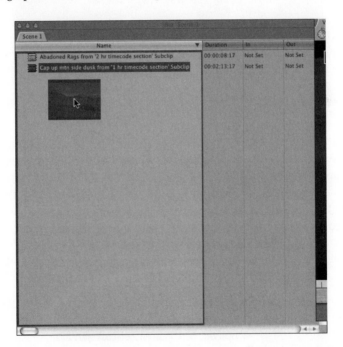

FIGURE 4.10   *Dragging a clip from the Viewer.*

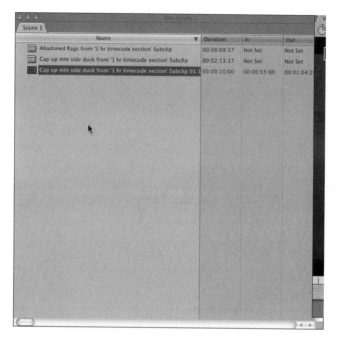

Figure 4.11   *A freeze frame clip after being dragged from the Viewer.*

10. Click the recent clips list in the lower-right corner of the Viewer, and select "Cap up mtn side dusk from '1 hr timecode section' Subclip," as shown in Figure 4.12. It reappears in the Viewer. Scroll through it to 1:14:33;14 and mark an In point. Either click the Mark In button or press I. Then click the Play button or press L until the end of this particular shot. Set an Out point there. This time, instead of dragging, choose Modify, Make Subclip or press Cmd+U. A subclip appears in the Scene 1 bin, ready to rename. Type **Pan of Mountains**. Double-click this new subclip's icon. The subclip opens in the Viewer. You'll find that it contains only the footage you selected.

Figure 4.12   *The Recent Clips shortcut menu.*

11. Take a look at the Pan of Mountains subclip. Reload the "Cap up mtn side dusk" subclip into the Viewer, but do it this time by highlighting the Scene 1 bin and using the up or down arrow keys to navigate to it. Highlight "Cap up mtn side

dusk from '1 hr timecode section' Subclip" and press Enter. The subclip reopens in the Viewer. There is a way to keep your hands on the keyboard instead of going back and forth between it and the mouse. If you type Cmd+4 to activate the Browser, you can navigate to any item in the Browser by using the four arrow keys to do so. The up and down keys do what you'd expect, and the right and left arrow keys will open an item with a disclosure triangle to navigate down or up through its contents. You may find you can navigate very fast this way. Where the position indicator (or playhead) is sitting is where you'll mark an In or an Out point if you press I or O. The Viewer must be the active window if you press L for play (or the spacebar, which also toggles play on and off), K for stop, or J to play backward. Holding down the K key and then holding down either the L key or J key plays a clip slowly. The right and left arrow keys advance or step forward and backward through a clip one frame at a time for precise movements. Using the mouse for this works too, but in the long haul it takes more time to get to exactly where you want to go.

12. Try the different methods of marking and creating subclips and navigating in the Viewer to find the In and Out points. I think you'll find that you will become more efficient using the keyboard commands to mark In, mark Out, and create the subclip. You can also drag the position indicator to scroll through the clip. Normally, you would subclip the two takes of Cap's walk up the hill, but later we'll edit the section that contains this shot as a pre-edited scene. When you get done trying things on your own, delete any subclips you've created so that your Scene 1 bin contains only the same clips as Figure 4.13. Just highlight any subclip and press the delete key to delete it.

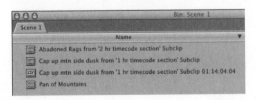

Figure 4.13   *The first four items.*

13. Create three more subclips of the shots that follow the last subclip the same way as earlier and name them Mountains 1, 2, and 3. When you are done, you should have a bin that contains the same six clips shown in Figure 4.14. When you are finished, delete the "Cap up mtn side dusk" subclip from the Scene 1 bin. (Be sure *not* to delete the freeze frame.) Don't worry; you still can access it from the Picture Clips bin. (There will be less to sort through later in the Scene 1 bin.)

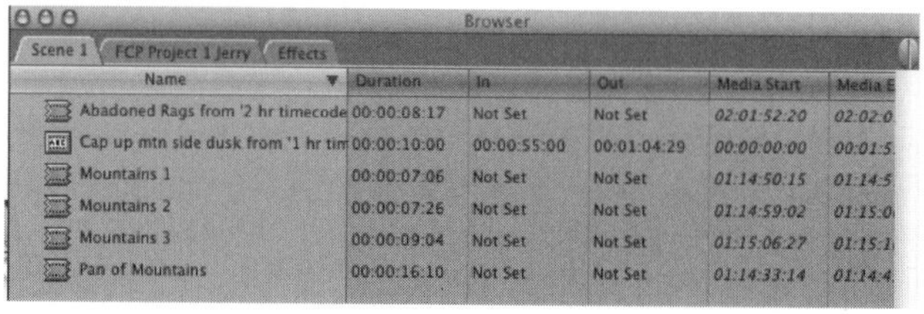

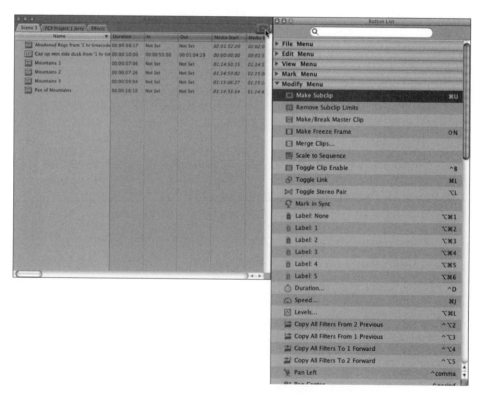

FIGURE 4.14   *The first six items.*

Work with the Button List, Button Bar, and Keyboard Layout

1. Press Opt+J to open the button list, or navigate to the Tools menu and select it from there. Then open the Modify menu's disclosure triangle by clicking it.

2. At the top of the list is the Make Subclip icon. Drag it to the button bar in the Browser, as shown in Figure 4.15.

FIGURE 4.15   *Dragging a button from the button list to the Browser's button bar.*

3. Ctrl-click the newly placed button, and change its color.

4. While you're here, take a close look at the button list. This is the same list that opens with the Keyboard Layout window. Note the organization of this enormous list of buttons. The menus across the top of Final Cut Pro 4's interface are repeated here, as are the commands on the pull-down menus.

5. Open the keyboard layout by pressing Opt+H or by navigating to it using the Tools menu. The button list closes, and the default keyboard layout opens. Click the cmd tab to reveal the default keyboard layout when the Command key is used. Note that Cmd+U is the default setting for the Modify, Make Subclip command.

6. Click the lock button in the lower left of the Keyboard Layout window to unlock it. Take some time to drag buttons from the list on the right and drop them on the keyboard so that you get a feel for how this works. When you are done, click the Reset button in the keyboard layout to reset the layout to the default settings for now. As soon as you get a handle on tasks you often perform (especially those with no default keyboard equivalent), you'll know when it's time to either learn a default keyboard shortcut or map a button to the keyboard or a button bar to ease your workflow. It will be when you navigate to a menu item repeatedly. When you are done experimenting and you've reset the keyboard layout to its default, close the Keyboard Layout window by clicking the close button in the top-right corner.

Discover Marker Shortcuts and Begin Working with Markers

1. Navigate to the Picture Clips bin and double-click the "1 hr timecode section" master clip to load it into the Viewer.

2. Press the Home key to bring the playhead to the first frame of the clip in the Viewer.

3. Press Shift+M to jump to the first marker. Pressing Shift+M repeatedly moves the playhead from marker to marker. Try this.

4. Press Opt+M to move the next marker earlier in the clip. Obviously, you could just edit from here, but your clip names in the Timeline would all be named the same as this master clip. This would be very inefficient later. Therefore, you'll continue to create subclips from these markers.

5. Open the "3 hr timecode section" master clip in the Viewer by double-clicking it. You'll create your own set of markers for this clip. To create one, you need to move the playhead to the starting frame of the marker by pressing M twice. A dialog box opens, allowing you to name the marker. (This name will also be used in the subclip you'll create from the markers.)

6. Navigate to 03:00:02:00, press M twice, name the subclip "Sam Asks Cap for Cremation tk 1 Pan," and press Enter. You see a marker in the scrubber bar and a disclosure triangle next to the master clip in the Picture Clips bin. Click the disclosure triangle next to the master clip's name to reveal the list of markers. You can change a marker's name if you need to by clicking it.

7. Next, using the following log, create a marker at each time-code number in the list, and name them accordingly. Don't deviate, because the way this works as you edit these clips depends on the exact positions of the subclips you'll end up creating.

Sam Asks Cap for Cremation tk 2 Pan	03:01:21;10
CU Sam looking at picture	03:02:38;15
CU over shoulder of Picture	03:03:00;14
Unusable footage	03:03:27;21
Wide angle Cap lights match in snow	03:03:35;28
CU Cap lights match in snow tk 1	03:04:34;28
CU Cap lights match in snow tk 2	03:04:44;26
Reverse Cap lights match in snow tk 1	03:05:09;25
Reverse Cap lights match in snow tk 2	03:05:29;22
Dog footage	03:06:07;04
Med shot Cap reverse on sled	03:10:58;14
CU Dog	03:11:33;03
Cap pulls body over ridge of snow	03:11:53;29
Dogs under trees resting	03:12:34;17
Cap looks at smoke tk 1	03:13:29;20
CU Lake Labarge Sign	03:13:45;27
Smoke coming from behind hill	03:13:56;26
Smoke bkg 1	03:14:12;06
Cap walks away LS	03:14:27;09

When you are done, opening the "3 hr timecode section" clip in the Picture Clips bin looks like Figure 4.16.

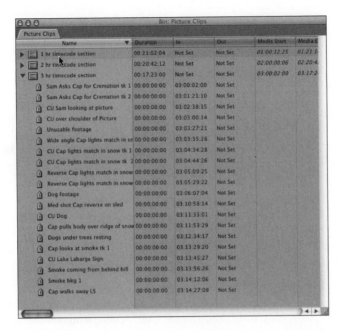

FIGURE 4.16   *The Picture Clips bin after you place the markers for "3 hr timecode section."*

8. Navigate to the Picture Clips bin. Open the marker named Lone Cross contained in the "1 hr timecode section" master clip in the Viewer by highlighting it and pressing Enter. Play the clip. Because it contains only this one shot, activate the Browser, make sure the Lone Cross marker is highlighted, and click the newly placed Subclip button in the Browser's button bar. Drag the new subclip to the Scene 1 bin.

   As explained in Chapter 3, these are reference files. They can also be thought of as aliases to a media file and, in this case, a portion of the actual media file. You didn't copy the media file; you created another pointer clip to it. Also keep in mind that each copy of a new clip is an independent reference to the media file it points to. If you change a clip, such as by setting an In point or Out point, any other clip that references this same media will not reflect the change you made in the first clip. Also be warned that if you delete the media associated with one of these matching clips, you delete the media to all these subclips and the master clip they were subclipped from.

9. Navigate back to the Picture Clips bin, and load the Dog footage marker in the "3 hr timecode section" clip into the Viewer. Create a subclip of the shot, and drag it into the Scene 1 bin.

10. Locate the Map Footage marker in the "2 hr timecode section" clip in the Picture Clips bin. Open this marker in the Viewer, and play it. This marker contains several shots, so we'll break it down. Create a subclip of the Map Footage marker, and drag it to the Scene 1 bin.

11. Double-click the new Map Footage subclip to open it in the Viewer.

12. Create subclips of the four shots contained in this subclip. Set an In point at 02:08:43;08, and mark an Out point at 02:08:59;04. Highlight the subclip in the Browser, and press Cmd+U or click the Viewer's button bar's Make Subclip button. The new subclip appears in the Scene 1 bin. Name this subclip "Reverse Cap and Sam look over the hill LS" (LS stands for long shot). The second subclip runs from 02:09:00;07 to 02:09:10;14. Name the second subclip "Cap walks through snow CU" (CU stands for close-up). The third subclip runs from 02:09:11;11 to 02:09:38;24. Name it "Cap and Sam look over the hill FS" (FS stands for full shot). The last subclip runs from 02:09:38;27 to the end of the shot at 02:09:55;23. Name this last clip "Cap looks at map CU." Delete the "Map Footage" subclip in the Scene 1 bin. It's been broken down further anyway, so you don't need it any longer.

13. Double-check your work. Your Scene 1 bin should contain the same clips as shown in Figure 4.17. Save the project by pressing Cmd+S. You can't save too often. I'll prompt you once in a while, but it's wise to save often and back up your project file to a medium not on your computer, such as a CD or Zip disc, at least at the end of each editing session.

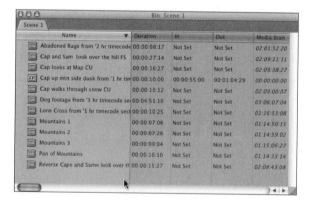

FIGURE 4.17 *The first 12 items.*

CHAPTER 5

Basic Editing

- Making Basic Edits
- Adding Transitions
- Working with Clip Overlays
- Working with Snapping
- Using Undo and Redo
- Workshop 5: Edit Your Subclips into a Sequence and Add Transitional Effects

Making Basic Edits

Final Cut Pro uses a *three-point editing paradigm*. Four points need to be determined to command any edit to be performed, but if you determine three of them, the fourth becomes a default calculation. The four points are the source clip's starting (or mark in) point, its ending (or mark out) point, and the In and Out points you set in your sequence that determine where in time this element is to be added to your sequence (the edit point).

You need to determine any three of these points. Final Cut Pro determines the fourth by using a bit of math. If you want a new source clip to start on a certain frame and end on a certain frame from the Viewer window, you only need to determine an In point *or* an Out point within the sequence and let the edit fall where it will be on the calculated fourth point. If you must keep a certain duration of an edit to be absolute in the sequence, you set that duration's In and Out points in the Canvas or Timeline window and set an In or an Out in the Viewer window.

There are several ways to perform an edit in Final Cut Pro. Different editors edit in different ways, but they all end up putting source clips into sequences using the method that seems best to them. I believe that there is no "best" way for everyone. The "best" way is what makes sense to you, the editor.

Most edits are either inserts or overwrites (see the section "The Canvas Window" in Chapter 3, "Understanding Final Cut Pro's Interface: An Overview"). To complete the edit, you have to either drag the marked clip from the Viewer to the Canvas Overlay or click one of the edit buttons in the lower left of the Canvas (press F9 for insert or F10 for overwrite). There are variations. You can press Shift+F9 to add the default transition at the head of the edit and insert the material. You can press Shift+F10 to add the default transition at the head of the edit and overwrite the material. "At the head of the edit" means that if your default transition is a dissolve, you dissolve *to* that clip and it *starts* with a dissolve from the edit before it. You can also simply drag a clip from the Browser directly to the sequence in the Timeline window and place it on the track you want it to be on.

As you learn to use Final Cut Pro, you'll find the way that suits you or the particular edit that works best for you. We'll use different methods in this chapter's workshop.

Targeting Audio and Video Tracks

You must select the target tracks you want Final Cut Pro to use in order to place these edits or clips in your sequence. When you click a source track's button, it toggles on or off (connecting it to the sequence's destination track, or not). You can Ctrl-click the button to assign it to a destination track, or simply slide it up or down to connect it to the destination track you want to place it in. If your source material contains video and audio, you can place them in your sequence together by targeting the audio and video tracks you want to put the new material on.

You also can take just the audio or video from a source clip to add it to your sequence. For example, if your source clip has audio and video, and you want only the video, simply clicking the source clip's audio track buttons to the left keeps them from being added to your sequence.

You can also target where each track of multitrack audio will be edited to in your sequence, as shown in Figures 5.1 and 5.2. In Figure 5.1, video and one track of audio will be edited to the adjacent tracks, and the other track of audio will not be edited into the sequence. You can also assign your source dual-channel audio to specific tracks, as shown in Figure 5.2. You Ctrl-click the source clip's button (in this case, the a2 track) to bring up a context menu and then select the A5 destination track. You also can do this by clicking the destination track's button. You might want to target only one of the two tracks even though you have more than one track of source audio. So you might want audio 1 or audio 2 only in a case where you've recorded only one track but have captured both. Another example is if you have two different audio levels (or two different microphones) recorded on your tape but you want only one placed in your sequence.

Monitoring Audio and Video Tracks

Selecting the green visibility lights (the round buttons) to the left of any track turns on or off the playback of that track in the Canvas. Selecting video or audio to be turned off might cause you to lose rendered files, though, so you must be careful here if you want to preserve them. If you want to turn off monitoring of a lower track of video, you can. However, if no changes are needed, it's best to turn monitoring back on by performing an undo (Cmd+Z), which relinks the render files to your sequence.

FIGURE 5.1
Targeting video and audio to adjacent tracks.

If you make changes to a clip that require rendering, it needs to be rerendered anyway, but only the clip(s) you've altered. All other renders in that track can be saved if you perform an undo after turning off a track that caused renders to be lost and *then* perform the changes. Using this method preserves all the renders you might have lost when you turned off the track. After you make the changes to just the area of the Timeline you want to affect, you only have to render the newly changed effect or composite.

FIGURE 5.2
Targeting video and swapping audio tracks.

Another way to preserve renders on a given track is to Ctrl-click a clip you might not want to see and select Clip Enable from the context menu. This causes any renders to be deleted, but only in the area in which the clip resides.

Adding Transitions

Transitional effects are those between two clips. Dissolves, wipes, and page peels are examples of these types of effects. Many different categories of programmable transitions are available. You select them from one of two places—from the Effects tab in the Browser, or from the Effects menu, as shown in Figure 5.3. Here, Cross Dissolve is selected. A cross-dissolve is an opacity change between clips. As the outgoing clip lowers its opacity, the incoming clip raises its opacity. These clips overlap during the effect.

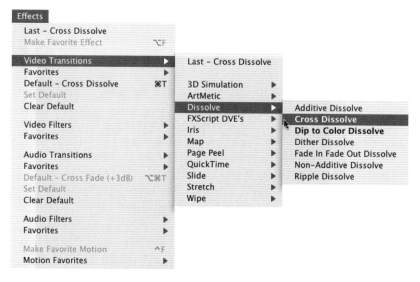

FIGURE 5.3
The Effects menu with Cross Dissolve selected.

The same set of effects is available at each location, and they are organized the same way. You can add third-party transitions as well. They show up in both places.

If you add a transition using the Effects tab in the Browser, you only need to drag the transition to the edit in the Timeline to add it to your sequence. To add transitions from the Effects menu, you must first select the edit you intend to add a transition to by clicking it with the Selection tool in the Timeline window.

warning   To add a transition of any type, you must have media available that is unused on both sides of the transition so that the transition will be centered on the edit point between two clips. For example, the outgoing clip must have 15 frames of video *past* the clip's Out edit point, and the incoming clip must contain 15 frames of video *before* the In point selected for its starting edit point to achieve a 30-frame transition that is centered on the edit point. You need even more unused media to perform longer effect durations. A transitional effect needs to have media unused originally before and after the cut point for the duration of the overlap of the two clips that are transitioning to each other.

Adding and Resetting the Default Transition

You can add the default transition to any edit point by Ctrl-clicking the edit point in the Timeline window and selecting Add Transition from the resulting pop-up menu. A 1-second dissolve is the default transition in Final Cut Pro.

To reset the default transition, Ctrl-click the transition you want to become the default transition in the Effects tab window of the Browser and select Set Default Transition from the pop-up menu (see Figure 5.4). When you Ctrl-click an edit point in the Timeline, right after the words Add Transition in this menu is the name of the default transition you have selected, as shown in Figure 5.5. This is useful if you have created a custom transition that you want to use over and over. It's easier than modifying one again and again the same way. You can create and save a custom transition in your Favorites bin or even the Browser and then select it as the default transition.

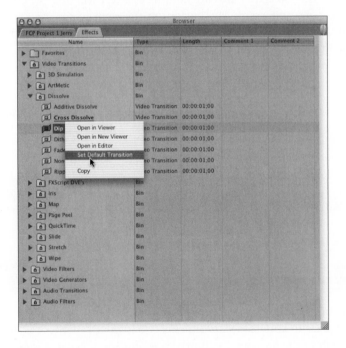

FIGURE 5.4   *Changing the default transition.*

FIGURE 5.5
Ctrl-clicking an edit point to add a default transition.

Modifying Transitions

There are two ways to modify a transition:

- Double-click it in the sequence after you've added it to open it in the Effects Editor (where you can modify all the settings for the transitions).

- Modify it directly in the sequence (where you can modify the duration).

Probably the simplest of these transitions is the one you'll use the most: a cross-dissolve.

If you double-click an effect in the Effects tab, its Effects Editor opens in the Viewer window, as shown in Figure 5.6. At the top of the Viewer, a tab contains the effect's name. Just below that is the effect's duration. Typing in a new duration changes the length. In the top center area are buttons to select whether the effect starts, centers, or ends at the edit point. The button on the right works the same as the Viewer's Recent Clips button. On the far right, the effect icon with the hand is called the drag handle. It allows you to drag this effect to a transition or to your bins for later use. You can also drag the transition's ends to lengthen it.

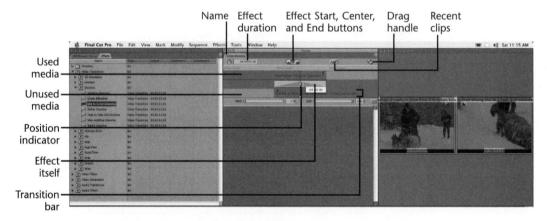

FIGURE 5.6   *The Effects Editor in the Viewer window.*

A good place to keep these custom effects is in your Favorites folder at the top of the Effects tab in the Browser. As shown in Figure 5.3, you can access these effects from the Effects menu.

Clicking in the ruler, which is beneath the top row of controls, allows you to scrub through the effect by clicking its position indicator, which corresponds to the position indicator in the Timeline window.

Beneath the ruler is the Transition Bar, which shows you the effect icon you are modifying. The outgoing clip is displayed on the top, with its available media past the edit point. The incoming clip is displayed on the bottom, with its available media before the edit point. You can see how the clips overlap this way. You must have overlap to perform any transitional effect.

The darker blue area represents the media used in the sequence, and the lighter blue area is the "unused" media. The light gray area (if there is any) shows where there is media past an edit point of an outgoing clip or before the start of the incoming clip.

Between them in the center row is the effect itself. If you have unused media past the edit point in the incoming clip, and/or if you have unused media before the In point of the incoming media, you can click and drag this transition and change its edit point. The Roll Edit tool is visible when you do this. While you move an edit point this way, a new two-up display appears in the Canvas window, as shown in Figure 5.7. In this case, it is a 3-second cross-dissolve that ends at the edit point.

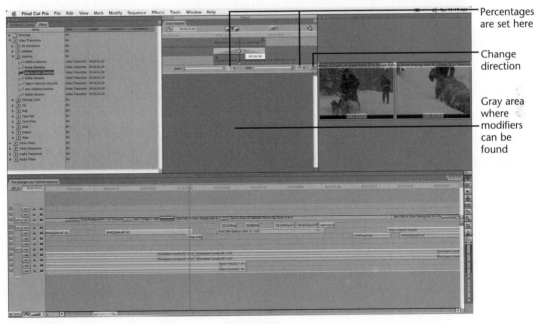

FIGURE 5.7   *Rolling an edit point in the Effects Editor window.*

The two-up display in the Canvas shows the current frame at the transition's start point in the outgoing clip in the frame on the left, and the current frame at the transition's end point in the incoming clip in the frame on the right. The name and source timecode are displayed in the respective clips as well. The timecode updates as you drag the transition's edit point right or left.

When you click and drag either end of the transition, you can change its duration by stretching it or squeezing it.

You can use the Transition Bar to perform not only roll edits but ripple edits as well. Move the mouse pointer to the start of the incoming clip or the end of the outgoing clip and drag in either direction. This is a great way to fine-tune not only a transition but also the edit point itself.

Below the Transition Bar you can select the percentages of the effect as it starts and ends. Just to the right is a button to change the effect's direction. In the case of more-complicated effects, the gray area is reserved for these modifiers. Modifiers such as the shape of a wipe and the color of an edge are found here. The red X button below this resets these changes only.

Any change made in the Effects Editor window is immediately applied to the effect as it exists in your sequence. If you double-click an effect from the Effects tab window and open its editor, you can program the effect. By dragging on the drag handle, you can either apply the effect to an edit point or save it for later use in your Favorites folder or any bin you want to store it in.

Working with Clip Overlays

As discussed in Chapter 3, the Timeline window has a button you can activate to show clip overlays. In the case of video, this overlay displays the video's opacity, and in the case of audio, it displays the audio's level or loudness. Keyframe indicators are added with the Pen tool. Dragging these indicators up and down changes these parameters.

You can also change the linear aspect of the opacity changes with the Pen Smooth tool. You activate it from the Tools Palette or by pressing P three times. You can use the Pen Smooth tool to modify how these keyframes act with each other, as shown in Figure 5.8. Here the fade-up on the clip starts quickly and slows as it gets near full opacity. You can also add a keyframe with the Pen tool and Ctrl-click it to transform it into a smooth version, as shown in Figure 5.9. You can also clear it using this menu.

You can also move these keyframe indicators by clicking them with the Selection tool. When you move the pointer to them, it changes to a crosshair tool to grab the indicators and move them later or earlier in the Timeline. Using this method of changing their positions lengthens or shortens the effect's duration.

Using the Selection tool, you also can drag the line up or down to adjust the parameters. Moving the line up sets higher levels, and moving it down sets lower levels in both audio and video clips (see Figure 5.10). Notice the Rollover tool, which appears when the Selection tool touches the clip overlay line. Also notice the yellow box indicating the number of decibels you are changing for playback of the audio clip.

Working with Snapping

As discussed in Chapter 3, snapping allows quick and precise moves to edit points and more with the position indicator. You can activate this feature by pressing N or by clicking it in the upper-right corner of the Timeline window. This feature also allows you to snap clips. You drag them from either the Viewer or the Browser directly to the sequence so that they are placed immediately next to clips already in your sequence. Dragging clips to the sequence with snapping activated leaves no space between them when you drop these clips with the snapping triangles activated.

Take a look at Figure 5.11 to see how the snapping indicators (the brown triangles at the edit point) look with this feature turned on and a clip being dragged into position next to another clip already in the sequence. Notice the Rollover tool that appears when you drag a clip into a sequence. The one in the figure indicates an overwrite edit.

FIGURE 5.8
Video clip opacity smoothed by dragging the blue bezier curve dots. Notice that the ramp of the opacity overlay isn't linear.

FIGURE 5.9
The keyframe pop-up menu.

FIGURE 5.10
Audio levels adjusted in the clip overlay.

tip

You can turn snapping on and off by pressing the N key even *while* you are dragging a clip to a new position.

Dragging clips without the snapping feature turned on is certainly possible, but you might leave space between them and the previously edited clip, or you might overwrite part of the previously edited clip. If you want to do this, you can, but if you don't, it's easier to use the snapping feature to apply clips when dragging them directly to the sequence.

FIGURE 5.11

Snapping clip indicators with snapping turned on.

tip

With the snapping feature turned off, it's easier to place a clip in the Timeline to *not* sit right next to a clip if you want to leave a blank space in the sequence, for example. Experimenting with turning this feature on and off will teach you a lot. Turning snapping on is great for adding clips where you want no space between them and the adjacent clips, but it's tough to use when you want to do any fine-tuning. It's best to turn snapping off if you will move a clip just a few frames, for example.

Using Undo and Redo

Undo and Redo are powerful editing tools. Undo allows you to try an edit and then view it. You can undo it if you don't like it or if you made a mistake. Feeling freer to try something knowing that you can simply undo it is a good idea. Because you are using a computer, *use this tool at will*. It's truly one of the advantages of using a non-linear editing system. You'll find that you feel more confident in your "tryouts." You activate Undo by selecting Edit, Undo or by pressing Cmd+Z.

Redo does the opposite. It lets you toggle between two edits in the Timeline or quickly go back if you have undone one or more edits and you want to keep them the way they were earlier. You activate Redo by selecting Edit, Redo or by pressing Shift+Cmd+Z.

You can keep undoing or redoing edits or changes you have made by continuing to use the Undo and Redo commands. They undo or redo in the order in which they were performed. The number of allowable Undo commands is set in the General tab of the User Preferences window. The maximum is 99. Keep in mind that setting this option to the maximum uses up RAM.

warning

You must be careful using the Undo feature. Be cognizant of exactly what you might be undoing! For example, you might have made a change that is not reflected in the current sequence that you don't want to undo. It might be best to make a copy of the Timeline if you will do some serious experimentation so that you can keep track of this new edit before you start doing many edits or changes you might want to undo. You can always add the new edits back to your sequence or just keep working on the copied sequence. You can even create sequences just for this purpose.

Workflow Issues and Duplicating Sequences or Clips

If you plan to make a massive "tryout" set of edits, you might want to create an entire sequence for them. That way, you can either delete the sequence or keep it as an alternative to possibly show a client, for example. You can duplicate an entire sequence in which to make these alternative edits by selecting the sequence in the Browser and pressing Opt+D; by selecting Edit, Duplicate; or by Ctrl-clicking a sequence and duplicating it using the resulting pop-up menu. Keep in mind that there is no limit on the number of sequences you can create within the same project.

You might use this technique to keep scenes in separate sequences until you are ready to marry them all into one sequence, especially if you have a lot of them. It's more efficient to navigate in a smaller sequence than in a larger one. You end up saving a lot of time if you break sequences with hundreds of edits into smaller sequences.

You can also use this method to create sequences that differ from each other only slightly. For example, you could create sets of commercials that are identical except for different addresses or phone numbers inserted in the same basic commercial to be aired in different markets. Just rename them with the names of the different phone numbers or addresses to keep them organized.

In a similar vein, you can duplicate, copy, and paste any object in the Browser to place a copy of it in another bin for quick access from a bin containing clips that relate to it. Remember that subclips first appear in the bin in which the clip you created them from resides. For that reason, you might want that longer master clip to be set either in its own bin or in other bins as well. You don't copy the media file; you simply create more pointers to it located where you might want to use it in multiple sorted bins. If you want to, you can delete this copied clip after subclipping from it just to have fewer objects to sort through in any given bin. Using copies of master clips is advisable so that you don't inadvertently delete the original master clip from your project. It's also possible to simply drag this master clip around from bin to bin, but I find it easy to keep duplicating it. Copy (Cmd+C) and Paste (Cmd+V) are quick keyboard commands. They allow quick copies to be made and require less scrolling around, opening and dragging windows to place the master clip where it should be. Another method is to hold down the Ctrl key while you drag a clip. This creates a duplicate while leaving the clip's original location unchanged.

Workshop 5: Edit Your Subclips into a Sequence and Add Transitional Effects

In this workshop, you'll begin to edit from the subclips already created and manipulate your views of the bins in the Browser. You'll learn to create more tracks in your sequence, edit a few clips into the sequence, and add some simple transitions.

Begin Editing Scene 1

Follow the steps in this workshop and do not deviate from them, because the entire book is predicated on the fact that you have followed these steps exactly. If you have trouble making things come out right, chances are you missed a step or didn't trim the video or audio as directed. Go back a step or two and check your work if you run into a problem. Also, "The Midnight Sun Finished Sequence" is included for reference purposes.

1. Open sequence 1 by double-clicking its icon. It should be an empty sequence. If it isn't, delete all clips from it by highlighting them and pressing Delete.

2. Open the Scene 1 bin by double-clicking it, or drag its tab away from the Browser window if you've left it there.

3. Enlarge the bin and Ctrl-click the gray area to the left of the clips. From the context menu, select View as Large Icons.

4. Enlarge the window to reveal all the video clips in it. Notice that some have slates or other pictures obscuring their view. You'll fix this before you make your first edits.

5. Double-click the "Abandoned rags" clip to open it in the Viewer.

6. Navigate to a frame that doesn't contain the slate. Select Mark, Set Poster Frame or press Ctrl+P. The representative frame in the bin is updated to be that frame. Do the same to all the subclips that have a slate at their head frame position.

7. When you are done experimenting, look at Figure 5.12, which looks more descriptive than when you started.

tip

Here's another trick you can do. Select the Scrub Video tool, and set a poster frame directly in the bin. (Click the Zoom tool in the Tools Palette, and select the hand with the arrows inside it or press H twice.) Scrub through the large icons (click and drag left and right on the pictures themselves with this tool) to quickly get a notion of what they contain. Then hold down the Ctrl key and release the mouse on the frame you want to park on.

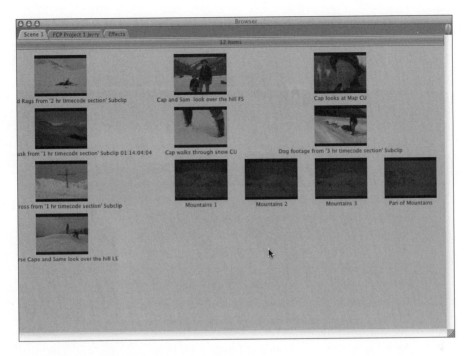

FIGURE 5.12   *The Scene 1 bin in the Large Icons View.*

Make the First Edits to the Movie

Many editors use their bins' List or Icons views to make it easier to locate clips. Sometimes pictures work better than a list of names, and sometimes they don't. It just depends on the project and its material. You'll make your first edits using the List view and then try some edits with the Large Icons view.

1. This movie has many tracks of audio, so start by creating a few more than the two that are currently in Sequence 1. Ctrl-click the A1 audio track label and select Add Track, as shown in Figure 5.13. This adds just one more track of audio. But if you want to add more than one track of audio or video, it's easy to do.

FIGURE 5.13
The tracks shortcut menu.

2. Select Sequence, Insert Tracks. The dialog box shown in Figure 5.14 appears.

3. Type 6 in the Audio Tracks box, and click OK. You should now have a total of nine audio tracks in Sequence 1. Having this many tracks is not uncommon. There are a couple of moments in the movie where nine audio tracks are used at once.

4. Open the Sound Clips bin. Double-click the clip titled "Wind, desert Lonely, 66_1-01" to open it in the Viewer.

5. Because you are trying to create a sequence of establishing shots, you'll establish sound to prepare for them. A great way to get the feeling of "cold" is to use wind; it's close to the feeling you want to establish, and wind also indicates loneliness. Scroll down through the audio tracks to reveal tracks 6 and 7. Select them as the target tracks by clicking their destination buttons, as shown in Figure 5.15. Play with this targeting a bit. You can click the source button (to the left of the destination button) to select the source footage to remap its track 1 to other tracks in the Timeline. But leave track 1 targeted to track 6 and track 2 targeted to track 7, as shown in Figure 5.15, after you are done experimenting. Note that you can also Ctrl-click the destination buttons to map source buttons to them.

6. Highlight the Viewer by pressing Cmd+1 or clicking it. Mark the whole clip by pressing X or by clicking the Mark Clip button. Make sure that the position indicator in the Timeline window is at the very head of the Timeline. Drag the hand-on-speaker icon in the top right of the Viewer to the Canvas window. The Canvas overlay reveals the Overwrite box. Drag the clip's ghost box to the Overwrite box in the overlay. The clip should now be in the Timeline on tracks 6 and 7.

FIGURE 5.14
The Insert Tracks dialog box.

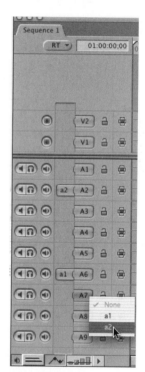

FIGURE 5.15
Targeting audio tracks.

7.   Open the Scene 1 bin and double-click the "Cap up mtn side dusk" freeze frame of the mountains you created earlier. It opens in the Viewer.

8.   Type **1001706** in the timecode display box in the upper right of the Canvas, and then press I to set an In point there for this shot. You needn't type the colons between the pairs of numbers. Final Cut Pro knows that when you type numbers in the timecode display boxes, you must be referring to timecode, so it puts in the colons for you.

9.   Type **910** in the duration timecode display box (the one on the left in the Canvas window) and press Enter. Again, no colons or semicolons are needed. If you type **910**, Final Cut Pro assumes that you mean 9:10, or 9 seconds and 10 frames. An Out point is created in the sequence, which creates a total duration of 9 seconds and 10 frames for the duration of the next edit.

Perform a Four-Point Edit

Now you will ask Final Cut Pro to perform a four-point edit. An In and Out point are selected in both the Viewer and the Canvas windows. When this happens, Final Cut Pro assumes that you want the duration of the edit to be that as selected in the Canvas and Timeline windows. It also assumes that you want the In point from the Viewer to be the edit's In point. It ignores the Out point selected in the Viewer, except in the case of a fit-to-fill edit (called a four-point edit in some applications). In this case, it calculates a new playback speed for the source clip to "fit" into the time indicated by the Canvas window's duration from in to out.

1.   Perform the edit by dragging from the center of the Viewer to the Canvas window overlay. Select Overwrite and let go of the mouse button. You can also perform this edit by pressing the F10 key. The still of the mountains is now in the Timeline.

2.   Turn on the Clips Overlays button in the Timeline window (it looks like a line graph). Little lines appear in the clips in the tracks. You might toggle this button on and off to watch the lines turn on and off. These lines indicate the level of opacity in video clips and the sound level in audio clips.

3.   Press Z to activate the Zoom tool. Zoom in on the "Cap up mtn side dusk" still frame clip in the Timeline window, and press P. The Pen tool is now active.

4.   Position the mouse pointer over the clip's line. The Pen tool appears. Move this tool to the line in the "Cap up mtn side dusk" still frame clip, and click about 2 seconds (judge this by looking at the timecode displayed in the Timeline window).

5. Click the clip right on the line to see the Pen tool. A keyframe is added, as shown in Figure 5.16. The small black dot is the keyframe indicator. It denotes that the frame it's over is a keyframe.

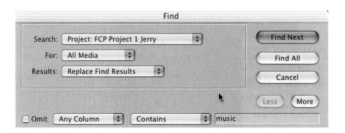

FIGURE 5.16
The keyframe indicator dot.

6. With the Pen tool still active, click the line at the very head of the same clip, and drag this new keyframe to the bottom of the clip, as shown in Figure 5.17. Notice the yellow box indicating the level of the keyframe as you drag it to 0.

FIGURE 5.17
Fading up from black.

7. The shot will now fade up from the keyframe at the beginning of the clip for a duration set from the beginning to the second keyframe. Try dragging the second keyframe with the Pen tool from left to right to change its duration. When the keyframe is being used correctly, a tiny + appears to let you know that you are on that keyframe.

8. Play the clip in the Timeline to see the "fade up" you created. Highlight the "Cap up mtn side dusk" still frame clip in the Timeline. Select Sequence, Render Selection, or press Opt+R. Save the project. (FCP 4 includes many changes to rendering options. We'll discuss them in Chapter 11, "Video Filter Effects and Basic Compositing.")

Add Music to the Clip

The wind is lonely-sounding, but you'll add even more sadness to the establishing shots by adding some music. This time, to get to the clip you want, you'll use the Find command.

1. Press Cmd+4 to activate the Browser, and then press Cmd+F. The Find dialog box opens, as shown in Figure 5.18.

FIGURE 5.18 *The Find dialog box.*

2. Select the Name column from the pop-up menu in the lower left. Type **music** in the bottom-right box, next to the word Contains. Click the Find All button. The Find Results window opens, as shown in Figure 5.19. It contains all the music in the movie.

   You can highlight the Music-Net116.4-04 clip and click the Show in Browser button to find the clip quickly. You can also double-click this clip to have it open in the Viewer too. While we're at it, let's create a bin just for these music clips.

FIGURE 5.19   *The Find Results window.*

3. Click the FCP Project tab in the Browser (or press Cmd+4). Create a new bin there (press Cmd+B), and name it Music. Then drag all the clips from the Find Results window to this new bin (see Figure 5.20). The next time you need some music, you can find it faster this way.

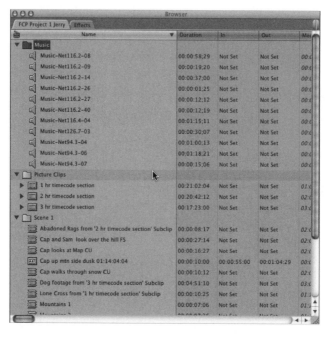

Figure 5.20   *The Music bin after step 3.*

4. Close the Find Results window.

5. Navigate to the Music-Net116.4-04 clip in the Music bin, and double-click its icon to open it in the Viewer. You'll use this entire music clip, so you don't need to mark any In or Out points within it.

6. In the Canvas window timecode position indicator box, type **1724**. Notice that I don't have you type **1001724** to indicate that the number you want has one-hour code assigned to it. FCP knows one-hour code is being used in the sequence, so it adds the extra numbers (100) at the head for you.

7. Press I, and then clear any Out point that might be showing in the Canvas by pressing Opt+O to clear it.

8. This time, instead of scrolling to the tracks to target them, click the expand window button in the top-left corner of the Timeline window to maximize the window. Target tracks 8 and 9, and then press the expand window button again to put the Timeline back in its "home" position. This might be the best way for you to work if you are using something other than a dual-monitor setup or a very large display such as a Cinema Display. It's quick and effective.

9. Drag the clip's hand-on-speaker icon to the Overwrite box in the Canvas window overlay, or press F10 (overwrite) to add the edit to your sequence. I use the function keys for editing as much as possible; it's faster. After this edit, the Timeline should look like Figure 5.21.

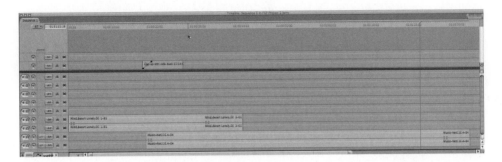

FIGURE 5.21   *The Timeline after the first three edits.*

10. Open the Lone Cross clip from the Scene 1 bin in the Viewer window. Set an In point at 01:16:53:26 and an Out point at 01:17:01:24.

11. Turn on snapping (press N or look at the button bar in the Timeline window to see if snapping is active). Drag the clip from the center of the Viewer directly to the Timeline, placing the clip next to the "Cap up mtn side dusk" clip that is already there. The Snapping tool makes this really easy. You'll know that you have set this clip right next to the "Cap up mtn side dusk" clip when you see the little triangles appear in the Timeline's position indicator, as shown in Figure 5.22. Experiment with this a moment to see how it works.

note

As we go along in the project, I'll dispense with the steps we've covered already. You've seen more than one way to create edits with Final Cut Pro, and you should begin to choose the one that makes the most sense for you. If an edit can be made easier using one method or another, I'll point this out.

FIGURE 5.22
Overwriting a clip from the Viewer to the Timeline.

note

In Figure 5.22, the arrow pointing down indicates an overwrite edit. If you raise the ghosted clip a bit, the arrow points to the right, which indicates an insert edit.

I purposefully edited this shot to cut out at the beginning of the next phrase of music. This tends to make the music drive the shots forward. When you edit your own material, this technique can be effective.

Add a Cross-Dissolve

To further add a matching feel to this edit, you'll add an effect that follows the sound of the cello's melody. A cross-dissolve that follows the length of this phrase of music is just right.

1. Click the Effects tab in the Browser window.

2. Open the Video Transitions folder by clicking the triangle next to it.

3. Open the Dissolve folder. Drag the cross-dissolve icon to the Timeline, placing it over the edit between the two video clips.

4. Release the mouse button to add the cross-dissolve to the edit point, as shown in Figure 5.23.

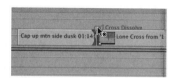

FIGURE 5.23

Adding a cross-dissolve from the Effects tab to the Timeline.

5. Play the edit. You'll see right away that it has problems. The first problem is that the frames *before* the cross-edit's In point show the slate footage. The other problems are that the dissolve's default position is center (starting too early), and its default duration is 1 second, which is just too short. This isn't what I had in mind, so let's modify the dissolve.

6. Double-click the dissolve in the Timeline to open the Effects Editor window in the Viewer, as shown in Figure 5.24. Click the Start on Edit button, as shown in the figure. This removes the frames with the slate and gets the dissolve to start where it should. There's no problem here, because the frames past the edit point of the outgoing Dawn Scenics clip are just part of the freeze you created. They will just continue through the dissolve.

7. The edit starts at the edit point, as I wanted, but it's only 1 second long and is shorter than the cello's music phrase. Therefore, in the duration time box, change this to 3 seconds by typing **300** or **3.**.

8. Now play the Timeline in this area to see the difference. The edit lasts the duration of the cello's phrase and leads into the shot of the cross. You should save the project again (press Cmd+S). This should become a habit.

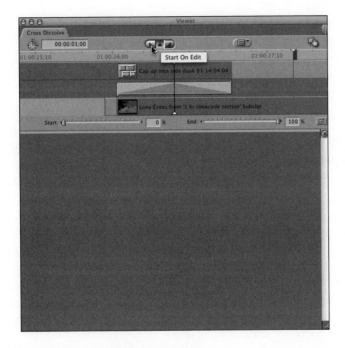

FIGURE 5.24 *The Transition Effects Editor in the Viewer.*

Add the Poem

It's time to introduce the poem. Its first line is also an establishing element. The poem is read by the actor who plays Cap. The phrases of the poem that are used in the film are all labeled with DANCLEAN.AIF and a number.

1. Open the Sound Clips bin to locate the poem files. You can also use the Find command to locate them. In the FCP Project 1 tab's window, create a new bin and name it Voice Over. Then drag all the DANCLEAN.AIF files to this bin.

2. Open the DANCLEAN.AIF-01 clip in the Viewer. Mark an In point in the Canvas at 01:00:32;19 and edit the entire DANCLEAN.AIF-01 there on track A3 (don't forget to target it). Pressing F10 is the quickest way to overwrite this edit.

3. Open the "Abandoned rags" clip in the Viewer. Its duration is too short for the next edit, so create a freeze frame of it. Navigate to 02:01:54:10 in the Viewer, and press Shift+N to create the freeze. The menu command for this freeze creation works too; it's under the Modify menu at Modify, Make Freeze Frame. You could even put a freeze frame button in the Modify set of buttons in the Viewer's button bar if you needed to perform this task often. (You won't do it much here, though.)

4. Drag from the center of the Viewer to the Scene 1 bin to save this freeze for possible use later. (You never know when you might want it again.)

5. Set an In point in the Canvas at 01:00:34;15 and an Out point at 01:00:42;21. Then overwrite this edit to the V1 track. Never forget to target the tracks you are getting ready to edit to.

6. Play back the sequence. The cut is abrupt, so add another 3-second dissolve between the two clips that *ends* on the transition. If you don't end it there, you run out of media in the Lone Cross clip, and you can't get it to be as long as 3 seconds.

7. Experiment with modifying this 3-second transition to be centered on the cut and to start on the cut. You'll see that you are constrained to using a shorter transition duration, because there isn't enough media in the Lone Cross clip to accommodate the extra 45 frames past the original edit point to create a 90-frame centered transition, let alone one that might start there.

warning

This issue is absolute. You must have enough media on *both* sides of the transition you want to add to an edit point. If you want to add a transition to any edit point, you must have enough media unused in the incoming shot and the outgoing shot to accommodate the extra duration that the transition calls for. If you use all the media on both sides of an edit point, you cannot add a transition to it.

Another way to think about this is that the clips must overlap each other so that they can be on the screen at the same time during the transition. If the transition starts at an edit point, you need frames past the original cut point of the outgoing shot. If you want to end the transition at the cut point, you must have frames before the original In point of the incoming shot to start seeing them during the transition, which will start *before* the original cut point. This issue is the same in any nonlinear editing application. When you are done experimenting, leave a transition that ends on the edit with a duration of 3 seconds.

8. Drag the Scene 1 bin's tab or double-click its folder in the Browser to open it in its own window.

9. Ctrl-click in the bin away from the clips to view this bin as Medium Icons or Large Icons. Take a moment to think about the next set of edits. You could use some of the unused mountain scenery, but I think it's better to get on with the introduction of the two heroes. After you've established the scene, you've established the scene, and it's better to get on with the story than to bore your audience with more shots that really don't add anything to the situation other than to say, "Here are some more mountains; they're cold too." Remember to move your story along. *Just because it was shot doesn't mean it should be used. This is the axiom you must live by as an editor.*

Establishing Edits in Sets of Odd Numbers

When discussion arises about just how many shots to use when establishing a time or place in your story, I really like an odd number of shots, especially three. Just as composition is more interesting when three objects are highlighted in the scene, so are odd-numbered sets of shots that relate to each other. The reason is that humans are *very* familiar with even-numbered things. We have two hands, two arms, two eyes, and so on. We have a mom and dad, aunt and uncle, and so on. When we encounter something that there are three of, it piques our interest, because it's "unfamiliar" or not quite "natural." Historically, the number 3 is found in many powerful symbols. The Trinity comes to mind. Even a single shot is better than two, and five shots are better than four. Again, this is more unusual and has a rhythm all its own, and it piques our interest.

Introduce the Characters

Four shots here contain the actors:

- Cap walks through snow CU
- Reverse, Cap and Sam look over the hill LS
- Cap and Sam look over the hill FS
- Cap looks at map CU

You'll use three of them to establish the heroes.

You've already heard one of the actors in the voice-over, so let's see him walking in close-up. Then you'll add a rather unrevealing shot just to tease the audience further. Next you'll use the reverse shot. Finally, you'll let the audience see the actors in the full shot. Then you'll go to the close-up of Cap, which starts the action after the three establishing shots.

1. Arrange the four shots just mentioned in the order in which they're listed by dragging them to a row of their own. This is one of my favorite ways to use this view of the bins. You have a storyboard of them to see how they will sort of cut to each other.

2. Double-click each shot one at a time to see them in the Viewer. Remove any In or Out points you might have put in them.

3. If you Ctrl-click the scrubber bar, you pull up a menu to remove edit marks, as shown in Figure 5.25. Or you can press Opt+X to eliminate both In and Out marks. Or press Opt+I to delete just an In mark, and press Opt+O to delete an Out mark. Add some In and Out points, and then play with these keyboard shortcuts to master

FIGURE 5.25
The scrubber bar shortcut menu.

them. You'll use them the rest of your editorial life with Final Cut Pro. But leave the clips without any In point or Out point selected in them.

Storyboard Editing

What's even more powerful than just arranging a storyboard is editing that story-board into the Timeline in one move.

1. Make sure that snapping is turned on. Shift-click each clip to highlight all four. If you drag the mouse across all of them, you can lasso them.

2. Drag one of the highlighted clips to the V1 track in the Timeline window and place it to the right of the "Abandoned rags" clip so that it comes immediately next. Having snapping turned on should make this easy. Keeping the Timeline's position indicator away from the Out point of the "Abandoned rags" clip should make things easier too. When you're done, your sequence should look like Figure 5.26.

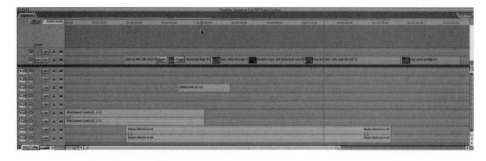

FIGURE 5.26   *The Timeline with the first 10 edits.*

3. Play back the sequence of these new shots. There are some problems such as slates at the beginning of them. And they don't cut together very well. We'll fix them one by one.

4. The first shot has a slate and a nonwalking actor. Move the position in the Timeline to 01:00:48;12 by typing in the Timeline's timecode position indicator box, as shown in Figure 5.27.

5. Press B or click the Razor Blade tool in the Tools Palette. It is available only when the mouse is positioned in the Timeline.

6. Position the Razor Blade on the current position indicator in Sequence 1, and click to create a new edit point. This new edit might end up with little red triangles indicating that it is a through edit. A *through edit* is one that has contiguous frames from the same media on either side of it. During playback, you do not

FIGURE 5.27
The Timecode position indicator box in the Timeline window.

see any change as you play through it. If you do not see the frames, turn them on. From the Sequence menu (or by pressing Cmd+0), access the Timeline Options tab in the Sequence Settings window, as shown in Figure 5.28. You can turn on frames by checking the Show Through Edits check box. This set of sequence settings acts only on the currently selected sequence, unlike the ones chosen from the Audio/Video settings, which affect only new sequences.

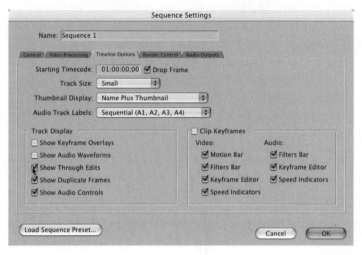

FIGURE 5.28   *Sequence Settings.*

7. Press A to activate the Selection tool again.

8. Highlight the first portion of this clip. Ctrl-click it to open the shortcut menu, and select Ripple Delete, as shown in Figure 5.29. This portion of the shot leaves the Timeline, and all shots past it move to the left. Ripple Delete is also available on the Sequence menu or by pressing Shift+Delete.

9. Ctrl-click the edit point at the end of the "Abandoned rags" clip to bring up yet another shortcut menu, and select Add Transition 'Cross Dissolve,' as shown in Figure 5.30. This shortcut menu adds whatever *default transition* you selected from the Effects tab in the Browser by Ctrl-clicking the desired transition from the list there. (A 1-second cross-dissolve is the default transition unless you change it.)

FIGURE 5.29
The Timeline clip shortcut menu.

FIGURE 5.30
The effect shortcut menu.

10. Ctrl-click the new dissolve in the Timeline. From the shortcut menu, select Transition Alignment, End On Edit, as shown in Figure 5.31.

FIGURE 5.31   *The transition shortcut menu.*

11. Using the same menu, select Duration to change the duration. You see the dialog box shown in Figure 5.32. Change the duration to 3 seconds.

12. Save the project.

FIGURE 5.32
The Duration dialog box.

Cutting Instead of Dissolving and Changing the Pacing

1. Using establishing shots with a series of dissolves leaves the viewer with a "general and nonspecific time" impression of the setup. Notice too that the three establishing shots have served the story, indicating cold, death, and loneliness (a great way to start a comedy). Now that the movie has introduced the characters, a series of cuts to bring the viewers to the "present" is in order. Cutting instead of using dissolves also serves to pick up the pace. We don't want to bore the viewers, so you'll "surprise" them with cuts. Navigate to 01:00:44;11 in the Canvas.

2. Razor blade (press B) the V1 track. Highlight the rest of the close-up of the walking (on the right side of the through edit), and select Ripple Delete.

3. Navigate to 01:00:51;05 in the Canvas. Razor blade an edit in the V1 track, and then ripple delete the left side of the through edit (Ctrl-click the clip). You need to match the footsteps of the close-up of the walk to the incoming reverse angle.

4. Take a look at the last frame of the close-up of Cap's feet. We've left him with his left leg down and the right one moving forward. Hold down the K key while pressing the L key to creep through the next (reverse) shot until you find a matching frame. There is a good one at 01:00:45;00 in the Timeline's timecode.

5. Select the Razor Blade again (press B). While you're parked on 01:00:45;00, slice another edit there and ripple delete the left side of this shot to pull up this frame next to the outgoing frame of the close-up.

6. Play from before the last dissolve through this cut. This works like gangbusters. This edit is called a *matching action* edit. You "matched" the action of the outgoing shot to that of the incoming shot and really put the viewers into the present with it.

7. Trim the Out point of the reverse shot. Move the Timeline indicator to 01:00:47;12 (so that Sam, the character following, just stops walking). Make a Razor Blade edit at that point, and then ripple delete the excess footage from there to the end of the clip.

View the Characters

You've seen where the heroes are and have placed them in the snowy mountains. Now it's time to see what they really look like. The next shot moves to the other side so that the viewers can see the characters' faces. We'll dwell on them for a moment to show that Cap is the "leader." The composition of the shot reinforces this. He is in front and on higher ground, and he also carries the all-important map to riches.

1. Move the Timeline's playhead to 01:00:50;20 and make another Razor Blade edit there.

2. Ripple delete the front portion of the shot with the slate in it. Then move the Timeline's position indicator to 01:00:51;14. Use the Razor Blade to slice an edit there.

3. Move only the footage past the new edit contained in the rest of the clip to the other side of the incoming close-up clip. You'll use it *after* the close-up to end the scene.

4. You can move the back half of this clip in the Timeline by pressing A and then highlighting and dragging the clip in the Timeline past the "Cap looks at map CU" clip. Turning on snapping (press N) makes it easy to ensure that you have not left a gap between the clips.

5. After you move the Cap and Sam clip, there is a blank space between the close-up and the last shot. Highlight both of the clips past this point, and drag them to the left to remove the gap. When the gap is closed, the Timeline should look like Figure 5.33. Again, using the snapping feature makes this a snap.

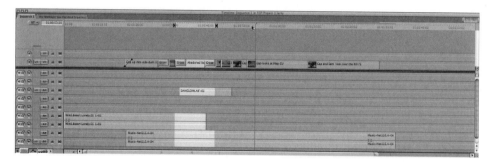

FIGURE 5.33   *The Timeline after the completion of step 5, viewing the characters.*

6. Move the position indicator to 01:00:57;02 in the Timeline and make a Razor Blade edit there. Ripple delete the first portion of the close-up, move the Timeline to 01:00:54;07, and make a Razor Blade edit there. Toggling between the Selection tool (by pressing A) and the Razor Blade tool (by pressing B) should be a habit by now. Ripple delete the section of the close-up clip on the right side of this new edit.

7. Move the Timeline position indicator to 01:00:57;12. Make a Razor Blade edit there. Ripple delete the first portion of this shot, move the Timeline position indicator to 01:01:09;22, and make a Razor Blade edit there. Delete the section of this clip on the right side by highlighting it and pressing Delete. Save the project file.

8. Save your project file. If you really want to protect your work, save a copy of it in another folder. Better yet, save it on a Zip or CD-R disc. Especially do this if you are in an environment in which many users share the same Mac.

Take a look at the sequence. You started with a series of three shots, establishing the location and atmosphere. You used music in a minor key to indicate sorrow and struggle. You spiced things up with the sound of wind, reinforcing the cold. Then you brought the viewers into the "present" by no longer using dissolves between shots that introduce the characters. (In the next chapter, you'll use dissolves for a different reason.)

CHAPTER 6

Audio Editing

- Audio File Formats
- Audio Mixing
- Real-Time Audio Mixing
- Examining an Audio-Only Clip
- Audio Transitions
- Workshop 6: Finish Editing Scene 1

Audio File Formats

Only two audio-only file formats are supported for editing within Final Cut Pro. Supported Audio formats include WAVE and AIFF files. To use a different file format, you must convert the original format, such as MP3 files, to a compatible format using the Pro version of the QuickTime Player (which is bundled with FCP 4 for free) or another audio application such as Pro Tools or even iTunes. You can even import a file, then export it as a supported file format from within Final Cut Pro choosing File/QuickTime Conversion, and selecting aiff and 48kHz as its file format. Then you import that file into Final Cut Pro for editing. Using compression is not a good idea. In fact, compressed audio files don't work with Final Cut Pro. Audio files are relatively small compared to the file size of video and graphics files in general. The higher the quality you preserve, the better the sound will be. Final Cut Pro converts these compressed files anyway, so just avoid using them.

The AIFF and WAV formats can be sampled at different rates. *Sampling* is the process used when you convert analog sound (like that which is created by a microphone) to digital audio files. The higher the sampling rate, the more samples that are taken, and thus the better the fidelity or sound reproduction of the audio files.

The different sampling rates are expressed as kHz settings. The higher the number, the better the sound. The most common rates of source files you will encounter editing with Final Cut Pro are 32kHz, 41.1kHz, and 48kHz. DV audio can be recorded as 12-bit or 32kHz (which contains four tracks of audio) and 16-bit audio. These *bit depths* represent the amount of information recorded in each sample. 12-bit recorded audio should be captured at 32kHz 16-bit, and 16-bit recorded DV audio should be captured at 48kHz 16-bit. Most CD audio files are sampled at 41.1kHz. So sound effect libraries and music CDs have this sampling rate and are always 16-bit recordings.

Some sets of audio sampling rates are lower than 32kHz; they range from 8 to 22.225kHz. They are strictly for use in multimedia projects. You should avoid them for editing within Final Cut Pro, because they aren't of a quality you want to work with. You can't improve their sound quality, and you want to edit in as high a quality as you can as long as you can, even if your final output destination is one of these formats.

The files you imported for use with "The Midnight Sun" that were recorded specifically for the movie were recorded in two ways. The sound sync (on-camera dialog) was recorded to a DAT while the film was shot. Then it was converted to AIFF format. The rest of the voice-over (the actor's read of the poetry) and foley (sound effects recorded in sync while the performers watched playback of the picture) were recorded in an audio studio and were saved as AIFF files. The rest of the files you imported were from sound-effects libraries and music CD libraries. These original files were also saved in the AIFF format. All the files have the same sample rate: 44.1kHz, the native format they were recorded in.

When mixing sampling rates within a project, it's best to up-sample rather than down-sample. If you mix 44.1kHz sampled audio, it will play better if you convert it to 48kHz to match the better rate recorded in the DV's audio. The reason is that you are asking your computer to up-convert these files in real time to the sampling rate you've set your DV Timeline to, for example. Faster Macintoshes (such as G4 dual-processor machines and the new G5 machines) up-sample these mixed formats in real time, but the demands on your computer are higher. This up-sampling might lower the number of real-time audio tracks that play back reliably. If you are working with many audio tracks (as you will while editing this tutorial), it's best to match sampling rates within your project with the sequence settings so that all the computer's processing power is used to play back your sequence and is not diverted to up-conversions.

If you mix 32kHz DV audio with 48kHz audio in the same sequence, you might experience popping sounds or other distortion. I highly recommend that you not record 12-bit audio DV in the first place. Mixing these two rates is problematic. 16-bit recordings have more information per sample and thus result in higher-quality audio. This is not quite as important in Final Cut Pro 4, because the quality of the resampling rates depends on the setting specified in User Preferences. Nevertheless, it's a good idea to match those settings by up-sampling them all to the same rates.

FCP 4 introduces clip-level rendering, which helps alleviate this problem. After you resample at the clip level, this resampled file moves with the clip and is rendered at the highest quality, saving repeated rendering of audio and giving the highest quality without losing tracks of real-time mixing. We'll discuss rendering in more depth in Chapter 11, "Video Filter Effects and Basic Compositing."

tip

If you're having audio such as voice-overs, automatic dialog replacement (ADR), or sound effects and original music recorded at a professional recording facility, you can often request that your source material be formatted as digital files and placed on CD instead of on tape. (This method was used in the development of this book, although the audio was mixed *originally* at the recording studio and was married to the picture there.) This way, you don't have to capture audio in Final Cut Pro from tape. You can just copy the audio files to your hard disk drive and then import them into Final Cut Pro. You don't want to import files directly from the CD. Instead, copy them to your scratch disk and import them from there into the Browser. Playback is more reliable from disk drives than from your computer's CD drive, and when you eject the CD, the files will be offline if they are connected to the CD and not locally stored on your scratch disk.

Audio Mixing

An entire book could be devoted to the art of mixing audio. It can be argued that an audio engineer who specializes in the art should always do your audio mixing. This process is commonly called *audio sweetening* or *sound sweetening*. So many different disciplines are involved with quality production that this argument can be made for each of them, but the democratizing nature of what's happening today in the area of video and film production runs contrary to this. It takes more money to hire specialists who might give you a better product. I recommend that you learn these tools and master their use. They can certainly improve the sound you add to your projects.

warning

There is no way to fix truly bad sound. If you have one voice among many (such as at a party) or a voice against wind or traffic noise, nothing can recover it.

The set of audio filters supplied by Final Cut Pro generally is for creating a better-sounding track and correcting errors. One thing is for sure: If you need a fix, there's probably a filter that can help if you learn how to use it properly.

You can hear various sources of audio at the same time by having audio files play "on top of" or "underneath" each other in the same moment, each residing in its own track or set of two tracks (for stereo clips) in your sequence. All frames of video and audio play at the same time if they are directly above or below each other, as you have seen already.

The number of clips you intend to hear at the same time determines how many audio tracks you need to create for them in your sequence. Stereo audio clips need two tracks per clip, and monaural tracks need only one.

Most users will use only two tracks of stereo audio for final output. So you need to determine which channel you want to hear each of your sound clips play from (left, right, or a combination, centered or not centered or even moving from side to side). You also need to determine each clip's volume and whether you want to add sound effects or filters to it. In Chapter 2, "Specifying Setups, Settings, Presets, and Preferences," see the "Audio Outputs" section for more information about setting up a system that uses more than two tracks of audio on output. You can have as many as 24 tracks of discrete audio output. The Final Cut Pro user's manual contains many pages on the use of multitrack recordings. Rather than repeat them here, I suggest that you read the discussion there. It is quite extensive.

Audio Aesthetics

When you edit audio into your sequence, it absolutely needs to be part of your story-telling. Each aspect of each element, whether audio or video, needs to enhance the part of the story you are telling. If it doesn't, it doesn't belong, and you shouldn't use it. This is one of the "live and die" rules of editing. When editing in additional elements, you must ask yourself if it's needed and if it's appropriate. Just because you recorded it doesn't mean you should use it. The same can be said of video edits.

Beginning filmmakers who edit the material they have shot or recorded themselves are especially prone to using an element that doesn't quite work because it's close, and the audience won't notice. Forget it. If you want a truly professional-sounding and -looking piece, don't show your audience your mistakes. As elementary as this sounds, it amazes me how often new filmmakers make this mistake.

Inappropriate audio elements especially get noticed when they have an unnatural or unsupportive sound or technical problems. For example, the moment you lose sync, you've lost the audience. On the whole, we are used to seeing lower-quality pictures, such as streaming video. We are not, however, used to hearing poor audio. The audience will hear a mistake or an inappropriate piece of audio sooner than they will notice a picture problem, and they won't forgive it as easily. Because you are trying to focus the audience on the feeling you want them to feel, keeping them in a mindset of fantasy or concentration on the subject at hand, don't jolt them back to reality by using audio that's not right or that has problems. It's better to simply leave it out.

Choose your elements solely on the basis of whether they paint a more-detailed picture of the portion of the story they appear in. If you show a mistake, you've blown it. If you don't show it, your audience will stay more focused. Although they won't hear that extra brush stroke of story, it's better than losing them because you used or left in something they noticed (and they *always* notice).

Sit back a bit from your direction, and tell your story anew when you start the editorial process. *Approach the material as if you are seeing and hearing it for the first time.* This is exactly why many producers don't allow their directors to edit the film they shot and choose an editor instead. Enhance the moments in your film only with edits that tell more story or add an adjective in film language. The moment you don't, your audience yawns.

Foley is the term used for recording sound effects that might or might not have been recorded when the film was shot. In the case of our movie, the entire sound effects track is either foley or effects taken from a sound-effects library. When you add this realistic and appropriate sound to your picture, it enhances the story. This might be done to get rid of inappropriate sound, such as cars or airplanes, or sync audio recorded with a technical problem. For example, it sure would wreck "The Midnight Sun" if we left in a 21st-century sound like an airplane. It would be better to use a different take or record ADR instead. This is also sometimes called *looping*.

Real-Time Audio Mixing

You can have up to 99 tracks of audio at one time within one sequence, but your computer's processor speed determines just how many of them you can play back in real time at the same time. This real-time audio mixing is set from the General tab of the User Preferences window, as shown in Figure 6.1.

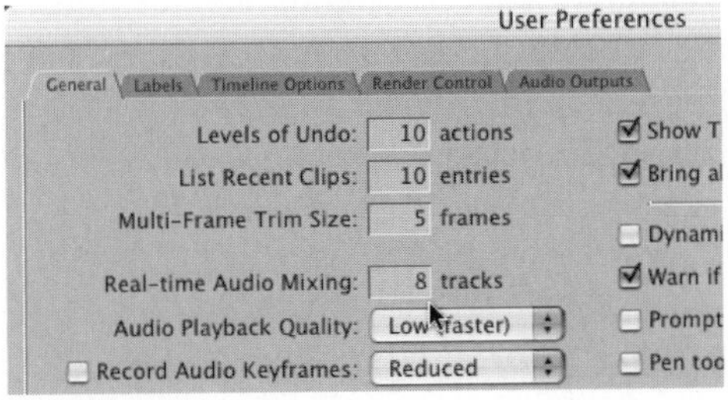

FIGURE 6.1   *The Real-time Audio Mixing setting.*

Experimentation is the way to find out how many tracks your computer will play back at the same time. Final Cut Pro has a default setting of eight tracks for real-time mixing. Faster machines, such as G4 duals, play back upwards of 20 or more. Most audio filters play back in real time, but "track costs" are involved with their use. Each machine is different, but it makes sense that if you ask your processor to process more data per track, fewer tracks will be available for monitoring at one time.

You can use a couple methods to increase the number of tracks you can play in real time:

■ You can render audio filters on a clip-by-clip basis. This lets you monitor more tracks, because you aren't asking your computer to apply the effect in real time.

■ If you render video effects that currently play in real time, you again relieve your computer from using computing power to show you these effects at the same time. To render an individual audio item in your sequence, highlight the clips in your sequence that have filters or transition effects added to them and select Sequence, Render Selection, Audio. You can select Sequence, Render All, Audio to render all audio effects.

If you render all the audio effects, you can still mix the pan and level settings in real time with the Audio Mixer (see "Understanding the Audio Mixer and Real-Time Mixing" later in this chapter). Furthermore, if you trim, move, or copy and paste a rendered audio clip, the audio-rendered file is preserved.

If you are experiencing poor performance, temporarily turn off tracks you don't need to monitor by clicking the green track-monitoring indicators. (Be aware that you might lose rendered files if you do this.) You also can set the number of tracks monitored at one time to a lower number in the General tab of the User Preferences. Or solo the track you want to hear against locked tracks. Monitoring too many tracks at the same time can cause dropped frames during playback.

When you are done mixing levels or adding audio effects, you can mix down your audio by selecting Sequence, Render Only, Mixdown or by pressing Opt+Cmd+R. This creates an invisible render file and allows you to hear all the files you've edited into your sequence and improve playback reliability. Because audio files are comparatively small, this process is relatively quick.

Examining an Audio-Only Clip

By double-clicking an audio clip placed in your sequence, you can open that clip in the Viewer window. This is an important distinction from loading clips into the Viewer from the Browser. When you make adjustments to an audio or video clip that has been opened in the Viewer this way, you affect only the clip *as it plays back in your sequence,* not the original file as it sits in the Browser. Remember that the clip in the Timeline window is not the same object that was in the Browser when you edited into the sequence. It is a *new* reference to the original media file. In this way, Final Cut Pro is *nondestructive.* It does not alter your original clip file, so you can feel free to experiment with it within a sequence without worrying about altering the original file. You can always go back to the original in the Browser and try different effects.

That said, it might be efficient to add effects or alter levels to clips contained in the Browser so that when you edit from them anywhere in your sequence, they have these changes each time you add them to your sequence. But Final Cut Pro still doesn't change the original media file itself (again, an instance of nondestructive operation). The same statements are true for video clips and their respective media files.

A Single-Track Audio-Only Clip

Take a look at Figure 6.2. Notice the "sprocket hole" dots in the scrubber bar. These dots let you know that you have loaded this clip into the Viewer window from your sequence by double-clicking it from the Timeline window. If you load an audio or video clip (or both) from the Browser, it will not have these dots. They are there to let you know you are working with audio or video as it is to be played back within your sequence.

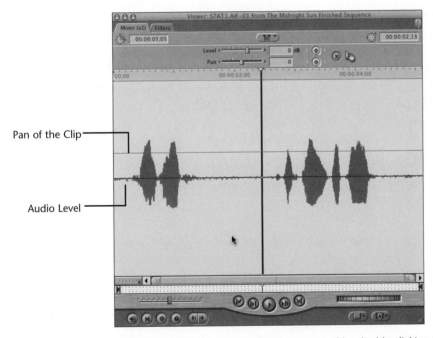

FIGURE 6.2   *A single-track audio-only clip in the Viewer, opened by double-clicking it from the Timeline window.*

In the center of the figure is a graphic representation of the waveform of the audio track you are working with. The higher the clip's level (loudness), the higher this gray waveform is. When there is no sound, the waveform collapses into a flat line.

There are two lines through the waveform. The lower line is pink and represents the audio level. The upper line is purple and represents the clip's pan. Figure 6.2 is set at a 0dB level and a pan of 0. These levels represent the audio panned to center and the volume of the clip set as recorded or captured. You can raise the audio level by raising or lowering the pink line. If you lower the purple line, you pan left. If you raise it, you pan right. You can use the Selection tool to lower or raise either line.

You can add keyframe indicators to these lines using the Pen tool, just as you did in the preceding chapter to the clip overlays line in the sequence in the Timeline when you faded up the opening shot. As long as you double-clicked the clip you are working with from the sequence currently in the Timeline window and not from the Browser, any change you make to level or pan settings is immediately reflected in the sequence that contains the clip. In the case of level changes, you see these added keyframe indicators mirrored in the clip's overlay in the Timeline window.

Take a look at Figure 6.3. You see four keyframe indicators. These determine from which point in time you want to start the lower level, fade the lower level, hold the level (–4dB), start the raise back, and then raise and hold it back up to 0, the recorded level. Notice that the position indicator when placed over this new level also shows in the level indicator slider and box the level you've lowered the audio to. If you played back this clip, you'd hear your changes immediately. To reset and undo these changes all at once, you can click the red X in the round button in the upper right of the Viewer window. This is the reset button. It removes all the keyframes you've added in that effect set. You'll find this button in every filter and transitional effect's controls used in Final Cut Pro.

FIGURE 6.3   *A single-track audio-only clip in the Viewer with keyframes.*

You can add keyframes to the current frame that the position indicator is sitting on by clicking the Add Keyframe buttons next to the Level and Pan sliders. The small triangles on either side of these keyframe buttons navigate to the previous keyframe (see Figure 6.4) or the next keyframe (see Figure 6.5). (You also can press Opt+K to go to the previous keyframe and Shift+K to go to the next keyframe.) If there are no more keyframes in the direction of the triangle, it is grayed out. When you are active on a keyframe, the diamond shape in the middle turns green, and the Level and Pan sliders change to that keyframe's Level and Pan settings.

FIGURE 6.4   *The previous keyframe navigational triangle.*

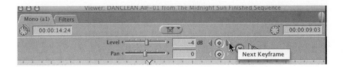

FIGURE 6.5   *The next keyframe navigational triangle.*

You can drag a keyframe indicator left to select an earlier frame or right to select a later frame. You can delete a keyframe indicator by Ctrl-clicking it and selecting Clear, as shown in Figure 6.6.

Notice the sliders at the bottom of the window. They work the same as the sliders at the bottom of the Timeline window. They allow you to zoom in or out on the waveform display. Zooming all the way in allows you to edit keyframe indicators within a single frame down to 1/100th of a frame, as shown in Figure 6.7. This is great for getting rid of a pop or part of a sound that exists within a single frame. The black area in the middle highlights a single frame, keyframed with an extremely fast drop in level, effectively cutting out a bit of the audio. More than once I've needed to delete an "s" sound to make a word singular rather than plural, for example. Holding down the Shift key while you scrub (drag the position indicator left and right) allows you to scrub in subframe increments. This can be useful for locating subframe points, such as the beginning and end point of an "s" within it.

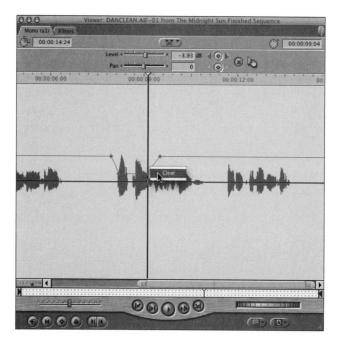

FIGURE 6.6   *The Clear Keyframe context menu.*

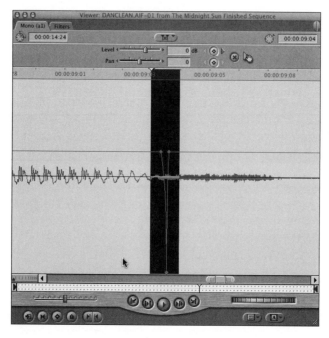

FIGURE 6.7   *A single frame of audio with keyframes within it.*

There are times when you might be working with audio recorded from a different source than the picture was recorded with, such as a film shoot where the audio was recorded on a DAT or Nagra, which is an audio recorder typically used in acquiring sync sound when shooting film. You also might notice a problem with music being in exact sync in a music video, or have a music beat within frames you want to edit to, or even have sync problems when you have recorded a speaker with a microphone placed some distance from the subject. Audio travels at a slower speed than light. You can actually move the audio tracks in subframe increments.

To move the sound that needs slightly better synchronization, move the playhead (position indicator) to an audio frame, and zoom completely in to that frame. Holding down the Shift key, move the playhead into the interior of the audio frame to a better sync point, and mark an In or Out point there. Final Cut Pro slips this audio clip's entire playback by this subframe amount.

The purple line, which represents the pan settings, is likewise keyframeable. As mentioned, lowering the level of this line pans the audio to the left, and raising it pans it to the right. It might be dramatic to have an arrow swoosh sound follow the screen direction, or a racing car's audio follow it across the screen. You can use a keyframe indicator and slide it up or down, use the sliders while activated on a keyframe, use the boxes and add values to them, or move the position indicator to a frame and type in a new value. All these actions accomplish the same thing. Again, I recommend experimentation to learn these tools. You'll find them quite intuitive.

> **tip**
>
> I've always found that using these sliders is not as intuitive as using the Zoom tool, activated by pressing Z to zoom in and ZZ to zoom out. Wherever you click with the Zoom tool, you zoom in or out on the position of the click. This is true in both this audio waveform and in the Timeline window's display.
>
> Pressing Shift+Z displays the entire clip you are viewing within the Viewer. In the case of the Timeline, Shift+Z fills the Timeline window with the complete sequence. I *really* like that one. Also, you can press A to activate the Selection tool. Notice that A and Z are next to each other on the keyboard. They are the first shortcuts you should learn and use consistently.

Multiple-Track Clips

Take a look at Figure 6.8. Notice that you are not constrained to a 4:3 window size when you are working with audio tracks in the Viewer window. If you use the pull tab in the lower-right corner, you can stretch out the window to see more of the track at once. This stereo music clip has two tracks of audio. The upper track is automatically panned to the left, and the right track is panned to the right. The pink line through each track represents the level of playback (as in the single-track clip discussed earlier). A pair of purple lines runs down the center of the two tracks (there are two if you've captured your material as stereo). They represent the pan of each track.

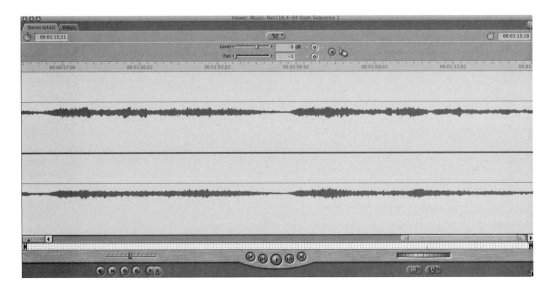

FIGURE 6.8   *Opening the Viewer to see more details of its waveform.*

Note too that if you open Sequence Settings (by pressing Cmd+0) and click the Timeline Options tab, you have two views of your audio tracks—Sequential and Paired. We will use Sequential throughout this book, but you might find it handy to organize your audio tracks as Paired if you are working with a lot of stereo clips. They operate the same as Sequential but give you a cue to use them to arrange mostly stereo clips.

In this case, the default pan setting is left channel of stereo to the left and right channel of stereo to the right. As with the single audio track, you can keyframe and change both these lines, except in the case of stereo pairs. Adding a keyframe indicator dot to either track adds a corresponding one on the other track, as shown in Figure 6.9. In this case, the track's audio level is lowered equally on both tracks at the same time to –12dB, as set by the four keyframe indicators.

Moving the second keyframe closer to the first (by simply clicking and dragging it) and the third keyframe closer to the fourth makes this "dip" in audio happen quicker, or more suddenly, as shown in Figure 6.10. You can think of this window as sort of a mini-Timeline, because it represents a clip from beginning to end over time.

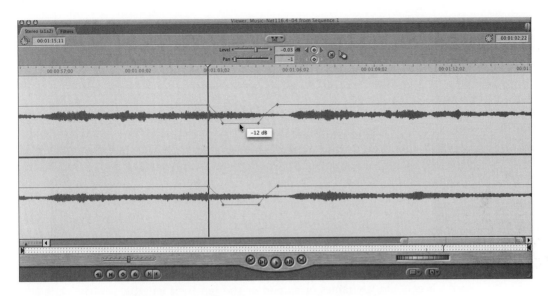

FIGURE 6.9   *Stereo pair "dual" keyframes.*

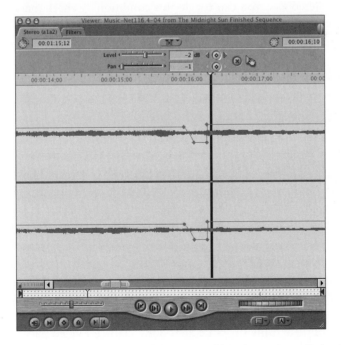

FIGURE 6.10   *Stereo pair "dual" keyframes with a more sudden change in audio level.*

If you want the entire audio clip to raise or lower its level, you don't need any keyframes. You simply drag the pink line down, use the slider, or type a positive or negative value in the box provided. Typing in a value here lowers the entire track at the same time. If a keyframe is already in the clip, FCP adds a keyframe to change the level to this new one over time between it and the previously added keyframe.

Notice that when you work with a stereo pair, the Pan slider is replaced with the Spread slider. The Spread slider allows you to begin swapping the left and right channels by sliding it from its default setting of –1 to 0 (when it's in the middle). This effectively makes this a mono mix, sending both the original left and right channels to both speakers. When this slider is all the way over to the right, it completes the swap, sending the original left channel to the right and the right channel to the left in your sequence as long as you have double-clicked the clip from the sequence and are effectively adjusting it from there. The rest of the controls in this window act the same as in the single-track audio clips window.

After it is edited into a sequence, a stereo pair continues working in tandem. In other words, if you add keyframes or extend or shorten their lengths, you can only edit them together as a pair. This condition can be changed, however, if you choose Modify, Stereo Pair. You can toggle this condition. A check mark next to this command tells you that the pair is locked as a stereo pair.

Audio Transitions

There are only two types of audio transitions:

- Cross fade (0dB)
- Cross fade (+3dB)

Both can be of any specified length. The difference between them is either no change in the levels during the transition, or a +3dB lift, which might sound better. During the fade, sometimes the audio sounds like it dropped in level. Audio sounds appear dropped in level with the 0dB transition because of the nonlinear nature of the human ear's response to audio. Without the +3dB cross fade, sound is faded linearly. That, to the ear, sounds like it dips.

Add audio transitions at edit points in your audio tracks using the same methods described for adding video transitions (drag the effect from the Effects tab to the clip or cut point you want to affect). You can change default transitions and save favorite versions of them using the same methods you use for video transitions. Simply highlight any audio effect in the Browser window's Effects tab (standard or customized, then saved in a favorites folder) and control click on the effect and select "Set Default

Transition" from the contextual menu that will appear. The default transition will be underlined in the Effects tab's list.

There is a different method of modifying audio transitions, though. If you Ctrl-click them, you see the contextual menu shown in Figure 6.11. You can cut, copy, and then paste them to other edit points in your audio. If you Ctrl-click an audio edit point, you can add your selected default transition to it, as shown in Figure 6.12.

FIGURE 6.11   *The audio transition context menu.*

FIGURE 6.12   *The audio edit point pop-up menu.*

Audio transitions are part of the set of real-time audio effects too, so you usually don't have to render them unless you reached the limit of what your machine can handle in the way of real-time audio mixing. You don't have to render them to listen to them externally, although it's highly recommended that you use the Mixdown Audio command before you print your masterpiece to tape.

Notice in Figure 6.11 that you can choose a duration. If you do, the window shown in Figure 6.13 opens. You can also open this window by double-clicking on an audio transition in the sequence in the Timeline.

You also can change an audio transition's duration by dragging either end of it in your sequence, as shown in Figure 6.14. Notice that it lets you know how much you have dragged it. It also displays a brown ghosted box to show you where it will sit if you let go of the mouse button. You also can click the center of an audio transition to drag its edit point using the Roll edit tool. It's similar to the Transition Effects Editor window for video effects, discussed in Chapter 5, "Basic Editing," in the section "Add a Cross-Dissolve."

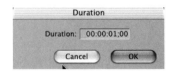

FIGURE 6.13
The Duration settings window.

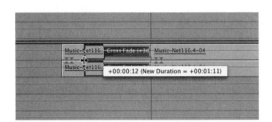

FIGURE 6.14 *Dragging an audio transition to change its duration.*

Understanding the Audio Mixer and Real-Time Mixing

New to FCP 4 is the *Audio Mixer,* shown in Figure 6.15. It appears in the Tool Bench with the other tools and their tabbed windows. If you are familiar with an automated hardware audio mixer, you'll feel right at home with this tool. Each audio track in the active sequence has a corresponding track strip. You'll find solo and mute buttons, a stereo panning slider, and a volume fader. You can change levels and pans of each track of your audio in real time. This means that you can play back the audio in your sequence and hear changes to the levels and pan adjustments you make with the Audio Mixer's controls as you play back your sequence. Changes in the level and pan settings are heard instantly. You'll find that this is faster than the manual adjustments described earlier in this chapter.

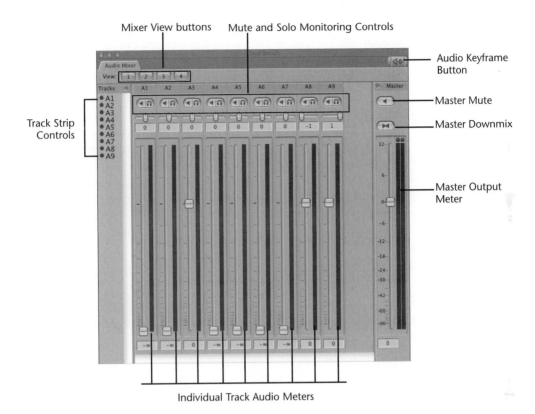

FIGURE 6.15 *The Audio Mixer.*

If you get close to the mix you want, it's probably best to keep the changes you've made with the Audio Mixer and do fine adjustments manually, as described earlier in this chapter. You can "rehearse" with this tool, though, because you have the option of either setting keyframes in your audio clips as they play, or not. A button bar at the top of the Tool Bench has a default button called Record Keyframes. Its default keyboard command is Shift+Cmd+K, which toggles the feature.

The Audio Mixer controls are as follows:

- Track strip controls provide real-time mixing and automation recording for volume and panning levels. You can hear the changes as you make them with these controls.

- Individual track audio meters allow you to see the levels of each audio track you are monitoring.

- Mute and Solo monitoring controls allow you to either mute a particular track or mute all other tracks. Soloing a track means playing it by itself. Muting a track temporarily disables that track's monitoring.

- The Master Level, Master Mute, and Downmix controls allow you to change global settings in the audio mix. Master Level controls change the level of the entire mix all at once. This doesn't change keyframed audio levels, but it does change Final Cut Pro's output level. It's used to control the output levels during a recording to tape, for example. The Master Mute control mutes all audio tracks during audio output. The Downmix button prevents dual mono tracks from being recorded too high when you lay back to tape or prepare a QuickTime movie of your sequence. When audio is mixed down to stereo tracks, the combined levels of dual mono tracks might overmodulate. The Downmix option's default setting (as set on the Audio outputs tab) is –3dB. This keeps the recording or QuickTime movie at the proper levels.

- Master output meters display the mixed output of your audio controls to show and hide individual track strips, allowing you to view only the tracks you want to adjust.

- Mixer View buttons allow for four different views of the Mixer. Hiding a few tracks whose audio needs no adjustment makes it easier to deal with just the tracks needing adjustment.

- The Audio Keyframe button allows you to enable or disable adding keyframes to your clips. It might be good for a "practice run" to keep these off.

Mixing in Real Time with the Audio Mixer

Using the Audio Mixer is very straightforward. Slide a slider up, and that track's audio level increases. Slide it down, and the level decreases. As long as you've clicked the Record Keyframes button, your changes will be recorded in the sequence.

The speed of your computer components dictates how many tracks of audio you can adjust in real time during playback with the Audio Mixer, but most dual G4s do many tracks at one time. It might help to individually render audio filters before you attempt a real-time mix. You can render effects individually by selecting the clips containing them and pressing Cmd+R. This goes for attempting playback of video clips that have real-time effects being processed for playback. Always think in these terms when trying to play back any real-time effects. The less you ask your computer to do at any one time in this regard, the more likely you'll get the real-time playback you want.

It's easier to use the Audio Mixer if your tracks are consistently arranged. Put music on one set of tracks, sound effects on another set, and voice-over or sync sound on yet another. Then you'll know which sliders affect which sound easier. Being as consistent as possible will help you in the mixing workflow.

To open the Audio Mixer, either select it from the Tools menu or press Opt+6. Much like the green track visibility lights on the left side of the Timeline window, the far-left side of the Audio Mixer has track visibility controls. There is a disclosure triangle on the left below the Audio Mixer tab. If you click it, it opens and closes the Tracks Selection pane. If there is a black dot next to an audio track name, its sliders are present in the Mixer.

Turning these track selectors on and off is how you select the four custom views of the Audio Mixer that are available to you. Not seeing all your tracks in this mixing tool might be a workflow advantage if you have a lot of them. After you select the tracks you want to work with, click one of the top four buttons and save this "view" of the Mixer.

note

If a track has been disabled in the current sequence in the Timeline window, it cannot be mixed in the Audio Mixer. Its slider will be grayed out.

If you Ctrl-click one of these tracks, a shortcut menu opens so that you can assign that channel's audio output track. The optional hardware installed on your specific machine for capturing and recording audio and/or video determines the number of tracks you can lay back to tape. At any rate, these output channels are sent to the device you've selected for output in the Audio Outputs tab of the User Preferences.

Workshop 6: Finish Editing Scene 1

It's time to finish Scene 1's audio tracks. Audio will enhance this story tremendously. You could watch a silent version of this film and get a grasp of what the story is about, but adding audio to it accents, defines, and brings the pictures to life. It further brings the audience into the story emotionally. It's important to add audio to further define the moments, but you must do this carefully, because an audio glitch is far more noticeable to an audience member than a rough video edit. We are very used to hearing high-quality audio in all forms of entertainment. Thus, we will forgive a mismatched shot sooner than we will an audio error.

When working with audio, be make sure that it transitions smoothly, is appropriate for the moment it enhances, and doesn't fight with the pictures it supports. Audio brings pictures to life.

Control the Sound of the Cold

You set up the audience with the sound of wind to indicate cold, which you hope will affect them emotionally, but there is a moment you should enhance and make feel even worse. The first shot established the where. Then you added some sorrowful-looking shots of the lone cross and the broken-down dog sled. Adding a bit more wind will make these shots even lonelier.

1. Open "Wind Light wind #2 2_1-01" in the Viewer. Mark an In point at 00:00:01:00 and an Out point at 00:00:15;22. You are placing this clip here to accent the cold (to tell more story with it), especially over the Lone Cross and Abandoned rags shots.

2. Overwrite this stereo clip to tracks A1 and A2 at 01:00:25;03 in Sequence 1. Don't forget to target the tracks.

3. Add the cross fade dissolve of your choice to the head of this audio edit in your sequence to each track. Ctrl-click the transitions in the sequence. Modify them to start on the edit point and to have a duration of 3 seconds. Alternatively, you can double-click them to open the Duration dialog box and change their durations there. Then play back the sequence.

4. It's too loud. It needs to be subtle. We're not in a blizzard; we're in a different place, so lower the level about 5 or 6dB. Double-click the pair to open the clip in the Viewer to modify it *as it is in the sequence*. You see the sprocket holes in the scrubber bar, as shown in Figure 6.16. Type in a new level, use the Level slider, or drag the pink line down. If you had *not* double-clicked the clip from the sequence, you would have lowered the original clip's audio and would not have changed it as it exists in the Timeline. The FCP user manual calls this type of clip a *Timeline clip*.

5. We have run out of "base" wind sound, so let's keep it going for now. Turn on snapping by pressing N. Locate the "Wind,desert Lonely,66_1-11" sound clip in the Sound clips bin. Drag the entire clip to tracks 6 and 7, right next to the earlier wind clip that's already there. It might be easier to do this if you click the green maximize button in the upper-left corner of the Timeline window to reveal all the tracks. It will look something like Figure 6.17. If you maximize the Timeline, clicking the same button after your edit puts the Timeline window back where you started.

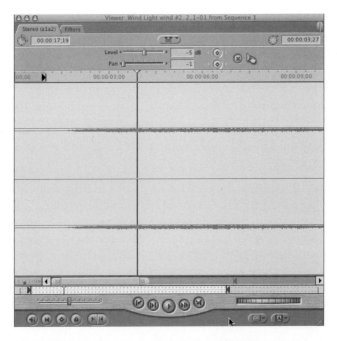

Figure 6.16   *A clip in the Viewer taken from the sequence. The sprocket holes represent the clip as it is in the sequence, not as it is in the Browser.*

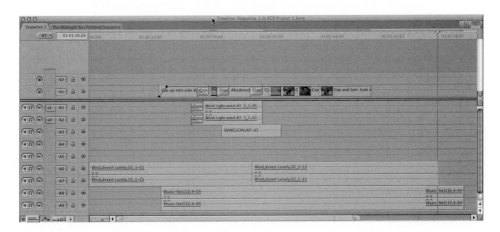

Figure 6.17   *In the maximized Timeline window, a clip is easily dragged from the Browser to the sequence in the Timeline.*

6. Turn off monitoring for all audio tracks except tracks 6 and 7 to check this new sound effect edit (click the green track lights off). Play the sequence through this edit. Listen to the wind noise by itself. It's fine. Don't forget to listen to tracks by themselves to make each element just right. Sometimes it might be necessary to put a dissolve between clips like this, for example.

7. Turn off monitoring for tracks 6 and 7, and turn on only tracks 1 and 2. The light wind edit cuts out too abruptly. You want it to fade away as the heroes begin to appear. At the same time, you should begin hearing their sound sync. However, there isn't any, because it wasn't recorded on the shoot. So we'll use the foley for it instead. Locate the clip named "Foley 1-FtStps Open-01" in the Sound Clips bin. There are a lot of foley recordings here, so create a new bin for them, but this time keep it in the Sound Clips bin as a sort of subset of sound clips. Scrolling through a larger bin wastes time, so creating subsets might save time in the long run. With the Sound Clips bin open, press Cmd+B. A new bin appears in this bin. Name it *Foley. Putting an asterisk next to the name causes this bin to automatically sort to the top of the Sound Clips bin—as long as the Name column is sorted alphabetically in ascending order. If it's sorted in descending order, this bin will be at the bottom of the list.

8. Using the Find command (Cmd+F), type **Foley** in the search box, and find all. The Find Results bin opens; all the foley recorded is in it. You can even edit directly from this bin. Select all the foley clips by pressing Cmd+A. With the Find Results window open, drag any one of the icons directly to the *Foley bin you just created.

    If the clips had not had the word "Foley" as their first word, they might not have been chosen if you were assuming that all foley clips start with "Foley." In this case, they do start with "Foley," but I never trust the naming conventions used by anyone else. I didn't name these clips; the sound recording engineer did. If you name your own clips, use names you can find later with the Find command, and be consistent with the names, because you'll save a lot of time searching for them later. Remember, sorting through clips is a big time-waster. The idea is to maximize editing time, not repeatedly search for clips. Form habits early.

9. Open the *Foley bin, and locate the clip named "Foley 1-FtStps Open-01." Double-click it to place it in the Viewer. Set an In point one frame from the first frame by pressing Home+right arrow. Play it to listen to it. It's quiet, so this time raise its level to +12dB. If this clip is ever needed again, this level will become the default level it contains. This exemplifies the difference between modifying clips as they play in the sequence and modifying them *before* you place them in the sequence. Each time you modify them when they were opened in the Viewer from the Browser window or an open bin window, they are modified as they are in these windows. This modification carries through to the sequence if and when you place the clips there. It's really efficient if you use them repeatedly modified in the same way. The same can be said for video clips and graphic clips.

10. Highlight the "Wind Light wind #2 2_1-01" clip in the Timeline window. Select Modify, Stereo Pair to turn this off. The reason you want to do this is that you will overwrite just one of the two tracks with the next edit, and you cannot do this if you are overwriting a stereo pair and you are not overwriting with *another* stereo pair.

11. Set a mark In point for this single-track edit at 01:00:39;11 in the sequence. Target track A1 and overwrite this edit. This time, use "overwrite with transition" by dragging the hand icon in the upper right to the Canvas Overlay window, or press Shift+F10 to add the audio and the aforementioned cross fade.

12. The problem is that this transition is only three frames long. This is because the audio you added (the foley clip) had only one frame of unused media before its edit point. There's an easy fix, though. Zoom into the Timeline, clicking this tiny transition, until you can Ctrl-click it and change it to have a different Transition Alignment. Change it to Starting on Edit. Next, change the cross fade's duration to 30 frames. Double-click the cross fade to open the Duration dialog box. Type **30** in the box and press Enter.

13. You need to fade out the other track of the Light wind clip, so add another 1-second audio cross fade to the outgoing sound on the A2 track by itself. Play back the sequence. The sound of the wind fades away too fast, so click the A2 track's wind audio transition, and change its transition alignment (by Ctrl-clicking the transition to bring up the pop-up menu) to start at the edit. Then click the end of the icon in the sequence, and drag it right until the transition is 2 seconds long, as shown in Figure 6.18. Play back the sequence. When you are done, your sequence should look like Figure 6.19.

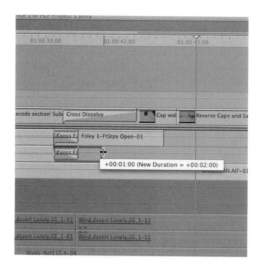

FIGURE 6.18 *Dragging an audio fade to extend its duration.*

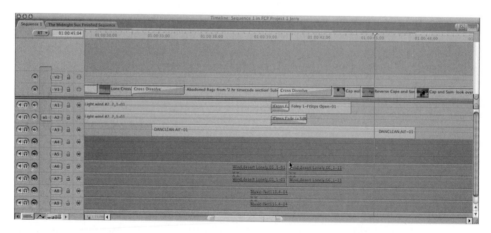

FIGURE 6.19 *The Timeline after step 13.*

Add Some Foley Sound

As defined earlier, *foley* is sound recorded by artists who watch the film and record sounds they make at the same time to create or replace audio that might have been recorded (or not recorded) when the film was shot. The footsteps in the snow you are about to add were created by artists with their hands crunching a box full of corn-starch on a foley stage! Whatever works, works.

1. Monitoring only audio tracks A1, A2, and A3, add the rest of the footsteps. Cap's (the older actor's) footsteps are rhythmic and even enough to reuse here, so add another "Foley 1-FtStps Open-01" clip to the A2 track and overlap it a bit. The first footstep sound is at 00:00:00;16, so, using the Viewer, mark an In point there, and mark an Out point at 00:00:03;14, where it sounds as if he plants a final footstep. Edit this into the sequence at 01:00:42;05 as an over-write edit, targeted to track A2.

2. Next, add some footsteps for Sam. Double-click "Foley 3-FtStps Open-03" to open it in the Viewer. Set an In point at 0:00:00;00 and an Out point at 0:00:02;21. On track A1, add the clip to the sequence at 01:00:44;19 by press-ing F10 (the keyboard shortcut for overwrite). Its Out is too loud, so set its level to +12dB for most of its duration. Add a keyframe about two-thirds of the way through and one on the very end of it. Lower the end keyframe all the way to the bottom of the clip. This effectively lowers the audio below the level at which you can hear it, dampening the outgoing sound of Sam's last step on the slope.

3. On track A2, add "Foley 2-FtStps Open-02" next to the end of the "Foley 1-FtStps Open-01" clip's Out point. (Use the Snapping tool.) Make sure that all the footstep edits are at +12dB. There is a single footstep in this last bit of foley to help accentuate Sam's struggle up the hill. Again, anything appropri-ate to enhance our story. Sam looks awkward, but Cap has been looking and *sounding* strong and even. Even sound effects can help tell our story. When you are done, this area of your sequence should look like Figure 6.20. Save your project by pressing Cmd+S.

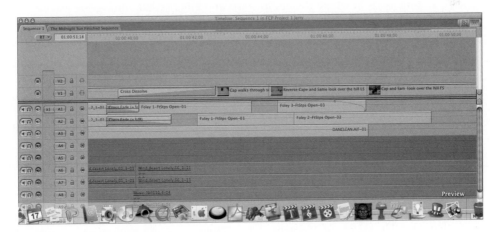

FIGURE 6.20   *The Timeline after step 3.*

Open and Close Cap's Map

Now that we are in a real-time situation in the story, the foley accentuates this. It started with the footsteps, and it continues with the sounds of the map being opened.

1. Load "Foley 4-Map 2" into the Viewer, and raise its level to +12dB. While it's in the Viewer, mark an In point at the very beginning and an Out point at 00:00:09;04. Then overwrite the marked clip onto A3 at 01:00:47;19. Don't forget to target A3 for your edit. This audio fills out the sound of Cap opening his map.

2. Load "Foley 4-Map Open -01" into the Viewer. Raise its level to +12dB. Mark the entire clip by pressing X. Drag its clip icon from the Browser right next to the tail of "Foley 4-Map 2" on A3. It's Cap putting the map away.

3. You need to add the footsteps of the two men again as Cap walks away. Open "Foley 2-Guy#2 Turn and Walk#-01" in the Viewer. Mark an In point at 00:00:10;23 and an Out point at 00:00:16;16. After raising the level to +12dB, overwrite it at 01:00:58;18 in your sequence on A1.

The Scene's Final Voice-Over

Next, you'll bring back the storyteller. You'll continue with a voice-over (VO) to move the story along. You are setting up what the story is about. You're also setting up the audience for what seems to be a horror story.

1. Open DANCLEAN.AIF-03 in the Viewer. It's Cap's final VO for the scene. This time, look at where the audio starts and ends by examining the waveform in the Viewer. Mark In just before it starts, and mark Out just after it ends. Overwrite the marked clip into the A2 track at 01:00:55;01 in your sequence.

2. Double-click the DANCLEAN edit you just put on track A2 so that it appears in the Viewer with the sprocket holes in the scrubber bar. Then play it in to out by clicking the Play In to Out button or by pressing Shift+\. While you listen, watch the levels on the audio meters. If they are not open, you can open them by selecting Window, Audio Meters, or type Opt+4. Cap starts a bit low and then really gets lower as he speaks. The meters bear this out.

    Start by raising the clip's level to +5dB. (Drag the pink line up to +5dB.) Use the sliders to reveal the entire waveform, as shown in Figure 6.21. Place the position indicator (playhead) somewhere near the middle of the flat line between the actor's two speeches. Mark a keyframe on the pink level line and another one about 15 frames later. Drag the second keyframe up another 3dB. The level will be raised a total of 8dB from the original recording level, as shown in Figure 6.22. Play back the clip while watching the meters. It's much more even and peaks around –12dB. Save the project file.

FIGURE 6.21   *The DANCLEAN audio raised evenly to +5dB.*

FIGURE 6.22   *The DANCLEAN audio with keyframes after step 2.*

View the Entire Scene

Turn on all the tracks and watch the Timeline from the beginning through Scene 1.

Since you added the foley, it's a different movie. The viewers are brought into the present earlier with the cuts that introduce the characters. You helped this feeling along by adding the sound of these fellows. You even went to the extent of adding sound that indicates a strong stride for Cap and a clumsier-sounding one for Sam. The three early shots foreshadow things to come.

Only one thing isn't quite right—the music. It feels just a bit too loud—especially where the poem's second stanza begins at the point of Cap's second voice-over. The music is fighting with the voice-over.

1. Enlarge the Timeline window so that you can see all nine tracks of audio. Expand the track height by clicking the third box from the bottom-left corner of the Timeline window, and press Opt+Cmd+W. This lets you see the waveforms in the Timeline. Make sure that the Timeline overlays are turned on (the second button in the bottom left of the Timeline window, next to the track height indicators).

2. You will lower the music *right before* the DANCLEAN.AIF-01 clip begins with the Audio Mixer. Select Window, Arrange, Audio Mixing. This opens the Audio Mixer and arranges the windows. The music level is fine until Cap's first reading of the poem, but as soon as the voice-over begins, the poem fights with it. Position the playhead well before the DANCLEAN.AIF-01 clip. Be sure that the Record Audio Keyframes button is turned on in the Audio Mixer (it will look pressed), and press Play. Click and hold the mouse over the A8 slider, which is at 0. While the sequence is playing, lower the music track near the beginning of the voice-over during the long hold of the music there. Gradually lower it to –7dB, and then let go of the mouse button. It might take you a couple of tries to get this just right, so if you goof up, just use my favorite keyboard command, Undo (Cmd+Z), and try again until you are satisfied with the result.

3. Keyframes are added to the music clip automatically just after you stop playing back. If you need to, use the "manual" method of deleting or adding them to clean up any mistakes. Also be aware that if you loop this playback (by setting an In and Out point and selecting View, Loop Playback), each time the loop begins again, it overwrites any keyframes made previously.

4. Click the Timeline window's green expansion button. You can make the entire sequence fit the Timeline window by pressing Shift+Z. It should look like Figure 6.23 if you have the track height clips in the same size. Save the project. I have only two keyframes in the music clip; you might have more. You might remember that in the User Preferences is a setting to control how many keyframes are added when you add them automatically with the Audio Mixer.

Figure 6.24 shows how I set this preference. Experiment with this particular audio mix with the different settings to learn the differences. You can have many, fewer, or only audio peak's keyframes recorded.

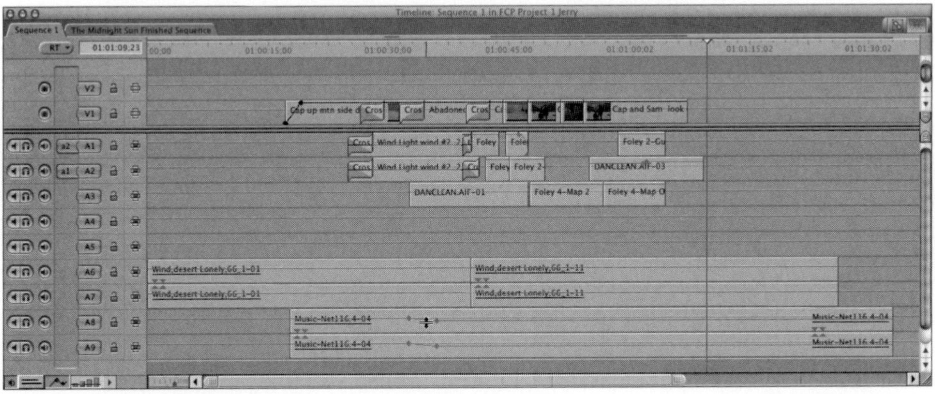

FIGURE 6.23   *The Timeline at the end of Workshop 6.*

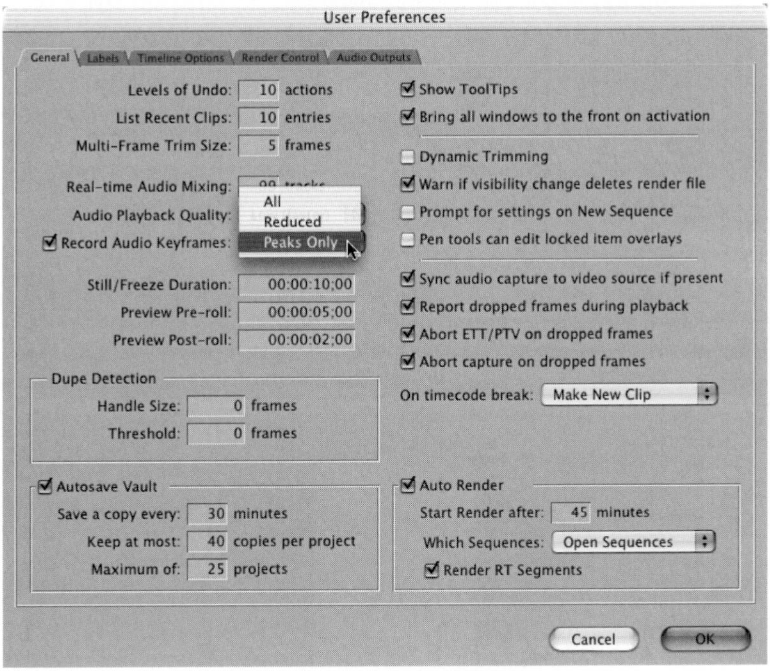

FIGURE 6.24   *The User Preferences Record Audio Keyframes setting.*

CHAPTER 7

Advanced Trimming: Beyond the Razor Blade

- The Trim Edit Window
- Slipping and Sliding Clips in the Sequence
- Workshop 7: Use More-Advanced Trimming

The Trim Edit Window

One of the best-designed features of Final Cut Pro is the Trim Edit window.

Trimming is the act of fine-tuning your edit points down to an exact frame. The Razor Blade is not as useful for the purpose, because it takes longer to make precision edits. For example, you can make small trims one frame at a time and immediately review and accept them, or you can further change them very quickly. The Trim Edit window keeps track of these changes as you make them. Furthermore, it gives you a side-by-side comparison of the outgoing clip's last frame and the incoming clip's first frame. This is most important when you're trying to match action between a medium shot and a close-up shot.

You can open the Trim Edit window three different ways. You can double-click the audio and/or video edit you want to trim. You can press Cmd+7 when the track(s) you want to trim are targeted by being the auto-selected track(s). Finally, you can use the Edit Selection tool. When you press Cmd+7, which is the default keyboard command, the Trim Edit window opens, ready to trim the edit point closest to the position indicator in the Timeline window unless an edit is selected in the Timeline.

If an edit is selected, pressing Cmd+7 opens the Trim Edit window with the selected edit. You can use the Edit Selection tool to lasso a group of edit points to trim all at once. When you do this, the Trim window opens, ready to trim the lassoed edit point(s).

As shown in Figure 7.1, when the Trim Edit window is open, you are presented with two windows that represent the last frame of the outgoing clip (on the left) and the first frame of the incoming clip (on the right). If you are trimming an audio-only edit, speaker icons replace these frames of video. A green line runs across the top of each window. When the green line can be seen, it lets you know which side (or both sides) of the edit point you are set up to trim.

FIGURE 7.1   *The Trim Edit window.*

By clicking anywhere on one of the two pictures, you select which side of this edit you want to trim, turning off the green line in the opposite window. In this way, you can add or subtract frames on just one side of the edit point and perform a ripple edit. If both sides are selected, you perform a roll edit. To reselect both sides if you have started the trim on one or the other, click the line between them. You can also cycle through the three different conditions of this selection (incoming, outgoing, or both) by pressing U repeatedly.

Rippling an edit point (selecting one side) shortens or lengthens your sequence. Rolling an edit point (selecting both sides) adds frames to one side of the edit while subtracting frames from the other side of the edit. This maintains the original duration of your sequence.

When you make an edit with this tool, it is immediately reflected in your sequence.

The Trim Edit Window's Playback Controls

Many of the controls in the Trim Edit window are familiar (see Figure 7.2). The Jog and Shuttle controls work with the window they are directly under, and they operate the same as they do in the Viewer and Canvas. The Play button under each window plays the clip on either side of the edit. The right and left arrows on either side of these buttons advance or rewind the clip in their respective windows a frame at a time.

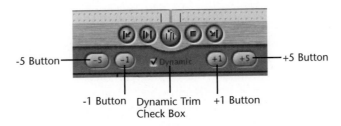

FIGURE 7.2   *The Trim Edit window's playback controls.*

The central six buttons are the transport controls for this window. From the left, they are as follows:

- Previous Edit jumps to the previous edit point in the sequence and makes the Trim Edit window ready to trim it. You can press the up arrow key on the keyboard to perform the same function.

- Play In to Out plays the entire clip of the outgoing shot through to the last frame of the incoming shot. When you use this function, the video plays in the right window, and the left window is dimmed.

- Play Around Edit Loop plays around and through the edit point with pre-roll and post-roll times determined by the preview pre-roll and post-roll times set in the General tab of the User Preferences window. You can press the spacebar to stop this loop. Just like the Play In to Out button, the video plays on the right.

- Stop stops the edit point's looping playback, leaving the position of the playhead on the edit point.

- Next Edit jumps to the next edit point in the sequence, making the Trim Edit window ready to trim it. You can press the down arrow key on the keyboard to perform the same function.

- With the Dynamic trim check box checked, you can use the J, K, and L keys to find a new edit point and trim the edit. This feature is new to FCP 4. When you use this mode, selected from the General tab of User Preferences or by clicking the Dynamic Trimming button, press L when you see a new edit you'd like to use. Pressing K then updates the edit point. Similarly, pressing J plays the edit backward, and pressing K then performs the edit. You set the playback's pre-roll and post-roll from the General tab of User Preferences. If you need to see more video (during the looping playback, for example), give yourself more time by changing this preference. Repeatedly pressing the L or J key increases the playback speed during the edit preview.

tip

Jumping from edit point to edit point lets you very quickly trim those 30-second TV spots whose first cut is too long, or that scene that just drags. You'll be amazed how quickly you can increase the pace of a whole scene this way. Or possibly a series of stills in a documentary, or any number of situations in which you need to quickly compress time in a scene and you don't know where to start. I've found this to be an amazing time-saver. You'll find places to trim and make a bit snappier just doing this.

If you are using the Dynamic Trim mode, you'll see a teal-colored light on the central preview button in the center, or on one of the individual play buttons just underneath each of the two windows. For example, if you move the mouse between the outgoing shot and the central button, you see the highlighted button change. If the central preview play button has the teal highlight, using the J, K, and L keys dynamically trims. If the highlight is on one of the other individual playback buttons, J, K, and L play back these clips only, and pressing I or O trims the edit. Playing around with this is the best way to understand the behaviors.

Another way to perform changes or trims in the Trim Edit window is to drag the handles in the scrubber bars. You can drag the Out point indicator to affect the outgoing shot or drag the In point indicator to change the edit point of the incoming shot. You can also use the J, K, and L keys to reposition the playhead within these two shots as long as the teal light is on in the proper place (see Figure 7.1). Press O to reset the Out point of the outgoing shot, or press I to reset the In point of the incoming shot. You can also reset these points by clicking the Mark Out button or the Mark In button on the far left and far right of the transport controls, which are shown in Figure 7.1.

Yet another way to make trims is to just type them in. With the Trim Edit window open and active, typing **30** moves the edit point 30 frames to the right, or later in time. Alternatively, typing **-30** moves the edit point 30 frames to the left, or sooner in time.

In the far bottom left and far bottom right of Figure 7.1, you see the Out Shift counter and In Shift counter. They keep a running total of the minutes, seconds, and frames of the trims you have performed on the outgoing clip (on the far left) and the incoming clip (on the far right). Use this to judge what you have done. Or, if you change your mind after previewing a change, you can quickly reset these numbers to 0s by typing in the opposite number for the trim. Thus, if you've added 22 frames to the head of the incoming shot, you see –22 in the In shift counter. Typing **22** (a positive number) resets this edit point to 0, leaving it the way you had it in the first place. Using Undo (Cmd+Z) is useful here as well.

Matching Action and Storytelling Using the Trim Edit Window

The real creative power of editing with Final Cut Pro and other nonlinear editors is the fact that nothing is "written in stone" until you have recorded your sequence to tape and deleted the media associated with the project. Changing your mind, trying different edits, and accepting or rejecting them is the key to finding a better treatment of the material and giving your story more impact. I mean story in the broadest sense. Even selling toothpaste in 30 seconds takes a story. Whiten your teeth to attract love—needs a story, right?

Undo should be used for the purpose of trying all the what-ifs. The Trim Edit window is one place this *really* comes into play. Does the matching action edit work better if you do it this way or that way? Remember that you want to make edits look seamless. You don't want the audience to notice that, in most cases, shots of matching action were not recorded simultaneously. Rather, they were shot with a single camera from a different angle and from different takes, as in the case of "The Midnight Sun."

The language of film has taught us that we as viewers can look at a scene from any angle. But the time that takes place between shots in a sequence of continuous action is instant, and the audience loses their focus either consciously or unconsciously the moment things don't match. It's better to avoid a sequence of shots that almost match. Otherwise, the story gives the impression that it's not true. The audience loses their involvement because they don't believe it's happening "right now." They quit being emotionally involved, because they are suddenly aware that they are watching a movie. It's partly your job as an editor to keep them under the ether.

Working with scenes that contain animals or cigarettes is a matching-action nightmare if they were shot with single cameras. It takes a very strong continuity person on the set to watch for the problems inherent in scenes like this and a very clever editor to cut around the problems that inevitably come up. The Trim Edit window is a powerful tool to make these shots seamless as they cut to each other, or to move an edit point to hit an audio cue of some sort and make your sequence a better marriage of picture and sound. It's also the quickest way to determine that the shots don't cut to each other and you possibly need to change the shot order. You might not always get everything to match perfectly. Much depends on the production team's efforts. But you will end up with a better edit of the material you were presented with if you use the Trim Edit window effectively.

There will be times that you simply cannot match action, for any number of reasons. The fix here, though, is to pay very close attention to the rhythm of the scene. (You should be doing this as much as you can. Most editors will tell you that this is more important than matching the action anyway.) Where would your own eyes move during a particular moment? Find that moment by possibly looking at a wide angle of the entire area shot. Pay close attention to your eye movements. Mirror them in the cut. They'll feel quite natural to your viewers, and they will probably overlook some of the mismatched cuts, because they too would do the same in real life. Matching action is certainly important. A balance must be achieved between matching the action and cutting to the rhythm of the scene. Maybe you shouldn't cut a two shot at all. If the story is being told in the best possible way by not cutting, don't cut. In most cases, it's more important to cut to the rhythm of the scene rather than cut just because you can. Don't make choices based on matching action unless they *also* mirror what you would be doing with your eyes if you were actually there. When watching student editors' work, I see cuts just for the sake of cuts way too often, and I see no cuts when there should be cuts, so I think the suggestions here must not come easily.

Just remember that if you cut a close-up of a character from a close-up of another character, for example, *a motivation has to be there*. All edits need motivation, and when they are cut to the rhythm of a scene, they become much more seamless and keep the audience "under the ether." In short, then, it's more important to cut with motivation and rhythm than it is to cut perfectly matched action.

The Trim Edit Window's Transport Controls

There are incremental buttons just under the transport controls, as shown in Figure 7.3. They trim the selected clips in lower and exact increments. The +1 and –1 buttons trim a frame at a time. In the case of an outgoing clip, –1 takes off one frame, and +1 adds a frame. In the case of an incoming clip, –1 adds a frame, and +1 takes a frame away. This might sound confusing, but you should think of these trim buttons as moving the edit point and not just adding or subtracting frames. If you click the –1 button, selecting either or both clips for the trim, it moves the edit point earlier. If you click +1, it moves the edit point later.

Next to the +1 and –1 trim buttons are the +5 and –5 buttons. They do the same thing as the others but trim five frames for each click of the mouse instead of just one. In the General tab of the User Preferences, you can customize them to be anything between 1 and 9 frames. They are called the *multiframe trim buttons*.

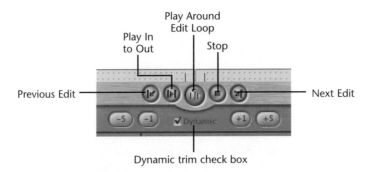

FIGURE 7.3   *A detail of the transport controls in the Trim Edit window.*

At the top of the Trim Edit window you'll find a plethora of information. Take a look at Figure 7.4. There are five timecode numbers. From the left, they are the duration of the outgoing clip, the timecode number of the last frame of the outgoing clip, the position in the Timeline that the edit is sitting on, the duration of the incoming clip, and the timecode number of the first frame of video in the incoming clip.

FIGURE 7.4   *A detail of the top of the Trim Edit window.*

The center button, labeled Track V1, opens a menu that changes the viewing point in a multitrack trimming situation. This is very handy for multiple tracks of audio and video in a complex edit.

tip

The great thing about the Trim Edit tool that sets it apart from all the other trim tools I've ever seen is that it allows you to take another look at edit points by scrubbing or playing either side of the shots without actually making any change to your sequence. That is, you can park on a new side-by-side comparison of the two clips' edit points by simply clicking either side's playhead, or playing either side and stopping, to look at whether these two frames are likely to cut to each other well (a previsualization). This is perfect for matching action edits. You can play the shots individually within their respective windows and park them wherever you want. Until you set a new Out or In point, you make no changes to the edit point. The arrow frame-at-a-time buttons and the jog wheel are great for this. For example, you can search shots that are currently active in the Trim Edit window without making a change to see if there isn't another edit point you could use.

When the Shots Aren't Quite Perfect

There are times when the footage shot just isn't perfect. There will be flaws in continuity, or times when a stunt person might have shown too much of himself, or shots that you must use but that just aren't perfect for any number of reasons. It's your job as an editor to minimize the problems. In the upcoming scene I'll show you examples of this sort of problem and how to minimize the issues involved as much as possible.

One of the things that loses your audience's attention or suspension of disbelief is if you in any way aggravate the problem by showing too much of it or use part of a shot that really points out the problem. Of course, the best solution is to reshoot, but in the real world of tight budgets, that's not always possible. It's becoming a very common production technique to capture footage on the set just after or even when it's being shot and to rough out a cut to double-check for these sorts of errors. Final Cut Pro is definitely up to the task.

The technique of doing rough cuts on the set familiarizes the editor with the footage. It also serves as a "live" storyboard to help with previsualization for everyone on the set, if for no other reason than to help everyone understand how the shots cut to each other. With the advent of editing on portable computers, this technique is becoming a mainstay.

Francis Ford Coppola used this technique for the first time when he shot "One from the Heart." In those days, he needed an *entire truck* on the set for the purpose, and he used the video assist feed from the film cameras to capture video. We've come a long way from those days. Now all you need when shooting film is an A/D converter and the video assist, a portable Mac and Final Cut Pro.

Slipping and Sliding Clips in the Sequence

Slipping and sliding clips contained in your sequence are very powerful ways to trim their edit points. In both cases, you trim two edit points at the same time without changing the sequence's duration. Slipping changes the frames used within one clip without changing the clip's duration. Sliding changes the edit points on both sides of the clip at the same time but does not change the frames used in the selected clip—nor does it change the clip's duration. Rather, it changes the duration of the clips before and after it, adding and subtracting frames to and from them *at the same time,* maintaining the duration of the sequence itself. In neither case can you slip or slide a frame farther than over the clips on either side of it.

For example, slipping can be used when a certain duration is best but the original footage you put in the sequence ends in the wrong place. If you slip the footage to the left until you get to the "right" frames, you are usually done with the trim you need to do.

Sliding works similarly but moves the clip earlier or later in the Timeline. For example, when you watch the first version of your edit, you see that your cut should use the same footage but should come earlier or later in the sequence. If you slide this clip, it trims the incoming and outgoing clips at the same time. Again, this is a time-saver, and it is very intuitive as well.

Using the Slip Item Tool

You activate the Slip Item tool, shown in Figure 7.5, by clicking it or by pressing S. Slipping an edit moves the edit points on both ends of it at the same time, allowing you to change the frames used for the clip while not moving its position in the sequence. To use slipping, you click a clip in the sequence in the Timeline window and drag it left or right. Figure 7.6 shows some ghosted boxes running around the selected clip. They represent the unused media from the clip or subclip you've decided to slip; therefore, they also show just how much unused media you have to work with. The ghost outline is brown in your sequence. If you drag to the right or left, the clip remains in the same location in the sequence. It also retains the same duration it began with. What you are doing is adding frames to one side while taking away frames from the other side *within the clip itself,* using a different part of the selected clip.

FIGURE 7.5
The Slip Item tool.

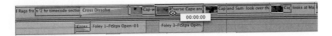

FIGURE 7.6   *The Slip Item tool's ghosted boxes in the sequence.*

In the Canvas window, the first and last frame of the selected clip are displayed in a *two-up* display. Notice that the source clip's timecode is displayed, along with the clip's name. The timecode and the two pictures of the first and last frame update as you slip the clip in either direction from the Timeline window. Slipping or dragging to the left uses frames contained later in the clip, and slipping to the right uses frames from earlier in the clip. Figures 7.7 and 7.8 show what happens if you slip all the way to the left and all the way to the right of a selected clip, respectively. This move is also a trim of sorts and is a very quick way to fine-tune an edit.

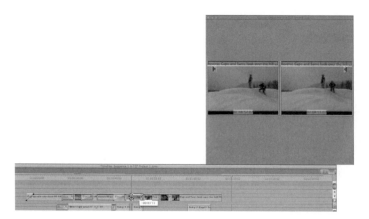

FIGURE 7.7   *A clip being slipped to the left.*

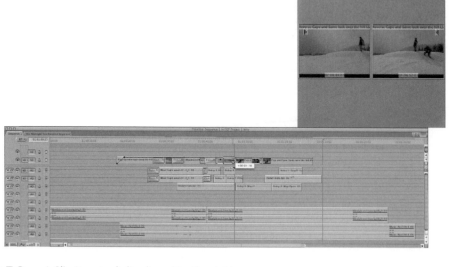

FIGURE 7.8   *A Slip Item tool clip slipped to the right.*

tip

You might encounter times where within a clip you find a frame you'd rather have be the first or last frame of the edit. Set the position indicator to that frame in the Canvas or Timeline window, and click there with the Slip Item tool active. Under the Slip Item tool, you see a vertical brown line. It represents the frame you clicked. So simply sliding to the beginning or end of the clip's position moves this frame to the edit point of your choice. Snapping helps you snap to the edit point when you want to make this move. You might or might not want to trim the other end of the clip, because you've not only changed one edit point, you've also changed the other. Or you can just look at the two-up display to check what the new default edit point will be to decide whether you need to trim it differently. The Trim Edit window is where you go next to possibly take a look at this new (and default) edit point and fine-tune it.

To accomplish this same task with the Trim Edit window, you'd have to take frames from one end of a clip and then jump to the other end of the clip and add the same number of frames, thus keeping the clip the same duration in your sequence. Another way to do this is to move the position indicator anywhere within the clip and click Match Frame in the Canvas window to pull this clip into the Viewer. Then you press X in the Canvas to mark the original clip contained in the sequence. Finally, you readjust the source footage by changing its In or Out point and overwrite the previous instance of this clip or shot. Hopefully, these two alternative methods show you just how powerful slipping really is. Many more steps are needed to do the same thing another way.

Using the Slide Item Tool

You activate the Slide Item tool, shown in Figure 7.9, by clicking it in the Tools window or by pressing SS. Similar to the Slip Item tool, this tool trims a clip contained in the Timeline without changing its duration. However, it's different in that it doesn't change the contents of the selected clip. Instead, it moves the clip earlier or later in the sequence and inserts it in a different place, maintaining the sequence's total duration. It's a very unusual insert edit, though. When you slide the clip to the left, the shot after it adds frames to its In point, and the shot preceding it removes frames from its Out point, because the shot you are sliding is overwriting it. When you slide the clip to the right, the shot before it adds frames to its Out point, and the shot after it is overwritten, removing frames from its In point.

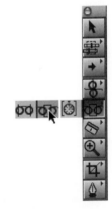

Figure 7.9
The Slide Item tool.

In other words, you are trimming both edit points at the same time, but you're changing only the frames used by the shot before and after the one you are sliding. This same move can be done in other ways, but again, it would take many steps to achieve the same result.

In Figure 7.10, you see that the clip has a similar ghosted brown box on either side of it, but when the Slide Item tool is activated on it, there are two vertical brown lines. These lines represent the edit point at the clip's head and the edit point at the clip's tail. The two-up display now shows the last frame of the outgoing clip at the selected clip's In point and the first frame of the incoming clip at the selected clip's Out point. The timecode of these source clips (the ones on either side of the sliding clip) and their respective names are contained in the Canvas window with their constantly updating edit point frames. When using the Slide Item tool, you are trimming shots, with equal numbers of frames being added to one side of the sliding shot and being subtracted from the other side of the sliding shot.

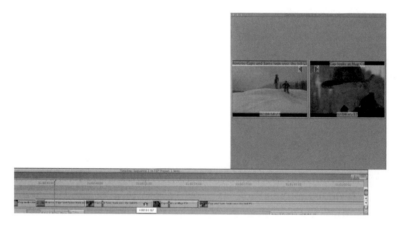

Figure 7.10   *The Slide Item tool and the two-up display.*

tip
You can swap clip positions quickly. When you move the clip in a track, hold down the Option key after you've started the move, and then release it in the new position. The clips all move up to swap the clip's position. Turn on snapping to ease the clip's new position in the Timeline between two other clips. It is inserted in the new position, and all clips past the old position pull up to close the gap it used to reside in.

Workshop 7: Use More-Advanced Trimming

This workshop introduces using more-advanced trimming techniques as you edit the next scene. Remember to take a look at the finished sequence if you need to refer to where you should end up. There are many ways to get away from the Razor Blade tool, and you'll find that as you leave it behind, you'll speed up your editing. At the same time, you'll make better edits, because you are using more-powerful tools to judge the changes.

Begin with Scene 2

Start by sorting the footage up front. Create a new bin in the Browser, and name it "Scene 2."

1. From the Picture Clips bin, click the disclosure triangle next to the 2 and 3hr timecode section master clips. Command-click these nine markers to highlight them:

   - Dog footage from the 3 hr timecode section at 03:06:07;04
   - Sam Falls in Snow chasing sled tk 1 from the 2 hr timecode section at 02:06:39;01
   - Sam Falls in Snow chasing sled tk 2 from the 2 hr timecode section at 02:06:55;06
   - Sam on Sled tk 3 from the 2 hr timecode section at 02:17:10;21
   - Sam Falls tk 3 from the 2 hr timecode section at 02:13:59;00
   - Sam falls in Snow med tk 2 from the 2 hr timecode section at 02:15:02;24
   - Cap walks to sam tk 2 from the 2 hr timecode section at 02:15:58;03
   - Sam in Snow CU delivers line to Cap from the 2 hr timecode section
   - Dog Footage 2 tracks in snow from the 2 hr timecode section at 02:18:22;23

2. Press Cmd+U to create subclips of these markers. Close the disclosure triangles to easily drag the new subclips in the Picture Clips bin to the Scene 2 bin. When you are done, your Scene 2 bin should look like Figure 7.11.

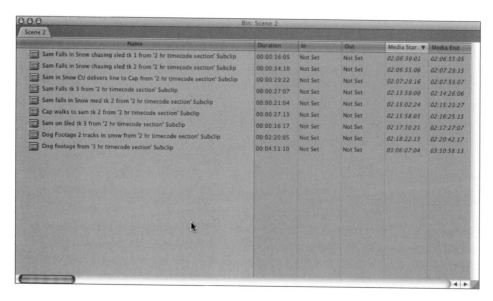

FIGURE 7.11   *The Scene 2 bin after step 2.*

Begin Editing Scene 2

Open the "Dog footage" from the Scene 2 bin in the Viewer. Take a look at this footage. Some of it was shot for slow motion in camera.

1. Set an In point just as the slow-motion shot begins at 03:06:38:25, and set an Out point at 03:07:22:29 in the Viewer just past the last frame of the sled on camera. Drag this selection to the Timeline, and butt it next to the "Cap and Sam look over the hill FS" clip. Don't forget to turn on snapping. Place it from the right side of the V1 track, and slide left until it snaps next to the last outgoing shot.

2. Double-click the edit at the head of "Dog Footage clip i" in the Timeline window to open the Trim Edit window, with its head frame on the right and the last frame of the previous shot, "Cap and Sam look over the hill FS," on the left. Play the slow-motion shot. Notice that there are a lot of dog tracks in the snow ahead of Cap. They sort of destroy the feeling that our heroes are in the middle of nowhere. To minimize this, click the window on the right to activate the green upper line to be only on the incoming shot. Move the playhead on the right side of the Trim Edit window to 03:07:04:28. Press I to trim this shot in the sequence.

3.   While the Trim Edit window is still open on these two shots, add a cross-dissolve centered on this edit point. Either Ctrl-click the edit point, pull it from the Effects tab, or select it from the Effects menu after highlighting the Timeline window. The Trim Edit tool closes automatically. Try the different methods, and decide which works best for you. One of the nice things that happens if you leave the Trim Edit window open and add the transition before you close it is that the Trim Edit window closes automatically, and the Transition Editor can be opened with a quick double-click on the transition in the Timeline, all ready to modify. After you have added the dissolve, double-click it to open the Transition Editor window. Another nice thing is that if you have added the default transition by using the context menu (Ctrl-clicking the edit point to add it) or you've dragged the transition from the Effects window to the edit point, the pointer sits near the new transition, and you can double-click it.

4.   Drag either end of the newly added dissolve icon in the Transition Editor window until its new duration is 2 seconds.

Create the Harsh Environment

Take a look at the playback from before the dissolve through to the end of the Dog Footage.

Not bad, but not perfect. There isn't much footage of the dog team in fresh snow (there's almost none), and you need a new shot here to further introduce the characters and their environment. This one minimizes the non-virgin snow the most. The characters definitely need to be shown in the harsh environment to tell the story with emphasis on their struggle.

1.   Double-click the "Dog Footage 2 tracks in snow from '2 hr timecode section' Subclip" to open it in the Viewer. You want to reveal the two men trudging through the snow, so navigate to 02:20:17:03 and set an In point there. Next, drag the clip directly from the Viewer to the Timeline, and butt it up next to the "Dog footage" shot with snapping turned on. Then double-click the head of this shot's edit point in the Timeline window. This opens the Trim Edit window.

2.   Take a look at the current edit by playing it in the Trim Edit window or the Timeline. The outgoing shot of the dogs seems to go on forever. Click the left side of the Trim Edit window to activate it alone, or press U repeatedly until it is set that way. Drag the position indicator in the left window to 03:07:12:14 and press O to trim the Out of the dogs shot. You keep the action going a bit faster by showing only a smaller portion of this shot, which really only serves to introduce that our heroes have a dog sled with them. This trims the edit –00:10:15, as shown in Figure 7.12.

FIGURE 7.12 *The Trim Edit window after step 2.*

3. Click the incoming shot to activate its green line. Play the shot in its window. You can see some preceding sled tracks in the snow.

4. Minimize the tracks a bit by trimming this shot's In point to 02:20:17:18 so that the sled is near the bottom of the frame, as shown in Figure 7.13. You might save some time by just clicking into the shot in the Trim Edit window's scrubber bar beneath it, moving the position indicator to the right, and then using the +1 or +5 button to creep up on the proper edit point.

FIGURE 7.13 *The Trim Edit window after step 4.*

5. Notice that you trimmed the incoming shot +00:00:15, as indicated in the bottom right of the Trim Edit window. Even though you took off frames, they don't show up as being a negative number. You've moved the edit point 15 frames *forward* into the shot—thus the *positive* number. The clip doesn't look like it minimized the preceding tracks much, but you'll put a dissolve here from the outgoing shot, which minimizes it further.

6. Add a dissolve centering on the edit point, and make its duration 2:15.

7. Double-click the subclip "Sam Falls in Snow chasing sled tk 1," and play it in the Viewer. Notice that most of Sam's body is cut off at the top of the frame. Compare this to the subclip "Sam Falls in Snow chasing sled tk 2."

8. This is a better take, but the actor who plays Cap was replaced by a stunt man. Use the lesser of two evils and add the first take in its entirety to the Timeline as the next V1 shot. Double-click the edit point between "Dog Footage 2 tracks in snow" and "Sam Falls in Snow chasing sled tk 1."

9. Trim the outgoing shot –19:20 and the incoming shot +5:16, as shown in Figure 7.14. Add another 2-second cross-dissolve centered on the edit point. You'll see that Sam is following the sled, but you can't tell who is driving it. The audience will assume it is Cap.

FIGURE 7.14   *The Trim Edit window after step 9.*

10. Save your project file.

11. Double-click DANCLEAN.AIF-05 from the Voice Overs bin. Listen to the read. It's a bit quiet, so raise its level to +4dB. Then add all of it to the sequence on the A2 audio track at 01:01:14;03 in the sequence's timecode. Don't forget to target the correct track.

Go to Our Heroes in Real Time

Now we will go "live" to our heroes. In other words, we are with them in time; we are watching things *as they happen*. Hopefully we'll begin to get the audience emotionally involved with the characters, identifying with them. One thing that must be done is adding realistic sound effects to the scene.

1. Add the clip "Foley 1-Guy#2 Run#1-02" to A3 at 01:01:25;06 in the sequence. You'll find it in the *Foley bin you created earlier.

2. Add to the end of "Wind,desert Lonely,66_1-11" the sound clip "Wind,desert Lonely,66_1-01" to extend the cold wind sound, leaving no gap between the clips (snapping helps). Use the entire clip by simply dragging it to tracks A6 and A7. Again, you must target the tracks to even drag clips to them in the Timeline window. Ctrl-clicking the source track allows you to quickly change tracks.

3. Turn off monitoring for all audio tracks except these two. The easiest way to do this is to click the headphone icons on the far left of the Timeline window. If you don't see them, open them by clicking the speaker button in the bottom-left corner of the Timeline. Then listen to the edit point of the wind sounds. The incoming sound is quiet and then sort of takes off.

4. Double-click this new audio cut point to open it in the Trim Edit window. Notice the speaker icons.

5. On the incoming clip only (cycle through the green line changes by pressing U), trim 2:07 into the sound, and start the incoming shot there instead. You can trim audio just as you trim video.

6. Listen to the new sound edit by clicking the Play Around Edit Loop button, or press the spacebar. It should now sound flawless.

7. Drag the "Sam in Snow CU delivers line to Cap" subclip from the Scene 2 bin directly to the sequence in the Timeline. Place it on V1, butted against the end of the "Sam Falls in Snow chasing sled tk 1" clip there.

8. Open the subclip's In edit point in the Trim Edit window, revealing an edit point with a slate on either side of it.

9. Trim the last 2:24 frames of the outgoing shot and the first 3:18 frames of the incoming shot. When you're done, the Trim Edit window should look like Figure 7.15.

FIGURE 7.15   *The Trim Edit window after step 9.*

Listen to Sam's Thoughts

While Sam lies in the snow, we need to know what he is thinking. Adding his thoughts via sound is a great way to do this. The "language of film" lets us change our view of the characters instantly and listen to their thoughts. I wish we could do this in real life!

1. Locate the "City, 19th Century 19th 13_1-01" clip in the Sound Clips bin. Add all of it to the A2 track at 01:01:29;08. This clip sets up "where" Sam is thinking about—his home in Tennessee.

2. Locate in the Sound Clips bin the clip "VO Girlfriend Tk#4-04." Edit the whole clip into the Timeline at 01:01:29;23 on track A1. This makes your edit to the CU of Sam a motivated one. It's motivated because we want to look closely at Sam's face when we "hear" his thoughts.

3. Edit the clip "SAMSDIALOG.AIF-02" into A1 at 01:01:33;03.

4. Locate in the Sound Clips bin the clip "VO Girlfriend Tk#4-05," and edit it into the sequence on A1 at 01:01:37;02. Locate the clip "VO Girlfriend Tk#1_3-12," and edit it into A1 at 01:01:40;04. Locate the clip "sam mic 3.aif-02.L," and edit it into A1 at 01:01:43;06. You've edited a flashback scene that precedes the movie itself—a memory of Sam's. Cap's boisterous voice (the first audio that was recorded on the set live) brings Sam back to reality.

5. Play back this new area of sound you've added to check its mix. The background city sound is too loud, and the dialog needs to be brought out. Because these are very short clips, it's best to not use the Audio Mixer to attempt a mix. Manually lower the city sounds to –4dB. Raise the girlfriend's audio on all three of her VO clips to 8dB. Raise SAMSDIALOG.AIF-02 to 5dB. Listen again. This is much better. Cap's voice is just about right.

6. Double-click the City sounds from the Timeline window to open it in the Viewer. Place a keyframe on both ends of the Viewer's audio level line in the waveform. Place another matching set about 1 second in from the beginning and about 1 second before the end.

7. Drag the very first keyframe indicator to the bottom of the window. Do the same with the last keyframe indicator. When you are done, your Viewer and Timeline should look like those shown in Figure 7.16.

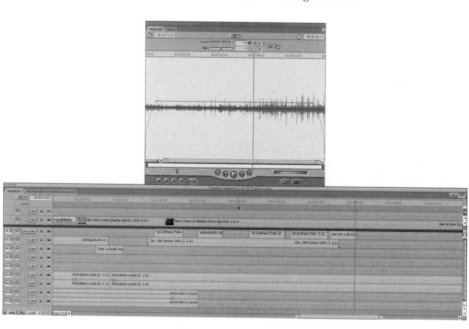

FIGURE 7.16   *The Timeline and Viewer after step 7.*

Add Synchronized Sound

Locate the clip named "S7AT1.AIF-01." This sounds like an esoteric name, but it actually contains some information. It's from the original scene number 7, angle "A," and it's take 1. This naming convention was used to digitize the clip as it was recorded originally from a Nagra recorder on the set. Because the Telecine (the process of transferring the film to video) was done without syncing the sound, it's your job to sync it in Final Cut Pro. It's not as hard as it sounds.

Rather than have you worry about it, I'll give you the sync point. If you edit the entire clip onto the A3 track at 01:01:47;24 in the Timeline window, it syncs perfectly. I'll show you some techniques for making these sorts of edits in the next chapter.

1. Relocate the clip "Sam Falls in Snow chasing sled tk 2" from the Scene 2 bin, and double-click it to open it in the Viewer. It's the clip that was rejected the first time we looked at it, but it's a complete take. The first take ended before Cap re-entered the scene.

2. Set an In point in it just past Sam's line at 02:07:19:21, and then edit to track V1 to the end of Sam's close-up. Trim the Out point of the close-up in the Trim Edit window by removing the last 3:14 from it, as shown in Figure 7.17. You can simply type **–314** with only the outgoing clip's window active. You'll trim 3 seconds and 14 frames from its Out point. Notice Sam's head position in Figure 7.17. It matches the head position in the incoming shot. You create a seamless edit when you pay attention to details like this. You also keep that suspension of disbelief you are trying to achieve with the audience.

FIGURE 7.17   *The Trim Edit window after step 2.*

3. Locate the clip "Foley 1-Guy#1 Away#1." It's the foley recorded for this moment in the movie. As Cap walks away, we need to hear him. Edit this clip in the sequence on track A2 at 01:01:52;12. Use it all, and then raise its level to the maximum of +12dB.

4. Edit "DANCLEAN.AIF-07" from the Voice Overs bin into track A3 at 01:01:54;07.

5. Locate the three "Sam on Sled" takes in the 2 hr timecode section clip in the Picture Clips bin. You can double-click the markers themselves to open them in the Viewer. Compare them. They seem about the same as far as the actor's performance, but there is a much better take here. You're trying to show Sam wishing that he'd "sooner be in hell." I picked the third take because it has more snow falling in it, and Sam looks much colder because of it.

6. Edit "Sam on Sled tk 3" into the Timeline on V1 butted against the previous clip. Load its In edit point into the Trim Edit window by double-clicking it. Trim the outgoing shot (Cap leaving Sam in the snow) –30 frames and the incoming shot +5:06, as shown in Figure 7.18. Add a 2-second dissolve that *ends* on the edit point so that we see Sam dissolving in, trudging along over the completely white snow. Again, this dissolve was programmed with this in mind. Make Sam really look as if he's buried in the snow, which, as we will see, is his worst nightmare. This moment is foreshadowing. That is, it's a hint of things to come. The previous shots of Sam's falling also were a sort of foreshadow. Sam will freeze to death, and this area of the story is preparing the audience for this. As we will see in a moment, he almost is completely buried in the snow.

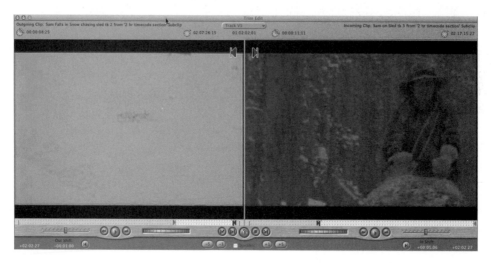

FIGURE 7.18 *The Trim Edit window after step 6.*

7. You've run out of wind, so locate "Wind,desert Lonely,66_1-03." Edit it into the sequence next to the end of the earlier wind sound (on tracks A6 and A7). Trim the first 30 frames of the incoming sound for the same reason as before. This time you can quickly do that by double-clicking the edit point between the two wind sound effects, pressing U, and clicking the +5 button six times

quickly. Listen to the playback by pressing the spacebar. To stop the looping playback, press the spacebar again. There's no "right" way to trim with this window. I think the best way to use this tool is the way that makes the most sense to you or the task you need to perform.

8. Locate the three markers titled "Sam Falls," takes 1 through 3, in the 2 hr timecode section master clips. Take a look at each one by double-clicking its marker. They are very similar, but more snow is falling in take 3, and the performance is better as well.

9. Edit the entire "Sam Falls tk 3" subclip from the Scene 2 bin into the sequence next on V1 butted up against the "Sam on Sled tk 3" clip. Trim the last 5:25 of the outgoing clip, "Sam on Sled tk 3," and trim the first 5:11 of the incoming clip, "Same Falls tk 3." The Trim Edit window should look like Figure 7.19.

FIGURE 7.19   *The Trim Edit window after step 9.*

10.   Place a 2-second centered dissolve between the two shots.

A Few Aesthetics While You're Editing

Take a look at the picture edits between the scenes of different places using dissolves between them. Dissolves can make a dramatic statement if you pick shots where the movement is either similar in direction or constantly dissimilar. In this case, dissimilar directions between shots seem to make the action more disjointed, adding to the feeling of helplessness on Sam's part. It's almost as if he's going nowhere, as if he's even retracing his steps. If the shots were similar in direction, they might propel the viewer forward in time in a smoother fashion, leaving the impression that things are moving forward evenly and in an orderly fashion.

The idea here is to get the shots' directions not smooth and moving in different directions, reflecting the feeling that all is *not* going well for Sam. Subtle choices like this are part of the aesthetics of the language of film. No one will take note particularly, but it adds a touch of tension—a feeling that things are not OK. Emphasize the emotions in your story even when picking directions of movement between shots that dissolve to each other. Emphasize emotion in any way that's not distracting to the viewer. Keep it subtle, though, almost on a subconscious level. You'll affect the audience's emotions, manipulating their feelings. They will be unconscious of it if you are subtle, and you'll keep their rapt attention.

11. Locate the markers named "Sam Falls in Snow med tk 1" and "Sam Falls in Snow med tk 2" in the 2 hr timecode section master clips. Compare them. Take 1 seems fine, but it looks a bit like Sam falls into a downy pillow. Take 2, on the other hand, looks a bit harsher, and more snow flies when he falls, so it tells the story better. This is why the shot was used. Edit "Sam Falls in Snow med tk 2," and butt it up to the end of the last shot, "Sam Falls tk 3." Prepare to trim between them with the Trim Edit window. Double-click this new edit point, and open it in the Trim Edit window.

12. These two edits are matching action, meaning that they cut to each other in real time. Matching action needs to look seamless, so trim the outgoing shot to 02:14:22:11 or take off the last 3:25 frames of it. What should happen is that Sam just leaves frame. I fudged here just a bit. I held a couple of frames past his last frame on camera to extend the duration and length of his fall. Trim the incoming shot to 02:15:08;13, taking off the first 5:19 frames. I also left a few frames before Sam enters the shot for the same reason.

13. You can experiment with this edit if you want to see what happens as you trim each side, but end up with the edit as the preceding step directed so that the rest of the movie works as planned. Try editing between them before Sam leaves frame on the outgoing shot and after he enters frame in the incoming shot. He doesn't seem to fall as far. Use the spacebar to start and stop the looping playback as you adjust. You'll begin to see the power of the what-ifs I've been talking about. When you're done experimenting, the Trim Edit window should look exactly like Figure 7.20. Perform Undos (Cmd+Z) if needed to get back.

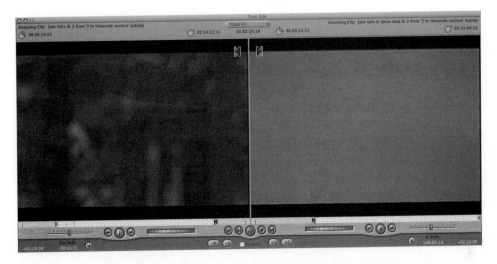

FIGURE 7.20   *The Trim Edit window after step 13.*

14. These shots are similar to Sam's earlier falling experience; he's almost hallucinating now. To enhance his desperate feeling, add some totally "opposite" memory experiences to this moment by hearing his childhood recollections of a hot summer's day swimming in a pond back in Tennessee. Add the foley first, just to be certain that it is in sync with the picture. From the *Foley bin, add "Foley 1-Sam Dog Sled #4-16" to the A4 track at 01:02:09;07 in the sequence. Raise its level to +10dB. At 01:02:25;18 in the sequence, add "Foley 1-Sam Dog Sled #4-18," also on the A4 track, and raise its level to +10dB as well. Play back through these new edits to check to make sure that they sound correct. You might need to slightly move the foley clip of Sam falling in the snow to sync exactly with the action if you altered the last edit point.

15. Add the following clips from the Sound Clips bin at 01:02:10;14 to the sequence:

    "GIGGLI~1.AIF-02 Verb" as a whole into A1

    "Children Swimming 40_1-03 Verb" into A2 and A3 (it's a stereo pair). Don't forget to target *both* tracks of audio.

16. Locate the "COMEIN~1.AIF-02" clip in the Sound Clips bin, and edit it into A1 at 01:02:25;02. This clip invites Sam to fall. You'll match its audio quality to the earlier reverb clips in the next chapter, which covers the use of audio filters.

17. Compare the two markers of "Cap walks to sam tk 1" and "Cap walks to sam tk 2." In take 1, Cap walks up and kicks Sam. In take 2, he just admonishes him with his hand. The first one is too rough, so edit "Cap walks to sam tk 2"

into the sequence by butting it up against the end of the "Sam Falls tk 3" clip on track V1. You can do this directly from the marker double-clicked in the Viewer, or create a subclip and edit it into the sequence from that. Trim them in the Trim Edit window by clicking the new edit point between them and trimming –8:06 to the outgoing edit and 5:08 to the incoming edit (see Figure 7.21).

FIGURE 7.21   *The Trim Edit window after step 17.*

18.   Locate the "Foley 1-Guy#1 Approach#3" clip in the *Foley bin in the Sound Clips bin, and double-click it to open it in the Viewer. Set an In point at 7:00 (1 second in from the beginning), and set an Out point 30 frames from its end. (To do this quickly, press the End key and type **–30**.) Edit the clip to track A1 at 01:02:27;03. Raise its level to the limit of +12dB. Fade up its audio level with keyframes from the beginning for about a second or so to give the effect that Cap is walking toward Sam. You can do this by adding keyframes to the clip's level overlay after you have double-clicked the clip to view these keyframes in the Viewer.

19.   Edit the sound sync lines. Locate "S8DT2.aif-01" in the Sound Clips bin, and double-click it to open it in the Viewer. With the Viewer active, press Shift+Z to reveal the clip's entire waveform. Play through it to see that last bit of Cap's line. It's a bit too hot. Zoom in a bit on it by pressing Z and clicking the clip with the Zoom tool. Press P to activate the Pen tool. Add a set of four keyframes on either side of the waveform representing Cap's last line. Press A to activate the Selection tool, and drag the middle section down to –4dB. Set an In point at 00:00:01;02 and an Out point at 00:00:11;22. Overwrite this shot to the A1 track in the sequence at 01:02:37;03. When you're done, the Viewer should look like Figure 7.22.

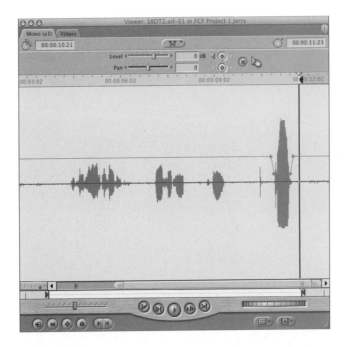

FIGURE 7.22   *The Viewer after step 19.*

20.   Find the clip named "Foley 1-Sam Away #2-01" in the *Foley bin. Load it into the Viewer. Mark an In point at the very beginning and an Out point at 7:15. Edit the clip into the sequence at 01:02:44;22 on A2. Raise its level to +12dB.

The Timeline for this new area should now look like Figure 7.23.

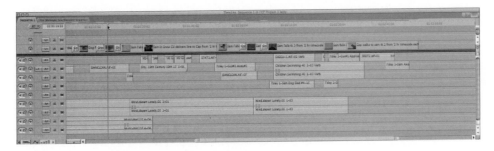

FIGURE 7.23   *The Timeline of Scene 2 after step 20.*

CHAPTER 8

Audio Filters, Timeline Editing, and Keeping Sync

- Audio Filters
- Editing in the Timeline Window
- Linking and Merging Audio and Video Clips
- Syncing Issues
- Workshop 8: Finish Scene 2 and Edit Scene 3

Audio Filters

Audio filters are effects (reverb and echo), equalizations (EQ), compression and expansion, or noise reduction applied to entire audio clips or portions of audio clips. They are used to enhance a clip's sound quality to add some punch to the telling of your story. Or they can be used to correct errors made in the recording process.

To add filters, highlight the audio clip from the sequence in the Timeline window, and select a filter from the Effects menu, as shown in Figures 8.1 and 8.2. You can also drag from the list in the Browser's Effects tab and drop one or more filters by Ctrl-clicking your choices. You can drag this set of filters to the Viewer, or you can drag them to the clip or set of clips you want to add them to in the Timeline that contains the sequence you are working with (see Figures 8.3 and 8.4). Alternatively, you can highlight an audio clip in the Timeline window and double-click an audio filter's icon from the Effects tab of the Browser window. This filter is added to the clip as it plays back in the sequence.

Figure 8.1   *The Apple Audio Effects menu.*

Figure 8.2   *The Final Cut Pro Audio Effects menu.*

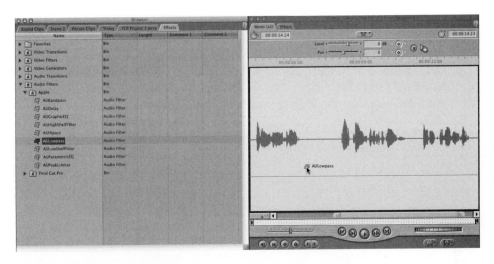

FIGURE 8.3   *Dragging an audio effect from the Browser to the Viewer.*

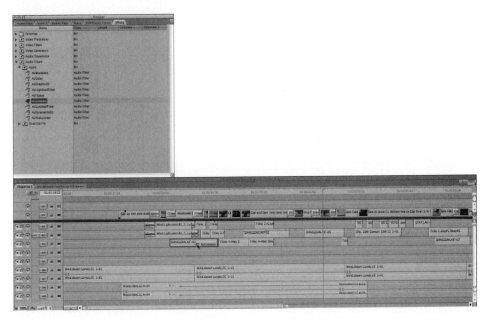

FIGURE 8.4   *Dragging an audio effect from the Browser to the Timeline.*

The Filters tab is shown in Figure 8.5. It contains filters and their controls after they are applied to a clip from either the Browser's Effects tab or the Filters menu. You can add a whole range of filters to audio clips. You are not limited to just one. You can add as many as you want, including the same one more than once, but keep in mind that Final Cut Pro addresses them in the order you have added them, which might affect the way they sound in concert with each other.

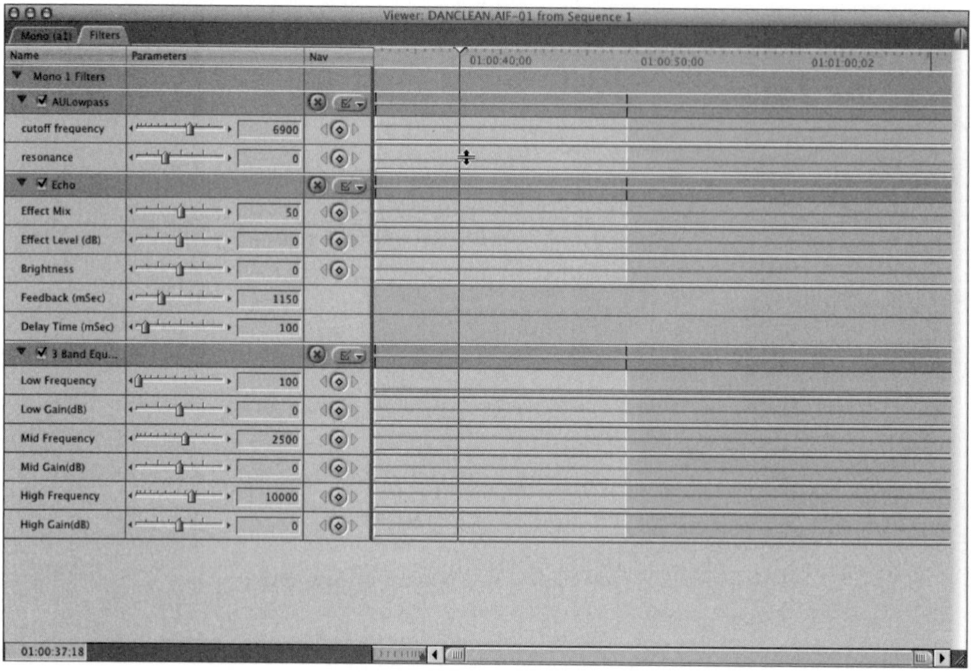

FIGURE 8.5   *The Filters tab in the Viewer window.*

To change their order, it's simply a matter of clicking their names and rearranging them by dragging them up or down the list.

If you apply a filter to a stereo pair, all filters you add to the pair are applied equally *if* linked selection is on. In the case of Audio 1 and 2 clips, if linked selection is not active when you apply an audio filter, it is applied to only the selected track, or the track you drag it to. This becomes important if you are working with audio that was recorded with one actor to one track and another actor to another track, or a set of two different microphones on the same subject. You might need to enhance one track, but not the other, or apply different filters to each track.

Keep in mind that a filter's effect is applied to the entire clip. To limit this condition without keyframing its entrance and exit, you can use the Range Selection tool to select just the portion of the audio clip in the Timeline window you want to affect.

You can also use the Razor Blade tool to "slice" a clip into sections. For example, you might need to limit an effect to the center section of a given audio clip. If you add an edit point with the Razor Blade tool before and after the section you want to affect, you apply the effect to this new section only, not to the entire clip. Both techniques can also be used to save some rendering time. You also save the disk space that would be used for an entire clip's render file.

Alternatively, if you open the Viewer to display the keyframe display areas next to the various parameter adjustments in a filter's controls, to the right of the filter's name is a band with two black vertical lines. These lines indicate the part of the clip being used in the sequence. You can drag them to minimize the duration of the filter's effect.

What's more, each filter you apply to a clip can have a different duration, because each filter has its own set of trimming lines. You might want to add an EQ filter to begin at the head of a clip and then start a reverb filter later as a character walks into a tunnel, for example. This same technique can be used with video filters. In effect, you can have one clip with many filters and control just when these filters make their entrances and exits.

A Second Place to Adjust Audio Filters

New to FCP 4, there are two different areas you can access to adjust the filters after they are applied—the Viewer's Filters tab and the keyframing area of the Timeline window (see Figure 8.6). To pull up the context menu shown in Figure 8.7, you Ctrl-click beneath the clip. You can select the individual parameter of each filter through this context menu. After they are selected, Figure 8.6 shows the keyframes as they change the parameter over time. Also note that changes made in the Timeline's keyframe area are reflected in the Viewer's keyframe area.

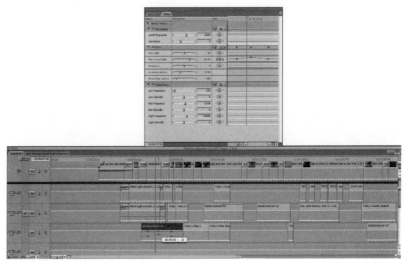

FIGURE 8.6   *The two keyframing areas.*

FIGURE 8.7   *Choosing the parameter to add keyframes to.*

You might find it easier to keyframe in one place or another, depending on your own sensibilities or workflow. However, note that you can make the keyframe area in the Viewer taller than the standard height by dragging the bottom of the parameter's keyframe area in the Viewer, as shown in Figure 8.8. You can do this in the area beneath the clip in the Timeline as well by placing the mouse over the keyframe edit size bar, located to the right of the Auto Select button. Put the mouse over the second vertical line. When it changes to an adjust cursor, drag up or down as you hold down the mouse button. Making the keyframe area for a specific parameter taller makes your adjustments more precise.

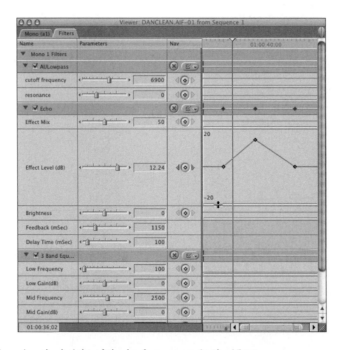

FIGURE 8.8   *Changing the height of the keyframe area in the Viewer.*

Adding and Smoothing Audio Keyframes

To add a keyframe, click the diamond button on the right of the parameter you want to change, use the Pen tool (press P), or change the parameter during playback. All the audio filters can be modified in real time as long as you are working with a fast-enough computer. (Officially, you need any 500MHz G4 or faster, but dual CPUs perform more real-time effects at one time.)

You can delete a keyframe in three ways. You can navigate to it using the arrows on either side of the diamond button and then click the diamond button to delete it. You can Ctrl-click the keyframe and select Clear. Finally, you can use the Delete Pen tool (press PP).

You can change from a linear line to a curved and therefore "ramping" change over time in either keyframe area in two ways. You can create a keyframe by using the Smooth Pen tool (press PPP). You also can Ctrl-click a keyframe that was added with the Pen tool to reveal a context menu (see Figure 8.9). Smoothing a keyframe adds a bezier curve handle with a blue dot that you can drag to change the way the curve looks, and thus the way the parameter's effect changes over time. You might want to change the effect to ramp quickly, as shown in Figure 8.10, and then slowly reach its peak level. Or you could do the opposite—slow the change early and then ramp quickly to its peak level. Either way, the curve can be seen in both keyframe areas in the Viewer and in the Timeline beneath the clip. To change the curve, drag the blue dot on the bezier control.

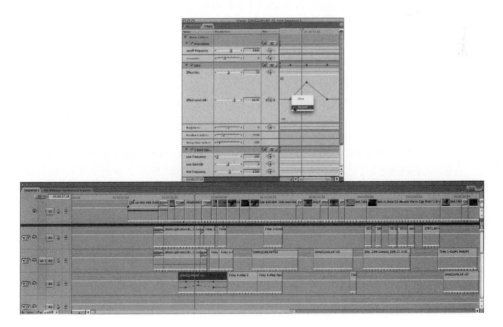

FIGURE 8.9   *The context keyframe menu.*

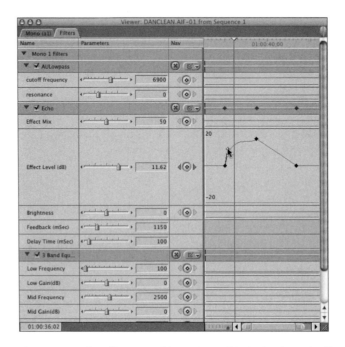

FIGURE 8.10 *Using bezier curve handles to modify or "smooth" the keyframe's effect over time.*

The Audio Filters Supplied in Final Cut Pro 4

This following sections describe the complete set of standard audio filters. As shown in Figures 8.1 and 8.2, they are broken into two sections:

- New to FCP 4, the Apple filters are supplied by the OS itself. These filters start with AU, which stands for audio units.

- The other set is the older "standard" set of filters supplied by Final Cut Pro.

Both sets of filters operate basically the same way. Adding and modifying them also is done in basically the same way. As soon as your computer has reached its capacity to play back these filtered clips in real time, you hear a beeping sound. At this point, you can render the files you are happy with to add additional filters. As a side note, the audio unit filters come from Logic, Apple's professional audio application. They also appear in SoundTrack, where the Logic interface is optional.

AUBandpass

AUBandpass, shown in Figure 8.11, changes a single frequency band. By selecting the center frequency slider, you can modify the boost or cut level. You also can change the bandwidth value to narrow or widen the frequency range that is heard and the level of accentuation at the center of the band. A low bandwidth value results in less accentuation and wider audibility across the band. A high bandwidth value focuses more sharply on the center of the band you've chosen with the center frequency slider, screening out more of the frequencies above and below it. AUBandpass can be used to quickly attenuate a range of frequencies in a clip. It can be used to create effects, like the sound of someone talking over the telephone.

FIGURE 8.11   *AUBandpass.*

AUDelay

AUDelay, shown in Figure 8.12, adds repeats to the audio clip. You can also set the level (amount) of the effect (using the dry/wet mix), brightness using the lowpass cutoff frequency, feedback (duration of repeats), and delay (time between repeats.) The AUDelay filter is useful for creating a "slapback" or the sound you'd hear in a canyon sort of effect for the selected audio.

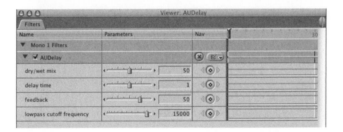

FIGURE 8.12   *AUDelay.*

AUGraphicEQ

AUGraphicEQ, shown in Figure 8.13, separates the audio into 31 frequency bands, ranging from 20Hz to 20,000Hz. You can set the center frequency for each band. This filter applies equalization in 31 bands of your clip at the same time rather than requiring you to apply multiple filters. It separates the EQ controls much like an audio mixing board does.

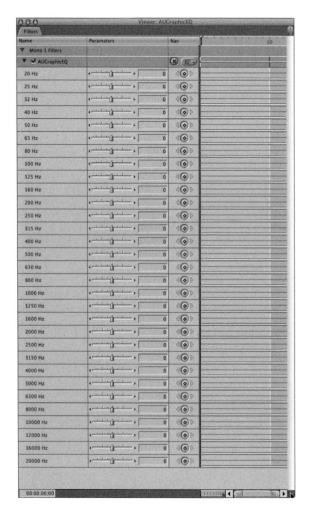

Figure 8.13   *AUGraphicEQ.*

AUHighShelfFilter

AUHighShelfFilter, shown in Figure 8.14, is much like the AUBandpass filter, but the higher end of the frequency range is sharply cut off. The lower-end frequencies are unaffected. You can use the gain setting to raise or lower the volume in the higher end of the frequency range.

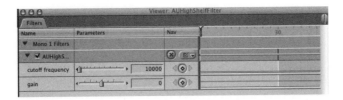

FIGURE 8.14 *AUHighShelfFilter.*

AUHipass

AUHipass, shown in Figure 8.15, is also similar to the AUBandpass filter, but it modifies the low-end frequencies, leaving high frequencies alone. The AUHipass filter can be used to minimize sounds such as traffic rumble or an airplane's sound mixed with a voice, for example.

FIGURE 8.15 *AUHipass.*

AULowpass

AULowpass, shown in Figure 8.16, is another AUBandpass-type filter that reduces high-end frequencies, leaving low frequencies alone. This filter can be used to reduce bright-sounding noises such as tape hiss.

FIGURE 8.16 *AULowpass.*

AULowShelfFilter

AULowShelfFilter, shown in Figure 8.17, is another AUBandpass-type filter. The lower end of the frequency range is cut off, but high frequencies are unaffected. You can use the gain setting to boost or cut the sound at the lower end of the frequency range.

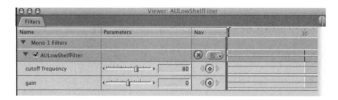

FIGURE 8.17   *AULowShelfFilter.*

AUParametricEQ

AUParametricEQ, shown in Figure 8.18, allows you to control a single frequency band. It combines the effects of the Bandpass, Notch, and Shelf filters. You set the Q value to narrow or widen the frequency range that is heard and the level of accentuation at the center of the band. A lower Q value gives less emphasis and wider audibility across the frequency band selected. A higher Q value focuses more sharply on the center of the band, screening out more of the higher and lower frequencies around the selected frequency.

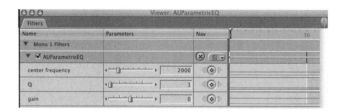

FIGURE 8.18   *AUParametricEQ.*

AUPeakLimiter

Similar to a normalization filter, applying AUPeakLimiter levels out inconsistent volume levels in an audio clip, as shown in Figure 8.19. The attack and decay settings determine how quickly the effect changes the volume level.

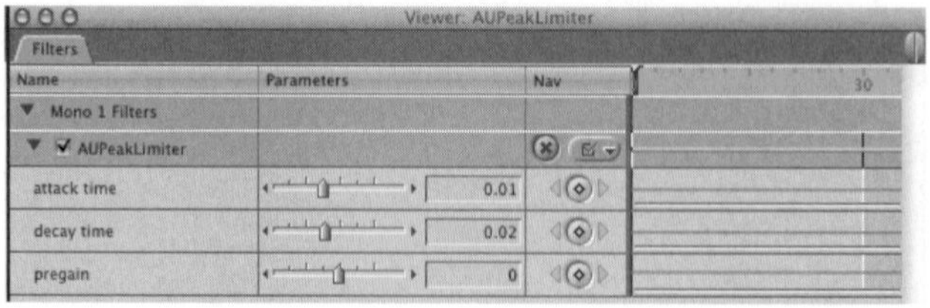

FIGURE 8.19   *AUPeakLimiter.*

3 Band Equalizer

The 3 Band Equalizer, shown in Figure 8.20, divides the audio spectrum into three frequency bands: Low, Mid, and High. Low frequency adjusts between 80Hz and 2,000Hz, Mid Frequency adjusts between 400Hz and 8,000Hz, and High Frequency adjusts between 5,000Hz and 20,000Hz. Notice that they overlap.

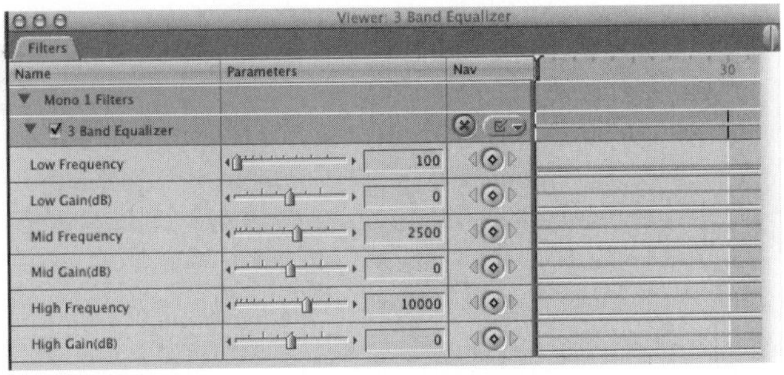

FIGURE 8.20   *3 Band Equalizer.*

You can set the center frequency for each band and change the volume of each band relative to the others by modifying the Gain setting for each frequency. This is much like the EQ controls on most mixing boards. This filter equalizes three bands of your clip at the same time. You might use this control to add more bass, treble, or midrange to bring out the quality of the audio you want to hear more clearly. As with all the audio filters, each slider is keyframeable over time. If you open the Viewer window, you can see another set of "mini-Timelines" used for this purpose. Keep in mind that you should err on the side of not enough rather than too much. There are an endless number of reasons to use this filter. You might have to match an ADR reading when the original microphone is unavailable, for instance, or give a spokesperson a little more presence.

Band Pass Filter

Band Pass Filter, shown in Figure 8.21, lets you alter a single frequency band. By choosing the center frequency, you can change the boost or cut level. Unlike the 3 Band Equalizer, this filter has a Q slider, which determines a range value.

You can alter the Q value to narrow or widen the frequency range that is heard or "passed" and the level of emphasis at the center of the band. A lower Q value gives less prominence and wider range across the band. A high Q value narrows the effect on the center of the band, eliminating more of the higher and lower frequencies.

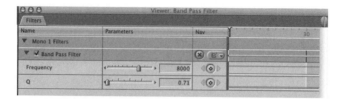

FIGURE 8.21   *Band Pass Filter.*

Band Pass Filter quickly makes a range of frequencies within a clip thinner (attenuates them). It's good for creating intense effects, such as the sound of someone's voice over the telephone.

Compressor/Limiter

Compressor/Limiter, shown in Figure 8.22, evens out inconsistencies in volume levels over time. It acts across all frequencies. Compression of volume reduces the dynamic range so that the audio level does not become too high. The more a level exceeds the limit you set, the more it is lowered in volume, depending on the Ratio setting. After making settings, you can click the Preserve Volume check box to keep the overall level close to the original. The Threshold setting determines the level at which the effect is initiated. The Attack and Release settings determine how fast or slow the change is initiated and then brought back to its original setting. This is especially useful for an actor who keeps moving to and from a microphone or whose delivery level is inconsistent.

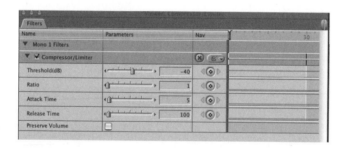

FIGURE 8.22   *Compressor/Limiter.*

DC Notch

DC Notch, shown in Figure 8.23, compensates for a specific type of error in your audio track caused by DC current leakage. It allows you to remove a DC offset component, which might happen during recording. This filter is either on or off.

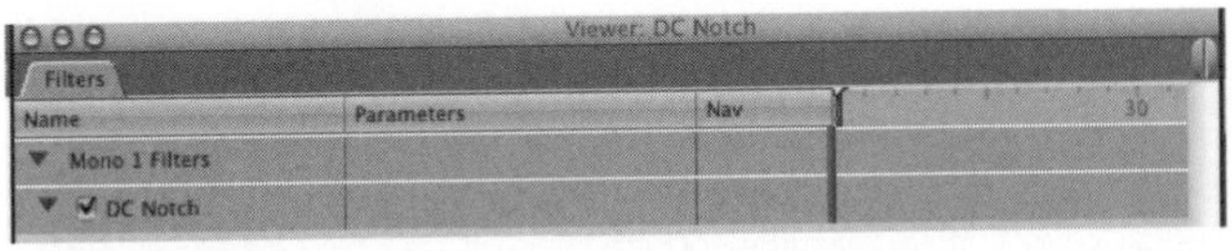

FIGURE 8.23 *DC Notch.*

Echo

Echo, shown in Figure 8.24, adds an echo. You can adjust the mix of the original source signal with the repeating sounds created by this filter. You can also set the level (amount) of the effect, brightness, feedback (duration of repeats), and delay (time between repeats). You can use the Echo filter to create the sound of someone walking in a canyon, for example. You need to add extra material beyond the end of the echo for the echo to fade out. The same is true of Reverberation. Keyframe the volume down before the clip ends.

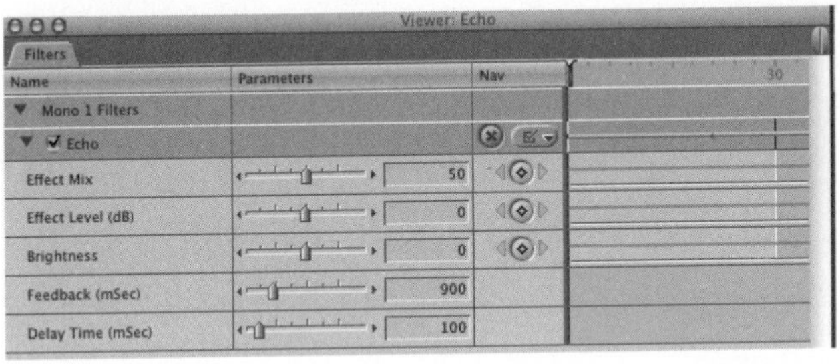

FIGURE 8.24 *Echo.*

Expander/Noise Gate

Expander/Noise Gate, shown in Figure 8.25, evens out inconsistencies in volume levels over time by raising the volume if it drops below a specified level. The lower a level is relative to the highest level, the more it is increased to compensate, depending on where you've set the Ratio slider. Noise Gate silences all sound below the specified volume threshold. Like the Compressor/Limiter filter, you can adjust the attack time and release time. Doing so alters the amount of time between this filter's commencement and deactivation. This filter is similar to the Compressor/Limiter, but instead of lowering the loud levels, it raises the levels that are too low.

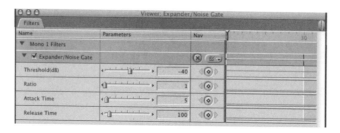

FIGURE 8.25   *Expander/Noise Gate.*

High Pass Filter

High Pass Filter, shown in Figure 8.26, is optimized to reduce low frequencies, leaving high frequencies alone. This filter is useful for reducing low noises such as rumbles or consistent low-pitched sounds such as air conditioners. To use it, you find the frequency of the offending noise and then adjust the Q slider to widen the range that will be affected.

FIGURE 8.26   *High Pass Filter.*

High Shelf Filter

With the High Shelf Filter, shown in Figure 8.27, the high frequencies are cut off, and the low frequencies are allowed to remain. You can use the Gain setting to boost or cut the volume in the higher end of the frequency range.

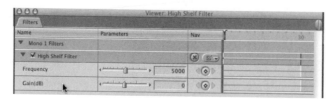

FIGURE 8.27   *High Shelf Filter.*

Hum Remover

Hum Remover, shown in Figure 8.28, is a notch filter that can compensate for cycle hum. Various things such as power lines can cause these hums. This filter's frequency usually matches the AC current used in the country you are recording in. So in Europe, it's likely around 50Hz, and in the U.S., around 60Hz. You can also specify up to five related harmonic frequencies to screen out as well by clicking the various buttons. Final Cut Pro sets them, but by clicking the various buttons, you can add to this notch filter additional frequencies that might be in your audio signal.

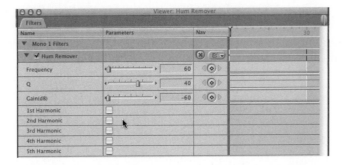

FIGURE 8.28   *Hum Remover.*

tip

You are more likely to find an offending hum on the harmonic frequency than on the primary main's frequency—particularly the third harmonic. Notch out the minimum harmonics for the problem to be solved, because the harmonics are within audible audio and degrade the content.

You might have to use the Q slider to narrow the range if the sound frequencies you want to preserve are near the hum's frequency.

Low Pass Filter

Low Pass Filter, shown in Figure 8.29, is a Band Pass filter optimized to lower the level of high frequencies, leaving low frequencies alone. This filter is useful for dulling down a sound that is too "bright," reducing things such as tape hiss and machine noise from a clip. Similar to the High Shelf Filter, it leaves some of the high frequency instead of cutting it off.

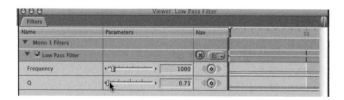

FIGURE 8.29   *Low Pass Filter.*

Low Shelf Filter

Low Shelf Filter, shown in Figure 8.30, is similar to the Band Pass filter, but the lower end of the frequency range is sharply cut off, whereas high frequencies are allowed to pass. You can use the Gain setting to boost or lower the volume at the lower end of the frequency range.

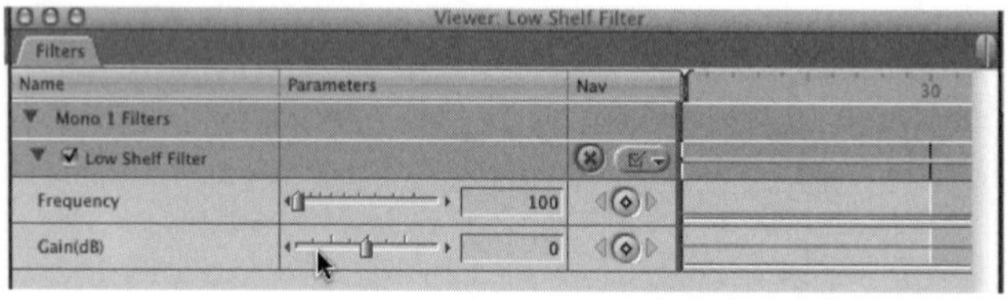

FIGURE 8.30   *Low Shelf Filter.*

Notch Filter

Notch Filter, shown in Figure 8.31, cuts out frequencies in a specific range. As opposed to the other notch filters, this one works on a narrow range of frequencies. The Notch filter is useful for easing a specific frequency of sound that is overly loud. This effect is the opposite of a Band Pass filter. For example, if you have a sound that has a reverberating frequency that draws attention to itself, you can use the Notch filter to attenuate just that frequency so that it doesn't stand out.

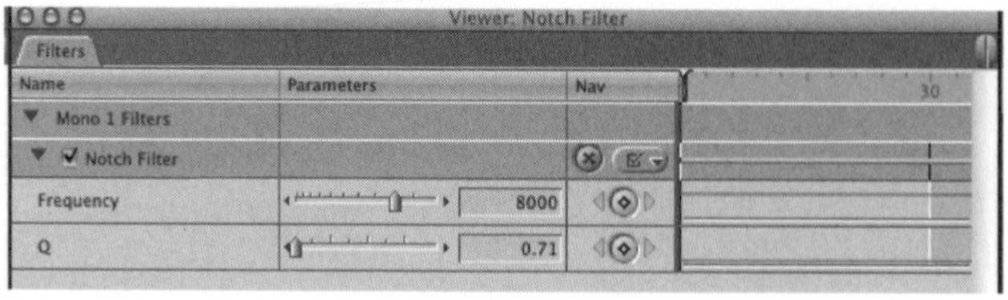

FIGURE 8.31   *Notch Filter.*

Parametric Equalizer

The Parametric Equalizer, shown in Figure 8.32, is the most accommodating of Final Cut Pro's EQ filters. It allows you to control various aspects of a single frequency band. It combines the features of the Band Pass, Notch, and Shelf filters. It works the same as other EQ filters that contain a Q slider. You can set the Q value to narrow or widen the frequency range that is heard and the level of prominence at the center of the band. A low Q value results in less accentuation and wider audibility across the band. A high Q value focuses more sharply on the center of the band, screening out more of the frequencies above and below it.

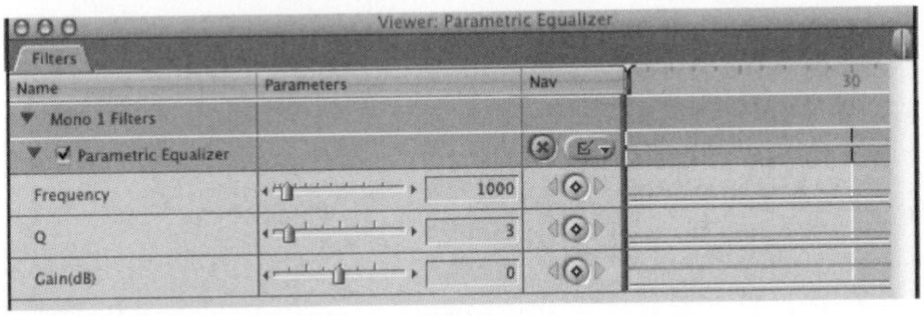

FIGURE 8.32   *Parametric Equalizer.*

Reverberation

Reverberation, shown in Figure 8.33, adds the effect of being in various rooms, simulating the acoustic effect you would hear if you were in them. You might have recorded some sound in a booth with no room acoustic sound, creating a more-or-less dead sound. You can mix this recorded signal and the effect, as well as the effect's level (amount) and brightness. This effect provides a list of predefined room types or spaces that can be applied to your audio clip. You can start with one of the "preset" room ambiences and alter it to fit the sound that fits the picture or effect you are trying to create. As with the Echo filter, you need to leave some extra frames for a Reverberation filter to fade.

An obvious use of the filter is when you have shot your actors against a green screen and will key them in a huge room for a composite shot. You need to make them sound as if they are really in this huge room or tunnel to complete the total effect. Take a look at the "preset" rooms you can put them in. Sometimes this filter is useful when you need to match an ADR recording done in a sound booth to a shot where the original recording was done in one of the preset rooms. You can also use this as an effect filter, to have a voice-over recording sound as if it's from the past, for example.

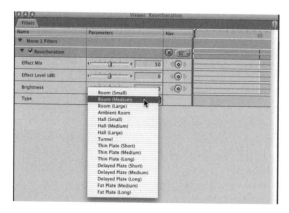

FIGURE 8.33   *Reverberation.*

Vocal DeEsser

Vocal DeEsser, shown in Figure 8.34, is a special-purpose filter that controls and reduces sibilant ("s") sounds. Some actors or voices overemphasize these sounds. The Vocal DeEsser reduces them. Experimenting with the various settings on this filter usually helps this condition.

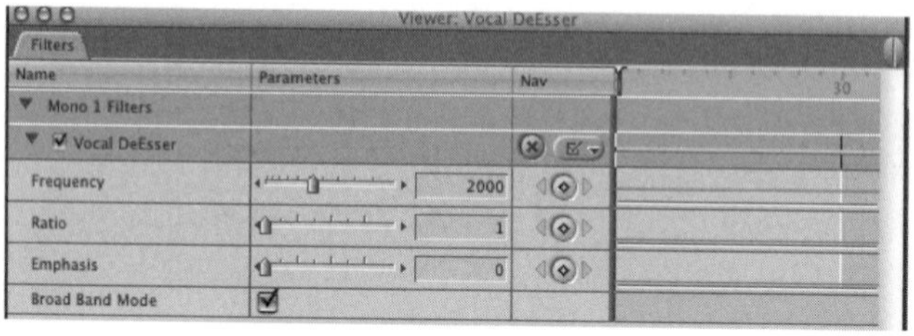

FIGURE 8.34   *Vocal DeEsser.*

Vocal DePopper

Sometimes, especially if a microphone is not placed properly or the speaker or actor moves it during a performance, a wind noise is recorded. It's caused by a "p" sound that "pops" across the microphone because of a sudden puff of air being converted to noise picked up by the microphone. The Vocal DePopper, shown in Figure 8.35, controls and reduces this unwanted noise. Microphone screens don't always catch this, and you might not be able to stop a performance in progress.

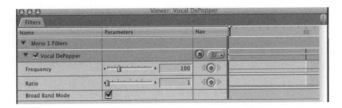

FIGURE 8.35   *Vocal DePopper.*

Editing in the Timeline Window

There's more than one way to edit your clips in Final Cut Pro. You can trim them directly in the Timeline window without using the Trim Edit window. All the same trimming functions available with the Trim Edit window are also available for use in the Timeline window. Ripple, Roll, Slip, and Slide can be done directly on the clips as you see them in the Timeline. You might find editing this way to be more logical or easier to understand. In the NLE world, this is called *Timeline editing*.

Dragging and Dropping in the Timeline Window

It's easy and intuitive to simply drag clips around within the Timeline window. You can drag and drop video edits to any video track, and you can do the same with audio clips. You can highlight a clip from the Browser and then drag and drop it in the sequence you've done already. You can rearrange clips there as well.

Take a look at Figure 8.36. In this chapter you'll examine the first three shots of the movie again. I've simply dragged the series in order from a Large Icons view of them from the Scene 1 bin in the order you have them right now in your Sequence 1 sequence. If you click the first shot, you can drag it past the third, as shown in Figure 8.37. If you have snapping turned on, you drop precisely next to the shot of your choice. If you need to drop a shot *between* two shots, keep snapping turned on. When you are in position between the shots (with the snapping indicators showing in the sequence), hold down the Option key and start dragging. The curved arrow tool appears to indicate that you will insert between the two shots. You can also insert in the middle of a shot. This is easy to do with snapping turned off.

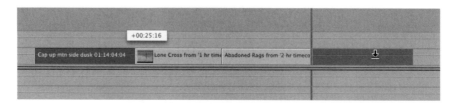

Figure 8.36   *Moving a clip directly in the Timeline window.*

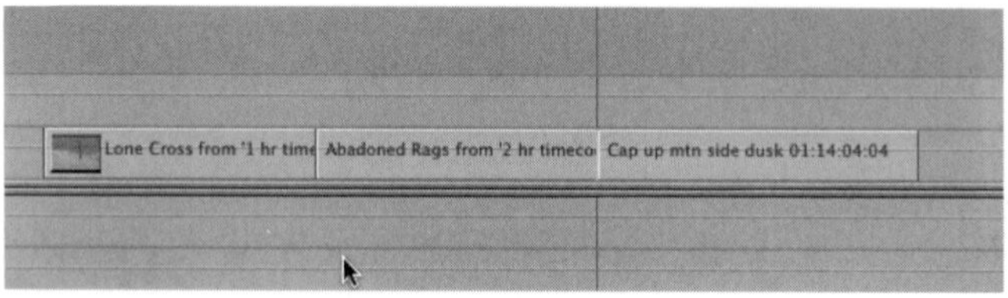

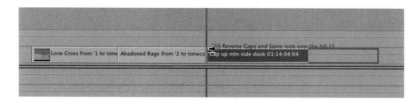

Figure 8.37   *The Timeline after you move a clip in the Timeline window.*

When dragging from the Browser or the Viewer to the Timeline window, you can choose between inserting the shot and overwriting the shot by selecting the area where you release the mouse button. If you drop the shot on the top third of the track, you insert it (see Figure 8.38). If you drop the shot on the bottom two-thirds of the track, you overwrite it (see Figure 8.39). Notice the arrow's display for inserts and overwrites. It's how you can tell that you're ready to drop this clip. If the arrow points right, you insert the shot. If it points down, you overwrite it.

Figure 8.38   *Inserting a shot from the Browser or Viewer (the arrow points to the right).*

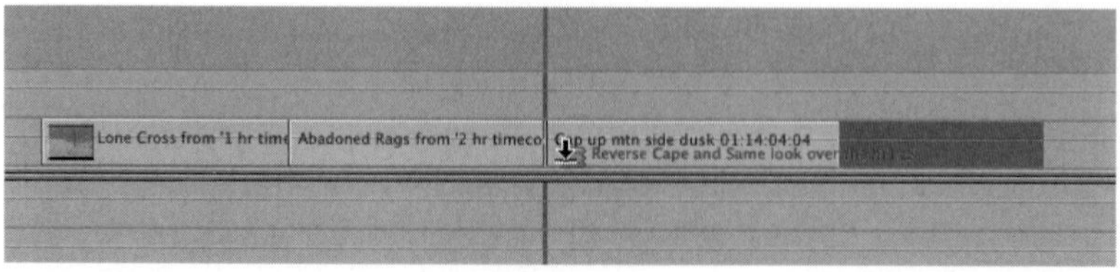

Figure 8.39   *Overwriting a shot from the Browser or Viewer (the arrow points down).*

You can also drag a shot up or down. If you have only one track of video, you automatically create another track by dragging above the first track. The same thing happens with audio clips; dragging them down creates a new audio track if necessary for them to reside in.

Ripple and Roll Trims in the Timeline Window

By activating the Ripple (press RR) or Roll (press R) edit tools from the Tools window, you can perform ripple and roll edits in the sequence itself in the Timeline window. I've found that if you zoom in on the sequence, you get better control. You can perform ripple and roll edits on video or audio clips. Remember that with a ripple edit, you take frames off or add frames to one clip, pulling the clips past it to come sooner or later in the sequence (rippling the sequence). With a roll edit, you take frames off as you add frames to either side of the edit point. A roll edit doesn't change the length of the Timeline in any way, because it adds an equal number of frames on one side of the edit point while you are taking away frames from the other side of the edit point.

To perform a ripple edit, select the Ripple tool (press RR), highlight the edit point you'd like to trim, and drag it (see Figure 8.40). Notice the "mini two-up" display that appears in the Canvas window. The left frame is the new last frame of the outgoing clip, and the right frame is the first frame of the incoming clip. Also note the counter in a yellow box, showing you the amount you are trimming. When you let go of the mouse button, the edit is performed. The sequence now looks like Figure 8.41. The Abandoned Rags clip is shortened, and the incoming clip is moved to the left.

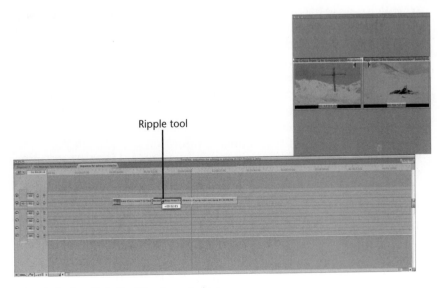

Ripple tool

FIGURE 8.40   *A ripple edit in the Timeline window.*

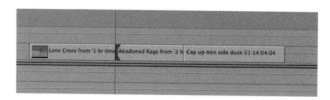

FIGURE 8.41   *The Timeline after the ripple edit.*

The "Cap up mtn side dusk" still frame clip was moved to the left an equal number of frames that were taken away from the "Abandoned rags" clip. Thus, it was moved sooner in the sequence. As frames were removed from the "Abandoned rags" clip, the incoming clip past it was moved left in the sequence with the edit point. By clicking the other side of the edit, you could perform a ripple edit on the incoming clip—in this case, the "Cap up mtn side dusk" clip. If you do this, any clips *past* it (right now there are none) are pulled sooner, and no hole is left in the sequence.

A roll edit is performed the same way. If media is available on both sides of the edit, you may perform a roll edit in the Timeline window. The two-up display appears in the Canvas window when you perform a roll edit. You add frames to one side of the edit point as you take away the same number of frames from the other side of the edit.

Linking and Merging Audio and Video Clips

Linking keeps together video clips that have audio associated with them (such as sync sound). It also keeps stereo audio tracks together. For example, if you move a linked video clip that has a sound you want to keep in sync with it, the linked track is selected at the same time. If you have a linked clip but the audio and video cannot be selected with one click, linking might be turned off. You can activate linking using the Linked Selection button, the chain-link button in the upper right of the Timeline window, as shown in Figure 8.42. (Figure 8.43 shows linking turned off.) You also can toggle linking back on by pressing Shift+L or by selecting Sequence, Link.

FIGURE 8.42
The Linked Selection button in the Linked position.

FIGURE 8.43
The Linked Selection button in the Unlinked position.

If you trim an actively linked clip, the material that is linked to it is also trimmed with the same number of frames. If you change an audio level within a stereo paired audio track, both tracks are affected. If you have captured clips as audio CH1 and CH2 clips, though, they still act independently of each other. When working with a capture that is video and audio, Final Cut Pro automatically links these clips.

The audio can be captured as ch1+ch2, where it behaves as linked-but-independent audio tracks, or as stereo audio, where it behaves as one audio track with two channels (all levels and filter settings are applied identically, regardless of linked selection).

You need to understand the difference between linking clips and linked selection. Linking clips creates a link between two or more clips, such as a video clip and an audio clip. After you perform this command, the clips are linked, meaning that if you select one, you select the other *unless* you've temporarily defeated this behavior by turning off the Linked Selection button. You can turn linked selection on or off at any time.

Merging Audio Clips to a Video Clip

New to FCP 4 is the ability to merge more than two tracks of audio to a single track of video, up to a total of 24 individual or 12 stereo tracks of audio. A *merged clip* links to more than one media file. For example, you might want to use a merged clip to create a single clip of video and audio in a case where the audio wasn't recorded on the camera's tape or film (when recording audio on a DAT, for example). After they are merged, these audio and video clips behave as if they were an audio/video clip in the first place.

You can use this new feature to sync audio and video even though you didn't use the same tape to record both (or if you used a film camera, which doesn't record audio). You can capture the video and audio as separate clips and then merge them into a single clip, which becomes a master clip and behaves as such.

When you capture audio you intend to merge with a separate video clip, it's important to use "house sync" (by connecting an independent video signal such as a black burst generator to your video deck and audio deck) to keep the audio deck synchronized with your system. You should also make sure that the timecode on the audio and video clips is accurate. If you don't use house sync, your audio sync can drift out of sync over time within the merged clip.

Creating Merged Clips

You need to synchronize your audio to your video before you merge the clips. You can do this in several ways. If the timecode on the videotape and the timecode on the audio tape have been "slaved" or are the same, you needn't do anything special. Just highlight the audio and video clips you want to merge in the Browser, Ctrl-click one of them, and select Merge Clips to open a dialog box that asks you how you want to synchronize the clips.

Figure 8.44 shows your choices. You can sync the clips by selecting In points that you've determined are in sync (such as the close of a clapstick and the sound that was recorded on your DAT at the same moment). You can also select Out points, Timecode (if the timecode matches on the two clips), Aux Timecode 1, or Aux Timecode 2. *Aux Timecode* is timecode you've added to a clip. You can determine what the sync point is, for example, and then assign timecode to the two clips that matches. You'll find these columns for this purpose in the Browser as part of each clip's information.

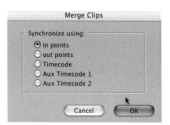

FIGURE 8.44
The Merge Clips dialog box.

Using a clapstick on the shoot to create a sync point is the best way to prepare for merging clips later in postproduction if you cannot sync or "slave" the timecode to the respective recording devices. This makes the process of syncing the audio to the video using In or Out points very easy.

All you need to do is find the first frame of picture where the clapstick closes and the first bit of sound recorded on your audiotape. Set In points on each clip. Highlight both clips. Ctrl-click one of the clips and select Merge Clips from the contextual menu. Select "in points" in the dialog box. You should be in sync.

If you've used an end slate instead of a head slate, put Out points on the two clips where this moment in time was recorded. The sound of the clap and the first frame of the closed clapstick are at the end of the recording in this case, and you select "out points" as the synchronization method. After being created, merged clips act as if they came from the same capture.

Syncing Issues

With linked selection turned off, moving one of two items that originally were in sync with each other causes an out-of-sync indicator to be displayed. By Ctrl-clicking the red box (the out-of-sync indicator) containing the number of frames by which the clip is out of sync, you can either move or slip the item into sync, as shown in Figure 8.45.

FIGURE 8.45
The original video is out of sync, as shown by the out-of-sync indicators.

If you choose Move into Sync, the clip returns to its original position, as shown in Figure 8.46. This command moved the clip with the frames it was originally using. If you choose Slip into Sync, the video (or, in the example, the audio) slips itself into sync, actually changing the frames used for the clip, not its position. And the video can still be offset visually from the audio, as shown in Figure 8.47. In the case of Figure 8.46, you'd hear the audio *before* you'd hear the video, but when you saw the video, it would be in sync with the audio track it was captured with. In Figure 8.47, you'd hear the audio as you saw the video. In both figures, the audio would be in sync with the video when you see it.

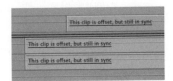

FIGURE 8.46
The video moved back into sync.

FIGURE 8.47
The video slipped into sync, leaving a visual offset.

To *temporarily* turn linked selection on or off, hold down the Option key. Linked selection is disabled (if it's on) or enabled (if it's off) for as long as you hold down the Option key. For example, if linked selection is turned on, and you hold down the Option key while clicking the video item of a linked clip, only the video item is selected. This is a quick way to select only one item of a linked clip for editing, trimming, or deleting.

You can establish a link whether or not it was originally captured as an audio/video clip. For example, in the case of "The Midnight Sun," all the sound sync audio, such as Sam and Cap's lines, was recorded separately from the picture. The picture was shot on film and was not synced in a session after the Telecine (film to tape) session. Therefore, it came to the editing session as an element separate from the videotape that was created from the film. After establishing the separate audio clip's sync point to the picture, you can link these two clips in case you want to move the clips later or earlier in the Timeline or trim them in some manner. Another use of this feature might be to keep a video associated with a music clip.

To link audio to video that isn't already linked, select the clips in the Timeline, and then select Modify, Link or press Cmd+L.

Syncing shots with a clapper is a snap. Simply listen for the sound of the clapper and press M in the Viewer to put a marker there (you'll read more about markers in the next chapter). Locate the frame of film or video where the clapper closes, and place a marker there. Edit either the video or the audio into the Timeline, and drag one of the clips until the markers

tip

You can use the same techniques to sync cameras that do not have the same timecode associated with them. Using a clapper is best, but you can also just shoot someone doing a single, fast handclap and achieve the same result. If you are off a frame or two, use the Slip tool to slip things until you achieve sync.

line up. If you don't have a clapper, you can simply shoot a flash from a still camera (shooting a wedding, you might find lots of these), or look for an identifying sound in the sound clip that you could easily find in the video clip, and use the markers to line them up.

Avoiding Sync Problems Now and Forever

Many new nonlinear editors have a problem understanding how to keep in sync. It's easy to get out of sync if you add a clip or extra frames of a clip to one track and then don't add to the other tracks if the clips involved are not linked.

Nonlinear editing lets you get out of sync when you trim video without trimming its accompanying audio. If you add or subtract audio or video without adding or subtracting an equal number of frames of video or audio, you *will* go out of sync. Therefore, remember to follow this hard-and-fast rule: If you remove frames from the audio, you must remove the same number of frames from the video, and vice versa. If you add frames of video to your sequence, you must also add frames of audio. If you follow this rule, you will *never* go out of sync.

For example, assume that you have very carefully edited some video to appear over a specific audio moment (not original sound sync, but, say, from a music video). If you add frames to a video shot without taking an equal number of frames from the following shot (as is the case with a ripple edit), you push or pull the video past this point away from the audio it was originally edited with. To keep this from happening, you must trim the next shot (or the one following it) by the same number of frames. This keeps the duration of the video track as a whole the same as it was before. The only other way to stay in sync later in your sequence is to add some audio to the tracks that are being pushed or pulled out of sync.

There will be times when you *want* the audio to be out of sync. For example, you might have captured a long clip that contains many takes of a given scene from many angles. If you use audio from one take to go under video from some other take (such as when you see a close-up of a reaction of a character who isn't speaking), you see the out-of-sync indicators. You can ignore them, or you can select the video and audio reported to be out of sync and then select Modify, Mark in Sync to make the warnings disappear.

Split Edits Made Easy: When, Why, and How to Make Them

A *split edit* is any edit in which the synchronized audio precedes or is heard later than the accompanying video. When the audio precedes the edit, this is called an *L cut*. When the video precedes its audio, this is called a *J cut*. The easiest way to do this sort of edit is to edit the sound sync audio and video as you want to *hear* it, starting with the video cutting at the same time as the audio edits. As soon as you're satisfied with the audio's pacing, use the Roll edit feature to move the video to the right or left of the audio's edit point to make your split edit. You need to turn linking off so that you roll only the video above the synced (and typically linked) audio. Therefore, you have to unlink the video clips from the audio clips they are linked to before this technique will work. Use this technique to give a much more natural delivery to a dialog scene, for example.

When editing a dialog scene, think about where *you* might look if you were watching the scene from an angle where you had to look at one of the characters who are talking to each other. What would motivate you to change your view, even if you only had to move your eyes? A person who starts talking and draws your attention to him *after* he starts speaking? Or maybe you're hearing a speech that you already know something about, and you want to change your point of view to include the other character to view his or her *reaction*. In this case, you'd continue to hear the outgoing audio and switch your point of view to the other character *before* he or she speaks.

This form of editing is quite commonly used, because it does the "unnatural" action of possibly jumping the viewer's point of view back and forth as each of the two characters speaks. As in real life, you don't know when a person's speech is finished, and you don't know to change your point of view *as the speeches are delivered*. When you view any conversation for the first time, you naturally look at a given character *after* he or she begins to speak, or before a reactionary speech is given to the person currently speaking. Always think of what would *motivate* you to change your point of view. Rarely do dialog scenes work smoothly and naturally if all the video edits happen at the same time the audio edits are happening. Sometimes it's not even necessary to see the person who's talking, especially when the person who's listening has the more important moment to show the audience.

In the case of a documentary, the same principles hold true. It's quite acceptable to hear an interview begin before the speaker is seen, for example. It's what draws the viewer in and leads the viewer to the scene or change of shot. Even when documenting a wedding, there might be times you can use this technique.

Workshop 8: Finish Scene 2 and Edit Scene 3

In this workshop, you will edit the rest of Scene 2 and all of Scene 3. Now that you have a bit of a handle on things, it's time to speed things up. You will begin with the remaining edits you need to finish Scene 2 and then will close this workshop by finishing Scene 3.

Rearrange Your Windows

If you haven't already done this, try a new arrangement for your windows. If you've been using the two-up arrangement, try a standard arrangement, or vice versa. You can also create a custom arrangement by simply dragging the windows around the screen until you are satisfied with the new arrangement and then saving this arrangement for later use.

Quickly arranging your windows with these preset or your custom views is a great way to keep them from overlapping. For example, if the Viewer is overlapped by another window, playback might stutter. Playback also might stutter in the Viewer or Canvas if they are not set to Fit to Window or smaller. You cannot easily play back material if you are cropping the video because you've zoomed in on the image. You can quickly get the image to be set to Fit to Window by activating the Viewer or Canvas and then pressing Shift+Z.

You can drag the double gray line in the Timeline window up to reveal more of the multiple audio tracks.

You might want to save this new view you've created by holding down the Option key and selecting Window, Arrange, Set Custom Layout 1. By pressing Shift+U, you can reset to this arrangement later.

In the top left of the Timeline window, click the far-right button with the plus sign on it. This lets you see more or even all of your audio and video tracks in one view. Don't forget to use this during the workshops, especially if you are working with a smaller single-computer display, such as what is found on a PowerBook or iMac.

Add an Audio Filter to an Audio Clip

1. Navigate to 01:01:29;23 in Sequence 1. On the A1 track is a series of four speeches between Sam and his girlfriend. They need an effect added to them to match the style used when we hear what's going on in Sam's memory later in the scene (remember the reverberation that the later clips use?). The "City, 19th century" sounds clip on A2 needs this effect as well.

2. Double-click the first speech ("VO Girlfriend Tk #4-04") so that it appears in the Viewer.

3. Click the Effects tab in the Browser to pull it up front, and open the Audio Filters>Final Cut Pro folder. In that folder, locate the Reverberation filter. Drag it to the Viewer window, and then click the Filters tab in the Viewer to reveal the Reverberation controls.

4. The default setting for this filter is an Effect Mix of 50 with no change to Brightness or the Effect Level. The Type is set to Room (Medium). To give the effect a more dramatic and appropriate feel, select Tunnel from the pop-up Type menu, as shown in Figure 8.48.

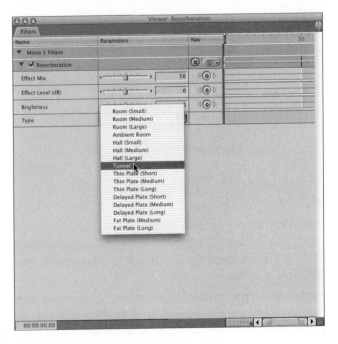

FIGURE 8.48   *The room type selection pop-up menu.*

5. Play back the clip.

6. It doesn't match the less-prominent reverberation heard later, so set the Effect Mix to 22, the Effect Level to –11, and the Brightness to 36. Play it back in the Canvas. Notice too that you can mark this clip in its entirety (mark an In point on the first frame and an Out point on the last frame). Select View, Looping Playback, or press Opt+L. Click Play In to Out. You can change the filter's settings as you listen to the changes.

7. Spend some time changing this filter's settings. Change rooms, change Brightness and Effect Mix levels, and see the results. Most of the time, you'll need to do this sort of experimentation to achieve just the feel you're going for.

Figure 8.49 shows how your filter's settings should be set when you are done.

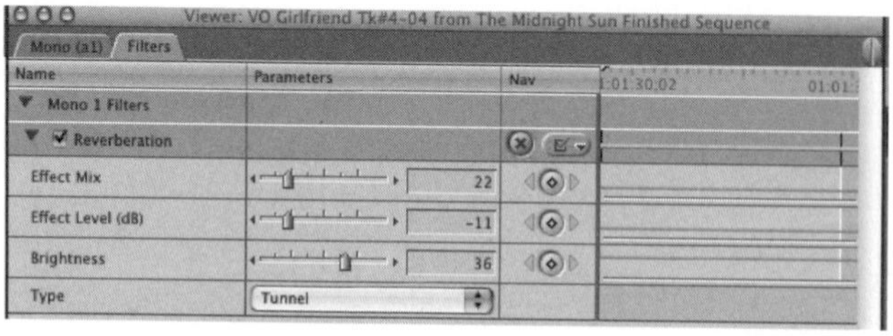

FIGURE 8.49   *The Filters settings after step 6.*

Copy the Reverberation Filter to Other Clips

There are several ways to apply this same newly programmed effect without adding and reprogramming a fresh Reverberation filter for each clip you need to add it to:

- Drag the filter directly from the Viewer to each of the clips (by clicking and dragging its name).

- Select all the clips, and drag the filter to the highlighted set. You can save it for further use later by dragging it from the Viewer to any bin in the Browser.

- Drag the filter to the Favorites folder contained in the Effects tab. This makes it available for use from the Effects menu, and you can select it when you want to use it. It will be contained in your audio Favorites list located just under the Audio Filters selection.

- A very powerful tool to learn is the Paste Attributes command. You can copy (Cmd+C) a programmed clip in the Timeline, Ctrl-click one or more selected clips, and select Paste Attributes from the context menu that opens. With this command, you can take any number of complex effects, filters, and other attributes you've programmed in one clip and apply them to as many clips as you want. Figure 8.50 shows your choices. Included here is the choice to even paste the contents, which replaces the selected clip or clips you've chosen for pasting with the actual shot or audio clip you have copied.

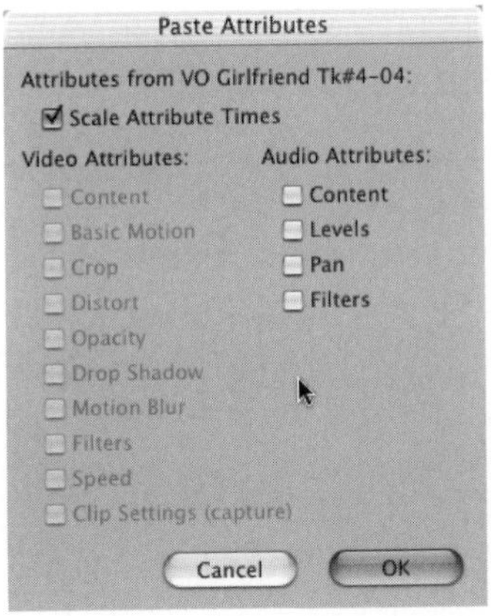

Paste Attributes

Attributes from VO Girlfriend Tk#4–04:

☑ Scale Attribute Times

Video Attributes: Audio Attributes:

☐ Content   ☐ Content

☐ Basic Motion   ☐ Levels

☐ Crop   ☐ Pan

☐ Distort   ☐ Filters

☐ Opacity

☐ Drop Shadow

☐ Motion Blur

☐ Filters

☐ Speed

☐ Clip Settings (capture)

(Cancel)   (OK)

FIGURE 8.50   *The Paste Attributes window.*

For this exercise, highlight the remaining three speeches and the City sounds clip
beneath them, as shown in Figure 8.51. You can command-click them to select them
individually and keep the earlier selection highlighted. From the Filters tab, drag the
effect to the set of selected audio clips. When they are active, you see a change in
their highlight to be "boxed"-looking. When you see the boxed look, release the
mouse button. All the clips will have this added (and programmed only once)
Reverberation filter. Play them back.

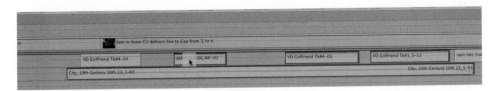

FIGURE 8.51   *Dragging the filter to the highlighted clips.*

Add Reverberation to the COMEIN Clip

You need to add reverberation to one more clip—the clip at 01:02:25;02 in the A1
track named "COMEIN~1.AIF-02."

1. Drag the Reverberation filter again, but this time, drag it to the Favorites folder
    contained in the Effects tab in the Browser.

2. Select the clip. Apply the filter by selecting Effects, Favorites, or drag the filter
    from the Favorites folder in the Effects tab of the Browser to the clip in the
    Timeline. You can rename it here as well to further specify what the filter is used
    for, such as Reverb for Memories or something like that. If you rename it, its new
    name is reflected in the Filters tab of the clip you applied it to. Play back the clip.

Create Scene 3

Start by creating a Scene 3 bin.

1. Open the Picture Clips bin, and open the disclosure triangle next to the 1 hr timecode section master clip. The last three markers are the ones you'll use to edit the next section of our story. Create subclips of these markers by highlighting them and pressing Cmd+U. Drag these subclips to the newly created Scene 3 bin.

2. Open the disclosure triangle next to the 3 hr timecode section clip in the Picture clips bin. Create subclips of the first four markers you made, from "Sam Asks Cap for Cremation tk 1 Pan" through "CU over shoulder of Picture." Drag these four subclips to the Scene 3 bin as well.

    When you are finished, your Scene 3 bin should look like Figure 8.52.

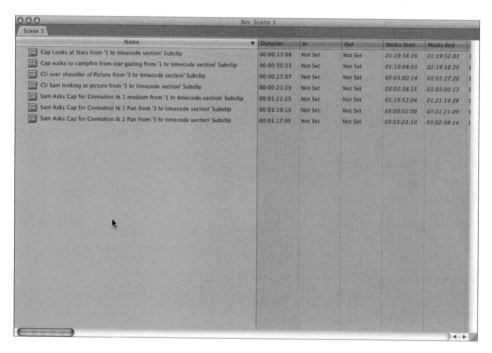

FIGURE 8.52 *The Scene 3 bin after step 2.*

3. Option-double-click the Scene 3 bin to open it and place its tab in the Browser window.

4. Make sure the Scene 3 bin is sorted in alphabetical order, starting with "Cap Looks at Stars." (Just click the Name column in the bin's List view to make it so.) Select the first four clips and drag them to the Timeline window. Place them on the V1 track right next to the "Cap walks to Sam tk 2" clip, as shown in Figure 8.53.

   Notice the +3 shadow, showing you the first clip's name and then adding the three additional clips in the ghosted name. Also notice the down-arrow indicator. It lets you know that you are overwriting, not inserting.

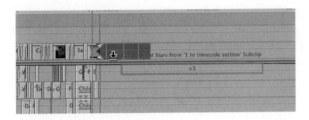

FIGURE 8.53 *Four clips overwriting.*

5. Take a look at the sequence of shots. The way it is, we start with two shots of Cap (the reverse of him looking at the stars, which we can't see, but we'll fix later), then a wide angle of the scene, followed by an over-the-shoulder of Sam, followed by a close-up of Sam. It's not too inspired. We'll start by changing the order of the shots.

6. Turn on snapping by pressing N. Place the playhead in the Timeline at 1:03:20;13. Use the arrow keys to be exact.

7. Click the CU of Sam shot (the last one in the current series of four), and then begin to drag it directly to the left. When you start to drag it, hold down the Option key so that you can see the insert curved arrow pointing down. Drag the shot until it sits over the "Cap walks to campfire from star gazing" clip and its head snaps to the playhead's position. Release the mouse button. When you are done, this area of the sequence should look like Figure 8.54.

FIGURE 8.54 *Detail of the Timeline after step 7.*

8. First you establish night with the close-up of Cap looking at the stars. Then you establish more of the scene with the wide angle. *Then from the wide* you go to Sam's close-up (detailing this from the wide angle). It still needs some help, because we are motivated to see what Sam is intently looking at next, not the moment where Cap walks over. So you need to swap the last two shots. Using the same method as before, drag (while holding down the Option key) the last shot of the over-the-shoulder of Sam to insert it between his close-up and the second instance of the wide angle on the scene. When you are done, your sequence should look like Figure 8.55.

Notice the two red triangles now present between the third and fourth shots. They appear because this is continuous footage. In other words, the last frame of Sam's CU and the first frame of the over-the-shoulder shot are next to each other in the source media file (3 hr timecode section), and they are also next to each other on the tape that captured this footage. This is called a through edit.

If you don't see the red triangles, check the Show Through Edits check box in the Timeline Options of the User Preferences (found on the Final Cut Pro menu). You can also press Opt+Q to open the User Preferences.

FIGURE 8.55   *Detail of the Timeline after step 8.*

Trim the Shots

The shots definitely need some trimming. This time, you'll trim them in the Timeline window.

1. Use the Zoom tool (press Z) to zoom into the Timeline so that you'll have better control over the next five trims. You'll find that this works better when you trim in the Timeline window.

2. Press RR to activate the Ripple edit tool, and snapping off by pressing N.

3. With the Ripple edit tool active, first trim the outgoing shot of Sam lying in the snow. Click its Out point, and then drag to the left until the two-up display shows 02:16:21:29 as its Out point. Figure 8.56 shows the final point where you should release the mouse button after the dragging. You'll find that you can ramp down the Ripple and Roll edit tools in the Timeline to achieve a more accurate trim if, while you are dragging the tools and trimming, you hold down the Command key. This allows for a slower and more precise handling of the trim, and you can be very accurate with the trims that way. When you release the mouse button, the trim is instantly reflected in your sequence.

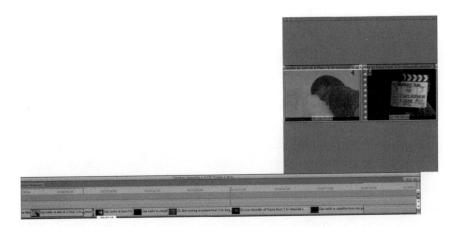

FIGURE 8.56   *A ripple edit trim in the Timeline after step 3.*

4.   Click the incoming shot (Cap's reverse looking up at the stars) at the same edit point and drag it to the right until you've trimmed it to have it start at 01:19:39:27. Then trim its Out point to be 01:19:43:24, again with the Ripple edit tool in the Timeline window. The last frame of "Cap Looks at Stars" should now sit on 1:02:55:14 in the Timeline's timecode.

5.   The wide-angle shot now coming in should be trimmed at its head to 01:19:16:18, and its Out point should be trimmed to 01:19:20:04. To do this, you have to drag the Ripple tool on the shot's Out point to the right this time. Don't forget to hold down the Command key to make this easy.

6.   Trim the "CU Sam looking at picture" shot's In point to be 03:02:40:20 and its Out point to be 03:02:46:01.

7.   Trim the "CU over shoulder of Picture" clip's In point to be 03:03:01:24 and its Out point to be 03:03:13:20.

8.   Trim the incoming shot's ("Cap Walks to campfire from star gazing") head to 01:19:19:07, dragging the Ripple edit tool to the left to add a few frames. Note that you are repeating frames. If your User Preferences are set to show all duplicated frames, you'll see a colored line at the bottom of the two instances of this clip in the Timeline, indicating the duplicated frames. The reason for the duplication is that the audience will not notice the double use of a few

frames, and it's Cap's head move that should start this edit. Furthermore, using this same head turn earlier motivated the cut to the close-up of Sam in the first place. Cap began to look at Sam, and this draws attention to him. Whenever you can, you should start and end an edit with a cut on action. In this case, you cut out on the head turn and then cut back to the angle repeating the same head turn. Detecting these repeated shots would be almost impossible when your audience sees the edits.

9. Trim the Out of the last shot in the sequence to 01:19:30:25. When you are done with this step, your sequence of these five shots should look like Figure 8.57.

FIGURE 8.57   *Scene 3 after step 9.*

10. Place a 2;00 dissolve that begins at the edit between "Cap walks to Sam tk 2" and "Cap looks at stars."

11. Open the Sound Clips bin, locate the "Wind,desert Lonely,66_1-04" clip, and double-click it to open it in the Viewer. Mark an In point at 3:11 and an Out point at 22:29. Overwrite it at 01:02:32;27, right next to the outgoing wind sounds on tracks A6 and A7.

12. Locate "Campfire Small crackling 77_1," and load it into the Viewer. Set an In point at 00:00:02:23, and edit it directly to tracks A6 and A7 next to "Wind, desert Lonely,66_1-04." Lower its level to –12dB. Add a 2-second audio fade that ends on the edit between the wind and campfire sound effects to match the duration of the video dissolve between the scenes. With the campfire sound effect still loaded in the Viewer, remove the mark In by pressing Opt+I. Drag the entire clip to the Timeline, and place it on Tracks 6 and 7 right next to the earlier edit. Lower its level to –12dB. The reason you put the In point in the first instance of this edit was in preparation for the cross-fade. You couldn't have had the cross-fade end at the edit point without unused media available for the task.

13. Navigate to 01:02:59;20. Set an In point there in the Canvas. Locate the sound clip "Train, steam, station 23_1 Verb" in the Sound Clips bin. With snapping turned on, drag the icon with the hand and speaker in the Viewer to the In point created in the Timeline on tracks A2 and A3. With the Roll edit tool (press R), drag the clip's Out point to match up with the edit at 01:03:16;11 in the sequence so that it ends with the "CU over shoulder of Picture" clip on

the V1 track. Raise its level to +12 dB, and create a fade-out at its end with the Pen tool for a duration of 2 seconds. There is no need for a fade-up at the head, because it's built into this sound effect.

14. Move the playhead in the Timeline window to 01:03:01;26. Turn on snapping if it's off. Locate the "MOTHER~1.AIF-02 Verb" clip in the Sound Clips bin. Drag it directly to the playhead on Track A1 (you don't have to have an In point to snap to). Trim this clip's Out point by 1 second with the Roll edit tool. Raise its level to +12 dB.

15. Move the playhead forward in the Timeline to 01:03:07;14. Locate "SAMSDIIA-LOG.AIF-14" in the Sound Clips bin, and place its head at the playhead's position on the A1 track. Raise its level to +7 dB.

16. Move the playhead forward in the Timeline to 01:03:11;28, locate "SAMSDIIA-LOG.AIF-15" in the Sound clips bin, and place its head at the playhead's position on the A1 track. Raise its level to +7 dB. Create a 15-frame fade-out at the end of this clip and one at the end of Sam's mother's line.

17. Locate the Reverberation filter you saved earlier, and add it to the first of Sam's lines. Play it back to see if it works. It's a little too much and doesn't quite match the lesser reverb already built into the train and the mother's speech. So change the Type to Hall (Large) and lower the Effect level to –16 on both clips. It's now much more like the mother's line. After modifying the new version of this filter on the first clip, drag its name in the Filters tab now open in the Viewer to the second of Sam's lines. Play back the affected audio clips.

18. Load the "Foley 1-Cap'n Campfire #1" clip in the *Foley bin. Set an In point at 00:00:22:01, and edit it to the A3 track in the sequence at 01:03:18;00. Raise its level to +12dB. It's Cap's footsteps.

Sync the Sound

So far, you've been supplied with the sound sync already figured out for you. It's time you did one for yourself to learn the techniques used. Create a new sequence with the OfflineRT NTSC (Photo JPEG) as its setting, and name it Sound Sync (press Cmd+N). If the Select Sequence Preset dialog box does not open, highlight this new sequence and press Cmd+0 to open this particular sequence's settings. Click the Load Sequence Presets button, and make sure it is set to OfflineRT NTSC (Photo JPEG).

1. Locate the "S9FT2.AIF" sound sync clip in the Sound Clips bin. Drag it in its entirety to the new sequence 10 seconds from its start point (at 1:00:10:00 in the Timeline's timecode).

2. Locate the clip named "Sam Asks Cap for Cremation tk 2 Pan" in the Scene 3 bin. Place it on the V1 track with its In point directly above the audio edit's In point.

3. Enlarge the Track Height by pressing Shift+T until it is at its widest. Turn on the waveforms in the audio track by highlighting the Timeline window and pressing Opt+Cmd+W. The Timeline should look like Figure 8.58.

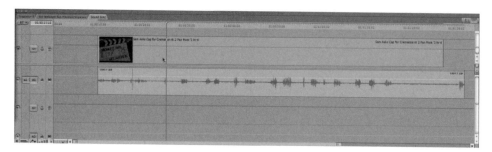

FIGURE 8.58   *The sound sync sequence ready for syncing.*

4. Play the sequence. At its start you see the closed clapstick, but you don't hear it close until much later. This indicates that we are out of sync. You can see where the clapstick's sound is, though. It's the spike in the audio waveform 7:25 in from the start of the audio clip.

   But there is a problem. The clapstick is already closed at the beginning of the video subclip. Because it was the whole subclip used, you cannot just trim back some frames to locate this point in the video to match it up with the sound, because Final Cut Pro behaves as if there is no more media in a subclip before its start point or after its end point. But there is a way to sort of "unsubclip" this clip to remove its limits.

5. Highlight the video clip in the sequence, and select Modify, Remove Subclip Limits. After you do this, no longer is there a limit to how much you can trim this subclip, except for the actual length of the original master clip's media file it came from. Double-click the video clip's In edit point to open it in the Trim Edit window. Click the –5 button three times to add 15 frames to its head. You see the clapstick open.

6. Close the Trim Edit window.

7. Locate the first frame where the clapstick is truly closed, and with the clip highlighted in the Timeline window, place a marker there by pressing M. (It actually *was* the first frame of the video, but you had to make sure it was the frame at 3:01:21:10 in the source clip's video. Turning on Show Overlays with Show Timecode Overlays checked in the far-right oval button near the center top of the Canvas window reveals this in the Canvas window.)

8.   Highlight the audio clip, and place a marker at the spike in the audio wave-form (the sound of the clapstick closing). The production audio person can be heard saying "Mark" right before the sound of the clapstick closing. To be exact, though, zoom into the audio at this point to make sure you've put the marker at the head of this sound.

9.   Drag the video clip until the marker in it and the marker in the audio clip line up perfectly. Then take a look at the clapstick's sync. It should be right on.

There are many ways to perform this syncing exercise. You could also have set In points in both the picture clip and the sound clip and merged the clips just for the experience. Try it.

10. Play the sequence all the way through to make sure it looks and sounds in sync. Use the Slip tool (press S) to slip it one way or the other until you are satisfied with the sync. It probably is within a frame or so if it's off at all. By experimenting with slipping the video left or right by a frame at a time, you'll begin to get a feel for syncing yet another way and pay attention to the Slip tool and how it acts on the clip. Think of those times when you don't have a clapstick—the Slip tool might become your best friend!

11. When you are satisfied with the sync, trim the video's In point to 1:00:22:10, and trim the video's tail until it lines up with the end of the audio clip, using the Roll edit tool with snapping turned on. Then trim the audio's In point to match that of the video's In point. Finally, link the clips by highlighting them and pressing Cmd+L. Their names will become underlined after they are linked.

12. Double-click the head of these clips. Notice that because they are linked, both the audio and the video are trimmed at the same time.

13. Trim the last 1:07 of the outgoing media. The clip should be 1:08:11 in total length now. If it isn't, trim the Out or In point so that it is this duration.

14. Copy the linked clips (highlight them and press Cmd+C), and paste them at 01:03:28;01 to the V1 and A1 tracks (don't forget to target the tracks) in your Sequence 1 sequence.

15. Close the Sound Sync sequence in the Timeline window by Ctrl-clicking its tab.

16. Add a fade-out at the end of the audio and video of the "Sam Asks Cap for Cremation tk 2" clip and the accompanying sound sync clip on track A1, which lasts 4:15. A long fade-out is used to accentuate the gravity of the moment. The easiest way to do both at once is to Ctrl-click the Out edit and add a cross-dissolve to both. Double-click them to change the durations of both in the Viewer's transition editor when it opens.

17. Trim the end of the fire sound effect to line up with the shots above it (about 21 frames), and then add a cross-dissolve of 4:15. But because you just made one of this duration, simply copy it and paste it to the stereo sound effect of the fire. Notice that because the campfire sound is a stereo pair, you need to add the dissolve only once for both tracks. When you are finished, the sequence should look like Figure 8.59.

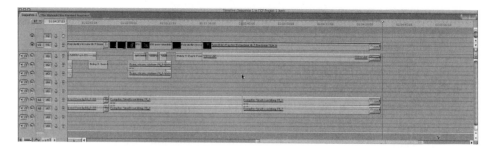

FIGURE 8.59 *The sequence after step 17.*

Edit the Middle of the Film to Sequence 1

Rather than being too redundant by having you edit the entire movie, because much of the next section would be repetitive editorial actions, the next edit takes you through the next few scenes.

1. Position the playhead at 01:04:30;18. Locate the clip "Midnight Sun Full Mix center" in the Sound Clips bin, and edit it to tracks A8 and A9 in its entirety at 01:04:30;18. Here, you'll start the music at the point of Cap's promise, indicated by his head shake, to cremate Sam in the event of his death. The reason for the music's starting here instead of in the following scene is to accent this huge moment in the story and to use an L cut to smooth the way to the next scene.

2. Position the playhead at 01:04:36;13. Turn on snapping. Open the sequence "The Midnight Sun finished Sequence" if it's not already open. (If it is, just click its tab to bring it forward.) Highlight all the video clips above the edit you just made, and copy them (press Cmd+C). The first of these clips is named "Sam Dies tk 1," and the last is named "Cap sees boat full shot." Paste the video shots in your sequence (press Cmd+V). When you are finished, your sequence should look like Figure 8.60. Save your project file (press Cmd+S).

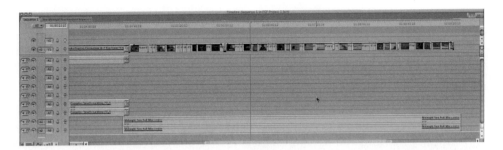

FIGURE 8.60   *The center section of the sequence after step 2.*

3. I've purposefully let you skip this portion of the edit. There really isn't any point in repeating the mechanics of editing this portion of the footage, because they are the same as what's preceded the edit up to the end of these scenes.

4. Save your project file.

The Aesthetics of the Middle of the Film

Sam is going to die. Cap's promise to cremate him will give him quite an adventure that involves a tremendous amount of struggle and pain. Where *does* one cremate a body in the middle of the snowy Klondike?

The use of a fade-out and then a fade-in at the beginning of this section is also an accent. We've consistently used dissolves for transitional effects, but these fades punctuate the moment much better than a dissolve between clips would, just *because* it's different. A page turn or some other digital effect or wipe is not organic enough for the feel of our turn-of-the-century movie; it's simply the wrong style. A fade to black and back is very organic, much like closing and opening your eyes. In actuality, it's in the same family as a dissolve—it's a dissolve to black and back.

Sam's death scene sets up the creepiness of the following night scene where Cap can't light a match. A sense of horror is being emphasized here (and the music is just right). Notice the point of view (POV) shots cut between the closer shots of Cap attempting to light the match. The editorial construction here was thought out to make you think that something awful is about to happen. Hopefully the viewers get little hairs standing up on the backs of their necks.

When you watch this center section, notice how Cap's scenes cut where they are real-time and dissolve when we go to another location or time. You should aim for consistency of style throughout any piece, and that's what's happened here. Notice too how little the voice-over actually drives the story. The *pictures* are driving the story.

The action is pushing us forward, not the words, and it's the music that draws emotion. Anytime action can dominate your storytelling, I suggest you choose it. Film is a visual medium, even when you're editing industrial training films. Repeating theme music is also used in this set of scenes.

Pay particular attention to the scene where Cap has to destroy the dogs because he's out of food for them. This scene uses a series of jump cuts called a montage. A *jump cut* is an edit between two shots where there is a change in time or a scene location (in this case it was time). A *montage* is a series of these jump cuts, a series of shots that separately don't seem to relate to each other, but as a whole and in a certain order (such as chronological order) they tell a story. They cut only when a new bit of information is told, and as a *group* they tell the story of only *one* scene. That's why no dissolves are used or needed here. As a group, they tell the story of Cap losing his dogs.

CHAPTER 9

Using Markers

- Understanding the Use of Markers
- Using Timeline and Canvas Window Markers
- Workshop 9: Experiment with Markers

Understanding the Use of Markers

There are five general types of markers:

- Clip and sequence markers, used to mark a location, usually for an editorial purpose
- Chapter and compression markers, used to create DVDs
- Scoring markers (new to FCP 4), which transfer to Soundtrack

Clip markers have many uses. You might want to mark several frames that you want to use as In or Out points. You can use clip markers to quickly mark different takes of a scene, much as you've been doing already. You can use them to align an audio cue to a video cue (like the sound syncing we did in the preceding chapter). Set a marker to remind you that you need to add an effect later, or replace a shot later, or any number of reasons you find helpful. Maybe place a marker for each beat of a piece of music to cue you where you might place video edits that cut to the music.

Each project or task you use clip markers for creates a visual reference point usually used for some purpose later. In and of themselves they don't really do anything like alter a visual or audio clip, but they give you a "bookmark" of sorts to remind you of something later, or they help you organize your material. They are very helpful indeed, because you can easily and quickly navigate to them, and they serve as a visual reminder of a note you've given yourself.

To set a marker in a clip, press M with the playhead positioned on the frame you want to reference when it's in the Viewer. When the frame is highlighted in the Timeline, or with the Timeline window highlighted, you can create a Timeline marker. You can press M during playback at any speed and set a marker on-the-fly. This might be great for a quick reference to different takes or scenes, or you can mark beats of music on-the-fly. Another way to add markers is with the Add Marker button in the Viewer.

Take a look at Figure 9.1. The Browser contains a copy of the "1 hr timecode section" master clip in the Picture Clips bin. Notice the disclosure triangle next to the master clip. When you activate it by clicking it, it opens much like a bin does, revealing the markers it contains in the Browser.

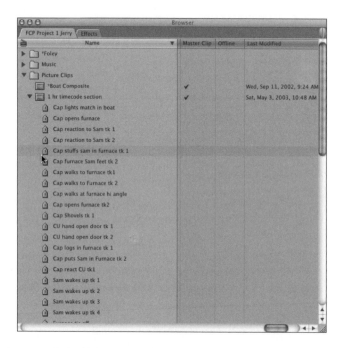

FIGURE 9.1   *Markers revealed within a clip in a bin.*

Figure 9.2 shows these same markers in the scrubber bar. They show you where you have placed the markers along the clip's duration. When the playhead is positioned on the frame you've marked, its name shows up in a box that overlays the picture. During playback, these boxes are invisible, so you needn't remove them if you don't want to.

FIGURE 9.2   *Markers in the Viewer.*

You can rename these markers just as you can any other clip in the Browser. The marker's new name is instantly visible in the Viewer when you are sitting on the frame it references. Unlike clips or subclips, where the timecode they reference is displayed in the Media Start and Media End columns, a marker's timecode position is displayed as an In point in the Browser. You can delete a marker by highlighting it in the Browser and pressing Delete. The keyboard equivalent is Cmd+` when the playhead is parked on the marker and it is highlighted. It changes color when it is an active marker.

To do more than just rename a marker, position the playhead on the marker in the Viewer, and select Mark, Markers, Edit, as shown in Figure 9.3. You also can press M when you are positioned on the marker. The Edit Marker window appears, as shown in Figure 9.4. From here you can change the marker's name and add more information in the Comment box. (This information shows up with the name change in the overlay and in the Name and Master Comment columns in the Browser.) You also can set a duration for the marker so that whenever you are parked on its starting frame or any frame contained in its duration, you see the name and comments you've added in the Viewer or Canvas displayed in its overlay (but only when you are paused).

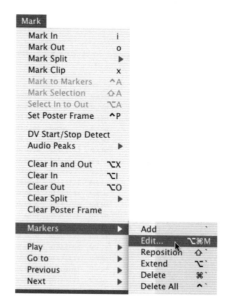

FIGURE 9.3   *The Markers submenu.*

FIGURE 9.4   *The Edit Marker window.*

From Markers submenu you can add, reposition, delete, delete all, extend, and edit.

To reposition a marker, move the playhead to the position you'd like the marker to move to and select Mark, Markers, Reposition. The marker to the left of the playhead moves to the playhead's position. You can only reposition *forward* in time.

You can delete one or all of the markers. To delete one marker, select Mark, Markers, Delete. To delete all of them within the active window, select Mark, Markers, Delete All. You can delete them if you have used them as a reminder, for example, or delete them all because you just can't hit the beat when adding them for music beat notation, and you need a break! When you are active on a marker, it turns yellow in the scrubber bar. By pressing M, you can delete the marker from the information window, or you can delete it by pressing   .

Extending a marker gives it duration. Position the playhead past the marker (later in time) and select Mark, Markers, Extend. This shows an extension of the marker visually in the active window.

Figure 9.5 shows an extended marker whose duration was set by placing the playhead past a marker and choosing Mark, Marker, Extend Marker. When you set a duration with this method or by typing a duration in the marker's Edit Marker window, its Out point is reflected in the Browser, with the addition of its Out point timecode. The name and comment that were entered into the Edit Marker window also are added to the overlay display when you are parked anywhere within this marker's duration.

FIGURE 9.5   *An extended marker in the Viewer.*

Figure 9.6 shows a sequence of a source clip or subclip you have added markers to. When you edit source material that contains markers, the markers are also added to the sequence clip in the Timeline window. The beauty of this is that you can snap to markers. When you do, you can use these markers to set In points or Out points—for a title, for example.

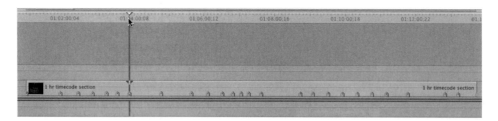

FIGURE 9.6   *Markers contained in a clip in the Timeline. Snapping to markers is a time-saver.*

From the marker's Edit Marker window, you can transform this marker to a chapter marker for use with DVD Studio Pro or iDVD. You can also transform the clip marker into a compression marker in the Edit Marker window. This forces a new MPEG-2 I frame (or keyframe) if you feel this is required, possibly because there is fast action on this frame. Scene changes automatically get "I" frames if you are using the QuickTime encoder, but when you have fast action in the middle of a shot, it's wise to add an I frame or two. This forces the MPEG-2 file you'll create later to record this entire frame, helping the scene play smoother. You can export these types of markers for use in DVD Studio Pro 2.0 or later or iDVD 3 or later by selecting them for export from the QuickTime Movie export dialog box, shown in Figure 9.7. Chapter markers also export to QuickTime movies and become QuickTime chapter markers.

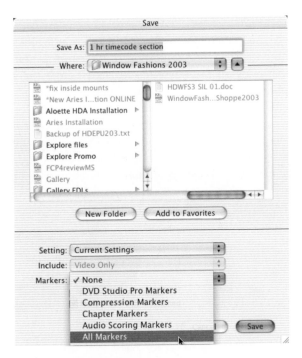

FIGURE 9.7   *Exporting markers in a QuickTime movie export.*

Navigating to Markers

You can navigate to markers in several ways. Select Mark, Markers, Next or Mark, Markers, Previous to jump to a later or earlier marker. You can also press Shift+M to go to the next marker or Opt+M to go to the previous marker. Finally, you can press Shift+up arrow to navigate to a previous marker and Shift+down arrow to navigate to the next marker. You don't have to be sitting on a marker to navigate to the next or previous marker. When you are active on a marker, pressing M opens that marker's Edit Marker window. You can add a marker and open its Edit Marker window by pressing MM.

You can use the scrubber bar in the Viewer or Canvas to click and snap to markers that are in these windows. When navigating to Timeline markers, you can use a context menu as well. See the section "Using Timeline and Canvas Window Markers."

All markers use the same keyboard shortcuts in their respective or active windows. The commands on the Mark, Markers menu work with the active window containing markers, as well as those selected using Mark, Next or Mark, Previous.

Subclips and Markers

Markers can be used much like subclips. Take a look at Figure 9.8. If you double-click the icon for the first marker, the portion of the clip that starts at the first marker's frame and that ends on the frame immediately before the second marker's frame opens in the Viewer. You can edit from this marker's "subclip," and it will act just like any other actual subclip. You can even remove its subclip limits. In the case of the third marker, this extended marker opens a clip in the Viewer whose first frame is that of the position of the third marker and whose Out point is the end of the extension. The next marker's In point is ignored. In other words, extended markers (those with a duration defined by their extension) have a duration of the extension only.

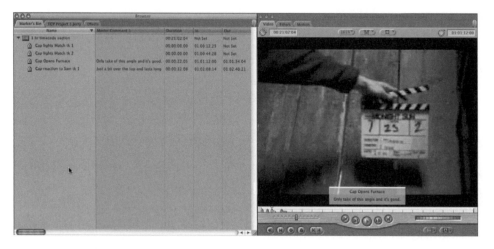

FIGURE 9.8   *Extended and nonextended markers contained in a master clip.*

About the only shortcoming of using markers only for your "subclipping" is that you cannot sort them in the Browser. (You can use the Find function to locate one, but you cannot use the Find All function with them added to the Find Results list.) You can make "true" subclips from markers by highlighting them and selecting Modify, Make Subclip, or press Cmd+U. In this way, you can sort the resulting sub-clips. Another way to turn markers into subclips is to drag them from their bin to the Browser or to a different bin. If you do, though, the markers themselves disappear from the clip they were created in. In either case, you can do this one at a time, or you can highlight as many markers as you want and create subclips from them.

tip

If you set the playhead between two markers in a clip contained in the Viewer, pressing Ctrl+A sets an In point and Out point on the two markers.

Using DV Start/Stop Detection

If you've shot your footage with a DV camera, there is a way to automatically create markers at each point at which you have paused or stopped the camera. In fact, in this way, Final Cut Pro can mark where subclips should be in *entire tapes* automatically. Highlight the clip you've captured from a DV camera master, and select Mark, DV Start/Stop Detection. A marker is placed at each place you've paused or stopped the camera. You can create subclips from them by highlighting them and pressing Cmd+U. A subclip created from a marker starts at a marker's timecode point and ends at the last frame before the next marker's point. If there is no marker past the selected marker, the subclip created from it sets its media Out point to the end of the clip it was contained in.

A caveat should be mentioned here about DV Start/Stop Detection. To have this function work properly when capturing whole tapes, you should not have any timecode breaks on your tape. Appendix A, "Capturing Footage," discusses how to add markers to clips during the logging process.

Final Cut Pro 4 has a new feature: creating new master clips automatically when timecode breaks are encountered during a capture process. You'll find this mode of capturing in the User Preferences in the General tab. You can have FCP create clips in this manner whose timecode is accurate. When this option is selected, a new master clip is created up to the point of the timecode break, and then FCP moves past the timecode break and starts another capture of material. This next clip then is given the same name you chose for the original clip, with a numerical extension added to the name. If the timecode breaks but is numerically higher, only the clip's name is changed. If the timecode is reset to 0, the reel's name is also incremented. This is helpful, because if you need to recapture from the same physical tape, you are cued to position a tape in the next section of possibly identical timecode numbers.

tip
It's best to avoid timecode breaks in the first place. There are two ways to accomplish this with DV cameras. You can "black" a tape (put a lens cap over the lens and record the whole tape this way) before you use it as a shoot tape and create a continuous timecode track in the process. Or you can make sure that each time you powered down the camera between takes, you record the new take just over the end of the last take. You need to cue your camera to make sure that you are recording over previously recorded video. Only a few frames are needed. What happens is that each time most DV cameras sense completely blank tape, they start their timecode numbering over at 0. If previously recorded timecode is read, they continue recording with contiguous numbers. It's probably better to use this method of keeping timecode breaks at bay, because it results in a lot less wear and tear on your camera or deck and the tape itself.

Creating Markers to Mark Beats of Music

Many editors find it effective to cut to the rhythm of the music that accompanies the video. To make this task quick and easy, set markers in the music clip as you listen to it.

1. Play the music clip in the Viewer or Timeline (from the Timeline window markers are added as sequence markers), and get a feel for the beat you want to be able to add a set of markers to.

2. Press the Home key to return to the beginning of the clip. This time, as you play the clip, press M to set markers to the beat of the music (just as if you were tapping your finger on the table when you are listening to music). If you need to reposition a marker to hit a certain beat, you can do so after you've set the first markers. Don't worry about the first pass. You can always delete this first set and try again.

Using Timeline and Canvas Window Markers

Sequence markers can be added with either the Timeline or Canvas window active. When they are added in the Timeline, they appear in green along the ruler, as shown in Figure 9.9. These can be used for anything you want to reference, such as marking music or audio cues, using them as bookmarks for later reference, adding them to force an I frame for an MPEG export to DVD Studio Pro, keeping a note for further editing or adding a title later, exporting to Soundtrack, and so forth.

When adding markers to the sequence, you can Ctrl-click the ruler and quickly jump to any marker by selecting its name from the context menu that appears, as shown in Figure 9.9. You can see the marker's name as long as Clip Overlays is turned on in the Canvas window. You can also press M when a sequence's marker is active to see more information about it in the Comments area of the Edit Marker dialog box.

If you add a marker to the Canvas, it appears in the Canvas window's scrubber bar and in the Timeline's ruler. When a marker is added to the Canvas, its name appears as long as canvas overlay is turned on.

FIGURE 9.9

Sequence markers and context menus.

---

tip

If you Shift-click the Add Marker button in either the Canvas or the Viewer, you can add a marker and at the same time open its Edit Marker window to add more information about this new marker.

Workshop 9: Experiment with Markers

In this workshop you'll experiment and have firsthand experience with the use and functions of markers. Their uses are practically endless. You'll find them to be a real time-saver if you master their uses.

Create an Extended Marker

1. Create a new bin in your Browser called "Marker Bin." Opt-click it to open it with its tab contained in the Browser.

2. Copy (Cmd+C) the "3 hr timecode section" master clip, and paste it (Cmd+V) into the Marker bin. Double-click it to open it in the Viewer. Click its disclosure triangle to reveal the markers you placed in it earlier.

3. Create a new sequence in the Marker bin. Set its settings to be NTSC OfflineRT, and name it "Marker's sequence." Double-click it to open it in the Timeline window, and then drag the entire "3 hr timecode section" master clip into it.

4. Highlight the Viewer (press Cmd+1). Press the Home key to place the playhead in the Viewer at the first marker at the head of the clip, highlighting the first marker as you do this. Press M to open this marker's Edit Marker window.

5. In the Duration box, type **11805** to give this marker a duration of 1:18:05. The colons are added automatically. Click OK. Notice that the marker now has a duration in the Viewer's scrubber bar. It also appears in the clip in the Timeline. In the Browser, it now contains the duration noted in the Duration column.

6. Place the playhead in the Viewer anywhere within the extended marker. Note that its overlay remains visible anywhere within this duration as long as you are not playing the video. Notice too that if you play the video, the marker disappears.

7. Highlight this extended marker in the Browser, and press Cmd+U to create a subclip from it. This subclip will appear in the Marker bin. Note that this subclip has a duration of 1:18:05 and ignores the second marker (this is much different from the behavior you've seen earlier in the book).

8. In the Viewer, press the Home key, and then press M to open this extended marker. Add a comment in the Comment box. Note that this is now a comment in the marker's Master Comment column. Note too that these comments do not come forward into a subclip created from the marker, so if you want to have a comment in the marker's subclip, just type it there instead.

Navigate to Markers and Observe Their Behavior

1. With the Viewer active, press the Home key to put the playhead on the first marker. Press Shift+M repeatedly to navigate to successive markers.

2. Press Opt+M to repeatedly go back to previous markers.

3. Turn on snapping, and click about in the Timeline window to snap to markers contained in the clip there. Notice that clip markers' names don't show up in the Canvas window, nor do they appear in the Canvas scrubber bar. (You probably wouldn't want them to anyway, because they relate to the clip, not the sequence.)

4. In the Viewer, click any marker, and note that you are instantly active on that frame. Pressing M when you are active on a marker's head frame opens its Edit Marker window. Do this to experience the behavior. It's a great way to add information or extend a marker, creating a new duration for it. Try some of these. Press M on an active marker with no duration and give it a duration of any length, even longer than the duration between it and the next marker.

5. When you park the playhead over any part of the extension, the marker's name appears in the Viewer. Only when you are actually parked on the head frame of this marker can you open its Edit Marker window. Therefore, navigating using Shift+M to go to the next marker or Opt+M to go to a previous marker, or clicking a marker in the scrubber bar, are the easiest ways to get there.

6. Create some markers in the Timeline or Canvas window. Navigate to anywhere in the Timeline, and press M without the "3 hr timecode section" clip actively highlighted. Navigate to the markers and rename them. Note that you can change them to be chapter markers or scoring markers by pressing MM to open their Edit Marker window. Try some. When you modify them to be chapter markers, in the Comment box you see <CHAPTER>, as shown in Figure 9.10. If you create a compression marker, you see <COMPRESSION> in the Comment box. If you create a scoring marker, you see <SCORING> there. Note too that you can create *all* of these for the *same marker,* as shown in Figure 9.10.

FIGURE 9.10   *Compression, scoring, and chapter markers displayed in the Edit Marker window.*

> **note**   When you create Timeline markers, and then highlight the sequence you've added them to in the Browser, and then choose Export, For LiveType, they appear in the video track in LiveType. When you export your sequence with scoring markers using the Export, For Soundtrack command, they appear in Soundtrack, giving you a notation where you want to create a special audio event of some sort.

7. Double-click the "3 hr timecode section" clip in the Timeline to open it in the Viewer. Note that the markers you originally put in this clip are displayed in the Viewer.

8. Extend a marker by clicking past the 11th marker (the Dog footage marker) and anywhere near the next marker. Press Opt+` (the ` key is just above the Tab key). Play the footage over this extended marker. It disappears during playback but reappears whenever you stop playback and are still within this extended marker. Note too that this extended marker is not reflected in the Browser clip; it is available only in the sequence clip. This is another instance of nondestructive editing. The sequence clip is not the same object as the Browser clip it came from, but both reference the same media file.

Adding Information to Clips

Whenever you add information about any clip in your project, you are creating a powerful tool. You can use the Find command (Cmd+F) to search for keywords you've used that are contained in any of the columns. Final Cut Pro highlights a clip or marker that contains this keyword. If you are searching through a large project that contains many clips, this is an invaluable way to save a lot of time searching later. Don't forget to use this feature. It's one of the reasons that editing with an NLE such as Final Cut Pro can be a joy rather than a slow and tedious process.

continues

It's simply a matter of entering words that group, delineate, describe, or otherwise allow you to find clips later. Use the Comment columns to find close-ups of everything or the Name columns to sort alphabetically. The uses go on and on. If you make a habit of accurately describing clips with marker or subclip comments, you will save a lot of very tedious searching time. Typing a short description is a lot faster than searching for a specific clip from among hundreds or even thousands. Imagine if you were sorting clips of various types of flower families or bug species. Literally thousands of them could be quickly sorted according to color, genus, or any other search term if these descriptions appeared in the Name or Comment columns of your clips. The name or comment doesn't have to be lengthy, but it does have to be consistent. Use the same words to describe related clips. It then becomes easy to find all "red" flowers, or all "8 legs" of a type of insect, for example.

How about sorting for scene numbers, or names of actors? How about searching for all the comments made at your client's wedding by Aunt Sue so that you can edit them into a montage later? To find each of the clips of Sue, you'd only have to type her name each time she was on camera.

This is one of the difficult and tedious lessons I learned a long time ago. My being able to be this organized and ready to edit and to find clips *extremely* fast has made my clients very happy and *very* impressed.

Observe More Marker Behavior

1. Double-click a number of marker icons in the Browser. As they load into the Viewer, notice that they open into the Viewer with *only* the media between the marker and the next marker in the Viewer window, all ready for you to edit from if you want to.

2. Notice that when you click the Recent Clips button, the *only* "recent clip" is the master clip. This is a possible shortcoming of editing from markers. With the Browser active, press Cmd+F to open the Find dialog box. Search for All Media. In the Results area, choose Add to Find Results. After typing **furnace** or **Cap** in the box next to the Contains selection, you can find the word "furnace" or "Cap" one at a time by clicking Find Next. You can keep pressing Cmd+G to keep finding clips whose name contains the search keyword. If you type **Cap** as the keyword in this dialog box and then click Find All, the master clip with *all* its markers appears in the Find Results window. If you can work with these limitations, there's nothing wrong with editing from these markers and using them as a subclip technique. When you edit from them, they act like any subclip, and they retain their names in the sequence they are added to.

3. Create a comment next to any clip, subclip, or marker in any bin. Give it a meaningful name, and then search for this with the Find command. Imagine using this to find all instances of anything you can think of. Using the power of your computer will make you a much happier and more productive editor.

With the master clip "3 hr timecode section" disclosure triangle closed so that you don't see the markers in the Marker bin, you can also find the specific subclips in the Find Results window. Try finding all clips that contain the word "Cap." You'll see that this works a bit better if you use the Find command to find these true subclips. Save the project file. DV Start/Stop Detection also works much the same. After you highlight a master clip that might contain many different shots, applying this command using the Mark menu creates a complete set of these markers, which you only have to rename. You can make subclips from them the same way.

CHAPTER 10

Putting a Workflow Together

- The Basic Workflow
- The Best Workflow
- Workshop 10: Edit Scene 9

The Basic Workflow

Most of the time, workflow is at least slightly different between one project and the next. Very likely, today's editor is not just doing narrative films, commercials, or corporate videos. Nearly every day a new form of the medium is being used. It's more likely that a successful career is being built around a combination of project types. So the process changes often between one project and the next. Moreover, not everyone's brain works the same way. What seems to be intuitive to one person feels counterproductive to another. Teaching hundreds of different editors over the past few years has opened my eyes to this. This chapter attempts to get you to start working the way that makes the most sense to *you*. It's far more important to finish a project that is successfully completed on time and that meets its goals than it is to use a certain method (or even software application) to get there.

When you are editing with any nonlinear editor, there are definite similarities between projects. You acquire the footage first, bring it into your computer using various methods, and then edit it, refine it, and deliver it. Some projects have all the source material ready to edit, and some do not. This is the beauty of a nonlinear editor. It doesn't matter in what order you edit each scene, and it doesn't matter that you have all the source footage or material at one time. Especially when you work with feature film, rarely is all the film shot before the editor starts working.

Feature film scripts typically are not shot in chronological order. The editor's job in these instances is to work on the material as it is shot. Probably never does this process begin with the editor working on Scene 1 first, and then Scene 2, and so forth. In the case of this book, you were given all the material you would edit into a movie up front. This is one reason I chose to edit it in script order. This is definitely not the case with not only feature films, but also documentaries, and even corporate or commercial work. Sometimes it's best to edit certain areas of a show before you shoot other areas, just to see how this next shoot needs to be performed, for example. Remember that there are no rules.

The Best Workflow

There isn't one. There's not a *right* or *wrong* way to work with Final Cut Pro. There's *your* way. As you've already seen, Final Cut Pro offers many different ways to accomplish the same task. For example, you can get source material that is contained in the Browser to your sequence in at least five different ways!

- Drag the clip directly from the Browser to the sequence in the Timeline window.
- Drag the clip from the Browser to the Viewer, (optionally) mark In and Out points, drag the clip to the Canvas overlay, and insert or overwrite it to the track of your choice.
- Drag the clip from the Viewer directly to the Timeline.
- Double-click the clip in the Browser, (optionally) mark In and Out points, and press one of the F9–F12 keyboard keys to place the clip in your sequence.
- Press Cmd+4 to make the Browser active. Use the up and down arrow keys in combination with the Enter key to open bins or load clips into the Viewer. (Optionally) create In and Out points. Press Cmd+2 or Cmd+3 to highlight the Canvas or the Timeline. Use the J, K, and L keys to navigate to an In point, and press one of the function keys to place the clip where you want it. This method does not use the mouse at all.

Any of these methods gets material from the Browser to the sequence. There are even more ways this single task can be described and achieved, and there are just as many ways to trim, add effects, navigate windows, or accomplish any other task you might need to perform.

One thing is certain, though. As you get your footage together, organization is key. The first thing you need to do is create bins and clips that are organized in such a way that you can find the source material quickly. Then the process of putting the material into a sequence can begin more efficiently. The biggest time-waster is looking for clips in poorly organized bins or, even worse, no bin structures and no organization at all. If you don't have a lot of clips, this really isn't a problem, but if you do, a very tedious edit session is in store for you.

Following that, the process you use to get those clips into your sequence can and should be *your own*. I find that double-clicking a clip to open it in the Viewer, marking an In and Out point, and then dragging the clip from the Viewer to the Timeline is the most intuitive method for me most of the time. Sometimes I'll even put the clip on a higher video track to hold it there for a moment until I drag it into a position between clips. There are even times that I'll grab a section of clips in the Timeline I've already edited, put them later in the sequence, overwrite a clip or set of clips into the blank area of the sequence, and then pull the moved clips back. There's nothing wrong with this. It might not be the quickest way, but for me, this particular edit just feels right. This might feel totally wrong for you, though, and I'm not here to tell you that there is only one way to do anything. I don't think I ever lock tracks so that I can't make a mistake with them. This would be heresy from another editor's point of view.

Some editors like to use keyboard commands for everything. I find this somehow less intuitive than a combination of techniques that at times uses the mouse. Some editors *never* use keyboard commands and *always* use the mouse to edit. With the addition of the button bars in FCP 4, I think this will become more and more common. It's probably slower, but it makes more sense for some people, and it's better than not having your source material organized. I seem to use a combination of mouse and keyboard; I find that most editors do. You'll know you've begun to arrive at your particular "best" workflow when you are editing with confidence and not making too many undos!

As you begin to learn Final Cut Pro, you will discover keyboard shortcuts or some other form of working with the software, such as using the Find command or sorting columns in the Browser, that eases your particular brand of editing.

Whenever I've watched other editors using the same application, they all seem to use a combination of the mouse and keyboard, but each seems to have his or her own method of accomplishing the same task. There's nothing wrong with using different methods to do the same task, but it could be argued that fewer mouse moves and keyboard commands to accomplish the same task is better.

The reasoning is that once you've made a mental edit decision, you want to preview it as fast as you can or trim it as fast as you can so that the time you spend working on a given project is allocated more to previewing *edit decisions* and not actually getting you and the computer to perform the edit. Spend your allotted time working with the material; don't spend it just getting a particular task done. The more time you spend previewing different approaches to the same project or scene, the better the edit, communication, or achievement of the project's goal.

In my experience, I've never sat back and said, "No matter how much more time I spend with this project, I can't improve it anymore." There's always just one more change that might improve things. You as an editor usually have an allotted amount of time to finish the project, and you are also the *last* person in the process: The project is written, and then shot, and *lastly* edited. It's the editor who is up against the wall in the process. Unfortunately, it's also the editor who sometimes has to fix it in post. You're up against a release date, a trade show, or an airtime for an ad campaign. Don't make your significant other an "editor's widow or widower." You have to have a life. Philip Hodgetts said, "An edit is never finished, only abandoned when the editor runs out of time." How true that is.

I find that completing a rough cut of the entire sequence serves me well. It gives me a feeling for the timing, pacing, and placement of scenes. Whether I'm working on a narrative, training, or marketing film, knowing where I need to get to helps. It also apprises me of what is yet to be done. Sometimes, when watching the first cut, I place markers in areas that need further refinement or make notes that shots are missing or need to be shot. Then I start over at the head of the program and start refining as I take another pass at it. I repeat this process until I'm out of time or am satisfied that it's ready to show a client. Changes are almost always made after a client sees the program for the first time, and the process continues to evolve.

Think about this. How many ways can a movie or program be edited? Let's do the math. Assume that you have 10 hours of useable source footage. If there are 30 frames of video per second (in NTSC video—the numbers for PAL would be different), that's 1,080,000 unique frames. You could cut on any of these frames, right? The number of possible combinations of edits is astronomical. But let's assume that there are just 100 video edits. The number of *possible* different combinations of edits based on a unique In point and Out point is then 1,080,000 to the 100th power times 2!

Of course, this is an extreme example bordering on the ridiculous, because I'll wager that 99% or more of the *possible* combinations of edits could be discarded out of hand. However, this makes the point that there *must* be more than one way to edit any particular project, and you will never have enough time to try them *all*. If you spent your entire lifetime working on this single project, you still wouldn't have enough time to preview them all.

That said, it is important to voice a point of view held by many an experienced editor. If you are faster with your editing system, you will create more time to try all the what-ifs I mentioned early on. It takes much longer to use a menu command than it does to use its keyboard shortcut. Over time, these little moments begin to mount up. So learning and using the keyboard commands makes you work faster with Final Cut Pro and creates more time to be, well, creative. In most professional jobs, you have a certain allotted time to finish, and it's far better to try more ways of telling your story than to wait on your physical movements to get to those "trial" edits. Each time you access a menu command that takes you 3 or 4 seconds, that's 3 or 4 seconds lost to mechanics, and therefore less time for creativity.

Discovering shorter and quicker ways to accomplish the same task takes time. Very few editors learn to master *any* NLE in a short amount of time. Probably six months of working 40 hours a week with any given editing software is sufficient time to master it. Final Cut Pro was designed to accommodate many different ways to accomplish the same thing so that many different sensibilities or practical situations can be catered to. You'll know that you are approaching proficiency when you don't even think about how to perform a task, and more and more of your time is being spent thinking about different edit decisions to make your program more effective.

The bottom line is that the best way for you to approach the workflow of editing your material is only limited by your imagination. The beauty of a nonlinear editor is that you can edit in any way that makes sense to you. If you like the idea of working in a linear fashion, (much like you've been editing while working with this book), you can. If your sensibility is that you want to work on different areas in the order of your choice, you can do that too. It might make sense to edit the climax of your story so that you can see where you are headed before you choose the path to get there, for example.

Techniques You Should Use

There are some habitual techniques in your workflow you should always use. One usually begins after the first or second cut of the material. When these early cuts are done, to get the most effective rhythm for your piece, you need to watch it beginning to end with fresh eyes (this is no easy task). It's also beneficial to view your project in the format in which it will be delivered. If it will be shown on a 70-foot movie screen, this might not be practical, but it's best to see it as close as you can to the final format.

You'll be surprised when you see your project in a large format. (My students are amazed the first time they see their films projected on a large screen.) I think it's because your brain doesn't always take in what you thought it would. Your film looks quite different on a wide screen than it does on your computer's display. You need to take into account this difference when you are editing for a format other than the 5- or 6-inch Canvas you are using for your edit decisions.

It's also wise to show your film to people who haven't seen it to *truly* have a fresh set of eyes watch it. *Your piece must stand by itself.* Giving any information about what the story is about will taint reactions, so avoid it. Don't tell them anything about the piece up front, other than its title and that it's a rough cut. They'll understand that they aren't looking at a finished movie and will forgive a lot of blemishes such as color timing or audio level problems. Watch them as they watch the movie, and see where interest lags or confusion arises. After your friends have viewed this early cut, ask them what they think, and ask them to be brutally honest.

You'll find that perhaps there are areas they don't understand. Remember, *you* know the material very well, and you even have a script with off-camera notations in front of you. Just because *you* get it doesn't mean that they will. The whole point of communication through storytelling is to be understood and to move your audience emotionally, keeping their involvement. If you don't accomplish this, the audience will be off to the popcorn stand, thinking about their troubles, or just sitting there feeling uninvolved. They *certainly* won't be motivated to buy your product, right?

I'll give you an example. In the middle of "The Midnight Sun," when it was first cut, I didn't put in the very quick shot of Cap pulling out the gun. Some first-time viewers thought he *ate* the dogs! Once the gun was shown, this reaction went away. Wrong reactions like this can really minimize the story. He loved the dogs too much to let them suffer from starvation, so he shot them. This was the real story I wanted to depict. If the audience thought he ate the dogs, they would lose some of their identification with Cap. Thus, the tension in the final scene would be lost, and the audience might lose their emotional reactions, all for the want of a single 2½-second shot.

You can't pace an entire movie very well without *seeing* the entire movie. You won't know that a scene is too fast or too slow without watching the whole film end to end. You might be watching the movie when a scene comes along that slows down the story. Or you might find some frames of a single shot that just don't need to be there. Today's "sound bite MTV" audience wants information fast and direct. If you want success, keep them involved. These same statements hold true for any piece you might be working on, including a training film or a documentary. It just doesn't pay to bore or confuse your audience when the goal is to communicate something to them. The more emotionally involved the audience becomes, the more likely you'll achieve the goal you set out to achieve.

Starting a scene with a long beauty shot of the location is OK, but repeating it at the end of the scene is boring. We've seen it already; we don't need the same information over and over. Keep your story in action. Never slow it down with superfluous shots that *you* might like just because they are pretty. Don't show us material we don't need to see, and don't forget to show us information we *must* have in order to understand what's going on. Cut when the information has been given about that shot and only when more information can be gleaned from the incoming shot.

If a scene drags, shorten it. If a scene is too fast and thus confusing, lengthen it; rewrite it with pictures and sound to make it clearer. It takes time to learn how to "forget" what you know about the story, but you must strive to gain this invaluable asset and constantly look at your project with fresh eyes, as if you know *nothing* about it and are seeing it for the *first time every time you watch it*. Remember that cuts are faster, and transitional effects tend to slow things down. And now for the biggie....

Don't involve your viewers in *anything* that doesn't move the story forward. Keep it coming at a crisp pace so that they don't have time to think about the popcorn stand. Don't show them the mundane. If a character says he needs to go to the grocery store, it's totally unimportant to show him getting into his car, turning the key, backing out of driveway, and so on. It's usually better to just cut to the moment that the character enters the store if what happens there moves the story forward and is an integral part of the story. *Never bore your audience with material that they can easily just assume happened.* Just because it was shot doesn't mean it needs to be there. Cut out the ordinary; give us the extraordinary. Also refrain from showing us mistakes. If it doesn't work exactly right, don't show it to us. The audience will never know you made a mistake if you don't show it. The moment you think they won't notice, trust me, they will. If you see an error, so will they.

When editing narrative film, most editors cut the audio first, just letting the picture fall where it may in sync with the sound, and changing it after the pacing has been set by the audio. The beauty of nonlinear editing is that you can change things at will anywhere and at any time during the process. If you need to add time in the audio track later for a reaction shot, it's not a problem. That's what insert editing was made for.

If you're stuck, and you aren't happy with the way a scene or moment is going, *move on*. Leaving it for another time will give you time to think, and many times it will dawn on you later how to approach a section of your piece. You'll be amazed how difficult it is to make wise decisions at the end of the day when you're tired. The next morning, that same scene will just fall into place. Trust me—you work better and smarter when you are rested and have taken a break from the work physically and mentally.

tip

Every day you spend editing without backing up the project file *away from your computer's hard drives* is a day closer to disaster. If your hard drive takes a dive, you can lose all your work to date. Imagine a feature edit you spent six months or more working on. Or a documentary that's been in post for two years! Losing a hard drive certainly doesn't happen often, but you should count on it happening, because it *does*. CD-Rs are probably the best way to handle this. You can always recapture the footage automatically if it has time-code associated with it. If it doesn't, such as VHS or graphics files, dub the VHS first to a format that does handle timecode, make copies of any other computer-generated media, and keep them in a different place from your editing bay. This should be part of your daily routine.

Minimize the Rendering; Maximize the Editing Time

When you are working on a program that involves a lot of rendering of effects or corrections, wait until the end to render them as much as you can. Put proxies in place of effects that you eventually need to perform to get the timing of your whole piece down first. Why render things that won't be used? Of course, this isn't always possible, but minimize rendering as much as you can.

Final Cut Pro 4 comes to the rescue here for a lot of situations with RT Extreme, but you'll still have times when you need to render if you are working on complicated effects, as you will in upcoming chapters. Do it at lunch, or at breaks, or overnight instead of during the precious time when you are fresh and are more effective creatively. Watching the render bar isn't my idea of a good time. Always save the project before rendering. I've seen machines crash during a long render, and thus lose work. What if the power goes out?

You can cancel rendering at any time too. Final Cut Pro saves what was rendered so far and commences rendering from where it left off. Turn on rendering automatically, just in case you forget to start the process manually and have taken a two-hour lunch.

Color correction should usually occur late in the process. Why work on color when you aren't sure that the shot will be used? Audio sweetening sound that ends up being cut is a big time-waster as well. Manage your time effectively by rendering at times away from the computer whenever you can. It will serve your edit well because you won't be using your allotted time on renders you don't end up using, and you won't waste your fresh and rested self on watching the render bar. Computers don't get tired, but you do.

A last word here about this book. In no way was this movie edited in the order the book has followed. So the linear fashion that is used here isn't the best way to edit the film. Rather, I found this linear approach to be the most effective way to teach the software.

A Change of Pace: Accenting the Horror Editorially

The following scene you'll edit in this chapter's workshop starts with a montage of shots where Cap tears up the floorboards and builds a fire. Its form is similar to that used when Cap has to kill his dogs rather than let them starve. There's one exception to the series of cuts, though. It's the dissolve used between the two shots of Cap as he loads wood and then uses the shovel in the furnace. In this case, I used it because the two shots might have appeared mismatched in action. A dissolve lets the viewer know it's later in time, so it's OK that Cap suddenly has a shovel in his hands.

We quickly go outside with Cap to wait while Sam's body burns, building some tension (that's Sam's body burning; the smoke is what's left of Sam). Then, to create even more tension, the pace of the next set of shots is the quickest in the film. Cutting back and forth between Cap approaching the hot furnace and the furnace itself creates tension. Faster cuts reflect nervousness, heightened fear, or even terror. They always reflect a fast heartbeat. Whenever you have to do something you really don't want to, or are afraid of, doesn't time seem like it will *never* pass? (How about the dentist's chair while he shoots you up with painkiller?) Every moment feels like an eternity. The technique used to create this horrific, can't-get-it-over-with-quickly-enough moment is intercutting between Cap's POV (point of view) of the furnace and the furnace's POV of Cap as he creeps toward it.

Keeping the moment feeling even longer, and extending the tension, the furnace never gets closer. Cap moves, but the furnace does not. The idea here is to convey the feeling that Cap doesn't want to open it. The moment of moving toward what Cap thinks might be a grisly sight (and hopefully the audience thinks this as well) doesn't come quickly or easily. The shots of Cap finally opening the door extend this tension even further. Will we *ever* get to see what's inside? The intercutting just reflects Cap's own feelings of trepidation. Then, instead of seeing what's in the furnace, we see Cap's reaction to it *first,* the paramount moment of horror, accented with a surging music cue. Hopefully, the audience will close their eyes in fear of seeing too much gore or something. It's just another way to add to the story. Cut the scene to *reflect the feelings of the character* we now know and hopefully are identifying with and feeling emotionally involved with and care about. The creepy music helps here too; pay attention to it and its accents. Each moment of this scene was thought about moment by moment to set up the surprise.

When we suddenly see Sam happily sitting up in the fire, the shock and surprise are complete. Once the film's "punch line" is over, it's best to get out of the movie quickly. We do so with only two more shots past the end of Sam's move to close the door: a shot of Cap's confused reaction, accenting the fun, and, of course, the shot of Cap as he "walks off into the sunset." It's an appropriate ending to a classic American tale.

Workshop 10: Edit Scene 9

This workshop first has you create and organize the Scene 9 bin, and then you'll edit Scene 9. Hopefully, you'll begin to find the workflow that works best for you. Rather than prompt your every move, I'll leave much of this up to you. Begin to experiment with different ways of editing the footage into the sequence, finding what makes the most sense to you (and at the same time gives you more practice with the everyday, every-edit situations you'll find yourself in).

Create and Organize Scene 9

1. Create a new bin, and name it Scene 9. Double-click it to open it in its own window, because you will drag subclips from the Picture Clips bin to it.

2. Open the Picture Clips bin, and reveal the markers in the "1 hr timecode section" clip.

3. Create subclips from the first 25 markers, from "Cap lights match in boat" through "Sam wakes up tie off tk 2." Highlight them, press Cmd+U, and drag them all to the Scene 9 bin.

4. Open the "3 hr timecode section" clip to reveal its markers. Create subclips of the last three markers and the "Cap looks at smoke tk 1" marker. Drag these new subclips to the Scene 9 bin. When you are done, your Scene 9 bin should look like Figure 10.1.

Name	Duration
Cap furnace Sam feet tk 2 from '1 hr timecode section' Subclip	00:00:10:07
Cap lights match in boat from '1 hr timecode section' Subclip	00:00:16:19
Cap logs in furnace tk 1 from '1 hr timecode section' Subclip	00:00:21:03
Cap looks at smoke tk 1 from '3 hr timecode section' Subclip	00:00:16:07
Cap opens furnace from '1 hr timecode section' Subclip	00:00:08:08
Cap opens furnace tk2 from '1 hr timecode section' Subclip	00:00:24:04
Cap puts Sam in Furnace tk 2 from '1 hr timecode section' Subclip	00:00:06:14
Cap react CU tk1 from '1 hr timecode section' Subclip	00:00:21:23
Cap reaction to Sam tk 1 from '1 hr timecode section' Subclip	00:00:24:23
Cap reaction to Sam tk 2 from '1 hr timecode section' Subclip	00:00:23:26
Cap Rips boards tk 1 from '1 hr timecode section' Subclip	00:00:02:00
Cap Shovels tk 1 from '1 hr timecode section' Subclip	00:00:10:22
Cap stuffs sam in furnace tk 1 from '1 hr timecode section' Subclip	00:00:19:11
Cap walks at furnace hi angle from '1 hr timecode section' Subclip	00:00:28:20
Cap walks away LS from '3 hr timecode section' Subclip	00:02:57:21
Cap walks to Furnace tk 2 from '1 hr timecode section' Subclip	00:00:51:28
Cap walks to furnace tk1 from '1 hr timecode section' Subclip	00:00:55:01
CU hand open door tk 1 from '1 hr timecode section' Subclip	00:00:14:05
CU hand open door tk 2 from '1 hr timecode section' Subclip	00:00:12:29
Furnace fire Tie off from '1 hr timecode section' Subclip	00:01:03:13
Furnace tie off from '1 hr timecode section' Subclip	00:00:25:01
Sam wakes up tie off tk 1 from '1 hr timecode section' Subclip	00:00:21:26
Sam wakes up tie off tk 2 from '1 hr timecode section' Subclip	00:00:32:24
Sam wakes up tk 1 from '1 hr timecode section' Subclip	00:00:25:12
Sam wakes up tk 2 from '1 hr timecode section' Subclip	00:00:24:05
Sam wakes up tk 3 from '1 hr timecode section' Subclip	00:00:25:13
Sam wakes up tk 4 from '1 hr timecode section' Subclip	00:00:24:25
Smoke bkg 1 from '3 hr timecode section' Subclip	00:00:15:03
Smoke coming from behind hill from '3 hr timecode section' Subclip	00:00:15:10

FIGURE 10.1   *The Scene 9 bin after step 4.*

Begin Editing Scene 9

1. Following Table 10.1, edit the beginning of Scene 9 (using any set of commands you want, trimming it any way you want, and so on). Begin to develop your own workflow, but don't vary from the finished video, or you will have problems later finishing the movie. Practice using the Find command, the trimming methods you've learned by dragging the whole clip from the Scene 9 bin to the Timeline (or the Viewer) and then trimming it there, marking In and Out points, and so on. Don't be afraid to try different methods of achieving the same results. You'll find

your way of editing during this workshop. Do what makes the most sense to you. But end up with the shots as they are listed, or your sound sync will not work. Also, the rest of the instructions are dependent on your placing the edits as I edited them. This workshop is designed to make you comfortable and faster. You can be as creative as you want later, because you are more than welcome to do your own edit of this movie. Everything that was shot for it is included on the DVD.

Table 10.1   On the V1 Track from the Scene 9 Bin

Clip	In Point	Out Point	Sequence In Point
Cap lights match in boat	01:00:48:05	01:01:04:23	01:09:21;24
Cap opens furnace	01:01:18:06	01:01:26:13	01:09:38;12
Cap Rips boards tk 1	01:10:34:18	01:10:36:01	01:09:46;20
Cap puts Sam in Furnace tk 2	01:07:22:23	01:07:27:28	01:09:48;04
Cap Rips boards tk 1	01:10:50:22	01:10:52:21	01:09:53;10
Cap puts Sam in Furnace tk 2	01:07:28:20	01:07:33:11	01:09:55;10
Cap shovels tk 1	01:05:51:01	01:05:54:17	01:10:00;02
Cap puts Sam in Furnace tk 2	01:07:51:29	01:07:55:05	01:10:03;19
Cap Shovels tk 1	01:05:54:20	01:06:05:11	01:10:06;26
Cap puts Sam in Furnace tk 2	01:07:04:17	01:07:11:00	01:10:17;18
Cap furnace Sam feet tk 2	01:02:56:07	01:03:06:13	01:10:24;02

After you've finished, you can check the timecode of each new clip in the sequence by selecting Overlays and Timecode Overlays to be turned on from the Canvas's View pop-up menu, as shown in Figure 10.2. Take a look at Figure 10.3. It's what you would see if you navigated in Sequence 1 to 01:02:21;21. In the Video Overlay is the *source* timecode of this point, and in the Audio Overlay, you see the audio timecode on all tracks that contain audio. Use this to check that you have followed along. If you go to the first frame of any given edit, this view allows you to double-check that you've done the edit as the lesson calls for it. The sequence timecode is in the upper right of the window, and the source timecode that is contained at this point is displayed as well. If things aren't working right, you can check for mistakes in this manner.

FIGURE 10.2 *The Canvas View pop-up menu.*

FIGURE 10.3 *Timecode overlays at 01:02:21;21 in Sequence 1.*

For example, take a look at Figure 10.4. This is the correct information you should see at the first frame of the "Cap furnace Sam feet tk 2" edit. Notice the gray-green L indicator in the Canvas window in the lower-left corner of the picture. It indicates that you are sitting on the first frame of a video clip, which would be how you'd check this particular edit. When you are done checking your edits, the Timeline looks like Figure 10.5.

FIGURE 10.4   *The correct view of the first frame of the "Cap furnace Sam feet tk 2" edit.*

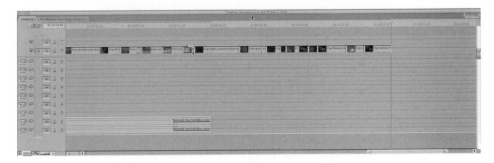

FIGURE 10.5   *The Timeline after step 1.*

2. Add a 45-frame fade-up at the beginning of the "Cap lights match in boat" clip to come out of the black. Use the Pen tool on the clip opacity overlay. Add a 30-frame centered cross-dissolve between the "Cap puts Sam in furnace tk 2" edit and the "Cap Shovels tk 1zz" clip at 01:10:00;02 in the sequence.

Add Audio to Scene 9

1. It's time to add some audio to this sequence. As you did earlier, use Tables 10.2 and 10.3 to add the audio clips. Save your project often!

Table 10.2   On the A1 Track from the Voice Overs Bin (Leave Them All at 0dB)

Audio Clip (No Level Change)	In Point	Out Point	Sequence In Point
DANCLEAN.AIF-23	00:00:00:00	00:00:04:16	01:09:53;16
DANCLEAN.AIF-25	00:00:00:00	00:00:04:15	01:09:58;16
DANCLEAN.AIF-27	00:00:00:00	00:00:03:09	01:10:03;12
DANCLEAN.AIF-28	00:00:00:00	00:00:03:24	01:10:06;28
DANCLEAN.AIF-29	00:00:00:00	00:00:06:19	01:10:24;00

Table 10.3   On the A2 and/or A3 Tracks from the *Foley and Sound Clips Bins; in the Case of Clips with Only One Track, Use Track 3

Audio Clip and Level	In Point	Out Point	Sequence In Point
Stove, wood burning Cast 46_1-01 +9dB	00:00:00:00	00:00:00:08	01:09:31;08
Telephone,antique Pick 29_5-01 –12dB	00:00:00:00	00:00:00:04	01:09:35;16
Footsteps,creaky flr 42_1-28 –7dB	00:00:00:00	00:00:01:27	01:09:36;18
Footsteps,creaky flr 42_2-02 –4dB	00:00:00:00	00:00:00:09	01:09:38;26
Metal,squeak Large ship 38_2-01 –4dB	00:00:00:00	00:00:01:18	01:09:41;12

Audio Clip and Level	In Point	Out Point	Sequence In Point
Footsteps,creaky flr 42_2-02 0dB	00:00:00:00	00:00:00:09	01:09:47;10
Construction,nail 14_2-04 0dB	00:00:00:00	00:00:00:09	01:09:47;25
Construction,nail 14_2-05 0dB	00:00:00:00	00:00:00:06	01:09:48;05
Fire,fireplace Moving 10_1 +5dB	00:00:01:15	00:00:02:17	01:09:51;02
Squeak,wood Short wood 13_5 -010dB	00:00:00:00	00:00:01:22	01:09:53;05
Snap,wood Wood break95_2-01 −12dB	00:00:00:00	00:00:00:12	01:09:54;28
Fire,fireplace Moving 10_1 +2dB	00:00:01:15	00:00:02:17	01:09:57;17
Fire,fireplace Moving 10_1 +2dB	00:00:02:17	00:00:03:14	01:09:59;04
Foley 1-Cap'n Shovel Ship#1-01 On Track 2 +12dB	00:00:02:19	00:00:10:03	01:10:00;19
Foley 1-Cap'n Shovel Ship#2 On Track 3 +10dB	00:00:02:13	00:00:09:02	01:10:00;24
Footsteps,creaky flr 42_2-14 0dB	00:00:00:00	00:00:02:23	01:10:15;20
Foley 1-Cap'n Body Ship#1	00:00:05:10	00:00:15:26	01:10:18;15

continues

Table 10.3   On the A2 and/or A3 Tracks from the *Foley and Sound Clips Bins; in the Case of Clips with Only One Track, Use Track 3

Audio Clip and Level	In Point	Out Point	Sequence In Point
Twice on Tracks 2 and 3 +12dB on both!			
Explosions Small, fiery 1_4-01 –4dB	00:00:00:00	00:00:01:15	01:10:30;15
Door,metal Furnace door 15_3-01 +2dB	00:00:00:00	00:00:00:22	01:10:32;19

Notice how the scene begins to come alive as you add voice-overs and sound effects. If you want to change the mix, do so and experiment with how it affects the feeling of the scene.

At the end of this step, your sequence should look like Figure 10.6.

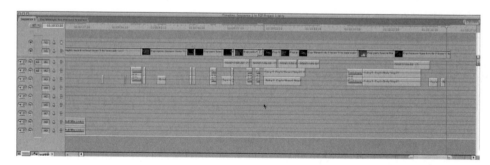

FIGURE 10.6   *The Timeline after you add the first audio clips to Scene 9.*

   2. Edit the rest of the audio for the first part of this scene on the tracks specified in Table 10.4. You'll use six different tracks. The music is in the Music bin, and the effect is in the Sound Clips bin.

Table 10.4   Audio Edits First of Scene 9

Audio Clip and Level	In Point	Out Point	Sequence In Point
Music-Net116.2-08 (the whole clip) Tracks 6 and 7 –4dB	00:00:00:00	00:00:59:00	01:09:28;11

Audio Clip and Level	In Point	Out Point	Sequence In Point
Fire,fireplace Wood 6_1-01 (the whole clip) Tracks 4 and 5 −4dB	00:00:00:00	00:00:46:28	01:09:46;22
Music-Net116.2-09 Tracks 8 and 9 0dB	00:00:04:20	00:00:19:19	01:10:26;15

Where the two music tracks cross over each other, fade out the outgoing clip "Music-Net116.2-08" as the incoming clip "Music-Net116.2-09" fades in, as shown in Figure 10.7, in the clip overlays using keyframes. This is a way to cross-fade. As tracks 6 and 7 fade out, tracks 8 and 9 fade in. This is an *audio loop*. Because the first clip of music is a little short, just repeating a section of it works great to fill out this section of the scene. It takes a bit of practice to learn to do this consistently, but matching beats and looping near musical phrases often works to create a longer length to your music beds.

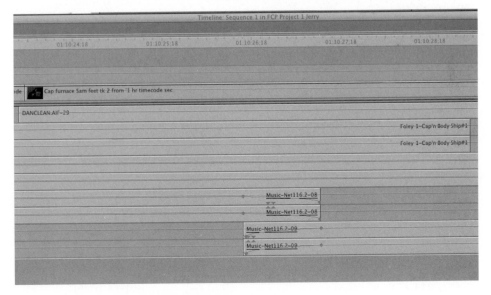

FIGURE 10.7 *Cross-fading the music tracks.*

Continue Editing Scene 9

1. You're in the home stretch. Hang in there and finish! Try using the recent clips list (at the bottom of Viewer window) to pull up repeated clips when you can. Add the clips listed in Table 10.5.

Table 10.5   On the V1 Track from the Scene 9 Bin

Clip	In Point	Out Point	Sequence In Point
Cap looks at smoke tk 1	03:13:31:09	03:13:33:09	01:10:34;09
Smoke bkg 1	03:14:18:24	03:14:22:03	01:10:36;10
Cap looks at smoke tk 1	03:13:33:24	03:13:35:09	01:10:39;20
Cap walks to furnace tk 1	01:03:16:06	01:03:25:22	01:10:41;06
Cap walks to Furnace tk 2	01:04:08:16	01:04:10:09	01:10:50;23
Furnace tie off	01:10:09:13	01:10:11:05	01:10:52;17
Cap walks to furnace tk 1	01:03:33:19	01:03:37:07	01:10:54;10
Furnace tie off	01:10:11:28	01:10:13:09	01:10:57;29
Cap walks to furnace tk 1	01:03:47:03	01:03:50:15	01:10:59;11
Furnace tie off	01:10:20:13	01:10:21:27	01:11:02;26
Cap walks to Furnace tk 2	01:04:48:18	01:04:49:13	01:11:04;11
Furnace tie off	01:10:19:29	01:10:20:27	01:11:05;07
Cap walks at furnace hi angle	01:05:10:12	01:05:12:12	01:11:06;06
Cap walks to Furnace tk 2	01:04:51:08	01:04:52:05	01:11:08;07
CU hand open door tk 2	01:06:27:04	01:06:28:24	01:11:09;05
Cap react CU tk 1	1:08:08:28	1:08:11;02	1:11:10;26
Cap walks at furnace hi angle	01:05:21:06	01:05:23:00	1:11:13;01
Cap react CU tk 1	01:08:12:25	01:08:15:00	01:11:14;26

Clip	In Point	Out Point	Sequence In Point
Sam wakes up tk 4	01:09:44:12	001:09:53:23	01:11:17;02
Cap react CU tk1	01:08:17:09	01:08:20:17	01:11:26;14
Sam wakes up tie off tk 2	01:12:51:27	01:12:53:17	01:11:29;23
Cap reaction to Sam tk 2	01:02:17:12	01:02:28:22	01:11:31;14
Cap walks away LS	03:15:06:24	03:15:32:24	01:11:41;25

Explain Time in the Scene with Dissolves

1. Place a 1-second cross-dissolve between the clip "Cap furnace Sam feet tk 2" and "Cap looks at smoke tk 1." The reasoning here is that this is a different time *and* *place*. The jump cuts, like the previous ones, indicate a jump in time, but they are in the same place (inside the boat). Here, the audience is told that we've gone even more forward in time—and furthermore, to a different place (*outside* the boat).

2. Place another 1-second cross-dissolve after "Cap looks at smoke tk 1" as it cuts to "Cap walks to furnace tk 1." This allows for the time and space lost while Cap walked outside for a bit and watched the smoke.

3. At 01:11:41;25 in the sequence, create a 2-second cross-dissolve between the interior of the boat as Cap leaves and the long shot of him walking away to cover the time missing. A longer dissolve is used to begin the final shot and slow the pacing back down. It's a nice way to slow the pacing down to match the upcoming title sequence.

4. At 01:12:05;21 in the sequence, place a key frame in the "Cap walks away LS" shot in the clip overlay in the Timeline window. Then, at the end of the shot, place another keyframe and drag it to 0. This accomplishes the fade-out at the end of the sequence.

   When you are done with this portion of the video edit, this area of the sequence should resemble Figure 10.8.

FIGURE 10.8   *The sequence after step 4.*

Add the Voice-Over Clips

1. Open the Voice Overs bin and arrange it so that you can quickly access its contents. Remember that you can click the green expansion button to open it and click the button again to put it back into its original position. Add the clips listed in Table 10.6.

Table 10.6   On the A1 Track from the Voice Overs Bin (Raising Levels Where Noted)

Clip	In Point	Out Point	Sequence In Point
DANCLEAN.AIF-33	00:00:00:00	00:00:04:14	01:10:34;21
DANCLEAN.AIF-34	00:00:00:00	00:00:05:15	01:10:39;15
DANCLEAN.AIF-35	00:00:00:00	00:00:05:06	01:10:47;22
DANCLEAN.AIF-37	00:00:00:00	00:00:06:19	01:11:42;11
DANCLEAN.AIF-39 +5dB	00:00:00:00	00:00:05:21	01:11:49;10
DANCLEAN.AIF-41 +5dB	00:00:00:00	00:00:03:00	01:11:55;13
DANCLEAN.AIF-42 +5dB	00:00:00:00	00:00:11:25	01:11:58;27

2. At 01:11:46;12 in the sequence, place a keyframe in the A1 "DANCLEAN.AIF-37" clip in the level overlay in the Timeline. Eight frames later, set another one and raise it to 7dB to quickly raise the level in the middle of the clip. The actor's level drops off in the recording, so you add the keyframes to keep a consistent level. It's easiest to zoom in on this area of the sequence to do this. You might want to double-click this audio clip and do it between 00:00:04:00 and 00:00:04:08, as shown in Figure 10.9.

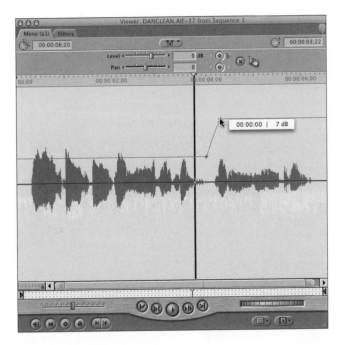

FIGURE 10.9   *Raising audio levels midway through the "DANCLEAN.AIF-37" clip.*

Add Sound Effects and Music to the Scene

1. Open the Sound Clips bin and arrange it so that you can quickly access it. Then add the clips that are listed in Table 10.7.

Table 10.7   On the A2 and/or A3 Tracks from the Sound Clips Bin
(Note the Audio Levels)

Clip	In Point	Out Point	Sequence In Point
Telephone,antique Pick 29_5-01 Track A3 −12dB	00:00:00:00	00:00:00:04	01:10:50;09
Footsteps,creaky flr 42_1-28 Tracks A2 and A3 −12dB	00:00:00:00	00:00:01:10	01:10:54;10

continues

Table 10.7   continued

Clip	In Point	Out Point	Sequence In Point
Footsteps,creaky flr 42_1-28 Tracks A2 and A3 0dB	00:00:00:00	00:00:01:27	01:10:55;21
Footsteps,creaky flr 42_2-24 Tracks A2 and A3 0dB	00:00:00:00	00:00:03:17	01:10:58;04
Footsteps,creaky flr 42_2-02 Tracks A2 and A3 0dB	00:00:00:00	00:00:00:09	01:11:01;24
Footsteps,creaky flr 42_2-24 Tracks A2 and A3 0dB	00:00:00:20	00:00:02:08	01:11:05;15
Footsteps,creaky flr 42_2-04 Tracks A2 and A3 0dB	00:00:00:00	00:00:01:00	01:11:07;04
Footsteps,creaky flr 42_2-07 Tracks A2 and A3 0dB	00:00:00:00	00:00:01:04	01:11:08;10
Stove,wood burning Cast 47_1-01 Track A3 0dB	00:00:00:00	00:00:00:16	01:11:10;09
B-Last Poem Clean Track A3 0dB	00:00:00:00	00:00:12:11	01:11:17;24
Metal,squeak Large ship 38_2-01 Track A2 0dB	00:00:00:00	00:00:01:18	01:11:30;13

Clip	In Point	Out Point	Sequence In Point
Doors,Elevators, Squeaks,51_1-01 Track A2 0dB	00:00:00:00	00:00:03:17	01:11:32;06
Wind,desert Lonely,66_1-01 Tracks A2 and A3 +10dB	00:00:00:00	00:00:29:28	01:11:40;25

2. In this last wind clip, fade it up at its beginning for 2 seconds (so that it fades with the dissolve). Then, at its tail, start a fade 5 seconds and five frames before its end, so that it starts with the "Cap walks away LS" fade and ends with the end of the "DANCLEAN.AIF-42" clip on the A1 track. The sound fades out with the picture and leaves a softer end to the scene, suggestive of the walk off in the distance. After this step, the sequence should look like Figure 10.10.

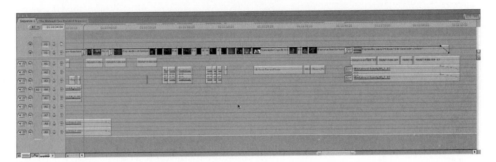

Figure 10.10   *The sequence after step 2.*

Add the Final Set of Sound Effects and Music

1. Locate the Music bin and the Sound Clips bin and have them ready. Then add the clips that are listed in Table 10.8.

Table 10.8   On the A4 Through A9 Tracks from the Sound Clips Bin
(Note the Audio Levels)

Clip	In Point	Out Point	Sequence In Point
Fire,fireplace Wood 6_1-02 Tracks A4 and A5 –8dB	00:00:00:00	00:00:20:29	01:10:41;06
Fire,fireplace Wood 6_1-03 Tracks A4 and A5 –8dB	00:00:00:00	00:00:30:12	01:11:02;08
Fire,fireplace Wood 6_1-04 Tracks A4 and A5 –8dB	00:00:00:00	00:00:10:14	01:11:32;21
Music-Net1 16.2-14 Tracks A6 and A7 0dB	00:00:02:14	00:00:37:01	01:10:41;05
Music-Net1 16.2-27 Tracks A8 and A9 –1dB	00:00:03:29	00:00:10:10	01:11:10;26
Music-Net1 16.2-26 Tracks A8 and A9 +4dB	00:00:00:00	00:00:01:25	01:11:17;08
Music-Net1 16.2-40 Tracks A6 and A7 0dB	00:00:00:00	00:00:12:20	01:11:18;17
Music-Net 126.7-03 Tracks A6 and A7 –5dB	00:00:00:00	00:00:30:07	01:11:35;22

2. In the "Music-Net116.2-14" clip (Tracks A6 and A7), fade up for 15 frames at its head to ease its entrance. Use keyframes in the clip's overlay.

3. At 01:11:10;26 in the sequence, place a keyframe in the "Fire, fireplace Wood 6_1-03" clip's level overlay line. At 01:11:11;04, place another. Move the position indicator to 01:11:14;14, and place another keyframe. At 01:11:14;26, place the

fourth keyframe, all in the "Fire, fireplace Wood 6_1-03" clip. With the Selection tool activated, drag the center of the line between the four keyframes to raise the level to +7dB. This way, as Cap is looking inside the furnace, the sound of the fire goes up.

4. Fade up (on the beginning) for 1 second and out (at the end) for 1 second on the "Music-Net116.2-40" clip with keyframes in the clip's level overlay line.

5. In the "Music-Net126.7-03" clip (Tracks A6 and A7), at 01:11:39;28 in the sequence, add a keyframe. In the same clip, add another at 01:11:42;11. Lower this second keyframe to −12dB to accommodate the voice-over. Because this is a stereo pair, you need to add a keyframe in only one track to automatically add it to the other.

6. At 01:12:01;22 in the sequence, place a keyframe in the "Music-Net126.7-03" clip (Tracks A6 and A7). At 01:12:05;14, place another in it, and lower this to -infinity dB. Even if a bit of audio is left in the Timeline past the -infinity keyframe, you won't hear it. Notice that you drop the music completely before Cap says, "I cremated Sam McGee." *Not* having this Irish jig playing punches up this last line, which also is accentuated because it's mostly said over black. Sometimes less is more.

When you are done, the last half of Scene 9 should look like Figure 10.11.

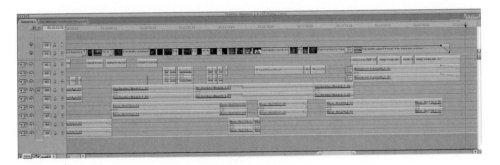

FIGURE 10.11   *The last half of Scene 9 after step 6.*

This Workshop took a lot of concentration on your part. No less concentration should be used when you are editing your programs. This craft and art form requires concentration. When you are properly concentrating, time flies!

If you want to, you might try your own edit of this movie, because all the source footage shot is included on the DVD. Try different takes; tell the story as you would tell it. See just how creative you can get. Enjoy the art form.

CHAPTER 11

Video Filter Effects and Basic Compositing

- Effects Editing
- Composites and Renders
- Video Filters
- Using the Video Scopes and Color-Correction Tools
- Real-Time Previewing
- Workshop 11: Work with Composites

Effects Editing

In this chapter, you will begin to investigate special effects that can be applied to your video clips. Many effects are available, but this book can't cover them all. In fact, there are so many, you'd need a set of books just to work with each of them and combinations of them. (You'll find more detailed information in Appendix F, "Video Filters List.") Using effects properly is possibly the most complicated area of Final Cut Pro or any NLE, but they are not in any way impossible to master. However, it can be said that it takes a special and different set of skills to effectively work with them.

It also can be argued that there are better programs than those contained in *any* NLE to achieve the best results for the effect you're after. However, Final Cut Pro gives you many fine tools to work with, and you could spend years honing the art and craft of using them effectively. Just take a look at the number of credits in a Hollywood big-budget feature such as *Star Wars* or *Titanic* given to the effects artists. Chances are with big-budget effects films like these, the larger part of the entire production crew is, in one way or another, a part of the effects team.

Just a few years ago, doing what you can do now with Final Cut Pro would have cost hundreds of thousands of dollars. Isn't technology great?

Composites and Renders

Whenever you combine more than one image to create a single image, you are *compositing*. You can composite a title over a background, for example. You can combine two or more images in any number of ways to create a composite of all of them.

A *render file* is a single composited or filtered video or audio file. It's a *separate* media file made from the originals, which stay untouched. In this way, Final Cut Pro does not change the original capture. Instead, it creates a new media file that is a combination of your original images, or a single image or audio file with a filter applied to it. The faster your computer is, the less time it takes to render this new file. With the advent of FCP 4's new rendering engine, RT Extreme, extremely fast computer setups might not need to render at all to record the video back to tape. Some capture cards, such as Pinnacle's Cinewave system or AJA's SD capture card, allow for real-time playback of some composites or affected clips.

If you are working in DV, however, you can gain more real-time effects capability with a faster computer by using FCP 4's real-time rendering capabilities. Audio effects real-time playback has been greatly improved in FCP 4.

Renders are stored in one of two folders on your scratch disk. *Audio renders* (such as those with effect filters added to them) are stored in a folder named Audio Render Files, created when you select a scratch disk for your media file storage. *Video renders* are stored in a separate folder named Render Files. In each of these folders is another set of folders that are automatically given the same name as the project they are associated with. Each time you create a new rendered file, it is placed in this folder named for the project files you created it in. If you select a hard disk as your scratch disk, both folders are created on the top of that disk's hierarchy. This allows Final Cut Pro to keep you organized.

> **tip**
>
> I recommend selecting a *disk* as a scratch disk rather than selecting a folder. A scratch disk then contains only three folders on the top of its folder hierarchy. Within each is a folder containing specific projects' captures, audio renders, and video renders. It's easy to find your renders and captures if you do things this way. Final Cut Pro organizes this set of project-named folders for you automatically.

To help you understand what you might have to render, Final Cut Pro provides a visual clue as to a clip's render status. Colored render status bars are contained in the Timeline window directly above the clip they relate to, as shown in Figure 11.1.

Figure 11.1 *Colored render status bars in the Timeline.*

There are two rows of bars. The upper bar reports the status of the video clips it is over, and the lower bar reports the status of the audio clips it is over. The following list describes the bars' meanings. Depending on the color, you might or might not have to render the items beneath the render bar.

- Dark gray—No rendering is needed.
- Blue-gray—The clip has been rendered, and a render cache file will be played back.
- Red—Sections of the Timeline contain audio items that cannot play in real time and that must be rendered. You hear beeps when audio cannot be played in real time. Red can also be present over video sections that cannot be played in real time and that must be rendered.
- Dark green—Shows a real-time effect you've added that doesn't need rendering and that should play back in full quality.
- Green—The shot or audio will play back in real time on your computer's display. If you have a third-party capture card or a fast-enough computer, this effect plays in lower quality without having to be rendered. You would want to render this kind of file to deliver your final master.
- Yellow—The clip will play without rendering but is a proxy of what has been affected. In other words, you see some of the effects you've applied to the medium, or an approximation of the effects parameter you changed. When you pause over one of these frames, however, you see the full effect you've applied. Rendering this sort of material also is done before you deliver your final master. In all cases, a rendered version of the effect plays back in high quality with all the parameters you've modified.
- Dark yellow—A rendered effect rendered at a lower frame rate or quality than the currently selected frame rate or quality, as set in the Render Control tab of the Sequence Settings. Render files are preserved even if these settings are changed back to 100 percent.
- Orange—When you've set your computer to play back unlimited real-time effects and there are effects that exceed your computer's ability to play back reliably, they are indicated with an orange line over them. Unlimited real-time playback lets you play more effects but increases the chances that your sequence will drop frames during playback. You will find this mode effective in allowing you to see a preview of your effect, even though it might not play back without dropping frames.

- Blue—One or more unsupported real-time enabler files are installed. Blue render bars indicate areas of real-time playback that might drop frames as a result.

Effects rendering is controlled from three submenus on the Sequence menu. These settings relate to and are governed by the settings you've made in the Render Control tab contained in the Sequence Settings window, which control the quality and speed of the render files you create. If you lower the quality of the files, for example, a *proxy* file is created. You need to rerender in a high-quality setting before you finish, but using these proxy files while working speeds up your rendering time.

The first submenu's name changes according to what you have selected in your sequence for rendering. If a range of clips is selected, this submenu is called Render Selection. If an In point and Out point are selected, this submenu is called Render In to Out. If nothing is selected in the Timeline window, this menu says Render.

This menu controls a selection of a clip or set of clips you've chosen in the Timeline window to render. If you select Both (press Cmd+R), you render both the audio and video regions of your selection. If you select Video or Audio, only the video or audio is rendered. Figure 11.2 shows check marks next to the various colored bars in this menu. By checking on the options of the red or other colored status bars you see over your selection, you can choose what will and won't be rendered. Only clips with checked status bars are rendered. You might want to render only effects you cannot play back in real time (the red bar), for example.

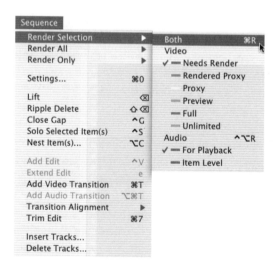

FIGURE 11.2   *The Rendering status bar.*

The second rendering submenu is Render All. The only difference between this submenu and the first one is that it is what you select when you want to render the entire sequence, not just a selection.

The last submenu is Render Only. It operates on a selected set of clips or on an entire sequence if no selection is made. There is a notable difference between this submenu and the first two. It contains the Mixdown command for audio. This command takes all your audio tracks and mixes them into a single stereo file, making playback easier for your computer to perform, because it doesn't have to find all the different audio clips you might be working with and mix them for you in real time. This might give you a better playback of real-time video effects if you mix down your audio tracks, for example.

New to FCP 4 is the Item Level option, found on the Render menus in the Audio area. If you choose item-level rendering, any audio with a different kHz setting (such as most CD music) is rendered or *up-converted* to the kHz setting your sequence contains. Most DV audio, for example, is recorded and set up to be edited in a 48kHz sequence. If you add CD audio to the mix, it typically is recorded at 41.1kHz. Selecting item-level rendering of audio resamples this audio to match the sampling rate of your sequence setting.

If you'll recall, you can listen to 41.1kHz audio in a 48kHz sequence in real time, but you might have problems if you set your audio playback quality to High in the User Preferences. You could set this to a lower quality to give your computer an easier time with the up conversion it does without rendering. If you perform item-level rendering, though, it is mixed in High quality no matter what you've set the audio playback quality to be.

To create a render file so that you can see specific effects play back, first highlight the clip or set of clips you want to render. Press Cmd+R, or select Sequence, Render Selection, and select the appropriate command from there. Keep in mind that only the status bars you selected from the menu will be rendered.

You can also select Sequence, Render All or press Opt+R. All the clips in the entire sequence whose status is checked on in the Render All submenu start rendering. In this case, you create a separate render file for each clip that needs one in your current sequence. When you start a render, the status bar keeps you informed of its progress, as shown in Figure 11.3.

FIGURE 11.3 *The Writing Video status bar.*

Some of these renders might be visual effects created by adding a filter to your clip. An example of a filter is a color correction or a blur (sort of like a defocus). Video filters differ from transitions in that they affect the whole clip or a selected part of a clip rather than combine an outgoing clip with an incoming clip (such as cross-dissolves, which are actually *composites* of the two images for the duration of the transition).

Video Filters

You can add a *video filter,* such as a color correction, to any video clip. If you add them to clips in the Viewer before they have been edited into your sequence, they are added to the sequence as you edit the clips that contain them. Be careful when doing things this way, though. What if you don't want the effect each time you use material from that clip? As soon as a filter is added to a clip that was opened from the Browser to the Viewer, it is attached to the clip in the Browser. Each time you edit that clip into a sequence later, it gets effects added to it. It is usually best to add effects to clips after you've edited them into your sequence. In reality, as soon as a clip is in a sequence, it is not the same reference clip or Browser clip it came from. Instead, it is another reference clip to the original medium. You can think of it as a copy of the original reference clip that might still reside in the Browser. These clips in a sequence are sequence clips, and those in the Browser are Browser clips. They might reference the same medium, but they are not the same object.

After they are rendered, though, they can be moved from sequence to sequence, or elsewhere in the current sequence. They maintain the link to their rendered files as long as you don't put them over another clip or affected clip that asks FCP to rerender them. An example of this is a picture-in-picture effect, where you move just the video of the picture clip that has been resized and rendered over one background and then copy it to another location with a new background. In this case, you'd have to rerender.

Unlike Avid's NLEs, Final Cut Pro always goes back to the original files to create new rendered files, keeping the highest quality possible, because FCP doesn't use already-rendered files to source in its rendering process. This could cause a lower-quality render, so FCP avoids using renders of rendered effects.

There can be some definite advantages to adding a filter to a clip in the Browser before you edit it into a sequence. One is that a color-correction filter needs to be added to any instance of certain clips. This way, you will have that correction already there and used if needed. Adding a second filter to an individual use of it is still possible after that instance of the clip is edited into your sequence.

Filters are usually applied to clips already edited into your sequence. As you work with them, you can see the results of your changes as you make them in the Canvas window as long as the position indicator in the Canvas or Timeline is parked over the clip you are affecting. The same can be said of altering some titles, as discussed in the next chapter.

There are three general areas of use for video filters:

- Enhance image quality—You can adjust a clip's image quality, such as color balance, brightness, contrast, and color saturation. You might need to correct a shot that is too dark or too light or that was shot with the wrong color temperature or white balance. You might need to match the look of one shot to the next, especially if the lighting changed. You can also stylize the look of the clips in your project.

- Generate visual effects—You can use filters to create sophisticated visual effects. You can apply and combine these filters to create effects such as spinning your clip in simulated 3D space, blurring, pond ripples, or flopping a clip's picture.

- Produce transparency effects and combine images—You can use filters to produce and control alpha channel information for clips in your project. An *alpha channel* is a mask between an image and its background. It determines an image's opacity. It may be completely opaque, which shows the foreground image, or completely transparent, which allows a background to show through. It can even be partially transparent. The keying filters create alpha channels based on white, black, and any specified color areas of the image. When you create an alpha channel, the Viewer window displays the transparent areas with a checkerboard background, as shown in Figure 11.4.

You can select the representation of the transparency in other ways. You can select View, Channels. You can also change the background display from the default checkerboard using the pop-up View menu in the Viewer. The list of background displays for transparency includes two checkerboard displays, white and black.

Other filters allow you to further manipulate the areas of transparency in a keyed clip, expanding, contracting, and feathering the area of transparency to fine-tune the effect. Other filters generate a new alpha channel based on simple geometric shapes or apply an alpha channel from one clip to another.

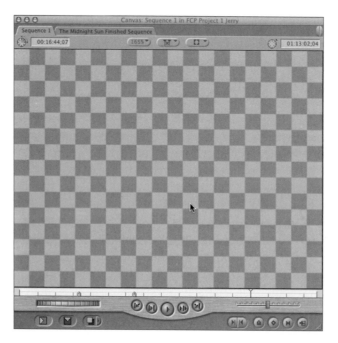

FIGURE 11.4 *An alpha channel displayed as a checkerboard pattern.*

Adding Video Filters to Clips

You can add as many filters as you like to a clip; the order in which they're applied determines the final result. For example, if you add a Gaussian blur to a clip and then add a border, you see something like Figure 11.5. If you apply the border first and then the blur effect, the result in the Canvas looks like Figure 11.6. In this case, because the border was added before the blur, the blur affects the border as well as the picture. Pay close attention to this fact. Final Cut Pro renders in the order you specify by putting the effect you want to be first at the top of multiple effects applied to the same clip. So FCP adds each effect to the clip with all the earlier effects already applied. If you nest clips, the effects applied inside the nest are addressed before those added to the nested clip. Nests and nesting are explained more in Chapter 13, "Working with Advanced Composites, Nests, and Exported QuickTime Movies."

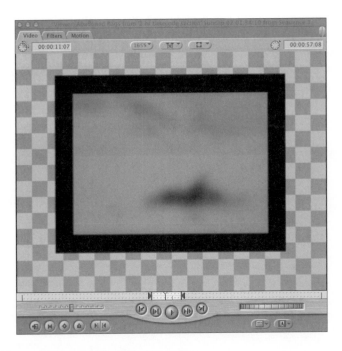

Figure 11.5   *A blur and then a border added to a clip.*

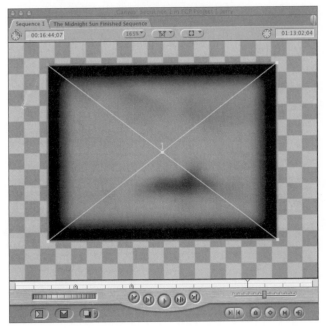

Figure 11.6   *A border and then a blur added to a clip. Notice that the border is blurred as well.*

To add a filter to a video clip in your sequence, double-click the clip in the Timeline window to open it in the Viewer. Select Effects, Video Filters and then the filter of your choice, as shown in Figure 11.7. Much like adding audio filters, you adjust a video filter from the Filters tab in the Viewer. You can also apply a filter directly to the clip in the Timeline by highlighting it and making your selection. However, you still have to double-click that clip to make any adjustments to it, because they are done from the Filters tab of the Viewer window *after* you've added them.

FIGURE 11.7   *Adding a video filter from the Effects menu.*

You can also add a filter to a clip by dragging it from the Effects tab listing in the Browser window. They are listed there just as the audio effects are.

Using the Viewer's Filters Tab

Each filter has its own set of controls, but some are common to all of them. They are shown in Figure 11.8 and described in the following list.

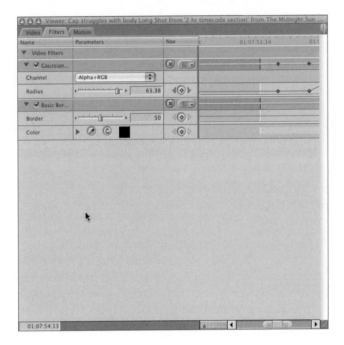

FIGURE 11.8   *The Viewer Filters tab with two filters applied to the same video clip.*

- Filter category bar—Video filters appear at the top of the Filters tab and audio filters at the bottom if the clip contains both audio and video. Click the Video Filters disclosure triangle or the Audio Filters disclosure triangle to select all the filters in that category.

- Name bar—Each filter has a name bar with a disclosure triangle next to it. By clicking the disclosure triangle, you can access the filter's controls. There is also a check box to turn the filter off and on for a before-and-after preview. If it is left off, the filter is not be rendered. You can drag the filter's name to move it up or down the list.

- Keyframe graph—The keyframe graph shows all the overlays and keyframes associated with each parameter displayed in the Viewer. Think of this as a sort of Timeline that shows the duration of the clip as it is in your sequence if you have double-clicked the clip from the Timeline. Each parameter has a sort of "mini-Timeline" associated with it.

- Filter start and end points—If a filter is applied to part of a clip, filter start and end points appear in the clip's keyframe graph area. Notice the start and end points in the filter shown in Figure 11.8. To apply a filter to part of a clip in a sequence, do the following:

  1. Select the Range Selection tool in the Tools Palette (or press GGG).

  2. Drag across the part of the clip you want to affect in the Timeline.

  3. Apply the desired filter to the highlighted portion of the clip. Double-click the clip to open it in the Viewer to further refine the filter.

note   You can also use keyframes to accomplish the same result. This is especially useful when you add multiple filters within one clip that might not start or end at the same time.

- Parameter controls—Each filter has its own set of parameter controls. Different filters have different controls. See the later section "Using Video Filters" for more information about each filter.

- Keyframe button—The keyframe button places a keyframe on the corresponding overlay at the playhead position in the keyframe graph. You need two of them to create an effect to change over time, much like a fade-out or fade-up of audio or video you've been doing in the Timeline window's clip overlays. When you are active on a keyframe, the keyframe button lights up with a green indicator. Clicking it again removes the active keyframe.

- Keyframe navigation buttons—These buttons navigate the playhead from one keyframe to the next on the corresponding overlay. They are the arrows on either side of the keyframe button.

- Reset button—This button deletes all keyframes for the corresponding parameter or parameters. It also resets those parameters to their original or default value.

- Keyframe graph ruler—The keyframe graph ruler corresponds to either the clip's duration or location in a sequence:

  If a clip is opened in the Viewer from the Browser, the keyframe ruler shows the clip's duration. The playhead in the Viewer window does not follow the movement of the playhead in the Timeline or Canvas window.

  If a clip is opened in the Viewer from a sequence in the Timeline, the keyframe ruler shows the section of the Timeline that the clip is edited into. The playhead in the Viewer window follows the movement of the playhead in the Timeline or Canvas window.

- Zoom control—This control zooms in and out on the duration displayed on the ruler in the keyframe graph area, expanding and contracting the keyframe graph ruler much the same way it does in the Timeline window. The zoom keyboard shortcuts, Cmd++ and Cmd+-, center the view on the playhead's position when zooming in or out. The Zoom tool from the Tools Palette also works like it does in the Timeline window. Wherever you click on the keyframe graph with it active, you either zoom in or zoom out of the position you click. Also, if the Filters tab is the active window, pressing Shift+Z automatically fills the available space with the clip's duration, as displayed in the keyframe graph.

- Zoom slider—The Zoom slider zooms in and out of the duration displayed in the keyframe graph ruler. It too works much the same as this control does in the Timeline window. Dragging a thumb tab at either end zooms in or out, moving the visible area in the direction you drag. Shift-dragging a thumb tab zooms both tabs and leaves the visible area centered. After you've set up the size of the keyframe graph you want to see, dragging the center of the slider to the left or right scrolls through the keyframe graph.

- Timecode navigation field—This field displays the position of the playhead in the keyframe graph area. Entering a new timecode number moves the playhead to that time within your clip.

- Section of clip not currently used—These are the frames of the clip displayed in the Viewer's Filters tab that are outside the duration set by its In and Out points. They are darker gray than the part in use. You'll want to set your keyframes within the lighter gray area, because this is what will be seen in your sequence.

Using the Clip Keyframe Area of the Timeline Window to Adjust Filters

New to FCP 4, you can adjust filters right in the Timeline window. Take a look at Figure 11.9. Here, I've added a Gaussian Blur filter to the clip displayed. Note that you can change its radius. First you click the clip's keyframe button in the lower-left corner of the Timeline window. Then you Ctrl-click the area that opens to display the context menu shown in Figure 11.9. You also can adjust the parameters set by the Motion tab using this pop-up menu, whether or not a filter has been added. If multiple filters are added to a clip, they all are listed in this pop-up menu. You see a submenu when you click a filter in this list, or a motion parameter opens so that you can select a single parameter to adjust.

After you've selected a parameter to adjust, a thin line appears. The line is green if you're adjusting a filter, as shown in Figure 11.10, and blue if it's a motion effect. You can add keyframes to change a parameter's values over time as well, much like you have been doing with the opacity overlay in the Timeline's clips to fade in and out of black. Figure 11.10 shows the blur's radius changing over time. Ctrl-clicking a keyframe (like the third one in the figure) smoothes the filters with a bezier curve that you can change to have the effect change in a nonlinear way. Experimenting with this is the best way to see the results of using a smoothed keyframe.

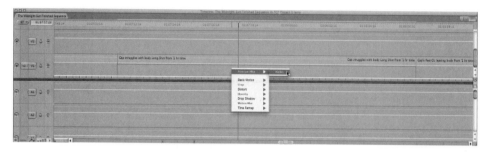

FIGURE 11.9   *A Gaussian Blur's Radius parameter is accessed from the context menu in the Timeline's Clip Keyframe area.*

FIGURE 11.10   *A thin line appears so that you can set a value, or you can add keyframes to change these values over time.*

Notice in Figure 11.11 that the keyframes added to the parameter in the Timeline are also reflected in the Filters tab. The keyframe indicators show up at the top of the Filters tab and also in the colored line above the parameter you adjusted. Often you'll have more than one parameter start or stop an effect at the same time, so having these keyframe indicators in the bolder line above them helps you navigate to where you've set earlier keyframes. Pressing Shift+K or Opt+K moves the playhead from keyframe to keyframe, much like Shift+M and Opt+M navigate to the next or previous marker.

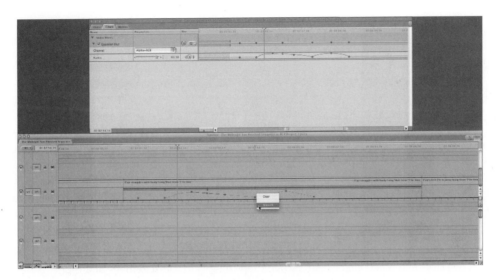

FIGURE 11.11 *Keyframes in the Timeline's Clip Keyframe area.*

Using the clip keyframes in the Timeline allows you to quickly navigate from parameter to parameter and also from filter to filter or motion effect.

Using Video Filters

Final Cut Pro includes many video filters, grouped into 11 categories.

The following is a discussion of the effects used in this chapter's workshop. Appendix F lists all the effects and their functions. Rather than sorting through them all now, use Appendix F to learn them as you need to know them.

The more interesting uses of these effects might come from changing them over time. That is, you can animate them from one setting to another using keyframes in the corresponding keyframe graphs to the right of each control. Some of these filters can be used on single tracks of video, such as those that affect color. Others are meant to be used to composite more than one clip. In the case of composites, the clips must be edited on different video tracks directly above one another. The clip on the bottom track becomes a background to the clips layered above it, the topmost clip is in front of those below it, and so forth. Also be aware that you can change the exact placement of the clips. In other words, you might run across effects where the first layer starts before the second layer, such as a ghost appearing over the background after the background shot begins. Clips might not be the exact same duration, but they still have to be placed one on top of the other.

Use Effects to Tell More of the Story

I've already discussed using transitional effects and how they enhance and affect the storytelling process. Using a dissolve to transport the viewer later in time or location is an example of this. Filters and composites can have the same general use. They can enhance the story and should reflect a mood. They also can be used as transitional effects, such as simulating a rack focus, increasingly blurring to the end of a shot, cutting to another blur at the beginning of the incoming shot, and then reducing the blur to the focused shot. The use of filters and video effects is endless. They can create composites that are impossible or impractical to shoot, such as the landing of a spaceship.

Filters and video effects can also be used to reflect the excitement of a moment—especially in music videos. But they should be limited to enhancing or telling more about the moment in the story and painting another brush stroke. They shouldn't be used to the extent that they take precedence over the story. New editors have a tendency to overuse them. Resist the temptation to use an effect that does not add to the story. Cheesy video effects only make the product, the information, and the story just that—cheesy. Just because you *can* use them doesn't mean you *should*. Typically, less is more. For every edit decision you make, ask yourself whether it enhances this moment in the story appropriately. If it doesn't, *don't do it or use it*. It will only get in the way and become what the audience pays attention to, taking them out of the ether you want to keep them in.

The Video Filters Used in "The Midnight Sun"

Four different filters are used in this chapter's workshop. This section describes these filters and their uses, as well as details of their particular controls.

Blur filters defocus or blur your video in various ways. Used to the extreme, they can create an interesting smear of color and shape that you might use as a background for a bulleted list or other title.

You might also want to use Blur filters in conjunction with other filters, such as a Four- or Eight-Point Garbage Matte filter (discussed later in this section) to hide a person's identity, for example. In this case, you'd put identical clips on top of each other, apply the blur to the lower clip, and use the garbage matte to reveal only the area you want to blur on the upper clip (see Figures 11.12 and 11.13).

FIGURE 11.12   *Gaussian Blur controls: Cap's shot out of focus on V1.*

FIGURE 11.13   *A Garbage Matte applied to a duplicate clip on V2.*

What's happening is that you cut a hole in the upper clip to reveal only a portion of the blurred lower clip. The hole cut is an alpha track added to Cap's face. You see a checkerboard pattern to let you know it's there. An Eight-Point Garbage Matte with smooth edges was applied to create the alpha track. It looks seamless until the person moves. At that point, you need to place a new set of keyframed positions of the Eight-Point Garbage Matte to track the person's movements. First you outline the move's beginning frame, and then you outline the move's ending frame. The blurred part of the image changes its position over time. If the matte move needs refining, you add keyframes for the matte's position between the starting and ending move, for example.

A Gaussian Blur defocuses the whole frame of a clip's video. The pop-up menu allows you to choose which channel to blur, as shown in Figure 11.12. You can blur one or all of the color and alpha channels together or separately, creating a different look to the blur. A radius slider allows you to select how much to blur the clip. The more you move the slider to the right, the more radical the blur. Setting a keyframe at 0 and then setting one later in your clip at a higher level creates the illusion of a rack focus, for example. This one is probably the most used of the group of Blur filters.

Matte filters can be used by themselves to create alpha channel information for a clip to composite it against other layers to mask areas of a clip. Matte filters can also be used to make further adjustments to layers with keying filters applied to them. For example, you might need to create a matte to recover areas of an image that are keyed out by a chroma key because they match the background key color, such as a blue tie on a person who is being keyed over a blue background. In this case, you'd put a duplicate of the clip on top of the keyed clip and use a matte to cover the blue tie area that's being keyed out with the same footage above it with a matte applied to it.

The Eight-Point Garbage Matte, shown in Figure 11.13, generates an eight-point mask that you can use to crop out areas of a clip. Eight-point controls allow you to draw this matte. When you click one of the crosshairs in the filter's controls, the Selection tool changes into a crosshair. You use it to create a new position for one of the eight points by clicking a new area of the picture in the Canvas window. The Smooth slider rounds off the shape's corners to create rounder mattes, the Choke slider allows you to expand or contract the matte in its entirety, and the Feather slider allows you to soften and blur the edges. The Invert check box reverses what's matted and what's transparent. The Hide Labels check box hides the number labels, which indicate which point of the matte corresponds to which filter point control.

Various third-party plugins can be added to Final Cut Pro to give you more than just four or eight points to map complex matte shapes. See `http://www.chv-plugins.com/`, `http://www.scriptgeek.netfirms.com/` (this one has links to all sorts of free plugin filters), `http://www.artmetic.com/plugins/`, and `http://www.cgm-online.com/`.

Video filters are generally used to create more "functional" effects to clips in your sequence, such as a timecode print, although this category includes design-oriented filters as well.

Image Stabilizer stabilizes motion in a handheld or shaky clip. In most cases, you can do an effective job with shots that should have been stable in the first place or handheld shots that are just a bit shaky. The Source pop-up menu, shown in Figure 11.14, allows you to view the clip before and after image stabilization has been applied. The Center control allows you to select a particular element in your video clip to use as the target for stabilization. The selected target should be a high-contrast element with a clearly defined shape, such as the sign in Figure 11.14. The Scan Range slider allows you to define the area of your clip that will be analyzed to track the motion of the selected target. Clips with greater motion should use a larger scan range; clips with more subtle motion can use a smaller one. The Show Scan Area check box toggles the stabilization target box on and off.

FIGURE 11.14 *Using the Image Stabilizer.*

Using the Video Scopes and Color-Correction Tools

It takes a collection of controls and measuring tools to accurately measure and work with a shot's color correction. Final Cut Pro 4 gives you a set of very sophisticated tools to do the job.

These tools let you assess and control the brightness and color levels of your clips in preparation for output to tape. These tools include the Tool Bench window with the Video Scopes tab, new range-checking options in the Viewer and Canvas, and all-new color-correction filters.

You can use these tools to balance the shots in a scene to match, keep your video broadcast legal, correct for errors made during the production process, and achieve a new look for your program. You can even create special effects with them, such as a day-for-night look, or give a scene a warmer or colder feel just by manipulating filters.

Using the Tool Bench Window, Frame Viewer, and Video Scopes

You open the Tool Bench window by selecting Tools, Video Scopes or by pressing Opt+9. My favorite way to open it is by selecting Window, Arrange, Color Correction, because this automatically resizes the windows so that you can see the Viewer, Canvas, and Tool Bench windows, including the new Frame Viewer. They are all neatly arranged across the top of your computer's display. See Figures 11.15, 11.16, and 11.17.

tip

The color range displayed on a video monitor is much narrower than what can be displayed on a computer. Colors that appear vivid and clean on NTSC or PAL video can look dull when viewed on your computer's display. Resist the temptation to overcorrect for this. Perform color correction while viewing your output on an NTSC or PAL monitor only. Otherwise, you won't really know how the corrections you're making will look on your finished tape. You might accidentally oversaturate your image, causing bleeding into other areas of the frame and a color range that is too "hot" for broadcast. The range-checking tools are great for this, but never assume that what you see on your computer's display is how it will look in the end on TV or on a video monitor.

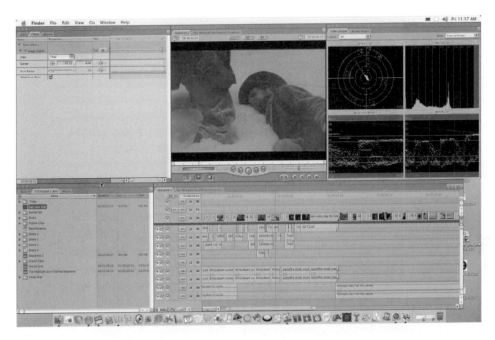

FIGURE 11.15 *Color Correction Arrangement.*

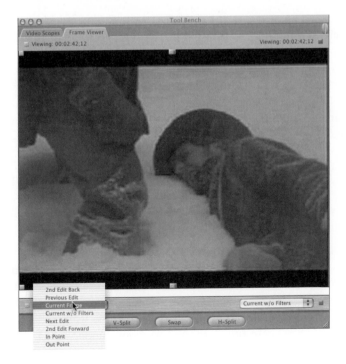

FIGURE 11.16 *The Tool Bench window with the Frame Viewer tab selected.*

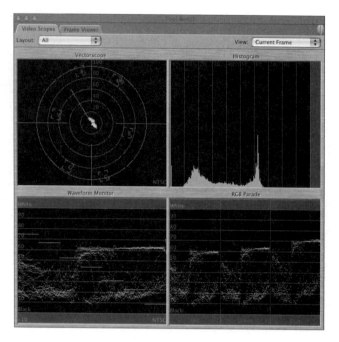

FIGURE 11.17 *The Tool Bench window with the Video Scopes tab selected.*

There are four different but related scopes here. Learning to read them will give you a leg up in setting proper levels for your video clips. Before you can effectively read them, you must understand what they show you. They all measure your image's luminance and chrominance. *Luminance* (also called *luma*) describes the image's relative brightness. *Chrominance* (also called *chroma*) describes the amount or saturation of the image's color and that color's hue. The absence of color is either black, white, or a shade of gray.

New to FCP 4, the Frame Viewer allows you to view two different video clips side by side to match color correction, and more. You can set the pop-up menus near the bottom of this video Viewer to show you the current frame, as well as frames of video on either side of the edit. This very useful tool expedites color correction, filter adjustments, and more.

Another great way to set yourself up to color-correct is to select Window, Arrange, Multiple Edit. To see this arrangement, your computer display must support higher resolutions. You can't see this arrangement on 12- and 15-inch PowerBooks. As shown in Figure 11.18, the multiple edit arrangement allows you to have two Frame Viewers, a Viewer, Canvas, and Video Scopes at the ready. Selecting what you want to view side by side in the Frame Viewer from the pop-up menus near the bottom determines the frames you see for comparison. For example, you might select a frame from a clip on either side up to two edits back or forward from your current position in the sequence to match color from one shot to another.

Figure 11.18 *The multiple edit window arrangement.*

Measuring Luma (Luminance) Levels

Final Cut Pro measures luma as a digital percentage from 0 to 100, where 100 is absolute white and 0 is absolute black. FCP also lets you see superwhite levels. Analog video is measured in increments called IRE levels. On the IRE scale, NTSC video black is measured at 7.5 IRE (except in Japan and territories that are away from the U.S., where it's measured at 0 IRE). The broadcast standard of the brightest (broadcast-legal) white is measured at 100 IRE. In PAL, legal black is measured at 0 IRE, and legal white is measured at 100 IRE. If you are in the U.S., black is measured at 7.5 IRE, but in many places that use NTSC it's measured at 0, so it is best to find out what your area uses by contacting a local broadcaster.

Final Cut Pro lets you see brighter images than what is considered legal if your images contain these superwhite levels. *Superwhite levels* are luminance levels greater than 100 IRE as measured by the Waveform Monitor. Many cameras (especially DV cameras) record these levels. They range from 101 IRE to 109 IRE and are not considered broadcast-legal in any broadcast video system. However, many broadcasters allow levels higher than 100. Notably, though, PBS stations in the U.S. do not allow levels greater than 100 IRE.

Technically, FCP's Waveform Monitor measures a percentage of luma, not IRE levels exactly, but for all intents and purposes, thinking of these measurements as IRE levels is fine. If you are worried about these levels, simply add a Broadcast Safe filter, found on the Color Correction submenu of the Video Effects menu, and you will definitely be legal everywhere.

Measuring Chroma Levels

Chroma levels describe hue and saturation. Hue describes the color itself—whether it's blue or red, for example. It's measured as an angle on a color wheel. In the case of color bars, red is at –13 degrees, yellow is at –77 degrees, green is at –151 degrees, cyan is at 167 degrees, and blue is at 103 degrees.

Saturation describes the intensity or amount of color, whether it's vivid and intense blue or pale blue, for example. Saturation is measured on a color wheel as well, but as the distance from the center of the wheel. If color intensity is measured at the center, it has no color. As it approaches the wheel's outer rim, it becomes more intensely saturated.

So how do you first detect problems with these levels? The Range Check tools are where to begin.

Using the Range-Checking Options in the Viewer and Canvas

You activate the Range Check tools by selecting View, Range Check, as shown in Figure 11.19. You can select to monitor luma or chroma or both from this menu. When they are active, and if you have an area of luma or excess chroma, zebra stripes appear as an overlay on the picture.

Figure 11.20 shows that there is too much luma in the shot. (There's not really too much in the shot supplied with this book; the levels have been raised for this example.) The zebra stripes over the sky area of the shot are red, and they are accompanied by a triangle with an exclamation point. This lets you know that something is amiss. The red stripes indicate that luma levels are over 100% as measured by Final Cut Pro. You see green stripes if the levels are between 90% and 100%. In either case, they are broadcast-legal, and you shouldn't need to correct them. When the range-checking is on and a clip is measured to be broadcast-legal, you don't see zebra stripes, and the triangle with an exclamation point is replaced with a green dot and a check mark, as shown in Figure 11.21.

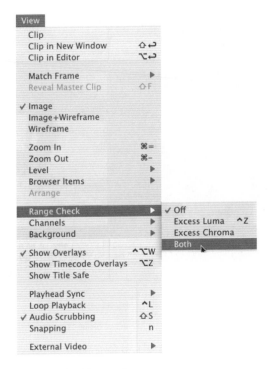

FIGURE 11.19 *Activating the range-checking tools.*

FIGURE 11.20 *Zebra stripes indicating a broadcast-illegal level of luma with the Range Check tool.*

FIGURE 11.21 *A green dot with a check mark indicates legal luma and chroma levels.*

If the chroma levels (the amount of color saturation) are too high, the Range Check tool places red zebra stripes in the areas where it is illegal. Bringing these under the legal limit is as easy as lowering the saturation slider in a color-correction filter. Depending on the setting of the Range Check control, if Range Check luma is on, you get only luma checking. If Range Check chroma is on, you get only chroma checking. If both are on, you have to have both luma and chroma in range to get green stripes or no stripes. The green striping is a warning that you are approaching the limit, not an indication that you have exceeded it.

> **tip**
>
> These excess chroma and luma indicators are great to keep on when you are correcting clips whose levels are legal. You might want to push up the levels to create a more pleasing picture, for example. If the indicators come on, you've gone too far with raising luma or chroma. Be aware that you might have a problem with having the indicators on when exporting QuickTime movies. They seem to make QuickTime movies come out all white in some versions of Final Cut Pro! So turn them off when you aren't checking or changing levels or you want to export a QuickTime movie. If you add a Broadcast Safe filter to a clip whose luma and/or chroma levels are illegal, Final Cut Pro instantly corrects them to the proper levels.

Using the Video Scopes

You have another precise way to check your levels—the four Video Scope readings.

Final Cut Pro supplies four different Video Scopes—the Waveform Monitor, Vectorscope, RGB Parade Scope, and Histogram. The first three work pretty much the same as those used in an online edit suite. The Histogram is a bit different; it measures the *distribution* of luma in your clips.

By comparing one clip's luma and chroma values to another with scopes, you can clearly spot all the hues, saturation, and luminance levels that might distinguish one clip from another. This lets you make more informed decisions about adjusting Final Cut Pro's color-correction filters to more closely match the levels from one clip to the next. Using the scopes also keeps you from just relying on what your computer display looks like. These scopes accurately measure levels and help you keep things matching, better looking, and broadcast-legal.

When you are paused on a clip, that current frame is the one being monitored by the scopes. You can select different displays of the various scopes by selecting an individual scope or a set of scopes you want to view from the Layout pop-up menu. If you choose one of the eight different combinations, you can monitor as many as all four of the scopes, a smaller combination of them, or just one of them at a time.

A View pop-up menu appears next to the Layout menu. Here you can select various frames for the scopes to get different readings. If you select Current, the Canvas and Timeline's playhead position is read. If you select Viewer, the scopes read the playhead position's frame in the Viewer. New to FCP 4, you also have a quick way to view previous frames, later frames, or frames with or without any effects added to them (much like you can with the Frame Viewer).

You should be very careful viewing scopes before effects are added (which could make your levels illegal), because they can lead you to make false decisions about legal level or color. Constantly monitoring these levels when you are adding filters to your clips is best.

The different display options in each of the scopes have pop-up menus. You activate the menu by Ctrl-clicking the scope.

Understanding the Waveform Monitor

The Waveform Monitor displays a clip's levels of brightness and saturation. They are displayed from left to right, mirroring the frame of video you are currently monitoring. You must Ctrl-click the display itself to see the saturation levels or to defeat them. You compare the relative saturation levels by looking at the waveform's thickness, as shown in Figure 11.22. The left side reflects the darker areas of Cap and Sam, and the right side reflects the brightness of the snow. Also note the pop-up menu, which you activate by Ctrl-clicking the monitor. A yellow line follows your cursor movement on the scope. Notice that it shows an absolute value of its position in the green box in the upper-right area of the display, just above the scope itself.

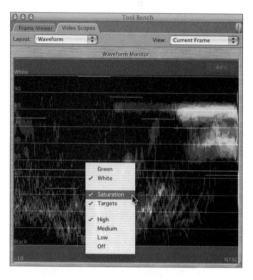

FIGURE 11.22 *Viewing a clip's waveform. Ctrl-click to open the context menu, which can be seen anywhere within the monitor.*

It's easy to change these levels and watch the results as they are displayed by choosing a color-correction filter and adjusting the levels with it. The color-correction filters are discussed later, in the section "Using the Color-Correction Filters."

Understanding the Vectorscope

The Vectorscope displays the distribution of color and its value in the monitored frame. The angle of this display around the circular scale represents the hue values. Small boxes mark the points of red, green, blue, yellow, cyan, and magenta. These are the same colors used in the color bars generated from the Generator pop-up menu. Color targets match the color bars. Correctly adjusted bars (and therefore source) fall on the targets. Saturation errors move the bars inside or outside the targets, and phase errors move them around. If you measure the color bars generated by Final Cut Pro with this scope, you'll see that the targets hit exactly in the Vectorscope. The outer rings of the scale represent maximum saturation, and the center point represents zero saturation. After you've identified the intensity and hue of a color in one clip, you can quickly see where another (which should be a matching clip) varies from the first one. The color targets of the Vectorscope scale match the controls of the Color Balance of Final Cut Pro's color-correction filters. After you've determined that you need to make a change in hue, to match another shot, for example, you can move the balance control indicators to properly match the two shots.

Figure 11.23 shows a Vectorscope reading color bars. Note that the intense colors of the color bars are the vectors that the Vectorscope is reading. The color vectors red, blue, yellow, cyan, and magenta fall within the various boxes assigned to them on the scope. Figure 11.24 shows a superimposition of color bars over Final Cut Pro's color-correction tools' Color Balance wheels. It shows a relationship between the balance wheel and the Vectorscope's readings. Not only are red, blue, magenta, yellow, and cyan on this balance wheel, but they also fall in the same areas in which a Vectorscope represents them. Whatever color is being worked with on the color wheel is reflected in the Vectorscope in hue and intensity.

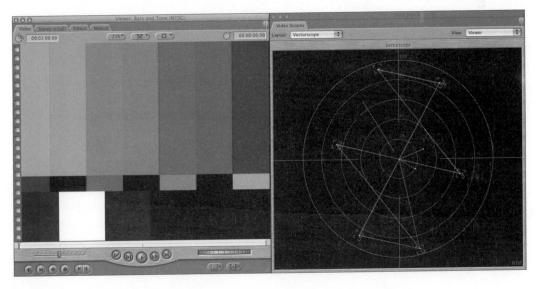

Figure 11.23 *The Vectorscope reading color bars.*

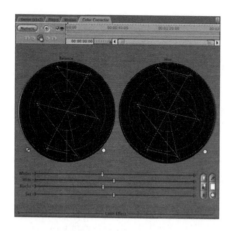

FIGURE 11.24 *The color bars superimposed over the Color Balance wheels.*

A helpful target line in the Vectorscope indicates the average flesh tones of every race. If your subjects' flesh tones are off, chances are you can correct them by lining them up to this indicator, as shown in Figure 11.25. Here you see the close-up of Cap. His flesh tones are tipped a bit to the right, toward red. In this case, you wouldn't change this, because his face should be a bit red from the cold. If you look at the shot, you'll see that it is red, but appropriately so. In contrast, Figure 11.26 shows Sam at the campfire. Notice how his flesh tones are right on the line. *All races' flesh tones fall very near this target line.*

Note that the intensity of the color is higher in Sam's shot. This is because there is more saturation of color in Sam's shot than in Cap's shot. You might want all your movie's color to match, so a color correction might be in order. But keep this in mind: In real life, you don't see the same amount of color all the time. The amount of color you see depends on lighting conditions, so it might also be appropriate to not change the intensity of color saturation to be the same from shot to shot in your entire movie. One thing is certain, though: Sam sure looks warmer in his shot than Cap does in his. And this makes perfect sense. Sam, after all, is next to a fire.

Saturation and luminance may vary from person to person, but unless they are little green men from Mars, the scope will indicate their relative hue, because all human flesh tones fall loosely around this indicator.

Because most shots are relatively low in saturation, the Vectorscope has a magnify mode to make the displayed area clearer. To activate this mode, Ctrl-click the Vectorscope and select Magnify from the context menu that appears.

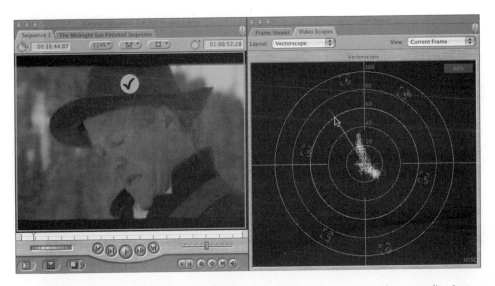

FIGURE 11.25 *Cap's red flesh tones as displayed on the Vectorscope. Note the target line just to the left of Cap's color indication.*

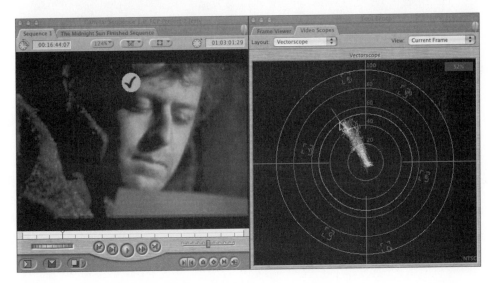

FIGURE 11.26 *Sam's close-up and flesh tone measurement in the Vectorscope.*

You should analyze each edit decision you make (including color) to ensure that it adds to your story at that moment. If it does add an appropriate nuance, it might be a good decision to do it. If it in any way detracts from the moment, it should be avoided.

Understanding the RGB Parade

The RGB Parade, shown in Figure 11.27, is a modified version of the Waveform Monitor. It works the same way, but it separates the red, green, and blue luminance values. It's great for comparing the relative color values that might differ between two clips you are trying to match. This can happen if two cameras were used to shoot a scene, and they don't match exactly in hue and luma values. Figure 11.27 has more red color than green or blue, and you can see this reflected in the RGB Parade's measurements. The levels of red luminance are around 87% in this frame, as indicated in the upper-left corner. You also can see this by placing the Selection tool near the dots at the height of the reds. The yellow line appears when you put the cursor over the scope.

FIGURE 11.27 *The RGB Parade Scope and Sam's shot.*

This tool might be very useful if you have an error in chroma level, indicated by the triangle with the exclamation point. Or you might just want to lower the red saturation, such as if this is the only offending level.

Understanding the Histogram

The Histogram is a bar graph that shows you the relative strength of all the luma values in the selected frame. Each pixel is measured on a scale of 1 to 110. Each bar that is shown in the display represents the number of pixels at each step of the scale. For each pixel brightness level as a percentage of the total, the number of pixels in the image at that brightness level is plotted up the graph.

This graph can be used to quickly compare the luma values of two clips you need to match. If you compare them to each other with this graph, you can quickly see where changes need to be made to bring them into the same levels of luminance.

Take a look at Figure 11.28. It is a black-and-white image whose contrast is spread completely throughout the image, but there is a spike in the number of pixels that peaks around 65. They are the light gray areas between the black centers of the soft squares. Notice too that this image is broadcast-legal, because it has no pixels over 100 and thus is considered superwhite.

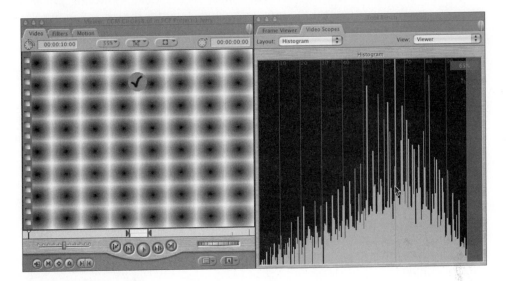

FIGURE 11.28 *The Histogram.*

This tool also is great for checking out an image's contrast. If the distribution of the pixels is high in one area, this represents a lower-contrast image. If they are more evenly distributed, a high-contrast image is being observed. You might want to keep the pixels the way they are, but if contrasts are too low, you might want to correct them to create a better-looking or more-detailed image. Again, you use the color-correction filters to do this. The scopes monitor the image's levels and ensure that you are correcting properly. They also are guides to help you get there quickly. All the scopes update as you change any setting.

In a well-exposed image, you can always expect to see a bell curve of values in the Histogram. Some images have the bell curve low, some have it high, and some spread it wide, but all well-exposed images should show a bell curve.

Using the Color-Correction Filters

Final Cut Pro includes a suite of color-correction tools. They are incredibly powerful. There are six in all:

- Broadcast Safe—This filter quickly brings clips into a broadcast-safe range in luma and chroma levels. It's a quick and easy fix. Simply apply it to a clip, and it's set to go.

- Color Corrector—A basic and intuitive color corrector.

- Color Corrector 3-way—This is similar to the Color Corrector, but it offers more-precise control and supplies separate tools for the correction of color in a clip's low range, mid range, and whites. The Color Corrector 3-way is one of two real-time effects supplied by Final Cut Pro. However, on slower computers, massive adjustments made with the Color Corrector 3-way might not play back in real time.

- Desaturate Highlights—The application of a color correction can at times result in unwanted color in the image's highlights. This filter lets you eliminate those colors. If you select Unlimited RT from the pop-up menu in the Timeline window, this filter's effects play in real time.

- Desaturate Lows—The application of a color correction can at times result in unwanted color in the image's lower luminance areas. This filter lets you eliminate those colors. If you select Unlimited RT from the pop-up menu in the Timeline window, this filter's effects play in real time.

- RGB Balance—This allows you to control your image's reds, greens, and blues independently. It breaks down each of these areas of color into controls for manipulation of your image's highlights, midtones, and blacks. If you select Unlimited RT from the pop-up menu in the Timeline window, this filter's effects play in real time.

> **note**
>
> When you select Unlimited RT from the Timeline's RT pop-up menu (located in the upper left of the Timeline window), keep in mind that even though you might drop frames, it's incredibly useful to view your playback without having to render these effects beforehand. However, you will probably want to render these effects after you are satisfied with the settings you've chosen.

To add a color-correction filter to a clip in the sequence, double-click the desired clip, and select Effects, Video Filters, Color Correction. You can add a filter to the Viewer or directly to a sequence clip from the submenu there. Alternatively, you can drag a filter from the Color Correction bin in the Filters tab in the Browser to the Viewer or directly to a clip in the Timeline window. You can also highlight a clip or series of clips in the Timeline window and double-click a filter from the Filters tab in the

Browser to add it to the clips in the sequence. After they are applied, you control these filters from the Filters tab of the clip that should now be in the Viewer or by clicking the keyframe graphs button (in the lower-left corner of the Timeline window) or by pressing Opt+T. Ctrl-clicking in the keyframe area underneath the clips allows you to select an individual control and modify the filter.

Similar to all other filters, you can click the disclosure triangle next to a filter's name in the Viewer's Filters tab and open the numeric set of controls. Unlike other filters (except for the Chroma Keyer), the Color Corrector 3-way and the Color Corrector have a set of visual controls that you activate by clicking the Visual button next to a filter's name in the Viewer's Filters tab or by clicking the tab that appears after a filter is added to the clip in the top of the Viewer.

In short, you can control the Color Corrector and Color Corrector 3-way from the Viewer's numeric display in the Filters tab, from the visual display from the tab with the filter names on it, or from the keyframe area of the Timeline. Any changes you make in any of these areas are reflected in all the areas. The other color-correction tools can be controlled in the Viewer's Effects tab or from the Timeline's keyframe area.

I recommend that when you're learning to use these filters, you start by working with the visual display. After you've mastered it, using the numeric controls and adjusting parameters in the keyframe area will be easier. It's also easier to use the numeric and keyframe area controls for more precise control. If you have a lot of screen space, you'll find that enlarging the visual display increases your control of them, just as it does when you work with edit points in the Timeline window. Keep in mind that professional colorists make a living using only tools similar to these, and it takes a while to learn all their ins and outs.

All these filters affect chroma and luma in your video, but probably most of the time you'll use the Color Corrector and the Color Corrector 3-way for everyday color-correction jobs. Experimenting with filters not discussed in this book will teach you much. The following is a discussion of these two most important tools.

Common Controls Between the Color Corrector Filter and the Color Corrector 3-Way Filter

Both these filters use similar controls that would be familiar to a professional colorist in an online bay or Telecine suite. The controls for each of these fabulous tools are similar. The intuitive visual controls are discussed first. Be aware that their numeric counterparts adjust the same parameters. A couple of extra controls are found only in the numeric controls.

Take a look at Figure 11.29. These controls are identical in both filters. There is a button in both the numeric and visual controls to change the view in the Viewer window to toggle between the two sets of controls. In the visual control it's in the upper left, as shown in Figure 11.29.

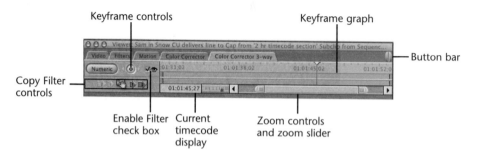

FIGURE 11.29 *Top area controls of both the Color Corrector and the Color Corrector 3-way.*

The controls in the visual displays of both filters are as follows:

- Keyframe controls—A set of three controls that allow you to set keyframes that control all the filter's parameters at once. If you want to control them individually, you must access the numeric controls and set individual keyframes for each parameter. You might want a more-precise change of color over time using these instead.

- Enable Filter check box—Enables or disables the filter. Great for checking the before and after display of your adjustments. Pressing Ctrl+1 toggles this condition.

- Copy Filter controls—This section of the controls has five buttons. They are as follows from the left:

  Copy from 2nd Clip Back copies the Color Corrector settings used on the clip that is two clips before the current one. You'd use this when correcting a cut between two actors, for example, where one needs this particular correction and you are cutting between two close-ups of the two actors every other cut.

  Copy from 1st Clip Back copies the Color Corrector settings from the immediately preceding clip. This could be used to correct two clips that must have the same correction applied to them.

  Drag Filter allows you to copy this color correction to any clip in the sequence by simply dragging this icon to another clip in your sequence. You also can drag this setting to your Favorites folder or anywhere in the Browser to store it for later use.

  Copy to 1st Clip Forward copies the color correction to the following clip.

Copy to 2nd Clip Forward copies the color correction to the second clip forward. Say you have the same shot edited with an insert of a close-up or cutaway shot between the beginning and the end of this first shot. This button could quickly make both sides of this shot match.

- Current timecode display—Works the same as the one in the Viewer.

- Keyframe graph—Works the same as the others, but controls all parameters at once.

- Zoom controls and zoom slider—Works the same as the ones that are in the controls of the video filters.

- Color Balance control—The Color Balance control is shown in Figure 11.30. It's common to both filters. It's a color wheel that allows you to change the mix of red, green, and blue that falls within three different ranges of luma in the Color Corrector 3-way tool and in the Color Corrector; it affects all ranges of luma. The wheel's angle of distribution corresponds to the same angle of degrees that a set of color bars uses in the Vectorscope.

Dragging the white center button toward the outer areas changes the balance of your clip's color toward the color you are dragging toward. Holding down the Shift key while dragging keeps the button moving in the same direction of color. Holding down the Command key while dragging allows it to gear up and move faster. Holding down *both* the Command and Shift keys allows it to move faster *and* maintain the same direction. The eyedropper in the lower left allows you to quickly white-balance a shot by selecting it and then picking something in the shot that is supposed to be white. The circular button in the lower right resets this control.

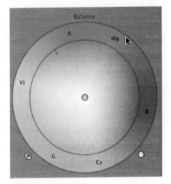

FIGURE 11.30
The Color Balance control.

- Limit Effect tools—Again, both filters have these controls, shown in Figure 11.31. These controls let you select specific values of hue, saturation, and luma and apply color correction to only the areas of the picture you've selected for change. For example, suppose you have a scene with a person wearing a red coat. Then you decide you want to change the color of that red coat to blue. Assuming that nothing else in the picture has the same values of red, you can use the Limit Effect controls to selectively make this change. If another color is the same, you might be able to block it out by using a Garbage Matte, much like the identity blur mentioned earlier in the discussion of the Eight-Point Garbage Matte. There is a check box next to each of the three major controls to activate them, as well as a reset button to put them back to their default settings. A common use of this filter is to reduce reds only, which typically can become oversaturated in video. Limiting the changes to the red areas keeps saturation levels on the other areas of color in your image.

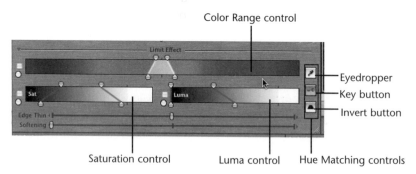

FIGURE 11.31 *Limit Effect controls.*

- Color Range control—Selects the color range you want to limit the effect to:

  Top handles select the color's range. They correspond to the numeric display's Chroma Width.

  Bottom handles select the tolerances of the keying range. They correspond to the Chroma softness in the numeric display.

  Color Gradient lets you click between the two sets of handles and drag left or right to change the hue of the limiting color.

  Saturation (Sat) control works the same as the Color Range controls but affects only the saturation of the selected limiting color.

  Luma control works the same as the Saturation control but affects only the luma range selected.

  Eyedropper lets you select the color within the clip by activating it and clicking the color in the Canvas you want to limit the effect to. Zooming in on the Viewer or Canvas might help you get a more accurate selection. Just press Z and continually click with the Zoom tool on the area you want to zoom into. After it is selected, press Shift+Z to set the Canvas or Viewer to Fit to Window.

  Key button allows you to change the view from full-color to reveal just a black-and-white view of what you are limiting the ranges to. (It shows you the alpha channel or key you are creating by using the Limit Effect set of tools.) The areas of black on this view are unaffected by the change, and the areas of white are affected. This is very useful for fine-tuning the limit's keyed or affected area. It also toggles to a state of showing you the video without the filter's effect applied to it so that you can see a before-and-after effect.

Invert button inverts the limiting effect to affect everything but the color and range selected by the Limit Effect controls. For example, if you set up a color to be limited and you change it to black-and-white, clicking this button turns everything else in the picture to black-and-white and leaves the selected color unchanged, much like the red coat on the child in *Schindler's List*. How about turning everything in a shot of roses to black-and-white except the roses themselves?

Hue Matching controls are new to FCP 4. This color-matching tool allows you to pick a color in one shot and match it to another color in a different shot. You can match the color of flesh tones from one shot to another shot of the same character, for example, when the lighting might have changed between the two shots. This filter changes the color balance of the entire shot so that it matches another. This works best as a starting point when you're correcting between two shots. You'll most likely use the other controls in the Color Corrector or Color Corrector 3-way to make fine adjustments. However, the Hue Matching controls can be controlled by using the Limit Effect controls.

Auto Black Level button sets the clip's black areas to 0 in the Histogram.

Auto White Level button sets the white levels to a maximum of 100 in the Histogram.

Auto Contrast button does the same as the Auto Black Level and Auto White Level buttons combined with one click.

The Auto Contrast set of three buttons resides along the right side of the Color Corrector and in the central area of the Color Corrector 3-way filter, as shown in Figures 11.32 and 11.33. The single white arrow is the Auto White Level, the single black arrow is the Auto Black Level, and the dual-arrows button is the Auto Contrast button. Using these controls first in your color-correction process maximizes the contrast in your pictures, but keep in mind that they assume that you have proper exposure levels to begin with. You can try this as a starting point. If it's too much of a change, you'll see it immediately and can always perform an Undo to start over.

To reset the controls in either filter, activate the numeric display and click the red reset button next to the filter's name. All changes are reset to their default settings, and you delete any keyframes you might have created.

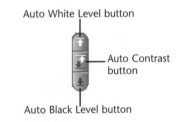

FIGURE 11.32
Auto Contrast buttons in the Color Corrector filter.

FIGURE 11.33
Auto Contrast buttons in the Color Corrector 3-way filter.

Other Controls in the Color Corrector Filter

Figure 11.34 shows the Color Corrector's remaining controls. They are as follows:

- Hue—Rotating the triangle here changes the video's overall hue.

- Hue Reset button—Resets the hue to its default setting.

- Whites slider—Drag the slider to adjust the maximum white levels between 25% and 100%. Clicking the arrows at either end moves the slider up or down in small increments.

- Mids slider—Dragging this slider redistributes the video's midtones (between 25% and 75%). Using this slider might bring out details in shadowy areas, leaving the brightest and darkest areas untouched. Clicking the arrows at either end moves the slider up or down in small increments.

- Blacks slider—Dragging this slider adjusts the minimum levels of the video's black areas (between 0% and 75%). Clicking the arrows at either end moves the slider up or down in small increments.

- Sat slider—Raises or lowers color saturation.

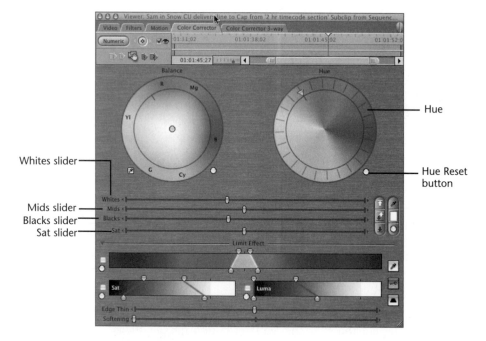

FIGURE 11.34 Controls in the Color Corrector filter.

You need to understand the differences between the Whites, Mids, and Blacks in Final Cut Pro's color filters. They overlap each other in each area of luminance they affect. The Blacks balance controls and sliders affect from 0% to about 75% of the luminance scale, the Mids balance controls and sliders affect the middle 75% of the luma scale, and the Whites controls affect the top 75% of the scale. Keep in mind that they overlap each other. This is true of the sliders in the Color Corrector and the balance and slider controls in the Color Corrector 3-way filters.

tip

To match the color of two clips, you must first match their luma levels using the Whites, Mids, and Blacks sliders. Only then can you match their hue and saturation levels properly.

Other Controls in the Color Corrector 3-way Filter

The primary difference between the Color Corrector and the Color Corrector 3-way filters is that the 3-way version has separate color balance controls for the Blacks, Mids, and Whites, as shown in Figure 11.35. The Color Corrector 3-way's remaining controls are described in the following list.

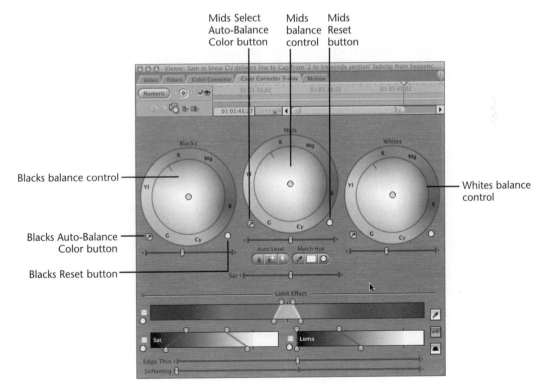

FIGURE 11.35 *The remaining controls in the Color Corrector 3-way filter.*

- Blacks balance control—Changes the balance of color in the blacks of your clip.

- Blacks Auto-Balance Color button (the eyedropper)—Clicking the Blacks Auto-Balance Color button turns the pointer into an eyedropper when it's moved into the video in the Viewer or the Canvas. Click the tip of the eyedropper into what is supposed to be the blackest area of your image. The color value of the pixel you select is analyzed, and the Blacks balance control is automatically adjusted to turn that pixel into true black. This affects all the black areas of your picture.

- Blacks Reset button—Clicking this button resets the Blacks balance control to its default settings. Holding down the Shift key while clicking this button resets the Blacks, Mids, Whites, and Saturation controls to their default settings.

- Mids balance control—Click and drag in the Mids balance control to move the balance control indicator and change the mix of red, green, and blue in the mids of your clip.

- Mids Select Auto-Balance Color button (the eyedropper)—Clicking this button turns the pointer into an eyedropper when it's moved into the video in the Viewer or the Canvas. Click the tip of the eyedropper into what is supposed to be an area of neutral gray. The mid area of luma is shifted into the correct balance.

- Mids Reset button—Click this button to reset the Mids balance control to its default settings and restore your clip to the original color balance.

- Whites balance control—Click and drag in the Whites balance control to move the balance control indicator and change the mix of red, green, and blue in the whites of your clip.

tip

When color-correcting a clip, the Blacks Auto-Balance Color eyedropper is usually the *second* step you take. First you use the Auto Contrast controls and the Blacks, Mids, and Whites sliders to maximize the contrast of your image and use the Histogram as a monitoring device to see exactly what you are doing. Using an external video monitor is a must as well to accurately see results.

note

The areas of your picture affected by the Mids balance control overlap the areas affected by the Blacks and the Whites balance controls, so adjustments to the Mids affect adjustments you might have already made to the Blacks and Whites. Usually it's best to tread softly. Also, the Blacks control overlaps the Whites, and the Whites control overlaps the Blacks control. I find it easy to adjust the Mids first and then the Blacks and/or Whites. Also keep in mind that you can add multiple instances of a color-correction filter and use limiting controls on each of them to achieve the look you are after.

Real-Time Previewing

Without additional hardware, Final Cut Pro attempts to play back composites and transitional effects *without* rendering them first, depending on your hardware configuration. Again, the faster your setup, the more-reliable and more-complex real-time effects you can achieve. Depending on your computer's speed, you might have to render effects eventually to print them back to DV tape in any case if they are DV. Real-time (RT) effects are being done with capture card additions such as those from Aurora, Matrox, AJA, and Pinnacle. They might add real-time effects that you cannot achieve with RT Extreme alone.

If you click the RT button in the upper-left corner of the Timeline window, you can set your playback of real time to Unlimited RT. Using this to preview effects you've added to your sequence allows you to see them in real time as long as they are real-time effects with their names in bold.

They might not play back smoothly, but they allow you to see changes before you waste time rendering them if further changes are required. For more information, see Figure 3.21 in Chapter 3, "Understanding Final Cut Pro's Interface: An Overview," and the render bar discussion in the section "Composites and Renders" earlier in this chapter.

There are some additional caveats here. Not all effects play back in real time. Only the bold effects in the list of filters and transitions will work in a preview without rendering. Not all Macintoshes can play back real-time effects. The faster your computer's processor is, the more real-time playback you can achieve. Dual-processor machines show more RT previews than single processors. Only 500MHz G4s or faster show you *any* RT effects, according to Apple, but slower machines *might* show you *some*. What's more, if you are working in one of the OfflineRT modes, you can get more effects to preview. Confused? Join the club. Here's the last caveat: Typically only on the faster dual G4 computers can you get more than one RT preview effect at a time.

The bottom line is that if you can get some of the effects to preview for you in RT, great! It's not the end of the world if you can't. There are some nifty tricks you can do to look at the effect as it plays even if you're working on a G3, if you want to preview the effect and continue monitoring your video externally, or if you're working with effects that have no real-time preview.

Nifty Tricks When Real-Time Playback Isn't Enough

The first of these tricks is the Opt+P keyboard command. It renders *any* effect or set of effects and shows you the frames in the Canvas as it builds them. The faster your computer, the faster it shows you this preview. It's really great when you want to check a middle section of a composite or effect and you don't want to wait for a rendering to get there. Rendering starts with the first frame of the selected clip and goes frame by frame until it gets to the area of interest. Opt+P, on the other hand, shows you a slow playback from anywhere you place the position indicator in the Canvas or Timeline windows. If this area can be played in real time, it will be.

The second trick is to drag the position indicator through the effects or jump through them every few frames by clicking in forward steps in the Timeline window. You'll be able to see if you have indeed set up that flying move of 10 layers of picture-in-picture clips properly or if that background of a video transitional page turns just right.

Another tool to help you preview unrendered material is the QuickView window. It's discussed next.

The QuickView Window for Previewing Effects

The QuickView window gives you another way to preview your effects before you render them. As you play a specified area of your sequence, video is cached to RAM as it's played. If you are familiar with After Effects, it is a RAM previewing tool. As soon as the duration of the sequence you've specified for QuickView playback has played all the way through, subsequent loops of it play at the full frame rate because they're being played back directly from RAM.

The QuickView tool stores in RAM as much of the sequence between the In and Out points set in the Timeline as possible (determined by how much RAM you have installed) for accelerated playback. If only an In point is set in the Timeline, Final Cut Pro caches video from the In point for the duration you specify in the Range slider for playback in the QuickView window. If no points are set in the Timeline, Final Cut Pro uses the playhead's position, caching half of the duration specified by the Range slider before the playhead's position and half after the playhead for display in the QuickView window. When you choose an In and Out point in your sequence, the Range slider is defeated.

To activate QuickView, choose Tools, QuickView or press Opt+8. It opens in the Tool Bench and resides there with the Video Scopes. You can click the tabs there to switch between them or drag either tab to keep them both open.

Figure 11.36 shows this window's controls. The pop-up menu in the upper left allows you to cache the video in full, half, or quarter resolution. Using the lower-resolution modes not only lets you play back sooner than a render to disk and render the preview faster, it also lets you load more time into RAM. The View pop-up menu in the upper right allows you to select which window to view with or to automatically switch to the Viewer or Canvas window for a QuickView playback.

Figure 11.36 *The QuickView window.*

To activate the play button under the picture area, click it or press the spacebar to toggle it on and off. The Range slider slides from left to right, selecting more or fewer seconds to work with in the looping playback. You can click the position indicator just above the play button to scrub through the loop.

You can also select a specific range you want to preview in your sequence by setting an In and Out point within the sequence. When you do, the QuickView window assumes that this is the range you want to preview.

tip
If you lower the playback's resolution, this tool becomes more powerful. Even though the picture becomes somewhat fuzzy, if you are animating titles or watching many layers of video play through, you can at least check positions of your clips to see if you have indeed programmed them correctly. It's much better than discovering that after you've waited for a long render, you have to rerender because you made a mistake. Unlike working with RT settings in the Timeline window, QuickView works with every effect you can add to a clip in Final Cut Pro, whether it's a bold RT effect or not.

note
Composite modes are discussed in detail in Chapter 13. They provide extremely powerful and useful effects. You'll discover some of their uses while editing the movie. They calculate differences between pixel values when you place images above each other. Using these modes gives you all sorts of interesting effects.

Workshop 11: Work with Composites

All the color correction for "The Midnight Sun" was done during the Telecine (film-to-tape) process, so it doesn't really require a lot of correcting from the point of view that it wasn't shot well (in this case, the footage was carefully exposed). However, taking the time to match each shot used in the same location in the story might improve the overall look of the movie. Nevertheless, to make the composites used in the storytelling process more realistic, you need to use the color-correction tools, filters, and more.

As mentioned, composites amount to any two or more visuals combined into one. We'll start with the composite of the boat Cap finds on Lake Lebarge and then move on to a set of stars for Cap to look at.

Build the Boat Composite

Because the producer couldn't afford to build a turn-of-the-century steam-powered boat for this shot, you need to build one for him.

1. If you have a video monitor that can monitor Final Cut Pro output, you should be looking at it for color adjustment. (Refer to Chapter 1, "Essential Equipment.") After you've connected the monitor, select View, External Video, All Frames or press Cmd+F12. If you don't have a way to monitor externally, it's not a problem; the results will be the same.

2. Create a new bin named Composites in the Browser. Option-double-click it to open its tab in the Browser.

3. With the Composites bin active, press Cmd+I and import these files (Command-clicking them one at a time allows you to pick and choose files):

    Cap Sees Boat
    Smoke bkg 1
    Cap looks at stars hi res
    Universe.jpg
    Boat.tga
    Boat1.tga
    Boat2.tga
    Boat3.tga
    Boat4.tga
    Smoke1.mov

    You are adding all the source clips for the composites for the movie now, but you will work on only the Boat and Stars Composites during this workshop. You'll create the smoke composite in Chapter 13.

4. Create three new sequences in the Composites bin (press Cmd+N). Select all the new sequences to be the standard Sequence Presets of DV NTSC 48kHz. Name the sequences "*Boat Composite," "*Smoke Composite," and "*Stars Composite." You put an asterisk in front of each name to have them sort at the top of the Composites bin. Another way to organize these special sequences is to put them in their own bin contained in the Composites bin. With this few clips, though, it's just as easy to keep them in the top of the bin hierarchy.

Highlight the sequences one at a time and press Cmd+0 to look at their settings. From the resulting window, you can check the sequence settings. If they are correct, click OK. If they are incorrect, click the Load Preset button and select the DV NTSC 48kHz preset. The compositing clips are not in the same format as the rest of the project's clips. You must match the sequence preset to the clip's properties to not have to render the clips just to play them in the sequences.

tip

This is how you can import files that might have come from another software application. All the boat's .tga files are targa files created by another company on a PC and sent to me. They could just as easily have been sent to me as logos or some other sort of file from an ad agency or another client. It's best to keep these files stored in the folders where you keep other media files that are associated with this project so that you can remember where they are. Also keep in mind that if you'll ever need these files again, you might want to back them up on a CD-R or Zip disc for reimportation and later use, because they did not all come from timecoded videotape and cannot automatically be captured later. You can, however, reconnect to them again later if you need to restore your project for any reason. LiveType and Soundtrack files can be treated the same way.

Create the Boat Composite

1. Double-click the Boat Composite sequence to open it in the Timeline window.

2. Drag the "Cap Sees Boat" clip from the Composites bin onto the head of the sequence on the V1 track. Double-click the "Boat.tga" file to open it in the Viewer.

3. Pretty funny-looking boat, eh? Looks like a cartoon—not photorealistic at all. You'll hide this problem, but first experiment with the view options pop-up menu near the top of the Viewer and below the tabs (the one with the square). Look at the different ways to view the alpha channel that this targa file contains. In this case, viewing with one of the checkerboard backgrounds is best. Keep in mind, though, that these are only views. You are not changing the track in any way.

4. Place the position indictor in the Timeline anywhere within the "Cap Sees Boat" clip, and press X to mark it from In to Out.

5. Ctrl-click the area just above the V1 track indicator in the Timeline, and add a video track to the sequence. Then overwrite the "Boat.tga" file onto the V2 track (don't forget to target it!). It should be directly over Cap's clip. Unfortunately, now the boat is impaled on the sign's post! You'll fix this in a moment. The boat needs to match color more closely first, and it's easier to see your results doing this while the boat is still large.

6. Double-click the "Boat.tga" clip in the Timeline window to open it in the Viewer. Notice the sprocket holes in the scrubber bar, indicating that the clip is from the Timeline window and no longer is the one that's from the Browser. You must think of these as separate elements, because, in fact, they are. Each references the same media file, but other than that, they are different elements.

7. Apply a color-correction filter to the clip. Making sure that the Viewer is active or the Boat.tga clip is highlighted in the Timeline window, select Effects, Video Filters, Color Correction, Color Correction 3-way. Notice that the Color Corrector 3-way tab appears in the Viewer. Click it. Toggle back and forth between the Numeric button and the corresponding Visual button, which are in the Numeric controls in the Viewer's Filters tab. Also note the red X button in the Numeric controls. By clicking it, you can start over when you need to. You can start the next step with the Visual Display active. It's probably more intuitive to use. However, as you change parameters in either display, they are instantly reflected in both.

8. The snow on the boat is where to start. It's too bright and white and doesn't have the same bluish look as the snow in the shot. First things first, though. Set your computer's display to be the Color Correction arrangement by selecting Window, Arrange, Color Correction. Set the Video Scopes' Layout pop-up menu to be the Vectorscope. If you want to, you can use the QuickView window to preview the effect in playback at any time by activating the QuickView window from the Tools menu (or by pressing Opt+8). It becomes a tab when you want to use it, but keep the Video Scopes tab selected to start with.

    Change the color to a bluish tint by dragging the center button on the Whites color wheel directly toward the B (the blue) until it's about halfway there. Then lower it just a bit toward the Cy area of the wheel. You can hold down the Command key while you drag to speed things up (on slower computers, it's mandatory that you do so). As you do this, notice the line shown on the Vectorscope. It's the color of the white being adjusted. You'll know that you have matched hue when it's along a similar angle as the rest of the picture, as shown in Figure 11.37. This figure shows a detail of how the Whites color wheel should look when you are done. Because it's more saturated and bright, it sticks out. When you are there, it should look too bright and too saturated; the Vectorscope reflects this (see Figure 11.38). Notice the matching angles of the color correction as it is shown between the Whites selector and the color wheel.

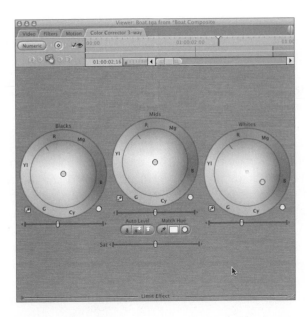

FIGURE 11.37 *The Whites color wheel detail.*

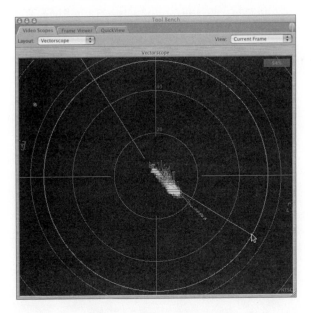

FIGURE 11.38 *A zoomed-in detail of the Vectorscope reading of the Boat.tga clip after the initial color correction.*

Keep in mind that you won't limit this effect to the whites, because this change in color also cools down the color of the whole boat and helps it begin to match Cap's shot. You are attempting to match the frozen feel of the composite to the whole boat, and you're using white as your reference. Notice how the boat just got colder-looking.

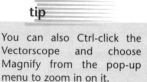

9. Lower the saturation by dragging the Sat slider to the left not quite halfway between its default position and its left side. Watch the Vectorscope move the line closer to the area of the rest of the colors displayed.

10. Change the Video Scopes display to the Waveform Monitor. Notice the tiny dots above the arc of the whites represented in the background. These dots are the bright white of the boat. Lower the Brightness control directly under the Whites controls in the Viewer until these dots fall into the big arc. You have just matched the luminance to the other whites in Cap's shot. When you are done, the Color Corrector 3-way tool should look like Figure 11.39.

The boat matches Cap's background shot pretty well now as far as color correction goes, but you need to place it where it realistically works in the composite to fool everyone into thinking it's really there. You also need to further reduce the boat's graphic look.

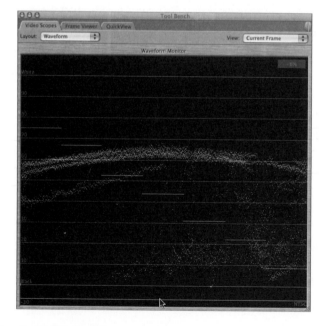

FIGURE 11.39   Waveform after step 10.

11. Reset your window arrangement to Standard by selecting Window, Arrange, Standard, or press Ctrl+U. The Video Scopes window closes.

12. From the Canvas View options pop-up menu (the one with the box on it between the timecode displays near the top of the Canvas), select Image + Wireframe. Image + Wireframe mode lets you resize and reposition a clip that it's active on as selected from the Timeline. So be sure to have "Boat.tga" selected in the Timeline window.

13. With the Selection tool active (press A), put the cursor over the Canvas window and drag any corner to make the boat much smaller—about half its current size. You'll know when to click and drag when the big crosshair tool turns into a much smaller plus sign. The idea is to put the boat off into the distance. When you are done, your Canvas window should look somewhat like Figure 11.40.

Figure 11.40 *The Canvas window after step 13.*

14. After the resize, click inside the blue bounding box, away from the corners, and drag it to the left so that the boat's roof is just below the mountains in the distance. It looks better already, but it still looks like you pasted it there. And it doesn't really match the depth of field of the background shot. The mountains are out of focus, and the apparent focus of the boat should match.

15.   Apply a Gaussian Blur to the boat from the Effects tab in the Browser. (If you
      don't see the Effects tab, press Cmd+5 to open it.) Drag the Gaussian Blur to
      the clip in the Timeline window or up to the Viewer (either way, it gets
      applied). Or you can apply the effect by selecting Effects, Video Filters, Blur,
      Gaussian Blur. Click the Filters tab in the Viewer to adjust the effect. Set its
      radius to 4. Now it looks much more in the distance, but it still looks a bit like
      a drawing, mainly because it doesn't reflect the haze that's in the scene.

16.   Make the clip's overlay button active in the Timeline window. It's the one
      with the line graph with two points in the lower left of the Timeline window.
      Lower the opacity of the "Boat.tga" clip until it blends into the background
      at 35%. Holding down the Command key at the same time makes for an
      easier fine adjustment. The problem is, as you did this, the boat's luminance
      went up.

17.   Click the Color Corrector 3-way tab or click the Visual button next to the fil-
      ter's name in the Viewer's Filters tab to open it. Lower the clip's luminance by
      adjusting the slider under the Mids controls, sliding it about halfway to the
      left. Do the same with the Blacks luminance slider.

18.   If you haven't noticed already, the smokestack has created a small problem
      too. It's blacker where the mountains are behind it. The mountains being seen
      through the smokestack causes this. There are two ways to fix this—either
      lower the boat's position, or crop the boat with the Crop tool. If you want to
      crop it, press C to activate the Crop tool. Lower the upper blue bounding box
      with the "Boat.tga" file highlighted until it's cropped just at the mountain's
      edge. I rather like the boat with a shorter smokestack, but it's got a hard edge
      to it. Not a problem. Just click the Motion tab in the Viewer, and click the dis-
      closure triangle next to the Crop parameter. Soften the edge of the crop by
      sliding the Feather Edge slider to the right a bit until you are satisfied. Figure
      11.41 shows the final result.

19.   Render the effect by highlighting the "Boat.tga" clip and pressing Cmd+R.
      When you're done, take a look at the playback. Experiment with different
      placements of the boat. Also experiment with the different views of the boat
      using the other targa files you imported in step 2. You might find a better-
      looking composite. Use the color-correction tools in concert with the Video
      Scopes and see how each move you make with the color correction is reflected
      in the Video Scopes. Learning about their interaction just takes a little prac-
      tice. This composite is only here to introduce the boat to the story. It really
      doesn't matter where it is in the shot. You can even place it behind the sign
      by cropping its bottom and then using the Distort tool (press D) with its
      Wireframe active to make the crop exactly match the angle of the top of the
      sign. The sign's top edge lowers very slightly on the left side. By pulling down

the lower-left corner of the boat's bounding box with the Distort tool a bit, you can hit it right on. Use the different Zoom controls to zoom in and out of the Canvas if you need to. It's up to you how to complete the composite. Play around with this, and most of all, have fun.

FIGURE 11.41 *The final boat scene composite.*

If you want to, you can save all your experiments in the Boat Composite sequence to compare them to each other. Just keep adding the background clip "Cap Sees Boat" over and over in the sequence, placing different views of the boat over each one.

If you decide that you have the "definitive" color correction for all clips, you can copy these corrections quickly by highlighting the clip that contains them and pressing Cmd+C. Then Ctrl-click the newly- and un-color-corrected clip and select Paste Attributes. You see the Paste Attributes dialog box, shown in Figure 11.42. Select Filters to paste just the filters from the previously copied clip. You can also select Opacity to apply the copied opacity settings to this new clip as well.

There's another way to copy the Color Correction 3-way filter to a clip next to it, or even two clips forward or backward from it. Use the arrow-shaped Copy to 1st Clip Forward or Copy to 2nd Clip Forward button in the top-left area of the Visual display.

FIGURE **11.42**   *The Paste Attributes window.*

20.   Save the project when you are finished.

Create the Stars Composite

Remember the shot of Cap looking up at the sky, which opens the night camp scene? It's time to enhance this moment by compositing some stars into the shot.

1.   Close the Boat Composite sequence from the Timeline window by Ctrl-clicking its tab and selecting Close Tab. Notice that the Canvas window closes at the same time. If it doesn't, close any sequences the same way by Ctrl-clicking their tabs. Remember that Final Cut Pro assumes that if you don't have a sequence active in the Timeline, you don't need the Canvas window, because that is what the Canvas window displays—the active sequence.

2.   Open the Stars Composite sequence by double-clicking it in the Composites bin. Notice that the Canvas window reopens with it. Double-click the Boat Composite sequence in the Composites window. Notice that *both* are open in the Timeline window. Also notice that there is a tab for each in the Canvas. Clicking the tabs in either the Canvas or Timeline toggles between them in both the Canvas and Timeline windows. When you are done experiencing the changes, close the Boat Composites tab by Ctrl-clicking it. This leaves just the Stars Composites sequence in the Timeline window. This time, you didn't lose the Canvas window, but you did lose the tabs to the Boat Composite sequence.

3. Drag the "Cap looks at stars hi res" clip to the Timeline above the V1 track, and create the V2 track at the same time. Be sure to place it at the very beginning of the sequence.

4. Drag the "Universe. jpg" clip directly under "Cap looks at stars hi res." Trim it to be the same duration as Cap's shot by clicking the Out point and dragging it left. It helps to have snapping turned on (press N).

5. Zoom in on the clips with the Zoom tool (press Z). You also can Ctrl-click the A2, A3, and A4 tracks to delete them if you want to. You won't use any audio tracks. Final Cut Pro allows you to delete down to only one audio track, but it allows you to position the sequence in the Timeline window to see more tracks of video when you have no need for the audio tracks.

6. Double-click the "Cap looks at stars hi res" clip from the Timeline window to make it active in the Viewer.

7. Add an Eight-Point Garbage Matte to the clip from the Browser's Effects tab. Navigate to it by selecting Effects, Video Filters, Matte, Eight-Point Garbage Matte. Then drag its icon directly to the Viewer window. Notice the default position of the eight points.

8. Click the Filters tab in the Viewer to reveal the Garbage Matte controls. Click the triangle next to it if you don't see the controls.

9. Change the View Mode in the effect controls to Wireframe.

10. Click the Point 1 crosshair. Position the Selection tool over the shot in the Canvas. Click just to the left of Cap's collar on his right side, as shown in Figure 11.43. Notice that the coordinates of this point have changed in the effect controls, and there is a line showing you what you are cropping when you click the picture.

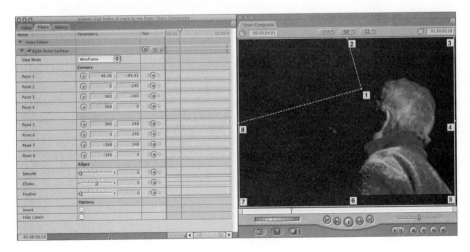

FIGURE 11.43 *The Wireframe view and Filters tab of the first point change in the Stars Composite.*

11. Change the View Mode in the effect controls to Final. The stars are beginning to reveal themselves.

12. Change the View Mode back to Wireframe. Click the 2, 3, 4, 5, 6, 7, and 8 Point crosshairs to surround Cap's head and shoulders. They should look somewhat like Figure 11.44. Raise points 5 and 6 just a bit.

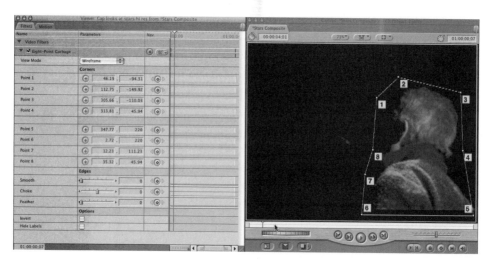

FIGURE 11.44 *The Wireframe view and Filters tab of the remaining point changes in the Stars Composite.*

13. Change the View Mode in the effect's controls to Final to reveal the composite. If you look closely, you can see the edges of the matte. To see them more accurately, drag this clip's Video tab from the Viewer to move it so that you can see it. (You can just cover up the Canvas with it.) Change the View Mode in the filter's controls to Preview. This reveals the alpha channel you are creating. If you need to, change the shot's View Mode to Checkerboard or White. Then use the Smooth slider (which rounds out the shape and makes it less noticeable), Choke slider (which makes the shape expand or contract), and Feather slider (which blurs the shape's edges to further hide it) until you are happy with the results. You can also change the points' positions by dragging them to a new position on the picture. Remember that if you were standing near Cap in real life, you would not perceive stars right next to his head, because your pupils would dilate to see his head, not the stars. When you are done, you should have something that looks like Figure 11.45.

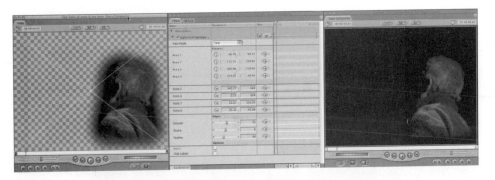

FIGURE 11.45 *The Preview view and Filters tab after step 13.*

14. Drag the Video tab back to the Viewer, and rejoin it with the other tabs there to reveal the Canvas again.

    If you look closely at the top and bottom edges of the frame in the Canvas, the stars also appear over the slightly letterboxed picture. Double-click the "Universe.jpg" clip to make it the active clip, and change the View Options in the Canvas to Image + Wireframe.

15. Activate the Crop tool (press C). Crop the top and bottom of the frame by dragging the blue edges of the bounding box until it hides the stars appropriately, lining up the bottom first and then matching the top to it.

16. With the Crop tool activated, double-click the "Cap looks at star hi res" clip to make it active. Crop it as well, but only along the bottom. You don't want that soft edge to appear at all along the letterbox.

17. Double-click "Universe.jpg" one more time. Then click the Motion tab in the Viewer. The next chapter discusses this tab in detail. For now, click the triangle next to the Crop parameter. Notice that there are values in the Top and Bottom parameters. It might be wise to set these equally. If you set them to be 6.81 each by typing the numbers in the boxes next to the sliders, you create a perfect crop. You placed the original values there when you used the Crop tool directly on the picture. Final Cut Pro entered the coordinates automatically. When you are done with this step, your composite should look like Figure 11.46.

Hopefully you've learned something during this introductory chapter on compositing images. First, you created some visual effects that added to the story. You didn't use anything that detracts (hopefully), and what you did add tells something more about the shots you added the effects to. Secondly, I hope your imagination is running wild with all the possibilities Final Cut Pro presents you with.

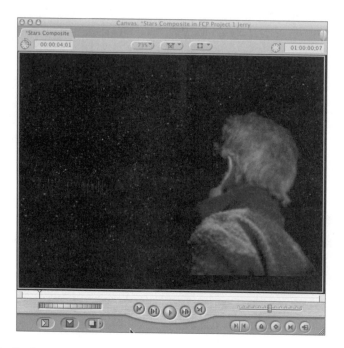

Figure 11.46 *The final composite of Cap looking at the stars.*

You might be wondering why the files for this chapter were given to you in a different format than the Photo-JPEG compressions of the rest of the material. It's because composites are better and more accurately made in higher resolutions. In fact, most color correction, titles, and effects are done in the project's final resolution. Offline/online workflow is discussed later, but know that you are better off working with the compositing tools in higher resolutions, because their color information and detail makes them easier to accomplish and creates better results.

You will add these composites back to your final sequence in a later workshop. You will also learn about changing compressions and nesting with these sequences.

Don't be afraid to experiment. You might find a way of compositing that really does a lot for your project. Most importantly, these composites were relatively easy to do mainly because they were thought out *before* the background and foreground shots were made. In the moment where Cap discovers the boat, the shot was set up with an area in mind for the boat to reside in. The same could be said of Cap's shot when he's looking up at the stars.

Originally, this movie's film transfers were done in a million-dollar Telecine suite. Color correction was decided there with realtime tools, but they weren't *that* much more sophisticated than those that come with Final Cut Pro. It would be a great exercise for you to color-correct every shot in the movie. Maybe your vision of the color is different from that of the movie's director, who wanted the look the way you see the files now. Maybe your vision of the snow is whiter, for example. One thing is for sure. If you want to make a change in the look of your project's color, there is every possibility that you can achieve the result you are after with Final Cut Pro.

The next chapter covers the title tools supplied by Final Cut Pro. We'll go into some more compositing techniques later. Think nonlinear. Nothing is finished until you've delivered the product. Nothing in your sequence has to be edited or modified in the order it will appear in the final sequence.

CHAPTER 12

Using the Title Tools and the Motion Tab

- The Title Generators
- Using Fonts
- The Text Generators
- The Calligraphy Title Tools
- Using Title Safe
- Using the Motion Tab
- Using Basic Motion
- Workshop 12: Create Titles

The Title Generators

Three sets of Title tools are supplied with Final Cut Pro 4. The first are the ones that have been with Final Cut Pro since it began: the Text tools. Final Cut Pro 4 also includes two tools supplied by the great folks at Boris FX. They are part of a plugin program. A *plugin program* is typically a third-party software company's program that "plugs in" to Final Cut Pro and runs from within it. The discussion here starts with the Text generators you run from within FCP. Later in this chapter, you'll investigate the Boris FX Title generators, collectively called the Calligraphy tools.

FCP 4 keeps in a project file all the various text-generating tools that earlier versions of FCP contained. I don't think you'll want to animate every title you ever generate, so the Text and Calligraphy tools are the main Text tools you'll use much of the time. The Text tools are bitmapped fonts, as are the titles created in Boris's Title Crawl. The Title 3D generator, however, creates vector-based titles. You'll find that they look better in many cases.

Using Fonts

Final Cut Pro's Text generators use TrueType fonts only. The Text generators include all the versions of the tools located in the Text submenu, which you access by clicking the Generator button in the lower-right corner of the Viewer. Most professionally generated fonts come in both TrueType and PostScript fonts. When you add fonts to your Macintosh, only the TrueType format works from within Final Cut Pro's Text generators.

It's a good idea to pick fonts that are not too thin or small. Because video is interlaced, one-pixel lines tend to flicker, so you achieve better results using larger font sizes. The smaller sizes look better with sans serif fonts such as Arial and Helvetica. Many editors tend to stay away from scrolling or serif-type fonts, but if they are large enough, they can work quite well.

The Calligraphy tools supplied by Boris FX in FCP 4 can use both TrueType and PostScript fonts. These tools include Title 3D and Title Crawl. They also can be found on the Generator button's pop-up menu.

To install fonts that can be used in Final Cut Pro, place them in the System>Library>Fonts folder. Where they can be used, they appear in the titler's font list. You can also put them in the folder User>Library>Fonts for use by individual users.

The Text Generators

You can access all the Text tools created from within Final Cut Pro using the Generator pop-up menu, located in the lower-right corner of the Viewer's Video tab. The limitation of using the basic Text tools is that you can use only one font, size, color, and style in each instance of them. Simple titles can be made quickly and easily from them, though, and they contain a subset of tools. The first of these is the Text generator.

Keep in mind that many of the parameters within the Text tools' controls allow you to animate the text, and all the parameters affect all the text with all the Text tools. So with these tools, you cannot change sizes of individual lines or create different colors for different words, for example. However, you can do this by creating different titles for each change you want to see in your final composite and layering these titles on higher video tracks above one another. When you create a title, it behaves like a regular video file as far as how it's edited into a sequence. It appears in the Viewer just as if it were video you captured from videotape.

Using the Text Generator

You can access the basic Title tool from the Generator pop-up menu of the Viewer's Video tab, as shown in Figure 12.1. Just click the Generator button and select Text, Text. In fact, all the Text generators are accessed the same way—from the Text menu. The Viewer window contains the words SAMPLE TEXT in the center when you select the Text generator. This is a placeholder title that you can drag to a track in the Timeline window. You can edit it the same as any other clip. You can preview it in real time (without rendering) if your Mac is fast enough. You can even see it externally on a video monitor.

FIGURE 12.1   *Accessing the Text generator.*

The Title tool comes supplied with an alpha channel to key over any background of your choice. It is represented by the checkerboard background you see when you first create the new text (see Figure 12.2). If you have selected black or white for the alpha channel display, you can change this using the Display Options button—the oval-shaped button in the center top area of the Viewer. You can modify this title immediately before placing it in the sequence. However, I find it best to simply edit this title as it is and then double-click it from the Timeline and modify it from there, because you can see any changes you make to it as they are applied. You see this title in the Canvas after you have edited it into your sequence. If you edit it to the V1 track, it appears over a black background (see Figure 12.2). If you edit it to a higher track with video clips under it, it appears over them as a composite.

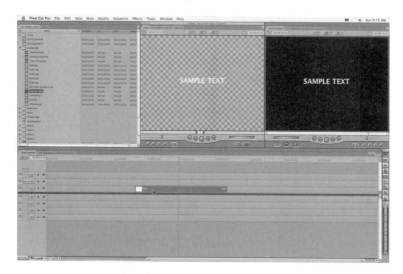

FIGURE 12.2 *Text edited to the Timeline over no background.*

Newly generated text defaults to a 10-second duration, marked as In and Out points in the middle of the clip out of the new source clip's 2-minute total duration. However, this can be edited just as if it were a 2-minute source clip that you edit to make it the duration of your choice. So edit this SAMPLE TEXT title for the correct duration you want it to end up being, in the proper place in your sequence.

Modifying the Text Generator

To modify the text after you've placed it in your sequence, double-click it and then click the Viewer's Controls tab. You see the text's controls, as shown in Figure 12.3. This figure is maximized to show you everything. When you first click the Controls tab, much of it probably will be hidden. You can move around using the scrolling buttons.

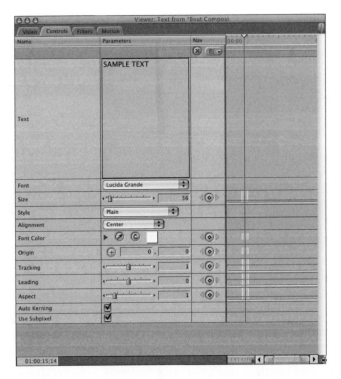

FIGURE 12.3   *The Text generator's controls.*

The Text generator's controls affect the entire title. They are as follows:

- Text—Highlight SAMPLE TEXT and replace it by typing the desired text. You also can copy and paste text here from any text file. Whenever you press Enter, you create another line within the same title.

- Font—The font you select is applied to all the text in the Text box.

- Size—You can type in the Size box any size of text you want, or use the slider to see the text size change in the Canvas window. It is keyframeable to change over time.

- Style—Select Bold, Italic, Bold/Italic, or Plain from the pop-up menu.

- Alignment—Select a Center, Left, or Right justification from the pop-up menu.

- Font Color—Font color can be selected in four basic ways:

  - By clicking the white square, you can choose from about 16.7 million colors. Keep in mind that luminance defaults to 100% in FCP measurements, which is superwhite on the Vectorscope and therefore illegal. To create titles with legal levels, lower the Brightness to 92 or less with the HSB slider, as shown in Figure 12.4, *before* selecting a color. When you do, *any* color will be broadcast-legal.

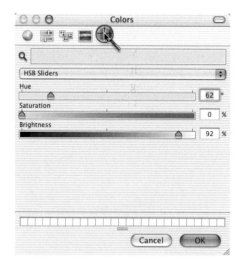

FIGURE 12.4   *The HSB slider set to 92% Brightness.*

- Clicking the magnifying glass icon in the Colors box changes the Selection tool to a magnifying glass with crosshairs. You can click anywhere in the Canvas and zoom in to see individual pixels to select a color for the title.

- Clicking the color wheel and the other color-picking tools in the top-left corner of the Colors box opens the various color pickers.

- The Font Color section of the Controls tab has a swirling symbol button (next to the eyedropper). It lets you select the direction on the color wheel that a keyframed change in color over time will take.

- Origin—Clicking the Origin button turns the Selection tool into a crosshair when placed over the Canvas window. When you click anywhere in the window, the center of the title clip moves to where you click. It's one of two ways that you can select where the title appears in the frame. See the section "Using the Motion Tab" for the other way of placing titles where you want them in the frame. It is keyframeable to change over time.

- Tracking—Much like a word processor, tracking changes the horizontal spacing between the letters in the title. For example, you could animate the letters to start far apart and then come together to form the word.

- Leading—Changes the vertical spacing between the lines of text. It is keyframeable to change over time.

- Aspect—Changes the letters' aspect ratio. Moving the slider to the right squishes them. Moving it to the left makes them taller.

- Auto Kerning check box—Automatically kerns the text (the spaces between the letters) to be correct. Its default setting is checked on.

- Use Subpixel check box—Final Cut Pro renders moving text with more smoothness when this option is checked on. When Use Subpixel is turned off, each move is in full-pixel jumps. Most movement is on "partial pixel" boundaries. Subpixel rendering allows a title, for example, to land on the "between" pixel. This can cause some softening of the text. It takes much longer to render. The Use Subpixel default setting is checked on.

Using the Crawl Generator

The Crawl generator, shown in Figure 12.5, creates horizontally scrolling text, much like a severe-weather warning or a ticker tape stream of stock market prices that moves left to right or right to left in a single row of text. The clip's length determines its speed as it is edited into your sequence. The longer the clip's duration, the slower the crawl's speed.

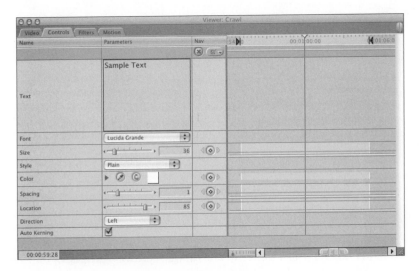

FIGURE 12.5   *The crawl's parameter controls.*

The parameters affecting the titles created with this tool are as follows:

- Spacing—This slider sets the spaces between letters. It is keyframeable to change over time.
- Location—This slider determines the vertical placement of the streaming words on the screen. The higher the number, the lower on the screen the crawl will be. It is keyframeable to change over time.
- Direction—This pop-up menu sets the crawl direction to the left or to the right.

Using the Lower 3rd Text Generator

The Lower 3rd generator, shown in Figure 12.6, creates titles like those seen under people being interviewed on TV. You can generate only two lines of text with an optional background. This tool's controls have the same names as the ones for the Text generator and work the same way. This Title tool can be played in real time if your computer is fast enough.

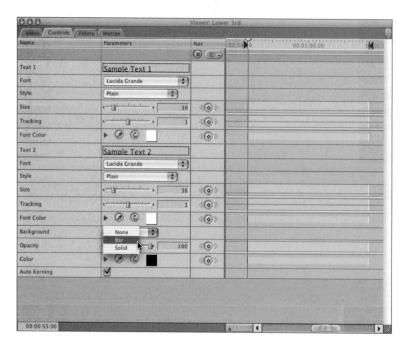

FIGURE 12.6   *Lower 3rd controls with a bar background selected.*

The Lower 3rd generator has only one unique control—the Background parameter.

The Background parameter creates a bar or solid that appears under both lines of text and goes across the entire screen, as shown in Figure 12.7. The Opacity slider affects only the opacity of the Background choice. The None selection leaves the Background option off. The Color selection controls the background's color.

FIGURE 12.7   *Lower 3rd controls with a solid background selected at 50% opacity.*

Using the Outline Text Generator

The Outline Text generator creates static text with an outline. What differentiates this generator is that you can fill (or not fill) the text and the outline it generates with any still clip you place in its set of wells. You can add a background that is generated by the tool, or you can put a clip in the background well. If you need to change the style of the row of letters, you can add another row of text with this same tool or use any other Text tool and layer that text above this tool's text. It's quite powerful. You could use this for your Lower 3rd titles instead of using the simpler Lower 3rd generator and create much more elaborate titles. If your computer is fast enough, this can be played in real time.

Figure 12.8 shows the unique parameters and how they were used to create the image you see in the Canvas. The parameters not discussed are identical to the ones in the basic Text generator.

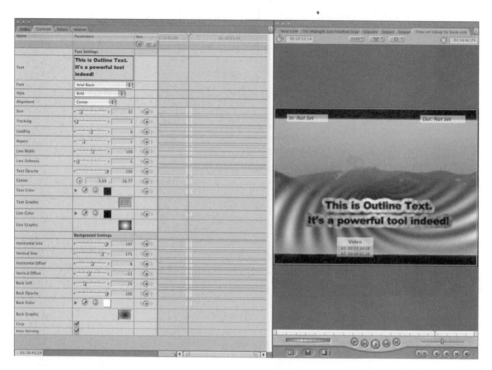

FIGURE 12.8   *The Outline Text generator.*

The control parameters that are unique to this tool are as follows:

- Aspect—Changes the aspect of all the parameters below it.
- Line Width—Changes the thickness of the outline.
- Line Softness—Changes the softness of the outline.
- Text Graphic—Any clip dragged to this well fills the letters with a still instead of color.
- Line Color—If no clip is placed in the Text Graphic well, the line around the text color is selected here.
- Line Graphic—Instead of a colored line, any clip placed here becomes the fill of the outline.

- Background Settings—These are as follows:
  - Horizontal Size—Changes the horizontal size of either the colored or Text Graphic background, masking the left and right sides, leaving the center area of the background in the picture.
  - Vertical Size—Adjusts the vertical size of the background, masking the top and bottom of the image or background color.
  - Horizontal Offset—Moving this slider to the right masks the left side of the background, and moving it to the left masks the right side of the background.
  - Vertical Offset—Moves the background up or down.
  - Back Soft—Softens all four sides of the background.
  - Back Opacity—Modifies the opacity of the background.
  - Back Color—The same color-selection tools for a colored background if a background graphic is not used.
  - Back Graphic—Any clip can be placed here for use as a background. The parameters are controlled with the Background Settings.
  - Crop—If this is checked on (the default), all the Background Settings work as described. If it is checked off, the Horizontal Size, Vertical Size, Horizontal Offset, and Vertical Offset controls squeeze the image instead of cropping or masking it.

Don't underestimate the power of the Outline Text generator. It's the easiest way to put a still inside text, for example. You simply type the text and drag video to the Text Graphic well. This is by far the most sophisticated of the Text tools. You can animate most of its parameters. Any parameter with a "mini-Timeline" next to its keyframe button is keyframeable to change over time. The possibilities are immense. It's one of the most underrated and least-understood tools in Final Cut Pro. Be sure to experiment with it.

Using the Scrolling Text Generator

Scrolling Text is the version of the Text tool that creates rolling titles, such as end credits for movies. You can scroll them up from the bottom (the default) or down from the top. It has a unique way to create center-justified dual columns of titles, as shown in Figure 12.9. You simply type the left column first, and then an asterisk, and then the right column. As you type in the text box, it automatically scrolls down. After you finish typing, you can use the keyboard's down arrow to scroll down through the text box if you need to make a change to a title that is below the visible area of the text box. If the alignment is set to Center in the Alignment pop-up menu, you get the result shown in Figure 12.9.

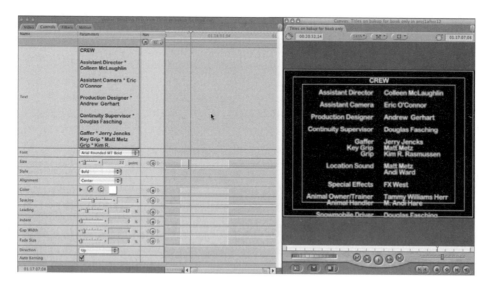

FIGURE 12.9 *The Scrolling Text generator.*

The longer you edit this effect's duration to be, the longer it takes to roll the entire list. The shorter you make this effect's duration, the faster the entire edit rolls or scrolls.

The parameters unique to the Scrolling Text tool are as follows:

- Spacing—The same as kerning. Spacing changes the horizontal space between letters.

- Indent—If the Alignment is Left, this moves all the titles to the right. If the Alignment is Right, this moves all the titles to the left. If the Alignment is Center, this does nothing.

- Gap Width—With two rows of text, this narrows or widens the gap between the two justified columns.

- Fade Size—Creates a fade effect at the top and bottom of the screen so that the rolling tiles fade in as they appear onscreen and fade out as they roll up or down. The higher the percentage, the wider and longer the fade effect lasts.

Using the Typewriter Generator

The Typewriter Text tool, shown in Figure 12.10, animates the letters as if they were being typed onscreen by a typewriter. The letters appear one at a time. This generator allows for more than one line of text.

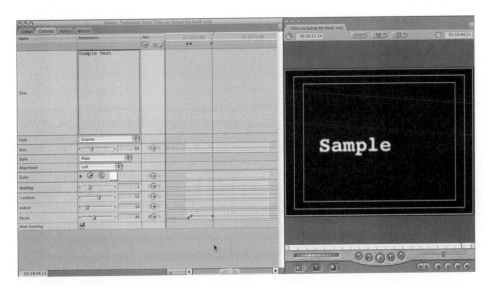

Figure 12.10   *The Typewriter Text tool.*

The parameters unique to the Typewriter Text tool are as follows:

- Location—Raises and lowers the vertical placement of the text.

- Indent—Changes the horizontal placement of the text.

- Pause—Speeds up or slows down the amount of time it takes for the letters to appear onscreen.

The Calligraphy Title Tools

The FCP installation CD has a plugin program written by Boris FX called Calligraphy. Calligraphy is an abbreviated version of Boris's title plugin, Graffiti. Calligraphy contains two more Title generators. You access them from the Generator pop-up menu in the Viewer or from the Effects tab in the Video Generators folder. I feel that the Calligraphy tools are much superior to the older Text tools. The earlier Text tools are included so that you can open project files from earlier versions of Final Cut Pro, and they certainly are useful for a quick title. They also allow you to see your changes over the background video, so they have that advantage.

After they are installed, the Calligraphy tools are named Title 3D and Title Crawl. They can be accessed from the Generator pop-up menu, as shown in Figure 12.11. Figure 12.12 shows the Title 3D Text tool.

Title 3D is a vector graphics-based generator. In that same menu you'll find Title Crawl. It's similar to Title 3D, however, this generator is a bitmap image-based generator, as are all the tools we've discussed so far. A *vector graphic* is a resolution-independent image. It's mathematically represented as a series of lines and curves. This means that if it is scaled larger, it looks good no matter what size it was originally created at. A *bitmap image* is based on images that are defined as a grid of pixels, each a specified color. If the images are scaled larger, they do not hold their quality, because the pixels become apparent. The vector graphics-based Title 3D plugin therefore has an advantage over the use of the native tools.

FIGURE 12.11
Accessing Title 3D from the Generator pop-up menu.

Color Ramp

FIGURE 12.12   *The Title 3D window.*

When either generator is active, you cannot go between its interface and Final Cut Pro's interface other than to choose the colors from your Mac desktop (such as a color in the video you are getting ready to overlay this title with). However, both generators' color-picking eyedroppers pick colors and values from the Canvas and Viewer, as well as from the Mac desktop.

Notice that the menu bar across the top of the screen has changed; it relates only to Title 3D. However, the operating system still reports Final Cut Pro as the application.

You can quickly apply either the Title 3D generator or the Title Crawl generator from the Video Generators bin contained in the Browser's Effects tab and drag either to the Timeline. When you do, the text entry window opens, ready to edit. If you access one of these generators using the Generator button, the text entry and style window opens. After the title is saved, it becomes a clip ready for insertion into your sequence. From the new title's Video tab, you can click the title itself and drag it to the Browser and use it just as you would any other video clip.

Remember that this generator's maximum duration can only be up to 2 minutes. Text entry and text style are done from either the Title 3D or Title Crawl windows. Other animations and parameter controls are contained in the Controls tab of the Viewer of any given title. Note that you can't save this title in any way except as a clip in the Browser or your sequence. After you delete it from the Viewer, it can be recalled only if you edited it into a sequence earlier or dragged it from the Viewer to the Browser, thus saving it there. You click the Apply button when you want to create a clip of this computer-generated image file.

After you create titles within either plugin program's window and save them by clicking either's Apply button, they become clips and can be edited in your sequence the same as any other clip.

tip

Title 3D and Title Crawl have the same duration limitation as any other generator in Final Cut Pro. Outline Text, Text, Scrolling Text, and so on are all limited to 2 minutes (as are a still, color matte, gradient, and so on) if they are dragged directly to a program. You can make any generator's duration longer by dragging it from the Viewer to the Browser after you've created it, and then modify its duration by changing the Duration field to the right of the name column and then adding it with this longer duration to your sequence.

Using Title 3D

The upper window in Figure 12.13 is where you type the text you want to create, and the lower window is where all formatting of any highlighted text is done. The tabs along the left side pull up various sets of controls.

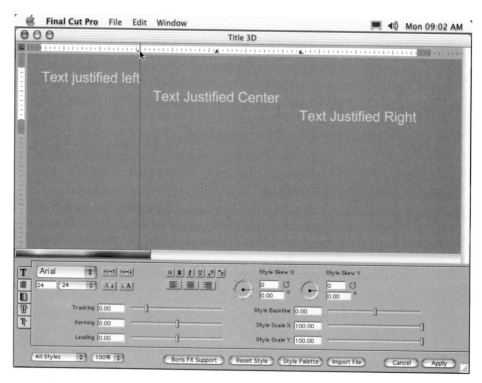

FIGURE 12.13   *Tabs and their justifications.*

The Text Preview Window

Figure 12.13 shows the text entry window. To enter your text, type it in this window. Any highlighted text here is affected by changes you make from the set of tabs in the lower window. Across the top is a ruler on which you can set tabs to help position your text. To create a tab, click the ruler and drag the tab to the desired position. To change the tab's justification, double-click it. Figure 12.13 shows the three justifications. To delete a tab, just drag it down and away from the ruler.

The white area of the ruler represents the page's boundaries, which are determined by the Page Width and Margin controls. In other words, this defines the text area. Page Width controls determine a page size *if* the Text Wrap pop-up menu is set to wrap.

The gray areas of the ruler indicate the margins determined by the Margin controls. See the section "Using the Page Tab" to learn how to work with these controls.

The rectangular color ramp in the lower-left (the rainbow colored bar across the left bottom of the text Preview window) is a quick way to pick a color with the eyedroppers available in the other tabs. If you simply click the colored version of this bar, it changes to a ramp from black to white to let you pick a luminance value between white and black for your title. Re-clicking it will change it back to the color ramp.

Keep in mind that you must select the text to be modified from the various tabs for that text to be affected. Also, unlike the "native" Text tools, you can select *any* text to be affected. Therefore, you can have as many different fonts and styles as you want within the same clip. You can even affect only one or more letters within words.

Using the Pop-Up Menus and Buttons at the Bottom of the Text Entry Window

Figure 12.14 shows the menus and buttons at the bottom of the window. They are the same in both the Title 3D plug-in application and the Title Crawl plug-in application.

FIGURE 12.14   *The menus and buttons common to Title 3D and Title Crawl.*

The two pop-up menus on the left are as follows:

- The style preview menu lets you preview all the styles you have applied. By selecting Basic Styles, you can preview the text without shadows, borders, and some text transformations. The idea is that you can preview the text faster, because the computer doesn't have to build all these styles in the Text Preview window.

- The scale selection menu lets you select a percentage of the actual scale of your text. Using a smaller percentage lets you see more text in the Text Preview window at one time. It also speeds up previews of the text.

The buttons across the bottom of the Calligraphy tools offer more options:

- Boris FX Support—Connects your Internet browser to Boris's website.
- Reset Style—Resets any highlighted text to the default setting. It does not change any page setup parameters you might have created, just the style settings you've used for the text itself.
- Style Palette—Opens the Style Palette (discussed in the later section "Using the Style Palette"). The Style Palette can store text styles that can be downloaded from Boris, plus any you create and want to use again. You can save a lot of work when you save a style you use repeatedly!
- Import File—You can import either a simple text file or a rich-text format file. A dialog box opens for you to locate the file for import. All basic text styles are applied to the imported text.
- Cancel—Cancels any changes you made and takes you back to Final Cut Pro.
- Apply—Saves the changes to any text and formatting you have created.

Using the Style Tab

When you first launch either Title 3D or Title Crawl, the Style tab is selected, as shown in Figure 12.15. This tab has a plain black T on it. It allows you to pick the font, size, and style of the text. It also allows you to set justification, tracking, kerning, and leading for the characters.

FIGURE 12.15   *The Style tab parameters.*

The Style tab parameters are as follows:

- The Font menu—You choose fonts and sizes here with the pop-up menus. You can also type a size into the size box, and you can click the two buttons with the As on them to quickly raise or lower the font size. This is very useful when you have different font sizes, because it doesn't change the sizes in a relative manner and doesn't assign the same size to all characters selected. The two buttons above the A buttons let you preview text by changing the font either up or down the font list without using the pop-up menu.

- The style buttons—Selected text can be styled with normal, bold, italic, underline, superscript, and subscript. These buttons toggle the style on and off.

- The justification buttons—Click here to justify all of the text on the page to the left, center, or right.

- Tracking—Sets the horizontal space between two or more selected letters on all of the text on the page.

- Kerning—Sets the distance between selected text.

- Leading—Sets the vertical space between all rows of text on the page.

- Style Skew X and Style Skew Y controls—With these controls you can distort the selected characters along the X- and Y-axes. Using these controls simulates turning the selected letters on an axis in 3D space.

- Style Baseline—Modifies the vertical position of the selected text. It lets you create text that appears above the text's baseline. This is used for effects such as pushing up a word or letter from the baseline of the other words or letters.

- Style Scale X and Style Scale Y controls—Sets the scale of selected text along the vertical and horizontal axes. For example, you might want to enlarge the first letter of a word whose letters are all-caps, or stretch entire words up, down, or sideways.

Using the Page Tab

The Page tab, shown in Figure 12.16, is used to set the margins and size of the page you are working with. This tab has a set of lines, which represents lines on a page.

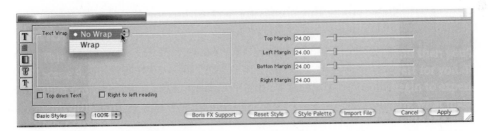

FIGURE 12.16   *The Page tab parameters.*

The Page tab's parameter settings are as follows:

- Text Wrap—Controls how the text is handled when it exceeds the width of the page. No Wrap lets you create a line of text that doesn't break or continue to the next line. Wrap creates additional lines of text as you create lines that come to the page width values. This should be turned on when you are creating many rows of text.

- Page Width—When Wrap is selected, this box and the adjoining slider set the width of the page.

- Top down Text—When this is selected, the text reads vertically.

- Right to left reading—When this is selected, text is read from right to left instead of from left to right, as if you're looking at it in a mirror.

- Top, Left, Bottom, and Right Margins—Selects the number of pixels for each of these margin-setting parameters.

Using the Fill Tab

The Fill tab, shown in Figure 12.17, determines how you will fill the text (with a color or with a gradient) and set its opacity. Its tab has a box with a gradient on it.

FIGURE 12.17   *The Fill tab parameters.*

The Fill tab's parameter settings are as follows:

- Fill On—Turning this on fills the text with color. Turning it off allows you to create an outline only of the text.

- Style Opacity—You can modify the opacity of the selected text by typing a percentage number in the box or using the slider control to its right.

- Text Fill menu—You can select Color, which is a solid color selected from the Style Color area, or select Gradient as a fill for the text. To activate the Gradient fill, select it from the Text Fill pop-up menu. When you select Gradient, the Click to Edit Gradient icon appears. Clicking it opens the Gradient Editor window, as shown in Figure 12.18.

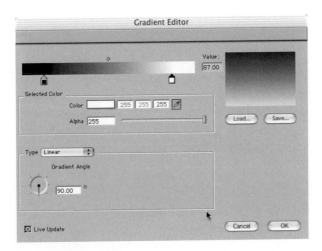

FIGURE 12.18   *The Gradient Editor window.*

- Color—Available when Color is selected in the Text Fill menu, Color sets the color of the selected text. Clicking the default white color box accesses the system color-picking controls, and you can set values in the boxes to its right. You can also use the eyedropper to select color anywhere on the screen, *including* the color ramp at the top of the Gradient Editor or in the Canvas window.

- Gradient Editor—When Gradient is selected in Text Fill, you can apply a graduated blend of two or more colors. You can edit their opacity, direction, and steepness by clicking the Gradient Editor button to open the Gradient Editor.

- Color stops—The squares under the gradient line in the top area of the Gradient Editor determine the colors and the positions of those colors in the gradient. To change them, click one of the boxes; the triangle above it turns black. The selected stop can then be modified for color and opacity. The Alpha box and slider adjust the opacity setting for that color stop. You can also drag the color stop right or left to modify the look of the ramp.

  The diamond above the gradient displays the midpoint between the colors. You can drag it left or right to change it.

  You can add as many color stops as you want by clicking just below the gradient line near the top of the Gradient Editor window next to the two that open in the default setting. In this way you can create multiple colors within a gradient. You can also drag these color stops left or right along the gradient to create a shorter blending area for your colors.

  Drag a color stop down away from the gradient to remove it.

- Shaping a gradient's direction—A set of controls in the lower half of this window changes the gradient's shape and direction. The pop-up menu lets you select whether the shape is linear (see Figure 12.18) or radial (see Figure 12.19).

  If you select Linear, The Gradient Angle controls the gradient's angle. If you select Radial, the controls determine the gradient's X or Y position, lowering, raising, and sliding left or right. The Radial gradient changes its relative position within the letters filled.

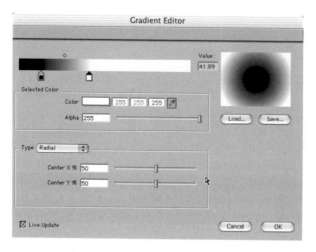

FIGURE 12.19   *The Radial gradient parameters.*

- Saving and loading gradients—Clicking the Save button saves a gradient for later use. It opens a dialog box allowing you to name and choose a location for that gradient to be saved to. Clicking the Load button opens a dialog box allowing you to load a previously saved gradient.

Using the Border Tab

Figure 12.20 shows the controls in the Border tab—the one with a bordered T on it. Notice that you can add up to five different borders by clicking the check box next to each. You can add more than one border to the same selected text. Each tab with a check box next to it contains these controls:

- Edge Style—This pop-up menu allows you to select whether the edge is Plain, Bevel, or Glowing.

- Position—Selects the border's location—Inside, Outside, or Center. The edge is put around the inside or outside of the selected letters, or even in the middle of the color fill.
- Edge Color—Selects the color of the edge.
- Edge Width—Selects the width of the edge in pixels.
- Edge Opacity—Selects the opacity of the edge.
- Edge Softness—Softens the edges of Glowing text.

FIGURE 12.20   *The Border tab parameters and controls.*

Using the Shadow Tab

The Shadow tab, shown in Figure 12.21, has a T with a drop shadow. Calligraphy adds up to five different shadow treatments to the same selected text. You cannot animate these shadows with this set of generators, but you can animate shadows in the Motion tab settings, as discussed in the section "Using the Motion Tab." Be aware that the Motion tab's shadows do not contain a cast or solid shadow.

FIGURE 12.21   *The Shadow tab parameters and controls.*

The controls for shadows are as follows:

- Shadow Type—Determines the type of shadow added to selected text:
  - Drop Shadow—Falls a specified distance from the letters.
  - Cast Shadow—Appears to fall on another object. The distance from the object and the shape of the object it falls on determine the shadow's appearance and shape.
  - Solid Shadow—Simulates 3D letters. It applies a gradient to a shadow. Keep in mind that these are still two-dimensional objects, and if you change the Z-axis of this generator, they will reveal that they are still two-dimensional objects. When Solid Shadow is selected, a second set of color tools appears. One set determines the shadow's highlight color, and the other selects the actual color of the shadow itself.

- Shadow Color—Determines the shadow's color. It works the same as the other color selectors.

- Shadow Distance—Sets the shadow's distance from the letters. A greater distance makes the letters appear farther from the background.

- Shadow Opacity—Sets the shadow's opacity.

- Shadow Softness—Blurs the shadow's edges, giving it the appearance of being lit by a softer light source.

- Shadow Angle—Determines the shadow's angle. By dragging around the dial, you can change the apparent direction of the light source.

Using the Style Palette

The Style Palette, shown in Figure 12.22, is common to both the Title 3D generator and the Title Crawl generator. Because both generators can program very sophisticated text parameters, it would be very cumbersome to have to repeatedly program a special set of looks that you might want to use again in the same project or future projects. This palette is the place to store font styles you have created so that you can retrieve them for later use.

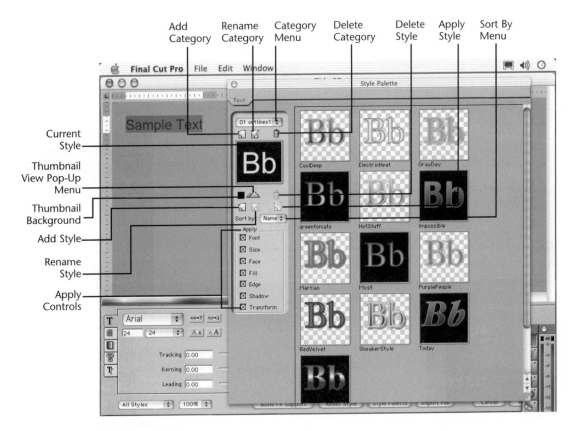

FIGURE 12.22   *The Style Palette.*

The features of this tool are as follows:

- Category menu—Stores sets of types of styles. When you change categories, the window on the right shows you previews of the different saved styles in that category.

- Add Category button—Displays a dialog box to name the new category. When you click OK, it is created and ready for use. You might create a category for use with certain shows, for example. They don't have to match each other in any particular way within the same category. When you save a new style, it is saved to the current category.

- Rename Category—Renames the current category.

- Delete Category trash can—Deletes the current category. A bit of caution is called for here.

- Current Style—Displays a thumbnail of the style of the characters currently highlighted in the text entry window. To update it, click the Thumbnail background under it.

- Thumbnail Background button—Allows you to change the view of the thumbnail background from black to checkerboard. The checkerboard background reveals a black drop shadow, for example.

- Thumbnail View pop-up menu—Changes the view of the thumbnails of the various selectable styles in the window on the right. You can size them or put them in a list. The list view shows their names as well as the dates they were created.

- Delete Style trash can—Deletes the selected style from the window on the right. This action cannot be undone, but a warning dialog box appears when you click this trash can.

- Add Style—Adds a style to the current category. To add a style, create one in the text window, highlight the text that uses the style, and then click this button. The check boxes below this area apply only the selected controls.

- Rename Style—Opens a dialog box where the saved and selected style is highlighted.

- Apply Style—Applies the style you've selected from the window on the right.

- Sort By menu—When you use the list view from the thumbnail pop-up menu, you can sort the list of styles by name or date.

- Apply Controls—When you apply or save styles, only the attributes checked here are saved or applied. You can apply just colors or shadows, for example.

tip　By registering Calligraphy with Boris (http://www.borisfx.com), you can download a large set of preset styles that, after being installed, show up here as presets you can use or modify to your liking. The preset styles are free just for taking a peek at Boris's site and registering!

The suggested workflow here is to select text in the Text window you want to apply a style to. You can select one character or all of them by pressing Cmd+A. Then double-click a selected style from the Style Palette.

Animating the Title 3D Generator

The Viewer's Controls tab contains the parameters of this Text generator's controls. These controls affect the entire title. Using keyframes, you can animate the text over time with most of the parameters. Only the check boxes do not allow any animation to take place. Using these controls to animate really brings your text to life.

The top half of these controls are shown in Figure 12.23 and are described next.

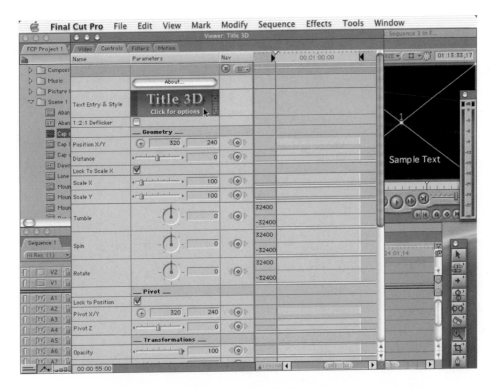

FIGURE 12.23   *The top parameter controls in the Title 3D Text generator.*

- Text Entry & Style—Activates the text entry window. After you've applied a title generated by this tool to the Timeline window, you can double-click it from the sequence for further modifications by clicking the Title 3D Click for Options box.

- 1:2:1 Deflicker—Applies a vertical blur to the title. It helps eliminate flickering in moving titles and smoothes hard edges. *It is especially useful with titles created in a DV sequence.*

- Geometry parameter settings:

  - Position X/Y—Sets the coordinates of the text block. It defaults to the center of the screen.

  - Distance—Modifies the apparent depth of the title in 3D space.

  - Lock to Scale X—Locks the Y and X axis parameters so that moving one moves the other.

- Scale X and Scale Y—Changes the size of the text block in percentages of the original text size.
- Tumble, Spin, and Rotate—Each modifies the text perspective along the X, Y, and Z axis, respectively. You can set keyframes and animate these parameters over time.

- Pivot:

    - Lock to Position—The text block revolves around its center point. If this box is unchecked, the Pivot X/Y and Pivot Z parameters are used.
    - Pivot X/Y and Pivot Z—Determines the coordinates of a point around which the Tumble, Spin, and Rotate parameters pivot.

Figure 12.24 shows the remainder of the parameters contained in the Viewer's controls for the Title 3D generator.

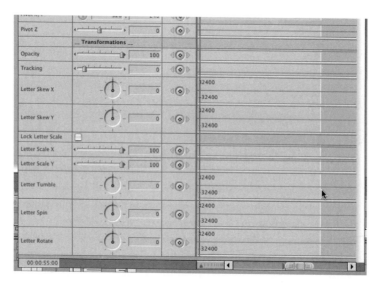

FIGURE 12.24 *The rest of the parameter controls in the Title 3D Text generator.*

note   All settings applied to individual letters are affected proportionally by the global transformations.

The remaining parameters are as follows:

- Transformations:
    - Opacity—Sets the global percentage of the title's opacity. Individual letters retain their relative opacity.
    - Tracking—Globally controls the distance between all the letters in the title.
    - Letter Skew X and Letter Skew Y—Distorts the text along the horizontal and vertical axis. Individual letter skew remains relative.
    - Lock Letter Scale—Locks the scale of the text along the horizontal and vertical axes. Individual letters scale proportionally.
    - Letter Scale X and Letter Scale Y—Sets the global settings of the size of the letters on the X- and Y-axes.
    - Letter Tumble, Letter Spin, and Letter Rotate—Rotates the letters around their baseline settings on the X-, Y-, and Z-axes, respectively.

Using the Title Crawl Generator

All the Text tools described for the Title 3D generator are the same for the Title Crawl generator as well. This tool's purpose is to create long title rolls and crawls. The difference between the Title 3D generator and the Title Crawl generator is that the latter has different animation controls. This generator can create text that *rolls* top to bottom or bottom to top, as with credits. It also can create a *crawl* of a single line or sets of lines from left to right or right to left, such as a constantly updating warning, a feature set, or a stock ticker. You choose a style of letters the same way you do with the Title 3D Text generator.

Animating Text with the Title Crawl Generator

Figure 12.25 shows the parameters of the animation controls available with the Title Crawl generator. Notice the Add Keyframe buttons too, because they denote that these parameters can be changed over time.

Figure 12.25   *The Title Crawl generator controls.*

The parameters in the Viewer's control tab are as follows:

■ Text Entry & Style—Clicking here opens or reopens the Text Style window.

■ 1:2:1 Deflicker—Adds a vertical blur to the text, smoothes the edges, and reduces flicker.

■ Animation Style—Specifies whether the title rolls or crawls. Be aware that it defaults to None.

■ Mask Start and Mask End—Sets the distance in pixels of masks where the titles begin to appear. In the case of a roll, they can be set to start from somewhere other than the bottom or the top and end before the bottom or the top.

■ Blend Start and Blend End—Softens the top and bottom or sides of the animations. They hide the text as it moves.

■ Reverse Direction—Changes the direction of a roll from bottom to top. In the case of a crawl, it changes the direction of the movement from right to left and then moves left to right.

■ Position X/Y—Clicking the crosshair and then clicking the Canvas window resets the position of the block up or down on the screen.

■ Opacity—Determines the title's opacity. It produces various transparencies.

note   A rolling or crawling block can be part of the title. There's no reason not to build a title with some rolling elements, static graphics, or bugs and other animations.

Using Title Safe

You should use the Title Safe overlay when you are creating titles. Final Cut Pro displays the entire *raster* of the video image. This means that it displays the *entire* recorded image from your tape, top to bottom and side to side. Many older television sets can crop up to 10% of the actual recorded picture all the way around. Final Cut Pro supplies the Title Safe overlay so that you can be positive that all titles will be seen on all television sets.

To use the Title Safe overlay, select Overlays from the View Options pop-up menu in the Canvas window. Then, with Overlays checked on, select Show Title Safe to be checked on as well, as shown in Figure 12.26. You then see the Title Safe overlay.

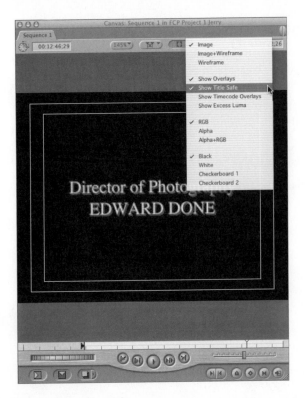

FIGURE 12.26   *Activating the Title Safe overlay.*

The Title Safe overlay is composed of two boxes, as shown in Figure 12.26. The outer box, called the *action safe,* is set 5% in on all four sides of the image. The second and inner box is drawn a full 10% in on all four sides of the image. You can rest assured that if your titles are set within this smaller area, they will be seen on all television sets. Remember too that this is a guideline. If you fudge a bit and place titles between the two boxes, they usually will be seen on all sets, but to be absolutely certain, you should stay within the inner box. Don't worry; this Title Safe overlay isn't recorded into your program. It's there to help you make sure that your titles will be seen and won't be cut off by a television set's cowling, which covers some of the picture tube.

The Action Safe box gives you a guide as to what will be seen on TVs as far as picture goes. On many TV sets, the curved tube might distort titles a bit, causing a small amount of geometric distortion, so it's best to keep titles a bit away from this edge of the area. Modern TV sets with flat screens don't cause this error at the edges of the viewable picture.

Using the Motion Tab

The Motion tab is the farthest-right tab in the Viewer window. It is available for use with *every* video clip you import or create with the Generator pop-up menu. Figure 12.27 shows its default settings when you click its tab in the Viewer window. With this window you can modify the parameters of a video clip's Basic Motion, Crop, Distort, Opacity, Drop Shadow, and Motion Blur settings.

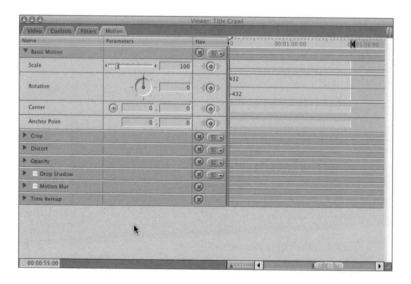

FIGURE 12.27   *The Motion tab default view.*

Each set of these parameter settings has a triangle next to its name. By clicking a triangle, you can open its individual controls. Keep in mind that you can close the triangles to hide other parameters' settings so that you don't have to scroll through the window as much. Also note that the Drop Shadow and Motion Blur settings have to be turned on by checking the box next to each of their names. The other settings take effect when you modify them. The Basic Motion settings are described first.

Using Basic Motion

The Basic Motion settings, as shown in Figure 12.27, determine the size, rotation, position, and anchor point around which the clip rotates.

As with all effect parameters, you can reset this to its default position by clicking the red X reset button. Each of the parameters is keyframeable to change over time by setting different parameters with keyframes in the associated parameter Timeline to the right of each parameter setting. The parameters are as follows:

- Scale—The slider and percentage box resize the clip up or down in size.
- Rotation—Rotates the clip on the Z-axis (like the traditional spinning newspaper/headlines shot might do).
- Center—Clicking the crosshair button and then clicking anywhere in the Canvas resets the clip's center position.
- Anchor Point—Sets the position of the anchor point that the rotation rotates around. Its default position is the center of the clip's frame.

Using the Crop Parameters

If you crop the edges of a clip with the Crop tool, as you did in the preceding chapter, the Crop parameters change. Figure 12.28 shows these controls. You can crop the frame's Left, Right, Top, and Bottom edges by using the sliders or by entering a number of pixels in the adjoining boxes. Note too that you can change the crop values over time and create a moving crop. You could use this in all sorts of ways, the most obvious of which would be a hard-edged wipe coming from one of the four sides and continuing across the screen. At the bottom of the set of sliders in this parameter control, you can soften the edges with the Edge Feather parameter control.

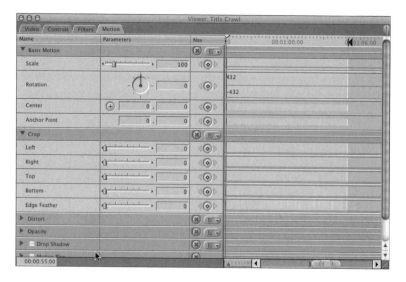

FIGURE 12.28 *The Crop parameter controls.*

Cropping is a percentage of screen width. If you crop more than 50% from two edges, the image reappears, so keep this in mind when you are cropping both sides of the image.

You can also use the Image + Wireframe view of the Viewer or Canvas and crop the sides with the Crop tool (which you activate by pressing C). When you use this method, your crop coordinates are reflected here.

Using the Distort Parameters

Each of the four corners of your video can be placed anywhere, including outside the raster of your image. When this parameter is not changed, you see the pixel coordinates from the center of each of the four corners, as shown in Figure 12.29. You can change them by typing in new coordinates, or you can change your view of the Viewer or Canvas to be Image + Wireframe and activate the Distort tool by pressing D. Wherever you drag a corner with the Distort tool, its new coordinates are reflected here. It's probably more intuitive to use the Distort tool than the Distort parameter controls. Each corner can be programmed to move over time with keyframes.

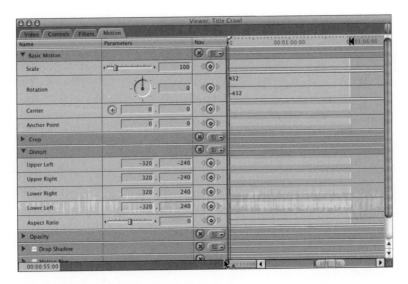

FIGURE 12.29   *The Distort parameter controls.*

The one exception to using the Distort tool in the Canvas is that it doesn't include the Aspect Ratio slider. By dragging the slider to the left, you squeeze the top and bottom edges of the video, and by moving this slider to the right, you squeeze the image's sides closer together. You can also distort the picture in the Viewer or Canvas by holding down the Shift key and using the Selection tool (press A) to drag a corner in the Image + Wireframe view.

Using the Opacity Parameter

The Opacity Parameter, shown in Figure 12.30, is as simple as it looks. You've already been setting keyframes for this parameter by adding keyframes to a video's opacity in the keyframe overlay of the Timeline window. If you check the sequence, you can double-click any video clip and see these keyframes mirrored here. The same is true if you set keyframes and values here—they are reflected in the keyframe overlay of the video in the Timeline window.

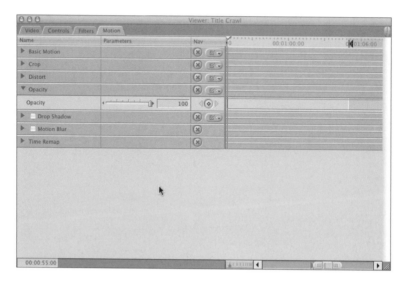

FIGURE 12.30   *The Opacity parameter control.*

Using the Drop Shadow Parameters

Figure 12.31 shows the Drop Shadow parameters in the Motion tab. Its use is pretty straightforward. You must turn it on using the check box next to its name for it to become active. The Drop Shadow can be used on titles as well as any other video clip, such as those used in a picture-in-picture effect. Keep in mind that its parameters are programmable to change over time. You could create an effect in which the light source of the drop shadow moves, for example.

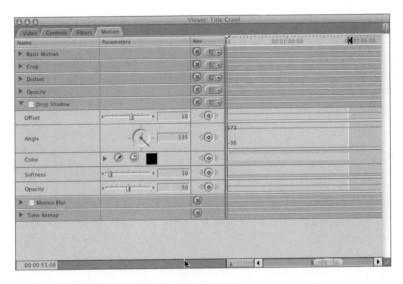

FIGURE 12.31   *The Drop Shadow parameter controls.*

The Drop Shadow parameters are as follows:

- Offset—Determines the distance between the shadow and the object it is a shadow of.
- Angle—Determines the angle of the shadow from the object.
- Color—Determines the color of the drop shadow and uses the same color controls as the native Title generators.
- Softness—Blurs the shadow around its edges to give the effect of a diffused light source.
- Opacity—Determines the opacity of the drop shadow.

Using the Motion Blur Parameters

When the Motion Blur parameter, shown in Figure 12.32, is checked on, it blurs any clip with motion applied to it. An example of this is a clip that has been programmed to move across the screen. This parameter does not add blur to motion within a frame. It uses the specified sample rate and amount of blur (%) you specify in its two settings. The higher the sample rate and the greater the percentage you apply to it, the more blurred the move becomes.

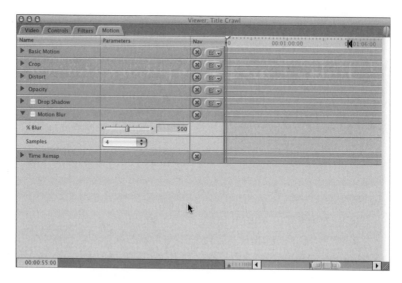

FIGURE 12.32   *The Motion Blur controls.*

This could be used to fly titles with blurs. As the title comes onto the screen, it becomes blurry, giving it a special effect.

Workshop 12: Create Titles

In this workshop you'll create the titles used in the film, as well as create some effects with them in another sequence. The workshop starts with titles created in the Text tools and then progresses into the Calligraphy tools. You'll also experiment with placing titles with the position parameters and use the Motion tab for some exercises.

Create the First Title

You'll create the first couple of titles that open the film with the native Title tool; in the next section you'll move on and work with both the Calligraphy tools.

1. Click the Generator pop-up menu in the lower-right corner of the Viewer's Video tab, and select Text, Text. A text clip appears in the Viewer.

2. Navigate to 01:00:03;03 in Sequence 1, and set an In point there. Then set an Out point at 01:00:09;14.

3. Overwrite the text clip onto track V1.

4. Double-click this new title to load it into the Viewer, and position the playhead anywhere within the SAMPLE TEXT default title. By doing this, you will see it update as you modify it.

5. Turn on Show Title Safe from the Canvas View options pop-up menu.

6. Click the Controls tab in the Viewer, and change the SAMPLE TEXT title to GRACE FILMS. Press Enter and type **presents**. Click outside the Text entry box to see the update happen in the Canvas. Note that Final Cut Pro doesn't let you view video if you have activated the Caps Lock on the keyboard. As soon as you release it, all becomes normal.

7. In the Viewer window's Font pop-up menu, select Times or a similar font. Notice that the alignment of the rows is centered as the default setting. If you want to, look at the other justifications available by selecting them from the Alignment pop-up menu, but leave the title centered.

8. Slide the Size slider to about 50. (You might want to hold down the Command key for more precise movement.) Notice the size change as you do this. Notice too how you could easily make this title "unsafe" by making the size too large. You can also type **50** in the Size box next to the slider to be accurate. The slider is more fun to watch, though, and it's also better for resizing titles when their size really matters.

Use the Motion Tab to Fade the Title

1. Click the Motion tab in the Viewer, and then click the triangle next to the Opacity parameter. Arrange your Viewer window so that you can see more of the parameter timeline similar to what you see in Figure 12.30. The idea is to see all of the parameter Timeline as well as the Opacity control. If you cannot see all of the light gray area of the parameter Timeline, press Shift+Z to fill the available area. Then position the playhead on the first frame of this title by clicking the Previous Edit button in the Canvas or by pressing Opt+E.

2. Click the Add Keyframe button in the Opacity parameter. Notice that a blue indicator appears above it next in the Opacity row. With the Viewer active, type **+45** and press Enter. The playhead moves 45 frames forward. Then add another keyframe there.

3. Press Shift+E to move to the next edit. Click the left arrow next to the keyframe button to put the playhead on the last frame of the title. Remember that when you jump from edit point to edit point using the buttons or the keyboard commands, you move the playhead to the first frame of the *next edit*. In this case, this is a frame past the end of the title clip, and a frame later than you want to be.

4. Set a keyframe on the last frame of the title, type **-45**, and press Enter. The playhead moves back in the title by 45 frames. Set another keyframe there. Click the left arrow next to the keyframe button twice to navigate to the first keyframe. Type **0** in the Opacity parameter box.

5. Click the right arrow next to the keyframe box three times until you stop on the last keyframe. This time, to lower the opacity to 0, click and hold on that keyframe as you drag it down. Play the title. Render it if you need to. Highlight it and press Cmd+R.

There's more than one way you could do this. You could have set the opacities as you added the keyframes, but you learned that you can navigate between them with the keyframe arrows. Notice too that the keyframes are reflected in your clip in the Timeline window if clip overlays are turned on, and you could just as well have done the fades as you have been doing so far.

Note too that aesthetically we still will hear the lonely wind begin before the first title. Setting the titles over a transparent background (in this case, it appears black) also keeps the cold in mind. You wouldn't want to put the titles over a bright happy color, would you? Keep titles simple when you can. Less is more, usually.

Create the Movie Title

1. By clicking the Generator button, create another title the same way you did the first one. Edit this title into the V1 track in Sequence 1 from 01:00:09;15 for a duration of 6:15 (type **615** in the duration timecode box in the upper left of the Viewer). This edit should leave an unused time of just over a second of dead space after this title and before the "Cap up mtn side dusk" opening shot of the film.

2. Double-click this title to load it from the Timeline to the Viewer. Click the Controls tab, and change SAMPLE TEXT to THE MIDNIGHT SUN (no quotes, all caps, and use the same font you used in the first title). Change the Size to 50, and then add opacity changes that will have the title fade up at the beginning and then fade down at the end for 45 frames. When you are done, Sequence 1 should look like Figure 12.33.

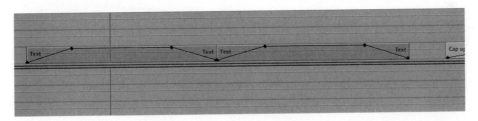

FIGURE 12.33   *The first two titles in Sequence 1 after step 2.*

3. There is a way to tell what these titles are just by looking at them in the Timeline. Ctrl-click the first of these and select Item Properties, Format from the pop-up submenu. The clip's Properties dialog box opens. You can change the name of the clip from there. Change the name to Grace Films Presents.

4. Change the name of the second title to The Midnight Sun. When you are done, your sequence should look like Figure 12.34. Notice that the title clips are a pale purple, and the other video clips are light blue to help you recognize the type of image they are.

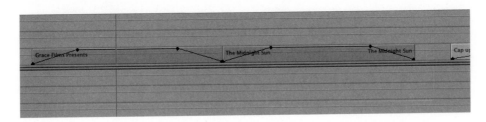

FIGURE 12.34   *Renamed titles after step 4.*

Create the End Titles

You'll use the Calligraphy tools to create the end titles. The first few are simple fade-ups and fade-downs using Title 3D, followed by a credit roll that uses Title Crawl.

1. Select Title 3D from the Generator pop-up menu in the Viewer. When you do, the Title 3D text entry window opens.

2. This time, you'll create the titles first and then edit them into the sequence. In the text entry window, type **Written & Directed** and press Enter. Type **by** and press Enter. Type **LARRY MCLAUGHLIN** (see Figure 12.35). Don't worry about matching the sample font in this step.

FIGURE 12.35   *The first end credit after step 2.*

3. Press Cmd+A to select all the text in the window. In the Font pop-up menu, select Times, or the same font you substituted before for the earlier titles.

4. Change the font size to 50 by typing it in the Font Size box. Click the Apply button in the lower-right corner of the text entry window. The text entry window disappears, and you now have a title clip you can see in the Viewer.

5. You can check to see if the title clip is broadcast-safe by turning on the Title Safe overlay in the Viewer's view options pop-up menu. Select Overlays, Title Safe.

6. The clip fits within the inner box, but it's pretty large. It might be a bit over the top, and it's not centered. It needs more work. Click the Controls tab in the Viewer. Then click the Title 3D logo in the Controls panel. The text entry window opens again, ready for a further modification.

7. Click the center justification button. The text centers automatically. It now matches the style you used earlier up front.

8. Press Cmd+A to select all the text. To decrease the size, click the button immediately to the right of the size pop-up menu (it has a big A and a smaller A on it). All the text drops in size 10 points for every click. If you go too far and click twice, you can click the next button over (the one with a small A and a bigger A) to jump back up in size 10 points at a time.

9. This is a little plain-looking, so add a three-dimensional drop shadow to it. With all the letters selected, click the Drop Shadow tab. Click the check box next to the T1 tab to add one layer of drop shadow. The default shadow is black. Because you will be putting this title over black, it won't be seen over a black background in the sequence unless it's a color other than black. If you click just past the N in Larry's last name to deselect the text, you'll see what I mean.

10. Select all letters (press Cmd+A) and click the Shadow Color box. Click the Color sliders (the second color icon from the right in the Colors Palette). Select either the Gray Scale slider or the HSB slider, and change the value to 70%. The original black color changes to gray. Click OK to accept the change. Deselect the letters by clicking just to the right of the N in Larry's last name.

11. It's hard to see this because the default background is gray. Ctrl-click the text entry window and select Change Background Color. Change the background color to a 0 value using the HSB color slider (black). Remember that you are not creating a background color; you are simply previewing the letters over something other than gray. Don't like it, do you? The problem is that it looks like you are seeing double!

12. Press Cmd+A. In the Shadow Type pull-down menu, select Solid Shadow. Click in the text entry box to create an outline around the selected text, revealing the new effect. Much better.

13. Play with the Shadow Distance control to set the letter thickness of this apparent 3D look. I like 6 or so. Decide for yourself where you want to leave it. Actually, I originally set the type to be plain with no drop, but this is a nice look too.

14. One last touch. Click the Highlight Color color box. Change the color from white to pale blue (reflecting the cold setting) just to give a touch of color to the white letters. When you are done, the text entry window should look like Figure 12.36.

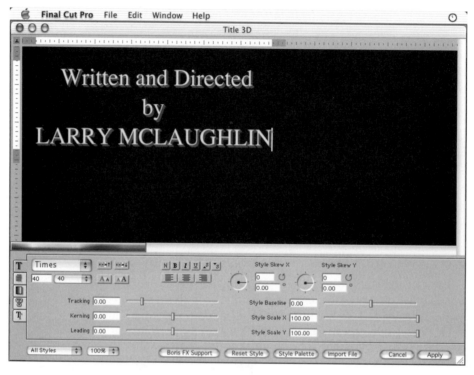

FIGURE 12.36   *The text entry window after step 14.*

Save the New Style

You now have a style you can repeat, so you'll save it for later use.

1. Click the Style Palette button to open the Style Palette. Make sure that all the check boxes in the Apply area are checked, as shown in Figure 12.37. Click the Add Category button in the upper-left corner. Type **Midnight Sun Styles** in the naming box and click OK.

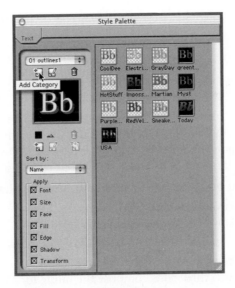

FIGURE 12.37   *Adding a new category to the Style Palette.*

2. Click the Add Style button, as shown in Figure 12.38. The style appears in this category and is saved for future use. Name this style anything you want. End Credits might be appropriate.

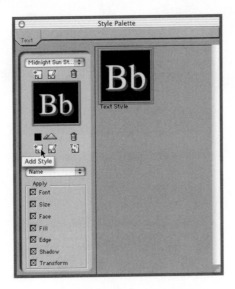

FIGURE 12.38   *A saved style in the Midnight Sun Styles category.*

3. Click the Apply button. Save your project.

Edit the First End Credit and Create a Music Track for the End Credits

1. With the first end title in the Viewer, edit it to the V1 track at 01:12:13;22 for a duration of 6;00. Its Out point should be at 01:12:19;21.

2. Fade the title up for a duration of 1 second at the beginning, and fade it down for 1 second at the end (30-frame durations for the fades).

3. With snapping turned on, locate the "Music-Net94.3-04" clip in the Music bin. Drag it directly to the A6 and A7 tracks (keeping the arrow pointing down by placing the clip in the lower two-thirds of the track to overwrite this edit). Place its head at the same position as the start of the "Written and Directed by" title.

4. Fade up its start for a duration of 1 second, mirroring the title's fade-up.

5. Add the "Music-Net94.3-06" clip in its entirety to the end of the "Music-Net94.3-04" clip on the same tracks.

6. Add the "Music-Net94.3-07" clip in its entirety to the end of the "Music-Net94.3-06" clip on the same tracks. Its Out point should be at 01:14:48;02. These three edits comprise the music for all the end credits. When you are done, this area of Sequence 1 should look like Figure 12.39.

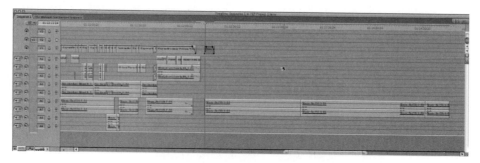

FIGURE 12.39   *The Timeline after step 6.*

Create Five More Fading Titles

1. Highlight the first fading title in the Timeline and press Cmd+C to copy it into memory.

2. Position the playhead at 01:12:19;22 in the Timeline. With the V1 track highlighted, press Cmd+V five times. Five more identical titles are added end to end on the V1 track.

3. Double-click the second title. Click its Controls tab in the Viewer. Click the Title 3D logo to change its contents to **Produced by COLLEEN MCLAUGHLIN**. Before you type, click the All Styles pop-up menu and change it to Basic Styles. This speeds up the typing process by using a basic style for text entry. When you apply the change, the styles are still applied. Keep the formatting the same (centered, size, and so on). Then click the Apply button.

4. Double-click the third title and change its contents to **Director of Photography** (first line) and **EDWARD DONE** (second line). Then click the Apply button.

5. Double-click the fourth title and change its contents to **Cap** (first line) and **DAN MUNDELL** (second line).

6. Double-click the fifth title and change its contents to **Sam McGee** (first line) and **SPENCER SEIM** (second line).

7. Drag the outgoing edit point of the last title to the right until its duration is 7:14. Drag the last keyframe until it is on the last frame of this (now longer) title. Drag the second-to-last keyframe over about 1:15 later in the clip to start its fade later.

8. Change this last fading title's contents to **Based on the** (first line), **Robert W. Service poem:** (second line), **"THE CREMATION OF** (third line), and **SAM MCGEE"** (fourth line). Leave the quotation marks around the poem's title. Lower the first two lines' point size to 36 (just highlight them and select 36 as the new size), as shown in Figure 12.40. After you click the Apply button, your sequence should look like Figure 12.41. Save your project file.

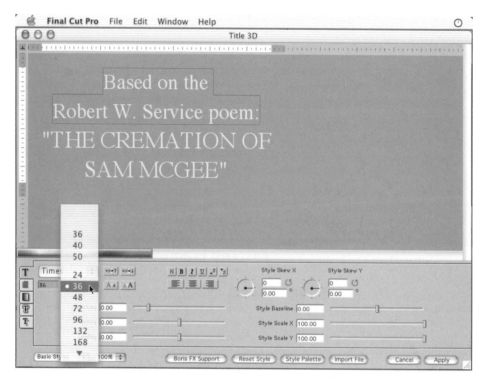

FIGURE 12.40   *The final title entry window after step 8.*

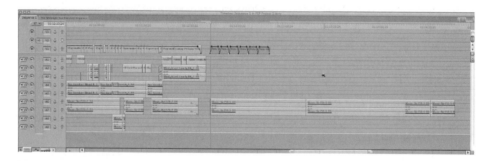

FIGURE 12.41   *The Timeline after step 8.*

Create Rolling Credits

There are two ways to create the rolling credits at the end of the film. You'll use the Calligraphy Title Crawl, but you could also create them with the Scrolling Text generator. You'll use the more-sophisticated tool to match the look of the fading titles at the end, though.

1. From the Generator pop-up menu, select Title Crawl (the last selection available on the list).
2. With Basic Styles selected, click the Import File button and locate the crew.txt file from the DVD. Select that file for importation.
3. Press Cmd+A to select all the text, and then open the Style Palette. Unclick the Size check box if it is checked. Double-click the saved style from the Midnight Sun Styles category. Even though you have applied the style, you will not see it just yet.
4. Change the font size to 24, and center the text.
5. Highlight each credit name (person or place, not crew position), and change each to a point size of 30, as shown in Figure 12.42. Leave the THANKS TO section at 24 points.

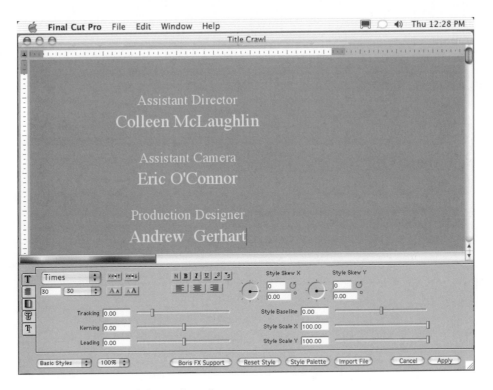

Figure 12.42   *Font sizing of the credits roll.*

6. When you are done, click the Apply button. Click the Controls tab. In the Animation Style pop-up menu, select Roll. Turn on the 1:2:1 Deflicker check box.

7. Set an In point in the Timeline at 01:12:51;06, and target the V1 track. Set an Out point at 01:14:20;29. The speed and duration of this roll are set by the duration in Sequence 1. In this case it is 00:01:29;22.

8. Clear the marks in the Viewer by clicking the Video tab in the Viewer and pressing Opt+X. Set the position indicator to the head of the rolling credits. Drag the "ghost box" of this title to the overwrite in the canvas overlay.

9. Highlight the Title Crawl clip in the sequence and press Cmd+R to render it. This might take some time.

10. Save the project.

CHAPTER 13

Working with Advanced Composites, Nests, and Exported QuickTime Movies

- Working with Composite Modes
- Working with Nests
- Working with Exported QuickTime Movies
- Workshop 13: Create Advanced Composites

Working with Composite Modes

This chapter introduces advanced composting techniques. You'll create and animate a sophisticated logo for the production company that produced "The Midnight Sun," Grace Films. You will also create two more composites for use within the movie. A discussion of composite modes begins this chapter.

Composite modes allow you to choose different ways you can combine images. Used in layered effects, they change how two or more images are combined into one image. Changing a composite mode changes how the pixel values are to be mixed between two or more images using different combinations of pixel values above and below each other in the Timeline's video tracks. Each composite mode uses a different mathematical formula that defines how pixel values in the affected layer are combined with the layer or layers beneath it. The resulting pixels are the composite you see.

To select a Composite mode other than the default mode, which is Normal, Ctrl-click in the Timeline the clip you want to affect, and choose the new mode from the resulting pop-up menu, as shown in Figure 13.1. Alternatively, you can select a clip, select Modify, Composite Mode, and then choose from the resulting submenu. You have 13 different choices.

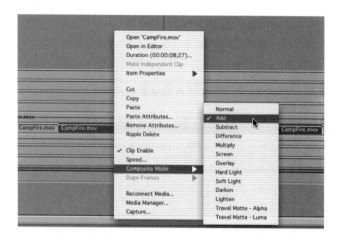

FIGURE 13.1   *Changing a composite mode by Ctrl-clicking a clip in the Timeline.*

- Normal—A linear mix of layers. This is the default mode. To mix layers, you must lower the opacity of the upper layer to see a mix of it with the layers beneath it. This looks the same as a dissolve and can be keyframed to act much like one.

- Add—Composites the color values of the affected clip with the ones in the layer or layers below it. The resulting image is brighter, but no pixels exceed absolute white. Selecting this mode adds a pixel's value in the affected layer to those directly beneath it.

- Subtract—Almost the opposite of Add. Composites the color values of the affected clip with the values in each pixel below it. You can darken the composite using this mode, but you can't go below absolute black.

- Difference—Similar to Subtract, but the resulting value of the each pixel is made positive and is an absolute value of this subtraction.

- Multiply—Calculates each pixel change in the resulting composite by multiplying each color channel's value by the corresponding one beneath it and then dividing this result by 255. Using this mode always darkens the image if it is light. This can be used to remove white areas of an image, leaving the dark areas to superimpose.

- Screen—Black or dark pixels are not added to the overlay. This composite mode inverts the brightness values of the colors in the layers and then multiplies the results. It's sort of like the opposite of Multiply: It loses the dark areas instead of the light areas.

- Overlay—Analyzes the values of the pixels' colors and applies Screen only to values greater than 128. If the value is less than 128, the Multiply composite mode is applied.

- Hard Light—Combines parts of Screen and Multiply with the approach of Soft Light. Like Soft Light, the action changes depending on the value of the underlying pixel. If the underlying pixel is brighter than 50% gray, the overlay pixel value is processed as if the two layers were combined using Screen mode. If the underlying pixel value is below 50% gray, the two layers are processed together as if the layers were combined with Multiply mode. The darker pixels darken. The result is usually quite dramatic. Hard Light simulates shining a harsh light (whose color is the light color or filtered output) on the source image. The source image and the light or filtered output contribute roughly equal amounts of detail to the final output.

- Soft Light—Similar to Hard Light, but the lighting effect is more diffused light, as if a "soft light" is hitting the image. Soft Light either darkens or lightens depending on the underlying color. If the underlying color is lighter than 50% gray, the value of the overlay pixel is added to the underlying pixel. If the underlying color is darker than 50% gray, the overlay pixel is subtracted from the underlying pixel. Some parts of the image lighten and some parts darken for a generally pleasing result that simulates shining a diffuse light (whose color is the light color or filtered output) on the source image. Most of the detail in the final output comes from the source image.

- Darken—Compares the values of the upper pixel with the lower one and selects the darker of the two to show in the resulting composite. The resulting image is always darker.

- Lighten—Similar to Darken, but the opposite happens—the lighter value is displayed. The resulting image is always lighter.

Two types of travel mattes also are available. A *matte* is a solid background color that is to be removed later and replaced with an image beneath it. It's as if a matte is a "hole cutter" in your image that defines an area that becomes transparent and thus reveals the image below it.

Mattes can also have semitransparent effects, depending on the brightness values of a given portion of them. Travel mattes usually (but not always) involve three tracks of video. The composite's foreground is the upper track, and the composite's background is the lower of the three tracks. The clip used as the matte is the middle track.

You change the composite mode to one of the two travel mattes to the uppermost track. The resulting composite uses the center track as the matting information to calculate the combination of images.

The two types of travel mattes are as follows:

- Travel Matte Alpha—Adds a matte to the selected clip. In the case of Travel Matte Alpha, RGB values are ignored, and the selected clip's alpha channel is used to create the matte (you must have an alpha channel in the clip).

- Travel Matte Luma—This matte is determined by averaging the RGB values contained in the clip. It changes the image to shades of gray and then uses this resulting image to define the matte. The different shades of gray determine the amount of transparency used in the resulting composite.

Figure 13.2 shows a two-layer Travel Matte Luma effect. The default "fill" is black because there is no bottom layer of video. Only the fire in the logo is shown. The white areas of the matte on V1 determine what part of the upper track is seen. The shades of gray in the matte shape file effectively soften the edges around the "hole" it cuts in the video. "FireGlowMatte.tga" was moved up, revealing an alpha track that was ignored. The V2 picture track has a Travel Matte Luma applied to it.

FIGURE 13.2   *A Travel Matte Luma revealing just the fire in the original picture.*

Working with Nests

Nests are sequences referenced by a single clip contained in another sequence. To create a nest in your current sequence, you highlight a selection of clips (possibly all of them) and press Opt+C or select Sequence, Nest Item(s). When you invoke the Nest Item(s) command, a dialog box opens for you to name this nested sequence. This nested sequence appears as a new sequence in the Browser window, creating a nest in your current sequence.

Nests can be used for a variety of purposes. A common use is to lower the numbers of video and/or audio tracks contained in a sequence for easier navigation. Another use of nesting sequences is to add audio and video filters or transitional effects to the entire set of clips contained in them. You can also use nests to repeat a sequence of shots within the same sequence. If you change the nested sequence, all instances of that nest change simultaneously. Rendering the nested sequence forwards this render into all instances of the nest.

If you drag a sequence to another sequence contained in the Timeline window, it appears as a single clip. When you double-click a nested clip, it opens the sequence it references in the Timeline window and displays itself in the Canvas window. Any changes made to the nested sequence are reflected in all occurrences of its nest (the single clip that represents it). As long as these single nested clips were not copied from another nested clip, they are unaffected by changes to the original nested sequence.

Any time you want to repeat sequences of clips you might want to change en masse, you must drag from the Browser or edit from the Viewer the nested sequence to a different sequence in the Timeline. If you copy the nest itself (the single-clip reference of the nested sequence) and then paste this copy again in any sequence, changes in the original sequence are not reflected in these copied single-layer nests. In other words, if you drag a sequence to a sequence, the nest corresponds to changes in the first sequence. If you copy the single-layer representation of the nested sequence and paste it into the same sequence or another sequence, changes in the original sequence are not reflected in these copied nests.

When you click a nest in a sequence and press Enter (or Option-double-click the nest), it opens in the Viewer to allow you to add and modify effects. For example, you might want to fade up an entire composite of many layers. By changing the opacity of a nest in your sequence, you change the opacity of all the layers contained in it at once. You can change all the Motion tab settings for a composite in this manner as well. Another example of using a nest is when you want to change the size of all the clips and position them as a group. This technique lets you add a letterbox effect to an entire sequence. Or you can reposition the clips on the screen to add text to the side of a picture-in-picture effect, which could be a series of clips or a composite of some sort.

You can also use nests to preserve renders. You can create a separate sequence for intensive composites, for example. When you add these rendered sequences to your main sequence, they maintain the renders even if you change the nest's In and Out points. However, you cannot add time to the In and Out points past the duration of the clips as they are edited in it, nor can you add the same sequence to itself. It's best to create a new sequence for this sort of work. You can create a sequence and add it to another sequence as many times as you want.

For example, you can place in a nest intensive effects done to a composite, render them, and then apply effects to the nest. This allows you to control how and the order in which the effects are applied. In other words, the effects applied to the nest affect all the clips in it after the individual effects are applied to those clips. You might want to add border or color correction to the entire nest after you have added a filter or composite mode to the individual clips contained in the nest.

You can also put nests *inside* nests. Using this technique, you can overcome the limitation of layering only 99 tracks of video on top of each other, but each nest can have only 99 tracks of video. Chances are this is enough for any project.

Working with Exported QuickTime Movies

QuickTime Movies (called Final Cut Pro Movies in earlier versions of FCP) come in two types. The first is a reference file, similar in concept to a sequence. It references the *original* media files and can be used to create a DVD in iDVD or DVD Studio Pro. It also can be used as a movie to be imported into Compressor or other compression software, such as Cleaner 6 or Sorenson Squeeze, for preparation for the Internet.

QuickTime Movie Exports Versus QuickTime Conversion Exports

You can convert or export your programs in many different file formats directly from Final Cut Pro. Depending on the format you want to use, you choose the file or set of files and then select either File, Export, QuickTime Movie or File, Export, Using QuickTime Conversion.

The main difference between QuickTime Movie exports and QuickTime Conversion exports is that QuickTime Movie exports are used primarily to make higher-quality movies, self-contained or not, that maintain their original quality. You would use this Export command for broadcast-quality movies, exchanging files with another workstation, and preparing files for other compression programs, such as DVD creation, because you can also include markers you've added in your sequence. Use QuickTime Movie exports to maintain the original quality of your original media.

QuickTime Movie exports prepare your program for other compression programs, such as Compressor, Sorenson Squeeze, and Cleaner. You would use QuickTime Movie exports to send a non-self-contained movie to Compressor (supplied with FCP 4) for an

MPEG-2 compression to be used in DVD Studio Pro 2 that includes chapter and compression markers. You cannot do this with QuickTime Conversion. However, you *can* prepare video for the web, CDs, and other multimedia uses.

Using QuickTime Conversion lets you export many more file formats than using QuickTime Movie exports. You also can use a myriad of codecs, compressions, frame sizes, still images, numbered sequences, audio formats, and more. Keep in mind that QuickTime Conversion always recompresses your movies, whereas QuickTime Movie exports might not, unless you check Recompress All Frames.

See Appendix B, "Output Options: Videotape, DVDs, and the Web," for further discussion of exporting files from Final Cut Pro to use with another compression program and creating files for use with Compressor.

QuickTime Movies that are non-self-contained also play in QuickTime. These are text files, somewhat like an Edit Decision List (EDL), which references the original media on the computer so that it is created quickly. The file size is much smaller than the self-contained type. To use it, the medium must be on the same computer you are playing it from.

The other type of QuickTime export is a self-contained one. QuickTime Movies that are self-contained are single-file QuickTime Movies that can be *exact* copies of your media files (including the renders). If you use the proper settings, these movies lose no quality whatsoever from the original clips or sequences you create them from. A self-contained QuickTime Movie can be a single clip of your whole project. You can also make self-contained movies of shorter versions of longer clips. In this manner, you can also turn subclips into master clips that contain only the material specified in the subclip.

In this chapter's workshop, you will use a self-contained QuickTime Movie to cut down on the amount of rendering you will do. These kinds of movies can also be used to create a single file of your whole project digitally on your computer in preparation for the web, for creating a DVD of your movie, or for transportation to another computer for viewing purposes. They play in any QuickTime player.

tip

Another use of a self-contained QuickTime Movie might be to simply cut down a complicated edit so that you have to render it only once and change only a title or other element for use in multiple versions of the same basic program. You might use this technique to create a set of television commercials for a chain of stores in different cities, in which the only difference is the store's phone number and address. Each time you make a change, you need to render only the title, for example, instead of a possible set of complicated and intensive effects.

Using this technique, you can then delete the media files associated with the original sequence, freeing up storage space. You simply import and use this new "clip" as you would any other clip. Unlike nests, though, this new clip has no reference to the original clips it was created with, and it mirrors the timecode from the *sequence* it was originally created from. Therefore, if you ever need to change its contents, you need to recapture the sequence the QuickTime Movie was created from.

To create a QuickTime Movie, highlight a clip or sequence in the Browser that contains an In point and an Out point (if you don't want to create a QuickTime Movie of the whole sequence or clip). Select File, Export, QuickTime Movie. Figure 13.3 shows the resulting dialog box. The various settings are discussed next.

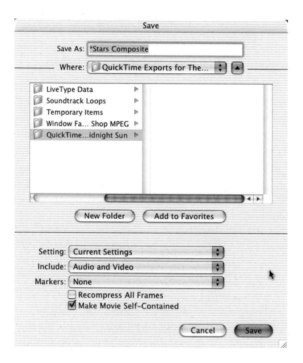

FIGURE 13.3   *The Save QuickTime Movie dialog box.*

- Save As—Type in a name for the file you are creating.
- Where—Navigate to the location where you want the file to be saved.
- New Folder—Creates a new folder for the file to be saved in.
- Add to Favorites—Adds to your Favorites location in OS X.
- Setting—Allows you to change the exported movie's sequence settings. If you leave it on Current Settings, no recompression occurs, and the movie doesn't lose any quality. You can change the setting using another codec. You can also create a custom setting from this pop-up menu, which opens the Sequence Preset Editor. A custom sequence setting created here is not saved for later use. However, you can create and save one for use before export, because any sequence presets you have created and saved are available from this pop-up menu.
- Include—Lets you select audio and video, video-only, or audio-only exports.

- Markers—Allows you to keep the markers you might have added to the sequence or clip, including chapter markers, which you might use to create a DVD in DVD Studio Pro 2.0 or later.

- Recompress All Frames—If you are working with an unrendered sequence that contains more than one source video file format, this selection is available to make all formats in the self-contained version of the movie the same data rate. If you are working in the same formats, you should *not* check this box for best results, because you will then recompress the video and lower the overall quality of the QuickTime Movie you are creating. You do want to use this setting if you will change file formats from the Settings menu.

- Make Movie Self-Contained—Creates a single QuickTime Movie that can be played in any QuickTime player, including Final Cut Pro. If this option is not checked, you create a reference movie for a quicker export. For this reference movie to be played, all the media must be on the same computer. Remember that this option is used for a quick export to iDVD, DVD Studio Pro, and other supported third-party applications such as Cleaner. I've found that most applications that work with QuickTime Movies also work with self-contained and non-self-contained QuickTime Movie exports.

note

A reference movie still copies the audio into the file and in some cases renders effects directly to the exported reference. A reference movie can contain *some* media itself, just not *all* the media. For example, if you export a sequence containing unrendered material, these renders have to be created to play a reference movie, and they are contained in a non-self-contained QuickTime Movie. However, you still have to have all the media it references on your computer, because it contains only media it could find no reference to. The smallest possible non-self-contained movie, then, is one made from a sequence that was completely rendered.

Workshop 13: Create Advanced Composites

In this workshop you will create more-sophisticated composites and add them to your sequence. You also will add the earlier composites you created with Cap, the stars, and the boat, and add some animation. Some rendering time is needed to complete this workshop.

Create the Smoke Composite

Cap leaves the boat after igniting Sam's body and then watches the smoke from outside. The problem with this shot as it is now is that there is no smoke. If you look at the earlier take of this shot, you see some smoke, but the director didn't think this was enough smoke. You'll add some computer-generated smoke and save the production crew from starting a larger fire.

1. Open the *Smoke Composite sequence in the Timeline. Drag the "smoke bkg 1" clip to the head of the sequence on the V1 track. (If you haven't created it, you can do so now. Just create a standard DV NTSC sequence and save it.)

2. Drag the "smoke1" clip to the Timeline, directly over *Smoke Composite, creating a V2 track at the same time. They are of the same duration, so you needn't trim them.

3. Ctrl-click the "smoke1" clip and select Composite Mode, Multiply, as shown in Figure 13.4. The smoke perfectly superimposes over the background. But there is a problem. It's coming from the bottom of the screen, not from behind the snowbank.

FIGURE 13.4   *Activating the multiply composite mode.*

4. Highlight the "smoke1" clip, and press D to activate the Distort tool. Select Image + Wireframe from the Viewing options button's pop-up menu in the Canvas.

5. Drag the four corners of the "smoke1" clip, as shown in Figure 13.5. You see the Selection tool change into the Distort tool when you touch one of the corners. Spend some time to suit your taste on just how the smoke rises, but keep in mind that it's coming from a smokestack, and you don't want it to appear over the top letterbox of the background image.

FIGURE 13.5   *Distorting the "smoke1" clip.*

6. Press Cmd+R to render the composite. Play it back to preview it and to make sure it really looks like it's coming from behind the snow and that it's coming from a smokestack. Save your project.

Create Fire in Front of Sam as He Closes the Furnace Door

In the first shot of Cap's point of view of Sam when he is seen in the furnace sitting up, there is fire between him and Cap. Fire also is prevalent in Cap's close-up from Sam's point of view just before this shot, but when Sam reaches over to close the door, there isn't any fire in front of him. The director didn't want to harm the actor. You need to make this shot match the earlier one by adding some fire to the shot.

1. Open Sequence 1 in the Timeline. Navigate to 01:11:29;24, which is the head of the shot you'll add the fire to.

2. Locate the "Furnace fire Tie off" clip in the Scene 9 bin, and double-click it to open it in the Viewer. Set an In point at 1:11:05:19, and edit it onto the V2 track directly above and for the duration of "Sam wakes up tie off tk 2," as shown in Figure 13.6. Change the "Fire only tk 1 from 'Footage inside boat' Subclip" composite mode to Add. The fire appears in front of Sam. With either clip highlighted, render the composite by pressing Cmd+R.

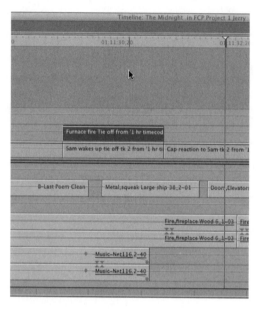

FIGURE 13.6   *The Timeline window after step 2.*

3. There is a problem. When Sam closes the door, you can still see the fire, and the door doesn't close in the "Fire only" shot. There is a fix. Double-click the "Fire only" clip to open it in the Viewer.

4. Click the Motion tab in the Viewer. Click the triangle next to the Basic Motion parameters to close them. Click the triangle next to the Crop parameters to open them. Change your window arrangement as shown in Figure 13.7. You will be adding keyframes to the Parameter Timelines.

5. Press C to activate the Crop tool. With the Image + Wireframe view active in the Canvas, crop the top, left, and right sides to hide the slight registration error in the shot, as shown in Figure 13.8. The right side of the fire-only clip is the crucial adjustment. Crop it just past the door to hide the registration error in the two shots on the right. If you want, you can type in **14** for the left crop, **15** for the right crop, and **20** for the top crop in the Crop Parameters boxes in the Motion tab.

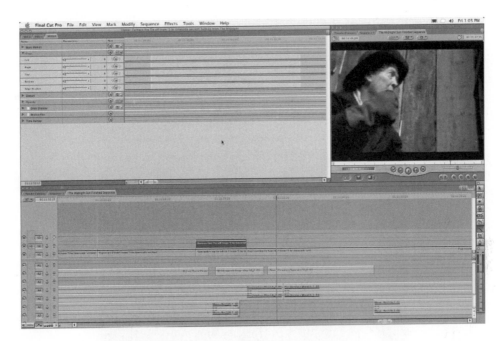

Figure 13.7   *The window arrangement after step 4.*

Figure 13.8   *Cropping the "Furnace fire Tie off" clip.*

6. Navigate to 01:11:30;18 in the Timeline. This is the point where the door begins to move. Click the add keyframe button next to the Right Crop parameter in the Viewer.

7. Navigate to 01:11:31;14 in the sequence. It's the last frame of this clip. Set another keyframe in the Right Crop parameter there. With the Crop tool active, crop the right side until the blue vertical line is just to the left of the door, as shown in Figure 13.9. It will be around 75.62 for the Right Crop parameter.

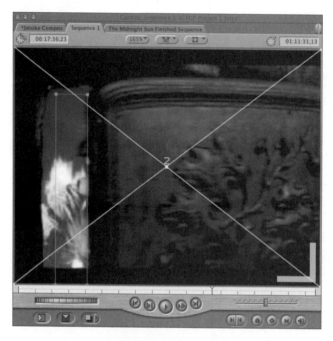

FIGURE 13.9   *Cropping the last frame of the composite.*

8. Click the position indicator in the Viewer to about halfway between the two keyframes. Notice that because the door doesn't close in a linear movement, you need to make one more adjustment. The first and last frames of the wipe work, but the middle one doesn't. Ctrl-click the last keyframe and select Smooth from the pop-up menu.

9. A blue dot appears in the line between the two keyframes. Click it and drag it down until the crop lines up with the door. This changes a linear movement of the crop to match the door's actual movement, which starts slowly and then speeds up from right to left toward the end of the clip. It's precise enough to fool the eye when you play the composite back, but in some cases, you might have to set more keyframes between the first and last to match up something like this. Render the clip. It looks much better. Save your project.

Create the Production Company Logo

This element is the most complicated set of edits, filters, and composites you will create for the movie. From a set of stills and short movies, you will create an entirely animated logo. Using just about every technique you have learned so far, this logo begins your process of learning how to coordinate many different editing techniques and elements into the same final element. The source clips for this logo were created in a variety of programs, including Combustion, Smoke, and Photoshop. All but one element (the strip of film footage, which was shot with a digital still camera) were created from computer-generated images.

By the time you have finished this exercise, you will have worked with 11 different layers of video, each of which needs a filter, a composite mode change, or an animation.

Create the Rock Wall Movie

1. Import the folder named Logo Material (inside the Compositing Material folder) into the Browser. Open it by Option-double-clicking it to have its tab appear in the Browser. You can select an entire group of clips this way for importing. Just select File, Import, Folder and navigate to the Compositing Material folder.

2. Open the Audio/Video Settings by pressing Opt+Cmd+Q, and then click the Sequence Presets tab. Duplicate the DV NTSC 48 kHz preset (click the Duplicate button in the lower area of the Sequence Presets window). The Sequence Preset Editor opens.

3. Change the name of this new preset you are about to create to Animation 720X486 CCIR 601/DV. Change the Description to "Use this for working with "The Midnight Sun" animation files." Select the following changes:

    Frame Size pop-up menu—CCIR 601 NTSC (40:27)

    Pixel Aspect Ratio—NTSC - CCIR 601 / DV

    Field Dominance—None

    Editing Timebase—Leave at 29.97

    Compressor—Animation. (Note that this compression setting is lossless. It is often used to transport media to another application. It maintains alpha channels.)

    Click the Advanced button under the Quality slider. Change the colors to Millions of Colors+, and then click OK.

    When you are done, the Preset Editor should look like Figure 13.10. If it does, click OK. The new preset is stored for further use. It is selected as the default preset after you click OK to dismiss the Audio/Video Settings window.

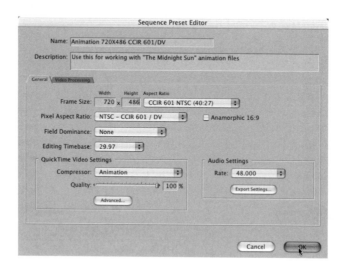

FIGURE 13.10 *The Sequence Preset Editor after step 3.*

4. Create a new bin inside the Logo Material bin. Name it Animation Sequences.

5. Create a new sequence in the Animation Sequences bin, and select the Animation 720X486 CCIR 601/DV Sequence Preset for it. If your General Preferences are set to show you easy setups (Prompt for Settings on New Sequence is selected), the sequence is selected from the Preset Settings dialog box that opens when you create a new sequence. Name the sequence "Rock Wall." Then open it in the Timeline window.

6. Zoom in on the Rock Wall sequence as far as you can. Double-click the "RockWall.0001.jpg" clip to open it in the Viewer. Press I and O to set a single frame as In and Out points, and then edit the clip onto the V1 track at the very head of the Rock Wall sequence. Alternatively, you can tab to the Duration field, enter **1**, and press F10 to edit this single frame into the new sequence.

7. Follow the same procedure for "RockWall.0002.jpg," except add its single frame after the first one. Then do the same with the "RockWall.0003.jpg" through "RockWall.0007.jpg" clips until you have seven single-frame edits in a row on the V1 track, as shown in Figure 13.11. Render these still frames and then play them back. A slight flicker appears in them, because each file has a very subtle difference in luminance, as if a light is flickering.

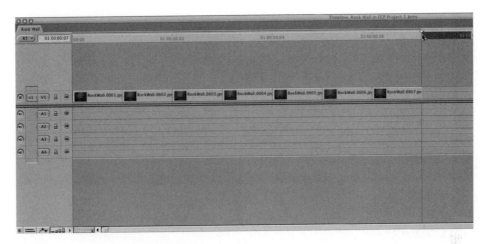

FIGURE 13.11   *The Rock Wall sequence after step 7.*

8. With the Timeline active, press Cmd+A to select all the clips. Copy (Cmd+C) and paste (Cmd+V) them several times past each other in the Rock Wall sequence, all on the V1 track. Keep copying and pasting the seven clips until you have created a Timeline that is exactly 27 seconds long. After you have copied the first seven clips a few times, select all of them in the Timeline again, copy them, and then paste more of them at once. Don't worry if you go over 27 seconds doing this. If you do, simply navigate to 01:00:27;00 in your sequence and delete all frames past this point (from 01:00:27;01 on). Use the track selector arrow pointing right to select them for deletion all at once.

9. Highlight the Rock Wall sequence in the Browser, and choose File, Export, QuickTime Movie. (Remember that you don't want to lose any quality doing this.) Select these options:

   Save as—Rock Wall Movie

   Where—Create a new folder named Animated Movies in the Logo Material folder in preparation for saving this movie (and more movies later) inside this new folder.

   Setting—Current Settings

   Include—Video Only

   Markers—None

Leave Recompress all Frames checked off (to save quality).

Check on Make movie Self-Contained (to make it a movie that contains media as a single file).

Click Save after you have set these options and have noted where you are saving this file (in the Save dialog box for a QuickTime Movie). (It's best to save this file on your scratch disk, where you've saved the rest of this project's files.) It will take a couple of minutes to render this movie, depending on the speed of your computer, but it would take more time to render this had you not rendered those first seven clips.

10. Ctrl-click the Rock Wall Sequence tab in the Timeline and select Close Tab. Save your project.

Create the River Rock, Leather, Horseshoe, and Grace Films Logo Movies

1. As you can see, there are several sets of files in the Logo Material bin. They are all named the same, except for the numbering at the end of their names. For each set of clips, create a separate sequence with the same new sequence setting of a 27-second loop for them, just as you did for the Rock Wall sequence. Save these sequences in the Animation Sequences bin. Name the new sequences as follows:

   Grace Films Logo

   Horseshoe

   Leather

   River Rock

2. Command-click each of these four new sequences so that all four are highlighted in the Browser (after you've built those 27-second sequences). Select File, Batch Export. You see the Export Queue window. Click the Settings button.

3. Click the Set Destination button (see Figure 13.12) and set the save destination as the Animated Movies folder you created earlier.

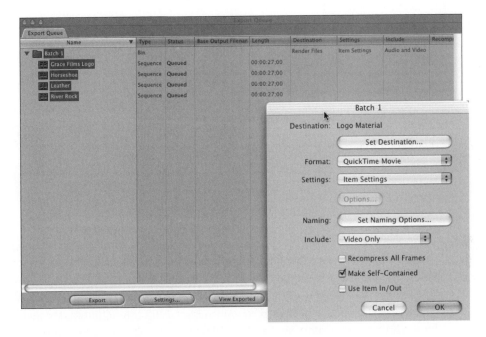

FIGURE 13.12   *The Batch dialog box.*

4. Set the Format to QuickTime Movie and the Settings to Item Settings. (This retains the sequence settings you're already using.)

5. Include Video Only, and check Make Self-Contained. Click OK and then Export. What you have done is simply use another feature of Final Cut Pro—the batch export function. Because you had more than one movie to export, it makes sense to use a batch export. It's just more efficient. This export takes about 2 minutes on a dual 533. A faster computer accomplishes the render faster.

> **tip**
>
> You should become more familiar with the Batch Export window and its uses. For example, you can export a number of clips whose audio needs looking after in another application such as Pro Tools or Peak. You can also use it to capture full-resolution DV or higher-quality clips. You could export them all at once to an OfflineRT for an offline of your program for use, say, on a laptop. Then you could use the media associated with the larger full-resolution files to reconnect your project file created on the laptop to these files on your tower, for example. The various settings in this dialog box let you export many files to the same format or even different formats in one batch export.
>
> Another recommended way to accomplish much the same thing is to use the Media Manager, as discussed in the next chapter.

Import the Movies and Begin the Composite

The reason that you've created Final Cut Pro movies of the sequences is to simplify the sequences you are getting ready to create. The smaller number of edits involved will make life easier for you. The total number of edits in the five sequences you just made was more than 4,000. By creating the single files, you've boiled that down to five.

Don't worry if you can't play these files on your computer right now. It takes a fast G4 and a fast set of hard drives to play these files. The idea is to keep their quality as high as possible for as long as you can. You can, however, scroll through them to see the animation of the flickering you've created. Next, you'll begin the composite. As you add the layers, start all edits of any new element at the head of the sequence, and end all layers to be the same length (27 seconds).

1. Ctrl-click the Animation Sequences bin, and select Import Folder from the context menu. Import the Animated Movies folder. Because you didn't put that first "Rock Wall" movie there, import it separately to the Animation Sequences bin.

2. Create a new sequence in it with the Animation 720X486 CCIR 601/DV Sequence Preset. Name it 1st Composite, and double-click it to open it in the Timeline.

3. Drag the entire "Rock Wall" clip from the Animated Movies bin onto the head of the V1 track. Create eight more video tracks by selecting Sequence, Insert Tracks. Then delete the A2 track from the 1st Composite sequence to help with viewing it. You will probably want to select the smallest track height setting. Click it in the lower left of the Timeline window.

4. Open the "Grace Films Logo" clip from the Browser into the Viewer. Add it to the V2 track directly above the "Rock Wall" clip. It composites perfectly because you have preserved the alpha track in the animation movie. If you see black instead of the checkerboard pattern in the Viewer, select Checkerboard from the Viewing options button in the Viewer to see it more clearly. Either way, the alpha track is still there. Double-click the "Grace Films Logo" sequence clip in the Timeline window to open it in the Viewer, and then click the Motion tab. Check the check box next to the Drop Shadow parameter. Doing so makes this metallic branding iron logo look like it's sort of away from the wall, as if it has posts hidden behind it.

5. Drag the "FireGlowMatte.tga" file from the Logo Material bin to the head of the V3 track, and extend its duration to the end of the layers. Change its composite mode to Add. You'll adjust its whiteness later, because this composite mode brightened it up. Start saving your project file often. This area of the workshop is taxing on your computer. If it crashes, at least you won't lose work.

6. In the Logo Material bin, double-click the "CampFire.mov" clip to open it in the

Viewer. Notice that it has a duration of only 8:27, so add it four times to the V4 track. Trim the fourth instance of it from the end so that it lines up with the end of the tracks beneath it. Change the composite mode of each of these repeated clips to Add. You can do this in one move. Highlight all four of the fire clips, and then Ctrl-click any of them to change the composite mode from the context menu. They all composite perfectly over the other clips.

Screen mode would be a more normal way of creating the transparency on this clip. But it gives a less punchy

note
look. Screen mode is most commonly used to make black transparent (similar to an unmultiply filter). Screen keeps more of the content's subtlety. Add works in this instance only because the background is very dark. The fire would look very odd if composited over a midtone using Add.

7. Double-click the "Smoke.mov" file, located in the Logo Material bin. It too is only 7 seconds long, so add it to the V5 track four times, and then trim the last instance of it to match those of the clips below it. Select all four clips in the sequence, and change the Smoke.mov composite mode to Screen. Using the Add mode works too, but Screen seems to give the smoke a softer look.

8. Add the "River Rock" clip from the Animated Movies folder to the V6 track. You'll fix the problems later.

9. Add the "Leather" clip from the Animated Movies folder to the V7 track.

10. Add the "Horseshoe" clip from the Animated Movies folder to the V8 track.

11. Add the "FilmStrip.tga" file to the V9 track and extend it to the end of the 27-second sequence, as you did with the "FireGlowMatte.tga" file. When you are done with Step 11, the 1st Composite sequence should look like Figure 13.13. Save your project.

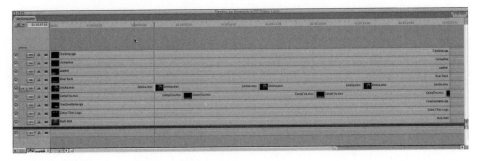

FIGURE 13.13   *The 1st Composite sequence after step 11.*

Setting Up Source Material for Compositing

One of the things to keep in mind when you do compositing such as what you just did is to prepare the source material in such a way as to make the composite go easily. In the case of the files with the alpha information kept in them, a quick and perfect composite was created by just adding them to the layers. Alpha information is absolutely the easiest way to composite something, but it's not always possible to create.

In the case of the fire and filmstrip elements, the black backgrounds were absolute 0 in their luminance values, so the composite mode worked well. The same can be said of the smoke element, absolute white was used as its background, making the composite easy to do.

When you are working in DV especially, the luminance information is all recorded in its compression scheme. DV is recorded in a 4:1:1 color space; the 4 is the luminance information. Attempting a blue or green screen key with DV is far more difficult, because not all the color information is recorded in the camera masters in the first place. Luminance-based keys are cleaner in DV than chrominance-based keys for this reason. If you must shoot DV in preparation for a composite, try to use a white or black background. Carefully light the object or subject of your foreground so that it won't be a difficult key to create.

New to FCP 4 are two Color Smoothing filters that primarily help you prepare and improve the quality of chroma keys from captured source clips. They are specifically designed to be used with either DV-25 clips (Mini DV, DVCAM, DVCPRO25) or clips from DVCPRO50, 8-bit, and 10-bit uncompressed video clips. Use the Color Smoothing - 4:1:1 filter on the DV-25 clips and the Color Smoothing - 4:2:2 filter on the DVCPRO50, 8-bit, and 10-bit uncompressed video files.

Add the appropriate filter to the file you want to key *before* you add a chroma key filter to it. With any subsequent filters added, keep this smoothing filter on the top so that it is addressed first in the rendering process.

These same filters may also be used to smooth out any stair-stepping you might see in video clips that contain areas of high-contrast color.

When you work with higher-quality video formats such as Digital Betacam, DVCPRO50, or IMX, video is captured (and originally recorded) in a 4:2:2 color space. There is twice as much color and hue information as DV-25 formats record. You'll find that chroma keys and other composites are much easier to perform in these higher-quality formats, and the results of a chroma key look better in general.

Rearrange and Color-Correct the Composite

You put all the elements together first to make it easier to rearrange them into a more-pleasing position. This workflow is typical for this sort of work. You'll start with the bottom and move up through the sequence's layers to rearrange things a bit.

1. Double-click the "Rock Wall" clip in the sequence, and turn on the Image + Wireframe viewing mode in the Canvas window. Place the position indicator in the Timeline anywhere in the first couple of seconds of the sequence to view things from there.

2. With the Selection tool active (press A), drag the "Rock Wall" clip straight up in the Canvas window to reveal the interesting darker area of the wall, as shown in Figure 13.14. Open the Motion tab. After you've done the raising, change the first box in the Center parameter of the Basic Motion parameters to 0 (the horizontal position) and the second box to –80 (the vertical position).

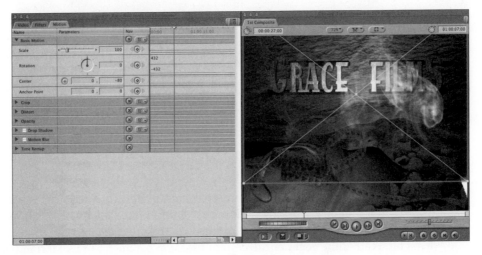

FIGURE 13.14   *The "Rock Wall" clip raised, and the Motion tab settings.*

3. Double-click the "FireGlowMatte.tga" clip in the V5 track. Click its Motion tab, and match the Center positions as you did with the "Rock Wall" clip in step 2. Add the Color Corrector filter to this clip. Set the balance almost (but not quite) to the red by dragging the button in the center of the Balance color wheel to the R. Hold down the Command key to drag it faster. Move the Whites slider about three-fourths of the way down to reduce the glaring brightness. When you are done, the Color Corrector should look like Figure 13.15.

FIGURE 13.15   *The Color Corrector settings for the "FireGlowMatte.tga" clip after step 3.*

4. The glow from the fire looks a bit hot, so lower the opacity of the "FireGlowMatte.tga" clip to 50% in the Motion tab's Opacity parameter.

5. Double-click the first instance of "CampFire.mov" in the sequence. Drag it with the Selection tool up and to the right until the tips of the flames are seen only in front of the glow in the creased area of the rock background. Crop the left side just a bit. Feather the edges of the crop in the Crop parameter of its Motion tab, as shown in Figure 13.16. If you don't soften the crop, the straight edge of the movie shows.

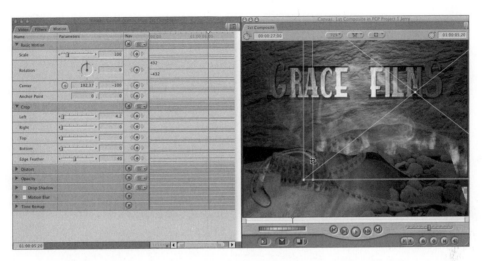

FIGURE 13.16   *Repositioning and cropping the "CampFire.mov" clip.*

6. With the "CampFire.mov" clip highlighted and the Timeline window active, press Cmd+C to copy this clip into memory. Highlight only the *remaining* three instances of this clip in the Timeline window, Ctrl-click one, and select Paste Attributes. In the Paste Attributes window, click Basic Motion and Crop, and then click OK. In this manner you add the same programming from the first instance of the clip (the one you copied) to the clips past the first one in the sequence. The Paste Attributes command is a very handy tool. Be careful, though. If you use this tool on the first clip by keeping it highlighted, you double its attributes. In this case you wouldn't have changed anything, but if you'd pasted filters as well, you would have doubled them up on the first clip—probably not a good idea.

7. The smoke is a little too much, so lower its opacity to 50%. Copy it and then paste its attributes to the other instances of the clip, but this time, copy only the opacity setting.

8. The fire reveals the edge of the "River Rock" clip. Double-click the "River Rock" clip in the Timeline and set its Center position in the Motion tab to 325 in the first box and 0 in the second box. This clip is sort of bland, so add some color to it using the Color Corrector. Again, drag the Balance control's centered button almost to the R in the color wheel, lower the Blacks slider a bit, and raise the Whites slider a bit to add a little more contrast. It begins to pick up the color of the leather. It's very western-looking, but a bit too oversaturated to look natural, so lower the saturation 15% or so until you think it looks more natural. When you are done, the Canvas and Viewer should look like Figure 13.17.

FIGURE 13.17   *The Viewer and Canvas after step 8.*

9. The river rock adds some interest and texture, so reveal more of it. Double-click the "Leather" clip in the movie, and drag it just a bit to the left to just about split the screen space with the river rocks.

10. The horseshoe looks as if it's floating in space. Double-click it and lower it so that it is completely over the leather. In its Motion tab, open the Drop Shadow parameter and check it on. Change the offset to 4 in the Offset parameter box. Because this is a very dense object, raise the Softness to around 50, and raise the Opacity to about 75 (see Figure 13.18). This places the object in the picture.

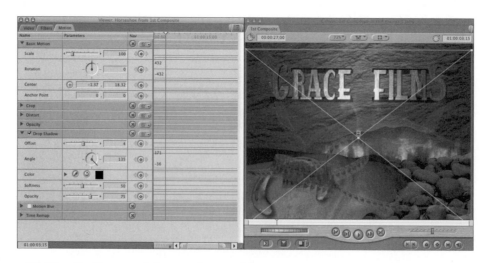

FIGURE 13.18   *The Viewer and Canvas after step 10.*

11. Double-click the "FilmStrip.tga" clip in the sequence to open it in the Viewer. It's too large, it covers too much of the horseshoe, and it too looks a bit like it's floating and not resting on anything. Plus, a filmstrip that close to a fire would probably melt! Click the Motion tab and set the scale to 75. Rotate it left by setting the rotation to –12, and set the center to 70 in the second (vertical) box. Click the Drop Shadow parameter check box, and open its parameter controls by clicking the triangle. Change the Offset to 2, Softness to 30, and Opacity to 75. By clicking the Drop Shadow parameter check box on and off, you can see how this places the filmstrip in the scene (see Figure 13.19).

Figure 13.19   *The Viewer and Canvas after step 11.*

12. Double-click the Grace Films Logo, and click the Drop Shadow parameter's disclosure triangle. Check on the Drop Shadow, and set the Softness to 50 or more. Notice again how this marries the graphic to the scene.

13. Everything looks pretty good now, except for the dull gray wall behind it all. It's best to repeat the colorization here too to warm up the entire look of the logo. Click the "River Rock" clip and press Cmd+C. Paste the filter, now in memory, using the Paste Attributes command to the "Rock Wall" clip. Click the Color Corrector tab. The contrast here is a bit too much, so adjust the Blacks slider up a bit to bring out the sides of the rock wall. Save your project file.

Build the Last Touch of Animation to the Scene

The fire and smoke give the logo life, but it needs another bit of animation to set it off. You'll next export this composite as a single clip to save some rendering time later. Then you'll build an animated reveal simulating someone coming upon the scene with a lantern of sorts, using tools right in Final Cut Pro. To do this animation, you need two full layers of this logo, so rendering them as a nested pair would take quite some time. In fact, doing this will save about 40 minutes of rendering time on a dual 533 G4, and possibly hours on a G3. Keep this technique in mind when you need to repeat a rather complicated sequence composite like this.

1. Make sure that there are no In or Out points in the 1st Composite sequence. Pressing Opt+X with the Timeline or Canvas window active deletes any marks.

2. Highlight the 1st Composite sequence in the Animated Movies folder, and select File, Export, QuickTime Movie. Save it to the Animated Movies folder, leave the name alone, use current settings, use Hi Res (1) in the Quality setting, Markers None, and check on Make Movie Self-Contained. Then click the Save button. This will take some time to render. On a dual 533 running on OS X, it takes about 10 minutes. If you don't want to wait for the render, it is supplied on the DVD. Look for it in the Logo Material folder. It's called 1st Composite. It might be fun to use this as a clocking method. I've found this to be a good test of your machine's ability. The rendering time for this render was half of FCP 3's time on the same machine.

3. Ctrl-click the Animated Movies bin, and select Import File to import the file you just saved in the Animated Movies folder on your hard drive, or be sure to have imported the one supplied in the Logo Material folder. Close the 1st Composite sequence in the Timeline window (Ctrl-click the tab). Create a new sequence in the Animation Sequences folder with the Animation 720X486 CCIR 601/DV sequence preset, and name it Final Composite. Double-click it to open it in the Timeline.

4. Edit the 1st Composite clip you just imported onto the V2 track, starting at its head, and then again onto the V3 track directly above it. Change the V2 track version's composite mode to Travel Matte Luma.

5. On the V1 track beneath the pair of 1st composite clips, edit the FireGlowMatte.tga file for the same duration, but this time (just to learn something new), Ctrl-click it, select Duration, and change its duration to 27:00. Turn off Monitoring Track 3 (click the green light on the far left of the Timeline window on its track).

6. Double-click the "FireGlowMatte.tga" clip in the Timeline window. Click its Motion tab to change the Scale parameter to 120. Change the Center point parameter to 0, –100. You'll use this matte to reveal only the fire on the fade-up of the animated logo.

7. Now for the lantern-approaching effect. Double-click the 1st Composite clip on the V3 track. Turn on its green track light to see it. Add the Softwipe video filter to it. It's located under Effects, Video Filters, FXScript Layered DVEs. It's also found in the same set of folders in the Effects tab in the Browser.

note

If you have not installed the FXScript additions that came with FCP 3, or you don't have FCP 3, locate the file named CGM Softwipe.sit and drag it to your desktop. Unstuff it by clicking on it. Then locate folder Macintosh HD/Library/Application Support/Final Cut Pro System Support/Plugins and drag the the unstuffed folder named "CGM Softwipe" into your Plugins folder. The CGM Softwipe is now installed on your system and will be available *after restarting* Final Cut Pro. While you are there, be sure to take a look at CGM's demo of there filters. The "readme" files are where to start.

8. Click the Filters tab in the Viewer to reveal the parameters for the Softwipe pattern. Set the playhead at the very first frame of the clip. Set a keyframe for each of the following changes in each of the parameters. Set the Phase parameter to 100. Set the Softness to 40. In the Method pop-up menu, set the parameter to Radial. Click the Invert option (neither the Method nor Invert selections allow keyframes to be set, however). Set the Width parameter to 0.

9. Type **1000328** in the Timecode Navigation box in the bottom left of the Filters tab. Type **73** in the Phase parameter. (Notice that it sets a keyframe for you.) Type **-514**, **330** in the Center parameter.

10. With the playhead at the head of this clip, set a keyframe in the Center parameter. Type **1000726** in the Timecode Navigation box. Type **200**, **166** in the Center parameter.

11. Type **1001307** in the Timecode Navigation box. Set a keyframe in the Phase parameter (click the button in the parameter with the diamond on it), but don't change it from 73. Type **5**, **35** in the Center box.

12. Type **1002026** in the Timecode Navigation box. Type **20** in the Phase parameter. Save your project. When you are done, your Parameter settings should look like Figure 13.20.

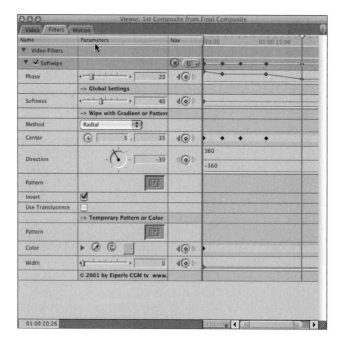

FIGURE 13.20   *The Softwipe parameters after step 12.*

13. Highlight all three clips and select Sequence, Nest Items or press Opt+C. In the resulting naming box, change the name of this nest to Final Composite 2 and click OK. Notice that this new "nested" sequence not only collapses into one layer, but it also is saved as "Final Composite 2" in the same bin that the original sequence resides in—the Animated Sequences bin. Double-click the single-layer nest in the Final Composite sequence. The Final Composite 2 sequence opens. Any changes you make here are reflected in the nest of this sequence in the Final Composite sequence. Ctrl-click the tab of the Final Composite 2 sequence to close it from the Timeline window.

14. Highlight the Final Composite 2 nest in the Final Composite Sequence and press Enter. It opens in the Viewer. At this point, if you wanted to, you could add color correction or any other filter or Motion tab parameter change, and it would affect all three layers nested in this sequence. Click the Motion tab. Program a 30-frame fade-up at the head of the clip and a 45-frame fade-down at its tail in the Opacity parameter. (You can also do this with the clip overlays using the Pen tool in the Timeline window.)

15. Double-click the nest in the Timeline to open its associated sequence (Final Composite 2). Add a Color Corrector to the V3 clip named 1st Composite. Double-click that clip to open it in the Viewer. Drag the centered Balance control toward the Y or the yellow to give the light a bit of a yellow cast. Dragging it about one-fourth the distance to the Y on the wheel is about right. This makes it more like a lantern (and less like a flashlight). But it's not enough. It just doesn't work. You need more—something else.

16. Try using the Color Corrector 3-way filter instead. You also can play around with these controls using the Video Scopes to match colors between elements.

CHAPTER 14

Managing Large Projects

- Media Management
- Organizing a Large Project
- Using Final Cut Pro's Media Management Features
- Workshop 14: Add the Effects to Sequence 1
- Conclusion

Media Management

You can use various techniques to manage large projects. The tools supplied by Final Cut Pro include a way to capture smaller media files and a way to capture more media than you would otherwise (with the OfflineRT mode, for example). FCP also has tools to delete media you no longer need (such as the Media Manager, the Make Offline command, and the Render Manager). But there is more to keeping you as lean as possible when working with large and complex projects. You need to be well-organized in the first place. Refer to Appendix A, "Capturing Footage," for tips on becoming organized. Logging clips properly and sorting them into bins keeps searching through a large number of files at a minimum, and it allows you to more quickly find media that needs managing in the first place. One thing to keep in mind is that that the clips in your sequences and Browser are not the media files; they are references to them. If you simply delete a clip from your Browser, you don't delete its media. It's best to do that with the Make Offline command, or the Use Existing command in the Media Manager, discussed later in this chapter.

This chapter gives you a foundation to work with when the job gets big and complex and you need to keep yourself together and as lean as possible. The discussion starts with the DV to OfflineRT mode of working (although the discussion also applies to any lower-resolution editing). This mode exists so that you can capture much more footage per gigabyte of storage space, losing resolution for editorial decision-making, and then allowing for a recapture only of the source footage actually used in your sequence in full resolution.

Using the OfflineRT Mode

It's best to use the OfflineRT mode of saving storage space when you have a lot of media to work with and when you know you don't have enough storage space for media files to work in high resolution. See the storage space requirements for various video formats discussed in Chapter 2, "Specifying Setups, Settings, Presets, and Preferences." The idea is to capture footage in a lower resolution, make your edit decisions in this lower resolution, and then recapture only the footage required to re-create your sequence in full resolution. This method requires that all your source tapes have timecode. However, if your source material was generated by a computer, such as video and audio files created in any other application, FCP knows that you can't recapture this footage from tape. It brings the footage forward into the high-resolution sequence you create with the Media Manager and doesn't take it offline.

For example, suppose you've added a graphics file from LiveType to your OfflineRT sequence. When you use the Media Manager to create a new sequence in higher resolution, Final Cut Pro automatically puts this LiveType file into the sequence and keeps it connected to the original file you created. All other items with a tape name assigned to them need to be recaptured, but it can be a very fast recapture if you logged things correctly in the first place.

Planning to use this "offline-to-online" method of working also requires that all your source videotape and audiotape footage have timecode. Otherwise, you won't be able to recapture all the footage and have it all edited properly in your sequence automatically. You wouldn't have to remake edit decisions without timecode, but you would have to manually reconform the higher-resolution material clip by clip, which is not an inviting prospect.

If you have material that doesn't have timecode associated with it, such as files from other computer programs, graphics, and the like, it's not a problem. These files can be used in higher resolutions. They should be created in higher resolutions from the beginning, because they edit into an OfflineRT project without problems. If you have source footage on videotape that does not have timecode associated with it, you have to dub this footage as cleanly as possible to DV or to the final videotape format you will finish your edit master in, such as DVCPRO50. In any event, you need to dub it to the same videotape format that your camera masters use when creating a timecode track, and then use these dubs as your source tapes instead of the originals before you start logging and capturing in OfflineRT.

The OfflineRT mode allows you to capture and store your material in about one-eighth the resolution of DV, taking up about one-eighth the storage space of full-resolution DV. Any Macintosh will play this resolution. Slower disk drives might play back this lower resolution when they cannot deal with full-resolution video. This is the same resolution you have been working in with this book, in fact. Its picture quality is certainly good enough to use for edit decisions. And instead of about 4.7 minutes of video and audio per gigabyte of drive space, you can store 40 minutes of footage per gigabyte. This means that instead of 470 minutes (about 7.8 hours) you could have over 66 hours! This sounds like more than you would ever need, but when you're working on a long documentary or a feature film, it's not unheard of to have that much footage. I once did a 4-minute short that was edited from more than 30 *hours* of footage, and the only way to edit it effectively was to have it all online in my computer. Using this mode becomes more crucial the less storage space you have available.

Offline editing is the process of editing your material just to make edit decisions with. The idea is to either save money by editing in a less-expensive system for an EDL export to be used in an online or finishing edit system, or to simply capture and be able to store more footage in the media storage space you have available. After finishing your edit with this lower-resolution footage, you can recapture *only the footage used in your sequence* in high resolution. Thus, it becomes your finished program or *online edit*.

There are other not-so-apparent benefits of using the DV-to-OfflineRT mode. Renders are much faster, and the video plays back more reliably, because the data rate needed to play the movies is so much lower than full-resolution DV or uncompressed video. Final Cut Pro comes with presets to capture in either NTSC or PAL in this lower-resolution mode with source material shot on DV. If you have a capture card such as those from Aurora, Pinnacle's Cinewave, or AJA, you will be supplied with a different method of doing basically the same thing—capturing offline resolutions. The techniques described here also are relevant to these other lower-quality resolutions.

You are all set to use OfflineRT if you are capturing from a DV deck or camera via FireWire. All DV formats contain timecode information. If your source material is on Betacam, you might consider using this format and capturing with a DV A/D (analog-to-digital) converter. This lets you convert the video and its associated timecode (with an appropriate serial port, USB serial adapter, or PCI card with serial ports installed). In this case, you would convert your Betacam source tapes to DV with the converter. Then, in real time (as you capture and transcode this signal to DV OfflineRT), you would create the lower-resolution files for your offline edit.

note

It's highly recommended that you use this resolution on portable computers such as a PowerBook. You can play back these files on its internal hard drive. This might work in many circumstances where portability is required and the addition of an external FireWire hard drive is not desired, or even possible, because most of them require an A/C power outlet, which might be unavailable where your edit is taking place. However, the Pocket Drives from LaCie work quite well. At any rate, this format's lower data rate can help anyone's situation.

After you've captured or converted your footage to this codec, you simply edit your program as you normally would. When you are finished, you use the Media Manager (discussed later) to create a copy of your sequence. The difference is that it contains clips whose referenced media contains *only the footage that you actually used in the sequence,* plus any *handles* (extra footage on either end of the actual used media you might want for minor adjustments). You then can highlight this new sequence and batch-capture it in full resolution for completion of your *online edit* (see Appendix A).

Organizing a Large Project

When you are working with a project that contains many scenes and edits, it's very efficient to break these different areas of your project into smaller sequences that you marry at the end for your final output (see Appendix B, "Output Options: Videotape, DVDs, and the Web"). If your project is extremely large, you might even consider breaking it into more than one project file. This might be desirable because the more complex a project file gets, the larger it becomes, and the more likely your computer's response time will slow down. It's also easier to navigate to fewer media files for use in a given area or set of areas of your total project. The less you need to scroll through your project file, the more efficient the editing process becomes.

tip

Large, complex projects can really benefit from using an additional computer display. My own system includes two Cinema Displays and another, smaller display next to them. The reason is that, with a small display or only one display, you waste a lot of time maximizing the Browser to find things quicker, and then you might have to minimize it just to do each edit. As you've begun to see as you are working with this book, if you don't have a large display area (the screen captures were done on a 22-inch Cinema Display), a larger display would come in handy. A separate display just for the Browser would be even better. Another advantage of creating more workspace in this manner is a larger Timeline window. Over a period of months of working with an ever-growing sequence or set of sequences, your work can become very tiresome if your Timeline window is small. This problem becomes even more exacerbated if your sequence contains multiple layers of audio and video. I find it easier and more efficient to work with multiple monitors for these reasons. It's also common to work with other applications at the same time, such as LiveType, so having more screen space becomes even more of a necessity. Other applications that contain many layered Timelines, such as After Effects, can benefit enormously as well.

Working with Multiple Sequences and Project Files for the Same Program

Whenever you are working with truly large programs, it's best to break them into smaller sections, bins organized possibly by scene, and even separate sequences for different scenes. First, it's easier for you and your computer to work with less-complicated sequences at one time, and second, it's easier to keep yourself focused on the job at hand. You can access shots of a specific scene or area of your program more quickly if they are stored together in a single bin. There are two different techniques you can use and even combine to accomplish both tasks:

- Create smaller sequences that contain related sections or scenes.
- If your project is *really* huge, work with more than one project file.

Opening, working with, and saving smaller project files speeds up you *and* your computer. You'll know when you might benefit from creating another project file or sequence when your computer reports that it is "preparing to display video" each time you make a change to your currently open sequence, and it's beginning to slow you down. I find it irritating to wait on a computer to perform the command I've given, and I'll wager that you do too.

Creating Separate Sequences

In the preceding chapter, you created separate sequences, which you will insert into Sequence 1 of this project. It was a primer used to demonstrate that it's more efficient to do things this way. Why add another eight tracks of video to Sequence 1 just for the ending production company logo, for example? It would mean an even more-complex sequence than you already have. Instead of nine tracks of audio and a couple of video tracks, you would be navigating through a sequence that has nearly twice that many tracks.

Continually having to scroll around in one really long sequence wastes time. You have less time to make quality edit decisions and spend more time just getting them done. Your creativity is not high when you're hampered by inefficiency. Learning how to spend your time creatively instead of mechanically will serve your finished projects well. A more efficient organization provides more time for experimentation with different edits and all the what-ifs I spoke about in the Introduction of this book.

The project you have nearly finished originally had about 300 edits. This is about as large a sequence as I care to work with, for the reasons just mentioned. Navigating through this sequence is time-consuming enough. Navigating through one that has 20 times as many edits just to find that single clip you need to adjust or replace would be a daunting task indeed.

It's not necessarily a program's length that determines when you might break it into smaller sequences, but rather the number of edits it contains. For example, a 90-minute speech with a few cut-away shots of the audience probably won't contain anywhere near the number of edits in a 90-minute documentary. A 2-hour-long wedding video would probably contain less than the 2,000 edits of a 90-minute feature.

If you are shooting a program that might be of feature length but that doesn't have a huge number of edits, you might be better off leaving it as one sequence. However, if you are working with a project that contains many edits, consider finding appropriate scenes or areas of your project you can work on in their own sequences to save navigational time and to ease your computer's overhead. I once worked on a project that contained 1,700 edits but that was only 28 minutes long. I broke this project into a series of shorter sequences, which I married toward the end of the project. I'm convinced it saved me time in the long run.

After you have done at least one fine cut of a set of scenes, you should add these scenes to a "master sequence." You need to examine the overall tone, pacing, and timing of the entire piece. You also need to examine and possibly trim the edits that come between the earlier sequences. As you enter the final stages of a large program, you might need to adjust certain scenes because they are too slow, or the whole piece is too long, for example. The only reliable way to judge what should be trimmed in this case is to look at the finished program in its entirety.

In the case of a narrative film, it's mandatory to watch the movie in its entirety, if for no other reason than to see where a scene drags on too long and might cause restlessness in your audience. You want to keep your audience interested by moving the story along and not dwelling on a redundant element. You might find an entire scene that is unneeded. You can examine the consistency of tonal qualities in this manner from scene to scene. If you need to rework a scene, you can easily go back to its "subsequence" for the work, keeping your edit-to-edit fine-tuning work efficient, and then marry this new version back to your master sequence.

Creating Multiple Project Files for the Same Program

Creating different project files for different areas of your program can enhance efficiency. Remember that you can have as many different project files open at one time as you want if you need to begin combining them toward the end of your editorial workflow. You can always drag clips and sequences *between* projects at any time. New to FCP 4 is the ability to copy rendered clips from project file to project file. You can even drag smaller sequences to one big master sequence, creating nests of them for your master sequence, possibly in its own project file. It's easy to do this on a daily basis to keep your director, producer, or client apprised of your progress. Smaller project files save and open faster on any computer.

An average feature-length program can easily contain 2,000 edits. What's more, a feature film can have an average of five to 10 takes of each edit. So you could be working with as many as 20,000 clips! In a case such as this, I would consider breaking this into a smaller subset of projects. Chances are you won't work on all areas of this huge project at one time (until the end), and Final Cut Pro can drag and drop sequences from any project to any project as long as both projects are open.

If you are working on a gargantuan project such as this, you should create a "master project file." You will use it to capture and log with. In this manner you'll keep your media files all originally associated with *one* project. Even if you create new projects and copy or drag a clip to them to begin the sorting of your footage, you will still be working with media management that will be more manageable.

It might be rare for you to work on projects of this magnitude, but nevertheless, you should be aware that you can have more than one project file open at the same time. For example, you might have an industrial client who uses the same opening or company logo treatment in all the various video programs the company produces. You will save time and effort later by not re-creating them each time you create a new project. Having a project file that contains all the repurposeable elements, including music files or company logos used repeatedly, might make for a great workflow enhancement, even if you recapture the associated media files again and again.

If you're working on a *series* of programs at the same time for a client, it's best to keep each one in its own project file. You might even keep a separate project file for the elements that are common to all projects. Later, you might need to re-create just a couple of them, and it's easier to work with a single project file for a single shorter program from an efficiency point of view. Another example is that for *every* program you produce, your *own* company logo treatment might be used. Having a project file specific to this element is a great time-saver.

Using Final Cut Pro's Media Management Features

Part of keeping large projects under control is the use of the Media Manager. You might be in a situation where you need to delete media you no longer want because you need to create space for new captures, or you simply want to continue keeping media online to a minimum.

Final Cut Pro comes with powerful tools to help you manage, compress (to the OfflineRT format, for example), and delete media you no longer need because you decided not to use it in your finished program. This is especially useful if you want to create some storage space as you are running low, or you want to move your project and media to another computer. The discussion in this section covers deleting whole clips' media, trimming clips' media to only the media you have decided you want to use, moving media to another location, and using the Media Manager to prepare sequences to recapture in a higher resolution to finish your project.

Using the Media Manager

The Media Manager, shown in Figure 14.1, is a tool that manages media for clips, sequences, and whole projects. It can copy, delete, and create offline sequences and more using different media processing options. You can use it to move media, delete media that you no longer want to keep available, and create new projects that have media trimmed to the media that was actually used in the projects' sequences.

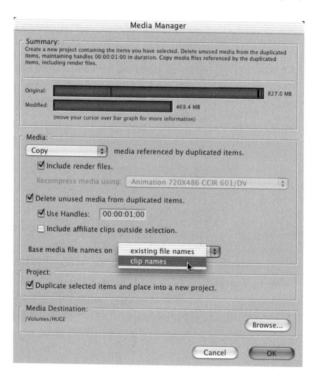

FIGURE 14.1   *The Media Manager window.*

You activate the Media Manager window by selecting File, Media Manager with the Browser window active. You also can Ctrl-click an item or items you've selected in the Browser and select Media Manager from the context menu that appears.

To perform media management on a clip, set of clips, or sequence, highlight the items you want to manage in the Browser, and choose the Media Manager. The best way to manage media is using this tool, because it can create new project files that reference the new, moved, deleted, or recompressed media as it is working its processes. If you move or delete media from the Finder, you will have to reconnect media when you reopen your project that might reference it. This becomes cumbersome, especially if you've changed the names of the clips from the Browser or bins that reference media that now do not have the same name.

Selecting Different Media Processing Options

To move and possibly trim the media used in a sequence or clip or in multiple sequences and clips, select them in the Browser, and activate the Media Manager. Figure 14.1 displays what happens if you copy Sequence 1 in your project to a new location (media file-wise) and delete media not used in the copied sequence.

The Media Manager's window has four areas:

- Summary—The area of the window where the Media Manager tells you exactly what you are getting ready to do. Notice that the original media in Sequence 1 contains 827.0 MB of space. By deleting the unused media and render files, you'll need only 469.4 MB of space for the trimmed copies. If you place the cursor over the green bars that show you the possible space savings you would get with this setup, you can obtain more-detailed information about the amount of media you are working with.

- Media—This section is where you specify what you want to do with the media you've selected in the Browser. Figure 14.2 shows a pop-up menu where you can select these different options:

  - Copy—Makes new copies of the highlighted media, leaving the originals untouched. It might be good to use this to make sure you've done the right thing before you delete the original media. It's also great for moving media to another computer.

  - Move—Moves the media. This process deletes the original files. It's undoable and permanent.

  - Recompress—Lets you change the media's file format. You might want to use this feature to turn a full-resolution set of media files into OfflineRT, for example.

  - Recompress media using:—Here you select the file format you will change the selected media to. There is even a custom option to create a format used for the recompression. It is active when you select Recompress for the process you are doing.

- Use existing—Performs the process on the original media files and saves the new, possibly used media only, or recompressed files in the same location that the original files were saved in. It deletes the original files. This process is undoable and permanent.

- Create offline—Creates a new project file that contains a sequence that is unconnected to any media. When this option is used with the "Delete unused media from duplicated items" check box, it references only the media (plus handles, if any) that the original sequence contained. You'd use this option in preparation for going from lower resolutions to higher resolutions, for example, when you batch-capture the new "offline" sequence. This option does not delete the original media. When you select this option, the Set Sequences To pop-up menu is available to set the new sequence to the resolution you intend to recapture with.

- Include render files—Does just that. Renders are included in the process you have chosen.

- Delete unused media from duplicated items—Eliminates media not used in the sequence.

- Use Handles—Adds the selected amount of media on both ends of the used media. You can select as much as you want by typing in the amount in the box next to the check box. For example, if you add 1 second of handle to a clip marked to be 10 seconds in length, you end up with a clip that is 12 seconds long with 1 second more media before the original In point and 1 second more after the original Out point.

"Include affiliate clips outside selection" when turned on, your new files will include these affiliate clips. *Affiliate clips* are those clips created from master clips, such as subclips or sequence clips. If a master clip has had a subclip made from it, it too is a clip with affiliation. Subclips and sequence clips maintain a relationship to the master clips you've created them from. Changing the name of a clip will also change the name of any affiliate clip. Also any changes made to a master clip such as a reel name, will also be made to any of its affiliated clips. Selecting this inclusion may dramatically increase the amount of footage you end up copying. Any affiliated clip will be included in the Media Manager process and the media maintained will be that media between In and Out points within the clip. It will include master clip media that you may not have used in a sequence for example. When checked on "Include affiliate clips outside selection" may also add clips from master clips affiliated with clips in the single sequence you want to perform an operation on that come from another sequence because they are affiliated.

If you want to preserve your current project file intact, and you want to create a new sequence that you may recapture in a higher resolution using only the media you actually used in the first place, simply copy the sequence you want to recapture into a new project file before you use the Media Manager to perform operations. This way all affiliated clips will not be included, and you'll get a better resulting management operation. No affiliation is ever maintained between different project files.

- Base Media file names on—This pop-up menu lets you either keep the existing media filenames for the new media being created or change these new media filenames to be the same as the clips they are created from. You might have changed the names of clips in your offline edit, for example, and you want to assign these new names to the new media files you might be creating.

- Project—This area of the Media Manager lets you select whether you want to create a new project file as part of processing. The check box lets you do just as it says—create a media bin in the new project file with clips that reference the new files. It is grayed out and selected when you're performing a "Make offline" process.

- Media Destination—Here you select where any new media will be stored.

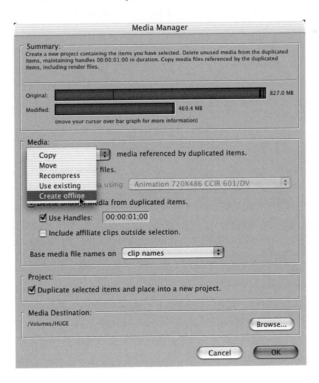

Figure 14.2 *Options for managing media.*

Outcomes and Considerations When Using Media Manager

As you can see, there are many ways to process media files with the Media Manager. Keep in mind that if you use certain features, you perform an irreversible process. Irreversible processes involve only the Moving and Use Existing commands. Undo (Shift+Cmd+Z) does not make any changes that were made to your media files after you have given these media management commands. If you choose to delete media files with any of the tools in Final Cut Pro, you are making a permanent change, and you are warned of this situation before you commit to the change.

When you copy, you need free disk space to copy to. When you recompress, you also need scratch disk space for the new media files. Using Create Offline creates a new offline sequence(s) or clip(s) when sequences or a set of new clips that will not reference any media are selected. The original media files remain on your hard disk and continue to be connected to their present project file. Using this command always creates a new project file to contain these offline clips.

The outcome of what you are getting ready to perform with the Media Manager is clearly explained in the Summary area of its interface. You should *always* take a look at this summary before you use the Media Manager.

I also highly recommend that you keep any existing media if you can until after you've used the Media Manager. This way, if you've made a mistake or a computer glitch (such as a power outage) has caused an error, you can always reperform the process. Of course, this assumes that you have enough space to perform copies or recompressions.

This leads to another recommendation: Perform media management that removes unused media before you begin running out of space. Keep your system lean in this regard. You can't have too much open disk space. Also, remember that deleting clips from the Browser doesn't delete the media files associated with them. So if you make a mistake when capturing, for example, delete the reference clip to it in the Browser *and* the actual media associated with it. Use the Make Offline command to do this from within Final Cut Pro.

If you need more room to perform the task you need to do, be careful about what you delete to create space on your hard disk. Using the Make Offline command is the way to delete the proper material.

Using the Make Offline Command

You can select clips and sequences within your current project to manage their media without using the Media Manager. You might want to use this feature because you don't want to open the space on your scratch disk, or when you are finished with your project and you need to delete its associated media.

When you select this feature on a clip or sequence, you don't create a new project. Instead, you can delete the media files that these items reference from the disk, you can lose the link to this media, or you can move them to the trash for a "temporary" deletion, which lets you recapture them and then delete the original media after a recapture. Figure 14.3 shows the straightforward window that appears when you Ctrl-click clips or sequences and select the Make Offline command from the context menu:

- Leave Them on the Disk—Leaves the media files untouched but disconnects the items selected in the Browser from them.

- Move Them to the Trash—Puts the media associated with the selected items in the trash. These files aren't actually deleted until you empty the trash. This might be useful if you are unsure of really deleting the files until you recapture them.

- Delete Them from the Disk—Does just that. It's permanent and undoable.

FIGURE 14.3   *The Make Offline window.*

In many instances this might very well be the easiest way to manage the space your media files are taking up. It's a quick way to take whole clips offline. You can create subclips from master clips, export them as Final Cut Pro movies in a batch export, reimport them as new master clips, and then delete the larger original master clip to create more space on your scratch disk. You can also perform this operation with the Media Manager (see the workshop). I find this a great way to quickly log footage.

It's faster to log footage digitally (as you have been doing so far) than to log takes individually from tape. It eliminates the slower shuttling time that videotape machines take. It also saves wear and tear on your source video machine or camera, because you are not shuttling it as much during the initial logging process and during the capture of logged clips (see Appendix A).

The quickest way to log a whole DV camera master is to capture whole sections or even the whole tape and then use DV Start/Stop Detection (found on the Mark menu) to create markers where the tape was paused during the shooting process. You can turn these markers into subclips to quickly sort and name them.

tip

It's a good idea to keep the offline clips you have spent time logging. (Offline clips are those that are logged but not captured. They are represented by an icon with a red slash through it.) *You never know* when you might need to take a second look at them. You can do this easily by creating a special bin or set of bins for the storage of offline clips. That way, they stay out of sight until you need to look at them. A batch capture of logged clips is *much* faster than having to relog them or search for them again on tape.

You can also control timecode-controllable videotape machines during this process to quickly park on a starting or ending point of the logged clip on its source tape. All you need to do is drag the offline clip to the Log and Capture window. The In and Out points there will be those of the clip. Press Shift+I to have the tape machine quickly search to the clip's In point for review. This too is faster than researching a tape to find that take you thought you didn't need. Additionally, you keep track of which tape that shot is located on. You'll never have to wonder (assuming that you've logged the tape name correctly) which one of the 100 source tapes a certain shot is on. The logging and capturing process is discussed in Appendix A.

I recommend that you use the Make Offline command to delete your media files after you've backed up any that have no timecode associated with them, such as files created in Photoshop or another application. This command is especially useful when your render files are spread over more than one disk.

Using the Render Manager

Final Cut Pro has a tool for managing renders in any open project or set of projects. It's called the Render Manager (see Figure 14.4). It's not often used, because any unused renders (renders that no longer are being accessed in any sequence) are automatically deleted when you close and save the project they were created in.

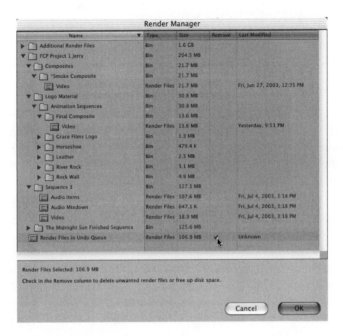

Name	Type	Size	Remove	Last Modified
▶ ☐ Additional Render Files	Bin	1.6 GB		
▼ ☐ FCP Project 1 Jerry	Bin	204.5 MB		
▼ ☐ Composites	Bin	21.7 MB		
▼ ☐ *Smoke Composite	Bin	21.7 MB		
▤ Video	Render Files	21.7 MB		Fri, Jun 27, 2003, 12:35 PM
▼ ☐ Logo Material	Bin	30.8 MB		
▼ ☐ Animation Sequences	Bin	30.8 MB		
▼ ☐ Final Composite	Bin	13.6 MB		
▤ Video	Render Files	13.6 MB		Yesterday, 9:51 PM
▶ ☐ Grace Films Logo	Bin	1.3 MB		
▶ ☐ Horseshoe	Bin	479.4 K		
▶ ☐ Leather	Bin	2.3 MB		
▶ ☐ River Rock	Bin	3.1 MB		
▶ ☐ Rock Wall	Bin	9.9 MB		
▼ ☐ Sequence 1	Bin	127.1 MB		
▤ Audio Items	Render Files	107.6 MB		Fri, Jul 4, 2003, 3:18 PM
▤ Audio Mixdown	Render Files	647.1 K		Fri, Jul 4, 2003, 3:18 PM
▤ Video	Render Files	18.9 MB		Fri, Jul 4, 2003, 3:18 PM
▶ ☐ The Midnight Sun Finished Sequence	Bin	125.6 MB		
▤ Render Files in Undo Queue	Render Files	106.9 MB	✓	Unknown

Render Files Selected: 106.9 MB

Check in the Remove column to delete unwanted render files or free up disk space.

Cancel   OK

FIGURE 14.4   *The Render Manager window.*

Nevertheless, you might want to free up disk space without saving, closing, and then reopening a project to accomplish a space-saving procedure. You also might want to put all renders in the same render folder if they aren't already. Simply select Tools, Render Manager to open the Render Manager window. Notice that Figure 14.4 has a file named Render Files in Undo Queue. These are renders you made during the current session that no longer are referenced by any sequence in the project. If you click in the Remove column, you can delete them from your disk drive and (in this case) save more than 106.9 MB of space immediately. If you were to close and reopen the project file, though, these files would automatically be deleted.

You might have renders in a lower resolution that you no longer need. The render resolutions are listed as part of the renders' names. You could use this to delete these renders too. Each folder contains the renders associated with the various sequences you currently have open for easy verification of exactly what renders are associated with each sequence.

When you are finished with a project, you use the Render Manager to delete the render files you used in the project. Keep them online. The Render Manager doesn't let you "reconnect" them later if you ever need to recapture the project's files again.

Workshop 14: Add the Effects to Sequence 1

In this workshop, you'll add the now-finished effects you've been creating in other Timelines. You'll experiment with using nested sequences to get a feel for how this feature works. You'll also work with the Media Manager.

Add the Final Logo to the End of the Movie

1. Locate the Final Composite 2 sequence in the Animation Sequences bin. With snapping turned on (press N), drag the sequence directly from the bin, and put it directly past the Title Crawl at the end of the movie.

2. Notice that the sequence is automatically converted to the OfflineRT mode you have set for it. Rendering this massive file will go much faster. You'll make one last change. Highlight this nest in Sequence 1 and press Enter to open it in the Viewer. Notice that you could add filters to the entire nest here if you needed to. Either set a 100 (3:10 seconds) frame fade-up in the Opacity parameter in its Motion tab, or use the Pen tool on the clip overlay in Sequence 1 to create the fade-up. Create a fade-down at the end of 45 frames. When you are finished, the end of Sequence 1 should look like Figure 14.5.

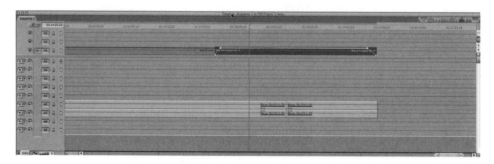

FIGURE 14.5   *The end of the sequence after step 2.*

3. Highlight the nest in Sequence 1. If you want to take the time now, render it (press Opt+R). Everything in your sequence will be rendered, but it will take a long time. Rather than take the time, as you normally would, open "The Midnight Sun Finished Sequence" and copy and paste the file already made for you there. It's the last video clip in the sequence named Final Composite 2. Just copy and paste it from the finished sequence to your sequence.

tip This is an example of a file you might want to back up if you ever wanted to bring this project back online in your computer, saving you the long render later. It was created by exporting the Final Composite 2 sequence to Compressor and using the Photo JPEG codec to create it. If you were actually doing a higher-resolution finish to this project, you could back up this file on a CD or DVD and save it for use later.

Prepare the Smoke, Stars, and Boat Composites

1. Locate the *Stars Composite, *Boat Composite, and *Smoke Composite sequences in the Composites bin. Highlight all three sequences and select File, Batch Export. They open in the Export Queue window.

2. Click the Settings button in the bottom of the Export Queue window. In the Batch window, set the Format to be QuickTime Movie. Change the Settings format to OfflineRT NTSC (Photo JPEG). Set Include to Video Only. Check the Make Self-Contained check box. When you have set things up correctly, the settings should be as shown in Figure 14.6.

FIGURE 14.6   *Batch 1 export settings after step 2.*

3. Look at the top of the window to see if the Destination is set to where you've been keeping the book's files. If not, click the Set Destination button, select the location you have been importing all the files from, and click OK.

4. Click the Export button. After the new files are created, the status column shows them as Done. With the Batch 1 folder still highlighted, click the View Exported button. Each clip opens in a separate Viewer window. Drag from the center of each Viewer to import these new clips, and place them in the Composites bin. Close each Viewer after you have imported the new files into the Composites bin. You'll note that you now have a clip that has the same name as the sequence it came from. This is OK, because they are different types of clips and are easily distinguished from one another.

5. Save your project file, and close the Export Queue window.

Edit the Stars Composite into Sequence 1

1. Navigate to 01:02:55;14 in Sequence 1; you should be sitting on the last frame of the "Cap reverse CU looks at stars" clip. Open the new "*Stars Composite" *clip* in the Viewer and press the End key on the keyboard. Drag from the center of the Viewer to the Replace overlay in the Canvas window. Render the 2-second dissolve to see the change.

2. Save your project file.

Edit the Boat Composite into Sequence 1

1. Navigate to 01:09:17;13 in Sequence 1. This should be the first frame of Cap looking at the boat that (so far) isn't there. Set an In point on the first frame of this shot and an Out point on the last frame of the Center Section clip, or use the shortcut (press X) to mark the clip for the same result. The duration window in the Canvas should be 3:17.

2. Double-click the *Boat Composite *clip* in the Composites bin to open it in the Viewer. Edit it (using the first frame as the In point) to Sequence 1, replacing the end of the "Center Section" clip on V1.

3. Create a 30-frame fade-out at the end of the new boat composite in the sequence. Use the Pen tool with the clip overlay turned on, or double-click to open this composite in the Viewer, and then change the opacity in the Opacity parameter.

4. Take a look at the series of shots in this area before the composited boat shot. The previous scene is very blue. The scene at the lake doesn't continue with the blue and very cold feeling of the previous scene, where Cap is dragging Sam's body up the slope.

5. Change your window arrangement to Color Correction, and then click the Frame Viewer in the Tool Bench window. Set the lower-right pop-up menu to Next Edit and the lower-left pop-up menu to Next Edit. Remove the dissolve at the end of the "Cap up mtn side dusk" shot and before the "Cap sees lake tk 1" shot. (If you don't do this, you'll see the first frame of the incoming edit displayed in the middle of the dissolve.) You'll add it back later.

6. Place the playhead in the Timeline window over the "Cap up mtn side dusk" clip. Note how green (and thus warmer) the "Cap sees lake tk 1" shot looks compared to the previous "Cap up mtn side dusk" shot. Add a Color Corrector 3-way filter to the "Cap sees lake tk 1" clip. Move the Mids color wheel button around a third of the way to the B (blue) until your display looks like Figure 14.7.

FIGURE 14.7 *Color correction after step 6.*

7. Add back the 2-second cross-dissolve. Click the 1 and 2 arrow icons next to the hand icon in the upper right of the "Cap sees lake tk 1" clip's color correction, as shown in Figure 14.8. Doing this adds this same color correction to the next two shots. All three match each other better, and they also look much colder. Furthermore, after the fade-out and fade-up, the contrast between the warm cabin in the boat and the cold exterior is accentuated, *emphasizing the story.* Cap has finally found a warm and dry-enough place to burn Sam's body.

FIGURE 14.8 *The two arrows that copy this filter to the next two shots.*

8. Change your arrangement to the Standard arrangement by pressing Ctrl+U. Save your project file.

Edit the Smoke Composite into Sequence 1

1. Navigate to 01:10:36;11 in Sequence 1. Press X to mark the "smoke background tk 1" clip.
2. Double-click the "*Smoke Composite" *clip* in the Composites bin to open it in the Viewer.
3. Using the first frame of the "*Smoke Composite" clip in the Viewer as an In point, overwrite it to the V1 track to replace the noncomposited clip.
4. Save your project.

Render Everything

1. With the Timeline window active, press Opt+R to render everything in Sequence 1 if you haven't already.
2. The render might take some time, so you might want to do it a bit later. When you're done, take a look at your handiwork from the beginning to the end of the film. Then pat yourself on the back. I hope you've learned a lot.

Prepare for a High-Resolution Recapture

If you were working in full resolution editing this movie, you would be ready to lay it out to tape now. There are no more edits to perform; you're finished. However, pretend that you have been working in OfflineRT and are now ready to recapture just the material actually used in Sequence 1 in full resolution. In the case of "The Midnight Sun," this is Digital Betacam—the format used in the Telecine (film-to-tape transfer).

We have a small problem. For educational purposes, this tutorial had to be edited using techniques to show features. It wasn't done as if it were going to be recaptured in high resolution. In reality, if this had been a true offline edit, you might *not* have created the three exported composite files you just edited into the sequence. Instead, you might have copied the sequences into Sequence 1 instead to *retain the proper timecode information.* The timecode now associated with these exported and then imported clips is *not the correct information at all.*

In fact, had this been a true offline, a better workflow would be to do the compositing after the offline was finished and *after* you had recaptured the files in full resolution (except in the case of the final company logo you created in higher resolution). The reason for this is that composites come out better in higher resolution. Assume, though, that the current composites are correct (you might have received them on their own Digital Betacam tapes done in a program like Apple's Shake), and follow along with a preparation technique and Media Manager exercise.

1. Undo the step where you added the prerendered clip for the company logo. Simply drag the Composite 2 sequence back into the Sequence 1 sequence to replace the clip used now. (You can undo this later if you want.)

2. Highlight Sequence 1 in the Browser. Ctrl-click its icon and select Media Manager from the context menu that opens. You see the Media Manager window.

3. Figure 14.9 shows how you should set each parameter in this window. In the pop-up menu "media referenced by duplicated items," select Create offline. This creates a new sequence with offline clips that have timecode and reel name information. In this case, it is the film footage. However, any clips such as audio files will be online in this new sequence and connected to the current media they are connected to now. If you will finish and recapture on the same computer, this isn't a problem. But if you are moving to another computer, you'll need to move these connected media files with the new project file you are creating to the new system. You won't need to recapture them, but you will need to use them for your online session.

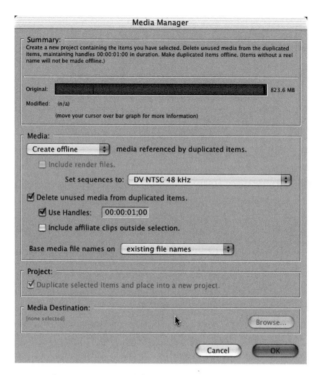

FIGURE 14.9   *Media Manager settings for online preparation.*

4. In the "Set sequences to:" pop-up menu, select DV NTSC 48 kHz. (I am assuming that your camera masters were DV and not the Digital Betacam they actually are.)

5. Check "Delete unused media from duplicated items." When you do this, you are not deleting media. Instead, you are creating a new sequence that doesn't reference any media not used in the sequence. So when you recapture this sequence, you capture only the media needed to re-create it, not all 55 or so minutes of tape that was shot for it. This could be important if you have 100 hours of source material for a 1-hour program. If you don't check this option, all the source material *originally captured* for each of the clips used in the sequence as it is now is captured in the online session too.

6. Check Use Handles and set it to 00:00:01:00. In this case, you will leave just a bit of fudge room in case you want to slip or trim just a bit of footage after you've seen the program in full resolution. You might want to change a bit of duration when you see this film projected full-screen (in a video projection system, for example). I've often seen movies that were edited on NLE software with those really small windows, and when I've seen the same film projected on a 30-foot screen, the whole feel of the pacing changed.

It will be nice to be able to easily add that extra beat needed for a moment in the film. Adding this extra second on either end of each clip's capture won't take up much space, and it will give you options you wouldn't have otherwise. How about if you needed to add a dissolve without deleting time with the new clips? You can add a new dissolve of up to 60 frames on either end of each shot if need be. You can shorten these new clips, but not lengthen them unless you add some handles.

> I strongly suggest that you never delete the lower-resolution media if you don't have to. If you do, you should check this new project file against the information your lower-resolution sequence provides *before you delete the lower-resolution media files.* Furthermore, I also strongly suggest that you *read the Summary.* If you make a mistake with the Media Manager, some options could permanently alter your current media files, such as selecting the "Use existing" option. Better safe than sorry.

7. After you have selected the proper settings, read what the Summary at the top of the window says about what will happen after you click OK. In this case, you'll create a new project file with a partially offline set of clips. They are partial because the audio files don't need to be reacquired from tape. Any other video files (such as the titles and the logo at the end) don't have to be reacquired from tape. Remember that they didn't come from tape in the first place, and FCP is smart enough to know this. FCP assumes that you need to recapture only items from tapes, so it creates a sequence with offline items that are only those associated with a reel name.

8. Click OK. A dialog box opens, asking you to create a new name for this new project file. Save it in a place you can find later, and name it "FCP Project 1 High Resolution." When you click Save, the project opens.

9. Rename the Sequence 1 sequence in the new project "High Resolution Sequence 1." Save your project file.

Examine the New Project

1. Ctrl-click theFCP Project 1 tab in the Browser to close it. If you are asked to save it, do so.

2. Double-click the High Resolution Sequence 1 sequence in the new project file.

3. Notice that all clips added by file in the first place are now linked to this sequence. All the audio is there, and new clips for it have been imported into the Clips bin you created when you checked the appropriate box in the Media Manager window.

4. Note that the nested sequence created from files you created for it at the end of the Timeline is still there, ready to render to DV.

5. Note that the high-resolution titles are ready for rendering. Also note that all clips with no tape name are still online. You have not deleted any of the media associated with your Project 1 file. All media online in this new sequence references the same media files, and they are of the same quality they were originally. None of the video files referenced in the new sequence are low-resolution.

6. If you had the original tape that the film transfer was done with, you could load it and batch-capture the rest of the sequence in this new project. You do this by Ctrl-clicking the High Resolution Sequence 1 sequence and selecting Capture. You can't perform this operation, because you don't have the original tapes, but you can see what the process involves.

Conclusion

If you were editing this particular project, you most likely would have started in full resolution, because not that much media was associated with it to begin with. You were supplied the files in an OfflineRT resolution for three reasons: That's all that would fit on the DVD, these files play back from any qualified Macintosh, and renders are much faster in this mode because the media files are so small. You were given high-resolution audio files because they simply don't take up the space that full-resolution video files do.

But consider how you could handle a very large project. You very well could capture much more footage per gigabyte of available storage. OfflineRT files take up only about one-eighth the storage space of full-resolution DV, which is only about one-fifth the size of uncompressed video files. So, in essence, if you were working in uncompressed video, you could capture 40 times as much media to create your program and have only enough storage space to recapture what was used.

There are some rules to live by here. You must have the original files (such as the audio and graphics files in "The Midnight Sun"). *All other files must come from a timecoded tape source.* You cannot recapture automatically or "bring online" any video or audio any other way. I again suggest that if you have source footage from a non-timecoded tape, you dub that tape to DV or another format that does have timecode, and start editing from that tape instead of the original. This new tape will become one you can batch-recapture from instead of the original.

If you had the tapes that the picture files came from, (there was only one, actually), you could recapture this new full-resolution sequence as fast as your machine can search the timecode and render it as fast as your computer can render. Note that dual processors count with those rendering times!

If the source material came from multiple tapes, Final Cut Pro asks for these tapes in a list it creates. You load the tape and tell Final Cut Pro which tape it is. The program captures from that tape all clips in their order of appearance on the tape, from first to last. It makes no difference where these new clips reside in your sequence. It's truly the fastest way to recapture in higher resolution only the media used in your sequence.

Appendix A walks you through the steps of bringing in media from tape (whether you are batching or just capturing for the first time in preparation for an edit). Appendix B teaches you how to lay your finished program back to tape or prepare it for the web or DVD.

APPENDIX A

Capturing Footage

So far, you've been working on footage that you imported from the DVD that comes with this book. But what of your own project's footage? This appendix thoroughly discusses the ways you can import footage from videotape, whether from digital or analog sources. The only thing you need to capture DV footage is a DV camera. If you have analog sources, you need to add to your system some sort of D/A converter in the form of a camera, deck, or stand-alone D/A converter.

If you want to work with higher resolutions than DV, you need a capture card or converter box, as well as a fast disk array to handle the data rate. Refer to Chapter 1, "Essential Equipment," for details.

The workflow involved in bringing footage into your computer to edit is straightforward. You simply set your capture and device control presets, log the footage from tape in Final Cut Pro, and then capture that footage.

Using the Log and Capture Window

Final Cut Pro uses a tool aptly named the Log and Capture window, shown in Figure A.1, to log, capture, and digitize footage and control your video source machine or camera. When you use its deck controls, you see your footage and hear audio from your source machine if you use the capture presets you made in Chapter 3, "Understanding Final Cut Pro's Interface: An Overview." To *capture* means to copy digital video into your computer, and to *digitize* means to change analog video such as VHS or Betacam SP into a digital file that your computer can deal with.

FIGURE A.1   *The Log and Capture window.*

To open the Log and Capture window, select it from the File menu or press Cmd+8. On the left side of the window is a Viewer used to look at your footage from videotape. On the right side of the window are three tabs:

- Logging
- Clip Settings
- Capture Settings

Using the Capture Settings Tab

It's important to set your scratch disk and capture preset settings first. This way, you won't make the mistake of capturing in the wrong resolution or to the wrong scratch disk location.

Figure A.2 shows the Capture Settings tab. Notice that you can quickly change Device Control preset settings. You also have Capture/Input settings and a "shortcut" button to pull up the Scratch Disk settings. This is the same window you pull up from the System Settings window, discussed in Chapter 2, "Specifying Setups, Settings, Presets, and Preferences."

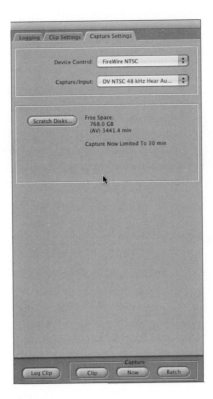

FIGURE A.2   *The Capture Settings tab.*

Any presets you have saved for Capture and Device Control presets are listed in the corresponding pop-up menu. If you need to create a new Capture preset or Device Control setting, you do so from the Audio/Video settings window. After you've saved the new settings, they show up in these two pop-up menus. This tab primarily is used to quickly access these three settings. It also contains the calculated time left on your current scratch disk to make sure that you have enough storage space for the captures you might be doing currently.

Logging and Capturing with the Log and Capture Window

Starting from the top of the Log and Capture window (refer to Figure A.1), you see a number for the total free space left on the current scratch disk selected and a calculation of how many minutes that space will hold using the current capture presets. In the case of Figure A.1, about 3,441 minutes of storage is available for the 768GB of storage open on the current scratch disk. The capture presets are set to DV NTSC in this figure. If you changed the capture preset to OfflineRT NTSC, you'd gain another 10,000 minutes of available storage space. If you were working in uncompressed video, you'd lower the available time to about 480 minutes. Remember that the lower the compression (DV being about 5:1), the greater the storage space requirements will be. Also remember that any resolution higher than DV requires a SCSI RAID array hard drive for proper capturing and playback.

The timecode box in the upper left of the Log and Capture window represents the duration of the clip you have set from its In point (set in the lower-left timecode box) to its Out point (set in the lower-right timecode box). To the right of the duration time indication is another box indicating the tape's current timecode. If you are not playing the tape, this box shows the current timecode of the frame you are stopped on.

The transport controls, used to control your camera or videotape machine, are under the preview area. They work exactly the same as those used in the Viewer and Canvas windows, except that on either end of the central buttons is a button for fast forward (on the right) and another to put the source machine into rewind (on the left). The slider scans the tape in either direction, and the wheel moves the tape very slowly in either direction. DV cameras and some DV decks might have a slow response time to these controls. However, RS-422-controlled machines have a much faster response time.

You'll know that you can control and capture from your deck or camera if Final Cut Pro reports "VTR OK" in the bottom of the Log and Capture window. If FCP can't communicate with the machine, a window opens, warning you that FCP has no communication with the deck that is specified in the device control settings and that you can log clips only. If you are sourcing DV and controlling it with FireWire, you need to restart FCP with your deck or camera connected and turned on. (Cameras have to be in VTR or VCR mode.) In the case of RS-422-controlled machines, however, you can simply turn them on, and communication with them begins immediately.

Beneath the transport controls are timecode boxes that display the In point and Out point of the material that you want to log as a clip. Clicking the button on the far left moves your source tape (in a camera or deck) to the selected In point, and clicking the button on the far right moves your source tape to the selected Out point. You can press I to set an In point at the tape's current position and press O to set an Out point, just as you do when setting points in the Viewer, Canvas, or Timeline. Or you can click the Mark In or Mark Out buttons. You can also type in timecode numbers, just as you do in the Viewer and Canvas windows' timecode displays.

Using the Capture and Log Clip Buttons

Figure A.3 shows the four buttons in the lower right of the Log and Capture window. The first is the Log Clip button. After you've selected an In point and an Out point for a clip, you can add the clip to your selected logging bin by clicking this button or pressing F2.

FIGURE A.3   *The Log Clip and Capture buttons.*

The Capture area next to the Log Clip button contains three buttons. Each starts a capture:

- The Clip button captures from the current In to Out point selected in the Log and Capture window.

- The Now button starts capturing immediately. You must have the source video-tape machine or camera in play to use this button. It captures timecode if the source material has it, but it is also used to capture material from a noncontrollable device such as a VHS machine. If you are using a noncontrollable device, you need to control it manually and set your device control settings to Non-controllable Device. Then click Now to capture footage.

- The Batch button starts a batch capture. A *batch capture* is when you have logged a clip or set of clips and you capture them all at once. This feature is available only with timecoded sources, however. Using batch captures is the best way to save wear and tear on your source videotape machine or camera, because the deck has to rewind only one time to its pre-roll point and through the clip you are capturing. It then goes forward to the next pre-roll point and captures the next clip on the tape, and so on. You end up shuttling with your machine less if you do things this way.

Using the Logging Tab

The Logging Tab, shown in Figure A.4, contains fields for you to add information about your clip. These fields include the tape (*reel* in Final Cut Pro terms) the clip is on and the bin you are about to log the clip into. You also get fields to specify more information about the clip you've set an In and Out point for:

- Description
- Scene
- Shot/Take
- Log Note

Any information you type in these fields shows up in the corresponding columns in your logging bin. If you check the check box next to the clapstick button, the field's information is included in the clip's name. The clip's name can have up to 31 letters and spaces. If the Mark Good check box is checked, you see a check mark in the Browser's Good column.

FIGURE A.4 *The Logging tab.*

A handy button in the Logging tab allows you to create a new bin. It's the button with a folder icon and a star. It's to the right of the Log Bin button. When you create a new bin with this button, it immediately becomes the logging bin as well. A *logging bin* is a user-specified bin where logged clips appear and are stored after you click the Log Clip button or Capture Clip or press F2.

To the left of the new bin button is another button with an up arrow on a folder icon. It changes your logging bin to be the next bin up in your organizational hierarchy. Whatever bin is shown in the large oval button is the logging bin. If you click that button, the bin opens in your Browser.

Notice the Prompt check box. When it is checked, if you click the Log Clip button or press F2, the window shown in Figure A.5 opens. It lets you name the clip, add information to a Log Note area, and mark the clip as being good. After you click OK, the clip shows up in the Browser in the bin set to be the logging bin. You can Ctrl-click any bin's icon in the Browser and, from the context menu that pops up, select it to be the logging bin.

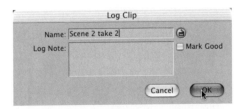

FIGURE A.5   *The Log Clip window.*

If you have several takes of a scene, you can use the same name and add a take number at the end. Each time you log a clip, Final Cut Pro automatically adds to the Name field the next number up from the last take. For example, if you have a scene named "Sally's closeup tk 1," after it is logged, the Scene, Shot/Take, or Description field automatically resets itself to be "Sally's closeup tk 2."

Note the clapstick button in this window. After you log a new clip, that clip's name might appear in the Name field with a 1 after its name. If you click the clapstick button, you change that number to the next-higher number. For example, suppose you name a clip "Mary kisses Tom." If there were more than one take of this clip, you could name the first one "Mary kisses Tom take 1." Then, each time you log another take of this clip, FCP adds a higher number. If you skipped take 2 and logged take 3, you could click this clapstick button, and a 3 would take the place of the automatic change to take 2. The program assumes that you will log and capture more than one take of any given shot. This facilitates renaming the same clip using just a different take number. The same behavior happens with the Description, Scene, and Shot/Take fields.

The bottom half of the Logging tab contains marker controls. If you click the disclosure triangle next to Markers, you see these controls. You can use them to create markers in clips as you log them. These controls are fairly straightforward, except for the Update button. You can change a marker's information by selecting it in the list of markers that appear in the list in the white area beneath the Markers controls. Highlight the marker you want to change, and after you've made changes, click Update to save the changes.

Using the Clip Settings Tab

Figure A.6 shows the Clip Settings tab. If your system has a capture card, the proc amp controls supported by the hardware, such as Hue and Brightness, become active, as well as the audio level controls. If you don't have a capture card installed, these are grayed out. If you have a digitizing or capture card, you can click the Use Digitizer's Default Settings button. When you do, the default proc amp setting set by the manufacturer moves the sliders accordingly. The audio level slider is unavailable if you are capturing digital video.

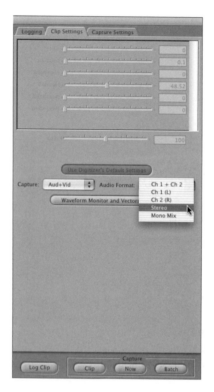

FIGURE A.6   *The Clip Settings tab.*

Beneath these controls are sets of controls that are available in all situations. Audio levels are displayed in the Audio Meters window in all cases, but you can control them only if you have a capture card installed or via the advanced audio settings in the Capture Settings preset. Don't be concerned if your recording levels here are low in DV. They should peak around –12dB on this meter. Digital Audio maintains dynamic range at much lower levels than analog audio does. If your peaks are around –12dB, you'll have plenty of volume and dynamic range. Some facilities even use –18dB or –14dB as their "house" reference level. If digital audio peaks at 0dB, it sounds distorted, unlike analog audio.

From the Capture pop-up menu, you can select which tracks you want to capture: audio only, video only, or both audio and video. Next to this pop-up menu is another pop-up menu. Here you select the audio tracks and the audio format you want to capture or log with the clip. The choices are as follows:

- Ch 1 + Ch 2 captures both tracks as independent tracks linked to the video track.
- Ch 1 (L) captures only the left track.
- Ch 2 (R) captures only the right track.
- Stereo captures tracks as a stereo pair.
- Mono Mix mixes two source tracks into a mono track.

Beneath the two pop-up menus is a large oval button to open the Waveform and Vectorscope, which you can use to monitor adjustment levels if you have a capture card installed. You can monitor the video levels from DV and other digital video formats, but you cannot adjust these levels unless you have a capture card installed and you are sourcing analog footage such as Betacam SP. In DV, you adjust levels with the color correction filters after you have captured your media. It also can be argued that you should never adjust footage "on the way in," or during the capture process. Instead, use Final Cut Pro's color correction tools on the clips in your sequences. If you correctly set your inputs from an analog machine with proc amp controls to view camera masters bars, any color correction you do from within Final Cut Pro remains in a backed-up project file. Later, when you recapture with the same method, these color corrections will match those done previously.

Log and Capture Strategy

If you have timecoded source material, it's highly recommended that you log everything available for you to use in your program. If you are working on something that has VHS or other nontimecoded material, I highly recommend that you dub this material to the format that the rest of your material uses and then log and capture these dubs. You probably won't lose any quality whatsoever, and you will be able to use OfflineRT mode editing and recapture all material automatically used in your program or recapture this material automatically later for a revision of the same program for a client.

tip

You might not believe up front that you will use every take you have at your disposal. However, time and time again you'll find that what you thought you wouldn't use, you need later to edit around a problem that might involve something like matching action. This is especially true when you're working with narrative film. I also think it's best for the editor to do the logging and capturing, because familiarity with the source footage is enhanced. You can use the Mark Good check box to sort only the clips you initially want to capture. Then you can put the offline uncaptured clips in a subfolder (that's best kept in the folder of the scene it relates to) for use later if you want. It's a lot easier to find a clip that's already been logged than to spend time (possibly with a client sitting next to you) searching for that sixth take. Not only that, but you also impress your client to no end when you locate a certain take from 30 source tapes in seconds.

The fastest way to log and capture your source material (if much of the tape will not be captured) is to log the portions of each tape you want to edit your sequence from (from end to end) and then capture the material logged *after* you have created offline clips by logging them first (by clicking the Log Clip button or pressing F2). The reason is that you will cause less wear and tear on your source machine or camera, because your workflow will usually involve only putting the machine in forward throughout the logging process. Then, when you batch-capture those offline clips (by highlighting them and pressing Cmd+H or clicking the Batch button), you send that machine into rewind one time. After that, it automatically captures or digitizes your source material from the first clip on any given tape to the last. This is actually faster than capturing each clip one at a time. (I love all things that are automatic, and you will too.)

If you intend to capture most of the tape's material, however, it's faster to simply capture the entire tape and log it digitally, much like you do in this book with the "3 hr timecode section" clip. It's especially useful to do things this way because, again, there is even less wear and tear on your source machine. If you are using DV camera masters, you can select Mark, DV Start/Stop Detection to find all the places you've restarted the camera's recording automatically. This saves you a lot of searching for these places on your tapes. However, this time-saving feature doesn't work with any tapes that are not DV camera masters, because it works with the time of day code these cameras record.

You can take a break while batch-capturing. In OS X, Final Cut Pro happily captures your footage while you work in another application or simply take a break. Of course, this assumes that all your source footage comes from timecoded sources.

Using the Batch Capture Window

It's at this point you should start to create your organization in the Browser. Start by creating new bins for the various scenes or portions of your program as you come across them, and log the appropriate clips into them. Even if clips are in different logging bins, you can highlight all of them in the Browser and click the Batch button. The Batch Capture window, shown in Figure A.7, opens. Here you can choose to capture only offline clips (those that are logged but not yet captured) or all selected items.

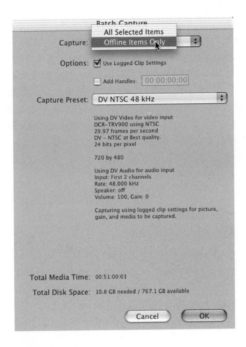

FIGURE A.7   *The Batch Capture window.*

When Use Logged Clip Settings is checked, any settings you have made as far as track settings, size, codec, frame rate, and any proc amp settings are used. When this is unchecked, you capture video and two channels of audio as Ch 1 + Ch 2 and any proc amp settings or gain settings you have logged. Leaving this option turned off uses the current Capture settings, so it can be dangerous to turn it on and off.

When Add Handles is checked, you can specify an amount of time to add to the front and rear of the logged timecode settings. You might want to add a second or so if you log very closely. It's better to have more media than you need than not to have enough and have to relog and recapture.

Last in this window is a pop-up menu to select a different Capture Preset. Note too that everything you are doing is displayed in the section below the Capture Preset pop-up menu. As you change things (just like the Media Manager does), Final Cut Pro lets you know what you are getting ready to do. If you have questions about your setup, just read this section to double-check that what you are about to do is what you want to do.

The Batch Capture also opens anytime you batch-capture a sequence. You might then use this for a "final" fine cut edit, so the handles you can add might be very appropriate to use in this case. I'm one of those folks who always wants any options I can have, so I usually add handles of a couple of seconds when batch-capturing sequences I might have made from an offline mode. However, adding handles requires that your tape has clean timecode without any breaks before and after the logged clip settings. To batch-capture a sequence, simply highlight it in the Browser, Ctrl-click its icon, and select Capture.

Making Sure You Are Set to Capture with the Proper Device Control

In the case of FireWire, if you don't have a FireWire source device connected, you see a window open just as you launch Final Cut Pro, telling you that you have a "missing FireWire device." Troubleshoot your connections with your camera or deck, and keep clicking Try Again until Final Cut Pro opens. Sometimes it's just a matter of turning on a device or unplugging and then plugging back in the FireWire or other connection, such as an RS-422 cable, to secure contact with your Mac.

You see this warning if you go out of FCP and back after turning off the device and leaving the Log and Capture window open.

I heartily recommend that you consult Apple's qualified device list at http://www.apple.com/finalcutpro/qualification.html *before* you invest in a device that won't work with the current version of Final Cut Pro. Don't be a guinea pig. Note too that some devices might need an extra or different capture preset. If they do, and if they have been qualified by Apple to work, this website shows you what you might need to do to get your particular device to work with Final Cut Pro.

Most RS-422-controlled devices work with the proper capture card or D/A converter and therefore might not be listed in the device list. Ask in the online discussion groups about any proposed addition to your system in this regard. Again, don't be a guinea pig. You'll find that most devices in this caliber of machine have been used successfully with Final Cut Pro.

If you are using an RS-422 device, be sure to select the appropriate RS-422 protocol in the Capture Preset editor. The RS-422 protocol varies somewhat between Sony and Panasonic devices. Simply experimenting with the various serial control settings in the Device Control settings will probably reveal the proper settings you need to use with your particular machine.

APPENDIX B

Output Options: Videotape, DVDs, and the Web

With Final Cut Pro you can output to any videotape format (with the proper hardware). DV cameras and decks allow analog recordings directly from your computer to VHS or other analog format passing the DV signal in from the FireWire input to your camera or deck and connecting your DV devices output to the input of the analog recorder. If you have a capture card, consulting with its manufacturer is the best advice I can give for more specifics of hardware setup. (Usually it's just a driver you need to install that supplies presets for your capture card.)

Exporting to a videotape from your computer when you are done editing is really accomplished in one of three ways. You can manually record your output to videotape when viewing video externally, you can use the Print to Video command, or you can use the Edit to Tape command. Each of these methods produces the same result—a copy of your program to tape. There is no advantage in picture quality between them, but you should perform an audio mixdown before you attempt a manual output to relieve bandwidth your computer needs to mix the audio tracks in real time.

Viewing Video Externally and Recording It

The first method is simply to view your video externally, record directly from the Timeline, and control your machine manually (put it into record and play the sequence in the Timeline). You can toggle this feature on and off by selecting View, External Video or by pressing Cmd+F12. (If you are working with a PowerBook, you need to press the fn key for any function key to work.) If you need a quick VHS dub, this method might be the fastest way. But you can even master for broadcast this way if you create a sequence with the appropriate bars, tone, and slate added to it. It's manual in nature, so you don't have the option of controlling the videotape machine to make a really precise edit, but in many circumstances, this is not necessary.

When recording a tape using this method, I highly recommend that you perform a Mixdown Audio command first. Highlight everything in your sequence that is open in the Timeline, and select Sequence, Render Only, Mixdown or press Opt+Cmd+R. Performing this mixdown frees bandwidth in your computer, because it creates a single two-track audio file (or more, depending on your capture card's ability, and as set by your A/V Devices settings) from all the audio tracks you've built into your sequence. This mixdown also keeps your media drives from having to search from audio cut to audio cut just to play the sequence.

Using the Print to Video Command

A second way to record videotape from your computer is to use the File, Print to Video command (you also can press Ctrl+M). Using this method, you still manually put your recording device into record and then proceed, but you gain the ability to have Final Cut Pro prepare and add elements to the recording with the options shown in Figure B.1. You are prompted to start the recording when the computer is ready.

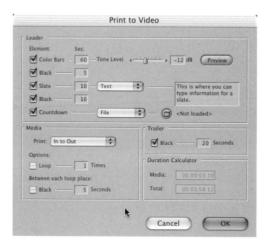

FIGURE B.1   *The Print to Video window.*

The Print to Video command, as seen in Figure B.2, includes a window of options you select for the entire recording, adding elements such as black video, color bars (and tone), a slate, a built-in or standard countdown, and some post program options such as black, and even looping the program. Again, you do not have to have device control to use this command. These options appear in the order they are in this window and for the selectable durations. Thus, the rest in the list follow Color Bars (which always include Tone).

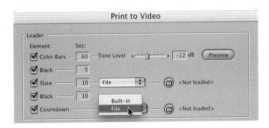

FIGURE B.2   *The Print to Video window.*

Print to Video Leader Options

All the check boxes in the Leader section of the Print to Video window (refer to Figure B.1) are relatively self-explanatory. By checking them, you can add color bars and tone, black (which would follow those bars), then a slate from text, a file (which needs to be a still file, such as a PICT or TIFF file) or the first clip's name as selected from the pop-up menu, then another option for black to follow the slate, and a countdown. There is an entry field next to each of these items for you to change the lengths of most of these elements except the Countdown. You can change the Countdown using your own QuickTime movie.

The Countdown can either be Final Cut Pro's built-in countdown or a custom one created from a file you select from the pop-up menu. In the case of the built-in countdown, the sequence begins 2 seconds after the countdown's last visible frame, so it's important to start your sequence on the first frame of the Timeline window when you use a countdown. If there is space in the Timeline window before the sequence starts, unless you have selected the actual start by setting an In and Out point for its playback, you record black video for the duration of this open space.

When you select File for the countdown's playback, a button with a file folder on it allows you to select the QuickTime movie file of your choice for this function. A custom countdown can be created for this use and stored on your computer in any location. If this QuickTime movie matches your sequence settings, it doesn't need rendering.

Note that you can loop playback, which is great for preparing tapes for trade shows, where you don't want to continually rewind a tape. You can also select how much black will be played between each instance of the repeated program or not. A trailer of black can be added, and a Duration Calculator keeps track of the math for you as you add the different extra options for your videotape to record, allowing you to make sure your tape has room on it for your recording.

After you've set the Leader options the way you want them, click OK. After Final Cut Pro creates the appropriate media files and mixes down your audio (if you have not done this already), a window opens, instructing you to start recording manually to your videotape machine or camera.

Using the Edit to Tape Command

The third and final way to output to videotape is the File, Edit to Tape command. Using this method, you have not only the Leader options that the Print to Video command adds to your output, but you also can control a qualified videotape device such as a camera or deck. If you can control and capture from your source device, you probably can use this method as well. But if you are having problems, you should consult the device qualification information from Apple (`http://www.apple.com/finalcutpro/qualification.html`). The Edit to Tape window looks much like the Canvas window, with some extra tabs at the top, as shown in Figures B.3 and B.4.

tip

If you perform a Mixdown Audio command before you record your program back to tape, Final Cut Pro uses this mixdown when doing a Print to Video or an Edit to Tape. It's very handy to do this first if you record multiple copies of your program, because you don't have to wait for this mixdown each time you record another copy. Performing an audio mixdown (by selecting Sequence, Render Only, Mixdown or by pressing Opt+Cmd+R) also opens up bandwidth and relieves your disk drives of searching for more than one audio file. You'll find that this creates a more reliable playback of your program.

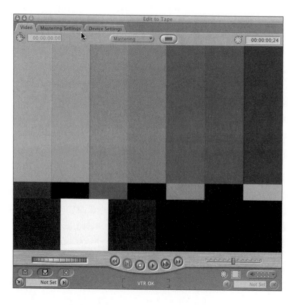

FIGURE B.3   *The Edit to Tape window.*

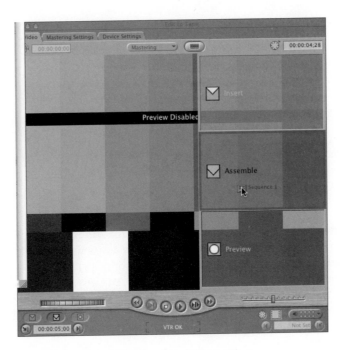

Figure B.4   *The Edit to Tape window showing its editing overlay.*

The shuttle controls control your videotape device just as they do in the Log and Capture window. They are much like those of a VCR.

To use the Edit to Tape function, which allows for precise control of where your program is put on the videotape, you must have a bit of black or other recorded video for the edit to take place. Using Final Cut Pro's Black and Code feature is the most common method of preparing a tape for an edit, but you only need some sort of pre-recorded video on the target tape to use the Edit to Tape function.

Using the Black and Code Button

The button with the filmstrip icon on it in the top area of the Edit to Tape window blacks and codes a tape in the format you are using. Figure B.5 shows the Black and Code window and its options. Mainly, from the pop-up menu you just select the file format for the output of the black signal if you are not using an RS-422-controlled machine. After you select the proper options, click OK. A window opens, warning you that you are about to erase a tape with black video and telling you to start your recording manually. After you start recording, click OK in the Black and Code window.

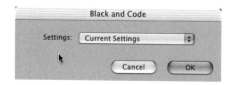

FIGURE B.5   *The Black and Code window.*

You need only a few seconds (10 seconds will do nicely) of recording to then edit your program to the front of a tape in assemble edit mode. To stop the black and code, press the Escape key.

Understanding Assemble and Insert Edits for Videotape Devices

Assemble edits erase all tracks of video and create a new timecode track as well. Just as you needed a bit of pre-roll when you capture from tape, you need a bit of pre-roll when you edit to tape to ensure a clean In point edit. After you have created an assemble edit, the Out edit is not clean. But you can cut back into the end of the recording just as you do with a camera, create another clean edit, and go on assembling edits until the tape is full.

An *insert edit* records only the tracks you've selected (from the track selectors in the lower right of the Edit to Tape window). An insert edit leaves the unselected tracks intact. An insert edit performs clean edits at both its In and Out points. Many professional analog videotape machines perform this sort of edit (but not all do, so check your manual for this specification), and Final Cut Pro can control them for this purpose. If your machine does not support an insert edit, the Out point selection in the Edit to Tape window is grayed out and unavailable for use, as is the Duration indicator in the upper left of the window. Most (all but the most expensive) DV cameras and decks do not perform insert edits (check your user's manual). To perform an insert edit, you must have RS-422 control of your source machine.

Using the Three Tabs in the Edit to Tape Window

The Edit to Tape window has three tabs. The second tab, Mastering Settings, is identical to the Print to Video leader options (see the earlier section "Print to Video Leader Options"). The third tab, Device Settings, is shown in Figure B.6. Here you select your Device Control setting and your Capture/Input setting (which doubles as an output). You should use the same settings here that you used for capturing in the first place.

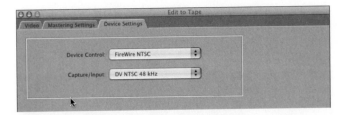

FIGURE B.6   *The Device Settings tab in the Edit to Tape window.*

After you've set up your record tape to have a bit of black and timecode at its head in the case of a new tape, and you have set up your leader options from the Mastering Settings tab, you can press I to set an In point where the recording starts. You can also type a timecode number in the lower-left timecode box. The transport controls work with your source device just as they do in the Canvas window to locate a specific place on the record tape. If you have a videotape machine that can perform an insert edit, you can also select an Out point in the bottom right of the Edit to Tape window. The duration of this edit is displayed in the upper-left timecode box.

Just above the In point selection are the familiar buttons that perform the editing functions. From the left, they are Insert, Assemble, and Preview. As explained in the sidebar, you must have a recorder that can perform an insert edit to use this first button. The Assemble button creates an assemble edit, and the Preview button creates a preview for you to check if you want to. You can view and preview the edit on an external video monitor that is connected to the output of your videotape machine or camera. Pressing the Escape key stops the preview or the actual edit during their execution.

To the right and left of the In point and Out point timecode boxes are familiar controls that set points and cue the videotape machine to the respective In or Out points. In the upper left of the Edit to Tape window is a duration box. The current videotape's timecode position indication box is in the upper right. They function the same as they do in the Canvas window.

One other pop-up menu appears just to the left of the Black and Code button. Here you can select whether you are mastering or editing. Selecting Mastering makes the system look at the Mastering Settings and include them in the recording process. Selecting Editing performs the edit and ignores them. Usually this is used to perform an insert edit, but it also can be used in the Assemble edit mode to start the edit without any of the leader options being used.

Note that in the Mastering Settings tab, you must either select to record an In and Out point within the sequence or edit all the sequence's media to tape. After you've selected the timecode to start your recording, you simply highlight the sequence you want to record to tape and click the appropriate button.

The Edit to Tape window has an edit overlay similar to that in the Canvas window, as shown in Figure B.7. You can drag your sequence from the Browser to the overlay window and start the process of recording it.

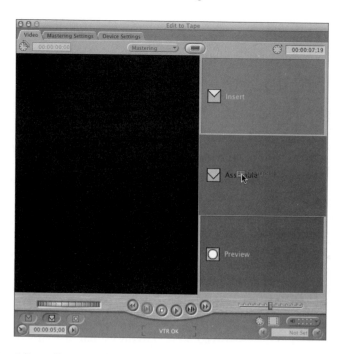

FIGURE B.7   *The Edit to Tape window overlay and a sequence icon dragged to the Assemble edit box.*

Outputting for the Web: Compressor and DVDs

When you want to output your movie to a medium other than videotape, you can output self-contained QuickTime movies, which do not recompress the original video files you captured. They make perfect copies of your original media files and marry them into one media file.

You can also output reference movies when you use a non-self-contained format. These movies appear to be single files to all applications that support QuickTime. They act like normal QuickTime movies when imported into these applications. These non-self-contained movies act like stand-alone media files, but in fact they are files that reference the original media files you edited the sequence from. They play in any QuickTime application only if those referenced original media files are on the same computer. They are not portable like self-contained movies are. Non-self-contained movies do not actually contain any media (picture and sound files). But it's helpful to use these when you can (when the media files they reference are on the same computer). These files are much smaller than self-contained movies and are created faster as well. You can also recompress your video with Final Cut Pro's QuickTime export features.

QuickTime export from Final Cut Pro includes various codecs you can choose to use in your exported file.

Final Cut Pro 4 includes a program called Compressor in addition to its own file compressions.

Preparing Your Video for iDVD

The easiest way to send your completed sequences to iDVD is via a QuickTime export. If you will burn your DVD to iDVD on the same computer your project file and media reside on, you can create a QuickTime movie export, which is non-self-contained. Chapter markers are exported to iDVD 3 or later as well if you include them in the QuickTime export dialog box.

You need to create a self-contained movie if you intend to create your DVD on another computer. Figure B.8 shows the correct setup for export to iDVD. You don't want to recompress your movie within FCP for this; rather, iDVD performs the MPEG-2 compression you need to do to ultimately burn your DVD.

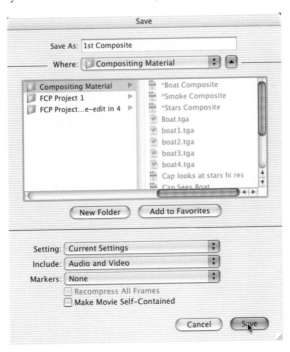

FIGURE B.8   *QuickTime movie export settings for a non-self-contained QuickTime movie.*

Preparing Your Video for DVD Studio Pro

You can choose from more options when exporting MPEG compressions for use with DVD Studio Pro. First, when you install DVD SP, you add an MPEG compressor to your list of available compressors using the Export, QuickTime Conversion dialog box, as shown in Figure B.9. This MPEG converter is supplied with DVD SP. The quality of this compression is probably a bit higher than that used by iDVD, because it is a professional-quality codec. When you install FCP 4, you get the MPEG-2 converter via Compressor, which is not available from QT Player for export. DVD SP 2 ships with Compressor as well. In either case, you get better-quality MPEG-2 files from Compressor's dual-pass VBR settings.

FIGURE B.9   *Using the QuickTime Conversion dialog box to create MPEG-2 files.*

Using Compressor

Figure B.9 shows the QuickTime Conversion dialog box. You open it after selecting MPEG2 as the file format from the pop-up menu and clicking the Options button. You can select the bit rate and format for your DVD's movie files.

The second and better (but possibly more time-consuming) way to create MPEG-2 files from Final Cut Pro is to use the supplied compression program, aptly named Compressor. Unfortunately, iDVD currently cannot accept files from Compressor.

Compressor lets you use a dual-pass compression algorithm called a two-pass VBR (Variable Bit Rate) compression. The first pass analyzes where the motion is in the file. Then, on the second pass, Compressor allocates bits where they're most needed while it does the encoding. No encoding is done on the first pass. There are two ways to use Compressor:

- You can export directly to Compressor from within Final Cut Pro by selecting File, Export, Using Compressor. Final Cut Pro then creates a temporary non-self-contained QuickTime movie. It opens Compressor on your computer and sends this information directly to Compressor so that you can choose from among several preset compression schemes or refine one of these presets into a custom preset. With Compressor, you can also change the video levels, crop the picture, and more. It also includes the ability to create a render queue and compress more than one sequence at a time and into more than one compressed format. You might want to prepare video for the web using an MPEG-4 compression or another QuickTime compression and at the same time create files for use in DVD SP. However, doing so "locks up" Final Cut Pro. In other words, you cannot edit in Final Cut Pro if you export directly from FCP to Compressor. There is a hidden advantage, though. When you use this direct-export method, Final Cut Pro's rendering engine is used, which might speed up the process.

- A second way to prepare sequences created in Final Cut Pro for use with DVD Studio Pro is to export a QuickTime Movie file as either a self-contained movie (which takes up more space, because it includes the actual picture and sound files but doesn't require that the original media files be on the same computer) or a non-self-contained movie, exactly as you would for iDVD. The difference is that you import this file into Compressor for the compressed-file creation.

Either of these methods results in the same quality files, but using the second method allows you to continue working in Final Cut Pro while you are compressing files with Compressor. You need a lot of RAM to do this with stability. A minimum of a gigabyte or more is recommended. It also might be wise to save your file from Compressor onto a drive you are not using for Final Cut Pro.

Using Compressor to Create MPEG-2 Files for DVDs

Compressor is a very sophisticated but intuitive program that compresses MPEG-2 files (used for DVDs), MPEG 4 files (used primarily for the web and CDs), and QuickTime movies that are compressed for the web, CD, or intranet use. It's outside the scope of this book to explain all the compressions and techniques used to create compressed video files, so the discussion here covers the use of Compressor to create files for DVDs.

DVD Studio Pro requires that audio/video assets used within it be M2v files (MPEG-2 files containing video) and AIFF files (containing audio). Using DVD SP with a Superdrive on your computer results in high-quality, professional-looking DVDs. You use Compressor to create the audio and video assets used by DVD SP. It can be as simple as importing your QuickTime movie into Compressor, choosing a preset, and clicking a button to start the compression. Figure B.10 shows the result of selecting Sequence 1 from the project file and exporting it using Compressor by Ctrl-clicking it.

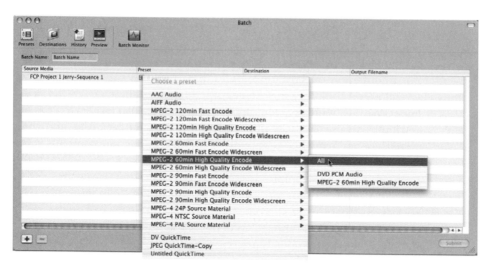

FIGURE B.10   *Compressor's Batch window.*

In this case, I've selected the 60min High Quality Encode preset by clicking the Preset selection button in the column to the right of the Name column and selecting a standard preset that comes with Compressor. I selected All from the menu to include audio and video. You then select the destination disk for your files to be saved on (the MPEG and audio file you'll use with DVD SP).

If you've placed chapter and compression markers in your sequence, they are included with the MPEG file you export from Compressor and are recognized by DVD Studio Pro 2.

It's then as simple as clicking the Submit button in the lower-right corner of Compressor's Batch window to start and save the encoding. The Batch Monitor window, shown in Figure B.11, opens to keep you apprised of the encoding's progress. You can stop and resume the encoding process and delete the batch as well.

note   DVD Studio Pro 2 has the capability to compress to MPEG-2 uncompressed files and do so in the background while you continue to work with the application. DVD Studio Pro 1.x does not and requires that you import MPEG files for use with the application. DVD SP 2 however uses the same software code during its "in the background" compressions, and doesn't require then an MPEG compressed file to begin with. However, I'd probably do the compression beforehand with Compressor for this if your computer isn't the fastest. Stability will be enhanced if you do so with slower computers or computers without a lot of RAM in them. As of this writing I've not tried this new feature on a G5, but predict that rendering in the background would be a better workflow with these super fast Macintoshes experimenting with your particular computer is advised.

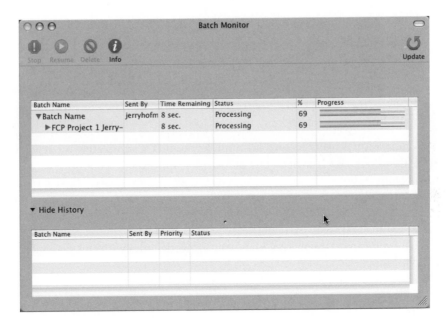

FIGURE B.11   *The Batch Monitor window.*

Learning to Compress High-Quality Video and Software Used for the Job

Describing all the compression techniques you can use to improve the quality of your compressed files would take an entire book. I suggest that you take the time to start using Compressor to its fullest capabilities by reading the PDF manual that comes with FCP 4 (you can access it from Compressor's Help menu). You can crop, change data rates, add filters, and more to your compressed video files, whether they are MPEG or other QuickTime compressions. You'll find Compressor very easy to use. The video it creates is of extremely high quality. It creates some of the best software-encoded files in the world. If you use the presets supplied by Compressor, you get very high-quality files, but the secret to the very best compressions is in preprocessing the files.

Another application I find extremely easy to use and whose results are world-class is Sorenson Media's Sorenson Squeeze 3 Compression Suite. As of this writing, it includes the ability to compress QuickTime, MPEG-4, and Flash movies using the highest-quality software codecs available. It supplies the Sorenson 3 Professional version of the Sorenson 3 codec, considered by most to be the best codec to use for QuickTime. After you install it, this Pro version of the codec is available in both Compressor and Final Cut Pro 4. You should import QuickTime Movie exports into Squeeze. It's best to ask questions about compression issues at the Creative Cow (http://www.creativecow.net). You'll find answers to issues with the latest software.

Cleaner 6 from Discreet Logic is another software application that is used to compress for the web and to create QuickTime files, Real Windows Media files, and more from Final Cut Pro. You use QuickTime movie exported files to import into Cleaner 6. However, by the time you read this, all the companies will probably have shifted their focus somewhat. It's best to ask questions about compression issues at the Creative Cow (`http://www.creativecow.net`) for definitive answers on issues with the latest software that's doing the best job.

Compression is really its own art form. Explaining it completely is outside the scope of this book. For further exploration of compression techniques, I suggest Ben Waggoner's book *Compression for Great Digital Video: Power Tips, Techniques, and Common Sense* from CMP Books. Keep in mind that there are professional compressionists whose sole occupation is compressing video for the web and DVDs. Final Cut Pro has made this job extremely easy with Compressor. You'll be amazed at just how easily you can create professional-quality encoded files with this extremely powerful application.

Appendix C

Solving Common Problems

You could write an entire library on how to troubleshoot a computer editing system, but this appendix provides some quick fixes that hopefully will save you a headache or two. Possibly more important, much of this appendix helps you understand how to troubleshoot in general. Understanding your computer's processes when working with Final Cut Pro is a valuable asset indeed. It's a necessary skill that all nonlinear editors should have.

System Problems and Playback Problems

Apple has a list of compatible and qualified third-party hardware that is updated constantly. Its web address is `http://www.apple.com/finalcutpro/qualification.html`.

Hardware interfaced with Final Cut Pro usually has some sort of software associated with it. Typically they are called drivers. Serial ports for control, SCSI card software, and more all usually have drivers associated with them. Be sure to check that you have the latest drivers for any third-party hardware you might be using. Especially be sure to keep up to date with drivers for equipment that is made to be used exclusively with Final Cut Pro, such as drivers for capture cards.

The manufacturers of this specialized equipment work very closely with Apple to write drivers that are compatible. Most of these manufacturers have a section on their website listing the latest drivers for their equipment, and you can download them from there. Because we live in a constantly evolving software environment (meaning that there are constant updates to software in general), if you encounter a problem you think is hardware-related, there might be a software/hardware conflict you can resolve simply by downloading an update from the Internet from the appropriate party.

Don't Always Be the First on Your Block

A savvy computer user usually is not the first one to download new software unless he or she *knows* that the update might cure a problem. Rarely (although it does happen), manufacturers post updates that can make matters worse. *Wait* if the update is brand-new. Check out the forums or tech sites listed in Appendix E, "Other Resources," to see how other (and braver) folks have fared with the update. Be extra cautious if you are *not* having problems and an update is posted. I've always held to the belief that if it's not broken, why fix it? Why be the guinea pig?

Remember that you are working with a *system* and not just a single piece of software. Even the simplest of setups, such as a single DV camera, Mac, or Final Cut Pro, can have issues that might or might not be resolved with a software update. Versions of QuickTime and FCP might work better in certain combinations with certain cameras, for example. Appendix E lists the places you should check before you jump in and update your software, purchase that new camera, and so on. Check the Creative Cow's Final Cut Pro forums (http://www.creativecow.com) or the Discussion group at Apple before you make any changes to a working system. Better safe than sorry.

Sometimes, just doing a *cold restart* of your computer clears up problems. A cold restart simply means that you shut down your Mac, wait at least 20 seconds, and then restart it. Many times this solution makes the problem disappear.

When a cold restart fails to fix the problem, the first thing to do in the case of external hardware problems such as a camera or videotape machine not showing up within FCP is to just turn it off, wait a few seconds, and then turn it back on. Some devices interact with their host machines and simply need to send a new signal or reinitialize themselves. It's best to have your source machine/camera powered on before you launch Final Cut Pro.

If this fails, suspect cables. Sometimes they go bad, get seated improperly, or have a bit of dust that keeps them from making a solid connection. Obviously, this isn't always the answer, but sometimes it is. Don't panic. Be persistent in isolating the problem. If the problem is intermittent, cables often are at fault. Always try substituting a suspect cable with a different one. FireWire cables are notoriously touchy. I particularly like the ones sold by Granite Digital (http://www.granitedigital.com), however. Never have I had one go bad, and I've been around many of them. The lighted connector is pretty cool, too. When you are solidly connected, it lights up. No guesswork!

When you are really in a bind for time and you must complete a project, think creatively. You'll almost always come up with a workaround that allows you to proceed. For example, a certain effect might not be working as you'd like, or a process of some sort isn't working well. Don't use up your precious time hitting your head against the wall. Stay calm. Think through the process step by step. Sometimes you'll realize what's getting in your way, and you'll solve the problem by coming up with a workaround. Check your System, User, and Audio/Video settings first if you have something going on like having to render every single edit you add to a sequence. The sequence settings have to match the properties of the clips you are adding to them. With Final Cut Pro 4, settings have become more complicated, and they can easily be set up incorrectly. Refer to Chapter 2, "Specifying Setups, Settings, Presets, and Preferences," for details.

note

I heartily recommend reading books on the subject of computers and Macintoshes in general. You can't know enough about your editing station. Learn its hardware; learn how it likes to be taken care of. Preventative maintenance will carry you far. There are many books on the subject, but take a look at the offerings from Peachpit Press and David Pogue's *Missing Manual*. Both sources are very readable and informative and are geared toward the less-technically-minded. Trust me: After reading them, you'll become more adept at using your computer, and you'll be a much happier editor. They also give you an idea of the processes your computer goes through, which in turn helps you troubleshoot any problems you might be having with *all* your software.

There is even an electronic troubleshooter for FCP! Sold at http://www.intelligent assistance.com, this application is an interactive program that you use on your computer. You tell it what your problem is, and it gives you step-by-step solutions for you to try. It's very cool and very accurate.

The OS X and hardware forums found at Apple's site and at the Creative Cow are a great place to check for solutions. The Knowledge Base articles found at http://www.info.apple.com/ are a wonderful resource. Sherlock can search these articles. New ones with suggestions for fixing things are posted all the time. If you click Sherlock and then click the AppleCare button at the top of the interface, you can search the Knowledge Base at Apple extremely fast, and you can preview the articles that your search finds in the lower pane of Sherlock's AppleCare window, much like most e-mail applications. By all means, look at Appendix E in this regard. There are a plethora of sites on the Internet for you to peruse.

Keeping Your Computer Happy

OS X introduced some new maintenance routines that you should run often. For example, you should run Repairing Disk Permissions on your startup disk about once a week and every time you install any new software. It's found in Apple's Drive Utility in the Utilities folder contained in your Applications folder. Just highlight your startup disk in the pane on the left, and click the First Aid tab. The rest is self-apparent.

Running Disk First Aid on all your hard drives at least monthly is also a good idea. Using third-party utilities also can save you a lot of headaches. There are some free ones on the Internet as well.

`http://personalpages.tds.net/~brian_hill/macjanitor.html` supplies a free utility that performs processes that are performed late at night by OS X. A Unix system performs daily, weekly, and monthly tasks. If you leave your computer running all the time (24/7), you have no need for MacJanitor. However, if you don't run your computer all the time, these processes might not get done. MacJanitor performs the relevant tasks for OS X on command.

Another site to visit in this regard is `http://www.MacFixit.com`. Here you'll find fixes to problems aplenty. Better yet, this site is a great place to visit before you update any software. You usually won't be the first person to try a new piece of software. Users who are early adopters of updates or new programs report their experiences at MacFixit.

All Macs have a Power Management Unit (PMU) switch that you can reset if you are having problems with power (such as if your Mac won't start up). I've seen the PMU switch fix "dead" FireWire ports and more. This tiny round button is labeled PMU and is found on the motherboard. Each Mac puts it on the motherboard in a different place, so consult the Knowledge Base (`http://www.info.apple.com/`) on your particular computer for the switch's location. This must be done with your Mac turned off and the power cord disconnected. It's also recommended that you wear a wrist grounding strap whenever you touch anything inside your Mac's housing. Read the articles about the PMU switch on Apple's website.

If your disks are extremely full, you might want to defragment them. Most defragmentation software is more or less equal. Several manufacturers sell them.

Do the prescribed maintenance, and you'll find you have a much happier Mac, and a much easier time keeping it from having problems. I'm not too surprised when I hear of problems coming from folks who don't do regular everyday maintenance on their computers. Regular maintenance goes with the territory. If anything, you'll save yourself some frustration. NLE software is probably one of the most taxing applications you can run on any computer. If it's not running on a happy and stable computer, you'll experience a lot of problems. Don't let your Mac get too far behind with its upkeep.

If you installed new software just before you encounter a problem, suspect the new software. There might be conflicts, or you might just find that running this software at the same time you run FCP isn't a good idea. Uninstall the new software and see if the problem goes away. Before you install any software, read the Read Me file that comes with it. Understand all the software's installation files and where they might be placed. Always err on the side of caution. Often, an Installation or Install log is made during a software installation. Locate it each time you add software, and give it a more-specific name if it's just called Install log. Keep it in a folder where you can locate it if you need to uninstall everything installed from an application.

Back up your project files to media away from the computer, such as a Zip or CD-R. Don't forget iDisk, a worthwhile service from Apple. Apple supplies iDisk as a web-accessed "disk" for your personal use. It is space kept on Apple's servers that's perfect for backups. To learn more about this disk space, go to http://www.apple.com and click the link to the Mac area. Always be prepared for the worst. I use iDisk as a place to back up daily saves of my current project. Then, when I'm finished with that project, I back it up on CD-Rs. It's easy enough to then delete the project from my iDisk to open up space if need be. Panther (OS X.3) has made iDisk so integrated into the OS that it's extremely easy to use and access. It's true that FCP has an Autosave folder containing backups of your project files (see Chapter 2), but what if it's on a hard drive that fails? Redundant backups are better.

Problems with Video Devices

If your camcorder or deck is not recognized, check your cables, make sure that the camera or deck is powered on, and make sure that your camera is in VTR or VCR mode. If the problem persists, check to make sure that you have set the proper device control settings for your particular device. Sometimes just restarting your computer and cycling your camera or deck's power clears up problems. Starting your camera or deck (after it is properly connected) before you launch FCP can also be of help.

Sometimes your FireWire port needs looking into. More than once I've seen resetting the PMU switch (discussed in the preceding section) bring it back to life.

If you can't control various functions of your camcorder or deck, make sure you've followed the previous instructions, and then try changing device control settings in an experimental manner. If you are using a DV device, try FireWire Basic for control instead of Apple FireWire. If your deck has a local/remote switch, make sure it's set to remote. Some extra scripts provided on your installation disk might be required to be installed with your particular camera or deck. Check the device qualification list at http://www.apple.com/finalcutpro/qualification.html to see if your device needs them.

This list of qualified devices is updated regularly. You should consult it *before* you decide to buy that new camera or videotape machine for use with Final Cut Pro. If it isn't listed, this doesn't necessarily mean it doesn't work. It probably just means that the good folks at Apple haven't tested it yet. Manufacturers of video equipment change their models rapidly, and it's impossible for Apple to keep up. You can post a question about the proposed device in the forums listed in Appendix E to see if someone has interfaced this particular device without problems. Being informed is better than hassling with a return of gear that doesn't work with your system. That said, most Sony equipment usually works quite reliably with Final Cut Pro. Nevertheless, it's a good idea to make sure that your proposed equipment will definitely work with Final Cut Pro 4.

Problems Playing Back Your Media

Sometimes improper settings can cause problems with playing back your picture and sound files in Final Cut Pro. The following sections explain the most common solutions to these sorts of problems.

You Can't View External Video or Hear Audio Playback

Make sure you have set your system to view externally. This setting is at the bottom of the View menu. Set it to be All Frames or Single Frames. All frames will play all the video as you play from Final Cut Pro. Single frames display the current frame you are parked on in the active monitor and allow you to hear audio from your computer's speakers during playback.

Check the settings in the A/V Devices tab of the Audio/Video Settings. They have to be set to the proper outputs during playback for you to see external video and hear audio from your selected device.

Remember that real-time playback of your DV material is more taxing on your computer when you view external video. It only previews effects supported by your computer. Rendering all your effects makes this much easier on slower G4s. G5 computers have an easier time with this feature. They also play back many more effects in real time.

The Media Has Become Offline

If you move media files on your computer from the location where Final Cut Pro last saw them, they are reported as "Media files Offline," and those pesky red lines run through the clips in the Browser. Don't panic; reconnect them. Highlight any and all clips whose media suddenly "disappears" from the Browser, Ctrl-click them, and select Reconnect Media from the context menu that appears. You did just that when you installed the media files used in this book. Final Cut Pro assumes that the media files referenced by the clips in the Browser are where you left them last. So it's easy to reconnect them if you move them.

New to Final Cut Pro 4, FCP warns you if scratch disks are missing during its startup, so you have a way to mount it or restart your computer (in the case of SCSI arrays).

Be aware that if you have media files on external drives, they must be mounted on your desktop for your project file in order for you to find them. If you need information about where your media files were "last seen," Ctrl-click a column header in the Browser (other than the Name column) and select Source to open this column in the Browser. The location where your media files were last located is shown in this column. Look there to see if you've deleted or moved them, or if you need to connect an external disk drive to bring them back online. This is especially useful if you have changed the names of master clips or used subclips that don't reference the master clips they came from. This column also lists the name of the media file these sorts of clips referenced originally. You can turn off the Matched Name Only option in the Reconnect Media window to manually attach unmatched media filenames to clips in your project file. This is very handy indeed.

Audio Sync Problems During Playback

Most of the time, audio sync problems are caused when you record audio on your camera at 12 bits per sample, and you have captured the material into FCP at 48kHz, 16-bit (or vice versa). If you record audio at the 12-bit setting with your camera, capture it with an audio capture preset setting of 32kHz, 16-bit. If you have recorded audio at 16-bit, capture it at 48kHz, 16-bit. It's not recommended that you record at an 8-bit setting. You can check the bit depth recorded (12- or 16-bit) from the viewfinder in your camera via its menu display, or from the playback deck's menu display. Some decks have lights on them to let you know what bit depth they are playing back.

Sometimes dropping frames during capture can cause audio to go out of sync with your video. See the next section to troubleshoot this specific problem.

If your audio is out of sync with the computer's display of video playback when you view video externally and monitor audio externally, your audio will be in sync with the external video monitor.

Turning off file sharing is also recommended. Having other computers access your FCP station can cause problems while you are running Final Cut Pro.

Dropping Frames During Playback

If your clip is not being displayed at Fit to Window or smaller, and you are cutting off some of its edges because you are zoomed in on the Viewer or Canvas window, you can experience audio playback out of sync. Check to make sure that nothing is touching either window. They should not overlap each other.

Make sure that you are running the proper version of QuickTime for your particular version of Final Cut Pro. Also check to make sure that you are running the proper OS for the version of Final Cut Pro you are using. Final Cut Pro does not run under Classic. Check Apple's website for the proper set of software to be running with your version of Final Cut Pro. The correct version of QuickTime is supplied on your Final Cut Pro installation disk. Depending on when you bought Final Cut Pro, there probably will be updates to it, to QuickTime, and to the current OS you are running. You will want to investigate these. Apple routinely updates professional applications, and there will no doubt be an update or two you should run on a new installation. Run Software Update from your System Preferences and see what turns up. Check with the sites listed in Appendix E for any information you can find, or post a question to the Creative Cow or in the Discussion groups about any updates and your specific computer setup.

I highly recommend reading Philip Hodgetts' article on the subject of installing Final Cut Pro 4. It's in the Articles section of the Creative Cow at http://www.creativecow.net/.

Reducing the number of real-time audio tracks being monitored or mixing them down can also improve audio playback problems. Also, it's easier on your computer if all your audio files are the same kHz, because it doesn't have to convert different audio files with different kHz recordings. This becomes more critical the more tracks of audio you ask your computer to play back. If your computer is slower, you need to use one of two techniques to relieve its CPU from doing more work than it has to: You can use Item Level renders and the Audio Mixdown command.

When you select Item Level Audio rendering by selecting Sequence, Renders, any audio clips are resampled to match the sample rate of the sequence they are contained in. Also, audio clips that you've added filters to are rendered. FCP saves them as item-level render cache files. Audio-level mixing can still be done in real time, and mixing performance improves, because audio resampling and audio effects no longer rely on real-time mixing and playback for you to hear them. This reduces computer overhead and improves performance playback.

You can use the Mixdown Audio option (found under Sequence, Render Only) to render *all* the audio in a sequence (or a set of sequences if multiple sequences are highlighted in the Browser) to a single group of render cache files, one for each audio output assigned to the selected sequence. This can improve playback performance by eliminating the need for Final Cut Pro to do any real-time mixing or audio effects playback.

In either case (using the Item Level or Audio Mixdown command), these renders are rendered at the highest quality, regardless of the setting chosen in the Audio Playback Quality pop-up menu in the General tab of the User Preferences. Using them also improves viewing video externally and lowers the instances of dropped frames during playback.

You will experience better performance in general with this problem if you are capturing to a disk drive that is separate from your startup disk. Ultra SCSI 160 systems (such as those from Huge Systems) and Apple's X RAID Fibre Channel drives are the fastest. You cannot get drives that are too fast to play back your media. ATA 7200rpm drives are certainly fast enough for DV, but they are not fast enough for higher-quality video by themselves. Using faster disk drives or disk drive arrays improves playback performance in any resolution. Even adding a new, faster computer display card improves playback of real-time effects. Open GL is used to enhance real-time playback in your computer, so the faster your video display card, the better the performance you'll see.

Your computer's monitor should always be set to a 75Hz or greater refresh rate.

Don't fill up your scratch disks. You might be able to improve playback by defragmenting them, but filling them up is not recommended. Keep at least 50 to 100MB free.

Don't keep too many sequences open at the same time. If you are having problems, close all but the sequence you are working with. If you have a lot of sequences open, Final Cut Pro uses more RAM resources. Keep much RAM available for use in playing back the sequence you are currently working on to improve playback reliability. This varies from one computer to the next, depending on how much RAM is installed.

Try turning off mirroring on the desktop during playback if you are having troubles with consistent playback through your FireWire output. In general, don't ask your computer to do anything tougher than it *has* to do to perform the task. Especially take a look at your RT Extreme settings. Higher-quality settings are simply more taxing on your computer. Setting them lower can make a huge difference in playback reliability.

Sometimes when you're having problems with dropping frames during playback, you can export the sequence as a self-contained Final Cut Pro movie, and this new file will play back without problems. Try this especially with complicated, many-rendered, multiple-edit sequences. Again, you are asking your disk drive to simply do less work, because it has to play back only one media file, not many. This problem is also minimized by using faster SCSI drives, because less drive latency is associated with them (they have larger buffers). This issue is exacerbated with ATA drives playing back DV files. If you add drives with larger buffers, such as IBM's 180GXP series hard drives and others, you'll have a drive that will play back DV media more reliably. When adding ATA drives, look for those with 8MB buffers. Avoid those with only 2MB buffers.

Don't run virus-checking utilities and the like while running Final Cut Pro. You'll experience a lot of problems running virus checking, especially when capturing video. Running these checks is always best done when you aren't running any NLE. Virus checkers are the number one cause of failed captures, it seems. Remarkably few viruses spread to Mac users anyway.

In general, the fewer applications you run at the same time, the better. However, you can run more applications at the same time if you install more RAM in your computer. You cannot install too much RAM. This is probably the single most important upgrade you should consider when you want a faster machine but you aren't ready to buy a new one. It will serve Final Cut Pro as well as *every other application you run*.

Broken Timecode

Broken timecode can cause problems. Final Cut Pro 4 has a new feature that can be activated from the General tab of the User Preferences. You can use a pop-up menu there to tell FCP what to do if it encounters timecode breaks. You can have FCP create a new clip automatically, abort the capture, or warn of these breaks after capture. I think the best route to take is to create new clips. (Even better, log all the clips first, or simply scan the tape to make sure it doesn't have any apparent timecode breaks.) If you choose to create new clips, these new clips always have the proper timecode attached to them. This is critical to a recapture process or an EDL creation for transfer to another NLE or linear online editing system.

However, it's best to avoid this problem when you shoot in the first place. If you rely on FCP's new timecode breaks feature, you will not get the first few seconds past the timecode break to come into your system. You can either record a new tape end to end with your lens cap on before you shoot with it, or always make sure that each new scene's recording starts *a few frames over the last scene shot*. Pausing between scenes rarely causes breaks in timecode, but rewinding to view scenes just shot or powering down the camera to move to a new setup might cause this problem. Lower-level DV cameras have no way to set timecode starting points, so it's best to record over the last frames of video you want to preserve rather than start again on unrecorded areas of your tape, which resets the timecode to 0.

If you have broken timecode on a DV camera master that resets to 0, when you log clips with identical timecode, from the same physical tape, it's best to rename that new set of timecode to be on a new reel. That way, you'll know which portion of the tape to recapture later. For example, name the first set of 0 hour code to be on tape 1, then the next set of matching code to be on Tape 1A, and so on. That way FCP will stop and ask for tape 1A to be put in your source deck camera. All you need to do then is fast forward to the next section of matching timecode on that same tape, and tell FCP that you've loaded a new tape in the machine.

If you are working with video formats other than DV, such as Betacam, as long as the timecode ascends from the beginning of the tape, you will have no problems batch-capturing material. But you don't want to capture over these jumps in timecode, and you won't be able to capture video before the length of your pre-roll settings, and possibly after the length of your post-roll settings. It's best to avoid these sorts of timecode breaks in the first place. Running Time of Day timecode causes these breaks and should be avoided altogether.

When All Else Fails

There are times when simply trashing the Final Cut Pro Preference file clears up problems. This file is located in your System folder in the Preferences folder. Keep in mind, though, that all favorites and custom presets have to be rebuilt if you trash this file. In OS X, it's located in Users>*your user name*>Library>Preferences>Final Cut Pro User Data>Final Cut Pro 4.0 Preferences. Just trash the file or put it in another folder temporarily. The next time you launch the application, Final Cut Pro builds a new one that has the FCP default settings.

If this fails, and you are positive you need to reinstall Final Cut Pro, an article in the Knowledge Base on Apple's website guides you through the uninstall process. You should uninstall Final Cut Pro before a "ground up" reinstall. You'll find this article at `http://docs.info.apple.com/article.html?artnum=93150`. In fact, many Final Cut Pro articles are posted. You should check them first when troubleshooting any problem. Go to `http://docs.info.apple.com` and search for "Final Cut Pro 4." You'll be enlightened by reading them.

Sometimes you just can't get things to work properly, and you are completely stumped. You can call AppleCare for support. You might even get your problem solved for free. The software warranty on Final Cut Pro is only 90 days from the date of purchase, but problems with new installations are always addressed for free. If the problem is directly related to your computer, and not third-party hardware, AppleCare is free during your hardware warranty period. I heartily recommend buying extended AppleCare for your computer and its Apple-purchased display. One computer repair can easily offset the cost of this extended warranty. Replacing a FireWire connector and bus can cost hundreds of dollars. It's not at all uncommon to replace CPUs, motherboards, and disk drives. All of these repairs are expensive. You can avoid the high cost for years if you add AppleCare to your order or if you add it when you purchase your Mac from any authorized dealer. Replacing a computer display when ordered with AppleCare could save you up to $2,000. A new motherboard is an expensive repair. This peace of mind is always welcome, especially if you are a professional who relies on your system to run properly at all times. You can add AppleCare to your computer anytime during the first year of its life. It's worth every dime.

Getting a system profile report might open your eyes to hardware problems. It's a piece of cake to do. Just select About this Mac from the Apple menu, and then click More Info to open the report. Try it just to become comfortable looking at it and what it tells you about your setup.

If you want to get help from other users, an amazing amount of support is available online from the various websites listed in Appendix E. Don't forget to post your problem with as much information about your computer setup as you can gather—which computer model, the amount of RAM, which OS, which version of QuickTime, which version of Final Cut Pro, which camera or input device, whether you have a capture card installed, and anything else related to your *complete* setup. The more you post about your environment, the sooner a helpful user will be able to determine your problem. Don't forget to thank someone who helps you solve your problem. Remember, no one is being paid to help you. The Final Cut Pro community enjoys a tremendous free online support system. Keeping posts friendly and supportive is probably a good idea for everyone.

Also remember to search the posts with keywords that relate to your specific problem. You'll quickly find answers to most questions this way, and you won't have to wait for someone to come to your rescue.

APPENDIX D

Keyboard Shortcuts

There are literally hundreds of keyboard shortcuts. I've included the most important ones in a *partial* list. Trust me—you'll like using them, and soon, using them instead of using the mouse will feel quite natural—just like riding a bike or learning to type.

Keep in mind that this list is of the default keyboard shortcuts. There's nothing wrong with mapping your own, but the default ones were carefully planned to be ergonomic and logical, so that's what is listed here.

Using these shortcuts will speed you along and save your wrist from repetitive strain using the mouse. If you find yourself using a menu command a lot, look at the menu to learn this command's keyboard shortcut. Most menu commands have keyboard shortcut equivalents.

If you want more, there *are* more! Just press Opt+H to see the default shortcuts. You'll be amazed at how many default shortcuts there are and how many *more* shortcuts you can map to the keyboard. In Chapter 4, "Organization and Basic Editing," see the section "Mapping the Keyboard" for instructions on how to do this.

The shortcuts in bold are the first ones to learn, because you'll use them almost every time you do any sort of project, and they will really speed you up.

General Shortcuts

Cmd+S	Save
Shift+Cmd+N	New project
Cmd+N	**New sequence**
Cmd+O	Open
Cmd+W	Close window
Cmd+I	Import files

Select, Copy, Cut, and Paste

Cmd+C	Copy
Cmd+X	**Cut**
Cmd+V	**Paste**
Cmd+A	**Select all**

Activating Windows

Cmd+1	Viewer
Cmd+2	**Canvas**
Cmd+3	**Timeline**
Cmd+4	**Browser**
Cmd+5	**Effects**
Cmd+6	**Favorites**
Opt+4	Audio Meters
Opt+5	Tool Bench
Cmd+7	**Trim Edit window**
Cmd+8	**Log and Capture window**
Cmd+9	Item Properties (for selected items and items under the playhead)
Cmd+0	Sequence Settings
Opt+Cmd+Q	Audio/Video Settings
Opt+Q	User Preferences

Activating Tools

A	**Selection tool**
G	Edit the selection
GG	Select a group
GGG	Select a range
T	Select tracks forward from the click point
TT	Select tracks backward from the click point
TTT	Select the entire track
TTTT	Select all tracks forward from the click point
TTTTT	Select all tracks backward from the click point
R	**Roll Edit tool**
RR	**Ripple Edit tool**
S	Slip Edit tool
SS	Slide Edit tool
B	Razor blade a single track
BB	Razor blade all tracks
Z	**Zoom in**
ZZ	**Zoom out**
H	Hand tool
HH	Scrub tool
C	Crop tool
D	Distort tool
P	**Pen tool**
PP	Delete point tool
PPP	Smooth point tool

Navigation

Right arrow	Forward one frame
Shift+right arrow	Forward 1 second (30 frames in NTSC, 25 frames in PAL)
Left arrow	**Back one frame**
Shift+left arrow	Back 1 second (30 frames in NTSC, 25 frames in PAL)
Up arrow	**Previous edit**
Down arrow	**Next edit**
J	**Play backward (repeated presses of J play backward faster)**
K or spacebar	**Stops playback**
L	**Plays forward (repeated presses of L play forward faster)**
Spacebar	**Toggles playback forward on and off**
Shift+Spacebar	**Playback backward**
L+K	Play forward in slow motion
J+K	Play backward in slow motion
Home	Go to beginning of medium
End	Go to end of medium
Opt+P	Play every frame regardless of whether it is rendered

Finding Items

Cmd+F	Find in the active window. Works in the Browser and Timeline.
Cmd+G or F3	Find again
Shift+F3	Find previous

Special Timeline Views

Cmd++	Zoom in
Cmd+-	**Zoom out**

Z	Zoom In tool. Can be dragged over just the area of the Timeline to fill the window. Very cool. Works in the Canvas and Viewer as well.
ZZ	Zoom Out tool. Works in the Canvas and Viewer as well.
Shift+Page Up	Scroll left in the Timeline
Shift+Page Down	Scroll right in the Timeline
Shift+Z	**Show the entire sequence in the Timeline. It also zooms your Canvas or Viewer to fit in the window.**
Shift+T	**Change track heights**
Cmd+Opt+W	Toggle the waveform display
Opt+W	Toggle clip overlays
Opt+T	Toggle clip keyframes

Editing

I	Set In
O	**Set Out**
X	**Mark In and Out points for the clip under the playhead**
Opt+I	Clear In
Opt+O	Clear Out
Opt+X	Clear In and Out
F9	**Insert edit**
F10	**Overwrite edit**
F11	Replace edit
Shift+F11	Fit to fill
F12	Superimpose
Cmd+U	**Make subclip**
Opt+U	**Use custom layout 2**
Cmd+Z	**Undo**

Logging and Capturing

F2	Log clip
Ctrl+C	Batch capture
Shift+C	Capture
Tab	**Advance to the next field in a dialog box that has multiple fields, such as in the Log and Capture windows**

Special Commands

N	Toggle snapping
Cmd+L	**Make a link or break a link for the selected clip(s) in the sequence**
Shift+L	Toggle the linked selection in the sequence

Markers

M	Add marker
MM	**Add and name marker**
Cmd+`	Delete marker
Ctrl+`	Delete all markers
Shift+M	Next marker
Opt+M	Previous marker
Opt+`	Extend marker
Shift+`	Reposition marker

Other Tools

NeoTron Design (http://lormiller.home.mindspring.com/) sells a wonderful tool—a really handy laminated key chart. It includes all the new default shortcuts available in FCP 4.

A very usable chart from Loren Miller (the NeoTron guy) is included on this book's DVD. It's based on the shortcuts that work in FCP 2. They're still valid in FCP 3 and 4. Check out this "demo" first and see just how useful this tool is.

Also, dedicated keyboards (with keycaps with the default shortcuts printed on them) are sold at http://www.promax.com. I really like them. They're built on Apple's Pro keyboard.

APPENDIX E

Other Resources

Many resources are available to you on the Internet. I find these to be very up-to-date, with the latest issues you might be experiencing or new techniques you want to learn. If you don't have an Internet connection, you'll want to get one just to visit these terrific sites! Never before has there been a better community of online resources connected with any software. It's truly amazing how much information you can find if you just know where to look. The sense of community surrounding Final Cut Pro is truly remarkable.

Sometimes editing is a solitary and lonely profession, so it's always great to interact with others using Final Cut Pro. It's a rare thing indeed to find anything free today, but the Internet has a wealth of free help, free demos, and free reading and learning tools. Here is a list of what I've found. Frequent these places and learn, talk, interact, and help others.

Websites, Discussion Groups, and User Groups

If you can't get an answer at one of these sites, there isn't an answer!

The Creative Cow

http://www.creativecow.net

This site contains a Final Cut Pro discussion group, as well as articles on editing and other software and hardware. It also has wonderful discussion groups for CineWave, AJA, Aurora, and more. The forum leaders in all the discussion groups are quite knowledgeable. This site is frequented by professionals. Just reading the posts is an education, but don't be afraid to post if you can't find the answer to your question. Searching the posts using the site's search feature works wonders. Philip Hodgetts, one of this book's technical editors, and I are forum leaders at The Creative Cow, as well as a group of the most knowledgeable folks on the Internet. Go there first for an answer to any question. Almost always, if your question isn't answered here, there isn't an answer in any forum anywhere.

Apple

`http://www.apple.com/support`

Free telephone help is available from Apple for 90 days after you've purchased your software and for at least a year for your hardware. Buying Apple Care from Apple is probably a good investment. The support site contains links to hardware and the vaunted Knowledge Base, which is a list of articles about all things Apple. Searching this base might bring you answers if you can't find them elsewhere.

Apple's support site contains hardware and software troubleshooting tips. You can access the discussion groups as well. The Final Cut Pro discussion group is a great resource. You can also access downloads of upgrades for all your Apple software. You'll want to get to know this site well. OS help, hardware, software, and even discussion groups on third-party software are available here.

A Feedback Form appears at the top of the Final Cut Pro forum in the Discussions at Apple. From there you can send feedback of hits and misses to the Final Cut Pro Team directly. They do read these, and they appreciate your sending them. This is one way bugs are found and fixed, so help the team help you!

2-pop

`http://www.2-pop.com`

An online resource for Final Cut Pro and famous for its forums. There is a dedicated teachers forum there.

The DV Guys

`http://www.dvguys.com`

Not every site has a weekly Internet radio show, but this one does! You can call in at the start of the show and get your questions answered, chat live, or just listen and absorb. The last 12 weeks of shows are archived on this site. Ron Margolis and Philip Hodgetts are the DV guys. They are a wealth of news, commentary, and general information about Final Cut Pro and more. They share tricks and tips. It's lots of fun.

Ken Stone's Site

http://www.kenstone.net

Ken Stone writes and posts a large number of articles related to Final Cut Pro. This site has a discussion group as well.

The Los Angeles Final Cut Pro Users Group

http://www.lafcpug.org

This is the largest Final Cut Pro users group in the world. It has a discussion group and a large number of articles, tips, and tricks. It's a great site, indeed. Mike Horton, who founded the LAFCPUG, is one of the Creative Cow leaders in the Final Cut Pro forum as well.

The San Francisco Final Cut Pro Users Group

http://www.sfcutters.org

This is a users group with tips, tricks, and a great links page.

The Boston Final Cut Pro Users Group

http://www.bosfcpug.org

The Boston group holds monthly meetings and has a dedicated discussion group at the Creative Cow site.

The Denver Final Cut Pro Users Group

http://www.dfcpug.org

This group meets monthly. It was founded by Justin Allen, Jerry Hofmann (the author of this book), and Brian Ercek.

International FCP Users Network

http://www.fcpugnetwork.org/

This site lists most of the user groups internationally. If you start one, let this group know so that they can list you too.

User Groups List at Apple

http://www.apple.com/software/pro/resources/usergroups.html

Apple's site has a list of user groups, including international ones.

Related Sites

http://www.res.com

This site is dedicated to the new wave of digital cinema. Be sure to check it out. I hear the "res" fests are the greatest.

http://www.dv.com

This DV-related site is associated with the popular industry magazine. dv.com is a great way to access current and past articles online. This site has articles about and reviews of cameras, software, decks, and all things DV.

http://dvforteachers.manilasites.com/

This site is designed for teachers using and teaching DV video production, but the information can be used by any user.

Online Reading About Digital Video on CD and DVD

http://www.disctronics.co.uk/technology/video/video_intro.htm

This site is full of information about formats. It has a glossary and more. It's a great read.

http://www.adamwilt.com

Adam Wilt's site is full of information on DV. It has tips on the format, using DV, titles, and more. It's probably the best resource on the net for practical information on the DV codec.

Hardware Manufacturers

http://www.aja.com

AJA manufactures the Kona SD and HD capture cards and the new Io converter box. High-quality products from a high-quality company.

http://www.auroravideosys.com

This company makes Mac-only capture cards. It's a super company too.

http://www.pinnaclesys.com

This company manufactures the CineWave Card system, including options for HD video—also very high-quality gear.

`http://www.digitalvoodoo.net`

This company manufactures SDI video capture cards as well as HD cards.

`http://www.canopuscorp.com`

A DV converter box works great with FCP. This "low-end" converter is great for VHS or any S analog input. ADVC-100 is the model number, and I highly recommend this box, because it is the best in its class.

`http://www.hugesystems.com`

Probably the best value in SCSI arrays out there.

`http://www.weibetech.com`

Super-fast FireWire drive equipment.

`http://www.granitedigital.com`

Also very good FireWire drives and especially great cables.

Specialized and Third-Party Equipment and Software

`http://www.geethree.com`

The place for RS-422 control (Stealth Port). Currently they have products for only G4 towers.

`http://www.keyspan.com`

The place to buy a USB/serial adapter. They make a PCI card that supplies multiple serial ports.

`http://www.contourdesign.com/`

Sells great mice and the famous ShuttlePro multimedia controllers.

`http://www.promax.com/`

Sells many things FCP. Take a look at the dedicated keyboard for FCP.

`http://www.bhphoto.com`

This site contains lots of professional video gear. This is an old, reliable company.

Software Companies

http://www.adobe.com

After Effects, Photoshop.

http://www.borisfx.com

All sorts of compositing software that integrates perfectly with Final Cut Pro.

http://www.discreet.com

Cleaner 5, Combustion, and more.

http://www.digitalfilmtools.com/

55MM is a unique set of filters from Digital Film Tools meant to simulate popular optical glass filters and specialized lenses.

http://www.intelligentassistance.com

DV Companion: Intelligent Assistance for Final Cut Pro and other Final Cut Pro tutorial guides.

http://www.joemaller.com/

Native FX script effects and filters for Final Cut Pro and great tutorials on how to program your own effects in FX Script Builder.

http://www.cgm-online.com/

Native FX script effects and filters for Final Cut Pro.

http://www.automaticduck.com/

Sells software to automate Final Cut Pro timeline transfers to After Effects. They also have other translator software. It's all very cool.

http://www.stagetools.com/

Sells MovingPicture, which is a tool for making smooth pans and zooms on hi-resolution stills. It is available as a stand-alone application or as a plug-in for Final Cut Pro.

Great Places to Visit

http://www.networkmusic.com/

This website sells some of the very best library music available. Do visit them.

http://www.natress.com/

Sells plug-in effects for FCP at a very reasonable price and some of them are included on this book's DVD.

http://www.chadroarkdesign.com/

The graphics wizard who designed the "Grace Films Logo" you created in this tutorial...ever need help with graphics and design, Chad Roark is your man! Truly talented fellow.

http://www.transmitmedia.com/

Paul Vachier's beautiful music website. This wonderful author was one of the technical editors for this book, and I must say his help was invaluable. His design work is first rate too!.

http://www.intelligentassistance.com/

Philip Hodgetts and company sell the coolest programs and help systems on the planet! Intelligent Assistance is just that, *very intelligent*. Look for his work in the Goodies folder on the DVD.

http://www.artbeats.com/

This fabulous site sells some of the very best stock footage and graphics around! They supplied the fire for the Logo for example. Way cool and not to be missed!

http://www.homepage.mac.com/fearless/

A website operated by the famous "fearless" who is one of the Helpers in the Apple Discussion groups and he hangs in the FCP forum there. A set of apple scripts designed for Final Cut Pro are available on his website. Check it out!

More Free Stuff

http://www.atomiclearning.com/finalcutpro.shtml

This site offers online training. Some is free, and you can subscribe to more.

http://www.macfixit.com

This is a great site on which to check out others' experiences with all things Macintosh. This site reports on user experiences with new OS updates and more. It's a super site.

http://www.info.apple.com/

The technical library is worth a search for sure.

http://www.videouniversity.com/

This is a great website dedicated to improving your video business.

http://www.finalcutproplanet.com/

This is a dedicated Final Cut Pro site that has some free tutorials and forums. It's a DV creators' information site with tips, tricks, and "tiplets."

http://www.rippletraining.com/

This is Steve Martin's Final Cut Pro information site. It contains free tutorials as well as inexpensive online tutorials. It's a great site.

warning When searching *any* forum beware of users who try to help but who have wrong information. A site's "guides" or leaders are usually right on the money with correct answers to your questions. Don't be afraid to post, but be sure you're getting the right scoop. Searching the forums (the Creative Cow's forum's search engine is wonderful) is a wise thing to do. Chances are that someone else has had the same question you want answered, so there's usually a post that answers your question.

APPENDIX F

Video Filters List

Final Cut Pro includes more than 70 video filters grouped into 12 categories. All of Final Cut Pro 4's video filters can be found in two places:

- The Effects tab of the Browser
- The Effects, Video Filters submenu

This appendix lists and briefly describes the standard video filters and what you might use them for. Experimenting with them is the key to learning their behavior. Also, if you look up these filters in the index, you can find their respective workshops if they were used to build "The Midnight Sun." You'll find more information about them there.

Be aware that interesting uses of these effects can be created by changing them over time. In other words, you can animate them from one setting to another using keyframes in the corresponding keyframe graphs to the right of each control. Any and all of these filters can be used in concert on the same clip, giving you even more ways to create effects. You might use a garbage matte to clean up a color key, for example. You'll learn to use them by using them, so experimenting will help you master their use. From an aesthetics point of view, though, you shouldn't use them just because you can. You should resist using them unless they tell more of the story. However, it can be argued that color correction should always be done. Paying close attention to this aspect of filter use is a must for a professional look to your program.

Some of these filters can be used on single tracks of video, such as those that affect color. Others are meant to be used to composite more than one clip. In the case of composites, the clips must be edited on different video tracks above one another. The clip on the bottom track becomes a background to the clips layered above it, and the topmost clip is in front of those below it.

note ≡≡≡≡ Some of these filters are listed in bold in the lists you see from within Final Cut Pro (in the Effects Tab or the Effects menu). These effects are real-time effects. Those that are not listed in bold have to be rendered unless your capture card supports them in real time.

Blur Filters

Blur filters are named much like they work or affect your video. They blur or defocus your video in various ways. Used to extremes, they can create an interesting image of colors and shapes. You might also want to use them in conjunction with other filters, such as a 4- or 8-Point Matte Filter, to hide a person's identity, for example. In this case, you'd put identical clips on top of each other, apply the blur to the lower clip, and use the Garbage Matte to reveal only the area you want to blur on the upper clip.

Gaussian Blur blurs the whole frame of a clip's video. You can blur one or all of the color and alpha channels together or separately, creating a different look to the blur. The pop-up menu it contains allows you to choose which channel to blur. The Radius slider allows you to select the amount of blurring you add to the clip. The more you move the slider to the right, the more radical the blur. Setting a keyframe at 0 and then setting one later in your clip at a higher level creates the illusion of a rack focus, for example. A *rack focus* is where you shoot two people or objects, and one is behind the other, in the distance. You can change focus during the shot to bring one or the other into focus. This one is probably the most used of the group of Blur filters. It's also often used as a way to blur a face using a Garbage Matte technique, much like you did with the clip of Cap looking at the stars. However, you use the same video on both layers and add the Blur and the Matte to one of them. Used at an extreme setting, a Gaussian Blur filter makes interesting backgrounds, because they become very abstract. Used with slowed-down footage, they can be very effective for title backgrounds or fills.

Radial Blur creates the effect that the image is swirling around a selectable point (the Center button). The Angle control adjusts the amount of the blur. The Steps slider smoothes the blur. You can specify the center point in the frame about which the blur rotates by clicking the Center button and then clicking any area of the frame, creating an anchor point to rotate it around.

Wind Blur creates the effect that the video is being blown by wind. You can adjust the direction in which the blur travels using the Angle control and specify the distance between each increment of blur with the Amount slider. The Steps slider determines how smooth the blur appears.

Zoom Blur creates the effect that the image is moving toward or away from you. A pop-up menu allows you to select whether the blur moves in or out. The Radius slider determines the distance between increments of blur, and the Steps slider determines the smoothness.

Border Filters

Border filters create borders around your clips.

Basic Border draws a border around the edges of the picture. The Border slider adjusts its width, and the Color control lets you select its color. You can add a drop shadow to it from the Motion tab to dress it up a bit. Basic Border ignores any alpha channels, which means that borders do not appear in cropped images, for example.

Bevel draws a beveled border around the edges of the picture. The Angle control allows you to change the direction of the light that reflects from the bevel. The Bevel Width slider changes the width of the border, the Opacity slider lets you change its opacity, and the Color control lets you change the color of the light that reflects from the border.

Channel Filters

Channel filters let you control the color and alpha channels of clips in your sequence to create a variety of visual effects.

Arithmetic blends a specific color channel of your clip with another color. From pop-up menus, you can choose the operator used and the channel it's applied to. The Color control changes the color with which the channel interacts.

Channel Blur allows you to apply different amounts of blur to a selected color and/or alpha channel of your clip independently. Sliders control how much blur is applied to each channel. Channel blurs create interesting color effects. The rack focus effect mentioned in the Gaussian Blur filter description can be taken to another level by garbage matting a subject onto a second layer and blurring one layer while unblurring the other layer.

Channel Offset offsets the position of one or all of a clip's channels within the frame. You can indicate the channel to be affected from the Channel pop-up menu. The Center Offset allows you to decide the amount and direction of the offset. You can select an edge from the Edges pop-up menu. You can animate this filter (using keyframes) and create some interesting effects. This might be great for a music video or for creating red/green 3D offsets.

Color Offset offsets the color of individual channels in the clip. Using this filter, you can create posterizing style effects. You've seen these; they look sort of like cartoons made from a live-action shot. Animating this filter reminds me of a Peter Max poster in motion; *Yellow Submarine* comes to mind. Sliders control the offset value for each color channel in your clip. You can either invert the image or wrap the colors. Experimentation is the key. Keep in mind that you can add more filters to really distort things. This one's fun.

Compound Arithmetic performs a composite between the first clip (the one you add it to) and one selected from the Browser and dragged to a well in the filter's settings. Several wells are available in other effects too; they all function similarly. To use them, just drag an image or clip to the well and release the mouse button there. You can adjust the operator (the way a composite is performed) and the channel it is performed on from two pop-up menus in the effect's controls. The well uses only the first frame of a video clip if it's put into the well. You can use stills to select the frame from video, or use a graphic image.

Invert inverts selectable channels of the selected clip. The result is like a negative image. The Channel pop-up menu lets you select which channel or channels to invert, and the Amount slider determines the amount of the inversion.

Color Correction Filters

Color Correction filters can be used to improve picture quality, adjust your video to proper levels, match shots that should match but don't, and more. But a huge caveat should be mentioned here. Don't use your computer's display to correct color that will eventually be delivered to a TV set or video monitor. The gammas are much different between your computer's display (which can actually show you a lot more color variations than a video monitor can). Use an external video monitor (or even a TV set with monitor inputs) to evaluate your color and luminance levels.

Broadcast Safe is a quick filter to add to bring your luma and chroma levels to a broadcast-legal level. It clamps any luminance to 100 IRE and lowers any chroma (color) levels to a legal amount as measured by a Vectorscope. It's easy to apply and saves time setting these proper levels. Broadcast Safe does a very gentle clamp, not as harsh as what a broadcaster or cable operator will do to your pictures down the line. It can be configured to cut off at any level, but the default is pretty much in line.

Color Corrector is a basic tool that can perform color corrections. It's more likely than the Color Corrector 3-way to be supported by real-time hardware. If you open the disclosure triangle near the bottom of this filter's visual display, you can limit the changes you make with this filter to selectable color and luma ranges. The eyedroppers select individual pixels, so it's helpful to zoom all the way in on your image to select the exact color you want. White Balance (color balance) can be quickly fixed with this tool. All you need to do is select the upper eyedropper and then pick a pixel that should be absolutely white in your image. All pixels that are this color then become white, and all other pixels become the color that they are supposed to be. The disclosure triangle near the bottom of the visual display opens the limiting tools, which are used to limit your correction to a selectable color range, starting with picking it with the eyedroppers there. This filter works in 16-bit if your sequence's video processing is set to 16-bit precision (this setting is found in the sequence's settings in the Video Processing tab).

Color Corrector 3-way is very similar to the Color Corrector, but it gives you more options to control the black, mid (much the same as a gamma control), and white levels somewhat independently of each other. Keep in mind that each of the color wheels and controls overlap the others' luma values a bit, so adjusting one might affect the others. The top of the luma is unaffected by the Blacks and the Mids. Conversely, the Whites and Mids do not affect the blackest area of the image you are working with. You can think of it this way: Each of the three controls affects about two-thirds to three-fourths of all the luminance values present. The Mids don't affect the top or bottom of these values, but areas in the Mids are affected by both the Whites and Blacks adjustments. This filter works in 16-bit if your sequence's video processing is set to 16-bit precision (this setting is found in the sequence's settings in the Video Processing tab).

Desaturate Highlights lets you lower the color levels in a picture's highlights when you apply either Color Correction filter. This filter works in 16-bit if your sequence's video processing is set to 16-bit precision (this setting is found in the sequence's settings in the Video Processing tab).

Desaturate Lows does the opposite of the Desaturate Highlights filter. It takes away color from the lows (blacker areas) of a color-corrected clip. This filter works in 16-bit if your sequence's video processing is set to 16-bit precision (this setting is found in the sequence's settings in the Video Processing tab).

RGB Balance lets you adjust your image's individual levels of red, green, and blue values. It also allows you to change these values in three different luminance areas of the image. I find this tool useful to match color between two clips that should match, monitoring the changes with the RGB Parade Videoscope.

Distort Filters

Distort contains a number of filters that are aptly grouped and named as distortions. Animating these distortions over time to apply them or take them away makes them dynamic.

Bumpmap offsets pixels in an image using the luminance of a second selected image dragged to its well. I've found that using grayscale images seems to work best. The well in this filter's settings accepts only still images. The image that the effect is applied to has a distortion done to it whose shape is determined by the luminance values of the image that you drag to its well. A black star on a white background distorts the image in the shape of a star, for example. You can use the Luma Scale slider, Direction Angle control, Outset slider, and Repeat Edges check box to further change the effect.

Cylinder distorts the clip as if it were being looked at through a cylindrical piece of glass, like a glass tube. You can adjust the Radius and Center sliders and the Vertical check box to change this filter's appearance. The Amount slider distorts the image even further.

Displace is similar to the Bumpmap filter. It contains a well to define the distortion's shape by dragging an image to it. The big difference between Displace and Bumpmap is the channels of video it uses. Whereas Bumpmap uses luminance, Displace uses the red and green channels. The horizontal offset uses the red channel for the distortion, and the vertical offset uses the green channel. Horizontal and vertical scales alter the offset's direction and amount. Luma scale and repeat edges change the look of the offset. Displace is useful for TV-style bugs or static Predator-style displace effects. Only static images work with this filter's well.

Fisheye distorts the clip as if it were shot with a fisheye lens. It's much like what you see when viewing a visitor through a peephole in your front door. Using the slider controls adjusts the amount and radius of the effect, and altering the position of the distortion is done by using the point control. Clicking the crosshair then clicking on the frame of video determines the center of the effect. You might use this effect to simulate the effect of looking through a peephole, for example.

Pond Ripple distorts the clip as if it were a rippling pond. A center point control allows you to set the center of this effect in the frame of your clip just like the Fisheye effect. You can change the size and number of the ripples it creates using the Radius, Ripple Amplitude, Acceleration, Highlight, and Decay sliders.

Ripple distorts the video in a wave pattern, both horizontally and vertically. You can make changes to both parameters independently using the Amplitude, Wavelength, Horizontal, and Vertical sliders. The Repeat Edge check box keeps black edges from appearing at the edges of the frame.

Wave distorts the picture in a simple zigzag pattern, either vertically or horizontally. You can adjust the amplitude, wavelength, and speed of this effect using sliders. The Vertical check box defines the effect's orientation. The Repeat Edge check box forces it to fill the frame.

Whirlpool distorts the clip in a swirling whirlpool pattern similar to watching water go down a drain. You can determine the center of this effect with the Center button. The Amount control defines the whirlpool's rotary motion. The Repeat Edge check box ensures that it fills the frame. You might use this to transition between shots, whirling one out and then cutting to another shot whirling in.

Image Control Filters

Image Control filters control changes in the levels of black, white, and color or chroma in your clips. They can be used to correct clips with exposure or color problems, to correct the color balance and brightness of a group of clips in a scene so that they all match, or to create color effects.

You'll probably use the Color Correction filters described earlier for most of your routine color-correction adjustments. However, it's a good thing that this older filter set is still included in Final Cut Pro. It lets you update projects created in earlier versions of FCP using these filters to the newer versions of FCP without a hitch. These filters do have some differences in their uses. Nevertheless, you might find them very intuitive. For example, examine the Proc Amp filter. Its adjustments are the same as those used by professional proc amps.

You use the **Brightness and Contrast (Bezier)** filter to alter a clip's brightness and/or contrast by percentages to lighten or darken the clip. Brightness and contrast affect all of a clip's colors and luminance values at once. Using this sometimes helps the washed-out look of VHS, for example.

Color Balance allows you to alter the amounts of red, green, and blue in a clip separately. You can select whether your clip's highlights (bright areas), midtones, or shadows (dark areas) are affected with the buttons in the Tones box. This filter can be used to correct white balance on video footage or to create color effects. It can also be used to help with key effect to boost a level that needs to be keyed out, such as green or blue. Remember that you can add more than one of these filters to adjust the three tone levels independently.

Desaturate removes color from a clip by percentages. A 100 percent selection would turn your image into shades of black and white (a grayscale image). You might want to correct oversaturation with it, or just give your image a dull look, reflecting depression, perhaps. Matching overall color levels might be another use of this quick and simple filter. But do not use Desaturate to make a black-and-white version of your footage. Use Tint instead at the default settings. It creates a much richer black-and-white version of your footage.

Gamma Correction changes a clip's *gamma* (the relative brightness of the midrange area of the image's luminance) by an amount you specify. The Gamma Correction filter can be used to pull details out of underexposed or overexposed footage without washing out your clip. It does not affect the brightest or darkest area of your footage.

Levels is similar to the Gamma Correction filter but offers greater control. You can specify a particular alpha or color channel of your clip to be affected using a pull-down menu. Adjusting the sliders alters the input, input tolerance, gamma, output, and output tolerance individually. It has more-sophisticated controls than the simpler but still quite useful Gamma Correction filter.

Proc Amp gives you control over your picture's black, white, and chroma levels, as well as the phase of your clip. Setup controls the black levels, Video controls the brightness, Chroma controls the amount of color, and Phase adjusts the image's hue. These adjustments are the same as those found on a professional analog video deck such as a Betacam SP machine. They have parallels to the controls found on most television sets. You'll find many uses for this filter. It's one of the best for correcting problems.

Sepia adds a tint of sepia to a clip as a *default setting*. You can change the amount of tint with the Amount parameter and the tint's brightness using the Highlight adjustment. You can select another color with the Color control. Giving a photograph an old, faded look is an example of its use. You might even add it to video for the same reason.

Tint tints the clip with the color of your choice. By clicking the triangle next to the eyedropper, you can specify values for the color's hue, saturation, and brightness. You can specify the amount of color from the slider next to the Amount parameter. It works much the same as Sepia but lacks the Highlight adjustment.

Key Filters

Key filters are used to remove backgrounds of elements, people, or objects to isolate these elements from their original backgrounds and composite them over a different or new background. An everyday example of a key is the one used in weather segments of newscasts.

The weatherman is not standing in front of a moving and ever-changing background. In reality, he is being shot in front of a green or blue screen most of the time. The sometimes-animated background of a storm front is supplied by an animated graphic from a computer system. To see what's behind him onscreen in the composite that viewers see at home, the weatherman watches this composite on monitors placed where he can see them. (Watch his eyes—it's sometimes a dead giveaway!) That's how he pinpoints certain things like the temperature of the area he is reporting on, even though his pointer is actually touching a green or blue screen.

Achieving Quality Keys When the Foreground was Shot on Tape

To achieve a good key, it's important to use footage that has been exposed properly and shot in as high-quality a video format as possible. Lighting a background evenly helps, and separating the foreground image as far as possible from the background helps too. Be sure to add a backlight to the foreground image to completely separate it from the background and to avoid color spill from a very saturated background. It's not a good idea for talent to wear the same color as the key color (such as a blue shirt shot against a blue screen background), because you are likely to key both the shirt and the background. (However, this technique could be useful for creating a key of just a head!) Keeping colors very distinct from each other in the first place makes keying easier in the postproduction process. It's a good idea to check out a key during the shooting process. This can point out an error you can avoid by simply changing a light or two and checking the key again. Many people create the key live for this same reason.

It's typically *very* difficult to use material shot with DV cameras to create clean and perfect color or chroma keys. This is because the color space that they work in does not record as much color information in the picture as a format such as Betacam does. In fact, only about half the color information about any given pixel is recorded in DV when compared to what a Motion JPEG compressed video signal contains, such as digital files created from Betacam SP or Digibeta. Typically, Betacam (or better) material is digitized or captured into this format with capture cards such as those from Aurora, Pinnacle, Digital Voodoo, and AJA. Unfortunately, using one of these cards to capture material shot with a DV camera does not add the color information that wasn't acquired by the format in the first place. You need to have shot Betacam SP or better (HD) to have the easiest time creating a key. This is because the algorithms used to create a key such as a color or chroma key determine what is to be kept (the foreground) and what is to be thrown away (the background) by very specific and detailed color information about each pixel. DV compression usually doesn't record enough color information to create a clean color key. The error occurs around the edges of the foreground as it composites over the new background. If you will do any keying work with NTSC DV source, use the 4:1:1 Color Smoothing filter first—every time.

continues

That said, luminance keys work much better in DV. This is because DV records as much luminance information as possible about a clip. The techniques used to set up a good luminance key (called the luma key in Final Cut Pro) are the same. Lighting only the foreground image and keeping the background absolutely black is the way to start. Remember that if the source footage is lit and exposed properly in the first place, it creates a fine key quickly in Final Cut Pro. Usually, if you have a lot of trouble keying, it's because it wasn't shot with the proper techniques in the first place. It isn't the fault of the software.

Even when you use a higher-quality acquisition format, compressing this signal in your computer when you digitize or capture it results in lower-quality keys. It's best to use the highest-quality digital image you can create to achieve the highest-quality results. The old saying applies—garbage in, garbage out. Rarely can you satisfactorily fix things in post.

When applied to an element that is shot against a blue or green background, **Blue and Green Screen** keys out the color background, allowing you to key the foreground over a different background. The View pop-up menu allows you to look at the source of the clip (the original clip), the matte created by the filter, the final matted image, or a special composite of the source, matte, and final image for reference. The Key Mode pop-up menu allows you to select blue, green, or a blue/green difference as the key color. The Color Level slider allows you to select the amount of blue or green in your clip to key out, and the Color Tolerance slider allows you to expand the key into adjacent areas containing other shades of the key color. The Edge Thin slider allows you to expand or contract the matte area to try to eliminate fringing, and the Edge Feather slider lets you blur out the edges of the matte to create a softer edge. Before you use these sliders, try using a Matte Choker filter. The Invert check box allows you to invert the matte, making what was masked solid and what was solid masked. I strongly suggest that you use the Chroma Keyer for your chroma effects instead of using the Blue and Green Screen filter. It is a legacy filter. It's still included in FCP because if you've created an old project—say, in FCP 1—you need this filter to translate your files into FCP 4 files.

Chroma Keyer is a more sophisticated filter that keys out any color, including blue and green. You can even use it as a luma keyer if you disable the color and saturation. When you perform a key with this filter, adjust the Color Range and Saturation controls to fine-tune the effect. The Chroma Keyer has the same settings as the Color Correctors Limit Effect controls. It also has spill suppression built in. Start with this keyer when creating chroma keys. It's much better than the earlier iterations of filters for this effect. The Blue and Green Screen filter is a legacy filter, included in FCP so that you can open previously affected clips from earlier versions of Final Cut Pro.

Color Key is similar to the Blue and Green Screen filter. It allows you to select any color for keying. The Color Picker control allows you to select which color you'd like to key out. It's great if what you are trying to key is blue or green, so using these colors as the background in preparation for a key doesn't work well.

Color Smoothing - 4:1:1 is new to FCP 4. You should apply this filter before you process chroma keys. The 4:1:1 version should be used with all DV25 formats (video captured in the 4:1:1 color space).

Color Smoothing - 4:2:2 also is new to FCP 4. You should apply this filter before you process chroma keys. It's the same as the 4:1:1 filter. However, you use this one if your source material is DVCPRO50 or 8- and 10-bit uncompressed video (video captured in the 4:2:2 color space).

Difference Matte compares two clips and keys out areas that are the same. The View pop-up menu allows you to look at the source of the clip (with no key applied), the matte created by the filter, the final matted image, or a special composite of the source, matte, and final image for reference. The Clip control allows you to specify another clip to compare to the current image for keying. The Threshold and Tolerance sliders allow you to adjust the key to try to isolate the parts of your image you want to keep. For example, consider video footage of a man walking next to a wall. If you use a video clip of the wall by itself shot before the man walked by as the specified difference layer, you can adjust the Threshold and Tolerance sliders to isolate the man as he walks, because he's the only element that's different.

Luma Key is similar to Color Key, except that Luma Key creates a matte based on the brightest or darkest areas of an image. Keying out a luminance value works best when the image has a wide variance between what you want to key out and what you want to preserve. For example, if you want to keep something that is bright, you should shoot it against a totally black background. The View pop-up menu allows you to look at the clip's source (with no key applied), the matte created by the filter, the final matted image, or a composite of the source, matte, and final image for reference. The Key Mode pop-up menu allows you to specify whether this filter keys out brighter, darker, similar, or dissimilar areas of the image. The Matte pop-up menu allows you to create alpha channel information for that clip. You also can create a high-contrast matte image applied to your clip's color channels, based on the matte created by this filter.

When you use the Blue and Green Screen key to key out the blue in a clip, there might be a bit of unwanted blue color around the edges of the key (called *spill*). The **Spill Suppressor, Blue** filter removes this spill by desaturating the edges where it appears. Use this filter *after* a Color Key in the Filters list that appears in the Viewer's Filters tab. It might have a slight effect on your image's color balance.

Spill Suppressor, Green works just like the Spill Suppressor, Blue, but it works on green edges instead of blue ones.

Matte Filters

Matte filters can be used by themselves to create alpha channel information for a clip to composite it against other layers to mask areas of a clip. Matte filters can also be used to make further adjustments to layers with keying filters applied to them. For example, you might want to color-correct only a small area of your image; you can do so with these tools.

4-Point Garbage Matte is similar to the 8-Point Garbage Matte, but it creates the matte using only four points.

8-Point Garbage Matte generates an eight-point mask that you can use to crop out areas of a clip. Eight point controls allow you to "draw" this matte. When you click one of the crosshairs in the filter's controls, the Selection tool changes into a crosshair. You use it to reposition one of the eight points by clicking a new area of the picture in the Canvas window. The Smooth slider rounds off the shape's corners to create rounder mattes. The Choke slider allows you to expand or contract the matte as a whole, and the Feather Edges slider allows you to blur its edges. The Invert check box reverses what's matted and what's transparent, changing it from what's inside the shape to what's outside the shape. The Hide Label check box hides the number labels, which indicate which point of the matte corresponds to which point control of the filter. This matte can be animated as well if what you are trying to matte is moving in the shot. This matte generator has a relative. It's a simpler version of this filter called the 4-Point Garbage Matte. You might want to use the 8- or 4-Point Garbage Matte to create a blur over someone's face to keep his or her identity secret, for example. If you have problems creating the shape with only eight points, you can add this matte to the image again to create a better-defined matte.

Extract creates a luminous matte around the clip. It's similar to a Luma Key. The View pop-up menu allows you to look at the source of the clip (with no key applied), the matte created by the filter, the final matted image, or a special composite of the source, matte, and final image for reference. The slider controls adjust the matte's threshold, tolerance, and softness. The Copy Result pop-up menu allows you to copy the luminance result to your clip's RGB or alpha channel, and the Invert check box allows you to invert the result of this filter. Adding this filter to a clip that is above another clip results in a combination of the images as programmed by the filter. Copying the result to alpha makes for some interesting results, which are quite different from simply superimposing two images. Extract, usually with a garbage matte, is excellent for pulling a key where no keyable color exists. It is also good for cleaning up a difference matte or other key by forcing it to black and white.

Image Mask creates the alpha channel or luminance from another clip you place in its well. Image Mask uses the clip to create a matte for the clip you apply it to. You could draw a black-and-white shape of some kind and then use this shape as a pattern for the matte. The Channel pop-up menu allows you to apply the matte to an alpha channel or luminance level. You can also click the Invert button to reverse the effect. Unlike the Travel Matte composite mode, the Image Mask filter attaches a matte to the selected clip. You can use motion effects to move the affected clip around; the matte stays in position with it.

Mask Feather blurs the clip's alpha channel by an amount specified by the Soft slider. You can add this filter to a masked clip and blur its edges as long as it's added after the matte, such as an Image Mask.

Mask Shape creates a mask shape to use to matte out a clip. A pop-up menu lets you choose from four separate shapes—Rectangle, Diamond, Oval, and Round Rectangle. The Horizontal and Vertical sliders adjust each shape's size and aspect ratio. The Center control allows you to place the matte anywhere in your picture. The Invert check box lets you reverse what's seen and what's masked.

Matte Choker is used in union with a keying filter to manipulate the key's edges. Instead of using an edge thin slider, try using this filter instead, because it looks more realistic and not as severe. If you move the Edge Thin slider to the right, slightly keyed areas of a clip are lengthened, spreading out the matte and filling in holes in your foreground image that might have been created by the keying filter you're using. Matte Chokers should be applied after a keying filter. Matte Chokers can be effectively used more than once on the same clip. The first Matte Choker might eliminate problems around an edge, but it also might create problems in the foreground image by keying part of it out. If you apply another Matte Choker in reverse, it can fill in these holes to make your foreground image key better. You can continue adding chokers until you are satisfied with the result.

Soft Edges blurs the four edges of a selected image independently by sliding or adding values to each of the four sliders (one for each side of the clip). The Dither and Gaussian check boxes change the quality of the blurred edge, and the Invert check box allows you to toggle between masking the edges and creating a hole in your image, revealing what might be underneath in a lower video track. You can use this filter to create a vignette effect, for example.

Wide Screen creates letterboxed images. The Type pop-up menu allows you to select the aspect ratio of the top and bottom mask using the standard film aspect ratios. Letterboxing helps you achieve a cinematic look. You can adjust the clip as it is revealed by this mask with the Offset slider. You might want to show just the top or bottom of the original 4:3 images, for example. The Border slider moves the top and bottom of the letterbox inward by up to 10 pixels at a time. You don't have to live with black for a border. You can use the Color controls to change the border's color. You can feather its edges by checking the Feather Edges check box. If you do, however, you lose the colored border.

Perspective Filters

Perspective filters allow you to move your clips spatially within their frames. The Motion Effects tab is used to move the entire frame of the Canvas. This set of filters moves the picture within that frame.

Basic 3D creates the effect that your clip is manipulated in 3D space. It is simulated, though. You can adjust the rotation around the X-, Y-, and Z-axes using the Angle controls. The Center control allows you to set the center of transformation. The Scale slider enlarges and reduces the size of the entire affected layer. You can keyframe this filter to move your clip in simulated three dimensions over time. Used in combination with the Motion tab, you can achieve some very interesting effects. For example, you can roll over a clip in what appears to be 3D space and then fly this frame from top to bottom with controls in the Motion tab. This results in the illusion that the frame is flying in from behind and then passing into infinity.

Curl curls the clip as if it were a piece of paper. This filter is much like a page peel transition effect, except that you can apply it to an entire clip. Adjustable parameters include the direction, radius, and amount of curl. The Peel check box toggles the effect between curling up in a roll or peeling it and not having the "paper" roll over itself. You can place an image in the well to be used as the backside of the curl.

Flop allows you to invert a clip horizontally, vertically, or both. You select the effect via its pop-up menu. It's like taking the picture and looking at it in a mirror; left is right, and so on. Sometimes you can fix screen direction using this filter, but you have to make sure that nothing in the picture would give this away, such as a sign whose words are suddenly printed backwards!

Mirror cuts the video in half and mirrors the right side of the picture on the left in its default setting. You can adjust the center of this reflection using the Reflection Center control. You can set the angle of the mirror effect using the Reflection Angle control.

Rotate rotates the affected clip by 90 degrees to the left or by 180 degrees (upside down). The Rotate pop-up menu lets you choose the angle of rotation. This filter scales the result to fit the frame size, distorting the clip if you use the 180-degree selection. You cannot keyframe this filter. It's used to do a quick rotation.

Sharpen Filters

Sharpen filters manipulate the contrast of clips and can result in an image that has more detail if used sparingly.

Sharpen increases the contrast between adjacent pixels, increasing the image's sharpness. Pushing it too far can create a grainy look.

Unsharp Mask actually is used for sharpening. This filter increases the contrast of adjacent pixels with greater control than the Sharpen filter. With individual sliders, you can adjust the amount, radius, and threshold of sharpness to soften this filter's effect. The Luminosity check box adds some luminance to the effect.

Stylize Filters

Stylize filters can be used to create extreme changes to the appearance of clips.

Anti-Alias blurs the clip's "stair-stepping" and high-contrast areas to soften the borders between elements in the frame. Use the Amount slider to soften the effect.

Diffuse randomly offsets pixels in the picture to create a texturized blur. The Angle control allows you to adjust the diffusion's direction. The Radius slider adjusts how extreme the offset becomes. The Direction pop-up menu allows you to specify whether the diffusion should be nondirectional (all directions), unidirectional (random on one axis), or bidirectional (random on two axes). The Random check box increases the amount of the effect, and the Repeat Edge selection eliminates any black that appears around the edge of the frame.

Emboss produces the look of raised edges where the clip has high contrast. The Angle control allows you to specify the effect's direction. The Depth slider allows you to raise or lower the apparent depth or height of the embossing. The Amount slider controls the blending between the original clip and the Emboss effect itself, making them look superimposed. This might make a nice addition to a freeze at the end of a moving shot. Adding a colorizing effect would further the look. Emboss is also good for creating bugs. Add the Emboss effect to a logo, and then add the logo clip to the sequence with (from memory) overlay mode. The gray disappears and creates a simple bug. Combine this with the solid logo and displace it to create a truly 3D logo bug.

Find Edges is an extreme-contrast effect used to outline the edges in the picture. The outline looks sort of like a neon sign. The Invert check box toggles between using a light-on-dark and dark-on-light version of the effect. The Amount slider controls the blending between the original clip and the effect itself. Overlay a copy with Find Edges on top of the original. Apply Multiply to the top copy to add outlines to the original. Adjust the opacity to taste.

Posterize limits a clip's color range by mapping the colors in it to a specified number of colors, creating an image with banding in areas of graduated color. You can adjust the amount of the effect with separate sliders for red, green, and blue.

Replicate repeats and multiplies the clip to create a video wall effect of the same picture. You can adjust the number of tiles independently for the horizontal and vertical, up to 16 repetitions on each axis. If the horizontal and vertical multiples are not the same, the images distort to fill the frame. This effect is particularly effective when animated from 1 to a very large number of tiles.

Solarize minimizes the midtones and maximizes the blacks and highlights, like a photographic negative of sorts. The Invert check box and slider let you adjust its amount.

Video Filters

Video filters are generally used to create more utilitarian effects to clips in your sequence, although design-oriented filters are included in this category as well.

Blink blinks the clip on and off. The frequency of the flashing can be adjusted independently with the On and Off duration sliders. You can also adjust the off duration's opacity. Used slightly, this effect can look sort of like a flashing of an old movie not quite registered.

De-Interlace can be used to remove either the upper (odd) or lower (even) field from an interlaced video clip. A pop-up menu allows you to remove either the upper or lower field. The remaining fields are interpolated to create a whole image, with marginal softening of the image as the result. The De-Interlace filter is useful when you want to create a still image from interlaced video clips of people or objects moving at high speed. Because each frame of video is a combination of two interlaced fields created sequentially over time, this can result in a flickering image. Another use of the De-Interlace filter is if you're outputting a QuickTime movie for computer playback or for streaming over the web. Interlacing can cause your video to have "banding" artifacts, which the De-Interlace filter can remove. This filter can also be used to eliminate flickering caused by interlacing in still frames, which have thin vertical lines, such as title pages with small text. However, the trade-off is that this effect reduces vertical resolution by half. Deinterlace upper on one track, deinterlace lower on an upper track, and set the upper track to 50% opacity to create progressive frames without losing resolution.

Flicker Filter reduces the flicker in images. This filter uses a vertical softening technique. You can adjust the amount using a pop-up menu. The different levels—Minimal, Medium, and Max—allow you to make the trade-off between flicker reduction and the amount of softness it applies. Flicker caused by still frames can be improved, as well as small letters in titles. This filter also works with scrolling titles to reduce flicker. It's also very useful when you're panning across images that have fine detail or horizontal lines (such as sheet music).

Image Stabilizer stabilizes motion in a clip that was handheld or that is shaking for some other reason. The Source pop-up menu allows you to view the clip before and after image stabilization has been applied. The Center control allows you to select a particular element in your video clip to use as the target for stabilization. The selected target should be a high-contrast element with a clearly defined shape. The Scan Range slider allows you to define the area of your clip that will be analyzed to track the motion of the selected target. Clips with greater motion should use a larger scan range; clips with more-subtle motion can use a smaller one. The Show Scan check box shows and hides the image stabilization target.

Stop Motion Blur blends frames within the clip. It sort of superimposes adjacent frames within each frame. This filter can be used to simulate the POV of a person under the influence of drugs or alcohol. It might also be useful for a time-warping sort of effect, because that is what it does—takes frames from earlier or later in the clip and superimposes them on current frames. You can adjust the time, steps, opacity, and operation used to blend the frames.

Strobe lowers a clip's visual frame rate by freezing the clip's frames for a selected amount of time. The Strobe Duration slider allows you to select the duration of each freeze frame. This filter is like a series of freeze frames that are sampled from the original video clip.

Timecode Print displays a clip's timecode to create a "window burn." You can adjust the timecode and the effect's look. This can be used to create a timecoded window burn of VHS approval copies of your work for a client's approval. If you nest your entire sequence in a new sequence, and then apply this filter to the nest, you can create a window burn that matches the timecode of your sequence. You then can make the changes noted by your client by timecode. This effect makes it easier to find specific areas to change. Timecode Print can also be used for all sorts of count-up and countdown effects. Crop and use just the numbers you need. Apply this effect to a slug that is as long as the event you want to time.

View Finder displays a viewfinder overlay much the same as you might find in a camera's viewfinder. Familiar elements can be included, such as record/play/pause mode, and even custom text, title/action safe, and a blinking lamp. You can adjust the text's color and mode as well.

APPENDIX G

What's on the DVD

The accompanying DVD is packed with all sorts of exercise files and products to help you work with this book and with Final Cut Pro. The following sections contain detailed descriptions of the DVD's contents.

For more information about the use of this DVD, please review the ReadMe.txt file in the root directory. This file includes important disclaimer information, as well as information about installation, system requirements, troubleshooting, and technical support.

Technical Support Issues

If you have any difficulties with this DVD, you can access our website at http://www.newriders.com.

System Requirements

This DVD was configured for use on systems running Mac OS 10.2.5 or later. Your machine needs to meet the following system requirements for this DVD to operate properly: any Macintosh G4 with a DVD player.

Loading the DVD Files

To load the files from the DVD, first insert the disc into your DVD drive. Then open its icon from the disk drive and drag all the files directly to your hard drive. It's best to use a dedicated media drive for this purpose, but it's not necessary. Just remember where you copied the files to, because you'll need to access them to work with the tutorial.

Exercise Files

This DVD contains all the files you need to complete the exercises in all the tutorials in this book. These files can be found in the root directory.

Third-Party Programs

This DVD also contains several third-party programs and demos from leading industry companies. These programs have been carefully selected to help you strengthen your professional skills in digital nonlinear editing.

Please note that some of the programs included on this DVD are shareware "try-before-you-buy" software. Please support these independent vendors by purchasing or registering any shareware software that you use for more than 30 days. Check with the documentation provided with the software on where and how to register the product.

Read This Before Opening the Software

By opening the DVD package, you agree to be bound by the following agreement:

You may not copy or redistribute the entire DVD as a whole. Copying and redistributing individual software programs on the DVD is governed by terms set by individual copyright holders.

The installer, code, images, actions, and brushes from the author are copyrighted by the publisher and the author.

This software is sold as-is, without warranty of any kind, either express or implied, including but not limited to the implied warranties of merchantability and fitness for a particular purpose. Neither the publisher nor its dealers nor distributors assumes any liability for any alleged or actual damages arising from the use of this program. (Some states do not allow for the exclusion of implied warranties, so the exclusion might not apply to you.)

Index

www.informit.com

YOUR GUIDE TO IT REFERENCE

New Riders has partnered with **InformIT.com** to bring technical information to your desktop. Drawing from New Riders authors and reviewers to provide additional information on topics of interest to you, **InformIT.com** provides free, in-depth information you won't find anywhere else.

Articles

Keep your edge with thousands of free articles, in-depth features, interviews, and IT reference recommendations— all written by experts you know and trust.

Online Books

Answers in an instant from **InformIT Online Books'** 600+ fully searchable online books.

POWERED BY

Catalog

Review online sample chapters, author biographies, and customer rankings and choose exactly the right book from a selection of more than 5,000 titles.

www.newriders.com